Research Instruments in Social Gerontology

Volume 2

Social Roles and Social Participation

Research Instruments in Social Gerontology

Edited by David J. Mangen and Warren A. Peterson

The editors and the University of Minnesota Press gratefully acknowledge the assistance of the Administration on Aging through contract number HEW 105-76-3107 and grant number 90-A-1370 to the Institute for Community Studies at the University of Missouri-Kansas City, and grant number 90-AR-0024-01 to the Minnesota Family Center at the University of Minnesota. Without the assistance of the Administration on Aging, this project would not have been possible.

Research Instruments
in Social Gerontology

Volume 2

Social Roles
and Social
Participation

Editors
David J. Mangen
Warren A. Peterson

With the assistance of
Toshi Kii and Robert Sanders

UNIVERSITY OF MINNESOTA PRESS

MINNEAPOLIS

Published by the University of Minnesota Press,
2037 University Avenue Southeast,
Minneapolis, Minnesota 55414
Printed in the United States of America.

Library of Congress Cataloging in Publication Data

Main entry under title:

Research instruments in social gerontology.

Includes index.
Contents: — v. 2. Social roles and social
participation.
1. Gerontology — Research — Addresses, essays,
lectures — Collected works. 2. Aged — Socioeconomic
status — Research — Addresses, essays, lectures —
Collected works. I. Mangen, David J. II. Peterson,
Warren A., 1922-   . [DNLM: 1. Aged. 2. Social
welfare — United States. 3. Sociology. 4. Health
services research — United States. WT 30 R433]
HQ1061.R44   305.2'6   81-16449
ISBN O-8166-1096-7 (v.2)   AACR2
ISBN O-8166-0991-8 (v.1)
ISBN O-8166-1112-2 (v.3)

Contents

Preface

Research Instruments in Social Gerontology: Social Roles and Social Participation is the second of a three-volume series of books designed to serve the needs of researchers, evaluators, and clinicians in assessing the instruments used in the field of aging. The length of this series and the amount of work involved in preparing the manuscript have greatly exceeded our expectations. Over 400 measures are reviewed in the three volumes, with topics ranging from formal demography to intelligence and personality. The measures reviewed in Volume 3 of the series address the concern of social gerontologists with the involvement of older persons in the major forms of social organization and social structure. Much of this work was done in response to the disengagement-activity theory controversy of the 1960s and 1970s, although use of the measures may not be limited to those theoretical perspectives.

The increasing size of the aging population in the United States has brought a corresponding increase in interest about the processes of aging and the effectiveness of social programs for the elderly. Now more than ever before, researchers require conceptually explicit instruments designed to assess individual and social behaviors, attitudes, and traits in the aging population. Measures are needed to help construct effective programs of social assistance and to evaluate those programs. It was in this spirit that we undertook this project, and, on the whole, we feel our efforts have been successful. To be sure, not every researcher will be able to find in this collection instruments ideal for his or her purposes. Indeed, such uncritical adoption of existent measures would reflect an intellectual stagnation that would endanger the growth of aging as a field of inquiry. We hope that *Research Instruments in Social Gerontology* will serve as a benchmark, helping the researcher who is developing measures to avoid reinventing the wheel. We also hope that our efforts will alert researchers to the necessity of clearly specifying their constructs and the differences between those constructs and other related measures. In short, we hope that our efforts will encourage researchers to use a theoretical basis—either deductively, inductively, or retroductively derived—in developing new measures.

However, many researchers may find useful measures through the reviews in these volumes. This collection of information about the instruments appropriate for work in aging should alleviate the burden of making a literature search. Still, the user of existing measures must recognize the implicit and explicit theoretical bases of an existing measure and contribute to knowledge about that measure. He or she should examine its reliability and validity and report those data in published accounts of the project. Each use of a measure constitutes only one case in the scientific development of a measure, and the importance of developing a cumulative body of knowledge about the use of measures in diverse populations and environments cannot be overstated. Responsibility for the scientific development of a measure lies not only with the original authors, but also with those who choose to use it.

In the interest of promoting the continued development of existing measures, the precise development of new ones, and the ready dissemination of all measures, one of us, the senior editor, David Mangen, will continue his efforts at compiling and evaluating measures. We also hope to update *Research Instruments in Social Gerontology* sometime in the future, a task that the community of scholars involved in aging can ease through correspondence about their development and uses of instruments. Undoubtedly, some instruments have escaped our attention. We intended to exclude no instrument, and we apologize for any oversights that may have occurred. Correspondence with the senior editor will ensure that these omissions will be rectified in the second edition, and his effort will be assisted if such correspondence includes the sorts of information contained within the instrument reviews together with copies of reprints, complete bibliographies, and research instruments.

We have been blessed with a high degree of cooperation from many persons throughout the life of this project. First, we thank the authors of the instruments who graciously provided us with information about their work and who allowed us to reproduce their materials. The journals and publishers who gave us permission to quote extensively from their publications have acted as true partners in the scientific process by recognizing both the utility of our work and the limitations of our budget. We thank them for their assistance.

A special note of thanks is due the members of the administrative committee for the project; they helped us develop the outline for the volumes and the methods for evaluating the instruments. We are further indebted to these esteemed colleagues—Donald McTavish of the University of Minnesota, Harold Orbach of Kansas State University, Edward Powers of Iowa State University and Ethel Shanas of the University of Illinois, Chicago Circle—for their assistance in finding appropriate contributing authors for the chapters. Furthermore, they used their own professional contacts to alert the discipline about the existence and importance of this project.

The individual chapter authors undertook a task that seemed to grow and to expand every day. Their efforts at searching the literature were monumental; indeed, some of their original contributions could almost qualify as books on their own. An enormous amount of editing was required to produce a manageable manuscript. We hope that we have not distorted their conclusions in the editorial process. Many of the contributors have pointed out that additional instruments have already emerged while we were editing. Unfortunately, we had to close off substantive revisions in order to finish the manuscript. To the chapter authors, therefore, we extend a hearty thank you. Your long efforts and devotion to detail were impressive, and the collegial bonds that developed remain a source of pleasure for us.

As is always the case with a massive undertaking such as this one, a number of people have provided vital assistance. Toshi Kii, now of Georgia State University, was one of the original research associates for the project as well as a chapter author. His assistance in developing the topical outline for the books and the format for evaluation must be acknowledged. After the initial chapter contributions were received and while the three-part editorial process was underway, Robert Sanders was in charge of disseminating information about our work on research instruments to scholars who wanted information prior to this publication. He, together with Julie Edgerton, was responsible for most of the work involved in securing permissions to use copyrighted materials. These were no small tasks in a project of this magnitude. Sanders and Edgerton were ably assisted by Nellie Lynde, the project secretary during the Kansas City phase of the project.

After the project was transferred to the University of Minnesota, two persons provided a good deal of assistance. Robert Leik, director of the Minnesota Family Study Center, arranged for clerical and secretarial support for preparing the final proposal to the Administration on Aging. After that proposal was approved, Pamela Adelmann joined the project staff. Nominally she was the project's secretary, but functionally she was a research associate who helped document sources, obtain copyrights, and conduct literature searches; she also prepared much of the final manuscript. To all of these people we extend our thanks.

The Administration on Aging of the U.S. Department of Health and Human Services has provided financial assistance through contract-HEW 105-76-3107 and grant HEW AoA 90-A-1370 to the Institute for Community Studies of the University of Missouri-Kansas City and grant 90-AR-0024-01 to the Minnesota Family Study Center of the University of Minnesota. A special note of thanks is due to David Dowd, the project officer throughout the life of the project.

Research Instruments in Social Gerontology is a product of the Midwest Council for Social Research on Aging, an interuniversity group of scholars devoted to increasing knowledge about aging. We would like to dedicate our efforts to the memory of two colleagues on the Midwest Council, Arnold Rose and Leonard Breen.

David J. Mangen
Los Angeles, California
Warren A. Peterson
Kansas City, Missouri

How to Use These Volumes

Almost every chapter in these books is composed of three parts. The first part is a concise narrative review of the major theoretical concerns and measurement strategies within that research domain. The second part of each chapter is a collection of abstracts. Each abstract presents a conceptual definition and description of a specific instrument, together with data about samples, reliability, validity, scaling properties, and correlations with age. Each abstract concludes with a list of references and, when the instrument is reproduced, a code number referring the reader to the instrument itself. The instruments themselves constitute the third part of most chapters. For a variety of reasons, not every abstract includes a separate instrument. At times, we were unable to secure permission to reproduce a copyrighted instrument. Other times, the length of an instrument precluded its publication. This was a difficult editorial decision to make, but it was one that was necessary in order to limit this work to three volumes.

The code numbers on the instruments reproduced in the section at the end of each chapter consist of four parts. The first part refers the reader to the volume in the three-volume series; the three volumes are represented by V1, V2, and V3. The second part of the code number refers to the chapter that reviews that instrument. Usually, the instrument is presented within the same chapter and volume. Occasionally, however, instruments are conceptually relevant to several chapters, and cross-referring is necessary. The third part of each code number is a roman numeral that refers to a subtopic of the general concept reviewed in the chapter. The final part of each code number is a letter code that is sequential after each roman numeral. The roman numerals and letter code correspond to the codes listed in the tables at the ends of the narrative reviews. The coding system is strictly hierarchical; for example, the code number V2.3.II.a refers to the second volume, the third chapter (by Mangen), subtopic II on role performance, power, and decision making. Instrument a is Kerckhoff's Task Sharing. (See Table 3-1.)

Some research instruments are missing from the instrument sections. This may be due to problems with copyrights or length or the necessity of using cross-references. Often, however, the simplest way to describe a very brief research instrument was to include the instrument in the abstract. When this is the case, a reference is usually made to the appropriate section of the abstract.

We recommend that readers review chapter narratives first and then go on to the abstracts. Only after the first two parts of the chapters have been read will the contents of the instruments sections be meaningful.

Contributors to Volume 2

Vern L. Bengtson
Andrus Gerontology Center
University of Southern California
Los Angeles, California

C. Neil Bull
Department of Sociology
University of Missouri-Kansas City
Kansas City, Missouri

Marshall J. Graney
Department of Sociology
Wayne State University
Detroit, Michigan

David J. Mangen
Andrus Gerontology Center
University of Southern California
Los Angeles, California

Charles H. Mindel
Graduate School of Social Work
University of Texas
Arlington, Texas

Angela M. O'Rand
Department of Sociology
Duke University
Durham, North Carolina

Barbara Pittard Payne
Department of Sociology
Georgia State University
Atlanta, Georgia

George R. Peters
Department of Sociology and
 Anthropology
Kansas State University
Manhattan, Kansas

Edward A. Powers
Department of Sociology and
 Anthropology
Iowa State University
Ames, Iowa

Sandi S. Schrader
School of Home Economics and
 Family Studies
University of Connecticut
Storrs, Connecticut

Research Instruments in Social Gerontology

Volume 2

Social Roles and Social Participation

Chapter 1

Introduction

David J. Mangen

Research instruments can be found in a surprisingly large number of publications in every area of social science, and the field of aging is no different than any other. Since many journal articles, books, dissertations, and unpublished manuscripts contain empirical instruments, the task of reviewing the measurement literature can be very difficult. Few scholars have access to all of the relevant literature, and the often limited amounts of time available during funded research sometimes preclude the exchange of information necessary for developing cumulative research strategies. For such reasons researchers often devise their own instruments, and knowledge about empirical measures is progressively fragmented.

This fragmentation of knowledge has important theoretical and empirical consequences for every area of inquiry in the social sciences. Researches who address similar theoretical questions but use different measurement devices are not able to build upon the work of others when they attempt to integrate their findings into theory. Their different findings may not be related to their use of different populations; rather, their findings may be a function of the different techniques of measurement they used. In addition, the routine development of a new measurement device for each new study would preclude the establishment of a cumulative record of reliability and validity for instruments already used, because each use of an instrument constitutes only one case in the scientific study of an instrument and many cases are required before validity and reliability can be shown to have been established.

There are many reasons for developing a central repository of instruments, and the three volumes of *Research Instruments in Social Gerontology* address such concerns. Volume 2 specifically examines instruments assessing the participation of older persons in important social roles as members of families and religions, as participants in leisure activities, and as workers, friends, and volunteers. The instruments reviewed differ widely in their scope and complexity. Though many of the measures reviewed are scales (i.e., sets of items that are homogeneous in content and are combined into summary rankings by mathematical decision rules), many of the instruments are batteries of possibly homogeneous items for which summary rankings have never been developed. Single-item indicators are also represented in the instruments reviewed.

Our intention was to develop a complete inventory of research instruments. Undoubtedly, we have omitted some that were in existence before our efforts began and still more that have been developed since we finished collecting instruments and began editing our findings. This is unfortunate, but it seems to be an unavoidable consequence of the magnitude of our effort. We feel confident, however, that most of the high-quality research instruments that have been used in aging are included in this compendium. It must be noted, though, that our inclusion of an instrument in these volumes does not constitute a recommendation for its use. Decisions to use specific instruments can only be made by scholars who are sensitive to the theoretical nuances of their own work and cognizant of the implications of their measurement strategies. We have tried to provide the information they need to make informed decisions.

Contents of This Volume

The introductory chapter in the first volume of *Research Instruments in Social Gerontology* explains the criteria we used during our evaluations of instruments, and it also includes an overall evaluation of the status of measurement in research in aging. We strongly urge readers to review carefully that chapter's discussion of psychometric theory and the criteria of instrument assessment.

In Chapter 2 of this volume, Marshall J. Graney reviews measures of social participation that simultaneously assess participation in multiple roles. The measures he reviewed include expert rating scales and self-reporting techniques. After reviewing these measures, he stresses the importance of developing middle-range theories that incorporate theories of measurement structure.

In Chapter 3, David J. Mangen reviews measures of husband-wife relations and aging. He reports that there are an inordinate number of instruments measuring the concept of marital satisfaction. Measures of power and task performance, among other instruments, are also reviewed, however. Mangen recommends that researchers expand the range of legitimate concepts for studying marital dyads and urges the use of a rational approach to measurement (Straus, 1964).

Measures of parent-child relations are reviewed by Vern L. Bengtson and Sandi S. Schrader in Chapter 4. They find that the study of parent-child relations in old age can be characterized by its emphasis on five concepts: family structure, associational solidarity, affectual solidarity, exchanges of assistance, and norms for "proper" relations among the generations. They recommend further attention to conceptualization and psychometric development.

Charles H. Mindel reviews 23 measures pertaining to kinship in Chapter 5. He discusses the three broad areas dealt with in most kinship studies: kinship structure (i.e., the number, proximity, and frequency of contacts with kin), kinship solidarity (i.e., the level of integration and the nature of kinship ties), and kinship norms and relations. He recommends further studies of the instruments' reliability and validity, clearer theoretical specification of the constructs the instruments are to measure, and more complete descriptions and documentations of the measurement procedures used in research into kinship.

In Chapter 6, Edward A. Powers reviews research and instrumentation in the area of work and retirement. He finds a lack of attention to systematic instrument development. Major research concerns reviewed include adjustment to retirement and attitudes toward work or retirement. Powers recommends that gerontological researchers examine scales in the area of personnel and work and occupations for further use in research in aging.

Angela M. O'Rand reviews measures of socioeconomic status and poverty in Chapter 7. She urges the use of objective economic and social status measures, as well as subjective class placements, in aging research. She suggests that measures in this area need to be improved in order to take into account female occupational attainments and household social standing.

Barbara Pittard Payne's review of religiosity in Chapter 8 notes the theoretical absorption of researchers with disengagement and activity theories. She urges considerable theoretical development and concurs with Riley and Foner's (1968) conclusion that knowledge of the religious role has as yet contributed little to the understanding of the aging process.

In Chapter 9, George R. Peters points out that measurements of relationships between friends, neighbors, and confidants are, in general, characterized by a low level of rigor and sophistication. He recommends further theoretical specification that differentiates the use of the terms *friend, neighbor,* and *confidant,* and he suggests that using balance models (Newcomb, 1961) or exchange theories (Homans, 1961; Emerson, 1972) might prove useful. He further recommends greater attention to the reliability and validity of the instruments used.

C. Neil Bull reviews 10 measures of participation in voluntary associations and volunteerism in Chapter 10. He notes the absence of a standard definition of a voluntary association and differentiates between the concepts of affiliation and active participation. He suggests that attention must be given to the growing number of age-specific organizations.

In Chapter 11, C. Neil Bull reviews instruments used in the area of leisure activities. He finds that leisure time is often considered to be residual, i.e., time that is free from work and other obligatory activities; and he points out that this defines as leisure virtually any facet of social participation. He urges greater attention to conceptualization and further studies of the measures of reliability and validity.

Summary

The 10 substantive chapters of Volume 2 provide an extensive review of research into social participation in the field of aging. Many other measures of social participation exist that have not been used on older populations and so are not included in this volume. Measurement compendiums by Miller (1970), Straus and Brown (1978), and Bonjean, Hill, and McLemore (1967) are useful sources for additional measurement devices that have been used in this general area of inquiry.

Nowhere in these three volumes do we review measures of social desirability and response set. Yet, these general measurement concerns are obviously relevant to the field of aging, and, indeed, evidence suggests that age is positively correlated with social desirability (Mutran and Burke, 1979). Edwards (1957) and Sudman and Bradburn (1974) provide useful starting points for reviews of this literature.

Although we could not possibly hope to cover all scales measuring a given concept or all scales that have relevance for the field of aging, we do believe that our efforts will assist researchers in further specifying and measuring their constructs. We hope that through this effort we will help reduce the unwarranted proliferation of research instruments and thus contribute to the growth of knowledge about the aging process.

REFERENCES

Bonjean, C. M., R. J. Hill, and S. D. McLemore. *Sociological Measurement: An Inventory of Scales and Indices.* San Francisco: Chandler, 1967.

Edwards, A. L. *The Social Desirability Variable in Personality Assessment and Research.* New York: Dryden, 1957.

Emerson, R. M. "Exchange Theory, Parts I-II." In *Sociological Theories in Progress* (vol. 2), J. Berger, M. Zelditch, Jr., and B. Anderson (eds.), pp. 38-87. Boston: Houghton Mifflin, 1972.

Homans, G. C. *Social Behavior: Its Elementary Forms.* New York: Harcourt, Brace, & World, 1961.

Miller, D. C. *Handbook of Research Design and Social Measurement* (2nd ed.). New York: David McKay, 1970.

Mutran, E., and P. J. Burke. "Personalism as a Component of Old Age Identity." *Research on Aging,* 1979, 1: 37-63.

Newcomb, T. *The Acquaintance Process.* New York: Holt, Rinehart and Winston, 1961.

Riley, M. W., and A. Foner. *Aging and Society* (vol. 1). New York: Russell Sage Foundation, 1968.

Straus, M. A. "Measuring Families." In *Handbook of Marriage and the Family*, H. T. Christiansen (ed.), pp. 335-400. Skokie, Ill.: Rand McNally, 1964.

Straus, M. A., and B. W. Brown. *Family Measurement Techniques* (rev. ed.). Minneapolis: University of Minnesota Press, 1978.

Sudman, S., and N. M. Bradburn. *Response Effects in Surveys.* Chicago: Aldine, 1974.

Chapter 2

Social Participation Roles

Marshall J. Graney

Many research instruments have been developed for measuring social participation activity, social roles, and social integration. The convenient term *social participation* can be used to represent all three of these research interests. Candidates for inclusion in this review of the currently available instruments were instruments that attempt to measure social participation in some general sense: in practice, such measures usually involve collecting subscores on two or more items, which are then combined in some way to yield a score that is said to be representative of an individual's placement on a more general scale of social participation. The subscale items can be drawn from observations, interviews, and questionnaires. Batteries of items that measure single dimensions or components of social participation but are not combined to yield a characteristic global score are reviewed elsewhere in this volume. In this chapter, only measurement instruments that have been developed to be representative of an individual's overall social life (or some general dimension of it) are reviewed. The 11 instruments that have been selected for this review are listed in Table 2-1. These include scales based on judges' ratings of nonspecific criteria, omnibus scales based on specific criteria, and scales of major dimensions of social participation also based on specific criteria.

Instruments Reviewed

Social participation scales have played an historically important part in research on the social aspects of human aging. These measures have figured prominently in several of the major studies that helped to place social research on aging on a scientific foundation. For example, Havighurst and Albrecht's *Older People* (1953), Cumming and Henry's *Growing Old* (1961), and Rosow's *Social Integration of the Aged* (1967) all used social participation scales. In these works instruments were used to develop findings and raise issues that have been subjects of ongoing research and have resulted in hundreds of published pages in the literature of social gerontology. During this same time, measurement technology has grown increasingly sophisticated, and research using existing or developing social participation scales continues in several academic disciplines and service institutions in several countries, especially in Canada, Sweden, and the United States.

TABLE 2-1
Instruments Reviewed in Chapter 2

Instrument	Author(s)	Code Number
I. Nonspecific Criteria		
a. Adjustment Rating Scales	Havighurst and Albrecht (1953)	V2.2.I.a
II. Specific Criteria, Omnibus Scales		
a. Role Activities in Later Maturity	Havighurst and Albrecht (1953)	V2.2.II.a
b. Participation Index	Bradburn and Caplovitz (1965)	V2.2.II.b
c. Social Participation Index	Phillips (1967)	V2.2.II.c
d. Comprehensive Role Loss Index	Rosow (1967)	V2.2.II.d
e. Activity Inventory	Cavan et al. (1949)	V2.2.II.e
III. Specific Criteria, Restricted Scales		
a. Social Participation Scale	Chapin (1939)	V2.2.III.a
b. General Community Participation Scale	Foskett (1955)	V2.2.III.b
c. Interaction Index	Cumming and Henry (1961)	V2.2.III.c
d. Role Count Index	Cumming and Henry (1961)	V2.2.III.d
e. Social Lifespace Measure	Cumming and Henry (1961)	V2.2.III.e

Three distinctly different research technologies have been associated with the measurement of social participation. The earliest research relied heavily on judges' ratings based on impressions formed through overall reviews of questionnaires and transcripts of interviews. The degree of subjectivity and invalidity in these ratings is uncertain, in part because the explicit empirical indicators used as a basis for judgment are only loosely specified.

Later research usually specified more carefully the precise empirical indicators in the process of operationalizing concepts. This has improved the credibility and the impression of objectivity in more recent studies. The most recent developments have emphasized measures of types of activities, or major classifications of social behavior, that are broader in scope than single observation/interview/questionnaire items. At the same time, these measures are less global than the omnibus social participation measures that dominated early research in this field. These historical developments will be briefly reviewed below, and this review will close with some observations and suggestions on topics that should be pursued in greater depth.

Social participation measures consisting of judges' ratings based on unspecified or global criteria are often considered subjective, and in the development of social research this kind of measurement has tended to fall into disuse (Graney and Graney, 1973). Nevertheless, there are at least two reasons why this measurement technique is still used by some researchers. One reason comes up in analyses of available data. A researcher may want to extract information that is implicit in the research protocols but is not explicitly represented by specific items or scales. Researchers disagree about whether or not scaling of this kind can be valid when precise empirical indicators are not specified. Another application of global judges' ratings can occur when the variable measured is such that respondents can provide data that are less reliable or valid than the judgments of others (for example, unconscious strivings toward cognitive consistency, yea-saying tendencies, and social desirability biases can arise in any interview situation). In this case, direct empirical indicators of the concept may reflect greater bias than global judges' ratings. Again, many researchers would question the validity of measurements based on unspecified criteria.

The Cavan Adjustment Rating Scales (Havighurst and Albrecht, 1953) are examples of scales developed for use in one or both of the research situations just described. The Adjustment Rating Scales are used as social participation instruments. One of the scales is a measure of primary association, and the other is a measure of secondary association. This follows the long-standing sociological distinction between these two categories of interpersonal relationships. Although the empirical indicators on which such ratings are based are not specified, both scales are exemplary judges' rating scales. Both are graduated as 10-step scales, and both are calibrated at 5 of the 10 steps with brief descriptions of general characteristics of the persons who are to be rated at different levels.

A second type of social participation instrument combines two or more questionnaire or interview items into an overall composite scale score. The composite score is designed to be an omnibus score representing social participation in a general sense. This technique has been used by a number of different researchers, and five such instruments have been identified and reviewed for this inventory.

Havighurst and Albrecht's index of Role Activities in Later Maturity (Havighurst and Albrecht, 1953) is an elaborately calibrated device requiring interviewers' ratings on 12 dimensions of the social role at the completion of the interview. A composite score is obtained by combining all 12 dimensions. The 12 role dimensions include: great-grandparent, grandparent, parent, home, kinship, social clubs, business clubs, church activities, peer relationships, clique activities, civic activities, and occupation. Ratings of these 12 social role dimensions are made according to 10 degrees of activity appropriate to each specific dimension. Each of these degrees is operationally linked to an empirical indicator that guides the interviewer's rating.

A second social participation measure that uses two or more item scores as components of an omnibus score is Bradburn and Caplovitz's (1965) Participation Index. This instrument combines seven interview items to yield a composite social participation score. The research subject is allowed to select a response from among several alternative categories for each of the seven items. The seven interview items used in the Participation Index include questions about the number of memberships in organizations currently held; the number of telephone calls received from, or made to, friends; the maximum distance traveled away from home; the frequency of attendance at meetings; the number of meetings with friends; the number of automobile trips; and the frequency of dining at restaurants.

A third omnibus social participation instrument is the Social Participation Index (Phillips, 1967). In comparison to the two scales already discussed, Phillips's scale is relatively crude in that only three items are combined in the composite scale. The small number of items may prove a disadvantage when reliability and validity are considered, but Phillips's scale is more easily incorporated into conventional questionnaire and interview schedules than the more cumbersome omnibus instruments. The three dimensions included by Phillips are key dimensions also included in more elaborate instruments: visiting with friends, neighborhood activity, and participation in activities associated with churches, clubs, and other associations. As was the case with Bradburn and Caplovitz's measure, respondents choose the appropriate item response on Phillips's scale.

The fourth omnibus social participation scale selected for this review is Rosow's (1967) Comprehensive Role Loss Index. Four dimensions are examined in Rosow's scale, which combines replies to questions about marital status, employment, income, and health. On each of the four items, replies were dichotomized in accordance with a priori cutoff points designating functionally significant role loss from middle-age to old-age. Further work is needed to establish intersample validity for the criteria of functionally significant role loss within each of the dimensions of this index. However, because of the parsimonious number of subscale component items and because it has been explicitly developed for research on aging, Rosow's index is an excellent prospect for further development as an omnibus social participation measure.

The last omnibus scale reviewed in this chapter is the Activity Inventory (Cavan et al., 1949), which combines 19 items into 5 subscales of activity and subsequently into 1 overall measure of activity level. Though Cavan and associates (1949) conceptualized this instrument as a measure of adjustment, the items tend to tap activity levels. One might question, however, the utility of including the health subscale as a *measure*, as contrasted to a determinant, of activity level. Finally, it is important to note that the subscales of the Activity Inventory have been used as independent constructs in some substantive research (e.g., Palmore, 1968). Because of this, other reviewers in this volume have commented on parts of the Activity Inventory. Interested readers are referred to the chapters by Pittard-Payne (Chapter 8), Peters (Chapter 9), and Bull (Chapters 10 and 11).

A third approach to measuring social participation does not attempt to measure social participation as an omnibus or global concept. Instead, instruments following this approach develop multiple-item scales to measure only one particular dimension of general social participation. Five measures of this kind are included in this review.

Chapin's (1939) Social Participation Scale is an instrument that is limited to measuring the number and intensity of involvements in groups and organizations, and it is a measure of secondary association. Five dimensions of organizational activity are weighted and combined in this scale: number of memberships, attendance, contributions, membership on committees, and holding office.

Foskett's (1955) General Community Participation Scale is designed for interview situations. This instrument measures formal and informal social participation of several kinds, but its primary focus is on educational, civic, and governmental affairs. Sixteen scale items allow relatively intensive measurement of behaviors such as voting; discussions with family, friends, and officials; memberships; and organizational activities.

The third, fourth, and fifth instruments included in this third section were developed by Cumming and Henry (1961). These include the Interaction Index, the Role Count Index, and the Social Lifespace Measure. The Interaction Index is based on judges' scoring of two open-ended interview questions, one about a "typical day" and the other about a "typical weekend." The Role Count Index is based on combining responses to eight interview questions concerning the number of people in the household and interaction with relatives, friends, neighbors, fellow workers; other specific interpersonal contacts; church activity; and other organizational activities. The intent is to measure the number of relationships in which an older person is currently active. The Social Lifespace Measure requires interview data, but it could be adapted for use with questionnaires. Six dimensions of interpersonal social contact are scored on the basis of frequency of contact over a month's time, and the items are combined to form a composite scale. The six items include questions about members of the household, relatives, friends, neighbors, fellow workers, and other specific interpersonal contacts. The intent is to provide a measure of the number of social contacts that an older person has over the course of a month.

Research on the social participation, roles, and integration of older people is a central concern in the social research on aging, whether the individual researcher thinks in terms of activity, disengagement, or some other theoretical perspective. One of the issues underlying research on social participation is concern about the use of rating versus scaling as an appropriate technique for obtaining quantitative data. Another of the principal issues is whether operationalization should be done in terms of scaling a global concept or measuring a particular behavior.

Both rating (using experts or judges) and scaling (multiple-item composites of measurements) have been used to generate quantitative data on social participation. The use of ratings tends to reflect a humanistic tradition in social research, in contrast to the somewhat mechanistic principles of scaling. However, scaling reflects a tradition of scientific measurement that emphasizes replicability and concreteness in operational procedure. The general resolution of this issue has been in favor of scaling in the sense that ratings are rarely used. There are situations in which ratings may be preferable to scaling, and two such situations have already been discussed in detail.

The other principal issue that needs to be addressed is whether operationalization should be done in terms of scaling a global concept or measuring particular indicators of individual behaviors. Favorable and unfavorable things can be said about both of these strategies. On the one hand, the global concept of social participation is heuristically rich because it is embedded in many theoretical perspectives, although omnibus scales suffer from operational ambiguities because the concept is relatively abstract. As long as the items combined in omnibus social participation scales have more in common internally than with measures of other concepts, it can be argued that a composite omnibus scale has better potential for reliability and validity than might otherwise be the case. However, studies of the convergent and discriminant validity of omnibus social participation scales have not been done. On the other hand, the use of single behavior indicators (alone or serially) does not compromise face validity by combining dissimilar indicators into a composite scale. Analyzing a single indicator, or even a series of indicators, in social participation research, however, is an ad hoc procedure that is unlikely to produce findings with theoretically interesting generalizability. It is fortunate that researchers are not faced with the dilemma of making an either/ or choice in this matter. Instead, a compromise that follows a sociological principle of long standing is available: that of trying to develop theories in the middle range.

Merton's emphasis on middle-range theories is important to conceptualizations and operationalizations in research on social participation. There is a sociological distinction between Gemeinschaft and Gesellschaft, or between primary relationships and secondary interpersonal relationships. This conceptualization is between the global concept and the individual behavior item indicators. This distinction was introduced into the gerontological literature with the Cavan scales of primary and secondary associations. In more recent work (Graney, 1975), the influence of ethnomethodology and phenomenology can be seen in the attempt to motivate inductively major classes of social behavior through detection of modes or clusters of social participation behaviors. The results of this inductive approach to a middle-range conceptualization of the social participation of older people fully support the distinction employed by Cavan. In addition, this work suggests that a third mode of social participation consists principally of the use of the mass communication media.

Summary

In addition to the Cavan scales, several other middle-range measures are reviewed in this chapter. More work is needed to refine and validate the scales developed by Cumming and Henry and by Rosow and to bring these scales into widespread use. Needed are new scales measuring social behaviors that are more specific than global scales and more general than individual indicators. In particular, new research that refines existing scales and develops new scales needs to focus on convergent and discriminant validity and to have sufficiently large and representative samples so that the results can be considered firmly established. Once this has been accomplished, it will be possible to develop social participation research that detects patterns of individual change in aging and differences between major subcategories of older people. In sum, the long-standing tradition of research on social participation and aging is still active, and new measurement strategies that focus on middle-range conceptualizations are likely to lead to more refined knowledge about relationships between aging and social integration and the relationship of this to intrapersonal happiness and interpersonal social adjustment.

REFERENCES

Bradburn, N. M., and D. Caplovitz. *Reports on Happiness.* Chicago: Aldine, 1965.

Cavan, R. S., E. W. Burgess, R. J. Havighurst, and H. Goldhammer. *Personal Adjustment in Old Age.* Chicago: Science Research Associates, 1949.

Chapin, F. S. "Social Participation and Social Intelligence." *American Sociological Review*, 1939, 4: 157-66.

Cumming, E., and W. E. Henry. *Growing Old.* New York: Basic Books. 1961.

Foskett, J. M. "Social Structure and Social Participation." *American Sociological Review*, 1955, 20: 431-38.

Graney, M. J. "Communication Uses and the Social Activity Constant." *Communication Research*, 1975, 2: 347-66.

Graney, M. J., and E. E. Graney. "Scaling Adjustment in Older People." *International Journal of Aging and Human Development*, 1973, 4: 351-59.

Havighurst, R. J., and R. Albrecht. *Older People.* New York: Longmans, Green and Company, 1953.

Palmore, E. "The Effects of Aging on Activities and Attitudes." *The Gerontologist*, 1968, 8 (4): 259-63.

Phillips, D. L. "Social Participation and Happiness." *American Journal of Sociology*, 1967, 72: 479-88.

Rosow, I. *Social Integration of the Aged.* New York: Free Press, 1967.

Abstracts

ADJUSTMENT RATING SCALES

R. J. Havighurst and R. Albrecht, 1953

Definition of Concept

Cavan's concept of adjustment included ratings of six specific dimensions. Two of these dimensions involved social participation and are rated independently from each other and from the other four dimensions. The social participation rating scales are: (1) "primary" or personal, intimate, contacts" and (2) "secondary or more formal and specialized contacts" (Havighurst and Albrecht, 1953, p. 408).

Description of Instrument

The instrument consists of two judges' rating scales, each calibrated in 10 subdivisions ranging from lack of activity in the behaviors (0) to relatively intense activity in the behaviors (9).

Method of Administration

Research subjects are judged by a panel of two or three raters, and a characteristic scale score is the median of these ratings.

Context of Development

These rating scales were developed as part of a research effort originating with the Committee on Human Development at the University of Chicago.

Sample

The sample was a representative stratified sample of 100 people aged 65 and over and residing in "Prairie City" (1953, p. 248).

General Comments and Recommendations

These simple ratings have an advantage in that they can be used ex post facto and do not require that time or space be reserved for them in the form of specific questionnaire or interview items. The subjectivity of ratings of these kinds has been critiqued elsewhere.

Reference

Havighurst, R. J. and R. Albrecht. *Older People*. New York: Longmans, Green and Company, 1953.

Instrument

See Instrument V2.2.I.a.

ROLE ACTIVITIES IN LATER MATURITY

R. J. Havighurst and R. Albrecht, 1953

Definition of Concept

According to Havighurst and Albrecht, "A social role is a coherent set of activities that is recognized and judged by others as something apart from the individual who happens to fill it" (1953, p. 43).

Description of Instrument

The instrument consists of a battery of 12 judges' ratings that are individually calibrated with 10 degrees of intensity. These degrees of intensity range from 0 (no activity) through 9 (relatively intense activity). The Role Activities in Later Maturity ratings measure the degree of activity in 12 roles, including role activities in family relationships (great-grandparents, grandparents, parents, home responsibilities, and kinship group or extended family), role activities in group and individual relationships (social clubs, business clubs, church activities, peer relationships, and single or married clique and small-group activities), and role activities in the community (civic activity and business or occupation) (1953, pp. 376-80).

Method of Administration

Following an interview in which the Burgess, Cavan, and Havighurst schedule Your Activities and Attitudes (Havighurst, and Albrecht, 1953, pp. 382-407) is completed, the interviewer rates the interviewee on the 12 items in the Role Activities in Later Maturity battery.

Context of Development

This battery was developed as part of a research effort originating with the Committee on Human Development at the University of Chicago.

Sample

The sample was a representative stratified sample of 100 people aged 65 and over and residing in "Prairie City" (Havighurst and Albrecht, 1953, p. 248).

Scoring, Scale Norms, and Distribution

A composite role-activity score for each interviewee is obtained by computing the arithmetic mean of the 12 items. The mean role-activity score for the original sample was 4.4. Means for the 12 scale items ranged from 1.10 to 7.12 (Havighurst and Albrecht, 1953, p. 366).

Formal Tests of Reliability/Homogeneity

Test-retest reliability averaged .90 across 11 of the 12 items, and interrater reliability averaged .75 (Havighurst and Albrecht, 1953, p. 267).

Usability on Older Populations

The scales are usable.

Sensitivity to Age Differences

Mean index scores have been recomputed from the original source, and they show moderate regression toward activity decline during aging (age 65-69, mean = 4.08; age 80+, mean = 3.87).

General Comments and Recommendations

The carefully calibrated items in this index can be used unobtrusively and without occupying interview time. The subjectivity of the ratings, particularly their vulnerability to halo effects, has contributed to their disuse. A critique of their validity has been offered elsewhere (Graney and Graney, 1973).

References

Graney, M. J., and E. E. Graney. "Scaling Adjustment in Older People." *International Journal of Aging and Human Development*, 1973, 4: 351-59.

Havighurst, R. J., and R. Albrecht. *Older People*. New York: Longmans, Green and Company, 1953.

Instrument

See Instrument V2.2.II.a.

PARTICIPATION INDEX

N. M. Bradburn and D. Caplovitz, 1965

Definition of Concept

Participation is conceptualized in a general way to include both interpersonal interaction and a broad range of other involvement with the sociocultural environment (Bradburn and Caplovitz, 1965, p. 42).

Description of Instrument

Seven questions from an interview schedule are combined as a participation index. Using a time frame of one week for reference, respondents were asked questions about: (1) the number of organizational memberships they currently held; (2) the number of telephone calls they received from, or made to, friends; (3) the maximum distance they traveled away from home; (4) the frequency of their attendance at meetings; (5) the number of face-to-face meetings they had with friends; (6) the number of automobile trips they made; and (7) the frequency of their dining at restaurants (Bradburn and Caplovitz, 1965, p. 45).

Method of Administration

The interview items selected for inclusion in the Participation Index were part of the 116-item National Opinion Research Center (NORC) Long Form Personal Interview (Bradburn and Caplovitz, 1965, Appendix 1, pp. 136-71).

Context of Development

The Participation Index was developed for use in a study of the empirical correlates of happiness. Evidence of the influence of socioeconomic status in scores on the Participation Index is available (Bradburn and Caplovitz, 1965, p. 44).

Sample

The analysis was based on a sample of 393 men aged 25 to 40 (Bradburn and Caplovitz, 1965, p. 43).

Scoring, Scale Norms, and Distribution

The exact technique whereby the seven items were combined into a single Participation Index score was not specified. It can be assumed that the item-response codes given in the instrument were additively combined with a unit weight accorded each item. After the initial distribution of scores (which has a theoretical range of more than 30 points) was developed, the index scores were grouped into four classes. Cutoff points were selected to make the frequencies of these four categories as nearly equal as possible.

General Comments and Recommendations

This is a short omnibus index that has some potential for further development as a scale and for application in research on aging.

Reference

Bradburn, N. M., and D. Caplovitz. *Reports on Happiness*. Chicago: Aldine, 1965.

Instrument

See Instrument V2.2.II.b.

SOCIAL PARTICIPATION INDEX

D. L. Phillips, 1967

Definition of Concept

According to Phillips (1967, p. 480), "Social participation has long been considered important as an index of social integration, reflecting common prescriptions and proscriptions for conduct and beliefs among individuals."

Description of Instrument

The instrument consists of three items that tap frequency of friendship interaction, knowledge of neighbors, and organizational memberships.

Method of Administration

Three items are embedded in an interview schedule. The complete interview schedule can be completed in approximately 60 minutes.

Context of Development

The original questionnaire items were developed for use by the NORC. Phillips (1967) combined the three interview items as a social participation index for use in research on the correlates of happiness.

Sample

The sample consisted of 600 New Hampshire adults, who were interviewed in their homes.

Scoring, Scale Norms, and Distribution

The three items were combined additively to form the Social Participation Index, with scores ranging from 3 to 8. Cutoff points were assigned to each open-ended response that differentiated two levels (organization activity: code 1 = none; code 2 = 1 or 2; contact with friends: code 1 = no contact; code 2 = 1 or 2; code 3 = 3 or more contacts; neighbors: code 1 = no neighbors known; code 2 = 1 to 3 neighbors; code 3 = 4 neighbors).

Usability on Older Populations

The index appears to be usable with older populations.

Sensitivity to Age Differences

"Sex and age were in no way related to social participation" (Phillips, 1967, p. 485).

General Comments and Recommendations

This compact index is well suited to applications involving secondary data analysis, but its reliability and validity have not been evaluated.

Reference

Phillips, D. L. "Social Participation and Happiness." *American Journal of Sociology*, 1967, 72: 479-88.

Instrument

See Instrument V2.2.II.c.

COMPREHENSIVE ROLE LOSS INDEX

I. Rosow, 1967

Definition of Concept

The Comprehensive Role Loss Index is an objective index of changes, resources, and functions in four areas of adult life: (1) marital status, (2) employment, (3) income, and (4) health.

Description of Instrument

The instrument is an index, but the language of individual items is not given in the source (Rosow, 1967).

Method of Administration

The data were collected within a longer interview schedule.

Context of Development

This index was developed as part of a study of social ties and age grading that was sponsored by grants from the Ford Foundation and the Social Security Administration (Rosow, 1967, p. vii).

Sample

A purposive sample of 1,200 apartment dwellers (918 women and 282 men) was drawn from residents of Cleveland, Ohio, to represent different degrees of age concentration. Only older people were sampled: women aged 62 or over and men aged 65 or over (90% of the total sample was over 65). Both working-class (326) and middle-class (874) persons were represented in the sample (Rosow, 1967, p. 44).

Scoring, Scale Norms, and Distribution

The Comprehensive Role Loss Index is based on four variables: marital status, employment, income, and health. According to Rosow (1967, p. 87), "For each of these variables,

TABLE 2-2
Scale Response Patterns for the Comprehensive Role Loss Index

Roll Loss Score	Pattern of Loss (MHWI)	Number of Cases	Score Frequency
4	− − − −	76	76
3	− − − +	66	
3	− − + −	0	
3	− + − −	155	
3	+ − − −	61	282
2	− − + +	0	
2	− + + −	187	
2	− + + −	2	
2	+ − − +	65	
2	+ − + −	13	
2	+ + − −	141	408
1	− + + +	13	
1	+ − + +	22	
1	+ + − +	255	
1	+ + + −	26	286
0	+ + + +	148	148

SOURCE: I. Rosow, personal communication, 1978.

NOTE: M = marital status; H = health; W = work; and I = income. A negative sign implies role loss; a positive sign implies no loss.

we established independent criteria of significant loss of function or status in old age as compared with middle age. The Comprehensive Role Loss Index simply expresses the number of significant losses which the respondent incurred in these four role areas. Consequently, the index varies between scores of zero and four." For analysis, this range was dichotomized to form two categories: low loss (scores 0-2, 842 persons) and high loss (scores 3-4, 358 persons). Table 2-2 lists the patterns of losses in the four roles that yield each index score, the frequency of each pattern, and the total frequency of each score.

Usability on Older Populations

The measure was designed for older respondents.

Sensitivity to Age Differences

Rosow (1967, p. 13) argued that after age 65 there is a steady erosion of social roles in the four areas of life measured by the Comprehensive Role Loss Index and that this erosion becomes relatively sharp after age 75. There is little reversal of role loss. According to Rosow (1967, p. 13), "Once a role is lost, it is seldom recovered."

General Comments and Recommendations

The principles underlying this index are readily adaptable to new research settings. This index has the virtue of providing an objective ex post facto method for measuring changes in the set of social roles that have primary importance in American society.

Reference

Rosow, I. *Social Integration of the Aged.* New York: Free Press, 1967.

Instrument

See Instrument V2.2.II.d.

ACTIVITY INVENTORY

R. S. Cavan, E. W. Burgess, R. J. Havighurst, and H. Goldhammer, 1949

Definition of Concept

The Activity Inventory and the Attitude Inventory (see chapter 5 in the first volume of *Research Instruments in Social Gerontology*), are used as measures of personal and social adjustment. Adjustment refers to the "reorientation of the attitudes and behavior of the person to meet the requirements of a changed situation" (Cavan et al., 1949, p. 10).

Description of Instrument

The Activity Inventory consists of 20 questions, 19 of which are used in the summated scale (questions 18 and 19 are gender specific). The questions address several topics, including leisure, religion, family, friends, economic activity, and health. Even though health status is a different concept than activity level, it was included in this schedule because of the impact of health upon activity (Cavan et al., 1949, p. 137).

Method of Administration

The Activity Inventory can be self-administered or used in a personal interview.

Context of Development

The Activity Inventory was developed as part of one of the earlier studies in social gerontology to examine readjustment (Cavan et al., 1949), and it has been used in the Duke Longitudinal Study of Aging (Jeffers and Nichols, 1961; Heyman and Jeffers, 1964; Maddox, 1965; Palmore, 1968). Though both the Activity Inventory and the Attitude Inventory were developed as holistic measures of adjustment, the separate dimensions of these measures have also been used in later research (e.g., Blazer and Palmore, 1976; Palmore, 1968).

Samples

The development sample included 499 white males and 759 white females over age 60. The median ages for men (73.5) and women (71.1) were somewhat higher than comparable census figures; however, all representatives from all major religious groups and regions of the country were included (Cavan et al., 1949, pp. 46-47, 174-75). An additional sample of 2,743 people was obtained through mail-questionnaire procedures (Cavan et al., 1949, pp. 170-71).

The Duke Longitudinal Study of Aging studied a volunteer panel that initially included 256 residents of the Durham, N.C. area (Busse, 1970, p.5). Attrition in this snowball sample reduced the panel considerably, with only 110 subjects returning from the fourth wave of data collection.

Scoring, Scale Norms, and Distribution

The Activity Inventory is scored as the simple sum of weights derived from a comparison of cases with high and low scores (Cavan et al., 1949, p. 138). In general, response weights (see the instrument) correspond to a simple ordinal scale of frequency, although two items on reading (items 3 and 8) deviate from this general pattern. Scores can range from 0 (low activity) through 50 (highly active).

Five subscales can also be constructed by a summation of response weights for the appropriate items. The subscales are: (1) leisure (items 1-5), (2) religious activity (items 6-8), (3) intimate contacts (items 9-13), (4) health (items 14-17), and (5) security (items 18-20; items 18 and 19 are gender specific in the original formulation). Scores on each of these subscales range from 0 through 10.

Cavan and associates (1949, p. 141) reported that the overall scores on the Activity Inventory ranged from 5 to 43 (with a mean of 25.5 and a standard deviation of 8.8) in their sample of 102 older persons. Palmore (1968, p. 260) reported that the average scores for males ranged from 26.1 to 28.4 across four waves of data in the Duke Longitudinal Study. The averages for females ranged from 28.8 to 31.1. Palmore also presented means for men and women for each of the subscales of the Activity Inventory (1968, p. 260).

Formal Tests of Reliability and Validity

Cavan and associates (1949, pp. 137-41) used an item analysis to eliminate six items that did not discriminate between high- and low-adjustment groups.

Split-half reliability (Spearman-Brown formula) was estimated as .66 (Cavan et al., 1949, p. 138). Palmore (1968, p. 261) reported correlations of activity reports over four waves (10 years) of data. These correlations range from .27 (waves I and IV) to .57 (waves I and II; II and III) for men and from .56 (waves I and IV) to .79 (waves III and IV for women).

Correlations of the Activity Inventory and the Attitude Inventory have been reported by several investigators. Cavan and associates (1949, p. 132) reported a correlation of .78 in a sample of 102 older persons. Havighurst (1951, p. 25) also reported a correlation of .78 in a study of 98 older residents of a small midwestern town. Jeffers and Nichols (1961, p. 68) obtained a correlation of .54 with 245 volunteers in the Duke Longitudinal Study of Aging.

Cavan and associates (1949, pp. 141-42) reported these correlations of the scale and subscales of the Activity Inventory with an observerated checklist and portrait score: (1) Activity Inventory (r = .65); (2) religion (r = .31); (3) security (r = .33); (4) intimate contacts (r = .37); (5) leisure (r = .38); and (6) health (r = .41).

Jeffers and Nichols (1961, p. 68) reported a biserial correlation of .39 between the Activity Inventory and a measure of physical functioning.

Usability on Older Populations

The instrument was developed and tested for use with older populations, and it appears to be sensitive to the unique concerns of older adults.

Sensitivity to Age Differences

Palmore (1968) presented data that indicate small reductions in activity over the 10 years of the Duke Longitudinal Study. These reductions are greater for women than for men. Maddox (1965, p. 121), in analyzing the relationship of age to activity level in each of two waves of the Duke Longitudinal Study, reported small declines in activity with age *at any one point in time* and yet consistency *across points in time*

General Comments and Recommendations

The Activity Inventory was one of the first multimodal measures of social participation constructed and used in gerontological research. It is also one of the few for which longitudinal data are available. However, one may well question the theoretical framework of this measure insofar as social participation is seen as a *component of adjustment*, rather than a *determinant of adjustment*. Furthermore, the utility of including a subscale on health status as a component of activity is unclear. This too might best be seen as a determinant of activity and adjustment.

Though social norms regarding women's participation in the labor force probably justified the use (in 1949) of gender-specific items in the security subscale, the long-term increase in female employment may well make this distinction obsolete or biased. One plausible resolution would be to use items 18 and 19 for both men and women. This, however, would change the distributional properties of the summated Activity Inventory.

Further analyses that examine and test the five-dimension conceptual structure of this instrument are certainly recommended.

References

Blazer, D., and E. Palmore. "Religion and Aging in a Longitudinal Panel." *The Gerontologist*, 1976, 16: 82-85.

Busse, E. W. "A Physiological, Psychological, and Sociological Study of Aging." In *Normal Aging*, E. Palmore (ed.), pp. 3-6. Durham, N.C.: Duke University Press, 1970.

Cavan, R. S., E. W. Burgess, R. J. Havighurst, and H. Goldhammer. *Personal Adjustment in Old Age*. Chicago: Science Research Associates, 1949.

Havighurst, R. J. "Validity of the Chicago Attitude Inventory as a Measure of Personal Adjustment in Old Age." *Journal of Abnormal and Social Psychology*, 1951, 46: 24-29.

Heyman, D. K., and F. C. Jeffers. "Study of the Relative Influence of Race and Socio-economic Status upon the Activities and Attitudes of a Southern Aged Population." *Journal of Gerontology*, 1964, 19: 225-29.

Jeffers, F. C., and C. R. Nichols. "The Relationship of Activities and Attitudes to Physical Well-being in Older People." *Journal of Gerontology*, 1961, 16: 67-70.

Maddox, G. L. "Fact and Artifact: Evidence Bearing on Disengagement Theory from the Duke Geriatrics Project." *Human Development*, 1965, 8: 117-30.

Palmore, E. "The Effects of Aging on Activities and Attitudes." *The Gerontologist*, 1968, 8 (4): 259-63.

————, (ed.). *Normal Aging*. Durham, N.C.: Duke University Press, 1970.

Instrument

See Instrument V2.2.II.e.

SOCIAL PARTICIPATION SCALE

F. S. Chapin, 1939

Definition of Concept

This scale was designed to measure both the number and the intensity of community social involvements.

Description of Instrument

Chapin's Social Participation Scale weighted together both the number of groups a family was involved in and the extent of their involvement in each group. Husbands' and wives' scores were combined to represent a total family score. The respondent lists the clubs and organizations in which some degree of participation is manifest. For each club or organization named, the respondent is asked to specify the kind of involvement (such as membership, attendance at meetings, financial contribution, committee membership, and offices held).

Method of Administration

Questions are asked in a personal interview. Questions related to the Social Participation Scale take only 10 to 15 minutes, but Chapin's complete interview schedule took approximately 60 minutes to complete.

Context of Development

Chapin's Social Participation Scale was developed as part of research on the correlates of social participation, funded by the Graduate School of the University of Minnesota. A number of studies done by Chapin and his associates pursued several different research questions, including the relationship between social participation and social intelligence.

Sample

Several purposive samples were collected by Chapin and his associates, primarily from among University of Minnesota students, residents of neighborhoods with diverse social-class characteristics in Minneapolis, and persons in various identifiable social positions in the Twin Cities community (Chapin, 1939).

Scoring, Scale Norms, and Distribution

The several levels of intensity of social participation were assigned integer weights as follows: (1) membership, (2) attendance, (3) contributions, (4) membership on committees, and (5) position as an officer. Cumulative scores for all the groups and organizations participated in were aggregated separately for husbands and wives, and they were averaged together to represent the extent and intensity of social participation by the family. Arithmetic mean scores for selected categories of interviewees ranged from 6.2 to 64.6.

Formal Tests of Reliability/Homogeneity

Test-retest reliability using a time interval of one week and 77 introductory sociology students was .89. Test-retest reliability using a time interval of several months and 171 slum families was .88. Correlations between scale items for 58 subjects ranged from .36 to .89 (Chapin, 1939, p. 159).

General Comments and Recommendations

This objective social participation scale is simple to administer and score.

Reference

Chapin, F. S. "Social Participation and Social Intelligence." *American Sociological Review*, 1939, 4: 157-66.

Instrument

See Instrument V2.2.III.a.

GENERAL COMMUNITY PARTICIPATION SCALE

J. M. Foskett, 1955

Definition of Concept

The General Community Participation Scale was developed as a way to measure formal and informal social participation of several kinds.

Description of Instrument

The General Community Participation Scale is an index based on 16 items: (1) voting in elections; discussion of educational affairs with: (2) family, (3) friends, (4) officials; discussion of governmental affairs with: (5) family, (6) friends, (7) officials; discussions of civic affairs with: (8) family, (9) friends, (10) officials; (11) membership in organizations; (12) membership in associations; (13) active on educational issues; (14) active on governmental issues; (15) attending community affairs meetings; and (16) associating with community officials and leaders.

Method of Administration

The 16 items are dispersed in an interview schedule. Interviewers were trained graduate students who were supervised in the field.

Context of Development

The General Community Participation Scale was developed as part of an interdisciplinary study of policy formation.

Sample

A random sample of 1,012 men and women aged from under 21 to over 70 years was drawn from two Oregon towns of 40,000 and 16,000 population.

Scoring, Scale Norms, and Distribution

Each item answered affirmatively or with frequency of activity above a criterion level (not specified) was scored 1 point on the 16-item index. Observed scores were highly skewed, with 66.9% of the sample reporting scales scores of 3 or less (Foskett, 1955, p. 432).

Usability on Older Populations

The instrument is usable with older samples.

Sensitivity to Age Differences

The significant inverse correlation between age and scores is substantially reduced when the educational level of participants is held constant.

General Comments and Recommendations

This index appears to generate considerable variance through its use of objective indicator items. Further scale development, including formal studies of reliability and validity, seems warranted.

Reference

Foskett, J. M. "Social Structure and Social Participation." *American Sociological Review*, 1955, 20: 431-38.

Instrument

This measure has not been published. For a general description of its contents, see the original source and the description of the instrument above.

INTERACTION INDEX

E. Cumming and W. E. Henry, 1961

Definition of Concept

According to Cumming and Henry (1961), "the Interaction Index is a subjective rating, assigned to each respondent, of the amount of each day spent in normatively governed inter-action with others" (p. 38) and "the Interaction Index is essentially an indication of the saturation of the daily life with interaction and says nothing about variety of roles or num-bers interacted with" (p. 243).

Description of Instrument

Two raters assign subjective judgments based on responses to two questions: "I would like you to tell me what a typical day is like for you" and "What is a typical weekend like?" Low scores reflect low levels of interaction.

Method of Administration

The two questions that formed the Interaction Index ratings were imbedded in a larger interview schedule.

Context of Development

This index was developed as part of the Kansas City Study of Adult Life.

Samples

Two samples were used. The first was based on a random sampling of 8,700 dwelling units in Kansas City. An initial panel of 172 (88 men, 84 women) was defined; it was re-duced to 129 by the fifth wave of interviews. Persons aged 48 to 68 were included in the sample, but blacks and persons who were chronically ill were not included. A second sample of 107 persons (50 men, 57 women) aged 70 years or older was added during the third wave of interviews to extend the age range of the original panel. Approximately 39% of the sec-ond sample reported impaired health.

Scoring, Scale Norms, and Distribution

The judges rating the interview protocols scored them on a scale from 1 through 5 in accordance with the relative amounts of interaction reported by the interviewees. Of the sample 58% were rated in the two lowest categories of interaction.

Formal Tests of Reliability/Homogeneity

A check on the agreement of the two judges yielded a contingency coefficient of .80.

Formal Tests of Validity

No formal analysis of the validity of this index was presented by Cumming and Henry. However, evidence of convergent validity is present in the strength of the correlations be-tween this measure and the other social participation measures reviewed in this section. Evidence of discriminate validity is available in the low correlations between these measures and measures of concepts that are unrelated to social participation. For a more detailed analysis, see Appendix 4 in Cumming and Henry (1961).

Usability on Older Populations

The instrument was developed specifically for use with an older population.

Sensitivity to Age Differences

Evidence of age-related differences in the scores of persons aged 50 and over was pre-sented by Cumming and Henry. The differences are most evident after age 65, where the proportion of interviewees with interaction scores of 3, 4, or 5 drops from approximately 60% to 45%, ultimately to decline to 15% in the 75-and-over age category (Cumming and Henry, 1961, p. 40).

General Comments and Recommendations

This simple ex post facto rating has the advantage of being usable without requiring a substantial amount of interview time or a large number of questions. Although evidence of reliability and validity demonstrates good potential, the rating is subject to all of the caveats usually associated with using subjective evaluations of behavior as scientific measurements.

Reference

Cumming, E. and W. E. Henry. *Growing Old*. New York: Basic Books, 1961.

Instrument

See the description of the instrument above.

ROLE COUNT INDEX

E. Cumming and W. E. Henry, 1961

Definition of Concept

The Role Count Index represents an inventory of the number of relationships in which an older person is currently active.

Description of Instrument

The Role Count Index involves eight items tapping the following roles: (1) household, (2) relatives, (3) friends, (4) neighbors, (5) fellow workers, (6) specific others, (7) church, and (8) organizations (Cumming and Henry, 1961, pp. 248-50).

Method of Administration

The questions that form the basis of this index were embedded in a larger interview schedule.

Context of Development

This index was developed as part of the Kansas City Study of Adult Life.

Samples

For a description of the samples used in the initial deployment of this index, see the abstract on Cumming and Henry's (1961) Interaction Index.

Scoring, Scale Norms, and Distribution

The Role Count Index is scored by combining the eight-item response scores. Of the sample of 211 respondents, 44% reported involvement in five or six roles (Cumming and Henry, 1961, p. 250).

Formal Tests of Validity

No formal analysis of the validity of this index was reported by Cumming and Henry. However, indirect evidence of convergent validity and discriminant validity is available in Tables 4-1 through 4-3 (Cumming and Henry, 1961).

Usability on Older Populations

The instrument was developed specifically for use with an older population.

Sensitivity to Age Differences

Cumming and Henry presented an extensive analysis of the sensitivity of the Role Count Index to age differences and of age-specific patterns of difference among component items. The age differences for the Role Count Index scores are most evident after age 65, where the proportion of interviewees with six or more roles declines from approximately 60% to 40%, ultimately to decline to only 8% for the 75-and-over age category (Cumming and Henry, 1961, p. 40).

General Comments and Recommendations

The Role Count Index provides a useful technique for measuring the range of social relationships in an older person's life.

Reference

Cumming, E. and W. E. Henry. *Growing Old.* New York: Basic Books, 1961.

Instrument

See Instrument V2.2.III.d.

SOCIAL LIFESPACE MEASURE

E. Cumming and W. E. Henry, 1961

Definition of Concept

According to Cumming and Henry (1961, p. 47), "Social Lifespace, is a composite . . . , a quantitative estimate of the numbers of discrete contacts with others which the respondent has in a month."

Description of Instrument

This measure was not operationalized until the third wave of a panel study, and for this reason the interview items refer to previous interviews. Six interview items assessed the following dimensions: (1) household, (2) relatives, (3) confidants, (4) neighbors, (5) work, and (6) specific others.

Method of Administration

The questions that form the basis of the Social Lifespace Measure were embedded in a larger interview schedule.

Context of Development

This measure was developed as part of the Kansas City Study of Adult Life.

Samples

For a description of samples used in the initial development of the Social Lifespace Measure, see the abstract on the Interaction Index (Cumming and Henry, 1961).

Scoring, Scale Norms, and Distribution

The six items were weighted in a composite measure in the following manner (Cumming and Henry, 1961, pp. 246-47).

1. Number of household:
   Assuming daily interaction with *each* other person in the household, each person (other than the respondent) listed is multiplied by 30 (days).
2. Relatives:
   Each relative mentioned is given a score as follows:

If seen every day	score 30
If seen once a week	score 4
If seen a few times a month	score 3
If seen once a month	score 1
If seen anything less	score 0

3. Friends:
   Each friend mentioned is given a score as follows:

If seen every day	score 30

If seen once a week   score 4
If seen a few times a month   score 3
If seen once a month   score 1
If seen anything less   score 0

4. Neighbors (based on neighbor seen most frequently):
   If seen every day   score 30
   If seen at least once a week   score 4
   If seen a few times a month   score 3
   If seen anything less   score 0

5. Fellow Workers:
   Number of fellow workers multiplied by 20. (This assumes daily interaction, approximately 20 days per month.)

6. Specific People:
   Number stated multiplied by 4. (This assumes that when asked this question, the respondents thought in terms of number seen per week. There is some empirical evidence for this assumption.)

Formal Tests of Validity

No formal analysis of the validity of the Social Lifespace Measure was reported by Cumming and Henry. However, indirect evidence of convergent validity and discriminant validity is available in Tables 4-1 through 4-3 (Cumming and Henry, 1961).

Usability on Older Populations

The measure was developed specifically for use with an older population.

Sensitivity to Age Differences

A regular regression to low values across age categories is evident in the data (Cumming and Henry, 1961, p. 40). A difference of 50% in mean score is evident in the comparison of the age category 60 to 64 (68 points) to the 65 to 69 age category (32 points). Among persons aged 75 and over, the mean Social Lifespace score reached a low value (18 points).

General Comments and Recommendations

This measure was developed to provide an objective way of estimating the number of social contacts an older person has on a month-by-month basis.

Reference

Cumming, E. and W. E. Henry. *Growing Old*. New York: Basic Books, 1961.

Instrument

See Instrument V2.2.III.e.

Instruments

V2.2.I.a

ADJUSTMENT RATING SCALES

R. J. Havighurst and R. Albrecht, 1953

1. Primary or personal, intimate contacts

0	1	2	3	4	5	6	7	8	9
Alone in world; no family, relatives, friends.	Infrequent contacts; perhaps lives alone; sees family sometimes; or lives with, but not closely incorporated.			Frequent contacts or lives with and is functioning member of intimate groups.		Almost daily contacts; helps determine group actions.		Daily contacts; group probably of long standing; closely incorporated into group life; important in determining group actions.	

2. Secondary or more formal specialized contacts

0	1	2	3	4	5	6	7	8	9
In no groups, no reading, no radio. Complete social isolation	Perhaps one group or irregular group contacts; occasional radio.			Several groups, regular participation, some reading or radio, probably favorite programs.		More than several groups; regular participation, chief interest is these contacts; much reading, radio, television.		Time filled with many groups, much reading, many radio programs. Always on the go or occupied with reading, radio.	

SOURCE: R. J. Havighurst and R. Albrecht. *Older People*. New York: Longmans, Green and Company, 1953, p. 408. Reprinted by permission of author and David McKay Company.

V2.2.II.a

ROLE ACTIVITIES IN LATER MATURITY

R. J. Havighurst and R. Albrecht, 1953

Role Activities in Family Relationships

Item 1:   Great-grandparents

0   No interest in great-grandchildren; rejects them.
1   No interest in great-grandchildren; too ill or too old to care.
3   Little knowledge of or interest in great-grandchildren.
4   Hears from or about great-grandchildren occasionally.
5   Sees and hears from great-grandchildren occasionally; some social participation.
6   Active communication with great-grandchildren by letters, messages, and some visits.
7   Active social participation but no responsibility.
8   Benevolent, gift-giving, or loving, with partial or occasional responsibility.
9   Shares or assumes most of responsibility for great-grandchildren.

Item 2:   Grandparents

0   No interest in grandchildren; rejects them.
1   No interest in grandchildren; too ill or too old to care.
2   Only conscious of existence of grandchildren; does not know them.
3   Little knowledge of or interest in grandchildren.
4   Hears from or about grandchildren occasionally.
5   Active social participation but no responsibility for grandchildren.
6   Occasional responsibility for grandchildren, e.g., baby-sitting.
7   Partial responsibility for care of grandchildren, e.g., while mother works.
8   Almost complete responsibility for grandchildren. One or both parents share responsibility.
9   Complete, full-time responsibility for grandchildren.

Item 3: Parents

0 Never visited by children. No interest in children; rejects them.
1 No interest in children; too old or too ill to care.
2 Knows little about children, where they are, etc. Seldom hears from them.
3 Sees children occasionally, or depends upon children.
4 Shares children's homes; somewhat burdensome.
5 Shares home of children; a help rather than a burden.
6 Slight dependence of children; some responsibility for them.
7 Responsible for children full- or part-time (child dependent).
8 Independent, occasional advice to children or needs their advice. Child may live with parent.
9 Mutual independence, but close social and affectional relationship.

Item 4: Home Responsibilities

0 In institution; care given by others. No responsibility.
1 In boarding or rooming house. No responsibility.
2 Lives with children or relatives; has no responsibility.
3 Lives with family or in institution; does odd tasks.
4 Assists children with upkeep or work in the home.
5 Shares home with children; also responsibility. If in institution, takes care of self.
6 Nominal head of household; responsibility carried by children or others.
7 Head of house; children or others take few responsibilities.
8 Shares responsibility for home with spouse or others, but has own tasks.
9 Independent; takes full responsibility for home.

Item 5: Kinship Group or Extended Family

0 No interest in or contact with any relative.
1 Has no living relatives.
2 Distant relatives; knows about them but shows little interest.
3 Little contact with relatives; correspondence, word of mouth, messages, etc.
4 Some social and affectional contact with nieces, nephews, brothers, sisters and other relatives.
5 Frequent contact with relatives for holidays, family reunions, etc.
6 Frequent social contact; more often than just special occasions.
7 Exchanges visits with or writes to relatives; close family feelings.
8 Close family feeling; help during illness, and frequent communication.
9 Very close social and affectional relationship with family and extended kinship group. Travel to visit, etc.

Role Activities in Group and Individual Relationships

Item 6: Clubs: Social

0 No memberships; no interest at all.
1 No memberships; passive interest, e.g., reads about meetings, etc.
2 Member; does not attend.
3 Member; seldom attends.
4 Member; attends frequently. Non-member but frequently visits.
5 Member; always attends, but says little.
6 Active participant; expresses opinion or works for organization, but holds no office.
7 Active participant; holds minor office, e.g., committee member.
8 Leadership position; active in more than one organization, e.g., officer or chairman of committee.
9 Leadership; holds important office in one or more organizations, e.g., president or secretary.

Item 7:   Clubs: Business

0   No memberships; no interest at all.
1   No memberships; passive interest.
2   Member; does not attend.
3   Member; seldom attends.
4   Member; attends frequently.
5   Member; always attends, but says little.
6   Active participant; expresses opinion, but holds no office.
7   Active participant; holds minor office, e.g., committee member.
8   Leadership position; active in more than one organization, e.g., officer or chairman of committee.
9   Leadership; holds important office in one or more organizations, e.g., president or secretary.

Item 8:   Church Activities

0   Rejects all church connections. No interest in religion.
1   No church affiliation or attendance.
2   Member of church; never attends.
3   Member; seldom attends.
4   Member; attends frequently, or nonmember but devout.
5   Member; faithful in attendance. No responsibility.
6   Member; active churchgoer. Opinion valued. No office.
7   Active churchgoer; holds minor office, e.g., committee member.
8   Responsible position; active worker. High office, e.g., deacon, president of Men's Club or Ladies' Aid.

Item 9:   Peer Relationships

0   No interest in peers or former friends.
1   Very seldom visits with peers or friends and acquaintances.
2   Seldom visited by acquaintances. (Once or twice a year.)
3   Occasionally visited by acquaintances.
4   Visited frequently. Hears from some friends via cards, etc.
5   Some exchange of visits with acquaintances. Exchange of Xmas greetings, etc.
6   Frequent exchange of visits. May take initiative in visiting locally.
7   Frequent exchange of visits with friends near home. (Within ten miles.)
8   Very active peer participation; keeps up by phone, mail, or personal visits within fifty miles of home.
9   Very active peer participation; keeps up by phone, mail, or personal visits locally and in distant places.

Item 10:   Clique and Small Group Activities

Single

0   Associates with no one.
1   Associates with few people; never in a social way.
2   Scattered social contacts in non-intimate groups, e.g., cigar store hangout.
3   Scattered social contacts in individual relationships. No clique groups.
4   Associates in social groups open to anyone; usually with people of own sex.
5   Visits families in their homes. No other social group activity.
6   Participation mainly in small same-sex groups.
7   Participation in organizations both sexes attended.
8   Participates freely in any social activity; without partner.
9   May initiate social activity. May attend social functions with partner.

Married

0 Never seen together.
1 Seen together occasionally; no social participation as a couple.
2 Scattered individual social contacts in non-intimate groups.
3 Scattered individual social contacts in small intimate groups.
4 Husband and wife may be visited by people in their home. Do not go out.
5 Husband and wife share fairly active social life; mutual friends. Visit others.
6 Extensive participation in social life; no clique groups.
7 Extensive participation in social life; couple-clique participation.
8 Busy and varied social life; always together.
9 Busy and varied social life; together or in separate interests, e.g., man to Rotary.

Role Activities in the Community

Item 11:   Civic Activity

0 No interest in community affairs; no participation.
1 Slight interest in community affairs; no participation.
2 Occasionally votes in local elections, e.g., when personal issues arise.
3 Always votes in national elections; no other participation.
4 Votes; never attends community meetings but keeps up by reading about them.
5 Occasionally attends open meetings; reads about and discusses community affairs.
6 Votes; will talk and work for special projects.
7 Will accept minor responsibility, e.g., committee member.
8 Holds position of leadership, e.g., alderman.
9 Holds high position of responsibility and fulfills its duties, e.g., mayor.

Item 12: Business or Occupation

0 Retired; unable to work.
1 Retired and/or does odd jobs occasionally.
2 Works regularly in job of lower rating, e.g., janitor or watchman.
3 Works as before but part-time, e.g., helps out at store.
4 Retired and living on fixed income, e.g., pension or savings.
5 Employed full-time, but is marginal to the job; retained because of long connection or employment.
6 Works full-time on a job which is fairly routine; or works as before with general diminution of responsibility.
7 Retired. Still managing own properties.
8 Works full-time in business or profession, diminution of responsibility.
9 Works at job or profession at peak plateau of career; no diminution of responsibility or activity.

SOURCE: R. J. Havighurst and R. Albrecht. *Older People.* New York: Longmans, Green and Company, 1953, pp. 376-80. Reprinted by permission of author and David McKay Company.

V2.2.II.b

PARTICIPATION INDEX

N. M. Bradburn and D. Caplovitz, 1965

Item 1:   "One of the things we'd like to know is how people spend their time. For instance, are you a member of any clubs, organizations, or community groups? (If yes) How many?"

Item 2:   "On the average last week, how many times a day did you chat with friends on the telephone?

None	0
Less than once a day	1
Once a day	2
Twice a day	3
Three times a day	4
Four or more times a day (write number)"	5

Item 3: "(During last week) what was the farthest distance you went from your home other than going to work? (Approximate number of miles one way.)

Did not leave house	0	50 - 99.9 miles	7
Less than 1 mile	1	100 - 199.9 miles	8
1 - 2.49 miles	2	200 or more miles"	9
2.50 - 4.9 miles	3		
5.0 - 9.9 miles	4		
10 - 24.9 miles	5		
25 - 49.9 miles	6		

Item 4: "One of the things we'd like to know is how people spend time. For instance, are you a member of any clubs, organizations, or community groups? (If yes) How many meetings did you go to last week?

None	0
One	1
Two	2
Three	3
More than three (specify)"	4

Item 5: "Now how about friends other than relatives? Did you get together with any friends—I mean things like going out together or visiting in each other's homes?

Not at all	0
Once	1
Twice	2
Three times	3
Four or more times (write number)"	4

Item 6: "Here are some things that people do. Would you tell me if you did any of them last week and, if so, about how often you did them?" Respondent is handed a card containing a list of ten items. The eighth item reads as follows: "Go for a trip in the car

Not at all	0
Once	1
Several times	2
Every day	3
More than once a day"	4

Item 7: "Here are some things that people do. Would you tell me if you did any of them last week and, if so, about how often you did them?" Respondent is handed a card containing a list of ten items. The tenth item reads as follows: "Eat in a restaurant

Not at all	0
Once	1
Several times	2
Every day	3
More than once a day?"	4

SOURCE: N. M. Bradburn and D. Caplovitz. *Reports on Happiness*. Chicago: Aldine, 1965, p. 45.

V2.2.II.c

SOCIAL PARTICIPATION INDEX

D. L. Phillips, 1967

Item 1:   "During the past few weeks how many times did you get together with friends — I mean things like going out together or visiting in each other's homes?"

Item 2:   "About how many neighbors around here do you know well enough to visit with?"

Item 3:   "How many organizations such as church and school groups, labor unions, or social, civic and fraternal clubs do you take an active part in?"

SOURCE: D. L. Phillips. "Social Participation and Happiness." *American Journal of Sociology*, 1967, 72: 480.

V2.2.II.d

COMPREHENSIVE ROLE LOSS INDEX

I. Rosow, 1967

Variable (with items)	"Loss" Response	"Stable" Response
1. *Marital Status* Are you now single, married, widowed, divorced, or separated?	Widowed, divorced, or separated *after* age 48	Married, single, OR young-widowed-divorced-separated *before* age 48
2. *Health* Has your health become better or worse in the last 5 years, or is it about the same?	Worse, with health scale* score 3-6	Better, same, OR worse with health scale* score 1-2
3. *Work* All respondents except stable *young-widowed-divorced-separated* (re: chief breadwinner). Is he usually working now? Full-time or part-time?	Deceased, part-time, not working	Full-time, question not applicable
Young-widowed-divorced-separated, respondent is chief breadwinner. As above.	Not working	Full-time, part-time, question not applicable
Young-widowed-divorced-separated, spouse is chief breadwinner. Are you working now or not? Full-time or part-time? Are you retired, too sick, or (women) haven't you ever worked?	Retired, too sick, temporarily not working	Housewife, question not applicable
4. *Income* All in all, are you better	Worse now	Better now, same, question

Variable (with items)	"Loss" Response	"Stable" Response
4. *Income* off now or worse off financially than you were 20 years ago?		applicable

SOURCE: I. Rosow. *Social Integration of the Aged*. New York: Free Press, 1967, p. 48.
*See Chapter 3 of Volume 3, Measures of Health by Sidney Stahl, for the Guttman Health Scale.

V2.2.II.e

ACTIVITY INVENTORY

R. S. Cavan, E. W. Burgess, R. J. Havighurst, and H. Goldhammer, 1949

1. What do you do in your free time?

Work in and around the house. . . _____
Work in garden or yard. . . . . . . _____
Farm work. . . . . _____
Attend movies. . . . . _____
Attend theatres, lectures,
   concerts . . . . _____
Shop . . . . _____
Attend clubs, lodges, other
   meetings. . . . . _____
Sew, crochet, or knit . . . . _____
Read . . . . _____
Just sit and think . . . . _____
Other (what?) _____

Work on some hobby. . . . . . . _____
Listen to the radio . . . . _____
Write letters . . . . _____
Write books, articles, poems,
   etc.. . . . . _____
Participate in community or
   church work . . . . _____
Play golf, other sports . . . . . . _____
Play cards or other table
   games. . . . . _____
Take rides . . . . _____
Visit or entertain friends. . . . . . _____

("Just sit and think [0] *; one to five items, exclusive of "Just sit and think" [1] ; six or more items, exclusive of "Just sit and think" [2] .)

2. List the hobbies or favorite pastimes you now have _____

(No hobbies listed or no reply [0] ; one to two items listed [1] ; three or more items listed [2] .)

3. How much time each day do you spend in reading?

Never read . . . .(0)
A few minutes. . . . .(0)
An hour or more . . . .(2)
Practically all day . . . .(1)

4. To how many organizations, such as clubs, lodges, unions, and the like, do you now belong?

None . . . .(0)
One. . . . .(1)
Two. . . . .(1)
Three . . . .(2)
Four or more . . . .(2)

5. How many club meetings do you usually attend each month?

None . . . .(0)
Less than one a month . . . . . .(0)

One or two a month . . . .(1)
One a week . . . .(2)
Twice a week or oftener . . . . . .(2)

6. How often do you attend religious services?

Never. . . . .(0)
Less than once a month . . . . . .(1)
Once or twice a month . . . .(2)
Once a week. . . . .(3)
Twice a week or oftener . . . . . .(4)

7. Do you listen to church services over the radio?

Never. . . . .(0)
Once in a while . . . .(1)
About once or twice a week. . . . (2)
Three or more times a week . . . .(3)

8. How often do you read the Prayer Book, Bible, or other religious books?

Never. . . . .(0)
Less than once a week . . . . . . (1)
Once a week. . . . .(3)
Every day . . . .(2)

9. With whom are you living?

With husband or wife. . . . . . .(2)　　　With parents. . . . .(0)
With husband or wife and children (2)　　With relatives . . . .(0)
With children alone. . . . .(0)　　　With friends . . . .(0)
　　　　　　　　　　　　　　　　　　　Alone. . . . .(0)
Others (who are they?)_____　　_____ (0)

10. How often do you see some of your family or close relatives?

Less than once a year. . . . . . .(0)　　Every day . . . .(2)
About one a month. . . . . (0)　　Have no family or relatives. . .(0)
Once or twice a week. . . . . . .(1)

11. If you have a family or close relatives, do they neglect you?

Yes, completely. . . . .(0)
A little . . . .(1)
Not at all. . . . .(2)

12. Do you see your friends more or less often now than when you were 55 years old?

Less often now . . . .(0)
About the same . . . .(1)
More often now. . . . .(2)

13. Do you often see or hear from children or young people who are friends?
(Include nieces, nephews, grandchildren.)

Less than once a year. . . . . . .(0)　　Every day . . . .(2)
A few times a year . . . .(0)　　Have no friends among children
Once or twice a month . . . . . .(1)　　　or young people . . . . . .(0)
About once a week . . . .(1)

14. What are your serious physical problems?

Poor sight . . . . ._____　　General rheumatic stiffness . . . ._____
Blind or nearly so. . . . . ._____　　Heart trouble . . . . ._____
Hard of hearing . . . . ._____　　Stomach trouble . . . . ._____

Deaf or nearly so . . . . High blood pressure. . . . .
Crippled arms, hands or legs. . . . . . No physical problems. . . . .
Other (what is it?) _____

("No physical problems" [4] ; one item checked, exclusive of "No physical problems" [1] ;
two ore more items checked, exclusive of "No physical problems" [0] .)

15. Below is a list of difficulties that people often have. Check those that trouble you.

Shortness of breath at night . . . _____ Difficulty in urination . . . . _____
Shortness of breath after   Constipation. . . . . _____
 slight exercise. . . . . _____ Aching joints . . . . _____
Heartburn . . . . _____ Backache. . . . . _____
Swelling of feet or legs . . . . . . _____ Gas pains. . . . . _____
Feeling tired. . . . . _____ Belching . . . . _____
Have had nervous breakdown . . _____ Headaches . . . . _____
              No difficulties. . . . . _____

("No difficulties" [2] ; one item checked, exclusive of "No difficulties" [1] ; two or more
items checked, exclusive of "No Difficulties" [0] .)

16. How many days did you spend in bed last year?

All the time . . . .(0)
A month or more . . . .(0)
Two to four weeks . . . .(0)
A few days. . . . .(1)
None . . . .(2)

17. Which of the following things often trouble you?

Sleeplessness. . . . . _____ Nervousness . . . . _____
Bad dreams . . . . _____ Dislike noise. . . . . _____
Tire too easily . . . . _____ Worry about my health. . . . . . _____
Food doesn't taste good . . . . . _____ Forgetfulness . . . . _____
Feel blue. . . . . _____ Troubled with none of these. . . _____

("Troubled with none of these" [2] ; one item checked, exclusive of "Troubled with none of
these" [1] ; two or more items checked, exclusive of "Troubled with none of these" [0] .)

18. Are you working now?

Yes, full-time . . . .(5)
Yes, part-time . . . .(2)
No . . . .(0)

19. If you are a woman, are you taking care of your home?

No . . . .(0)
Do a little or help someone else .(2)
Do everything myself. . . . . . .(5)
Other (what?) . . . .(0)

20. What things have you had to do since the age of 55 because of lowered income?

Gave up my home. . . . . _____ Gave up clubs . . . . _____
Moved to less expensive home. . _____ Bought less expensive clothes . . . _____
Stopped going to church . . . . . _____ Stopped taking vacations. . . . . . _____
Bought less expensive foods . . . _____ Gave up auto or bought cheaper
Couldn't keep home or fur-   car . . . . _____
 nishings in repair. . . . . . . _____ Have not had to do any of
Other (what?) _____ these. . . . . _____

("Have not had to do any of these" [5] ; one or more items checked, exclusive of "Have not had to do any of these" [0].)

SOURCE: R. S. Cavan, E. W. Burgess, R. J. Havighurst, and H. Goldhammer. *Personal Adjustment in Old Age*. Chicago: Science Research Associates, 1949, pp. 183-87.
*Scale values for each item are given in parentheses following responses.

V2.2.III.a

SOCIAL PARTICIPATION SCALE

F. S. Chapin, 1939

1. List by name the organizations with which the husband and wife are affiliated (at the present time) as indicated by the five types of participation No. 1 to No. 5 across the top of the schedule. It is not necessary to enter the date at which the person became a member of the organization. It is important to enter L if the membership is in a purely local group, and to enter N if the membership is in a local unit of some state or national organization.
2. An organization means some active or organized grouping, usually but not necessarily in the community or neighborhood of residence, such as club, lodge, business or political or professional or religious organization, labor union, etc.; subgroups of a church or other institution are to be included separately *provided they are organized* as more or less independent entities.
3. Recorded under attendance the mere fact of attendance or non-attendance without regard to the number of meetings attended (corrections for the number attended *have not* been found to influence the final score sufficiently to justify such labor).
4. Record under contributions the mere fact of financial contributions or absence of contributions, and *not the amount* (corrections for amount of contributions, *have not* been found to influence the final score sufficiently to justify such labor).
5. Previous memberships, committee work, offices held, etc., should *not be* counted or recorded or used in computing the final score.
6. Final score is computed by counting each membership as 1, each attended as 2, each contributed to as 3, each committee membership as 4, and each office held as 5. If both parents are living regularly in the home, add their total scores and divide the sum by two. The result is the mean social participation *score* of the family. In case only one parent lives in the home, as widow, widower, etc., the sum of that one person's participations is the score for the family (unless it is desired to obtain scores on children also).

SOCIAL PARTICIPATION SCALE

Address_____   Case No. _____
Age _____ Education _____ Race or Nationality _____
Occupation_____Income _____

Name of Organization	1. Member[a]	2. Attendance	3. Financial Contributions	4. Member of Committees Not Named	5. Offices Held
1. ___					
2. ___					
3. ___					

4. _____
5. _____
6. _____
7. _____
8. _____
9. _____
10._____
Totals
_____

[a]Enter L if purely local group; enter N if a local unit of a state or national organization.

SOURCE: F. S. Chapin. "Social Participation and Social Intelligence." *American Sociological Review*, 1939, 4: 169.

V2.2.III.b

GENERAL COMMUNITY PARTICIPATION SCALE

J. M. Foskett, 1955

This measure has not been published. For a general description of its contents, see the original source and the description of the instrument in the abstract.

V2.2.III.c

INTERACTION INDEX

E. Cumming and W. E. Henry, 1961

See the description of the instrument in the abstract.

V2.2.III.d

ROLE COUNT INDEX

E. Cumming and W. E. Henry, 1961

Item 1:   Number of household: If only one person other than the respondent who lives in the household, count 1. For two or more people, count 2.

Item 2:   Relatives: For each category of relatives mentioned in Interview 1, count 1. If none, count 0.

Item 3:   Friends: Count 1 if any friends are mentioned, 0 if none are mentioned.

Item 4:   Neighbors: As for friends (above).

Item 5:   Fellow workers: Score 1 if employed, 0 if unemployed.

Item 6:   Specific people (shopper, customer, etc.): Score 1 if any mentioned, 0 if none are mentioned.

Item 7:   Church: Score 1 for membership, 0 if not a member.

Item 8:   Organizations: Score 1 for each attended, 0 if none.
_____

SOURCE: E. Cumming and W. E. Henry. *Growing Old*. New York: Basic Books, 1961.

V2.2.III.e

SOCIAL LIFESPACE MEASURE

E. Cumming and W. E. Henry, 1961

Item 1:   When you were last interviewed, there were (number in household) living here. Are the same number of persons living here now?

Item 2:   Last time, you mentioned (whoever mentioned in interview 2) as the relatives you felt closest to. Is that right? How often do you get together with these relatives?

_____ every day
_____ at least once a week
_____ a few times a month
_____ about once a month
_____ a few times a year
_____ about once a year
_____ almost never—haven't seen in years

Item 3:   How many people that you know do you consider close friends—that is, people you can confide in and talk over personal matters with? Now take the friends you're closest to—about how often do you get together with any of them?

_____ at least once a week
_____ a few times a month
_____ about once a month
_____ a few times a year
_____ almost never—haven't seen in years

Item 4:   Last time, you mentioned (whoever was mentioned in interview 1) as the neighbors you know best. Is that right? How often do you get together with these neighbors?

_____ every day
_____ at least once a week
_____ a few times a month
_____ about once a month
_____ anything less

Item 5:   In the course of a day's work, about how many people do you see and talk to?

Item 6:   Now, about people you see for certain specific purposes—like storekeepers, bus drivers, waiters, salespeople, and so on. About how many of these do you see fairly regularly, would you say?

SOURCE: E. Cumming and W. E. Henry. *Growing Old*. New York: Basic Books, 1961, pp. 244-45.

Chapter 3

Dyadic Relations

David J. Mangen

The importance of family in the social lives of older persons is reflected in the amount of research that examines the family roles of
the aged. Broad-ranging reviews of the gerontological literature usually include sections devoted to the family lives of older people (e.g.,
Tibbitts and Donahue, 1962; Rose and Peterson, 1965; Riley and
Foner, 1968; Troll, 1971; Binstock and Shanas, 1976). Despite this
apparent interest, most of the research has focused on parent-child
relations or the interface of older persons with their broader kinship networks; less work has examined the dyadic relations of older
couples.

This chapter reviews those research instruments that have been
used in research with older husbands and wives. An instrument that
addresses the general issue of dyadic relations was included when it
met one of the following criteria: (1) the instrument was developed
and/or utilized in projects that examined the family patterns of older
(postparental and retired) family units, or (2) the instrument was
utilized in research examining couples of all ages or stages of the
family life cycle, and explicit analyses of age or family life-cycle effects were conducted. A total of 27 instruments were reviewed, 24 of
which are included in this chapter (Table 3-1). Most instruments came
from research examining the impact of the family-life-cycle stages
upon the functioning or quality of dyadic life. The family-life-cycle
concept is quite similar to the concept of age insofar as its stages are
delineated on the basis of the presence and ages of the oldest and
youngest children in the family (Duvall, 1962; Hill and Rodgers,
1964); therefore, the family life cycle serves as a useful concept

analogous to age, which may be used to study age-related effects.

TABLE 3-1
Measures Reviewed in Chapter 3

Instrument	Author(s)	Code Number
I. Marital Adjustment, Satisfaction, and Integration		
a. Short Marital Adjustment Test	Locke and Wallace (1959)	V2.3.I.a
b. Marital Satisfaction	Rollins and Feldman (1970)	V2.3.I.b
c. Marriage Adjustment Balance Scale	Orden and Bradburn (1968)	V2.3.I.c
d. Marital Role Adjustment Battery	Gurin, Veroff, and Feld (1960)	V2.3.I.d
e. Marital Need Satisfaction Scale	Stinnett, Collins and Montgomery (1970)	V2.3.I.e
f. Marital Satisfaction Index	Blood and Wolfe (1960)	V2.3.I.f
g. Marital Satisfaction	Gilford and Bengtson (1976; 1979)	V2.3.I.g
h. Marital Satisfaction	Burr (1967)	V2.3.I.h
i. Perceptions of Marriage	Stinnett, Carter, and Montgomery (1972)	Not available
j. Marital Satisfaction	Miller (1976)	V2.3.I.j
k. Ease of Role Transition	Miller (1976)	V2.3.I.k
l. Marital Communication and Agreement	Hill (1970)	V2.3.I.l
m. Marital Integration Index	Farber (1957)	V2.3.I.m
II. Role Performance, Power, and Decision Making		
a. Task Sharing	Kerckhoff (1965)	V2.3.II.a
b. Male Household Activities	Lipman (1961)	V2.3.II.b
c. Husband's Participation	Kerckhoff (1965)	V2.3.II.c
d. Household Task Performance	Ballweg (1967)	V2.3.II.d
e. Rationality in Decision Making	Hill (1963; 1965; 1970)	V2.3.II.e
f. Decision Power Index	Blood and Wolfe (1960)	V2.3.II.f
g. Division of Labor	Blood (1958); Blood and Wolfe (1960)	V2.3.II.g
III. The Family and Late-Life Transitions		
a. Anticipatory Socialization	Miller (1976)	V2.3.III.a
b. Support Systems of Widows	Lopata (1977)	V2.3.III.b
c. Relations-Restrictive Attitude	Lopata (1973)	V2.3.III.c
d. Sanctification of Husband	Lopata (1976)	V2.3.III.d

The instruments reviewed in this chapter address a range of conceptual interests and theoretical focuses, and yet the underlying content of most of the instruments is remarkably similar. Over half of the instruments measure the extent of husband-wife support, adjustment, or love; and another seven focus on family power, decision making, and/or task performance. Finally, included are four instruments that are not neatly subsumed under the other categories. Three of these focus explicitly on widowhood as the last stage of the family life cycle, and one focuses on anticipatory socialization processes. It is interesting that the review of general family measurement techniques done by Straus and Brown (1978) found the same levels of conceptual order in the broader family research. Thus, gerontologically oriented family research on the dyad appears to run parallel to the research tradition of family sociology, with some additional concern for the role transitions that occur during old age.

Measures of Marital Adjustment, Satisfaction, and Integration

Concern with marital adjustment and success has long been manifest in sociological studies of the family, and this concern is reflected in the review presented here. The majority of instruments reviewed are concerned with what might be broadly termed marital success. Only two of these instruments were specifically designed for use with aging populations (Stinnett, Collins and Montgomery, 1970; Stinnett, Carter, and Montgomery, 1972). Two others (Gilford and Bengtson, 1976; Hill, 1970) were designed and used in three-generation studies. Hill's study also included Farber's (1957) Marital Integration Index.

The remainder of the marital success instruments do not focus as explicitly on older persons, and the research that has used these instruments tends to be characterized by smaller samples of the aged. More information pertaining to the reliability and validity of these measures is available, but this information is most often based on samples of younger families. Moreover, the construct validity of some of these measures when used for older persons may be questionable since items pertaining to disciplining children and relationships with in-laws are included in the scales.

Specific data pertaining to the reliability and validity properties for research on older persons are available for only two of all the marital success instruments, the Marital Need Satisfaction Scale (Stinnett, Collins, and Montgomery, 1970) and the Marital Satisfaction scale of Gilford and Bengtson (1976). The former is a relatively long scale (24 items) that is hypothesized to measure six dimensions of marital need. Data are needed to verify this six-dimension structure, and information pertaining to subscale reliability and validity is needed. The measure designed by Gilford and Bengtson (1976) is relatively short (10 items) and has been shown to have a two-dimensional structure in *each* of the three generations examined in that study. Although this structure is consistent *across* the generations, several questions remain. The most important of these pertains to the construct itself. Since the 10 items define two dimensions and since each dimension consists of only *positive* or *negative* items, it is plausible that some elements of social desirability are manifest in this scale. However, the authors predict such a structure and use the basic reward-cost framework of exchange theory to support the emerging structure.

In sum, measures of marital success that have been used in research on the aging dyad have not given sufficient attention to ensuring or testing stimulus isomorphism across generations or stages of the family life cycle. Both the family development approach (Hill and Rodgers, 1964) and the sociology of age stratification (Riley, Johnson, and Foner, 1972) could realistically hypothesize that the unique structural constraints of age and/or family-life-cycle stage might influence the level or degree of the marital success phenomenon and *change the construct itself*. This is, of course, a researchable question, and one that the work of Gilford and Bengtson (1976) begins to test. Further efforts in this vein are recommended.

Measures of Role Performance, Power, and Decision Making

Although most of the research on marital success and aging stems from studies that examine the entire age range, the seven measures of role performance, power, and decision making focus more explicitly on the aging dyad. Four of the seven were used in studies examining only older couples. A fifth, Rationality in Decision Making (Hill, 1963; 1965; 1970), was developed for use in a three-generation study. This three-generation study also included two measures from Blood and Wolfe's (1960) study of families across the life cycle.

The four measures developed on older samples have been infrequently used, and formal testing of measurement models is nonexistent. No measures of reliability are available, and only scanty, inferred evidence of validity is presented. In contrast to this trend, the reliability and validity of the Blood and Wolfe (1960) Decision Power Index has been extensively examined, but this information is based on samples of younger adults. The greater amount of information available on this measure stems from the controversy that emerged in the family literature regarding what was really measured by the Decision Power Index.

Finally, Hill's (1963; 1965; 1970) Rationality in Decision Making measure questions a common assumption of decision-making studies and treats rationality as a variable. The reliability of this measure has been tested in each of the three generations included in Hill's study, with coefficients of reproducibility exceeding .87 in all cases. Furthermore, moderately strong positive correlations of rationality with goal achievement measures suggest the validity of Hill's approach.

Measures of the Family and Late-Life Transitions

Finally, several measures of family variables are included that do not fall into the other two classifications. Three of these focus on widowhood as the final stage of the family and are drawn from the work of Lopata (1973; 1976; 1977). The Sanctification of Husband measure addresses the tendency of the surviving spouse to idealize the deceased. The internal consistency of this measure is quite strong; however, validity tests should be conducted. On the one hand, it is methodologically sound to have an estimate of idealization tendencies insofar as this may reflect context-specific social desirability; on the other, idealization is realistically seen as an integral part of the grief process. In short, knowledge about the discriminant validity of this instrument would be useful so that its use as either a methodological or a substantive concept could be promoted.

The Relations-Restrictive Attitude Scale (Lopata, 1973) measures the degree to which widows perceive their social relations as restrictive and normatively bound, and the Support Systems of Widows (Lopata, 1977) measures the patterns of exchange between a widow and significant others in her social network. This latter measure taps five different dimensions of social support: (1) emotional-sentimental supports, (2) emotional-feeling states, (3) economic supports, (4) service supports, and (5) social supports. Both the Relations-Restrictive Attitude Scale and the Support Systems of Widows measure could benefit from detailed examinations of their measurement properties.

Miller's (1976) measure of Anticipatory Socialization for role change taps formal learning, role modeling, planning, and preparation through reading as components of socialization. Since scholars have increasingly expressed interest in adult socialization, including old age (Mortimer and Simmons, 1978; Rosow, 1974), this measure is included in order to suggest strategies for measurement of this concept.

Limitations on Measurement

In a review of the range of measures presented here, a number of issues pertaining to the role of measurement in the construction and development of theory emerge. Before the discussion turns to these broader issues, however, a cautionary note regarding what constitutes validity evidence must be advanced. Specifically, these reviews treat husband-wife correlations as a test of validity. The rationale advanced for this treatment lies in the assumption that, if a husband and a wife converge in their evaluation of a family property, then such agreement is an indicator of greater validity. One could also consider these correlations as a form of interrater reliability or as a substantive research question in their own right. Certainly, this "soft" approach to validity in no way approximates the rigor of the multitrait-multimethod approach to the assessment of validity (Campbell and Fiske, 1959; see also Alwin, 1974; Althauser, 1974; and Althauser, Heberlein, and Scott, 1971 for discussions of this technique).

The first basic issue concerning the role of theory in measurement addresses what some have called the rational approach to measurement (Straus, 1964; Guilford, 1954). Researchers interested in the aging dyad have all too often relegated theoretical definitions of concepts to implicit discussions, if indeed any discussion of theory occurred at all. Since these theoretical and conceptual concerns are of great importance in defining the nature of the item pool, as well as the rules of correspondence between indicators and constructs, failure to address these issues leaves a significant gap in knowledge. In a related vein, many measures are theoretically multidimensional, and yet operationalization most often consists of unidimensional constructs. As a result, important differences *between* constructs may be masked by combining multiple constructs in single scales.

A second issue pertains to the unit of analysis employed in the research. Family theory attempts to organize knowledge regarding the properties of the *family as a social group*, and yet the majority of research instruments measure properties of married individuals. Of the marital adjustment, satisfaction, and integration measures, only Farber's (1957) Marital Integration Index develops rules of correspondence between individual responses and a family scale score. A similar pattern is found with the measures of role performance, power, and decision making; researchers have attempted to measure family characteristics on the basis of individual data. Since husband-wife correlations are less than unity (and often much less), one can realistically question the validity of these data. Safilios-Rothschild (1969) has labeled this as the theoretical development of "wives' family sociology." The gender of the respondent may be irrelevant, but the basic issue remains. Measurement of group properties based on individual data may lead to fallacious results.

A third limitation of the measures of aging and the family presented here involves their complete reliance on survey research techniques. Experimental, observational, unobtrusive, and simulation methods have not yet been used in research on aging dyads. Use of such techniques in combination with survey research would allow some assessment of the validity of the survey measures if multitrait-multimethod analyses were conducted. When such research has been conducted with younger married couples, different results have been obtained (Olson, 1969; Olson and Rabunsky, 1972; Turk and Bell, 1972). This *should not* be interpreted as a wholesale endorsement of alternative research methods. Rather, I would suggest that knowledge about the aging dyad needs to be supplemented and that the use of alternative methodological approaches can, when guided by theory, provide not only important validation information but also substantive insight.

Summary

In closing these introductory remarks, this observer is struck by the limited range of conceptual issues deemed pertinent in the study of the aging dyad. Studies of marital conflict, problem solving, commitment, role strain, empathy, and normative sanctioning, to name just a few, remain to be conducted, with either total age-range samples or just older dyads. Such studies must be grounded within an explicit conceptual and theoretical framework.

As it was noted earlier, research on the aging dyad would benefit from considering, when theoretically appropriate, alternative methodological strategies. In addition to providing valuable cross-validation data, such strategies can provide relevant substantive insight into phenomena not yet examined by researchers interested in the aging family.

Researchers are urged to examine their theoretical orientations to determine whether the rules of correspondence between indicators and constructs are indeed the simple additive rules assumed throughout most of the measures included in this review. When theoretically justified, nonadditive measurement techniques (Blalock, 1975), magnitude-estimation procedures (Hamblin, 1974; Shinn, 1974; Stevens, 1959), and a number of multidimensional scaling models (Shepard, Romney, and Nerlove, 1972; Romney, Shepard, and Nerlove, 1972) are available for use in substantive research. In a similar vein, theoretically additive constructs should be tested to determine the uni- or multidimensional properties of such constructs and to determine the goodness of fit between theoretical construct and empirical data.

Confirmatory factor analysis (Jöreskog, 1969) as well as traditional exploratory factor analysis (Harman, 1976; Rummel, 1970) are valuable tools that can be employed in these measurement models.

Finally, regardless of the specific theoretical orientation that guides research efforts, greater attention to issues of standardization of measurement and documentation of reliability, validity, and norms is urged. Given such standards, researchers from similar theoretical orientations can then employ already-developed measures and allow knowledge in the field to become cumulative and unified.

REFERENCES

Althauser, R. P. "Inferring Validity from the Multitrait-Multimethod Matrix: Another Assessment." In *Sociological Methodology 1973-1974*, H. L. Costner (ed.), pp. 106-27. San Francisco: Jossey-Bass, 1974.

Althauser, R. P., T. A. Heberlein, and R. A. Scott. "A Causal Assessment of Validity: The Augmented Multitrait-Multimethod Matrix." In *Causal Models in the Social Sciences*, H. M. Blalock (ed.), pp. 374-99. Chicago: Aldine, 1971.

Alwin, D. F. "Approaches to the Interpretation of Relationships in the Multitrait-Multimethod Matrix." In *Sociological Methodology 1973-1974*, H. L. Costner (ed.), pp. 79-105. San Francisco: Jossey-Bass, 1974.

Binstock, R. H., and E. Shanas. *Handbook of Aging and the Social Sciences*. New York: Van Nostrand Reinhold, 1976.

Blalock, H. M. "Indirect Measurement in Social Science: Some Nonadditive Models." In *Quantitative Sociology: International Perspectives on Mathematical and Statistical Modeling*, H. M. Blalock, A. Aganbegian, F. M. Borodkin, R. Boudon, and V. Capecchi (eds.), pp. 359-79. New York: Academic Press, 1975.

Blood, R. O., and D. M. Wolfe. *Husbands and Wives: The Dynamics of Married Living*. New York: Free Press, 1960.

Campbell, D. T., and D. W. Fiske. "Convergent and Discriminant Validation by the Multitrait-Multimethod Matrix." *Psychological Bulletin*, 1959, 56: 81-105.

Duvall, E. M. *Family Development*. Philadelphia: J. B. Lippincott, 1962.

Farber, B. "An Index of Marital Integration." *Sociometry*, 1957, 20: 117-34.

Gilford, R., and V. Bengtson. "Marital Satisfaction in Three Generations: Positive and Negative Dimensions." Paper presented to the 29th Annual Meeting of the Gerontological Society, New York, October 13-17, 1976.

Guilford, J. P. *Psychometric Methods* (2nd ed.). New York: McGraw-Hill, 1954.

Hamblin, R. L. "Social Attitudes: Magnitude Measurement and Theory." In *Measurement in the Social Sciences*, H. M. Blalock (ed.), pp. 61-120. Chicago: Aldine, 1974.

Harman, H. H. *Modern Factor Analysis* (3rd ed.). Chicago: University of Chicago Press, 1976.

Hill, R. "Judgement and Consumership in the Management of Family Resources." *Sociology and Social Research*, 1963, 47: 446-60.

_____. "Decision Making and the Family Life Cycle." In *Social Structure and the Family: Generational Relations*, E. Shanas and G. F. Streib (eds.), pp. 113-39. Englewood Cliffs, N.J.: Prentice-Hall, 1965.

_____. *Family Development in Three Generations*. Cambridge, Mass: Schenkman, 1970.

Hill, R., and R. H. Rodgers. "The Developmental Approach." In *Handbook of Marriage and the Family*, H. T. Christensen (ed.), pp. 171-211. Skokie, Ill.: Rand McNally, 1964.

Jöreskog, K. G. "A General Approach to Confirmatory Maximum Likelihood Factor Analysis." *Psychometrika* 1969, 34: 183-202.

Lopata, H. Z. *Widowhood in an American City*. Cambridge, Mass.: Schenkman, 1973.

_____ . "Widowhood and Husband Sanctification." Paper presented at the 71st Annual Meeting of the American Sociological Association, New York, August 1976.

_____ . "Support Systems Involving Widows in a Metropolitan Area of the United States." Final report to the Social Security Administration. Chicago: Center for the Comparative Study of Social Roles, 1977.

Miller, B. C. "A Multivariate Developmental Model of Marital Satisfaction." *Journal of Marriage and the Family*, 1976, 38: 643-57.

Mortimer, J. T., and R. G. Simmons. "Adult Socialization." In *Annual Review of Sociology* (vol. 4), R. Turner, J. Coleman, and R. Fox (eds.), pp. 421-54. Palo Alto, Calif.: Annual Reviews, 1978.

Olson, D. H. "The Measurement of Family Power by Self-Report and Behavioral Methods." *Journal of Marriage and the Family*, 1969, 31: 545-50.

Olson, D. H., and C. Rabunsky. "Validity of Four Measures of Family Power." *Journal of Marriage and the Family*, 1972, 34: 224-34.

Riley, M. W., and A. Foner. *Aging and Society* (vol. 1). New York: Russell Sage Foundation, 1968.

Riley, M.W., M. Johnson, and A. Foner. *Aging and Society* (vol. 3). New York: Russell Sage Foundation, 1972.

Romney, A., R. N. Shepard, and S. Nerlove. *Multidimensional Scaling* (vol. 2). New York: Seminar Press, 1972.

Rose, A. M., and W. A. Peterson. *Older People and Their Social World*. Philadelphia: F. A. Davis, 1965.

Rosow, I. *Socialization to Old Age*. Berkeley: University of California Press, 1974.

Rummel, R. J. *Applied Factor Analysis*. Evanston, Ill.: Northwestern University Press, 1970.

Safilios—Rothschild, C. "Family Sociology or Wives' Family Sociology: A Cross-cultural Examination of Decision-Making." *Journal of Marriage and the Family*, 1969, 31: 290-301.

Shepard, R. N., A. Romney, and S. Nerlove. *Multidimensional Scaling* (vol. 1). New York: Seminar Press, 1972.

Shinn, A. M. "Relations between Scales." In *Measurement in the Social Sciences*, H. M. Blalock (ed.), pp. 121-58. Chicago: Aldine, 1974.

Stevens, S. S. "Measurement." In *Measurement: Definitions and Theories*, C. W. Churchman (ed.), pp. 18-36. New York: John Wiley and Sons, 1959.

Stinnett, N., L. Carter, and J. Montgomery. "Older Persons' Perceptions of Their Marriages." *Journal of Marriage and the Family*, 1972, 34: 665-71.

Stinnett, N., J. Collins, and J. Montgomery. "Marital Need Satisfaction of Older Husbands and Wives." *Journal of Marriage and the Family*, 1970, 32: 428-34.

Straus, M. A. "Measuring Families." In *Handbook of Marriage and the Family*, H. T. Christensen (ed.), pp. 335-400. Skokie, Ill.: Rand McNally, 1964.

Straus, M. A., and B. W. Brown. *Family Measurement Techniques* (rev. ed.). Minneapolis: University of Minnesota Press, 1978.

Tibbitts, C., and W. Donahue. *Social and Psychological Aspects of Aging*. New York: Columbia University Press, 1962.

Troll, L. E. "The Family of Later Life: A Decade Review." *Journal of Marriage and the Family*, 1971, 33: 263-90.

Turk, J. L., and N. W. Bell. "Measuring Power in Families." *Journal of Marriage and the Family*, 1972, 34:215-22.

Abstracts

SHORT MARITAL ADJUSTMENT TEST

H. J. Locke and K. M. Wallace, 1959

Definition of Variable or Concept

"Marital adjustment is accommodation of a husband and wife to each other at a given time" (Locke and Wallace, 1959, p. 251).

Description of Instrument

This is a relatively brief, 15-item scale that uses a differential weighting system. Items were chosen on the basis of their discriminatory power as well as to ensure that the important areas of marital adjustment (as defined by the investigators) were addressed by this instrument.

Method of Administration

The short marital adjustment test is a self-reporting questionnaire.

Context of Development and Subsequent Use

This instrument was developed to measure adjustment with a short protocol and without considerable reduction in reliability and validity. The instrument follows the tradition of Burgess and associates (Burgess and Wallin, 1953; Burgess and Cottrell, 1939), Terman (1938), Locke (1951), and Karlsson (1951).

The Locke-Wallace scale has been used extensively in marital adjustment studies. Of these one includes retired persons (Rollins and Cannon, 1974) and one, couples (Spanier, Lewis, and Cole, 1975); and the two explicitly analyze stage differences.

Sample(s)

The Locke-Wallace scale was developed on a sample of 118 men and 118 women who were married but not to each other. As a result, 236 marriages are represented in the sample. This sample was predominantly young (the mean age of the husbands was 29; the wives, 30), white, well-educated, Protestant, urban, and of higher social status (Locke and Wallace, 1959).

The Rollins and Cannon (1974) study employed a sample of 489 individuals representing all stages of the family life cycle, including 33 retired individuals. (See the abstracts in this chapter for the Blood-Wolfe measure of marital satisfaction and the Rollins-Feldman measure for a further description of the sample in the Rollins-Cannon study.)

The study by Spanier, Lewis, and Cole (1975) used three independent but coordinated samples from Iowa, Ohio, and Georgia. Stratified area probability samples were drawn in Ames, Iowa, and Neward, Ohio, and a systematic random sample was drawn from Classic County in northeastern Georgia. All ages were represented in these samples, but only a few retired couples were included in each of the community samples; 8 Iowa couples, 12 Ohio couples, and 13 Georgia couples were in the retirement stage.

Scoring, Scale Norms, and Distribution

Marital adjustment is scored as a weighted linear combination of an individual's responses to the 15 items. The weights are presented with the accompanying instrument. When this instrument is used as a self-reporting instrument (as it was designed to be), the weights should not be included in the instrument.

Possible scores on this scale range from 2 to 158. As is typical with marital adjustment scales, responses tend to be biased toward a positive evaluation of marriage.

Spanier, Lewis, and Cole (1975) reported average scores for retired males of 130.3, 115.6, and 119.4 and for females of 129.5, 124.1, and 124.4 in the Iowa, Ohio, and Georgia samples, respectively.

Rollins and Cannon (1974, p. 277) reported an average score of 125.54 for 23 retired males and 137.80 for 10 retired females.

Formal Tests of Reliability/Homogeneity

Locke and Wallace (1959) reported split-half reliability (Spearman-Brown formula) of .90.

Formal Tests of Validity

Locke and Wallace indicated that well-adjusted couples (mean 135.9) were significantly different from maladjusted couples (mean 71.7). Only 17% of the maladjusted group scored 100 or more, while 96% of the adjusted group achieved this score or better.

Hawkins (1966) reported that the Locke-Wallace scale correlates significantly with the Crowne-Marlowe Social Desirability Scale (Crowne and Marlowe, 1964) for husbands ($r = .31$) and wives ($r = .37$). The single item indicator of happiness correlated significantly with social desirability for wives ($r = .36$) but not for husbands ($r = .19$).

Edmonds (1967) reported a correlation of .63 between the Locke-Wallace scale and marital conventionalization; this indicates that social desirability positively influences scores on the Locke-Wallace instrument.

Edmonds, Withers, and Dibatista (1972) reported correlations between marital conventionalization and the Locke-Wallace scale in two other samples ($r = .53, r = .70$), which support the initial conclusions of Edmonds (1967). Furthermore, the individual Locke-Wallace items are all significantly correlated with marital conventionalization (rank order correlations ranged from .37 to .59 according to Edmonds, Withers, and Dibatista, 1972).

Usability on Older Populations

None of the 15 items in this index appear to be stage specific.

Sensitivity to Age Differences

Rollins and Cannon (1974) reported that the Locke-Wallace scale is significantly related to family-life-cycle stage in a curvilinear fashion, with greater marital adjustment reported in the extreme stages.

Spanier, Lewis, and Cole (1975) reported a significant U-shaped curvilinear relationship between the Locke-Wallace scale and family-life-cycle stage in their Ohio sample. In the data on their Georgia sample, the linear decline hypothesis is supported, although tendencies toward curvilinearity are noted. The data on the Iowa sample are not significantly related to family-life-cycle stage with linear or curvilinear techniques.

General Comments and Recommendations

The strong correlations between this instrument and social desirability should be addressed by family scholars using this scale, especially in light of evidence relating age and social desirability (Gove and Geerken, 1977). In addition, the dimensionality of this instrument should be assessed.

The weights for a given response may not be entirely applicable for older populations. Researchers should assess the relative importance of individual items for elderly populations. Assessment of the dimensional structure of the instrument would assist in validation of the relative weights given the items.

It is not clear why a wife's giving in during disagreements is more satisfying than a husband's giving in (item 10).

References

Burgess, E. W., and L. S. Cottrell. *Predicting Success or Failure in Marriage.* New York: Prentice-Hall, 1939.

Burgess, E. W., and P. Wallin. *Engagement and Marriage.* Philadelphia: J. B. Lippincott, 1953.

Crowne, D., and D. Marlowe. *The Approval Motive.* New York: John Wiley and Sons, 1964.

Edmonds, V. H. "Marital Conventionalization: Definition and Measurement." *Journal of Marriage and the Family,* 1967, 29: 681-88.

Edmonds, V. H., G. Withers, and B. Dibatista. "Adjustment, Conservatism, and Marital Conventionalization." *Journal of Marriage and the Family,* 1972, 34: 97-103.

Gove, W. R., and M. R. Geerken. "Response Bias in Surveys of Mental Health: An Emprical Investigation." *American Journal of Sociology,* 1977, 82 (6): 1289-1317.

Hawkins, J. L. "The Locke Marital Adjustment Test and Social Desirability." *Journal of Marriage and the Family,* 1966, 28: 193-95.

Karlsson, G., *Adaptability and Communication in Marriage: A Swedish Prediction Study of Marital Satisfaction.* Uppsala: Almqvist and Wiksells, 1951.

Locke, H. J. *Predicting Adjustment in Marriage: A Comparison of a Divorced and a Happily Married Group.* New York: Holt, 1951.

Locke, H. J., and K. M. Wallace, "Short Marital Adjustment and Prediction Tests, Their Reliability and Validity." *Marriage and Family Living,* 1959, 21: 251-55.

Rollins, B. C., and K. L. Cannon. "Marital Satisfaction over the Family Life Cycle: A Reevaluation." *Journal of Marriage and the Family,* 1974, 36: 271-82.

Spanier, G. B., R. A. Lewis, and C. L. Cole. "Marital Adjustment over the Family Life Cycle: The Issue of Curvilinearity." *Journal of Marriage and the Family,* 1975, 37: 263-75.

Terman, L. M. *Psychological Factors in Marital Happiness.* New York: McGraw-Hill, 1938.

Instrument

See Instrument V2.3.I.a.

MARITAL SATISFACTION

B. C. Rollins and H. Feldman, 1970

Definition of Variable or Concept

Satisfaction is defined as the "correspondence between the actual and the expected or a comparison of the actual relationship with the alternative, if the present relationship were terminated" (Burgess and Locke, 1945, p. 439).

Description of Instrument

This measure looks at four different dimensions of marital satisfaction: (1) general marital satisfaction, one item; (2) negative feelings from interaction with spouse, three items; (3) positive companionship experiences with spouse, four items; and (4) satisfaction with present stage of the family life cycle, one item, which varies depending upon the life-cycle stage of the respondent.

Method of Administration

Questionnaires were left for husbands and wives to fill out and were picked up within a few days. This instrument could be easily applied to an interview format.

Context of Development and Subsequent Use

The study was designed to examine life-cycle patterns of marital satisfaction for males and females.

Sample

An initial response rate of 85% from both spouses resulted in data for 852 couples. Fifty-three couples who were childless after five years of marriage were eliminated from the sample, yielding a working sample of 799 couples. Of the husbands 88% were white-collar workers; 68% of the husbands had received some college education. Fifty couples (100 individuals) were in the retirement stage.

Scoring, Scale Norms, and Distribution

The multiitem dimensions of negative feelings and positive companionship are summated across the items. Negative feelings has a conceptual range of 0 to 15; positive companionship ranges 0 to 20. Rollins and Feldman (1970, p. 24) reported percentage distributions for men and women at each stage of the life cycle.

Usability on Older Populations

The instrument appears to be usable since its questions apply to general marital phenomena and are not stage specific.

Sensitivity to Age (Including Social Age) Differences

The marital satisfaction of both husbands and wives is significantly related to family-life-cycle stage. The shape of the relationship varies, however, for each of the four indicators.

General Comments and Recommendations

This short battery seems to tap different facets of marital satisfaction. Further scaling work remains to be done, however, and researchers are cautioned about the lack of stimulus isomorphism for the "satisfaction with the present stage of family life cycle" question.

References

Burgess, E. W., and H. J. Locke. *The Family: From Institution to Companionship*. New York: American Book Company, 1945.

Rollins, B. C., and H. Feldman. "Marital Satisfaction over the Family Life Cycle." *Journal of Marriage and the Family*, 1970, 32: 20-38.

Instrument

See Instrument V2.3.I.b.

MARRIAGE ADJUSTMENT BALANCE SCALE (MABS)

S. R. Orden and N. M. Bradburn, 1968

Definition of Variable or Concept

Marriage adjustment is seen as resulting from the general dimensions of satisfaction and tension.

Description of Instrument

The MABS is an 18-item survey instrument designed to tap three dimensions of marriage happiness: marriage sociability, marriage companionship, and marriage tensions. Items are responded to on a yes/no basis. The scale was developed on the basis of a cluster analysis of the items.

Method of Administration

The MABS was administered as part of a larger interview examining psychological well-being.

Context of Development and Subsequent Use

The instrument was developed on the basis of previous work on the structure of psychological well-being (Bradburn, 1969; Bradburn and Caplovitz, 1965).

Sample(s)

Five samples including married and single persons were incorporated into the longitudinal study design: (1) Washington suburban county, $N = 1,001$; (2) residents of the 10 largest metropolitan areas in the country, $N = 208$; (3) Detroit suburb, $N = 427$; (4) Detroit inner city, $N = 350$; and (5) Chicago, $N = 177$. The MABS was developed on the 781 husbands and 957 wives (not couples) included in this wave of the longitudinal survey.

Otto and Featherman (1972a) reported on the use of the MABS with 216 couples; the mean age of the males was 48; the mean age of the females was 45 in a Wisconsin sample.

Scaling, Scale Norms, and Distribution

Each subscale is scored as the sum of the yes responses. Responses tend to be skewed toward favorable ratings of marriage, with companionship and sociability ratings concentrated at the positive end of the scale, and tensions generally skewed toward few reported tensions. Scale and item distributions are reported in Orden and Bradburn (1968, p. 719-23). A composite index can be computed by summing the companionship and sociability indexes and subtracting from that sum the score on the tensions index. This is then converted to a scale of 0 to 10 by adding 4 to the original MABS score.

Formal Tests of Reliability/Homogeneity

Average Q values of association for items in each dimension are: (1) companionship, males .62 and females .69; (2) sociability, males .48 and females .47; (3) tensions, males .47 and females .50 (Orden and Bradburn, 1968, p. 721).

Otto and Featherman (1972b) reported the following coefficients alpha: (1) companionship, .82 for males and .91 for females; (2) sociability, .86 for males and .84 for females; (3) tensions, .97 for males and .96 for females.

Formal Tests of Validity

Gamma coefficients of association among these three indexes and with a global evaluation of marriage are: (1) for men: companionship-sociability .34; companionship-happiness .44; sociability-tensions – .01; sociability-happiness .20; tensions-happiness – .36; companionship-tensions – .08; and (2) For women: companionship-sociability .37; companionship-tensions – .15; companionship-happiness .40; sociability-tensions .02; sociability-happiness .26; tensions-happiness – .41.

These findings are interpreted as evidence of convergent and discriminant validity for each of the separate indexes. The composite score correlates with the global marriage happiness question (gamma coefficient .47), thus providing evidence of convergent validity for the composite. Otto and Featherman (1972b) questioned the independence of dimensions in the context of data for couples (as opposed to the data for individuals on which the original scaling work was based) because between-partner correlations indicate a significant correlation between husband's sociability and wife's tensions ($r = - .17$).

The between-partner constellation of effects was tested by regression analysis. Male companionship *did not contribute* to female companionship ($\beta = - .006$). Female companionship influenced male sociability negatively ($\beta = -.149$); and the associations of male sociability to female companionship, and male companionship to female sociability, were not significant.

Marini (1976) suggested that satisfactions and tensions are only two of a class of variables related to marital happiness. Marital companionship (measured with one variable to assess the *amount of time spent together*) is suggested as a further dimension. Furthermore, three extra items are recommended for the measure of marital satisfactions, and two extra items are recommended for the measure of marital tensions.

Usability on Older Populations

This instrument appears to be usable, since items refer to behaviors and experiences that are relevant to couples across the stages of the family life cycle.

General Comments and Recommendations

Further analysis on the measurement properties of this instrument is needed, especially in light of Otto and Featherman's (1972a; 1972b) findings. Replication of the scale when used with older persons is also needed, as is an assessment of family-life-cycle effects on each dimension and the total score.

Marini (1976) suggested that some additional items that were asked of respondents in the original study but were not used in the Orden and Bradburn (1968) analysis should be included. One of these concerns disciplining children. Since the children of older adults have, in all likelihood, left home, the use of this item is questionable.

References

Bradburn, N. *The Structure of Psychological Well-being*. Chicago: Aldine, 1969.

Bradburn, N. M., and D. Caplovitz. *Reports on Happiness*. Chicago: Aldine, 1965.

Marini, M. M. "Dimensions of Marriage Happiness: A Research Note." *Journal of Marriage and the Family*, 1976, 38: 443-50.

Orden, S. R., and N. M. Bradburn. "Dimensions of Marriage Happiness." *American Journal of Sociology*, 1968, 73: 715-31.

Otto, L. B., and D. L. Featherman. "On the Measurement of Marital Adjustment among Spouses." Madison, Wis.: Center for Demography and Ecology, University of Wisconsin, 1972a.

_____. "A Critique of the Marital Adjustment Balance Scale in the Context of Couple Data." Madison, Wis.: Center for Demography and Ecology, University of Wisconsin, 1972b.

Instrument

See Instrument V2.3.I.c.

MARITAL ROLE ADJUSTMENT BATTERY

G. Gurin, J. Veroff, and S. Feld, 1960

Definition of Variable or Concept

This three-item battery taps the general affective tone of the marital relationship.

Description of Instrument

This instrument is a three-item battery of open-ended questions that measures the following areas of adjustment to marriage: (1) general satisfaction with marriage, (2) feelings of inadequacy in the role of husband or wife, and (3) experience of problems in the marital role. The general satisfaction dimension is scored on a four-point scale from "very happy" to "not too happy." Feelings of inadequacy are scored on a three-point ordinal scale of frequency, and experience of problems is a binary variable ("had problems" and "no problems").

Method of Administration

The battery was administered originally during personal interviews conducted by the Survey Research Center.

Context of Development and Subsequent Use

The battery was developed as part of national survey of mental health in the United States. Adjustment in three major roles (marriage, parenthood, and work) constituted one area of concern within this general survey.

Sample

The individuals in this sample constituted a representative cross section of adults aged 21 and older and who are living in private households in the United States. The total sample of 2,460 individuals was selected with a multistage stratified probability sample. In the sample, 15% of the men and 14% of the women were 65 years old or older.

Formal Tests of Reliability/Homogeneity

Cross-tabulation among the three items revealed that happiness is only slightly related to feelings of inadequacy, but a moderate relationship between inadequacy and problems was reported. Happiness is also moderately related to the reporting of problems (Gurin, Veroff, and Feld, 1960, pp. 92-94).

Usability on Older Populations

The items appear to be usable with older populations.

Sensitivity to Age (Including Social Age) Differences

Feelings of inadequacy and reports of problems consistently decrease with age. Only persons aged 65 and over deviate from this pattern in feelings of inadequacy, and then only a moderate increase is noted. Marital happiness is related to age in a U-shaped manner, with those persons aged 55 to 64 reporting lowest happiness (Gurin, Veroff, and Feld, 1960, p. 103).

General Comments and Recommendations

This short battery is included here because of the broad, representative nature of the sample and study behind it. In addition, the conceptualization of similar dimensions of adjustment across different roles and role changes represents a useful and systematic theoretical organization.

Further elaboration of these dimensions is desirable, both in terms of analyzing the items as components of a single adjustment as well as elaboration of the item pool for *each* dimension.

References

Gurin, G., J. Veroff, and S. Feld. *Americans View Their Mental Health*. New York: Basic Books, 1960.

Veroff, J., and S. Feld. *Marriage and Work in America*. New York: Van Nostrand Reinhold, 1970.

Instrument

See Instrument V2.3.I.d.

MARITAL NEED SATISFACTION SCALE

N. Stinnett, J. Collins, and J. Montgomery, 1970

Definition of Variable or Concept

The investigators defined their concept as "the extent of satisfaction which older husbands and wives express concerning the fulfillment of certain needs involved in the marriage relationship during the later years" (Stinnett, Collins, and Montgomery, 1970, p. 429).

Description of Instrument

This Likert-type scale includes 24 items and measures six different developmental needs in the marriages of older men and women. The six needs are: (1) love, (2) personality fulfillment, (3) respect, (4) communication, (5) finding meaning in life, and (6) integration of past life experiences.

Method of Administration

Data were collected as part of a mail questionnaire sent to both husbands and wives.

Context of Development and Subsequent Use

The scale was developed from a review of literature that suggested the specific need areas. The scale was modified, in part, on the basis of a factor analysis.

Sample

The sample consisted of 227 married couples over age 60 who were identified from the mailing lists of centers for senior citizens. Although the questionnaires were mailed to husbands and wives, the data presented here are based on individuals, not couples. Respondents ranged in age from 60 to 89; 49% were male; 79% of the men were retired, and 43% were skilled, semiskilled, and unskilled workers. Most were Caucasian, and most had been married for more than 40 years.

Scoring, Scale Norms, and Distribution

Responses are summed, with a favorable response given the higher score. This yields a scale ranging from 24 to 120. Six subscales with scores ranging from 4 to 20 can also be constructed. These dimensions are identified with the accompanying scale. Males received a mean score of 101.56 for the full scale; females, a score of 94.88.

Formal Tests of Reliability/Homogeneity

A split-half reliability coefficient (Spearman-Brown correlation) of .99 was obtained for the full 24-item scale. Trichotomization of the scale at the first and third quartiles was used for chi-square item analysis. All 24 items were significantly related to the trichotomized scale ($p < .001$).

Formal Tests of Validity

Analysis of variance indicated that those who perceived the "present as the happiest period of time" and those who "perceived their marriage as very happy" tended to score higher on this measure. Pearson correlations with self-image (.13), self-orientation (− .08), interaction orientation (.00), and task orientation (.03) were not significant. Correlation with an indicator of morale was equal to .37 ($p < .001$).

Usability on Older Populations

The scale was explicitly designed for use with older populations.

General Comments and Recommendations

The items in this test are all positively phrased, a factor that may influence response bias. Moreover, two items (numbers 15 and 16) are somewhat ambiguous as to the directionality of the stimulus; this is reflected in the relatively lower chi squares obtained for the statements in the item analysis.

This instrument holds promise for future work, but it needs more testing. Explicit factor analytic data would be helpful.

Reference

N. Stinnett, J. Collins, and J. Montgomery. "Marital Need Satisfaction of Older Husbands and Wives." *Journal of Marriage and the Family*, 1970, 32: 428-34.

Instrument

See Instrument V2.3.I.e.

MARITAL SATISFACTION INDEX

R. O. Blood and D. M. Wolfe, 1960

Definition of Variable or Concept

The instrument measures the marital satisfaction of women, which is seen as an evaluative judgment in comparison to an appropriate (undefined) reference group.

Description of Instrument

The Marital Satisfaction Index is a five-item, weighted index that combines responses to each of the following areas: (1) standard of living, (2) spousal understanding, (3) love and affection, (4) companionship, and (5) children. Responses for items 1 to 4 range from "enthusiastic" to "disappointed," and *congruity* of the expected and the desired number of children is the response set for the fifth item.

Method of Administration

The items were included as part of a larger interview of married women in Detroit and southeastern Michigan. Rollins and Cannon (1974) reported that an adaptation of this instrument as a questionnaire was "relatively easy."

Context of Development and Subsequent Use

The instrument was designed as part of a larger study to examine the factors that determine how husbands and wives interact and what effects the patterns of interaction have upon husbands, wives, and families in general.

Sample(s)

This instrument has been used on several different samples (see Table 3-2).

TABLE 3-2
Summary Description of Samples Using the
Blood-Wolfe Marital Satisfaction Index

Researcher(s)	Sample Size	Percentage over Age 60	Location	Comments
Blood & Wolfe	909	15%	Detroit & south-eastern Michigan	Principal analysis focuses on 731 married women[a]
Rollins & Cannon	489	6.7%[b]	Western mountain states	Mormon families
Safilios-Rothschild	250	NR	Athens, Greece	Random sample
Michel	550	NR	Paris & Bordeaux France	Random sample
Buric & Zecevic	117	NR	Kragujevac, Yugo-slavia	Random sample

[a]Further sample characteristics are available in Blood and Wolfe (1960, p. 271).
[b]Retirement stage families.

Scoring, Scale Norms, and Distribution

Several different scoring systems for this measure have been used. Blood and Wolfe (1960, p. 102) scaled a wife's marital satisfaction as the sum of her reported satisfactions with standard of living, companionship, understanding, love and affection, and congruity of expected and desired number of children weighted by the comparative importance attached to each of these five aspects. The exact procedure was not given; but mean scores by family-life-cycle stage range from 4.00 (for only 8 retired couples) to 5.26 (for 19 honeymoon couples).

Blood (1967, p. 256) reported the use of the following weights: (5) most important area, (4) second most important, (3) third most important, (1) fourth and fifth most important. These weights are multiplied by the item-response codes, which vary from 1 ("disappointed") to 5 ("enthusiastic"), and summed to yield a scale ranging from 14 to 70. Using this scoring system, Rollins and Cannon (1974, p. 274) reported a mean score of 55.46 for 23 retired males and 55.70 for 10 retired females.

Rollins and Cannon questioned the validity of the Blood-Wolfe scoring system (1974, pp. 278-79, Table 4). Use of the weighting procedure results in an illogical element in the index. A respondent who was very disappointed (code 1) with a most important area of marriage (code 5) would receive 5 satisfaction points. In contrast, a respondent who was very disappointed with a trivial aspect of marriage would receive only 1 satisfaction point. Rollins and Cannon (1974) argued that logic dictates that being very disappointed with a most important aspect of marriage should be less satisfying than being disappointed with a trivial aspect of marriage. To correct this illogical element Rollins and Cannon (1974) recommended altering the item-response codes to range from −2 ("pretty disappointed") through 0 ("it's all right") to +2 ("enthusiastic"). When weighted by comparative importance, scores for individual items range from −10 ("pretty disappointed with the most important area of marriage") to +10 ("enthusiastic about the most important area of marriage").

In addition to their reservations about the Blood-Wolfe scoring system, Rollins and Cannon did not recommend that these five subindexes be combined into one measure since the relationship of family life cycle to satisfaction with children exhibits a linear decline, though love and affection, understanding, and companionship exhibited a U-shaped pattern. Satisfaction with standard of living, although exhibiting some U-shaped tendencies, is primarily characterized by a linear increase. Hence, summation is problematic insofar as the trend in one variable could tend to cancel out the effects of trends in the remaining variables.

Formal Test of Validity

Buric and Zecevic (1967, p. 327, n.5) reported that 15.4% of the "husbands and wives do not agree, to a greater or lesser degree, about their marital satisfaction."

Usability on Older Populations

Rollins and Cannon (1974) reported that age was correlated with response rate to the items in this index. Less than 50% of the stage VII (postparental) and stage VIII (retired) couples submitted usable responses. Only 20% of stage-VIII women returned usable responses. Hence, any stage effects may be very nearly invalidated.

Sensitivity to Age Differences

Blood and Wolfe (1960) reported a nearly linear decline in marital satisfaction over the family life cycle. Rollins and Cannon (1974) reported an increase in satisfaction with standard of living, a decrease in satisfaction with children, and a U-shaped relationship with love and affection, understanding, and companionship.

General Comments and Recommendations

Use of this instrument as an index of marital satisfaction appears to be problematic. Given differential response rates to items as well as differential effects by age, one might question the scaleability of this index. The internal consistency and additivity of this scale have not been established for either general or aged samples.

It would probably benefit family researchers interested in the later stages of the life cycle to eliminate the questions dealing with children. Since this item is confounded with the other items dealing more strictly with the dyadic relationships, its elimination could allow scale construction. Questions of additivity must, however, be addressed.

References

Blood, R. O. *Love Match and Arranged Marriage: A Tokyo-Detroit Comparison.* New York: Free Press, 1967.

Blood, R. O., and D. M. Wolfe. *Husbands and Wives: The Dynamics of Married Living.* New York: Free Press, 1960.

Buric, O., and Z. Zecevic. "Family Authority, Marital Satisfaction, and the Social Network in Yugoslavia." *Journal of Marriage and the Family*, 1967, 29: 325-36.

Michel, A. "Comparative Data Concerning the Interaction in French and American Families." *Journal of Marriage and the Family*, 1967, 29: 337-45.

Rollins, B. C., and K. L. Cannon. "Marital Satisfaction over the Family Life Cycle: A Reevaluation." *Journal of Marriage and the Family*, 1974, 36: 271-82.

Safilios-Rothschild, C. "A Comparison of Power Structure and Marital Satisfaction in Urban Greek and French Families." *Journal of Marriage and the Family*, 1967, 29: 345-52.

Instrument

See Instrument V2.3.I.f.

MARITAL SATISFACTION

R. Gilford and V. Bengtson, 1976; 1979

Definition of Variable or Concept

Marital satisfaction is defined as the "spouses' evaluation of their relationship on two general dimensions: positive interaction and negative sentiment" (Gilford and Bengtson, 1979, p. 389).

Description of Instrument

This scale is a two-dimensional instrument derived from a factor analysis of 10 items. Respondents are asked to respond to a list of "some things husbands and wives may do when they are together" and to respond on a five-point ordinal scale of frequency.

Method of Administration

The 10 questions were asked originally as part of a longer self-reporting questionnaire.

Context of Development and Subsequent Use

The items in the scale are taken from Meyerowitz (1970) and Spanier (1976).

Sample

The sample of three-generation families was drawn from a population of 840,000 subscribers to a major medical plan (Bengtson, 1975). It was somewhat biased toward higher educational and income levels, and its members were primarily Caucasian.

Scoring, Scale Norms, and Distribution

Items 1, 3, 5, 6, and 9 define the positive interaction dimension. The remaining five items define the negative sentiment dimension.

Dimension scores are operationalized as regression-estimated factor scores with a mean of 0 and a standard deviation of 1. Mean scores by sex and generation are provided below.

Formal Tests of Reliability/Homogeneity

Item-to-item analysis indicated an average correlation of .53 for the items in the positive interaction dimension and an average correlation of .43 for the negative sentiment dimension (Gilford and Bengtson, 1976). Item-total correlations for the positive interaction dimension ranged from .62 to .77, and item-total correlations for the negative sentiment dimension ranged from – .51 to – .63 (Gilford and Bengtson, 1976).

TABLE 3-3
Bengtson's Three-Generation Sample,
a Summary Description

Generation	Average Age	Average Length of Marriage	Sample Size
Grandparent (G1)	67	41	383
Parent (G2)	44	21	501
Grandchild (G3)	22	3	172

Formal Tests of Validity

The two hypothesized dimensions emerged in a principal components factor analysis with varimax rotation conducted on the total sample and on each generation. Convergent validity is indicated in correlations with a single-item indicator of marital happiness. The positive interaction dimension correlates positively with avowed happiness (men: G1, $r = .44$; G2, $r = .46$; G3, $r = .39$; and women: G1, $r = .41$; G2, $r = .57$; G3, $r = .40$), while the negative sentiment dimension correlates negatively with avowed happiness (men: G1, $r = -.18$; G2, $r = -.2$; G3, $r = -.17$; and women: G1, $r = -.30$; G2, $r = -.47$; G3, $r = -.17$) (Gilford and Bengtson, 1976).

The positive interaction dimension was correlated with the Bradburn Affect-Balance Scale (Bradburn and Caplovitz, 1965; Bradburn, 1969). The positive interaction dimension was related to positive affect ($r = .20$), negative affect ($r = -.12$), and affect-balance ($r = .22$). The negative sentiment dimension was related to negative affect ($r = .22$), positive affect ($r = .07$), and affect balance ($r = -.25$).

Usability on Older Populations

The instrument has been shown to retain factor structure for each generation.

Sensitivity to Age (Including Social Age) Differences

The 10 items tap facets of the marital relationship that are not stage specific. Analysis of variance indicates that generation is significantly related to both indexes.

Grandfathers report highest satisfaction on the positive interaction dimension and lowest scores on the negative sentiment. Grandmothers, on the other hand, score slightly below average on the positive interaction dimension and well below average on the negative sentiment dimension. (See Table 3-4, which is from Gilford and Bengtson, 1976.)

Scale Development Statistics

Varimax-rotated factor loadings for the positive interaction dimension range from .53 to .79 for the combined sample and .58 to .83 for the grandparent generation. Loadings for

TABLE 3-4
Means of Each Factor Score on Marital Satisfaction
by Generation and Sex

Generation	Factor I Positive Interaction			Factor II Negative Sentiment		
	Male	Female	Both	Male	Female	Both
Grandparent	.30	−.06	.04	−.12	−.19	−.15
	(N = 175)	(N = 175)	(350)	(175)	(175)	(350)
Parent	−.13	−.08	−.10	.04	.01	.02
	(225)	(258)	(483)	(225)	(258)	(483)
Grandchildren	.11	.28	.22	.25	.26	.26
	(66)	(103)	(169)	(66)	(103)	(169)
All generations	.003	−.003	.00	.01	−.01	−.001
	(466)	(536)	(1002)	(466)	(536)	(1002)

SOURCE: R. Gilford and V. Bengtson. "Marital Satisfaction in Three Generations: Positive and Negative Dimensions." Paper presented to the 29th Annual Meeting of the Gerontological Society, New York, October 13-17, 1976.

the negative sentiment dimension range from .54 to .72 for the total sample and .50 to .78 for the grandparent generation. A high degree of factor congruence is present across generations.

General Comments and Recommendations

This instrument measures the marital satisfaction of individuals as two orthogonal dimentions. Further replication of this analysis is needed, as is testing on couples instead of individuals.

Though the investigators followed exchange theory on rewards and costs to predict the two-dimensional structure, the emergency of this structure could indicate that elements of response effects are operating in these questions. Scale correlations with measures of social desirability would be useful.

References

Bengtson, V. L. "Generation and Family Effects in Value Socialization." *American Sociological Review*, 1975, 40: 358-71.

Bradburn, N. *The Structure of Psychological Well-being.* Chicago: Aldine, 1969.

Bradburn, N. M., and D. Caplovitz. *Reports on Happiness.* Chicago: Aldine, 1965.

Gilford, R. and V. Bengtson. "Marital Satisfaction in Three Generations: Positive and Negative Dimensions." Paper presented to the 29th Annual Meeting of the Gerontological Society, New York, October 13-17, 1976.

_____. "Measuring Marital Satisfaction in Three Generations: Positive and Negative Dimensions." *Journal of Marriage and the Family*, 1979, 41: 387-98.

Meyerowitz, J. "Satisfaction during Pregnancy." *Journal of Marriage and the Family*, 1970, 32: 38-44.

Spanier, G. "Measuring Dyadic Adjustment: New Scales for Assessing the Quality of Marriage and Similar Dyads." *Journal of Marriage and the Family*, 1976, 38: 15-28.

Instrument

See Instrument V2.3.I.g.

MARITAL SATISFACTION
W. R. Burr, 1967; 1970

Definition of Variable or Concept

Marital satisfaction is defined as "a subjective condition in which an individual experiences a certain degree of attainment of a goal or desire" (Burr, 1970, p. 29).

Description of Instrument

This instrument is a six-dimensional, 18-item indicator of marital satisfaction. The six different dimensions of the marital relationship that are examined in this scale are: (1) finances, (2) couple social activities, (3) spousal performance of household tasks, (4) companionship, (5) sexual interaction, and (6) relationships with children. The six dimensions are each measured by three items: (1) tension in that specific area, (2) perception of room for improvement, and (3) general satisfaction.

Burr did not combine the six dimensions into one overall indicator of marital success, but he suggested that comparison of the trends of variation by age across dimensions can assist in subsequent theoretical development.

Method of Administration

The instrument is administered as part of a personal interview.

Context of Development and Subsequent Use

The instrument attempts to overcome measurement limitations in the marital success variable. One limitation is treating marital satisfaction as a unidimensional construct; another limitation is the fact that previous measures of success were predefined by the researchers. Marital satisfaction is a *subjectively defined, multidimensional construct* as it is measured by this instrument.

Sample

The sample was a random sample of intact dyads who lived in census tracts that had been selected in such a way as to eliminate the lower socioeconomic strata. It was felt that persons in lower socioeconomic levels would not be able to complete a complex instrument that dealt extensively with hypothetical situations (Burr, 1967, p. 131). Data were gathered from 116 couples representing all age-groups. The sample included 11 postparental and 10 retired couples (males' average age was 47.5, females' average age was 45.6).

Scoring, Scale Norms, and Distribution

The responses for each dimension are summed according to the weights provided. Scale scores range from 3 to 16, with high scores indicating greater satisfaction. Average scores are unavailable because data are presented in figures.

Usability on Older Populations

The instrument appears to be usable for older populations.

Sensitivity to Age Differences

Although the small sample size limits confidence in the findings, there appears to be a slight tendency for the couples with children of school age to report lowest satisfaction.

General Comments and Recommendations

The measurement strategy creates an explicitly defined multidimensional instrument. An empirical assessment of the conceptual structure and data pertaining to reliability and validity of the measure would be useful.

The limited sample size precludes a true assessment of the usability of this instrument with either the elderly or the lower socioeconomic strata. The dimension that examines relationships with children would not appear to be too strongly influenced by the absence of offspring from the home.

References

Burr, W. R. "Marital Satisfaction: A Conceptual Reformulation, Theory and Partial Test of the Theory." Ph.D. dissertation, University of Minnesota, 1967.

_____. "Satisfaction with Various Aspects of Marriage over the Life Cycle: A Random Middle Class Sample." *Journal of Marriage and the Family*, 1970, 32: 29-37.

_____. "An Expansion and Test of a Role Theory of Marital Satisfaction." *Journal of Marriage and the Family*, 1971, 33: 368-72.

Instrument

See Instrument V2.3.I.h.

PERCEPTIONS OF MARRIAGE

N. Stinnett, L. Carter, and J. Montgomery, 1972

Definition of Variable or Concept

Husbands' and wives' perceptions of marriage are measured by this instrument.

Description of Instrument

Perceptions of Marriage is a 10-item battery concerning present marital happiness, factors important to marital success, and recall questions about change in the marriage over time. Only the first 8 items specifically concern the marital relationship.

Method of Administration

The instrument is a mailed questionnaire.

Context of Development and Subsequent Use

This instrument was developed as part of a questionnaire sent to persons on a mailing list of senior centers in Oklahoma.

Sample

Questionnaires were completed by 408 older husbands and wives (not necessarily couples). These individuals were located from the mailing lists of senior centers in Oklahoma.

The age range of the respondents was 60 to 89; 36% of the respondents were aged 65 to 69. The sample was 96% Caucasian, and a plurality (38%) had less than a high school education. Approximately 50% of the sample had lived in small (less than 25,000 population) towns for most of their lives.

Scoring, Scale Norms, and Distribution

Item frequencies for the 10-item battery are reported in Stinnett, Carter, and Montgomery (1972). Older persons favorably evaluate their marital happiness, and 45.4% to 54.9% select the most favorable response option on the five ordinally scaled items. Almost half (48.6%) consider being in love to be the most important factor in achieving marital success, and a plurality consider respect to be the most important characteristic of a successful marriage.

Usability on Older Populations

None of the questions would appear to cause difficulty in use with older populations.

General Comments and Recommendations

The pattern of response to the items in this 10-item battery strongly suggests the possibility of response bias.

Reference

Stinnett, N., L. Carter, and J. Montgomery. "Older Persons' Perceptions of Their Marriages." *Journal of Marriage and the Family*, 1972, 34: 665-71.

Instrument

This instrument is not available in its exact form at this time.

MARITAL SATISFACTION

B. C. Miller, 1976

Definition of Variable or Concept

This instrument measures marital satisfaction as it is subjectively defined by the respondent.

Description of Instrument

This index of marital satisfaction is composed of seven items that assess satisfaction in the following areas of marriage: (1) finances, (2) recreation, (3) affection, (4) task performance in the household, (5) relations with in-laws, (6) sexual relations, and (7) religious beliefs. Respondents indicate their degree of satisfaction on a five-point scale of expressed satisfaction.

Method of Administration

The instrument is administered during personal interviews.

Context of Development and Subsequent Use

The items examine aspects of the dyadic relationship as identified by Hamilton (1929), Terman (1938), and Burgess and Cottrell (1939).

Sample

A representative sample of 212 Minneapolis adults was drawn. From this, 140 married individuals were selected for analysis. Females constituted 59.3% of the sample. Seven stages of the family life cycle were represented, with 7 couples in the launching stage and 10 couples in the retirement stage.

Scoring, Scale Norms, and Distribution

The seven items on the scale were standardized and summed with unit weighting, yielding an index with a mean of 0 and a standard deviation of 4.74. Retirement-age persons score between 1.0 and 1.5 (Miller, 1976, p. 652).

Formal Tests of Reliability/Homogeneity

Miller (1976) reported a Cronbach's alpha of .81 for the seven-item instrument.

Formal Tests of Validity

The items all loaded on the first factor in a principal-factoring solution with loadings greater than .40. Single factor structure was inferred from a screen test examining the discontinuity of eigenvalues.

Usability on Older Populations

This instrument appears to be usable with older populations.

Sensitivity to Age Differences

Marital satisfaction is reported as lowest in the second stage (from the birth of first child until the first child begins school), after which it climbs relatively consistently through the retirement stage. At the same time, individuals who were married for more than 36 years reported decreased marital satisfaction when compared to those married 26 to 35 years.

General Comments and Recommendations

The instrument seems to measure adequately expressed satisfaction with various aspects of marriage. As Miller hypothesized, the instrument exhibits properties of unidimensionality, but convergent and discriminant validity assessments are needed.

The variation in age-related trends in marital satisfaction according to stage of the family life cycle and length of marriage is disconcerting. The sample size at each of the stages may be too small to permit accurate estimates of mean index scores for each stage. The instrument should be tested more with samples of older adults.

References

Burgess, E. W., and L. Cottrell, Jr. *Predicting Success or Failure in Marriage*. New York: Prentice-Hall, 1939.

Hamilton, G. V. *A Research in Marriage*. New York: A and C Boni, 1929.

Miller, B. C. "A Multivariate Developmental Model of Marital Satisfaction." *Journal of Marriage and the Family*, 1976, 38: 643-57.

Terman, L. *Psychological Factors in Marital Happiness*. New York: McGraw-Hill, 1938.

Instrument

See Instrument V2.3.I.j.

EASE OF ROLE TRANSITION

B. C. Miller, 1976

Definition of Variable or Concept

Ease of role transition is "the degree to which there is freedom from difficulty in beginning to perform, or ceasing performance, in any particular role" (Miller, 1976, p. 644).

Description of Instrument

The first item of this six-item scale ascertains the most recent family role transition, and the remaining five items concern the ease of the transition. Respondents indicate their agreement or disagreement on a four-point scale to questions on the amount, ease, concern, and adjustment associated with the transition.

Method of Administration

The scale is administered during personal interviews.

Context of Development and Subsequent Use

Current marital satisfaction was the principal criterion variable in this study. It was hypothesized that the ease of the most recent transition would be positively related to marital satisfaction. The exact wording of the instrument varies slightly, depending on the stage of the family life cycle of the respondent.

Sample

From a representative sample of 212 Minneapolis adults, 140 married individuals were selected for analysis. Females made up 59.3% of the sample. Seven stages of the family life cycle were represented, with 7 couples in the launching stage and 10 couples in the retirement stage.

Scoring, Scale Norms, and Distribution

After reflection of the variables with negative loadings, responses to the five items on the ease of role transition index are standardized and summed with unit weighting. This yields a scale with a mean of 0 and a standard deviation of 3.51. Weights given with the instrument are those *after reflection*.

Formal Test of Reliability/Homogeneity

Miller (1975; 1976) reported a Cronbach's alpha of .75.

Formal Test of Validity

The five items load on the first factor of a principal-factoring analysis. Factor loadings are .65, −.70, .48, −.60, and .59, respectively, for the five items in question number 2 on the instrument.

Ease of Role Transition correlates positively (as the investigator hypothesized) with marital satisfaction ($r = .23$; $\beta = .172$).

Usability on Older Populations

No problems in using this instrument were noted by Miller. There would appear to be no problem in using this instrument with older samples; however, see the general comments below.

Sensitivity to Age Differences

Miller (1975; 1976) reported zero-order correlation ($r = .098$) and a path coefficient ($\beta = .20$, full path model) relating duration of marriage to ease of role transition. The path coefficient decreases ($\beta = .047$) in the trimmed version.

General Comments and Recommendations

This instrument is included in this chapter because it examines a concept of interest to researchers studying age-related phenomena. The explicit connection of the adjustment or ease-of-transition items to a specific role transition (such as widowhood) allows researchers to make comparisons about the relative difficulty of any given transition with a somewhat greater degree of confidence.

As Miller noted (1975; 1976), it is possible that a given transition might be more difficult or that the *structure* of the ease of transition might vary across the family life cycle. Researchers who wish to study a more limited sample of transitions in greater detail may want to expand the item pool with transition-specific items. However, insofar as this research has documented the appearance of a general ease of role transition dimension relatively distinct from marital satisfaction, it may represent a viable strategy for researchers to use in measuring adjustment as a distinct conceptual issue.

References

Miller, B. C. "A Multivariate Developmental Model of Marital Satisfaction." Paper presented to the meeting of the Midwest Sociological Society, Chicago, 1975.

_____. "A Multivariate Developmental Model of Marital Satisfaction." *Journal of Marriage and the Family*, 1976, 38: 643-57.

Instrument

See Instrument V2.3.I.k.

MARITAL COMMUNICATION AND AGREEMENT

R. Hill, 1970

Definition of Variable or Concept

Communication and agreement between spouses are seen as parts of the general domain of family organization.

Description of Instrument

This 13-item test examines a variety of family topics, such as finances, public behavior, religion, and household-task allocation. Respondents rate the frequency of discussion on a three-point ordinal scale and the extent of perceived spousal agreement on a five-point scale of agreement-disagreement.

Method of Administration

Hill used this instrument as a paper-and-pencil test. It could easily be used in an interview format.

Context of Development

The instrument was used in a three-generation, longitudinal study of family consumption patterns.

Sample

The unique three-generation sample included 312 couples, of which 100 were grandparents. The sample was drawn from the Minneapolis-St. Paul metropolitan area.

Scoring, Scale Norms, and Distribution

There are two separate indexes—the marital communication score and the marital agreement score. Each score is the simple sum of the item-response weights. (See Instrument V2.3.I.l.)

The median score for the grandparent generation on marital communication is 4.6; the median score for marital agreement is 36.5. Further data regarding all generations and all measures of marital organization are available in Hill, 1970 (p. 50).

Usability on Older Populations

The items are clearly worded and they appear to be appropriate for all age and educational levels.

Sensitivity to Age Differences

In the three generations studied by Hill, marital communication declines with age/generation and marital agreement increases with age/generation (Hill, 1970, p. 50).

General Comments and Recommendations

Although the measure appears to have a high degree of face validity for all ages/generations, further work on the reliability and validity of each of the separate indexes is needed. Factor analytic procedures could be employed to test the unidimensionality of each of the constructs.

Reference

Hill, R. *Family Development in Three Generations*. Cambridge, Mass.: Schenkman, 1970.

Instrument

See Instrument V2.3.I.l.

MARITAL INTEGRATION INDEX

B. Farber, 1957

Definition of Variable or Concept

The Marital Integration Index measures the "degree of family integration . . . by the extent to which family members agree on the rank-ordering of values and the degree of appropriate coordination of domestic roles" (Farber, 1975, p. 119).

Description of Instrument

The Marital Integration Index is composed of two dimensions: role tension and value consensus. Farber's original version (Farber, 1957; Farber and Blackman, 1956) consisted of 10 items on each of the subscales. The index of role tension included several "positive" or "neutral" traits that were not used in scale construction (Farber and Blackman, 1956).

The index of value consensus involves ranking items from 1 to 10 according to the importance of that item to the success of families (Farber, 1957).

The index of role tension involves the rating of self and spouse on 10 personality traits. Responses vary on a five-point scale of "very much" (−2) to "hasn't the trait at all" (+2) (Farber and Blackman, 1956).

Kerckhoff (1966) used a shortened version of the value consensus index that consisted of only seven items. His deletions are noted in Instrument V2.3.I.m.

Method of Administration

Personal interviews with both husbands and wives are held in separate rooms to avoid collusion.

Context of Development and Subsequent Use

The index of role tension was developed from the Burgess and Wallin prediction study (1953). Role tension is considered cumulative and mutually stimulating.

The index of value consensus assumes that integration as a value system is dependent on the consensus of family members as to the rank ordering of outcomes.

Samples

The index of role tension (Farber and Blackman, 1956) was developed with 211 couples, who provided information after 3 years and 14 years of marriage for the Burgess and Wallin prediction study (1953). It was later used in a sample of 99 married couples, the same individuals with which the index of value consensus and the composite Marital Integration Index were developed. Neither sample included older persons.

Hill (1970) employed this measure in a three-generation sample of residents of the Minneapolis-St. Paul metropolitan area. Goodman (1968) also reported on these data. The total sample numbered 312 couples, of which 100 were grandparents.

Kerckhoff (1966) used the two subscales in a sample of 135 retired white couples from the Piedmont region of North Carolina. Subjects were chosen in such a way as to maximize the occupational distribution of the sample. All subjects had at least one child who was either married or who was at least 25 years old.

Scoring, Scale Norms, and Distribution

The index of value consensus is scored as the Spearman rank correlation coefficient, rho, which indicates the degree of agreement between the rankings of husbands and wives.

Farber and Blackman (1956) scored the index of role tension by summing both husbands' and wives' ratings of the personality traits for self and spouse. The combination of these four ratings yields a scale that varies from −80 to 80.

Kerckhoff (1966) scored the index of role tension by summing only the negative traits attributed to the spouse. This combination of two scores yields a scale with a theoretical range from −40 to 40.

Farber (1957) created a composite index of marital integration by arranging scores on the two subscales in quartiles. For each subscale, the lowest quartile is assigned a score of 0 and the highest quartile, a score of 3. These are added to create a score, varying from 0 to 6, that measures integration.

Goodman (1968) reported a mean marital integration of 3.36 for 42 retired couples. The average for grandparents on the index of value consensus is 0.28. Grandparents average 31.9 on the tension index.

Hill (1970) reported grandparents' median scores of 0.25 for value consensus and 33.0 for the tension index.

Formal Test of Reliability/Homogeneity

Farber (1957) reported a test-retest correlation of .77 for the index of role tensions.

Formal Test of Validity

The 10 items on the index of role tensions were selected on the basis of a principal components analysis in which all 10 items loaded highly on the first factor. Refactoring of only 10 tension items indicates that 49% of the total variance was accounted for by the first factor.

Predictive validity is claimed insofar as marriage-adjustment scores obtained 3 years after marriage significantly correlate with tension scores achieved after 14 years (Farber and Blackman, 1956, p. 601).

Usability on Older Populations

Kerckhoff (1966) did not use three items from the index of value consensus because of difficulty encountered in having older persons rank the items. The items deleted were "healthy and happy children," "personality development," and "a home."

General Comments and Recommendations

This instrument utilizes an interesting approach to measuring value consensus; further justification for the selection of these value statements as representative of the item pool is needed. The relationship between the two subscales is not presented; hence, justification for the combination of the two indexes into one composite measure is needed.

References

Burgess, E. W., and P. Wallin. *Engagement and Marriage*. Philadelphia: J. B. Lippincott Company, 1953.

Farber, B. "An Index of Marital Integration." *Sociometry*, 1957, 20: 117-34.

Farber, B., and L. S. Blackman. "Marital Role Tensions and Number and Sex of Children." *American Sociological Review*, 1956, 21: 590-601.

Goodman, A. D. "Marital Adjustment in a Three Generation Sample." M. A. thesis, University of Minnesota, 1968.

Hill, R. *Family Development in Three Generations*. Cambridge, Mass.: Schenkman, 1970.

Kerckhoff, A.C. "Family Patterns and Morale in Retirement." In *Social Aspects of Aging*, I. H. Simpson and J. C. McKinney (eds.), pp. 173-92. Durham N.C.: Duke University Press, 1966.

Instrument

See Instrument V2.3.I.m.

TASK SHARING

A. C. Kerckhoff, 1965

Definition of Variable or Concept

The degree to which husbands and wives accept norms of task sharing or prefer task segregation and specialization is examined.

Description of Instrument

This nine-item, Likert-type index indicates the respondent's opinion of what activities are "proper" for husbands and wives.

Method of Administration

This instrument is administered in a personal interview.

Context of Development and Subsequent Use

The items were included as part of an extensive interview that examined nuclear and extended family relationships during the later years of life.

Sample

A purposive sample of 201 older white couples was drawn from the Piedmont region of North Carolina. The subjects were chosen in such a way as to maximize occupational distribution. All the subjects had at least one child who was married or at least 25 years old. Males in the sample had either retired or were within 5 years of retirement.

Scoring, Scale Norms, and Distribution

Responses are summed so that a high score indicates acceptance of task sharing. Scale scores can range from 9 through 45.

Kerckhoff reported average task sharing scores of 14.83 and 17.88 (extended family husbands and wives, respectively), 17.67 and 17.96 (modified extended), and 18.66 and 22.73 (nuclear family) in his sample (Kerckhoff, 1965).

Formal Test of Validity

Kerckhoff (1966) reported a husband-wife Pearson correlation of .327.

Usability on Older Populations

Since this instrument is a normative index, the use of item number 7 (disciplining children) should not distort scale scores insofar as recall of normative issues is less problematic than recall of affective states or exhibited behaviors.

General Comments and Recommendations

The measurement properties of this instrument need to be addressed more completely. The unidimensionality of the scale has not been demonstrated, nor has its internal consistency. Husband-wife correlation indicates a relatively low degree of dyadic agreement. Replication is needed.

References

Kerckhoff, A.C. "Nuclear and Extended Family Relationships: A Normative and Behavioral Analysis." In *Social Structure and the Family: Generational Relations*, E. Shanas and G. F. Streib (eds.), pp. 93-112. Englewood Cliffs, N.J.: Prentice-Hall, 1965.

_____. "Norm-Value Clusters and the Strain toward Consistency among Older Married Couples." In *Social Aspects of Aging*, I. H. Simpson and J. C. McKinney (eds.), pp. 138-59. Durham, N.C.: Duke University Press, 1966.

Instrument

See Instrument V2.3.II.a.

MALE HOUSEHOLD ACTIVITIES

A. Lipman, 1961

Definition of Variable or Concept

Male household activities are seen as indexing the degree to which a husband has retained an instrumental definition of himself following retirement.

Description of Instrument

This 12-item battery was designed to elicit information about whether the husband participates in household activities.

Method of Administration

The instrument is administered in a personal interview.

Context of Development and Subsequent Use

The instrument was designed to test the hypothesis that husbands adopt a quasi-instrumental role in the home after retirement.

Sample

The sample included 100 retired couples over 60 years of age and residing in Dade County, Florida (Miami). The respondents were mostly migrants from other states and of high socioeconomic status.

Scoring, Scale Norms, and Distribution

Since this instrument is a battery of items, it is not summated. Item frequencies were reported by Lipman (1961).

Usability on Older Populations

The battery appears to be usable; it was designed for use with an aged population.

General Comments and Recommendations

Although Lipman suggested that retired males adopt a quasi-instrumental role in the home, he presented neither longitudinal nor cross-sectional data.

This battery actually may tend to underestimate males' activities insofar as other traditionally defined household activities for males such as mowing the lawn, doing small repairs, etc., are not included in the instrument. However, to obtain a parameter estimate of male-female task participation, a *representative* sample of tasks must be presented.

References

Lipman, A. "Marital Roles of the Retired Aged." *Merrill-Palmer Quarterly*, 1960, 6: 192-95.

_____. "Role Conceptions and Morale of Couples in Retirement." *Journal of Gerontology*, 1961, 16: 267-71.

_____. "Role Conceptions of Couples in Retirement." In *Social and Psychological Aspects of Aging*, C. Tibbitts and W. Donahue (eds.), pp. 475-85. New York: Columbia University Press, 1962.

Instrument

See Instrument V2.3.II.b.

HUSBAND'S PARTICIPATION

A. C. Kerckhoff, 1965

Definition of Variable or Concept

Husband's Participation is "an index of the degree to which the husband had assumed responsibility for some of the tasks traditionally carried out by wives . . ." (Kerckhoff, 1965, p. 103).

Description of Instrument

This nine-item index focuses on "who does" a series of household tasks. Responses are coded on a size-point ordinal scale of frequency varying from 0 ("wife always") through 5 ("husband always").

Method of Administration

The instrument is administered in a personal interview.

Context of Development and Subsequent Use

This measure was developed as part of an extensive interview oriented toward an understanding of the contemporary American kinship structure. Items in this index are quite similar to those in Blood and Wolfe's (1960) Division of Labor index (which is reviewed elsewhere in this chapter).

Sample

A purposive sample of 201 older white couples was drawn from the Piedmont region of North Carolina. The subjects were chosen in such a way as to maximize the distribution across occupations. All the subjects had at least one child who was married or at least 25 years old. Males in the sample had either retired or were within 5 years of retirement.

Scoring, Scale Norms, and Distribution

Responses are summed so that a high score indicates a high degree of participation by husbands in family tasks. This is then averaged in order to adjust for variations in the number of tasks performed within each family.

Formal Test of Validity

Kerckhoff stated that the responses of husbands and wives were "generally quite similar" (Kerckhoff, 1965, p. 103).

Usability on Older Populations

The instrument appears to be usable; it was designed for use with an older sample.

General Comments and Recommendations

The tasks that were chosen for inclusion in this scale are biased toward traditional female roles in the family. Only one family role that is traditionally male is included (doing minor household repairs), and "paying bills" and "grocery shopping" are roles likely to be shared (Blood and Wolfe, 1960). The remaining six items tend to describe female-dominated roles. As a result, this instrument may tend to underestimate the husband's participation in the family. To obtain a parameter estimate of male-female participation, a *representative* sample of tasks must be examined.

The six response categories provided for the index may not be truly ordinal. The distinction drawn between "usually done together" and "sometimes one, sometimes the other" is not at all clear, and yet the latter response is arbitrarily deemed to be indicative of greater participation by husbands in family tasks.

Further work on this instrument is recommended, especially in addressing the dimensionality and related measurement properties of the instrument.

References

Blood, R. O., and D. M. Wolfe. *Husbands and Wives: The Dynamics of Married Living.* New York: Free Press, 1960.

Kerckhoff, A.C. "Nuclear and Extended Family Relationships: A Normative and Behavioral Analysis." In *Social Structure and the Family: Generational Relations*, E. Shanas and G. F. Streib (eds.), pp. 93-112. Englewood Cliffs, N.J.: Prentice-Hall, 1965.

Instrument

See Instrument V2.3.II.c.

HOUSEHOLD TASK PERFORMANCE

J. A. Ballweg, 1967

Definiton of Variable or Concept

"The extent to which a selected list of household tasks was performed by the husband, the wife, or hired help" (Ballweg, 1967, p. 278) is examined.

Description of Instrument

A total of 12 specific tasks were selected on the basis of a Q-sort of 30 different household tasks performed by 25 raters (middle-class husbands and wives). Respondents indicate the extent to which husband, wife, or hired help perform these taks, with responses varying on a five-point ordinal scale of frequency ranging from "never" to "always."

Method of Administration

These data were collected as a part of personal interviews with housewives.

Context of Development and Subsequent Use

The instrument was developed to assess the adjustments of the conjugal unit to the change in roles within the family brought about by the retirement of the husband.

Sample

Fifty-two couples from urban areas were selected for the study. In all cases, the husband was at least 65 years old. Invalids and institutionalized older persons were eliminated; all of the dyads included in the sample maintained independent housing arrangements. In 34.6% of the cases the husband was employed outside the home. The average age of husbands in the sample was 69; the average age of retired husbands was 71 years. The average age of wives with working husbands was 61 years; the average age of wives with retired husbands was 65 years. Having an education beyond high school was characteristic of 27.8% of the working husbands and 11.8% of the retired husbands.

Scoring, Scale Norms, and Distribution

Responses to the 12 items are summed separately for husbands and wives and then readjusted to a 5-point scale by dividing by the number of applicable items. A plurality of retired husbands and a majority of working husbands are reported as "never" participating in household tasks, while the opposite is true of housewives. Wives of working husbands report that they "always" fulfill household tasks in 44.9% of the cases.

Formal Test of Validity

Items were selected on the basis of a Q-sort of 30 potential items. The Q-sort was done on a limited sample of 25 middle-class husbands and wives.

Usability on Older Populations

The instrument appears to be usable with older populations; in fact, it was designed for use with an older group.

General Comments and Recommendations

The sampling of items reflects masculine, feminine, and administrative tasks and covers a range of household duties. No items are concerned with child-care responsibilities; this reflects the instrument's sensitivity to an older population.

The skewed responses may reflect a bias brought about through interviewing wives only. True data on couples, as well as further assessment of the measurement properties of this instrument, are needed. Longitudinal studies are needed in order to realistically assess the impact of retirement on household-task performance. Time-budget methodologies might be employed in order to provide validation data.

Item number 8 may be partially obsolete in some geographic areas where antipollution regulations forbid the burning of trash.

Reference

Ballweg, J. A. "Resolution of Conjugal Role Adjustment after Retirement." *Journal of Marriage and the Family*, 1967, 29: 277-81.

Instrument

See Instrument V2.3.II.d.

RATIONALITY IN DECISION MAKING

R. Hill, 1963; 1965; 1970

Definition of Variable or Concept

Rationality is defined as the degree to which families search for information, consult among themselves, and weigh the consequences of their decisions (Hill, 1970, p. 197).

Description of Instrument

This instrument is an eight-item Guttman scale that looks at information-search procedures, discussion within and outside the family, long- and short-term satisfactions, examination of the costs and benefits of a given decision vis-à-vis alternatives, and whether a family policy exists pertaining to decisions in this domain.

Method of Administration

This measure is based on interviewers' ratings of data elicited from couples. In the original Hill study, the rationality of a range of purchasing decisions was averaged for each couple to obtain the final rationality score. As a result, the instrument can be used for assessing a single, uniformly present decision or for assessing a sample of possible decisions.

Context of Development

The instrument was included as part of a longitudinal study of consumption patterns of three-generation families in the Minneapolis-St. Paul metropolitan area.

Sample

The three-generation sample included a total of 312 couples, of which 100 were grandparents. The sample was identified through previous polling of the population of the Twin Cities.

Scoring, Scale Norms, and Distribution

Rationality is scored as the number of correct responses to the scale items. Scores range from 0 through 8. When more than one decision is examined, scores are averaged across decisions.

The grandparent generation achieved a mean score of 4.61 on this instrument. Hill (1970, p. 205) reported the percentage distributions for the scale for each of the three generations.

Formal Test of Reliability

The coefficient of reproducibility was .874 for the grandparents, .889 for the parents, and .90 for the children.

Formal Tests of Validity

Rationality is moderately correlated with two indicators of specificity of plans ($r = .22$; $r = .14$), total number of actions ($r = .31$), percentage of actions preceded by plans ($r = .36$), and percentage of specific plans fulfilled on time ($r = .29$), thus suggesting that rationality will improve the likelihood of achieving goals (Hill, 1963, pp. 450-51).

The husband's education is positively correlated with rationality when all generations are pooled ($r = .21$). This relationship is negative for the grandparent generation. Hill suggested that highly educated grandparents may have formulated policies and rules to circumvent many aspects of rational decision making.

Usability on Older Populations

With proper training of interviewers, this instrument should be applicable for use with older populations. Specific difficulties may center around the weighing of the costs and benefits of alternative decisions (item 3 on the instrument).

Sensitivity to Age Differences

Grandparents score lowest on rationality, followed by parents, and then children (Hill, 1970, p. 205). The age of the husband and the age of the wife are positively correlated with rationality ($r = .28$ and $r = .25$, respectively); but within the grandparent generation a negative relationship emerges for the husband's age and a positive relationship emerges for the wife's age (Hill, 1970, p. 209).

General Comments and Recommendations

The instrument appears to tap a range of possible issues pertinent to decision making. The negative correlation between education and rationality in the grandparent generation is, however, counter intuitive. Researchers are strongly urged to examine the Guttman ordering of this instrument when it is used with samples of older adults.

References

Aldous J. "Family Continuity Patterns over Three Generations: Content, Degree of Transmission, and Consequences." Ph.D. dissertation, University of Minnesota, 1963.

Hill, R. "Judgement and Consumership in the Management of Family Resources." *Sociology and Social Research*, 1963, 47 (4): 446-60.

_____. "Decision Making and the Family Life Cycle." In *Social Structure and the Family: Generational Relations*, E. Shanas and G. F. Streib (eds.), pp. 113-39. Englewood Cliffs, N.J.: Prentice-Hall, 1965.

_____. *Family Development in Three Generations*. Cambridge, Mass.: Schenkman, 1970.

Instrument

See Instrument V2.3.II.e.

DECISION POWER INDEX (DPI)

R. O. Blood and D. M. Wolfe, 1960

Definition of Variable or Concept

Power is defined as "the potential ability of one partner to influence the other's behavior. Power is manifested in the ability to make decisions affecting the life of the family" (Blood and Wolfe, 1960, p. 11).

Description of Instrument

The respondent is asked to indicate who makes the *final decision* with regard to eight family decisions. Responses are given on a five-point scale varying from "(1) wife always" to "(5) husband always."

Method of Administration

This instrument is administered in personal interviews.

Context of Development and Subsequent Use

This instrument was designed and used in an extensive survey of the contemporary American family and in a three-generation study (Hill, 1965; 1970). There have been many revisions of this basic instrument, including cross-cultural revisions (Blood and Takeshita, 1964; Safilios-Rothschild, 1967; Michel, 1967; Buric and Zecevic, 1967).

Sample(s)

This instrument has been used on a number of different samples. (See Table 3-5.)

Scoring, Scale Norms, and Distribution

There are a number of scoring systems. Blood and Wolfe (1960) reported scoring the eight questions on a 10-point scale reflecting the husband's degree of influence on which a score of 4 is equivalent to "husband and wife exactly the same" (Blood and Wolfe, 1960, p. 23). Different scoring systems are used for the cross-cultural studies.

Wolfe (1959) developed four family power types based on the Decision Power Index (DPI) and scored through simple summation (ranging from 8 through 40) and a Shared Power Index (SPI). The SPI is a frequency count of the number of decisions for which husband and wife share responsibility (range of 0 through 8). The four family power types are: (1) syncratic families (SPI greater than, or equal to, 4), (2) husband-dominant families (SPI of 0 to 3 and DPI of 29 to 40), (3) wife-dominant families (SPI of 0 to 3 and DPI of 8 to 19), and (4) autonomic families (SPI of 0 to 3 and DPI of 20 to 28). This typology attempts to differentiate between a separate-but-equal power structure and a shared power structure.

TABLE 3-5
Summary Descriptions of the Samples Using the Blood-Wolfe Decision Power Index

Researcher(s)	Sample Size	Percentage over Age 60	Location	Comments
Blood and Wolfe	909	15%	Detroit & south-eastern Michigan	Principal analysis focuses on 731 married women
Hill	312	31.2%[*]	Minnea-polis-St. Paul SMSA	Intergenerational sample
Safilios-Rothschild	250	NR	Athens, Greece	Random sample
Michel	550	NR	Paris & Bordeaux, France	Random sample
Buric and Zecevic	117	NR	Kragujevac, Yugoslavia	Random sample

[*]Grandparent generation.

Formal Tests of Reliability/Homogeneity

Bahr (1973) reported coefficients of reproducibility of .86 for husbands and .88 for wives; coefficient alpha is reported as .62.

Formal Tests of Validity

Granbois and Willett (1970) reported a husband-wife correlation of .353.

Turk and Bell (1972) reported that each spouse tends to underreport his or her own score on the Decision Power Index and overreport the marital partner's (Wilcoxon matched-pairs, signed-ranks test, $p = .03$). Husbands and wives agreed on the distribution of power in 21.2% of the cases, and 28.3% reported disagreement ranging from 5 scale points to 16 scale points.

Turk and Bell (1972) also reported rank correlations (Goodman and Kruskal gamma) between the Decision Power Index and the following measures of power: (1) Heer (1958):$\gamma = .17$; (2) a single-item measure, "Who is the real boss in your family?": $\gamma = .54$; (3) Kenkel's (1957) outcome measure on a decision; to spend $300: $\gamma = -.19$; (4) revealed differences: $\gamma = -.17$; (5) relative number of units of action initiated: $\gamma = .11$; (6) relative number of instrumental acts initiated: $\gamma = .09$; (7) index of directive control: $\gamma = -.02$; and (8) relative number of interruptions initiated: $\gamma = .05$.

Turk and Bell (1972) reported that the Decision Power Index correlates with male dominance ideology (Hoffman, 1960) .54 for husbands and .34 for wives (Goodman and Kurskal gamma).

Usability on Older Populations

The eight decisions appear to tap those that most couples make in the course of a marriage. The salience and/or direction of the eight decisions for older persons might be questioned. For example, a decision about retirement might well be a more salient issue to older families than what job a husband should take.

Sensitivity to Age Differences

Blood and Wolfe (1960) reported that power is related to stage of the family life cycle. A husband's power increases slightly during the preschool stage and then declines until the postparental stage. A slight increase in the power of postparental males is reported; retirement-stage couples report decreased husband power (Blood and Wolfe, 1960, p. 42). A similar pattern is found in French data (Michel, 1967). Greek data (Safilios-Rothschild, 1967) show a nearly linear decline in a husband's decision-making power.

Hill (1965) reported that the grandparent generation was more likely to be wife dominated or husband dominated. Relatively few egalitarian marriages are reported among the grandparent generation.

General Comments and Recommendations

This instrument has been widely used and has stimulated much controversy regarding the face validity of the measure (Safilios-Rothschild, 1970; Bahr, 1972; Heer, 1963; Olson, 1969; Olson and Rabunsky, 1972).

Turk and Bell (1972) indicated low or negative correlations between the Decision Power Index and many behavioral measures of power, as well as strong correlations with male dominance ideology and reported boss. This suggests that the Decision Power Index may be tapping a normative "who should" component of decision making as part of the measurement protocol.

It is important to note that the Blood-Wolfe measure only examines the relative power of the husband compared to the wife. When using behavioral measures, Turk and Bell (1972) found that children possess power in families. Though the aging family often returns to a dyadic structure, this in and of itself does not preclude the possibility of children holding power. Indeed, if aging parents and their adult children *do* live together, then it becomes even more important to investigate the distribution of power among all members of a household.

Price-Bonham (1976) has suggested that the importance of making decisions should be considered in studies of family power. This consideration could be tested as part of a nonadditive measurement model.

References

Bahr, S. J. "Comment on 'The Study of Family Power Structure 1960-1969.'" *Journal of Marriage and the Family*, 1972, 34: 239-43.

_____ . "The Internal Consistency of Blood and Wolfe's Measure of Conjugal Power: A Research Note." *Journal of Marriage and the Family*, 1973, 35: 293-95.

Blood, R. O., and Y. J. Takeshita. "Development of Cross-cultural Equivalence of Measures of Marital Interaction for U.S.A. and Japan, " *Transactions of the Fifth World Congress of Sociology*, 1964, 4: 333-44.

Blood, R. O., and D. M. Wolfe. *Husbands and Wives: The Dynamics of Married Living*. New York: Free Press, 1960.

Buric, O., and A. Zecevic, "Family Authority, Marital Satisfaction, and the Social Network in Yugoslavia." *Journal of Marriage and the Family*, 1967, 29: 325-36.

Granbois, D., and R. Willett. "Equivalence of Family Role Measures Based on Husband and Wife Data." *Journal of Marriage and the Family*, 1970, 32: 68-72.

Heer, D. "Dominance and the Working Wife." *Social Forces*, 1958, 34: 341-47.

_____. "The Measurement and Bases of Family Power: An Overview." *Journal of Marriage and the Family*, 1963, 25: 133-39.

Hill, R. "Decision Making and the Family Life Cycle." In *Social Structure and the Family: Generational Relations*, E. Shanas and G. F. Streib (eds.), pp. 113-39. Englewood Cliffs, N.J.: Prentice-Hall, 1965.

_____. *Family Development in Three Generations*. Cambridge, Mass.: Schenkman, 1970.

Hoffman, M. L. "Power Assertion by the Parent and Its Impact on the Child." *Child Development*, 1960, 31: 129-43.

Kenkel, W. F. "Influence Differentiation in Family Decision Making." *Sociology and Social Research*, 1957, 42: 18-25.

Michel, A. "Comparative Data Concerning the Interaction in French and American Families." *Journal of Marriage and the Family*, 1967, 29: 337-44.

Olson, D. H. "The Measurement of Family Power by Self-Report and Behavioral Methods." *Journal of Marriage and the Family*, 1969, 31: 545-50.

Olson, D. H., and C. Rabunsky. "Validity of Four Measures of Family Power." *Journal of Marriage and the Family*, 1972, 34: 224-34.

Price-Bonham, S. "A Comparison of Weighted and Unweighted Decision-making Scores." *Journal of Marriage and the Family*, 1976, 38: 629-40.

Safilios-Rothschild, C. "A Comparison of Power Structure and Marital Satisfaction in Urban Greek and French Families." *Journal of Marriage and the Family*, 1967, 29: 345-52.

_____. "The Study of Family Power Structure: A Review 1960-1969." *Journal of Marriage and the Family*, 1970, 32: 539-52.

Straus, M. *Family Measurement Techniques*. Minneapolis: University of Minnesota Press, 1969.

Turk, J. L., and N. W. Bell. "Measuring Power in Families." *Journal of Marriage and the Family*, 1972, 34: 215-22.

Wolfe, D. M. "Power and Authority in the Family." In *Studies in Social Power*, D. Cartwright (ed.), pp. 99-117. Mich.: Institute for Social Research, 1959.

Instrument

See Instrument V2.3.II.f.

DIVISION OF LABOR

R. O. Blood, 1958; R. O. Blood and D. M. Wolfe, 1960

Definition of Variable or Concept

The Division of Labor instrument measures a number of different issues. Relative task participation refers to the degree to which a husband or a wife performs standard household tasks. Role specialization refers to the extent to which tasks are "performed exclusively by one partner but not necessarily by the traditional partner" (Blood and Wolfe, 1960, p. 50). Adherence to traditional sex roles refers to the extent to which spouses perform their culturally prescribed tasks.

Description of Instrument

Eight different household tasks are used as an example of all household tasks. The eight are: (1) making repairs, (2) mowing the lawn, (3) shoveling the sidewalk, (4) keeping track of the money, (5) shopping for groceries, (6) husband's breakfast, (7) straightening up the

living room, and (8) washing the evening dishes. Subjects respond on a five-point scale ranging from "(1) husband always" through "(5) wife always."

Method of Administration

These data are collected through personal interviews.

Context of Development and Subsequent Use

This instrument was developed as part of a larger study to examine the factors that determine how husbands and wives interact and the effect of their interaction on the husband,
the wife, and the family.

This instrument has been used in a number of studies, including a three-generation study
(Hill, 1965; 1970) and two cross-cultural studies (Silverman and Hill, 1967; Michel, 1970).

Sample(s)

See Table 3-6.

TABLE 3-6
Summary Descriptions of the Samples Using the Blood-Wolfe Division of Labor Measure

Researcher(s)	Sample Size	Percentage over Age 60	Location	Comments
Blood and Wolfe (1960)	909	15%	Detroit & south-eastern Michigan	Principal analysis focuses on 731 urban and subur-ban wives*
Hill (1965; 1970)	312	31.2% (grandparent generation)	Minnea-polis-St. Paul SMSA	Sample of intact generation families all living within 50 miles of Minnea-polis-St. Paul
Silverman and Hill (1967)	500	7.8% (retired couples)	Louvain, Belgium	Representative of households in the Louvain area

*Further sample characteristics are given in Blood and Wolfe (1960, p. 271).

Scoring, Scale Norms, and Distribution

Blood and Wolfe (1960) scored the task participation index as the sum of the unit-
weighted responses to all eight items, which yielded a score varying from 8 ("husband always does all tasks") to 40 ("wife always does all tasks"). Blood and Wolfe (1960) adjusted this to a scale from 1 to 10. The role specialization index is a frequency count of the
number of different tasks performed exclusively by either the husband or the wife, varying
from 0 to 8.

Silverman and Hill (1967) reported on the scoring of adherence to traditional sex roles,
which is a frequency count of the number of culturally approved tasks performed by the
spouses. The culturally approved tasks for the male are: (1) making repairs, (2) mowing the
lawn, and (3) shoveling the sidewalk; for the female: (1) buying groceries, (2) making
breakfast for husband, (3) straightening up the living room, and (4) doing the evening dishes.
The exact list of tasks used in the Silverman-Hill study is different because of pragmatic

(cross-cultural) nonequivalence in the development of their Louvain instrument (Silverman and Hill, 1967, p. 354).

Item frequencies for the eight different tasks are given in Blood and Wolfe (1960, p. 50).

Formal Tests of Validity

Granbois and Willett (1970) reported a husband-wife correlation of .61 (Pearson r). Analysis revealed that, when the husband's estimate of the task participation of the wife exceeds the wife's estimate of her task participation, the wife tends to have a high school education or less (Granbois and Willett, 1970, p. 70).

Usability on Older Populations

The instrument appears to be usable for older populations. The researcher should include responses that allow for the possibility of hired help or other kin performing some of these tasks.

Sensitivity to Age Differences

Blood and Wolfe (1960, p. 70) reported that the role specialization index exhibits a fairly consistent increase over the life cycle and peaks during the unlaunched, postparental, and retired stages. Silverman and Hill (1967), in a Belgian study, reported no significant variation in role specialization across the family life cycle. Hill (1965; 1970) reported greater role specialization from the married child to the parent to the grandparent generation.

The task participation index exhibits an increase in the wife's participation through the early stages of the family life cycle. Scores peak during the preadolescent stage and maintain a fairly high level through launching and retirement (Blood and Wolfe, 1960, p. 71). Silverman and Hill (1967) reported a significant relationship between stage of the family life cycle and wife's task participation in Belgium. In their study, scores rise through the early stages and peak at the adolescent stage, remaining high until retirement. Following retirement, the husband increases his task participation.

Adherence to traditional sex roles is related to family-life-cycle stage in the Louvain data (Silverman and Hill, 1967). Scores rise through the early stages of the family, peaking at the adolescent stage and declining through retirement. Hill (1965) reported that the grandparent generation is both *more conventional* and *unconventional* when compared to the other two generations.

General Comments and Recommendations

The eight tasks sample the item pool of household tasks, but questions remain as to the validity of the husbands' and wives' responses to the questions. First, the response options should allow for the performance of tasks by persons other than the husband or the wife. Second, the range of tasks could be expanded for older persons. Third, since there is a normative component to the division of labor in families, the instrument may measure that component. Fourth, validation studies involving the use of time budgets could be conducted. Finally, the unidimensionality, scaleability, and internal consistency of this instrument need to be addressed.

References

Blood, R. O. "The Division of Labor in City and Farm Families." *Marriage and Family Living*, 1958, 20: 170-74.

Blood, R. O., and D. M. Wolfe. *Husbands and Wives: The Dynamics of Married Living*. New York: Free Press, 1960.

Granbois, D. H., and R. P. Willett. "Equivalence of Family Role Measures Based on Husband and Wife Data." *Journal of Marriage and the Family*, 1970, 32: 68-72.

Hill, R. "Decision Making and the Family Life Cycle." In *Social Structure and the Family:*

Generational Relations, E. Shanas and G. F. Streib (eds.), pp. 113-390. Englewood Cliffs, N.J.: Prentice-Hall, 1965.

_____ . *Family Development in Three Generations*. Cambridge, Mass.: Schenkman, 1970.

Michel, A. "Working Wives and Family Interaction in French and American Families." *International Journal of Comparative Sociology*, 1970, 11: 157-65.

Silverman, W., and R. Hill. "Task Allocation in Marriage in the United States and Belgium." *Journal of Marriage and the Family*, 1967, 29: 353-59.

Instrument

See Instrument V2.3.II.g.

ANTICIPATORY SOCIALIZATION

B. C. Miller, 1976

Defintion of Variable or Concept

"Anticipatory socialization is the rehearsing or practicing of role behaviors and . . . learning about the norms associated with a given role prior to actually performing in that role" (Miller, 1976, p. 644).

Description of Instrument

Anticipatory socialization for the most recent role transition is measured as a four-item index that examines the following aspects: (1) socialization through formal learning, (2) socialization through observation, (3) planning with spouse, and (4) preparation through reading. Respondents indicate the relative amount of socialization derived from each area on a four-point ordinal scale.

Method of Administration

The instrument is administered in a personal interview.

Context of Development and Subsequent Use

The instrument was developed as part of a study examining marital satisfaction. Anticipatory socialization was expected to influence positively the ease of role transitions, which in turn was expected to influence positively marital satisfaction (Miller, 1976).

Sample

From a representative sample of 212 Minneapolis adults, 140 married individuals were selected for analysis. Females made up 59.3% of the sample. Seven stages of the family life cycle are represented, with 7 couples in the launching stage and 10 couples in the retirement stage.

Scoring, Scale Norms, and Distribution

The four items in the index are standardized and summed with unit weights to yield an index with a mean of 0 and a standard deviation of 2.71.

Formal Test of Reliability/Homogeneity

Miller (1976) reported a Cronbach's alpha of .74.

Formal Test of Validity

The four items in the index load between .47 and .56 on the first factor of a principal-factoring solution. A fifth item dealing with previous experience was eliminated due to a lower (.33) factor loading.

Usability on Older Populations

The instrument seems to be usable with older populations. In this study of transitions across the family life cycle, the items are recall items pertaining to the anticipatory socialization for the last transition. Hence, the stimuli are somewhat different for each stage of the family life cycle. Further work is needed to ascertain the congruence of this dimension across the entire age range and for older persons.

Sensitivity to Age Differences

Anticipatory socialization is correlated with duration of marriage ($r = -.195$).

General Comments and Recommendations

This instrument is included in this chapter because it holds promise for use with older populations, especially given the current interest in adult socialization (Rosow, 1974; Riley et al., 1969; Mortimer and Simmons, 1978).

Two points should be made. First, since anticipatory socialization *for the last role change* is measured by this instrument, all the questions are recall items and as such may be biased. Second, Miller (1976) reported that anticipatory socialization is *negatively* related to ease of role transitions, contrary to the theoretical hypothesis behind Miller's instrument.

Researchers interested in one specific role transition and the anticipatory socialization associated with that one could benefit by expanding the item pool to include transition-specific measures. The instrument should be tested before transitions, and comparability across transitions should be determined.

References

Miller, B.C. "A Multivariate Developmental Model of Marital Satisfaction." *Journal of Marriage and the Family*, 1976, 38: 643-57.

Mortimer, J.T., and R. G. Simmons. "Adult Socialization." In *Annual Review of Sociology* (vol. 4), R. Turner, J. Coleman, and R. Fox (eds.), pp. 421-54. Palo Alto, Calif.: Annual Reviews, 1978.

Riley, M.W., A. Foner, B. Hess, and M. L. Toby. "Socialization for Middle and Later Years." In *Handbook of Socialization Theory and Research*, D. A. Goslin (ed.), pp. 951-82. Skokie, Ill.: Rand McNally, 1969.

Rosow, I. *Socialization to Old Age*. Berkeley, Calif.: University of California Press, 1974.

Instrument

See Instrument V2.3.III.2.

SUPPORT SYSTEMS OF WIDOWS

H. Lopata, 1977; 1979

Definition of Variable or Concept

This instrument assesses "a set of patterned actions between or among people which either or both the giver and the receiver define as necessary or helpful in maintaining a style of life" (Lopata, 1977, p. 8).

Description of Instrument

Five components of support systems are measured by this battery: (1) emotional-sentimental supports, (2) emotional-feeling states, (3) economic supports, (4) service supports, and (5) social supports. For the two emotional support dimensions, respondents list up to three significant others who provided support prior to the death of the spouse and three potential significant others who provide emotional support at the present time. For the remaining three dimensions, respondents are asked who helps them and how often help is given; in addition, reciprocity of the support system is examined (i.e., who and how often does the widow *help* someone).

Method of Administration

Interviews were conducted by the Survey Research Laboratory of the University of Illinois at Chicago Circle.

Context of Development

The conceptual model of role theory was further differentiated to allow an examination of the dyads of interaction between a widow and other persons in her social circle that pertain to the dimensions of social support.

Sample

Five subsamples of widows of all ages who were or had been beneficiaries of the Social Security Administration and who resided in metropolitan Chicago were drawn. Each of these five sub-samples used different sampling ratios. The obtained sample of 1,169 was weighted by the sampling fraction to achieve a representative sample of 82,085. Of the sample 60% was aged 65 and older.

Scoring, Scale Norms, and Distribution

Responses to the individual items focus on the relationship of the giver or the receiver of support to the widow and the frequency with which support is received or given. The categories of significant others include present husband, boyfriend, children, siblings, parents, other relatives, friends, and other people or groups. Examination of the distributions of these categories of significant others in providing support constitutes the principal analysis and is too long to report here. However, only 2.9% to 8.4% of the sample reported a failure of significant others to provide minimum support in any of the five areas.

Usability on Older Populations

With properly trained interviewers, the difficulty of using the instrument with older populations should be minimized. Indeed, 60% of the original sample in this study was over age 65 and 28.2% was age 75 and over.

Sensitivity to Age Differences

Older widows are more likely to report reliance on self or no one in the area of emotional supports, and younger widows emphasize present husband, boyfriends, siblings, parents, and friends as providers of emotional support. Older widows are, in general, more apt to receive support from social services.

General Comments and Recommendations

This instrument presents an intuitively sound and theoretically based approach to measuring the components of the support system. Summary measures could be developed from these data. For example, the proportion of total support provided by family members, either within each dimension or across all dimensions, may well constitute a theoretically relevant summary measure. Other measures of this form could be developed. Information on reliability (test-retest) and validity is needed.

References

Lopata, H.Z. *Women as Widows.* New York: Elsevier, 1979.

————. "Support Systems Involving Widows in a Metropolitan Area of the United States." Final Report to the Social Security Administration. Chicago: Center for the Comparative Study of Social Roles, 1977.

Instrument

See Instrument V2.3.III.b.

RELATIONS-RESTRICTIVE ATTITUDE SCALE

H. Z. Lopata, 1973

Definition of Variable or Concept

The degree to which the social relations of widows are perceived as defined in restrictive, normatively bound terms is assessed by this scale.

Description of Instrument

The scale is made up of 36 attitudinal items concerning social relations with children, male and female friends, sexual relations, status, decision making, and independence in the role of widow. Responses are agree-disagree and true-false.

Method of Administration

Interviews conducted by the National Opinion Research Center were the basis of the study.

Context of Development

The scale grew out of exploratory work concerning the social roles of widows. Qualitative interviews preceded the construction of the scale itself.

Sample

A modified area probability sample of 301 widowed females residing in 60 neighborhoods of the Chicago SMSA (standard metropolitan statistical area) was drawn by the National Opinion Research Center. Fully 87.1% of the total sample was over age 55, with 49.6% age 65 or more. The average length of widowhood was 11.45 years.

Scoring, Scale Norms, and Distribution

Scores are summed across the 36 items, yielding a score with an observed distribution ranging from 0 (nonrestrictive) to 19 (restrictive). Lopata recoded these scores into low (0-6, 21.5%), medium (7-12, 65.7%), and high (13-19, 12.6%).

Formal Tests of Reliability

Though no formal tests have been reported, selected associations among items are presented in Lopata (1973, Appendix C). The pattern of these selected associations is one of moderate to high correlations.

Usability on Older Populations

The instrument is applicable for use in older samples.

General Comments and Recommendations

Though Lopata stated that the Relations-Restrictive Attitude Scale contains 36 items (1973, pp. 6-7, 214), this reviewer found 37 items. Item number 4 is set B on the instrument may be the additional item. Further tests of reliability and validity are needed. These data could be factor analyzed to provide further information pertaining to reliability and validity; such an analysis could also validate the conceptual scheme used in scoring the instrument.

Reference

Lopata, H. Z. *Widowhood in an American City*. Cambridge, Mass.: Schenkman, 1973.

Instrument

See Instrument V2.3.III.c.

SANCTIFICATION OF HUSBAND

H. Z. Lopata, 1976

Definition of Variable or Concept

The tendency to idealize the deceased husband is measured by this scale.

Description of Instrument

Fourteen items make up the sanctifiction scale. Seven of these items are bipolar, semantic differential items concerning evaluation of the deceased person; the remaining items are four-point agree-disagree attitude statements about life with the late husband.

Method of Administration

Personal interviews were conducted by the Survey Research Laboratory of the University of Illinois at Chicago Circle.

Context of Development

This scale grew out of the earlier work of Lopata (1973) concerning widowhood as a social role of older women. This earlier research suggested that widows were providing a picture of life with their husbands that reflected a reconstruction of memories that sanctified the husbands.

Sample

Five subsamples were made up of widows of all ages who were or had been beneficiaries of the Social Security Administration and who resided in metropolitan Chicago. These five subsamples each used different sampling ratios. As a result, the obtained sample of 1,169 was weighted by the sampling ratios to achieve a representative sample of 82,085. Sixty percent of the sample was aged 65 and older.

Scoring, Scale Norms, and Distribution

The semantic differential (SD) section of the instrument is scored separately from the life-together (LT) portion of the instrument. The cumulative scales are scored through simple summation of the items within each section. Lopata recoded each of the cumulative scores into four ordinal categories: extreme (SD = 45.7%; LT = 14.0%), high (SD = 19.8%; LT = 49.5%), medium (SD = 20.1%; LT = 30.2%), and low (SD = 14.4%; LT = 6.3%).

Item means for the semantic differential items all tend toward the sanctified end of the scale of 1 to 7 and range from 1.47 to 2.07. Item means for the life-together items also tend toward the sanctified response, with means ranging from 1.46 to 2.25 (Lopata, 1976). Mean scores for each item are listed with Instrument V2.3.III.d.

Formal Tests of Reliability

Gamma associations among the semantic differential items range from .60 to .90, with an average gamma of .80. Gamma associations among the life-together items range from .62 to .91, with an average gamma of .78. Between-scale gamma associations of the items range from .54 to .89, with an average gamma of .71.

Usability on Older Populations

The instrument appears to be usable with older populations. Of the original sample 60% was over age 65.

General Comments and Recommendations

Since sanctification refers to the tendency toward idealizing the deceased husband or giving a socially acceptable response, this scale can be seen as a context-specific measure of social desirability. Given the transition associated with widowhood, this factor is of substantive relevance.

Scale responses are definitely biased toward the sanctified response, and this limits the utility of the items. Researchers might benefit from a reversal of the bipolar anchors in the semantic differential portion of the scale, and some negative stimuli items in the life-together portion of the scale might improve item distributions.

The internal consistency of these items is high. Further dimensional analysis could be applied to verify empirically the conceptual structure of the widow's evaluation of her husband as a person and her sanctification of the couple's life together.

Although Lopata recoded the summated scales into four-point ordinal categories, use of the raw scale scores would appear to be feasible.

References

Lopata, H.Z. "Widowhood and Husband Sanctification." Paper presented to the 71st Annual Meeting of the American Sociological Association, New York, 1976.

_____ . *Widowhood in an American City*. Cambridge, Mass.: Schenkman, 1973.

Instrument

See Instrument V2.3.III.d.

Instruments

V2.3.I.a

SHORT MARITAL ADJUSTMENT TEST

H. J. Locke and K. M. Wallace, 1959

1. Check the dot on the scale line below which best describes the degree of happiness, everything considered, of your present marriage. The middle point, "happy," represents the degree of happiness which more people get from marriage, and the scale gradually ranges on one side to those few who are very unhappy in marriage, and on the other, to those few who experience extreme joy or felicity in marriage.

0	2	7	15	20	25	35
.	.	.	.	.	.	.

Very Unhappy	Happy	Perfectly Happy

State the approximate extent of agreement or disagreement between you and your mate on the following items. Please check each column.

	Always Agree	Almost Always Agree	Occasionally Disagree	Frequently Disagree	Almost Always Disagree	Always Disagree
2. Handling family finances	5	4	3	2	1	0
3. Matters of recreation	5	4	3	2	1	0
4. Demonstrations of affection	8	6	4	2	1	0
5. Friends	5	4	3	2	1	0

		Almost			Almost	
	Always Agree	Always Agree	Occasionally Disagree	Frequently Disagree	Always Disagree	Always Disagree
6.	Sex relations	15	12	9	4	1	0
7.	Conventionality (right, good, or proper conduct)	5	4	3	2	1	0
8.	Philosophy of life	5	4	3	2	1	0
9.	Ways of dealing with in-laws	5	4	3	2	1	0

10. When disagreements arise, they usually result in: husband giving in 0, wife giving in 2, agreement by mutual give and take 10.

11. Do you and your mate engage in outside interests together? All of them 10, some of them 8, very few of them 3, none of them 0.

12. In leisure time do you generally prefer: to be "on the go"_____ , to stay at home?_____ Does your mate generally prefer: to be "on the go"_____, stay at home?_____ (Stay at home for both, 10 points; "on the go" for both, 3 points; disagreement, 2 points.)

13. Do you ever wish you had not married? Frequently 0, occasionally 3, rarely 8, never 15.

14. If you had your life to live over, do you think you would: marry the same person 15, marry a different person 0, not marry at all 1?

15. Do you confide in your mate: almost never 0, rarely 2, in most things 10, in everything 10?

SOURCE: H. J. Locke and K. M. Wallace. "Short Marital Adjustment and Prediction Tests, Their Reliability and Validity." *Marriage and Family Living*, 1959, 21: 251-55. Copyrighted 1959 by the National Council on Family Relations. Reprinted by permission.

V2.3.I.b

MARITAL SATISFACTION

B. C. Rollins and H. Feldman, 1970

1. *General Marital Satisfaction* — "In general, how often do you think that things between you and your wife are going well?"
   - 5   all the time
   - 4   most of the time
   - 3   more often than not
   - 2   occasionally
   - 1   rarely
   - 0   never

2. *Negative Feelings from Interaction with Spouse* — "How often would you say the following events occur between you and your husband (wife)?"
   a. You feel resentful
   - 0   never
   - 1   once or twice a year
   - 2   once or twice a month
   - 3   once or twice a week
   - 4   about once a day
   - 5   more than once a day

b. You feel not needed
    0   never
    1   once or twice a year
    2   once or twice a month
    3   once or twice a week
    4   about once a day
    5   more than once a day

c. You feel misunderstood
    0   never
    1   once or twice a year
    2   once or twice a month
    3   once or twice a week
    4   about once a day
    5   more than once a day

3. *Positive Companionship Experiences with Spouse* — "How often would you say that the following events occur between you and your husband (wife)?"

a. Laugh together
    0   never
    1   once or twice a year
    2   once or twice a month
    3   once or twice a week
    4   about once a day
    5   more than once a day

b. Calmly discuss something together
    0   never
    1   once or twice a year
    2   once or twice a month
    3   once or twice a week
    4   about once a day
    5   more than once a day

c. Have a stimulating exchange of ideas
    0   never
    1   once or twice a year
    2   once or twice a month
    3   once or twice a week
    4   about once a day
    5   more than once a day

d. Work together on a project
    0   never
    1   once or twice a year
    2   once or twice a month
    3   once or twice a week
    4   about once a day
    5   more than once a day

4. *Satisfaction with Present Stage of the Family Life Cycle* — "Different stages of the life cycle may be viewed as being more satisfying than others. How satisfying do you think the following stages are?"

a. Before the children arrive (Stage I couples)
    3   very satisfying

a. Before the children arrive (Stage I couples) — *continued*
  2 quite satisfying
  1 somewhat satisfying
  0 not satisfying

b. First year with infant (Stage II couples)
  3 very satisfying
  2 quite satisfying
  1 somewhat satisfying
  0 not satisfying

c. Preschool children at home (Stage III couples)
  3 very satisfying
  2 quite satisfying
  1 somewhat satisfying
  0 not satisfying

d. All children at school (Stage IV couples)
  3 very satisfying
  2 quite satisfying
  1 somewhat satisfying
  0 not satisfying

e. Having teenagers (Stage V)
  3 very satisfying
  2 quite satisfying
  1 somewhat satisfying
  0 not satisfying

f. Children gone from home (Stages VI and VII)
  3 very satisfying
  2 quite satisfying
  1 somewhat satisfying
  0 not satisfying

g. Being grandparents (Stage VIII)
  3 very satisfying
  2 quite satisfying
  1 somewhat satisfying
  0 not satisfying

SOURCE: B. C. Rollins and H. Feldman. "Marital Satisfaction over the Family Life Cycle." *Journal of Marriage and the Family*, 1970, 32: 20-38. Copyrighted 1959 by the National Council on Family Relations. Reprinted by permission.

V2.3.I.c

MARRIAGE ADJUSTMENT BALANCE SCALE

S. R. Orden and N. M. Bradburn, 1968

F6. I am going to read you some things about which husbands and wives sometimes agree and sometimes disagree. Would you tell me which ones caused differences of opinion or were problems in your marriage *during the past few weeks?*

First, how about —

			Yes	No
(T)	A. Time spent with friends?	28–	3	2
	How about —			
(T)	B. Household expenses?	29–	6	5

				Yes	No
(T)	C.	Being tired?	30–	9	8
(T)	D.	Being away from home too much ?	31–	3	2
*	E.	Disciplining children?	32–	6	5
(T)	F.	In-laws?	33–	9	8
(T)	G.	Not showing love?	34–	3	2
(T)	H.	Your (husband's) job?	35–	6	5
(T)	I.	How to spend your leisure time?	36–	9	8
*	J.	Religion?	37–	3	2
(T)	K.	Irritating personal habits?	38–	6	5

F4. I am going to read you some things that married couples often do together. Tell me which ones you and your (husband/wife) have done together *in the past few weeks*.

				Yes	No
(S)	A.	Visited friends together.	20–	2	3
(S)	B.	Gone out together to a movie, bowling, sporting event or some other entertainment.	30–	5	6
(C)	C.	Spent an evening just chatting with each other.	31–	8	9
*	D.	Worked on some household project together.	32–	2	3
(S)	E.	Entertained friends in your home.	33–	5	6
*	F.	Gone shopping together.	34–	8	9
(C)	G.	Had a good laugh together or shared a joke.	35–	2	3
(S)	H.	Ate out in a restaurant together.	36–	8	9
(C)	I.	Been affectionate toward each other.	37–	8	9
(C)	J.	Taken a drive or gone for a walk for pleasure.	38–	2	3
(C)	K.	Did something that the other one particularly appreciated.	39–	5	6
*	L.	Helped the other solve some problem.	40–	8	9

*Items not utilized by Orden and Bradburn (1968) but suggested by Marini (1976).
T = Tensions Dimension
S = Sociability Dimension
C = Companionship Dimension

SOURCE: S. R. Orden and N. M. Bradburn. "Dimensions of Marriage Happiness." *American Journal of Sociology*. 1968, 73: 715-31. Reprinted by permission of author and publisher.

V2.3.I.d

MARITAL ROLE ADJUSTMENT BATTERY

G. Gurin, J. Veroff, and S. Feld, 1960

1. Taking things all together, how would you describe your marriage – would you say your marriage was *very happy, a little happier than average, just about average,* or *not too happy?*
2. Many men (women) feel that they're not as good husbands (wives) as they would like to be. Have you ever felt this way? (If Yes) Do you feel this way a lot of times, or only once in a while?
3. Even in cases where married people are happy there have been times in the past when they weren't too happy – when they had problems getting along with each other. Has this ever been true for you?

SOURCE: G. Gurin, J. Veroff, and S. Feld. *Americans View Their Mental Health.* New York: Basic Books, 1960, pp. 92-94. Copyrighted 1960 by Basic Books, Inc., Publishers, New York.

V2.3.I.e

MARITAL NEED SATISFACTION SCALE

N. Stinnett, J. Collins, and J. Montgomery, 1970

Rate your spouse's performance in each of the following areas of your marital relationship.

1. Providing a feeling of security in me.
   (5) Very Satisfactory (4) Satisfactory (3) Undecided (2) Unsatisfactory (1) Very Un-satisfactory
2. Expressing affection toward me.
   (5) Very Satisfactory (4) Satisfactory (3) Undecided (2) Unsatisfactory (1) Very Un-satisfactory
3. Giving me an optimistic feeling toward life.
   (5) Very Satisfactory (4) Satisfactory (3) Undecided (2) Unsatisfactory (1) Very Un-satisfactory
4. Expressing a feeling of being emotionally close to me.
   (5) Very Satisfactory (4) Satisfactory (3) Undecided (2) Unsatisfactory (1) Very Un-satisfactory
5. Bringing out the best qualities in me.
   (5) Very Satisfactory (4) Satisfactory (3) Undecided (2) Unsatisfactory (1) Very Un-satisfactory
6. Helping me to become a more interesting person.
   (5) Very Satisfactory (4) Satisfactory (3) Undecided (2) Unsatisfactory (1) Very Un-satisfactory
7. Helping me to continue to develop my personality.
   (5) Very Satisfactory (4) Satisfactory (3) Undecided (2) Unsatisfactory (1) Very Un-satisfactory
8. Helping me to achieve my individual potential (becoming what I am capable of becoming).
   (5) Very Satisfactory (4) Satisfactory (3) Undecided (2) Unsatisfactory (1) Very Un-satisfactory
9. Being a good listener.
   (5) Very Satisfactory (4) Satisfactory (3) Undecided (2) Unsatisfactory (1) Very Un-satisfactory
10. Giving me encouragement when I am discouraged.
    (5) Very Satisfactory (4) Satisfactory (3) Undecided (2) Unsatisfactory (1) Very Un-satisfactory
11. Accepting my differentness.
    (5) very Satisfactory (4) Satisfactory (3) Undecided (2) Unsatisfactory (1) Very Un-satisfactory
12. Avoiding habits which annoy me.
    (5) Very Satisfactory (4) Satisfactory (3) Undecided (2) Unsatisfactory (1) Very Un-satisfactory
13. Letting me know how he or she really feels about something.
    (5) Very Satisfactory (4) Satisfactory (3) Undecided (2) Unsatisfactory (1) Very Un-satisfactory
14 Trying to find satisfactory solutions to our disagreements.
    (5) Very Satisfactory (4) Satisfactory (3) Undecided (2) Unsatisfactory (1) Very Un-satisfactory
15. Expressing disagreement with me honestly and openly.
    (5) Very Satisfactory (4) Satisfactory (3) Undecided (2) Unsatisfactory (1) Very Un-satisfactory
16. Letting me know when he or she is displeased with me.
    (5) Very Satisfactory (4) Satisfactory (3) Undecided (2) Unsatisfactory (1) Very Un-satisfactory

17. Helping me to feel that life has meaning.
    (5) Very Satisfactory (4) Satisfactory (3) Undecided (2) Unsatisfactory (1) Very Unsatisfactory
18. Helping me to feel needed.
    (5) Very Satisfactory (4) Satisfactory (3) Undecided (2) Unsatisfactory (1) Very Unsatisfactory
19. Helping me to feel that my life is serving a purpose.
    (5) Very Satisfactory (4) Satisfactory (3) Undecided (2) Unsatisfactory (1) Very Unsatisfactory
20. Helping me to obtain satisfaction and pleasure in daily activities.
    (5) Very Satisfactory (4) Satisfactory (3) Undecided (2) Unsatisfactory (1) Very Unsatisfactory
21. Giving me recognition for my past accomplishments.
    (5) Very Satisfactory (4) Satisfactory (3) Undecided (2) Unsatisfactory (1) Very Unsatisfactory
22. Helping me to feel that my life has been important.
    (5) Very Satisfactory (4) Satisfactory (3) Undecided (2) Unsatisfactory (1) Very Unsatisfactory
23. Helping me to accept my past life experiences as good and rewarding.
    (5) Very Satisfactory (4) Satisfactory (3) Undecided (2) Unsatisfactory (1) Very Unsatisfactory
24. Helping me to accept myself despite my shortcomings.
    (5) Very Satisfactory (4) Satisfactory (3) Undecided (2) Unsatisfactory (1) Very Unsatisfactory

*Love items: 1-4; personality fulfillment items: 5-8; respect items: 9-12; communication items: 13-16; finding meanings in life items: 17-20; and integration of past life experiences items: 21-24.

SOURCE: N. Stinnett, J. Collins, and J. Montgomery. "Marital Need Satisfaction of Older Husbands and Wives." *Journal of Marriage and the Family*, 1970, 32: 428-34. Copyrighted 1970 by the National Council on Family Relations. Reprinted by permission.

V2.3.I.f

MARITAL SATISFACTION INDEX

R. O. Blood and D. M. Wolfe, 1960

A. Weighting Variable
    66. Thinking of marriage in general, which one of five things on this next card would you say is the most valuable part of marriage? (Card VII)
        1. The chance to have children.
        2. The standard of living—the kind of house, clothes, car and so forth.
        3. The husband's understanding of the wife's problems and feelings.
        4. The husband's expression of love and affection for the wife.
        5. Companionship in doing things together with the husband.
    67. Which would you say is the second most valuable? (Card VII)
    68. Which would you say is the third most valuable? (Card VII)
B. Satisfaction Items
    (wife 45 years or older)
    74. We are interested in the changing size of American families. To begin with, how many children had you had altogether?
    90. Considering how things have turned out, how many children would you want to have if you could start over again?

102. Here is a card that lists some feelings you might have about certain aspects of marriage. Could you tell me the statement that best describes how you feel about each of the following? For example, how do you feel about your standard of living—the kind of house, clothes, car, and so forth? (Card VIII)
    1. Pretty disappointed—I'm really missing out on that.
    2. It would be nice to have more.
    3. It's all right, I guess—I can't complain.
    4. Quite satisfied—I'm lucky the way it is.
    5. Enthusiastic—it couldn't be better.
103. How do you feel about the understanding you get of your problems and feelings? (Card VIII)
104. How do you feel about the love and affection you receive? (Card VIII)
105. How do you feel about the companionship in doing things together? (Card VIII)

SOURCE: R. O. Blood and D. M. Wolfe. *Husbands and Wives: The Dynamics of Married Living.* New York: Free Press, 1960. Reprinted by permission of the Free Press, a division of Macmillan Publishing Company, Inc. Copyright 1960 by the Free Press, a corporation.

V2.3.I.g

MARITAL SATISFACTION

R. Gilford and V. Bengtson, 1976; 1979

Please read this list of some things husbands and wives may do when they are together. Please indicate how often it happens between you and your spouse.
1. You calmly discuss something together.*
    (0) hardly ever (1) not usually but sometimes (2) fairly often (3) quite frequently (4) always
2. One of you is sarcastic.
    (0) hardly ever (1) not usually but sometimes (2) fairly often (3) quite frequently (4) always
3. You work together on something (dishes, yardwork, hobbies, etc.)*
    (0) hardly ever (1) not usually but sometimes (2) fairly often (3) quite frequently (4) always
4. One of you refuses to talk in a normal manner.
    (0) hardly ever (1) not usually but sometimes (2) fairly often (3) quite frequently (4) always
5. You laugh together.*
    (0) hardly ever (1) not usually but sometimes (2) fairly often (3) quite frequently (4) always
6. You have stimulating exchange of ideas.*
    (0) hardly ever (1) not usually but sometimes (2) fairly often (3) quite frequently (4) always
7. You disagree about something important.
    (0) hardly ever (1) not usually but sometimes (2) fairly often (3) quite freqeuntly (4) always
8. You become critical and belittling.
    (0) hardly ever (1) not usually but sometimes (2) fairly often (3) quite frequently (4) always
9. You have a good time together.*
    (0) hardly ever (1) not usually but sometimes (2) fairly often (3) quite frequently (4) always

10. You become angry.
    (0) hardly ever (1) not usually but sometimes (2) fairly often (3) quite frequently
    (4) always

*Refers to positive interaction dimension.

SOURCE: R. Gilford and V. Bengtson. "Measuring Marital Satisfaction in Three Generations: Positive and Negative Dimensions." *Journal of Marriage and the Family*, 1979, 41:
390-91.

V2.3.I.h

MARITAL SATISFACTION

W. R. Burr, 1967

The following questions deal with the way things are going in different areas of your life.
Each box deals with a different area.

FAMILY FINANCES

1. How often do I get mad or angry at something in regard to the way money is handled
   in our family?
   (1) very frequently.
   (2) frequently.
   (3) occasionally . . . . response set A
   (4) seldom.
   (5) very seldom.
   (6) never.
2. How much improvement could there be in the way money is handled in the family?
   (5) none.
   (4) very little.
   (3) some. . . . . .response set B
   (2) quite a bit.
   (1) a great deal.
3. How satisfied am I with the way money is handled?
   (5) perfectly satisfied.
   (4) quite satisfied.
   (3) satisfied. . . . . .response set C
   (2) a little dissatisfied.
   (1) very dissatisfied.

THE WAY MY HUSBAND GETS JOBS DONE
AROUND THE HOUSE

1. How often do I get mad or angry at something related to his getting jobs done?
   Response A
2. How much improvement could there be in the way he does his jobs or work around the
   house?
   Response B
3. How satisfied am I with the way he does his jobs or work around the house?
   Response C

RECREATIONAL OR SOCIAL ACTIVITIES
WITH MY HUSBAND

1. How often do I get mad or angry at something related to our social life?
   Response A

2. How much improvement could there be in the ways things are in our social life?
   Response B
3. How satisfied am I with the way things are going in our social life?
   Response C

THE AMOUNT OF COMPANIONSHIP I HAVE
WITH HIM

1. How often do I get mad at something in regard to our companionship?
   Response A
2. How much improvement could there be in our companionship?
   Response B
3. In regard to our companionship, I am . . .
   Response C

OUR RELATIONSHIP IN THE SEXUAL AREA

1. How often do I get mad or angry at something related to sex?
   Response A
2. How much improvement could there be in our sex life?
   Response B
3. How satisfied am I with our sex?
   Response C

THE WAY THINGS ARE GOING IN MY
RELATIONSHIPS WITH THE CHILDREN

1. How often do I get mad or angry at the children?
   Response A
2. How much improvement could there be in my relationships with the children?
   Response B
3. How satisfied am I with my relationships with the children?
   Response C

SOURCE: W. R. Burr. "Marital Satisfaction: A Conceptual Reformulation, Theory and Partial Test of Theory." Ph.D. dissertation, University of Minnesota, 1967.

V2.3.I.i

PERCEPTIONS OF MARRIAGE

N. Stinnett, L. Carter, and J. Montgomery, 1972

This instrument is not available in its exact form at this time.

V2.3.I.j

MARITAL SATISFACTION

B. C. Miller, 1976

Now I am going to ask you about certain aspects of your marriage. Could you please tell me how satisfied you are currently with each of these aspects? How satisfied are you currently with:

1. The way *money* is handled in your marriage?
2. The things you and your mate do *when you go out* for entertainment, fun?
3. The amount of *affection* in your marriage?
4. The way *chores* around the house are performed?
5. The way you and your mate deal with *in-laws* in your marriage?
6. *Sexual relations* in your marriage?
7. *Religious beliefs* and activities in your marriage?

Response options for all items are as follows:
(1) Very Dissatisfied, (2) A Little Dissatisfied, (3) Satisfied, (4) Quite Satisfied, (5) Perfectly Satisfied

V2.3.I.k

EASE OF ROLE TRANSITION

B. C. Miller, 1976

1. In nearly every family certain events happen. Which of these changes has happened most recently in your family?
   1) Marriage
   2) Birth of the first child
   3) The first child entering school
   4) The oldest child becomes a teenager
   5) The first child leaving home
   6) The last child leaving home
   7) The retirement of the breadwinner
   8) The death of a spouse
2. Now I am going to read some statements about how easy or difficult it was to adjust to (name of transition) in the first little while after it happened.
   a) After (name of transition) I was surprised that I had to change so many of the ways I was doing things.
      (1) agree strongly (2) agree somewhat (3) disagree somewhat (4) disagree strongly
   b) Going through the change was about as easy as I thought it would be.
      (4) agree strongly (3) agree somewhat (2) disagree somewhat (1) disagree strongly
   c) For a while after the change I was concerned about how things would turn out.
      (1) agree strongly (2) agree somewhat (3) disagree somewhat (4) disagree strongly
   d) I wasn't affected too much and my life stayed about the same.
      (4) agree strongly (3) agree somewhat (2) disagree somewhat (1) disagree strongly
   e) All things considered, I had a pretty hard time adjusting.
      (1) agree strongly (2) agree somewhat (3) disagree somewhat (4) disagree strongly

V2.3.I.l

MARITAL COMMUNICATION AND AGREEMENT

R. Hill, 1970

	We Discuss—			I Think We—				
Topic	Often	Once in a While	Never	Always Agree	Almost Always Agree	Occasionally Disagree	Frequently Disagree	Always Disagree
	2	1	0	4	3	2	1	0
a. Handling family finances								
b. Matters of recreation								

| Topic | We Discuss— | | | I Think We— | | | | |
	Often 2	Once in a While 1	Never 0	Always Agree 4	Almost Always Agree 3	Occasionally Disagree 2	Frequently Disagree 1	Always Disagree 0
c. Religious matters								
d. Showing affection								
e. Friends								
f. Caring for children								
g. Sexual relations								
h. Table manners								
i. Ways of acting in public								
j. Ideas about what is best in life								
k. Ways of dealing with your in-laws								
l. Wife's working								
m. Sharing household tasks								

SOURCE: R. Hill. Family Development in Three Generations. Cambridge, Mass.: Schenkman, 1970, p. 413.

V2.3.I.m

MARITAL INTEGRATION INDEX

B. Farber, 1957

Index of Value Consensus

Below are listed standards by which family success has been measured. Look through the list and mark 1 after the item you consider the most important in judging the success of families (in the column headed Rank). Look through the list again and mark 2 after the item you consider next important. Keep doing this until you have a number after each item.

There is no order of items which is correct; the order you choose is correct for you. Remember, there can be only one item arked 1, one item marked 2, one item marked 3, . . . one item marked 10.

Rank

A place in the community. The ability of a family to give its members a respected place in the community and to make them good citizens (not criminals or undesirable people) . . . . ____

* *Healthy and happy children* . . . . ____

Rank

Companionship. The family members feeling comfortable with each other and able to get along together . . . .——

*Personality development. Continued increase in family members' ability to understand and get along with people and to accept responsibility . . . .——

Satisfaction in affection shown. Satisfaction of family members with amount of affection shown and of the husband and wife in their sex life . . . .——

Economic security. Being sure that the family will be able to keep up or improve its standard of living . . . .——

Emotional security. Feeling that the members of the family really need each other emotionally and trust each other fully . . . .——

Moral and religious unity. Trying to live a family life according to religious and moral principles and teachings . . . .——

Everyday interest. Interesting day-to-day activities having to do with house and family which keep family life from being boring . . . .——

*A home. Having a place where the family members feel they belong, where they feel at ease, and where other people do not interfere in their lives . . . .——

*Items not included in the Kerckhoff (1966) analysis.

Index of Role Tension

To what extent is your spouse:

1. Stubborn
(−2) Very Much (−1) Considerably (0) Somewhat (1) A little (2) Hasn't the trait at all
2. Gets Angry Easily
(−2) Very Much (−1) Considerably (0) Somewhat (1) A little (2) Hasn't the trait at all
3. Feelings Easily Hurt
(−2) Very Much (−1) Considerably (0) Somewhat (1) A little (2) Hasn't the trait at all
4. Nervous and Irritable
(−2) Very Much (−1) Considerably (0) Somewhat (1) A little (2) Hasn't the trait at all
5. Moody
(−2) Very Much (−1) Considerably (0) Somewhat (1) A little (2) Hasn't the trait at all
6. Jealous
(−2) Very Much (−1) Considerably (0) Somewhat (1) A little (2) Hasn't the trait at all
7. Dominating or Bossy
(−2) Very Much (−1) Considerably (0) Somewhat (1) A little (2) Hasn't the trait at all
8. Easily Excited
(−2) Very Much (−1) Considerably (0) Somewhat (1) A little (2) Hasn't the trait at all
9. Easily Depressed
(−2) Very Much (−1) Considerably (0) Somewhat (1) A little (2) Hasn't the trait at all
10.Self-centered
(−2) Very Much (−1) Considerably (0) Somewhat (1) A little (2) Hasn't the trait at all

SOURCE: B. Farber, "An Index of Marital Integration." *Sociometry,* 1957, 20:117-34.

V2.3.II.a

TASK SHARING

A. C. Kerckhoff, 1965

1. Yard work is the man's job, and his wife should not be expected to help with it.
   (5) Strongly Disagree (4) Disagree (3) Don't Know (2) Agree (1) Strongly Agree
2. Unless it is absolutely necessary for the family support, a wife should not work.
   (5) Strongly Disagree (4) Disagree (3) Don't Know (2) Agree (1) Strongly Agree

3. Housework is for women. A man should not do housework.
   (5) Strongly Disagree (4) Disagree (3) Don't Know (2) Agree (1) Strongly Agree
4. A man should simply "stay out of the way" as far as housework is concerned.
   (5) Strongly Disagree (4) Disagree (3) Don't Know (2) Agree (1) Strongly Agree
5. Certain family tasks are "women's work" and other tasks are "men's work," and it is best to keep them separate.
   (5) Strongly Disagree (4) Disagree (3) Don't Know (2) Agree (1) Strongly Agree
6. Although fathers are concerned with their children's welfare, the raising of children is really the mother's job.
   (5) Strongly Disagree (4) Disagree (3) Don't Know (2) Agree (1) Strongly Agree
7. When the children need to be punished or scolded, the father should do it.
   (5) Strongly Disagree (4) Disagree (3) Don't Know (2) Agree (1) Strongly Agree
8. When it comes to money matters, what the man says should be the rule.
   (5) Strongly Disagree (4) Disagree (3) Don't Know (2) Agree (1) Strongly Agree
9. A woman's place is in the home, not on a job.
   (5) Strongly Disagree (4) Disagree (3) Don't Know (2) Agree (1) Strongly Agree

SOURCE: A. C. Kerckhoff, "Nuclear and Extended Family Relationships: A Normative and Behavioral Analysis." In *Social Structure and the Family: Generational Relations,* E. Shanas and G. F. Streib (eds.), p. 102. Englewood Cliffs, N.J.: Prentice-Hall, 1965. Copyright 1965 by Prentice-Hall. Reprinted by permission.

V2.3.II.b.

MALE HOUSEHOLD ACTIVITIES

A. Lipman, 1961

To what extent does your husband:
1. Take care of the garbage and trash?
   ( ) husband does not help ( ) husband helps ( ) husband does completely
2. Go grocery shopping?
   ( ) husband does not help ( ) husband helps ( ) husband does completely
3. Pick up and put away the clothes?
   ( ) husband does not help ( ) husband helps ( ) husband does completely
4. Wipe the dishes?
   ( ) husband does not help ( ) husband helps ( ) husband does completely
5. Clear the breakfast table?
   ( ) husband does not help ( ) husband helps ( ) husband does completely
6. Wash the dishes?
   ( ) husband does not help ( ) husband helps ( ) husband does completely
7. Make the breakfast?
   ( ) husband does not help ( ) husband helps ( ) husband does completely
8. Set the table for the day's main meal?
   ( ) husband does not help ( ) husband helps ( ) husband does completely
9. Hang up the laundry?
   ( ) husband does not help ( ) husband helps ( ) husband does completely
10. Clean and dust?
    ( ) husband does not help ( ) husband helps ( ) husband does completely
11. Do the laundry?
    ( ) husband does not help ( ) husband helps ( ) husband does completely
12. Make the beds?
    ( ) husband does not help ( ) husband helps ( ) husband does completely

SOURCE: A. Lipman. "Role Conceptions and Morale of Couples in Retirement." *Journal of Gerontology*, 1961, 16:267-71.

V2.3.II.c

HUSBAND'S PARTICIPATION

A. C. Kerckhoff, 1965

Who does each of the following tasks in your family?

1. *Washes and dries the dishes.*
   (0) Wife always (1) Wife usually (2) Usually done together (3) Sometimes one, sometimes the other (4) Husband usually (5) Husband always
2. *Pays the monthly bills.*
   (0) Wife always (1) Wife usually (2) Usually done together (3) Sometimes one, sometimes the other (4) Husband usually (5) Husband always
3. *Sweeps and scrubs the floors.*
   (0) Wife always (1) Wife usually (2) Usually done togehter (3) Sometimes one, sometimes the other (4) Husband usually (5) Husband always
4. *Does the grocery shopping.*
   (0) Wife always (1) Wife usually (2) Usually done together (3) Sometimes one, sometimes the other (4) Husband usually (5) Husband always
5. *Makes the beds on weekends.*
   (0) Wife always (1) Wife usually (2) Usually done together (3) Sometimes one, sometimes the other (4) Husband usually (5) Husband always
6. *Dusts the furniture.*
   (0) Wife always (1) Wife usually (2) Usually done together (3) Sometimes one, sometimes the other (4) Husband usually (5) Husband always
7. *Does minor household repairs.*
   (0) Wife always (1) Wife usually (2) Usually done togehter (3) Sometimes one, sometimes the other (4) Husband usually (5) Husband always
8. *Hangs out the clothes to dry.*
   (0) Wife always (1) Wife usually (2) Usually done together (3) Sometimes one, sometimes the other (4) Husband usually (5) Husband always
9. *Sets the table.*
   (0) Wife always (1) Wife usually (2) Usually done together (3) Sometimes one, sometimes the other (4) Husband usually (5) Husband always

SOURCE: A. C. Kerckhoff. "Nuclear and Extended Family Relationships: A Normative and Behavioral Analysis." In *Social Structure and the Family: Generational Relations*, E. Shanas and G. F. Streib (eds.), pp. 102-3. Englewood Cliffs, N.J.: Prentice-Hall, 1965. Copyright 1965 by Prentice-Hall. Reprinted by permission.

V2.3.II.d

HOUSEHOLD TASK PERFORMANCE

J. A. Ballweg, 1967

To what extent do you (husband/hired help) perform each of the following tasks:

1. Household dusting.
   (0) Never (1) Rarely (2) Sometimes (3) Frequently (4) Always
2. Moving furniture within a room.
   (0) Never (1) Rarely (2) Sometimes (3) Frequently (4) Always

3. Doing the family laundry.
   (0) Never (1) Rarely (2) Sometimes (3) Frequently (4) Always
4. Ironing.
   (0) Never (1) Rarely (2) Sometimes (3) Frequently (4) Always
5. Washing windows.
   (0) Never (1) Rarely (2) Sometimes (3) Frequently (4) Always
6. Fixing a leaky faucet.
   (0) Never (1) Rarely (2) Sometimes (3) Frequently (4) Always
7. Washing dishes.
   (0) Never (1) Rarely (2) Sometimes (3) Frequently (4) Always
8. Removing and burning trash.
   (0) Never (1) Rarely (2) Sometimes (3) Frequently (4) Always
9. Scrubbing floors.
   (0) Never (1) Rarely (2) Sometimes (3) Frequently (4) Always
10. Repairing a broken item of furniture.
    (0) Never (1) Rarely (2) Sometimes (3) Frequently (4) Always
11. Making beds.
    (0) Never (1) Rarely (2) Sometimes (3) Frequently (4) Always
12. Paying household bills.
    (0) Never (1) Rarely (2) Sometimes (3) Frequently (4) Always

SOURCE: J. A. Ballweg. "Resolution of Conjugal Role Adjustment after Retirement." *Journal of Marriage and the Family*, 1967, 29:277-81. Copyright 1967 by the National Council on Family Relations. Reprinted by permission.

V2.3.II.e

RATIONALITY IN DECISION MAKING

R. Hill, 1963; 1965; 1970

Interviewer Rating: (After each confrontation of places with actions taken, the interviewer is expected to elicit the data about the decisions made to make the rating below.)

ITEM[1]	GUTTMAN ORDER
1. Did couple discuss or confer:	
(a) within the family	2
(b) outside the family?	8
2. Was there a search for information about alternatives—shopping around?	6
. . . Yes . . . No	
3. Were relative costs and satisfactions weighed among alternatives?	
. . . Yes (costs)	5
. . . Yes (satisfactions)	3
4. Were long-range and immediate satisfactions taken into account?	
. . . Yes (long-range satisfactions)	4
. . . Yes (short-term satisfactions)	1
5. Is there a family policy?	7
. . . Yes . . . No	
What is it, if any?	

1. Items 3 and 4 have been slightly modified in format, not substance, in order to present the Guttman scale pattern (see Hill [1970, p. 387] for exact format).

SOURCE: R. Hill. *Family Development in Three Generations.* Cambridge, Mass: Schenkman, 1970, p. 387.

V2.3.II.f

DECISION POWER INDEX

R. O. Blood and D. M. Wolfe, 1960

1. In every family somebody has to decide such things as where the family will live and so on. Many couples talk such things over first, but the *final* decision often has to be made by the husband or the wife. For instance, who usually makes the final decision about what car to get?
   (5) husband always (4) husband more than wife (3) husband and wife exactly the same (2) wife more than husband (1) wife always
2. ...about whether or not to buy some life insurance?
   (5) husband always (4) husband more than wife (3) husband and wife exactly the same (2) wife more than husband (1) wife always
3. ...about what house or apartment to take?
   (5) husband always (4) husband more than wife (3) husband and wife exactly the same (2) wife more than husband (1) wife always
4. Who usually makes the final decision about what job your husband should take?
   (5) husband always (4) husband more than wife (3) husband and wife exactly the same (2) wife more than husband (1) wife always
5. ...about whether or not *you* should go to work or quit work?
   (5) husband always (4) husband more than wife (3) husband and wife exactly the same (2) wife more than husband (1) wife always
6. ...about how much money your family can afford to spend per week on food.
   (5) husband always (4) husband more than wife (3) husband and wife exactly the same (2) wife more than husband (1) wife always
7. ...about what doctor to have when someone is sick?
   (5) husband always (4) husband more than wife (3) husband and wife exactly the same (2) wife more than husband (1) wife always
8. ...and, about where to go on a vacation?
   (5) husband always (4) husband more than wife (3) husband and wife exactly the same (2) wife more than husband (1) wife always

SOURCE: R. O. Blood and D. M. Wolfe, *Husbands and Wives: The Dynamics of Married Living,* p. 282. New York: Free Press, 1960. Reprinted with permission of the Free Press, a division of Macmillan Publishing Company, Inc. Copyright 1960 by the Free Press, a corporation.

V2.3.II.g

DIVISION OF LABOR

R. O. Blood, 1958; R. O. Blood and D. M. Wolfe, 1960

We would like to know how you and your husband divide up some of the family jobs. Here is a list of different ways of dividing up jobs.
1. Now who does the grocery shopping?
   (1) Husband always (2) Husband more than wife (3) Husband and wife exactly the same (4) Wife more than husband (5) Wife always
2. Who gets your husband's breakfast on workdays?
   (1) Husband always (2) Husband more than wife (3) Husband and wife exactly the same (4) Wife more than husband (5) Wife always
3. Who does the evening dishes?

(1) Husband always (2) Husband more than wife (3) Husband and wife exactly the same (4) Wife more than husband (5) Wife always

4. Who straightens up the living room when company is coming?
   (1) Husband always (2) Husband more than wife (3) Husband and wife exactly the same (4) Wife more than husband (5) Wife always

5. Who mows the lawn?
   (1) Husband always (2) Husband more than wife (3) Husband and wife exactly the same (4) Wife more than husband (5) Wife always

6. Who shovels the sidewalk?
   (1) Husband always (2) Husband more than wife (3) Husband and wife exactly the same (4) Wife more than husband? (5) Wife always

7. Who repairs things around the house?
   (1) Husband always (2) Husband more than wife (3) Husband and wife exactly the same (4) Wife more than husband (5) Wife always

8. Who keeps track of the money and the bills?
   (1) Husband always (2) Husband more than wife (3) Husband and wife exactly the same (4) Wife more than husband (5) Wife always

SOURCE: R. O. Blood and D. M. Wolfe, *Husbands and Wives: The Dynamics of Married Living*, p. 282. New York: Free Press, 1960. Reprinted by permission of the Free Press, a division of Macmillan Publishing Company, Inc. Copyright 1960 by the Free Press, a corporation.

V2.3.III.a

ANTICIPATORY SOCIALIZATION

B. C. Miller, 1976

The questions I will ask you now apply to the change you just mentioned; that is (name of transition).[1] Keep this change in mind as I ask you these questions. We would like to find out how prepared you feel you were for (name of transition) *before* it actually took place.

1. Before this change happened, did you learn anything about what it would be like through *special classes* or schooling?
   (1) nothing (2) a little (3) quite a bit (4) a lot

2. How much did you learn about what to expect by *observing* friends or relatives going through the same thing?
   (1) nothing (2) a little (3) quite a bit (4) a lot

3. How much did you plan for this by *talking* about it ahead of time with your (husband/ wife)?
   (1) nothing (2) a little (3) quite a bit (4) a lot

4. How much preparation did you get by *reading* about what it would be like?
   (1) nothing (2) a little (3) quite a bit (4) a lot

1. See the instrument report on Ease of Role Transition (Miller, 1976).

SOURCE: B. C. Miller. "A Multivariate Developmental Model of Marital Satisfaction." *Journal of Marriage and the Family*, 1976, 38:643-57. Copyright 1976 by the National Council on Family Relations. Reprinted by permission.

V2.3.III.b

SUPPORT SYSTEMS OF WIDOWS

H. Z. Lopata, 1977

1. Emotional Support
   a. Sentimental

ASK EVERYONE

	Before	*Now*

39. In 19__before your husband's last illness (accident), what persons were closest to you? (What persons are closest to you now?) (Record each person's first name, relationship to R, and sex if not obvious.)

40. Whom did (do) you most enjoy being with in 19__(now)? (Record each person's first name, relationship to R, and sex if not obvious.)

41. To whom did (do) you tell your problems in 19__ (now)? (Record each person's first name, relationship to R, and sex if not obvious.)

42. Who comforted (comforts) you when you were (are) depressed in 19___ (now)? (Record each person's first name, relationship to R, and sex if not obvious.)

47. What persons made (make) you feel like an especially important person in 19__ (now)? (Record each person's first name, relationship to R, and sex if not obvious.)

48. What persons made (make) you angry most often in 19__(now)? (Record each person's first name, relationship to R, and sex if not obvious.)

49. To whom did you turn (do you turn) in a crisis in 19__(now)? (Record each person's first name, relationship to R, and sex if not obvious.)

   b. Feeling States

53. Now I am going to read some "feeling states" which many people think are important for a full life. What persons or groups made (make) you feel this way in 19__(now)? (Ask "before" and "now" for each lettered category. For persons, record first name and relationship to R. Record sex if not obvious.)

	Before	*Now*

a. Respected . . . .

b. Useful . . . .

c. Independent . . . .

d. Accepted. . . . .

e. Self-sufficient . . . .

f. Secure . . . .

2. Economic Supports

ASK EVERYONE:

90a. In addition to your regular income, are you presently *receiving* any of the following kinds of financial help? (Read each category and circle responses; then go back and ask Q.90b and c for each "Yes" response obtained. Record responses in table below.)
(If Yes)

90b. Who helps you? (For person, record first name, relationship to R, and sex if not obvious.)

90c. How often do you get this help? Would you say . . . (Show Card #2. Read categories and record answer code in table.)

Daily 01
Several times a week 02
About once a week 03
Several times a month 04
About once a month 05
Several times a year 06
About once a year 07
Less than once a year 08
Never 09

		a. Received help		b. Who helped	c. How often
		No	Yes	*(If Yes)*	
(1)	Gifts	2	1	_____	_____
				_____	_____
				_____	_____
(2)	Payment or help on payment of your rent or mortgage	2	1	_____	_____
(3)	Food or payment for food. . . .	2	1	_____	_____
				_____	_____
(4)	Clothing or payment for clothing	2	1	_____	_____
				_____	_____
(5)	Payment or help in payment of other bills such as medical or vacation expenses	2	1	_____	_____
(6)	Any other financial help (specify)	2	1	_____	_____
				_____	_____

91a. Are you presently *giving* any of the following kinds of financial help to anyone? (Read each category and record responses; then go back and ask Q.91b and c for each "Yes" response obtained. Record response in table below.)
(If Yes)

91b. Who are you helping? (For persons, record first name, relationship to R, and sex if not obvious.)

91c. How often do you give this help? (Show Card #2. Read categories and record answer code in table.)

Daily 01
Several times a week 02

About once a week 03
Several times a month 04
About once a month 05
Several times a year 06
About once a year 07
Less than once a year 08
Never 09

		a. Give help		b. Who helped	c. How often
		No	Yes	*(If Yes)*	
(1)	Gifts	2	1	_____	_____
				_____	_____
(2)	Payment or help in payment of your rent or mortgage	2	1	_____	_____
(3)	Food or payment for food	2	1	_____	_____
				_____	_____
(4)	Clothing or payment for clothing	2	1	_____	_____
(5)	Payment or help in payment of other bills such as medical or vacation expenses	2	1	_____	_____
(6)	Any other financial help (specify)	2	1	_____	_____
				_____	_____

3. Service Supports

92a. Now I will read you a list of things people often do for each other in daily life or in solving special problems. Does anyone do any of these things for you? Does anyone . . . (Read each category; circle responses; then go ask Q.92b and c for each "Yes" response obtained. Record responses in table below.)
 (If Yes)

92b. Who does this for you? (For persons, record first name, relationship to R, and sex if not obvious.)

92c. How often is this done for you? Would you say . . . (Show Card #2. Read categories and record answer code in table.)

Daily 01
Several times a week 02
About once a week 03
Several times a month 04
About once a month 05
Several times a year 06
About once a year 07
Less than once a year 08
Never 09

		a. Receives this		b. Who provides	c. How often
		No	Yes	*(If Yes)*	
(1)	Provide transportation or drive you places	2	1	_____	_____

		a. Receives this		b. Who provides	c. How often
		No	Yes		
(2)	Make minor household repairs for you............	2	1	_____	_____
(3)	Help you with housekeeping. . .	2	1	_____	_____
(4)	Help you with shopping	2	1	_____	_____
(5)	Help you with yard work	2	1	_____	_____
(6)	Help you with child care.....	2	1	_____	_____
(7)	Help you take care of your car	2	1	_____	_____
(8)	Care for you when you are ill . .	2	1	_____	_____
(9)	Help you make important decisions..............	2	1	_____	_____
(10)	Provide you with legal aid	2	1	_____	_____

93a. Do you do any of these things for others? Do you . . . (Read each category and circle responses; then go back and ask Q.93b and c for each "Yes" response obtained. Record responses in table below.)
(If Yes)

93b. For whom do you do these things? (For persons, record first name, relationship to R, and sex if not obvious.)

93c. How often do you do this? Would you say . . . (Show Card #2. Read categories and record answer code in table.)

Daily 01
Several times a week 02
About once a week 03
Several times a month 04
About once a month 05
Several times a year. 06
About once a year 07
Less than once a year. 08
Never 09

		(If Yes)			
		a. Provide this		b. For whom	c. How often
		No	Yes		
(1)	Provide transportation or drive others places	2	1	_____	_____
(2)	Make minor household repairs for others	2	1	_____	_____
(3)	Help others with housekeeping .	2	1	_____	_____
(4)	Help others with shopping....	2	1	_____	_____
(5)	Help others with yard work ...	2	1	_____	_____
(6)	Help others with child care ...	2	1	_____	_____
(7)	Help others take care of their car	2	1	_____	_____
(8)	Care for others when they are ill	2	1	_____	_____
(9)	Help others make important decisions..............	2	1	_____	_____
(10)	Provide others with legal aid. . .	2	1	_____	_____

4. Social Supports
94a. Now I would like to know some things about your social activities. I will read you a list

of social activities that people can do with others. Please tell me which of these activities you do. (Read each category and circle responses; then ask Q.94B through d for each as appropriate. Record responses in table.)

(If Yes)

94b. With whom do you do this? (Record first name, relationship to R, and sex if not obvious.)

94c. How often do you do these things? (Show Card #2. Record answer code in table.)

Daily 01
Several times a week 02
About once a week 03
Several times a month 04
About once a month 05
Several times a year. 06
About once a year 07
Less than once a year. 08
Never 09

(If No)

94d. Why aren't you doing these things now? Is it mainly because of your . . . (Read categories. Record answer code in table.)

a. Health 1
b. Lack of money. 2
c. Transportation difficulties 3
d. Lack of male escort 4
e. Lack of time or energy 5
f. Feelings and emotions 6
g. Something else (Specify in table). 7

		a. Does activity Yes No	(If Yes) b. With whom	c. How often	(If No) d. Why not
(1)	Go to public places, movies theater	1 2	_____	_____	_____
(2)	Visit	1 2	_____	_____	_____
(3)	Entertain in your home	1 2	_____	_____	_____
(4)	Go out to lunch or eat lunch with someone	1 2	_____	_____	_____
(5)	Go to church	1 2	_____	_____	_____
(6)	Engage in sports, cards, games. .	1 2	_____	_____	_____
(7)	Travel out of town	1 2	_____	_____	_____
(8)	Celebrate holidays	1 2	_____	_____	_____
(9)	Something else (specify)	1 2	_____	_____	_____

SOURCE: H. Z. Lopata. *Women as Widows.* New York: Elsevier, 1979, pp. 417, 419, 421, 440-45.

V2.3.III.c

RELATIONS-RESTRICTIVE ATTITUDE SCALE

H. Z. Lopata, 1973

Item Set A

	Agree Strongly	Agree	Disagree	Disagree Strongly
1. One problem with adult children is that they always want you to do favors for them—babysit, or sew, or things like that.	1	2	3	4
2. Sons are more help to a widow than daughters.	1	2	3	4
3. Relatives are your only true friends.	1	2	3	4
4. A widow has to make her own life and not depend on others.	1	2	3	4
5. A new widow should not move too soon from the place in which she was living before her husband died.	1	2	3	4
6. Other women are jealous of a widow when their husbands are around.	1	2	3	4
7. Many widows who remarry are very unhappy in that marriage.	1	2	3	4
8. Widows are constantly sexually propositioned even by the husbands of their friends.	1	2	3	4
9. One problem of being a widow is feeling like a "fifth wheel."	1	2	3	4
10. People take advantage of you when they know you are a widow.	1	2	3	4
11. Sharing one's home with anyone causes nothing but trouble for a widow.	1	2	3	4
12. Most widows prefer living near other widows.	1	2	3	4
13. It is all right for a widow to have sexual relations with a man without planning on marriage.	1	2	3	4
14. The hardest thing for a widow to learn is how to make decisions.	1	2	3	4
15. Women lose status when they become widows—they lose respect and consideration.	1	2	3	4
16. Old friends cannot be replaced no matter how one tries to make new friends.	1	2	3	4

Item Set B: In this next set of statements, please circle the number which shows whether each statement is true or false for you.

	True	False
1. My husband was an unusually good man.	1	2
2. My husband and I did not do too many things together; he had his activities, and I had mine.	1	2
3. I did not know anything about our finances when my husband died.	1	2
(IF APPLICABLE)		
4. My husband and I pretended we did not know how sick he really was.	1	2
5. My sexual relations with my husband were very good until his last illness.	1	2
6. I would do more things outside of the house if someone would come and pick me up.	1	2
7. I felt angry at the doctor and the hospital for not doing enough for my husband when he was ill.	1	2
8. My married friends have not been much help to me.	1	2
9. My present income makes it impossible for me to maintain old friendships.	1	2
10. My marriage was above average and no second marriage could match it.	1	2
11. I wish people wouldn't try to get me to go out and do things all the time.	1	2
12. My brothers and/or sisters became much more important to me after I became a widow.	1	2
13. I wish I had more male companionship.	1	2
14. I have trouble being nice to people who did not help during my period of grief.	1	2
15. I like living alone.	1	2
16. I wish I had more friends.	1	2
17. My faith helped me more than anything else after my husband's death.	1	2
18. Of the men I have dated, I have most in common with widowers.	1	2
19. I feel sorry for some of my married friends who have little freedom to do as they please.	1	2
20. This time of my life is actually easier than any other time.	1	2
21. I feel more independent and free now than before I became a widow.	1	2

SOURCE: H. Z. Lopata. *Widowhood in an American City.* Cambridge, Mass.: Schenkman, 1973, pp. 299-300.

V2.3.III.d.

SANCTIFICATION OF HUSBAND

H. Z. Lopata, 1976

Semantic Differential Evaluation of Deceased Spouse[1]

Adjective Pair	*Item Mean*
1. Good-Bad	1.62
2. Useful-Useless	1.68
3. Honest-Dishonest	1.47
4. Superior-Inferior	2.07
5. Kind-Cruel	1.56
6. Friendly-Unfriendly	1.53
7. Warm-Cold	1.61

Life-Together Items[2]

1. My husband was an unusually good man.	1.48
2. My marriage was above average.	1.76
3. My husband and I were always together except for working hours.	1.80
4. My husband and I felt the same way about almost everything.	1.98
5. My husband was a very good father to our children.	1.46
6. Our home was an unusually happy one.	1.67
7. My husband had no irritating habits.	2.25

1. Semantic differential range of 1 to 7.

2. Item responses: (1) Strongly Agree, (2) Agree, (3) Disagree, and (4) Strongly Disagree.
SOURCE: H. Z. Lopata. "Widowhood and Husband Sanctification." Paper presented to the 71st Annual Meeting of the American Sociological Association, New York, 1976.

Chapter 4

Parent-Child Relations

Vern L. Bengtson and Sandi S. Schrader

Assessment of family relations has been a part of most surveys examining the social aspects of aging. For many older individuals, family roles and participation constitute an important arena of social life. In examining the correlates of personal adjustment in old age, for example, many studies have suggested that family integration may be an important variable. Unfortunately, the conceptual analysis of family interaction in old age remains underdeveloped. Furthermore, the measures employed to describe that interaction have been somewhat informal, and, in many cases, they are idiosyncratic from one study to another.

At the construct level, many surveys have not differentiated parent-child relations from other kinship interaction. Few studies have made any attempt to distinguish conceptually various aspects of parent-child relations in terms of the type of interaction or the meaning of affective bonds. At the measurement level, very few studies report any information on the reliability, validity, or scaling properties of the items employed to measure interaction. Most information appears to be based on single-item indicators (for example, "When was the last time you saw one of your children?"), with measurement accuracy an untested assumption.

Some researchers have adopted an entirely different conceptual perspective by employing the construct of support systems, with spouse, siblings, children, and other kin—as well as friends and neighbors—being viewed as potential elements in interaction or service assistance (Lopata, 1973; Cantor, 1976; NCOA, 1975). Thus, there is considerable overlap (and some confusion) between this review and other sections of the measurement inventory, although each reflects distinct constructs in the evaluation of social roles, relationships, and potential interpersonal support. It is particularly useful, therefore, to differentiate among theoretically important constructs in investigating parent-child relations across the life cycle (Shanas et al., 1968; Bengtson and Black, 1973a; Bengtson and Cutler, 1976; Sussman, 1976).

Constructs and Variables

Careful construct definition can lead to more precise operationalization and measurement. From a review of the literature it appears there are six conceptually distinct but interrelated constructs that are useful in organizing previous studies and instructive in defining future research. The six constructs reflect *intergenerational family structure, associational solidarity, affectual solidarity, consensual solidarity, exchanges* of assistance and/or support (or functional solidarity), and *norms* or expectations regarding filial or parental behavior.

These constructs, and variables that have been used to reflect them, are summarized in Table 4-1 and nominally defined in the sections below. Before reviewing their use in previous studies, it is worthwhile to summarize some theoretical considerations regarding cohesion in social groups, with special reference to the family. This provides the conceptual background necessary for any thorough attempt to classify and measure parent-child relations in maturity.

TABLE 4-1
Critical Constructs in the Analysis of Family Intergenerational Relations
and Variables Reflecting Their Measurement

Construct	Variables to Be Operationalized
A. Family structure across generations: Parameters of social unions	A-1. *Number* of living family lineage members of the subject a. Children b. Parents c. Grandchildren or grandparents d. Lineal relatives by marriage (children-in-law, parents-in-law) e. Siblings and siblings' lineal relations A-2. Sex—lineage type (male-male; male-female; female-female; female-male) A-3. *Number and type* of lineal "fictive kin"

TABLE 4-1—*Continued*

Construct		Variables to Be Operationalized
	A-4.	*Geographical proximity* of each of the above to the subject
	A-5.	Household composition of the subject
B. Associational solidarity of integration	B-1.	*Frequency* of interaction between subject and lineage members in common activities
	B-2.	*Type* of common activities shared
C. Affectional solidarity or integration	C-1.	Perceived *quality* of interaction: sentiments of warmth, closeness, trust, understanding, communication, respect *toward* the Other
	C-2.	Perceived *reciprocity* of interaction: sentiments *from* the Other
D. Consensual solidarity or integration	D-1.	Degree of similarity or conflict in *general values*
	D-2.	Degree of similarity or conflict in *specific opinions* (socio-political or religous orientations)
	D-3.	*Perception* of similarity or contrast and/or conflict
E. Functional solidarity or integration	E-1.	*Degree* of exchange of services or assistance between lineage members
	E-2.	*Perception* of potential support or assistance between lineage members
F. Normative solidarity or integration	F-1.	Instances of norms enacted concerning associational, affectional, consensual, or functional solidarity
	F-2.	Perceptions of norms potentially *enacted*

Cohesion and Family Solidarity

The concept of social cohesion, or group solidarity, has been a concern of sociologists since the beginning of formal social analysis. Comte, Durkheim, Marx, and Weber developed theories of social organization based on both the division of labor and the development of cohesiveness among subunits. Contemporary functionalists such as Parsons (1951) have emphasized the importance of solidarity in analyzing both macro- and microsocial organization. Social psychologists such as Back (1951), Deutsch and Krauss (1965), and Festinger (1967) have discussed forces that act on members of a group to induce them to remain in the group. Cleland (1955) viewed solidarity as evidenced in "the extent of shared activities" (p. 242) in a group, and Cartwright and Zander (1960) and Brown (1965) emphasized solidarity as residing in the sharing of common needs and goals among group members. Thibaut and Kelley (1967) defined solidarity in terms of members' attraction to a group. These are but a few of the many definitions of *solidarity* as it is seen in small groups. Other observers have used terms such as *normative integration* and *value agreement, trust,* and *mutual expectations,* and *pressures* invoked in the management of conflict.

Solidarity and cohesiveness have also been frequently discussed by those interested specifically in the family as a small group. It is common for solidarity to be considered in horizontal role relations (for example, the husband-wife dyad), with outcomes labeled "adjustment," "happiness," or "satisfaction."

Many characteristics of kinship relations also reflect the construct of solidarity, though it is not explicitly named as such. Adams (1968) provided a good example in his differentiation between the objective and the subjective aspects of kinship. He defined the *objective aspects of kinship* as the occasions of actual interpersonal interaction: home visits, work together, ritualistic activities, and aid given and received. The subjective elements include affectional closeness, value consensus, identification, and obligation.

Nye and Rushing (1966) noted the multidimensional character of cohesiveness and solidarity and identified six dimensions that have frequently been considered (at least implicitly) in family research:

1. Associational integration: the frequency with which group members are in contact with one another and interact in common activities.
2. Affectional integration: the mutual positive sentiment among group members and their expressions of love, appreciation, respect, and recognition of one another.
3. Consensual integration: the degree of consensus among group members on beliefs and values.
4. Functional integration: the exchange of services among group members.
5. Normative integration: the group's control over individual members, as evidenced in conformity mechanisms.
6. Goal integration: the extent to which individual members subordinate their interests or goals to those of the group as a whole.

An important consideration in selecting dimensions for analysis of parent-child relations concerns the degree of fit with conceptual approaches used in understanding small-group behavior. The six dimensions reviewed reflect this concern. They integrate well, for example, with the work of Homans (1950; 1961) and other social exchange theorists, as well as with the ideas of balance in interpersonal relations suggested by Heider (1958). Future family research will probably construct such theoretical links more explicitly and formally as the field continues to develop.

Family Structure between Generations

Enumerating the structural characteristics of an elderly respondent's family is of interest as descriptive information for constructing theoretical connections to other variables and for assessing potential interpersonal support systems. In terms of parent-child relations, assessing three kinds of information is important: (1) the number of living children, grandchildren, and parents, (2) their geographic proximity, and (3) composition of the individual's household.

Family structure may seem the most simple of the various aspects of parent-child relations to measure by simply asking the age and sex of each child and then the number of miles he or she lives from the respondent (Rosow, 1967; Adams, 1968; Shanas et al., 1968; Streib and Schneider, 1971; Bengtson and Black, 1973a; Cantor, 1976; NCOA, 1975), but the issue is complicated by social, in contrast to biological, definitions of kin. For one thing, the respondent may have step-children whom she or he may or may not have raised and who may or may not be children in a relational sense. It should be noted that nongenetically related children may be of special importance for some ethnic groups. For example, in samples of black elderly people, the surviving elderly respondent may have parental relations with several members of younger generations who may not be related by birth and who may call her auntie or him uncle (Jackson, 1970). Second, children-in-law may be particularly important in intergenerational interaction. Both fictive children and children-in-law may or may not reflect potential elements of a support system or a sense of social bondedness.

Associational Solidarity between Generations

Solidarity is a construct that has been suggested by many sociologists, from Durkheim to Homans, as an attribute characterizing human groups. One indicator of solidarity concerns the activities and encounters that characterize human interaction. In studies of parent-child relations, such an association (with its several indicators) appears to be particularly important to assess (Bengtson, Olander, and Haddad, 1976).

One indicator of associational solidarity is simply the frequency of

interaction of any type between elderly individuals and their offspring. A second involves the type of activities in which they engage,
from telephone conversations to family gatherings. A third concerns
the frequency or quantity of specific types of interaction. Each can
be measured with relative ease by presenting respondents with activities checklists (Adams, 1968; Hill et al., 1970; Bengtson and
Black, 1973a; NCOA, 1975; Cantor, 1976). However, two precautions
must be noted.

First, the selection of activities (and their frequency) should be
based on previous research and/or theoretical considerations. The
types of interactions in which elderly parents and their children
might engage are numerous, and the investigator should choose those
that have substantive relevance to the particular problem being investigated *or* are reflective of some superordinate theoretical dimensions (e.g., instrumental versus expressive interaction).

Second, self-reports (even those of observable interactions) should
be interpreted with caution; it has been found that, although middle-
aged children and their aging parents generally agree about the frequency of their mutually shared activities, there may be a tendency
for each generation to overreport or underestimate some types of
interaction (Bengtson and Black, 1973b). (Other methods are discussed by Kerckhoff, 1965, and Bultena, 1969.)

Affectual Solidarity between Generations

The third major dimension of parent-child relations concerns subjective judgments of the quality of interaction. Often, this has been
treated as a global concept: the general closeness or warmth of the
relationship (Adams, 1968; Bengtson, 1971; Bengtson and Black,
1973b; Cantor 1976). Several traditions in social and behavioral theory (e.g., symbolic interaction, sociology of knowledge, attribution
theory) suggest that such subjective assessments may be the most important dimension in examinations of intersonal relations such as
parent-child interaction because "insofar as individuals define situations to be real, they are real in their consequences" (Thomas 1931,
p. 11).

Relations between parent and child across the life span can be characterized by positive sentiment, by negative sentiment (which must be
a consideration in any relationship, whether it is openly acknowledged
and revealed or not), and in terms of the global closeness or distance
that members attribute to the relationship. Although each of these
conceptual dimensions appears to be useful to both scientific and
applied questions in social gerontology, very few investigators have
attempted to operationalize them.

Consensual Solidarity

Consensus refers to the extent of agreement or similarity in general values or orientations, in specific sociopolitical attitudes, or in beliefs (Bengtson, Olander, and Haddad, 1976). Such values or opinions can be assessed by asking questions specific to one attitudinal domain, or by batteries reflecting a cross section of issues (Hill et al., 1970).

The degree of consensual solidarity can be measured by comparing *actual attitude responses* of the older respondent with those of his or her child, using some measure of absolute agreement or relative predictivity. Alternatively, the respondent may be asked to predict what responses would be given by the other family member, leading to a comparison of *attributions or perceptions of similarity or contrast*. A third approach is to ask directly about *global similarity or difference* as perceived by the respondent.

Functional Solidarity: Exchanges of Assistance and Support between Generations

Intergenerational relations between adult family members invariably involve some exchange of tangible goods and services in addition to (and perhaps as part of) the interactional and affectual solidarity exchanges already described. Two important types of exchange are financial and helping activities. Both can be assessed by checklists (Sussman, 1965; Rosow, 1967; Shanas, 1968; Adams, 1968; Hill et al., 1970; Lopata, 1973; Cantor, 1976; NCOA, 1975). Although these cross-generational exchanges appear to be of considerable salience to both parents and children, with all being quite conscious of the balance in terms of giving and receiving (see Streib and Thompson's 1960 discussion of the "norms of reciprocity" and Hill and his colleagues' 1970 description of boundary maintenance versus boundary crossing), they may be difficult to measure for three reasons.

One problem is the often-idiosyncratic calculus of exchange in a family unit; monetary or subsistence (housing) support may be given to the older or the younger generation in implicit exchange for helping services (e.g., babysitting, gardening, and cooking) in ways that are not easily identified in survey research. Another reason that exchanges may be difficult to measure is that exchanges may be given in implicit expectation of future benefits; testamentary dispositions, for example, often reflect an older family member's explicit attempt to reward the relative who has given him or her the most help during his or her last years (Rosenfeld, 1974). A third problem is that the flow of exchange may be perceived differently by each generation.

The amount of exchange may be perceived differently by each generation, too, and the amount of exchange must be balanced by the amount of resources available. From the conclusions of one study, it appears that elderly grandparents spend a disproportionate amount of their resources for gifts at Christmas and birthdays for children and grandchildren. Furthermore, the older generation is likely to underreport gifts and services they give, and their middle-aged children are likely to overestimate their receipt of such exchanges (Bengtson and Black, 1973b). Another study (Hill et al., 1970) presents data clearly indicating that the middle generation is the "donor" for the other two.

Norms Regarding Parent-Child Relations

A fifth dimension that may be of particular salience in some research focuses on the expectations, or presumed obligations, in intergenerational behavior involving an aging parent. Conceptually distinct from actual interaction, affect, and exchange, such perceptions of what should be involved in parent-child relations during maturity are reflected in some of the earliest research in social gerontology (e.g., Dinkel, 1944; Havighurst and Albrecht, 1953).

Operationalization and Measurement

Clearly, construct definition is underdeveloped in most studies of parent-child relations during old age, with relatively little attention given to identifying the various dimensions of interaction, affect, and norms that govern the relationship. However, many surveys have included measures of various aspects of primary group relations.

A variety of indicators have been used to assess the relationship between aged parents and their children. Relatively few actual scales have been reported in the literature; almost all instrumentation has used single-item indicators. Virtually no information is available concerning the reliability and/or validity of single-item indicators. Some investigators have employed what may be called batteries, sets of conceptually related single-item indicators not combined into a summary measure. Here, too, few data pertinent to reliability and validity are available.

Summary

The batteries, scales, and items presented on the following pages reflect one or more conceptual dimensions of the parent-child relationship. Questionnaire items from the various studies are grouped in the sections to follow according to the conceptual areas they reflect (see Table 4-2). Some of the instruments tap several conceptual areas and are represented accordingly. The use of the same items with exactly comparable wording in future studies will allow comparisons with previous findings.

TABLE 4-2
Measures Reviewed in Chapter 4

Instrument	Author(s)	Code Number
A. Family Structure (Number of children, geographic proximity, household composition)		
Contact between Generations Battery	Adams (1968)	V2.4.I.a
Cross-ethnic Battery of Familism	Bengtson and Manuel (1976)	V2.4.I.d
Family Mutual Aid and Interaction Index	Cantor (1976); Mayer (1976)	V2.4.I.e
Family Structure and Contact Battery	Lopata (1973)	V2.4.I.i
Family Structure and Contact Battery	Shanas et al. (1968)	V2.4.I.m
Family Structure and Interaction Battery	Streib and Schneider (1971)	V2.4.I.n
B. Associational Solidarity between Generations		
Contact between Generations Battery	Adams (1968)	V2.4.I.a
Interaction Index	Bengtson (1973)	V2.4.I.c
Cross-ethnic Battery of Familism	Bengtson and Manuel (1976)	V2.4.I.d
Familial Interaction Index	Bultena (1969)	V2.5.I.f
Family Mutual Aid and Interaction Index	Cantor (1976); Mayer (1976)	V2.4.I.e
Role Activities in Later Maturity	Havighurst and Albrecht (1953)	V2.2.II.a
Exchanges between Generations Index	Hill et al. (1970)	V2.4.I.h
Family Structure and Contact Battery	Lopata (1973)	V2.4.I.i
Social and Family Contact Scale	NCOA (1975; 1976)	V2.4.I.j
Emotional Dependence on Children Scale	Rosow (1967)	V2.4.I.l

TABLE 4-2—*Continued*

Instrument	Author(s)	Code Number
Family Structure and Contact Battery	Shanas et al. (1968)	V2.4.I.m
Family Structure and Interaction Battery	Streib and Schneider (1971)	V2.4.I.n
Married Offspring-Parent Adjustment Checklist	Stryker (1955)	V2.4.I.o
Dependence Checklist	Stryker (1955)	V2.4.I.p
Intergenerational Family Continuity Rating Scale	Sussman (1960)	Not available
C. Affectional Solidarity between Generations		
Contact between Generations Battery	Adams (1968)	V2.4.I.a
Positive Affect Index	Bengtson (1973)	V2.4.I.b
Family Mutual Aid and Interaction Index	Cantor (1976); Mayer (1976)	V2.4.I.e
Role Activities in Later Maturity	Havighurst and Albrecht (1953)	V2.2.II.a
Family Structure and Interaction Battery	Streib and Schneider (1971)	V2.4.I.n
Married Offspring-Parent Adjustment	Stryker (1955)	V2.4.I.o
Intergenerational Family Continuity Rating Scale	Sussman (1960)	Not available
D. Exchange of Assistance and Support		
Contact between Generations Battery	Adams (1968)	V2.4.I.a
Family Mutual Aid and Interaction Index	Cantor (1976); Mayer (1976)	V2.4.I.e
Role Activities in Later Maturity	Havighurst and Albrecht (1953)	V2.2.II.a
Exchanges between Generations Index	Hill et al. (1970)	V2.4.I.h
Mutual Support Index	Kerckhoff (1965)	V2.5.II.i
Family Structure and Contact Battery	Lopata (1973)	V2.4.I.i
Exchanges of Support and Assistance Index	NCOA (1975; 1976)	V2.4.I.k
Family Structure and Contact Battery	Shanas et al. (1968)	V2.4.I.m
Family Structure and Interaction Battery	Streib and Schneider (1971)	V2.4.I.n
Married Offspring-Parent Adjustment Checklist	Stryker (1955)	V2.4.I.o
Dependence Checklist	Stryker (1955)	V2.4.I.p

TABLE 4-2—*Continued*

Instrument	Author(s)	Code Number
E. Norms Regarding Parent-Child Relations		
Contact between Generations		
Battery	Adams (1968)	V2.4.I.a
Familism Index	Cantor (1976); Wilker (1976)	V2.4.I.f
Children's Attitudes toward supporting aged parents	Dinkel (1944)	V2.4.I.g
Mutual Aid and Affection Scale	Kerckhoff (1965)	V2.5.II.h
Family Structure and Contact Battery	Lopata (1973)	V2.4.I.i
Emotional Dependence on Children Scale	Rowow (1967)	V2.4.I.l
Family Structure and Contact Battery	Shanas et al. (1968)	V2.4.I.m
Family Structure and Interaction Battery	Streib and Schneider (1971)	V2.4.I.n
Dependence Checklist	Stryker (1955)	V2.4.I.p

It should be pointed out that most of the items and batteries reviewed in this chapter could be used in studies focusing on either parents (the aged) or children (the middle-aged). By a simple substitution of terms, assessments can be made of either generation's situation vis-à-vis the other. For simplicity the items below are phrased from the standpoint of a survey involving older respondents (e.g., geographic proximity to child, not to parents).

REFERENCES

Adams, B.N. *Kinship in an Urban Setting.* Chicago: Markham, 1968.

Back, K. W. "Influence through Social Communication." *The Journal of Abnormal and Social Psychology* 1951, 46: 131-45.

Bengtson, V. L. "Inter-age Differences in Perception and the Generation Gap." *The Gerontolotist,* 1971, 11 (4): 85-90.

———. "Progress Report on the Study of Generations and Mental Health." Unpublished report submitted to NIMH, 1973.

Bengtson, V. L., and K. D. Black. "Inter-generational Relations and Continuities in Socialization." In *Life-Span Developmental Psychology: Personality and Socialization,* P. Baltes and W. Schaie (eds.), pp. 207-34. New York: Academic Press, 1973a.

———. "Solidarity between Parents and Children: Four Perspectives on Theory Development." Paper presented to the Theory Development Workshop, National Council on Family Relations, Toronto, October 16, 1973 (b).

Bengtson, V. L., and N. E. Cutler. "Generations and Intergenerational Relations: Perspectives on Age Groups and Social Change." In *Handbook of Aging and the Social Sciences,* H. Binstock and E. Shanas (eds.), pp. 130-59. New York: Van Nostrand Reinhold, 1976.

Bengtson, V. L., and M. C. Lovejoy. "Values, Personality, and Social Structure: An Intergenerational Analysis." *American Behavioral Scientist*, 1973, 16: 880-912.

Bengtson, V. L. and R. Manuel. "Ethnicity and Family Patterns in Mature Adults: Effects of Race, Age, SES and Sex." Paper presented to the Annual Meeting of the Pacific Sociological Association, San Diego, March 25-27, 1976.

Bengtson, V. L., E. Olander, and A. Haddad. "The 'Generation Gap' and Aging Family Members." In *Time, Roles, and Self in Old Age*, J. Gubrium (ed.), pp. 237-63. New York: Behavioral Publications, 1976.

Blenkner, M. "Social Work and Family Relationships in Later Life with Some Thoughts on Filial Maturity." In *Social Structure and the Family: Generational Relations*, E. Shanas and G. F. Streib (eds.), pp. 297-305. Englewood Cliffs, N.J.: Prentice-Hall, 1965.

Brown, R. G. "Family Structure and Social Isolation of Older Persons." *Journal of Gerontology*, 1960, 15: 170-74.

————. *Social Psychology*. New York: John Wiley and Sons, 1965.

Bultena, G. L. "Rural-Urban Differences in the Familial Interaction of the Aged." *Rural Sociology*, 1969, 34: 5-15.

Cantor, M. H. "The Configuration and Intensity of the Informal Support System in a New York City Elderly Population." Paper presented to the 29th Annual Meeting of the Gerontological Society, New York, October 13-17, 1976.

Cartwright, D., and A. Zander (eds.). *Predicting Success or Failure in Marriage*. New York: Prentice-Hall, 1960.

Cleland, C. B. "Familism in Rural Saskatchewan." *Rural Sociology*, 1955, 20: 252.

Deutsch, M., and R. M. Krauss. *Theories in Social Psychology*. New York: Basic Books, 1965.

Dinkel, R. M. "Parent-Child Conflict in Minnesota Families." *American Sociological Review*, 1943, 8: 412-19.

————. "Attitudes of Children toward Supporting Aged Parents." *American Sociological Review*, 1944, 9: 370-79.

Festinger, L. "Informal Social Communication." In *Current Perspectives in Social Psychology*, E. Hollander and R. Hunt (eds.), pp. 34-89. New York: Oxford University Press, 1967.

Havighurst, R. J., and R. Albrecht. *Older People*. New York: Longmans, Green and Company, 1953.

Havighurst, R. J., J. M. A. Munnichs, B. Neugarten, and H. Thomae (eds). *Adjustment to Retirement: A Cross National Study*. Assen, the Netherlands: Van Gorcum, 1969.

Heider, F. *The Psychology of Interpersonal Relations*. New York: John Wiley and Sons, 1958.

Hill, R., N. Foote, J. Aldous, R. Carlson and R. MacDonald. *Family Development in Three Generations*. Cambridge, Mass: Schenkman, 1970.

Homans, G. F. *The Human Group*. New York: Harcourt, Brace and World, 1950.

————. *Social Behavior: Its Elementary Forms*. New York: Harcourt, Brace and World, 1961.

Jackson, J. J. "Kinship Relations among Urban Blacks." *Journal of Social and Behavioral Sciences*, 1970, 61: 5-17.

Kerckhoff, A. C. "Nuclear and Extended Family Relationships: Normative and Behavioral Analysis." In *Social Structure and the Family: Generational Relations*. E. Shanas and G. F. Streib (eds.), pp. 93-112. Englewood Cliffs, N.J.: Prentice-Hall, 1965.

————. "Family Patterns and Morale." In *Social Aspects of Aging*, I. H. Simpson and J. C. McKinney (eds.), pp. 173-94. Durham, N.C.: Duke University Press, 1966.

Komarovsky, M. "Functional Analysis of Sex Roles." *American Sociological Review,* 1950, 15: 508-16.

Lopata, H. Z. *Widowhood in an American City.* Cambridge, Mass: Schenkman, 1973.

Mayer, M. "Kin and Neighbors: Differential Roles in Differing Cultures." Paper presented to the 29th Annual Meeting of the Gerontological Society, New York, October 13-17, 1976.

National Council on the Aging. *The Myth and Reality of Aging in America.* Washington, D.C.: National Council on the Aging, 1975.

————. *Codebook for "The Myth and Reality of Aging,"* a survey conducted by Louis Harris and Associates for the National Council on the Aging; prepared by the Duke University Center for the Study of Aging and Human Development, 1976.

Nye, I., and W. Rushing. "Toward Family Measurement Research." Proceedings of the Family Measurement Conference, Department of Health, Education and Welfare, Washington, D.C., 1966, pp. 31-34.

Parsons, T. *The Social System.* New York: Free Press, 1951.

Ragan, P., and V. L. Bengtson. "Factors of Ethnicity and Aging." Unpublished report to NSF, 1977.

Rosenfeld, J. P. "Inheritance: A Sex-related System of Exchange." In *The Family: Its Structures and Functions,* R. L. Coser (ed.), pp. 326-34. New York: St. Martin's Press, 1974.

Rosow, I. *Social Integration of the Aged.* New York: Free Press, 1967.

Shanas, E. *The Health of Older People: A Social Survey.* Cambridge, Mass.: Harvard University Press, 1962.

————. "The Family as a Social Support System in Old Age." Paper presented to the 30th Annual Meeting of the Gerontological Society, San Francisco, November 18-22, 1977.

Shanas, E., P. Townsend, D. Wedderburn, H. Friis, P. Milhøj, and J. Stehouwer. *Old People in Three Industrial Societies.* New York: Atherton Press, 1968.

Streib, G. F. "Intergenerational Relations: Perspectives of the Two Generations on the Older Parent." *Journal of Marriage and the Family,* 1965, 35: 469-76.

Streib, G. F., and C. J. Schneider. *Retirement in American Society.* Ithaca, N. Y.: Cornell University Press, 1971.

Streib, G. F., and W. E. Thompson. "The Older Person in a Family Context." In *Handbook of Social Gerontology,* C. Tibbitts (ed.), pp. 447-87. Chicago: University of Chicago Press, 1960.

Stryker, S. "The Adjustment of Married Offspring to Their Parents." *American Sociological Review,* 1955, 20: 149-54.

Sussman, M. B. "The Help Pattern in the Middle-Class Family." *American Sociological Review,* 1953, 18: 22-28.

————. "Intergenerational Family Relationship and Social Role Change in Middle Age." *Journal of Gerontology,* 1960, 15: 71-75.

————. "Relationships of Adult Children with Their Parents in the United States." In *Social Structure and the Family: Generational Relations,* E. Shanas and G. F. Streib (eds.), pp. 231-42. Englewood Cliffs, N.J.: Prentice-Hall, 1965.

————. "The Family Life of Old People." In *Handbook of Aging and the Social Sciences,* R. H. Binstock and E. Shanas (eds.), pp. 218-43. New York: Van Nostrand Reinhold, 1976.

Thibaut, J. W., and H. H. Kelley. *The Social Psychology of Groups,* (2nd ed.). New York: John Wiley and Sons, 1967.

Thomas, W. I. *The Unadjusted Girl.* Boston: Little, Brown and Company, 1931.

Wake, S. B., and M. J. Sporakowski. "An Intergenerational Comparison of Attitudes Supporting Aged Parents." *Journal of Marriage and the Family*, 1972, 34: 42-48.

Wilker, L. "Ethnicity and Familism: The Congruency between Attitudes and Behavior." Paper presented to the 29th Annual Meeting of the Gerontological Society, New York, October 13-17, 1976.

Abstracts

CONTACT BETWEEN GENERATIONS BATTERY

B. N. Adams, 1968

Definition of Variable or Concept

Five types of variables are assessed: (1) family structure and household composition, (2) frequency and type of activities shared between middle-aged children and their aging parents, (3) closeness with parents, (4) exchanges of assistance and support, and (5) norms regarding why children keep in touch with parents.

Description of Instrument

The instrument consists of several batteries of items examining the frequency of types of kinship interaction and aid. No claims are made for these being any more than single-item indicators.

Method of Administration

The instrument is a fixed-alternative (closed) interview schedule involving a total of about 120 questions.

Context of Development and Subsequent Use

The battery was developed to explore the nature of kinship relations in an urban American area. Four specific questions guided the research program: (1) What are the occasions for, and kinds of, interaction between kin; what is their significance? (2) What are the subjective or attitudinal dimensions of urban kinship? (3) What is the characteristic relationship between adult siblings and more genealogically distant kin? (4) How does the kin network articulate with other societal systems?

Sample

Data are presented for a stratified random sample ($N = 799$) of white, once-married (for 20 years or less) persons with median ages of 34.5 years for males ($N = 332$) and 32.3 years for females ($N = 467$).

Scoring, Scale Norms and Distribution

No summary scores are developed. Item responses are variable, but most are coded in Likert-type categories. Items measuring frequency of kin activity were coded 1 for more than once a month, 2 for several times a year, 3 for once or twice, and 4 for never. Distributions are presented in Adams, 1968.

Formal Tests of Validity

Face validity is suggested since Adams developed each set of items in the battery after reviewing an extensive literature on types of kin contact.

Usability on Older Populations

This set of items was developed to measure the contact of young adults with their older kin. With some changes, however, the items would be useful on an older population.

General Comments and Recommendations

This useful, short, but comprehensive battery of items measures the four construct areas (structure, interaction, affect, and norms) that are important in kinship research. However, some care should be taken before assuming its reliability in future uses.

Reference

Adams, B. N. *Kinship in an Urban Setting.* Chicago: Markham, 1968.

Instrument

See Instrument V2.4.I.a.

POSITIVE AFFECT INDEX:
SUBJECTIVE SOLIDARITY BETWEEN PARENTS AND CHILDREN

V. L. Bengtson, 1973

Definition of Variable or Concept

The instrument assesses sentiment, or positive affect, among family members as it is perceived and reported by family members. Five dimensions of positive affect are included: the degree of (1) understanding, (2) fairness, (3) trust, (4) respect, and (5) affection. Additional questions reflect communication among family members and the general closeness of the relationship.

Description of Instrument

A scale of five items is repeated twice, with the target or referent changed from "other's feelings" to "your feelings." For example, in the first set, the respondent is asked, "How well do you feel your child understands you?"; on the next page, he or she is asked, "How well do you feel you understand this child?" Responses range from 1 ("not well") to 6 ("extremely well"). In addition, single-item indicators are used to assess global closeness, similarity, getting together, and communication.

Method of Administration

This self-administered, mail questionnaire could also be used in an interview format.

Context of Development and Subsequent Use

The index was developed as part of a large-scale study of three generations at the University of Southern California's Andrus Gerontology Center. Constructs were derived from Durkheim's assessment of solidarity and from an exchange-theory perspective on interaction.

Sample(s)

A sample of 2,044 members of three-generation families was drawn from a list of 840,000 members of a prepaid health plan. The response rate was 64%. The sample was of blue-collar (union) origin, but it evidenced considerable mobility in the second and third generations (Bengtson and Lovejoy, 1973). Grandparents ranged in age from 51 to 93 (mean age 67.0) and parents from 33 to 67 (mean age 43.8).

Scoring

Scores on the 10 items are summed to provide an index of positive affect, which ranges from 10 to 60. The simple, equally weighted sum was used in preference to factor weighting because of the similarity in loadings of items on the factor for positive affect; "thus it seemed that little information would be lost, and the benefit of simplicity gained, by using an equal-weighted sum" (Bengtson and Black, 1973, p. 17). Alternatively, however, factor weighting can be employed for greater reliability.

Formal Tests of Reliability/Homogeneity

Test-retest reliability was examined on a group of summer students ($N = 68$; age range 21-58 years) who filled out the form twice during an interval of 4 weeks. The correlation (rho) over the two time periods was .89.

Homogeneity/dimensionality was assessed on a sample of 100 parent-child dyads from the two oldest generations (100 G1, mean age 67; and 100 G2, mean age 43). Moderate-to-high homogeneity is indicated by interitem correlations that ranged from .73 to .41, with a Cronbach's alpha of .92. Factor analyses indicated the Positive Affect Index items to have relatively uniform loadings (.60 to .80) on the same factor (Bengtson and Black, 1973).

Formal Tests of Validity

Construct and discriminant validity were examined by combining the Positive Affect Index items with other items measuring interaction frequency (see the next abstract) and attitude similarity and by factoring this larger pool of items in a pooled G1-G2 sample. All the Positive Affect Index items loaded highly on the same factor, with relatively uniform loadings (see Table 4-3).

Further construct validity was examined by separating the generations in a factor analysis of G1 and G2 respondents' scores on Positive Affect Index items. This was done to test the assumption that, since each person's responses (e.g., a parent's) represent his or her subjective analysis of the relationship, these would be independent of the corresponding responses of the other dyad member (e.g., a middle-aged child's). If so, the factor analysis would yield one distinct factor for each dyad member. Results support this expectation (see Table 4-3).

Usability on Older Populations

The items were designed to measure parent-child subjective affect, regardless of age, and were employed on a three-generation sample.

Sensitivity to Age Differences

Increased internal consistency of items with age has been reported (Black and Bengtson, 1973).

General Comments and Recommendations

The emphasis on the conceptual definition of subjective affectual solidarity is important. Because the social desirability of responses is a potential problem in asking for assessments of intrafamily affect, the use of 10 items (rather than 1 global item) seems to be very important in order to enhance validity and distribution of scores. Skewed distributions remain a problem, with most respondents giving a highly favorable evaluation for each item. Concurrent validity data are needed, probably data utilizing observers' ratings.

References

Bengtson, V.L. "Progress Report on the Study of Generations and Mental Health." Unpublished report submitted to NIMH, 1973.

Bengtson, V. L., and K. D. Black. "Solidarity between Parents and Children: Four Perspectives on Theory Development." Paper presented to the Theory Development Workshop, National Council on Family Relations, Toronto, Ocrober 16, 1973.

Bengtson, V. L. and M.C. Lovejoy. "Values, Personality, and Social Structure: An Intergenerational Analysis." *American Behavioral Scientist*, 1973, 16: 880-912.

TABLE 4-3

Factor Loadings of Positive Affect and Associational Interaction Dimensions
and Factor Loadings of Positive Affect by Generation

Column 1	Column 2[a]	Column 3[b]	Column 4[b]
Item	Factor Loading Full Set	Factor Loading G1	Factor Loading G2
Factor I: Positive Affect:			
Respected by partner (i.e., by child)	.80	.81	.78
Respect partner	.79	.77	.75
Treated fairly by partner	.78	.82	.74
Trust partner	.74	.76	.72
Understand partner	.73	.74	.71
Liked by partner	.72	.84	.78
Like partner	.70	.80	.78
Trusted by partner	.70	.74	.71
Understood by partner	.67	.74	.71
Similar to partner	.62[c]	.60	.60
Treat partner fairly	.60	.71	.56
Factor II: Informal Interaction:			
His/her helping you out with chores or errands	.87	—	—
Your helping him/her out with chores or errands	.85	—	—
Brief visits for conversation	.80	—	—
Dinner together	.79	—	—
Talking over things that are important to you	.67	—	—
Recreation outside the home	.55	—	—
Small family gatherings for birthdays or anniversaries	.50[d]	—	—
Factor III: Ceremonial Interaction:			
Small family gatherings for birthdays or anniversaries	.66	—	—
Large family gatherings like reunions or holiday dinners	.59	—	—

a. Analysis of the pooled G1-G2 sample included items from the Positive Affect Index and the associational interaction dimensions (see the next abstract).

b. Analysis of the Positive Affect Index items alone in the pooled G1-G2 sample.

c. This item, reflecting a global assessment of perceived similarity to the other dyad member, was included in the analysis but is not part of the 10-item Positive Affect Index.

d. This item was loaded on both factors II and III, but, because of its higher loading on factor III, it is included in the ceremonial interaction dimension.

SOURCE: V. L. Bengtson and K. D. Black. "Solidarity between Parents and Children: Four Perspectives on Theory Development." Paper presented to the Theory Development Workshop, National Council on Family Relations, Toronto, October 16, 1973.

Bengtson, V. L., E. Olander, and A. Haddad. "The 'Generation Gap' and Aging Family Members." In *Time, Roles, and Self in Old Age*, J. Gubrium (ed.), pp. 297-305. New York: Behavioral Publications, 1976.

Black, K. D., and V. L. Bengtson. "The Measurement of Family Solidarity: An Inter-generational Analysis." Paper presented to the American Psychological Association, August 27, 1973.

Instrument

See Instrument V2.4.I.b.

INTERACTION INDEX:
ASSOCIATIONAL SOLIDARITY BETWEEN PARENTS AND CHILDREN

V. L. Bengtson, 1973

Definition of Variable or Concept

The instrument measures the type and frequency of activities that constitute intergenerational interaction. Two dimensions are reflected by the index: informal interaction and ceremonial functions.

Description of Instrument

This checklist of 12 items reflects: (1) interaction together outside the home; (2) visits and conversations; (3) family gatherings, large and small; (4) writing and telephoning; and (5) exchange of gifts and assistance. The respondent (e.g., the aged parent) is asked to check the frequency of activity with the other generation (e.g., the middle-aged child) on an eight-point scale ranging from "almost never" to "almost every day."

Method of Administration

This self-administered, mail questionnaire could also be used in an interview format. See the abstract on the Positive Affect Index for a description of the research context and sample.

Scoring

Several alternatives are presented. First, single items can be examined, with highly correlated sets of items combined. In cases where geographic distance from the parents is great, for example, some items carry more weight than others (writing, telephoning). Second, scores can be summed over the 12 items since the distance factor "averages out" because of the way the items were arranged. Third, factor scores can be used for applying weights reflecting informal and ceremonial functions (see Table 4-3).

Formal Tests of Reliability/Homogeneity

Test-retest reliability was examined on a group of summer students (N = 68; age range 21-58 years) who filled out the form twice over an interval of 4 weeks. Correlation over the two time periods, averaged over the 12 items, was .81.

Interitem correlations, when examined for the entire sample, are low to moderate, ranging from .71 (dinner together and visits for conversation) to .05 (visits for conversation and telephoning) when the item on letter writing is omitted. Correlations are reported to be higher when respondents who live more than 100 miles from each other are omitted from analysis.

Coefficient alpha for the six-item informal interaction dimension is equal of .89. The two items in the ceremonial interaction dimension correlate moderately (r = .58).

Formal Tests of Validity

Construct discriminant validity was examined by combining the items for this index with those of the Positive Affect Index. Two factors emerged, one reflecting ceremonial functions and the other, informal interaction (see Table 4-3). Bengtson and Black (1973) suggested that factor scores, rather than single-item indicators, should be used whenever possible in order to maximize measurement reliability.

Concurrent validity can be assessed by examining the responses of parents compared to the responses of children. The reports of the parent and the child are similar except for exchange of help, in which each generation overreports the assistance of the other.

Usability on Older Populations

The items were designed to measure parent-child interaction regardless of age and were employed on a three-generation sample.

General Comments and Recommendations

The two dimensions that emerged (informal versus ritualistic interactions) are probably important conceptual distinctions. The checklist format appears easy for respondents to answer and provides enhanced reliability. However, the universe of possible interaction activities may be inadequately sampled, and the meaning or importance of individual activities probably varies from family to family.

The problem of geographic proximity should be noted in any analysis of interaction items; samples should be grouped on the basis of proximity and norms established for those families who live together, within 15 minutes, within 60 minutes, within 300 miles, and farther.

Reports by one generation may differ from reports by the other, but the variation shows no consistent pattern except with respect to items on exchange of assistance, in which each generation overestimates receiving support and underestimates "helping out with chores or errands."

References

Bengtson, V. L. "Progress Report on the Study of Generations and Mental Health." Report submitted to NIMH, 1973.

Bengtson, V. L., and K. D. Black. "Solidarity between Parents and Children: Four Perspectives on Theory Development." Paper presented to the Theory Development Workshop, National Council on Family Relations, Toronto, October 16, 1973.

Bengtson, V. L., and M. C. Lovejoy. "Values, Personality, and Social Structure: An Intergenerational Analysis." *American Behavioral Scientist*, 1973, 16: 880-912.

Bengtson, V. L., E. Olander, and A. Haddad. "The 'Generation Gap' and Aging Family Members." In *Time, Roles and Self in Old Age*, J. Gubrium (ed.), pp. 237-63. New York: Behavioral Publications, 1976.

Instrument

See Instrument V2.4.I.c.

CROSS-ETHNIC BATTERY OF FAMILISM

V. L. Bengtson and R. Manuel, 1976

Definition of Variable or Concept

The instrument assesses family structure, interaction, satisfactions, and norms in a cross-ethnic comparative survey design.

Description of Instrument

Fifteen items are part of a structured interview lasting 60 minutes. Questions reflect four dimensions of parent-child relations: (1) family structure, (2) frequency of family interaction, (3) satisfaction with contact with children, and (4) expectations and opinions of intergenerational interaction. Special attention is paid to the problem of reliability across ethnic groups.

Method of Administration

Interveiws were conducted in English or Spanish, and the interviewers were matched to the respondents as much as possible by ethnicity and age.

Context of Development and Subsequent Use

Items from previous surveys were used to develop an item pool. In the process of developing the questionnaire with minority-group representatives, some items were deleted and others were modified slightly. The interviews were carried out in 1974 and 1975.

Sample

The 1,269 individuals were sampled from three age cohorts (45-54, 55-64, 65-74) and two occupational levels within three ethnic groups (black, Chicano, and Anglo). Because of the need to oversample in order to obtain sufficient numbers in some of the cells, a weighting procedure was employed to maintain the representativeness of the sample with respect to the population.

Scoring, Scale Norms, and Distribution

The items are used as single-item indicators; most are scored on a three-point alternative.

Formal Tests of Validity

Face validity across ethnic groups was informally assessed through consultation with a community research planning committee made up of representatives from the minority communities. The committee determined the final wording of the instruments so as to achieve broad comparability and to maintain (whenever possible) the ability to replicate items for comparison with other surveys. The interview was translated back into Spanish twice. Special attention was paid to the interviewers' comments regarding the meaning of the items for the respondents.

Usability on Older Populations

The battery was designed specifically for an older age-group in three racial-ethnic categories.

General Comments and Recommendations

The instrument is a sampling of constructs reflecting several dimensions of parent-child interaction amenable to survey techniques. The attempt to ensure cross-stratum equivalence is commendable, though not entirely convincing. The items are similar to those used in other studies; this allows for baseline comparisons and replications. Scaling procedures should be carried out to examine dimensionality.

References

Bengtson, V. L., and R. Manuel. "Ethnicity and Family Patterns in Later Life: Effects of Race, Age, S.E.S. and gender." Unpublished paper: Andrus Gerontology Center, 1976.

Manuel, R. "Familial Social Patterns: Ethnic and Cohort Differences in Middle and Old Age." Paper presented to the 30th Annual Meeting of the Gerontological Society, San Francisco, November 18-22, 1977.

Instrument

See Instrument V2.4.I.d.

FAMILY MUTUAL AID AND INTERACTION INDEX

M. H. Cantor, 1976a; 1976b; M. Mayer, 1976

Definition of Variable or Concept

The index assesses family structure and exchange or assistance and mutual-aid activities between parents and children in an urban setting.

Description of Instrument

The instrument lists 10 types of assistance from parent to child and 11 types from child to parent. Four broad categories of help are included: (1) crisis intervention, (2) assistance with daily chores, (3) advice giving, and (4) gift giving.

Method of Administration

The index is administered as a questionnaire. No time specifications were given.

Context of Development and Subsequent Use

This instrument was developed as part of a larger study undertaken by the New York City Department for the Aging. The study was designed to assess the characteristic life-style, service needs, and primary group relationships of older people living in inner-city New York. Of particular interest were: (1) the extent of the informal support system; (2) the differential roles assumed by kin, friends, and neighbors; (3) the congruence between attitudinal and behavioral indicators of the role of family and primary others; and (4) the division of support between the informal and the formal systems for white, black, and Hispanic ethnic groups.

The extent and specific nature of the interactions between the elderly and their children are examined, as is the degree of mutual assistance that occurs.

Sample

The study sample consisted of 1,552 elderly respondents aged 60 and over and living in New York City; 41% were male, 59% female; 49.4% were white, 37.4% black, and 13.2% Hispanic. Of the total sample, 1,020 respondents (65.7%) had one or more living children. The data on parent-child assistance patterns are based on the replies of these 1,020 respondents.

Scoring, Scale Norms, and Distribution

Two types of scoring are available: a help-no help dichotomy, with help scored 1 and no help, 0; and frequency of assistance, with a range from 0 to 3 (0 for never, 3 for very often). Four separate indexes of mutual aid are scored through simple summation: (1) parent-to-child dichotomy ($\bar{X}$ = 2.54), (2) parent-to-child frequency ($\bar{X}$ = 4.23), (3) child-to-parent- dichotomy ($\bar{X}$ = 3.85), and (4) child-to-parent frequency ($\bar{X}$ = 6.90).

Formal Tests of Reliability/Homogeneity

Coefficient alpha for the parent-to-child dichotomy was .759; for the parent-to-child frequency alpha equaled .784. For the child-to-parent dichotomy reliability was .811, and the internal consistency of the frequency score was .861.

Reliability was computed separately for each ethnic group. Greatest reliability was noted for the Hispanic sample (.812 to .892), followed by blacks (.773 to .864), and then whites (.720 to .833).

Usability on Older Populations

The items were designed for use with an elderly population.

Sensitivity to Age Differences

Most of the items were incorporated into the exchange of support and assistance index of the Harris survey (NCOA, 1975) and were used with a younger population.

General Comments and Recommendations

The emphasis on the mutual-aid patterns between parent and child and the assessment of each independently are important. The comparisons of assistance from kin and neighbors as they vary between ethnic groups is an area being newly documented. An assessment of the validity of the items is needed.

References

Cantor, M. H. "Life Space and the Social Support System of the Inner City Elderly of New York." *The Gerontologist*, 1975, 15: 23-27.

_____ . "The Configuration and Intensity of the Informal Support System in a New York City Elderly Population." Paper presented to the 29th Annual Meeting of the Gerontological Society, New York, October 13-17, 1976a. (Reprint available from the New York City Department for the Aging and the Center on Gerontology, Fordham University.)

_____ . "Effect of Ethnicity on Life Styles of the Inner-City Elderly." In *Community Planning for an Aging Society*, M. P. Lawton, R. J. Newcomer, and T. O. Byerts (eds.), pp. 41-55. Stroudsbourg, Pa.: Dowden, Hutchinson and Ross, 1976b.

Mayer, M. "Kin and Neighbors: Differential Roles in Differing Cultures." Paper presented to the 29th Annual Meeting of the Gerontological Society, New York, October 13-17, 1976.

National Council on the Aging. *The Myth and Reality of Aging in America.* Washington, D. C.: National Council on the Aging, 1975.

Instrument

See Instrument V2.4.I.e.

FAMILISM INDEX

M. H. Cantor, 1976; L. Wilker, 1976

Definition of Variable or Concept

The index assesses familistic attitudes and norms.

Description of Instrument

The familism scale consists of a set of eight items adpated from those of Leichter and Mitchell (1967). The factor scores reflect three dimensions: (1) a propinquity or proximity factor, i.e., the desirability for young married children and their parents to live close by; (2) a filial obligation factor, i.e., the belief that adult children should help their aged parents; and (3) a kin-oriented factor, i.e., the preferred turning to kin, rather than to friends or neighbors, for satisfaction of material and emotional needs.

Method of Administration

The respondents are handed a card that reads: "Here are some statements that people make about relatives and friends. As I read each statement, I'd like you to tell me if you *agree* or *disagree* with it."

For information on the research context and sample for this study, see the abstract on the Family Mutual Aid and Interaction Index.

Scoring, Scale Norms and Distribution

The items (scored 1 for agree; 2 for unsure; 3 for disagree) were factor analyzed, and indexes of each factor were created by summing those items on each factor that had a loading of .40 or greater. The proximity index consisted of the sum of items a and c; the filial obligation index, of items e and h; and the kin orientation index, of items f and g. Items b and d are not included in any of the subtest scores but are included in the total familism score.

The Hispanic respondents had the highest average score on this scale (11.1); the blacks, the lowest (9.3); and the whites were moderate (9.8).

Formal Tests of Reliability/Homogeneity

Coefficient alpha for the total sample was .68, which varied from a low of .53 for the Spanish-speaking respondents to a high of .72 for the black and .68 for the white elderly respondents. Factor loadings and communalities are included with the instrument.

Usability on Older Populations

The items appear to be usable on samples of older populations.

General Comments and Recommendations

This scale is one of a few that consider normative aspects of intergenerational relationships. It is also one of the more extensively examined in terms of factor analysis. The approach taken holds promise for further development. The relatively high response-error variance for Spanish-speaking elderly respondents should be noted. Further work on reliability—especially between ethnic groups—is recommended.

References

Cantor, M. H. "The Configuration and Intensity of the Informal Support System in a New York City Elderly Population." Paper presented to the 29th Annual Meeting of the Gerontological Society, New York, October 13-17, 1976. (Reprint available from the New York City Department for the Aging and the Center on Gerontology, Fordham University.)

Leichter, H., and W. Mitchell. *Kinship and Casework.* New York: Russell Sage Foundation, 1967.

Wilker, L. "Ethnicity and Familism: The congruency between Attitudes and Behavior." Paper presented to the 29th Annual Meeting of the Gerontological Society, New York, October 13-17, 1976.

Instrument

See Instrument V2.4.I.f.

CHILDREN'S ATTITUDES TOWARD SUPPORTING AGED PARENTS

R. M. Dinkel, 1944

Definition of Variable or Concept

The attitudes of children toward taking care of aged parents, particularly concerning home support, are studied.

Description of Instrument

The scale includes 20 agree-disagree items. Both overall sum-of-checked-item weights and individual item responses are used in the analysis.

NOTE: This abstract was prepared by Donald McTavish.

The scale was developed from an initial pool of 160 items that were rated on a five-point, agree-disagree scale by 14 social workers. The items (N = 66) receiving similar placement by 10 judges were retained, and these were assigned weights (−2 to +2) based on the raters' judgments. Two instruments with 20 items each were created from these 66 items, and they were tested on 440 college students, using a Likert response format. One form was administered again in an agree-disagree format; the correlation between the response formats was .86. Of the 40 items, 30 had satisfactory discriminability; from these 30 a balanced scale of 20 items was created.

Method of Administration

Administration has been to classes in a group, with a paper-and-pencil format. Verbal instructions make the following three points. (1) Assume that children, while able to give support, would suffer a moderate degree of financial sacrifice by doing so. (2) Assume that, if help were not extended, the parents would probably be able to get old-age assistance that would provide enough to live on but not the comforts to which they were accustomed. (3) Assume parents to be in reasonably good mental and physical health, being neither senile nor bedridden.

Context of Development and Subsequent Use

The scale was developed in connection with the Work Progress Administration. The investigator was concerned about children's willingness to support older parents. The assumption underlying the scale is that the satisfactory support of older parents depends partly on the younger generation's attitudes toward responsibility for the care of the elderly. Hypotheses about the differences that should be observed by religion, sex, residence, and education as well as potential physical and psychological hardships were advanced by the investigator (Dinkel, 1944).

Sample(s)

Other than the scale-development samples noted below, Dinkel's 1943 sample included 1006 college students (1939-1940) aged up to 45 years (summer-session students) from colleges and universities in and around Minneapolis (plus a summer session at the University of Wisconsin). These students apparently were members of entire classes. An additional 318 high school students (1939-1940) from rural and urban Minnesota were also sampled. Again, entire classes and YMCA farm camps seem to have been used.

Scoring, Scale Norms, and Distribution

The scores used are the sum weights (−2 to +2) that reflect the strength of favorableness or negativeness of an item in the opinion of the 14 social workers taking part in an early judgment task. The theoretical range of sum scores is 31 points (−15 to +16). Mean range of sum scores is 31 points (−15 to +16). Mean scores are given for the scale by sex, religion, rural/urban residence, and educational level; but, because of the nonrepresentative nature of the samples, these means are not reported here.

Formal Tests of Reliability/Homogeneity

The 20-item instrument was administered twice (with a three-week interval) to 90 sociology students at the University of Minnesota. Test-retest Pearson's correlation was .87.

Formal Tests of Validity

Eighty-six sociology students at the University of Minnesota were asked to take the test and to write essays on the topic of supporting aged parents. The essays were classified into five degree-of-belief groups. An F test comparing the scores and the classifications was significant at .001.

Case histories of 50 families (taken from college-student children who apparently had been given the instrument) were studied. Dinkel concluded that there was some relationship between parent/child opinion and conflicts (Dinkel, 1943), but in practice did not appear to be highly correlated.

Usability on Older Populations

Only use on student groups is reported (summer-session students were as old as 45 years). No special limitations are noted.

Sensitivity to Age (Including Social Age) Differences

Age-level differences within the high school to 45-year-old summer-session students were examined, but no systematic differences were found. Note that age and education may be confounded.

General Comments and Recommendations

The scale is among those that have been more extensively examined methodologically; however, these tests may be somewhat dated and/or period specific. The items appear to be of general use and tap an area not generally included in attitude scales (i.e., they are focused on a family context and on support issues). The scale is limited to general housing or living-in kinds of support and may not take account of different options for older parents or conditions under which different kinds of support might be forthcoming and effective. Note that social interaction support is not specifically differentiated in the scale.

References

Dinkel, R. M. "Parent-Child Conflict in Minnesota Families." *American Sociological Review*, 1943, 8: 412-19.
_____ ."Attitudes of Children toward Supporting Aged Parents." *American Sociological Review*, 1944, 9: 370-79.
Wake, S. B., and M. J. Sporakowski. "An Integenerational Comparison of Attitudes towards Supporting Aged Parents." *Journal of Marriage and the Family*, 1972, 34: 42-48.

Instrument

See Instrument V2.4.I.g.

EXCHANGES BETWEEN GENERATIONS INDEX

R. Hill, N. Foote, J. Aldous, R. Carlson, and R. MacDonald, 1970

Definition of Concept

The index measures associational interdependence among the generations (the extent of participation in common activities) and mutual exchanges. Exchanges questions pertain to help given or received involving money, goods, services, and knowledge.

Description of Instrument

Semi-structured interviews with wives that gave a retrospective record of the preceding 12 months were conducted. The respondents were interviewed in their homes in four waves (once every 3 months) over a 12-month period. The items are part of a much larger instrument on intergenerational contacts and exchanges.

Method of Administration

The 2-hour home interview was the fourth in a panel study of the families.

Context of Development and Subsequent Use

The instrument was developed to explore interfamily transactions among three interlinked generations and the extent of interdependence that bound them together (boundary maintenance versus boundary crossing).

Sample(s)

The sample consisted of 312 nuclear families of three generations living in the metropolitan area of Minneapolis-St. Paul. There were 100 grandparent families aged 71 to 80, 105 parent families with an age range of 46 to 55, and 107 young married children families aged 21 to 30, all of the same lineages. The socioeconomic status of families compared closely to the distribution of occupations and income within the SMSA of Minneapolis-St. Paul.

Scoring, Scale Norms, and Distribution

Frequency counts and frequency distributions (percentages) are used to assess contact between generations and the occasions and circumstances of intergenerational exchanges.

Formal Tests of Validity

Many of the self-reported items were collected by tests and scales already used in other studies. No formal tests have been reported. There appears to be a high degree of face validity.

Usability on Older Populations

No special limitations were noted for the three-generation sample.

Sensitivity to Age (Including Social Age) Differences

This set of items is not specifically sensitive to older populations per se, but it is applicable to them.

General Comments and Recommendations

This index is the most extensive assessment of intergenerational transactions in the field, but it is limited primarily to the exchange of services. Further examination of the reliability and validity of the items appears to be needed, although the response categories and questions appear to have a high degree of face validity. This approach to assessing exchanges among generations may hold promise for future development.

Reference

Hill, R., N. Foote, J. Aldous, R. Carlson, and R. MacDonald. *Family Development in Three Generations*. Cambridge, Mass.: Schenkman, 1970.

Instrument

See Instrument V2.4.I.h.

FAMILY STRUCTURE AND CONTACT BATTERY

H. Z. Lopata, 1973

Definition of Variable or Concept

This instrument measures the role involvements of widows, including their relations with their children.

Description of Instrument

The interview schedule includes items that can be analyzed singly and in cross-tabulations and that are combined into several scales. These scales are: (1) the role scale, in which all references to each of the major roles such as the role of the mother are combined and ranked in relation to the other roles; (2) the social isolation scale, which measures the extent to which a widow lacks the kinds of personal and community contacts normally available to widowed women; (3) the frequency of contact scale, which combines, for example, the number of phone calls and the number of letters received; and (4) the relations-restrictive attitude scale, which consists of 36 items that measure the degree of agreement of each widow with statements referring to various types of social relations. The relations-restrictive scale is included in Chapter 3 of this volume.

Method of Administration

The items are part of a much longer questionnaire and a more extensive data-gathering procedure that includes interviews, group discussions, and collections of diaries.

Sample(s)

Sixty neighborhoods in the Chicago metropolitan area were used in a modified area probability sample selected by the National Opinion Research Center. All of the 301 individuals were female and widowed; 87.1% of the sample was aged 55 and above.

Scoring, Scale Norms, and Distribution

The role scale included a role of mother that combined the number of living children, the distance from the mother, and the frequency with which a child, rather than a sibling or a friend, was named as a person providing help or companionship. The scores were often collapsed into high, medium, and low levels.

The social isolation scale combined selected answers to a set of 45 questions. The highest score on this scale could be 80 points, indicating a high degree of isolation. The scores were collapsed into high, medium, and low levels.

Formal Tests of Validity

No tests have been reported, although there appears to be a high degree of construct validity.

Usability on Older Populations

No special difficulties in using the scale with an older population have been reported.

General Comments and Recommendations

Although not specific to parents and their middle-aged children, this instrument provides a wealth of data. Further examination of the reliability and validity of the items is needed, as is an examination of the applicability of the items to the general population.

Reference

Lopata, H. Z. *Widowhood in an American City*. Cambridge, Mass.: Schenkman, 1973.

Instrument

See Instrument V2.4.I.i.

SOCIAL AND FAMILY CONTACT SCALE

National Council on the Aging, 1975; 1976

Definition of Variable or Concept

This scale assesses contact with family and friends as it varies by a person's age. Also included are measures of family structure, frequency of interaction, and mutual aid and assistance.

Description of Instrument

The structured survey included two questionnaires: one for respondents 18 to 64 years old and other for those 65 and older. The scale itself consists of two questions and is used to compare differences in contact with family and friends for those over 65 and those under 65.

Method of Administration

Personal interviews were conducted in the home; the timing for this scale was not reported since it is part of a longer schedule of items. There are no special administration requirements.

Context of Development and Subsequent Use

In 1974, the National Council on the Aging commissioned Louis Harris and Associates to conduct an extensive nationwide survey examining and documenting the public's attitudes toward aging and its perceptions of "what it's like to be old in America today" (NCOA, 1975, p. 1). The scale was developed to assess the degree of Americans' contact with friends and family members in an attempt to get an objective standard of loneliness.

Sample(s)

A total of 4,254 in-person, household interviews were conducted during the late spring and early summer of 1974 by trained Harris interviewers. The probability sample (a multistage, random cluster sample of the noninstitutionalized public aged 18 and over) had four parts: (1) 1,500 adults over 18, national cross-section sample; (2) 2,400 persons over 65, oversample; (3) 360 persons 55 to 64, oversample; and (4) 200 persons, black, over 65, oversample. The analyzed sample was weighted to reflect known (from the 1970 census) distributions and oversampling procedures.

Scoring, Scale Norms, and Distribution

The family contact index is a five-item scale with the following scoring procedure: 6 points were given for each friend or relative seen within the last day or so (including those living with respondent); 5 points were given for each friend or relative seen within the last week or two; 4 points were given for each friend or relative seen about a month ago; 3 points were given for each friend or relative seen two to three months ago; 2 points were given for each friend or relative seen longer ago than that; and 1 point was given each time the respondent had no friend or relative.

The scale ranged from 0 to 30. The general public received a median score of 13.3. The scores of the young and old were nearly identical. Distributions for the items by age were reported (NCOA, 1975, p. 166).

Usability on Older Populations

No difficulties have been reported for any of the noninstitutionalized respondents aged 18 to 80.

Sensitivity to Age (Including Social Age) Differences

The questions were not specifically designed to pick up age differences, although the differences in responses were reported for those under 65 years of age and those over 65. Age-related bias in understanding or responding to given items was not reported.

General Comments and Recommendations

The value of the Social and Family Contact scale is limited in that it does not account for the length of contact with the family members nor the quality of the contact. The scale was not specifically designed for an assessment of intergenerational relationships. The main advantage of this scale is the availability of the national cross-sectional data for 1974, with which specific samples can be compared.

References

National Council on the Aging. *The Myth and Reality of Aging in America.* Washington, D. C.: National Council on the Aging, 1975.

_____.*Codebook for "The Myth and Reality of Aging,"* a survey conducted by Louis Harris and Associates for the National Council on the Aging; prepared by the Duke University Center for the Study of Aging and Human Development, 1976.

Instrument

See Instrument V2.4.I.j.

EXCHANGES OF SUPPORT AND ASSISTANCE INDEX

National Council on the Aging, 1975; 1976

Definition of Variable or Concept

The exchanges of support and assistance among generations are measured by this instrument.

Description of Instrument

This battery of items is asked in the context of a household interview schedule. Timing for these items was not reported since it was a part of a longer schedule of items. (See the abstract for the Social and Family Contact scale in this chapter for a description of the research context and the sampling procedures.)

Usability on Older Populations

No difficulties were reported for use of the index with any noninstitutionalized respondents aged 18 to 80.

Sensitivity to Age (Including Social Age) Differences

The questions were not specifically designed to pick up age differences, although differences in responses were reported for those under 65 years of age and those 65 and older. Age-related bias in understanding or responding to given items was not reported.

General Comments and Recommendations

This is a good checklist with which to assess exchanges of support and assistance among generations. The main advantage of these items is their availability in a national cross-sectional study. The disadvantage is a lock of conceptual specificity. More information is needed on reliability and validity. Some items seem to be more specific than others; some appear to be vulnerable to the effects of social desirability.

References

National Council on the Aging. *The Myth and Reality of Aging in America.* Washington, D. C.: National Council on the Aging, 1975.
_____ . *Codebook for "The Myth and Reality of Aging,"* a survey conducted by Louis Harris and Associates for the National Council on the Aging; prepared by the Duke University Center for the Study of Aging and Human Development, 1976.

Instrument

See Instrument V2.4.I.k.

EMOTIONAL DEPENDENCE ON CHILDREN SCALE

I. Rosow, 1967

Definition of Variable or Concept

The scale measures the respondent's emotional dependence on his or her adult children.

Description of Instrument

This is a four-item Guttman scale that orders people on a continuum of emotional dependence.

Method of Administration

The instrument is administered as part of an interview.

Context of Development and Subsequent Use

Emotional dependence is seen as a set of sentiments in which: (1) children are the principal source of satisfaction in life; (2) they are perceived as reciprocating parents' love by their strong devotion and sustained closeness; and (3) parents are unusually demanding of filial solicitude, demanding attention well beyond the normal limits of children's obligations. Rosow developed a series of multiple-choice questions whose alternatives were graded on dependence. Analysis yielded four responses that together constituted a Guttman scale of emotional dependence on children. In order to facilitate analysis, the five scale types can be reduced to three by combining the two high groups and the two low groups.

Sample(s)

The sample was a purposive sample of 760 parents aged 62 and over from the Cleveland area. Included were both males and females from the working and middle classes.

Scoring, Scale Norms, and Distribution

Scores varied from 1 (lowest) to 5 (highest dependence) for this Guttman scale. Reducing the five types to three by combining extreme groups resulted in the following distribution of dependence: high, 35%; moderate, 37%; and low, 28%.

Formal Tests of Reliability/Homogeneity

The coefficient of reproducibility was .96. The positive responses on the four items were, respectively, 89%, 66%, 39%, and 13%; the percentage item error was, respectively, 6%, 10%, 12%, and 8%.

Usability on Older Populations

No unsatisfactory subject population was mentioned by Rosow.

Sensitivity to Age (Including Social Age) Differences

Rosow hypothesized that the comparative importance of the family as a support group should grow with the correlates of age. He found that emotional dependence was not particularly related to age or sex and was a basic (and probably stable) psychological variable. Emotional dependence was not significantly increased by marital disruption or widowhood, by serious deterioration of health, by comprehensive role losses, by living arrangements, or even by extended illness and children's absence.

General Comments and Recommendations

This construct appears to be highly useful, and it is one of the few scales actually developed in the area of parent-child relations. Its approach to the analysis of parent-child relations warrants further use.

Reference

Rosow, I. *Social Integration of the Aged*. New York, Free Press, 1967.

Instrument

See Instrument V2.4.I.l.

FAMILY STRUCTURE AND CONTACT BATTERY

E. Shanas, P. Townsend, D. Wedderburn, H. Friis, P. Milhøj, and J. Stehouwer, 1968

Definition of Variable or Concept

This battery is an assessment of the family life of older people that focuses on structure, interaction, exchanges of assistance, and norms.

Description of Instrument

The items included are part of a much larger (90-item) instrument. The family-life items include family structure, the numbers of children of old people, the physical proximity of relatives of old people, and the frequency and kind of contact among family members. The instrument was used three times in United States national samples (1957, 1962, 1975) and once in a cross-national study (1962).

Method of Administration

The battery was administered as part of a structured interview, with no time specifications reported.

Context of Development and Subsequent Use

The study was designed to determine the physical functioning of old people, how they use community services, their relationships with family and friends, and their economic position.

Sample

The initial sample (1957) was an area probability sample of private households in the United Sates. The study was repeated in 1962 on national probability samples in Denmark, Britain, and the United States (2,500 households were sampled in each country). Respondents were 65 and over, and they varied according to their socioeconomic status, marital status, and health status.

Scoring, Scale Norms, and Distribution

Frequency distributions and percentages are reported in Shanas et al. (1968, Chapters 6 and 7).

Formal Tests of Validity

In order to ensure a high degree of comparability among the samples, all concepts and variables were defined in the same way. The questionnaires used were developed jointly by research teams from each of the three countries.

Usability on Older Populations

The instrument was designed specifically for persons aged 65 and over.

Sensitivity to Age (Including Social Age) Differences

Although the entire instrument was designed for persons aged 65 and over, the items referred to here would not be limited to use with that age-group.

General Comments and Recommendations

The comprehensive, succinct, and well-tested items could be usefully replicated. There is evidence for face validity in these items, although further work on reliability and validity is recommended. This study was one of the first attempts to assess intergenerational relations comparatively, across cultures and at different points in history.

Reliability for these single-item indicators may be problematic. Conceptual dimensions have been stated, however, thus facilitating future assessment of reliability and validity.

References

Shanas, E. *The Health of Older People: A Social Survey*. Cambridge, Mass: Harvard University Press, 1962.

——— . "The Family as a Social Support System in Old Age." Paper presented to the 30th Annual Meeting of the Gerontological Society, San Francisco, November 18-22, 1977.

——— . "National Survey of the Aged." An unpublished report to the Administration on Aging, 1978.

——— . "Social Myth as Hypothesis: The Case of the Family Relations of Old People." *The Gerontologist*, 1979, 19: 3-9.

Shanas, E., P. Townsend, D. Wedderburn, H. Friis, P. Milhøj, and J. Stehouwer. *Old People in Three Industrial Societies*. New York: Atherton Press, 1968.

Instrument

See Instrument V2.4.I.m.

FAMILY STRUCTURE AND INTERACTION BATTERY

G. F. Streib and C. J. Schneider, 1971

Definition of Variable or Concept

Studied are the family lives of retirees, specifically the way in which they and their adult children perceive certain phases of family life: (1) definitions of family, (2) family help patterns, (3) effects of retirement on family relations, and (4) family structure.

Description of Instrument

The items presented here are a part of a 20-page questionnaire composed principally of questions with short-answer categories and opportunities for free responses on some questions. Within the section on norms regarding parent-child relations (see the instrument), several agree-disagree items were repeated. These have been deleted from the abstract.

Method of Administration

In their responses to this self-administered questionnaire parents and children were asked not to collaborate.

Context of Development and Subsequent Use

The questionnaires were administered in 1952-1953, 1954, 1956, 1967, and 1968-1969 as a part of longitudinal research on effects of retirement (Cornell study). The main focus of the study was on what happens when an older person's major role is dropped, disrupted, or altered.

Sample

The sample included 3,793 respondents who were born in 1887, 1888, and 1889 in urban areas. The older respondents, males and females, were contacted initially when all were approximately 64 years old and still employed. Most were contacted at their places of employment. Subsequently, four follow-ups were made by means of a mail questionnaire. Loss of the respondent population averaged about 20% at the time a follow-up contact was made. After the last follow-up questionnaires had been sent to the 1969, older participants (when all were approximately 69 or 70 years old), their adult children were contacted by mail. The study population of retired parents *and* their adult children numbered 291. The children were about equally distributed by gender.

Scoring, Scale Norms, and Distribution

Percentage distributions have been reported. In analyzing the data from the questionnaires, the investigators did not match parents and children. Attention focused on overall comparisons in the way in which the two generations, grouped separately, viewed the role of the older person.

Usability on Older Populations

The researchers discussed problems with using this kind of self-administered questionnaire with persons with limited reading skills. Respondents for this study were more educated than the general population, but it is unlikely this factor would affect responses (Streib, 1965).

General Comments and Recommendations

One major advantage of this instrument is its use in a large-scale, longitudinal research endeavor. Another advantage is the focus on feeling, sentiment and behavior between generations. This is an impressive and useful battery.

Longitudinal research in this area has been rare; the problem of item validity is more complicated in a longitudinal study. As change is reported in different waves of measurement, the investigator is faced with the dilemma of trying to decide whether a genuine change has taken place or whether there has been instability in the measuring instrument. The panel of respondents from whom these data were gathered probably did not constitute a representative cross section of America's population of like age. A more representative sample and reliability and validity assessments are needed.

References

Streib, G. F. "Intergenerational Relations: Perspectives of the Two Generations on the Older Parent." *Journal of Marriage and the Family*, 1965, 35: 469-76.

Streib, G. F., and C. J. Schneider. *Retirement in American Society*. Ithaca, N.Y.: Cornell University Press, 1971.

Streib, G. F., and W. E. Thompson. "The Older Person in a Family Context." In *Handbook of Social Gerontology*, C. Tibbitts (ed.), pp. 447-87. Chicago: University of Chicago Press, 1960.

Instrument

See Instrument V2.4.I.n.

MARRIED OFFSPRING-PARENT ADJUSTMENT CHECKLIST

S. Stryker, 1955a; 1955b

Definition of Variable or Concept

Four dimensions of married child-parent relations are measured: (1) affection, (2) intimacy, (3) tension, and (4) sympathy (defined in terms of ego-involvement).

Description of Instrument

There are a total of 40 true-false items in the checklist, with 10 items used as indicators for each dimension. The subjects respond to the checklist as it applies to each parent and parent-in-law (i.e., four times). The score is the number of positive adjustment items minus the negative. Along with these 40 items, a 10-item dependence index was randomly interspersed. (See the abstract for the Dependence Checklist.)

Method of Administration

The instrument is a self-administered questionnaire.

Context of Development and Subsequent Use

It was developed to test propositions in symbolic interaction theory concerning social distance.

Sample

The sample consisted of 51 married males and 53 married females living in university housing at Indiana University. The males ranged in age from 21 to 42 (mean 28.3); the females ranged in age from 20 to 39 (mean 25.1). The respondents had been married for from 1 to 12 years (males: mean 3.9; females: mean 4.2). The sample included 40 married couples.

Scoring, Scale Norms and Distribution

The means and standard deviations by sex of child and parent and by affinial versus consanguinial parents are reported in Stryker's article (1955a, p. 150).

Formal Tests of Reliability/Homogeneity

Split-half reliability with Spearman-Brown correction varies from .88 to .92, depending on the individual rated.

Formal Tests of Validity

Content: The items were selected from pool of 150 on the basis of high agreement among 10 judges (graduate students in sociology) on the variable measured.

Construct: Differences in adjustment vary according to the gender of child and the type of parental relationship as predicted from a functional analysis of sex roles (Komarovsky, 1950).

Convergent: Chi-square tests between dichotomized index scores and a single-item indicator of the quality of the parent-child relationship are significant for both males and females (Stryker, 1955b, p. 65).

Usability on Older Populations

Though they were developed for a young, married adult population with children, the questions appear to be quite appropriate for use with a sample of elderly parents.

General Comments and Recommendations

This useful index should be used in future research in gerontology. The four dimensions are conceptually important, and the measurement properties are attractive. It seems to be easy to administer.

References

Komarovsky, M. "Functional Analysis of Sex Roles." *American Sociological Review*, 1950, 15: 508-16.

Stryker, S. "The Adjustment of Married Offspring to Their Parents." *American Sociological Review*, 1955a, 20: 149-54.

————. "Attitude Ascription in Adult Married Offspring-Parent Relationships: A Study of Implications of the Social Psychological Theory of G. H. Mead." Ph.D. dissertation, University of Minnesota, 1955b.

Instrument

See Instrument V2.4.I.o.

DEPENDENCE CHECKLIST

S. Stryker, 1955

Definition of Variable or Concept

The degree of the superordinate versus subordinate relationship between parents and married children is measured by this instrument.

Description of Instrument

This set of 10 true-false items is scored by subtracting the number of items indicating subordination from the number indicating superordination. Scores range from −10 to +10. These items are usually used with the Married Offspring-Parent Adjustment Checklist.

Method of Administration

The checklist is part of a self-administered interview schedule. The time required for completing it was not reported.

Context of Development and Subsequent Use

Following Mead's proposition that taking the role the other presumes a common universe of discourse or a system of shared meanings, Stryker hypothesized that shared meanings will increase with more extensive interaction, with decreased difference in status and with greater commonality of interest.

Sample

The sample population included 133 eligible family units who were nominated by ministers in Bloomington, Ind., as being couples with married children; other names were taken from the *New Citizens* column from local newspaper files. From the couples nominated, 46 completed schedules. The sample consisted of white parental couples and married-child couples. A maximum age of 70 was reported for parents.

Scoring, Scale Norms, and Distribution

Frequency distributions are reported in Stryker's aritcle (1956).

Formal Tests of Validity

There is some evidence of construct validity for this measure: (1) females indicate greater dependence on parents than males do and (2) parents are more superordinate to their own married children than to their married children's mates.

Usability on Older Populations

The items seem to be appropriate for use with older populations.

General Comments and Recommendations

This useful instrument should be employed in further research.

References

Stryker, S. "Attitude Ascription in Adult Married Offspring-Parent Relationships: A Study of Implications of the Social Psychological Theory of G. H. Mead." Ph.D. dissertation. University of Minnesota, 1955.

———. "Relationships of Married Offspring and Parent: A Test of Mead's Theory." *American Journal of Sociology*, 1956, 62: 308-19.

Instrument

See Instrument V2.4.I.p.

INTERGENERATIONAL FAMILY CONTINUITY RATING SCALE

M. B. Sussman, 1960

Definition of Variable or Concept

Parent-child affect, contact, exchanges of help, and closeness are measured in this family continuity scale.

Description of Instrument

This interview schedule involving both open-ended and structured questions included these items: (1) feelings about children's marriage, (2) feelings about children-in-law, (3) closeness of family at present time, (4) children come for advice and take advice at present time, (5) family celebrations at present time (6) visits between parents and children at present time, (7) communication between parents and children at present time, and (8) help given to children at present time.

Method of Administration

The data were collected by means of a personal interview lasting 1 to 4 hours.

Sample

Two separate 2% random samples were drawn from a list of 12,000 marriages recorded in Cuyahoga County, Ohio, during 1956. Parents were traced through these married couples and selected on the basis of these criteria: (1) the marriage was of the last child living at home, (2) the couple was white, and (3) both parents were aged 45 to 60. There were 57 families, with a median age of 53.4 for the wives and 57.5 for the husbands.

Scoring, Scale Norms, and Distribution

Each part of the interview is rated on a three-point scale. The scores are assigned to one of four levels of family continuity: high, good, fair, or poor (a fifth possibility, "no family continuity," did not occur in the sample).

Formal Tests of Reliability/Homogeneity

Interrater agreement of .99 was noted (Sussman, 1960).

Usability on Older Populations

No problems were noted in using this technique.

Reference

Sussman, M. B. "Intergenerational Family Relationships and Social Role Changes in Middle Age." *Journal of Gerontology*, 1960, 15: 71-75.

Instrument

This instrument is not available at this time.

Instruments

V2.4.I.a

CONTACT BETWEEN GENERATIONS BATTERY

B. N. Adams, 1968

I. *Family Structure and Household Composition*

    A7.   How many children do you have?

        _____ 0. None.

        _____ (Simply write in number of children; if none, skip to q. A9.)

    A8.   Are any of your children three years of age or younger?

        _____ (Write in the number: 0, 1, 2, etc.)

    A9.   Does anyone live with you besides your wife (husband) and children?

        _____ 0. No one.

        _____ 1. Your parent(s).

        _____ 2. Your spouse's parent(s).

A34. Are your parents still living?
_____ 1. Yes, both are living.
_____ 2. Father only is living.
_____ 3. Mother only is living.
_____ 4. Neither parent is alive.
(If neither is living, skip to q. A38, and then to B11. If only one is living, ask questions pertaining to that one.)
A35. If both are living, are they living together?
_____ 1. Yes.
_____ 2. No. (If no, talk about the one with whom contact is most frequent.)
A36. Where are they (he, she) living?
_____ 1. In this city.
_____ 2. Within 50 miles.
_____ 3. 50-100 miles.
_____ 4. Elsewhere in North Carolina.
_____ 5. South Carolina or +100 miles in Virginia.
_____ 6. Another Southern state.
_____ 7. Northeastern U.S.

II. *Associational Solidarity*

A47. In the past two years or so, about how often have you seen your parents (or the one we are talking about)?
_____ 1. Every day.
_____ 2. More than once a week.
_____ 3. Once a week.
_____ 4. More than monthly.
_____ 5. About once a month.
_____ 6. Several times a year.
_____ 7. About once a year.
_____ 8. Less than once a year.
_____ 9. Never.
A48. If you have not seen them (him, her) at all, how long has it been since you have seen them? (Insert no. of years.)
(Skip to q. A63.)
A49. Whose idea is it usually that you get together?
_____ 1. Your idea.
_____ 2. Your spouse's idea.
_____ 3. Your parents' idea.
_____ 4. Sometimes your idea, and sometimes your parents'.
_____ 5. No one suggests it; we get together from habit or tradition.
A50-62. In the past two years or so (or since moving here, if less than two years), how often have you and your parent(s) engaged in the following types of activities together? (1 = more than once a month, 2 = several times a year, 3 = once or twice, 4 = never.)
_____ A50. Commercial recreation.
_____ A51. Home recreation, such as picnics, card playing, etc.
_____ A52. Outdoor recreation, such as fishing, hunting, or camping.
_____ A53. Brief drop-in visits for conversation.
_____ A54. Vacation visits.
_____ A55. Large family reunions (including aunts, uncles, cousins).
_____ A56. Emergencies of any sort (sickness, death, etc.).
_____ A57. Working together at the same location, or occupation.
_____ A58. Baby sitting.
_____ A59. Happy occasions, such as birthdays or Christmas.

_____ A60. Attending the same church or religious group.
_____ A61. Shopping together.
_____ A62. Other (specify: . . . .).

A64. How often do you (your spouse) write letters to your parents.
    _____ 1. Never.
    _____ 2. Only on special occasions, such as birthdays or Christmas.
    _____ 3. Several times a year.
    _____ 4. About once a month.
    _____ 5. Several times a month.
    _____ 6. Once a week or more.

A65. Do you ever talk to your parents on the telephone?
    _____ 1. No, never.
    _____ 2. Yes, on special occasions, or in emergencies.
    _____ 3. Several times a year.
    _____ 4. About once a month.
    _____ 5. Several times a month.
    _____ 6. Once a week or more.

(If never, omit q. A66.)

A66. Do you usually call them, or do they call you?
    _____ 1. You almost always call them.
    _____ 2. You call a little more often.
    _____ 3. You and they call equally often.
    _____ 4. They call a little more often.
    _____ 5. They almost always call you.

III. _Affectional Solidarity_

A39. How close would you say you are in your feelings toward your father?
    _____ 1. Not too close.
    _____ 2. Somewhat close.
    _____ 3. Fairly close.
    _____ 4. Quite close.
    _____ 5. Extremely close.

A43. How close would you say you feel to your mother?
    _____ 1. Not too close.
    _____ 2. Somewhat close.
    _____ 3. Fairly close.
    _____ 4. Quite close.
    _____ 5. Extremely close.

A42. Would you like to be the kind of person your father is?
    _____ 1. Not at all.
    _____ 2. In just a few ways.
    _____ 3. In several ways.
    _____ 4. In most ways.
    _____ 5. Yes, completely.

A46. Would you like to be the kind of person your mother is?
    _____ 1. Not at all.
    _____ 2. In just a few ways.
    _____ 3. In several ways.
    _____ 4. In most ways.
    _____ 5. Yes, completely.

A41. Do you and your father agree in your ideas and opinions about the things you consider really important in life?

_____ 1. Yes, completely.

_____ 2. Yes, to a great extent.

_____ 3. Yes, to some extent.

_____ 4. No, very little.

A45. Do you and your mother agree in your ideas and opinions about the things you consider to be really important in life?

_____ 1. Yes, completely.

_____ 2. Yes, to a great extent.

_____ 3. Yes, to some extent.

_____ 4. No, very little.

A63. Do you wish you could see your parents more or less often than you do?

_____ 1. Much less often.

_____ 2. A little less often.

_____ 3. You see them just often enough.

_____ 4. A little more often.

_____ 5. Much more often.

IV. *Exchanges of Assistance and Support*

A71-A78. In the past two years or so, how often have you received the following kinds of help from your parents? (Use 1, 2, 3, or 4.)

_____ A71. Advice on a decision you had to make.

_____ A72. Help on special occasions, such as childbirth, sickness.

_____ A73. Help in caring for your children such as baby sitting.

_____ A74. Financial assistance, such as money or a loan.

_____ A75. Gifts, other than the reciprocal occasions.

_____ A76. Hand work: such as garden produce, sewing, yard work.

_____ A77. Job placement.

_____ A78. Other (specify: . . . .).

B5-B8. In the past two years or so, have you given your parents any specific help you can think of? If so, how often? (1, 2, 3, or 4).

_____ B5. Help in their home or yard.

_____ B6. Taking them to the doctor, or caring for them when sick.

_____ B7. Financial aid.

_____ B8. Non-reciprocal gifts, or other miscellaneous.

V. *Norms Regarding Parent-Child Relations*

A67-A70. Now I want us to look a little deeper into your relations with your parent(s), to see if we can get at why you keep in touch. There are several reasons people might give for keeping in touch with their parents. As I read each of the following reasons, tell me if it is very important, somewhat important, or unimportant, in your relation with your parents:

	Very Impt.	Some Impt.	Unimportant
A67. First you feel you ought to, or have an obligation to keep in touch.	1. _____	2. _____	3. _____
A68. You need their help in some way.	1. _____	2. _____	3. _____
A69. They need your help in some way.	1. _____	2. _____	3. _____
A70. You simply enjoy keeping in touch.	1. _____	2. _____	3. _____

SOURCE: B. N. Adams. *Kinship in an Urban Setting.* Chicago: Markham, 1968, pp. 200-201.

V2.4.I.b

POSITIVE AFFECT INDEX

V. L. Bengtson, 1973

III. Affectual Solidarity
1. How well do you feel this child *understands* you?
   (circle the number)
   1. not well
   2. not too well
   3. some
   4. pretty well
   5. very well
   6. extremely well
2. How well do you feel your child *trusts* you?
   (same categories as above)
3. How *fair* do you feel this child is toward you?
4. How much *respect* do you feel from this child?
5. How much *affection* do you feel this child has for you?
6. How well do you *understand* him (or her)?
7. How much do you *trust* this child?
8. How *fair* do you feel you are toward this child?
9. How much do you *respect* this child?
10. How much *affection* do you have toward this child?

ADDITIONAL SINGLE-ITEM INDICATORS (NOT PART OF SCALE)
11. Taking everything into consideration, how *close* do you feel, in the relationship between you and this child?
12. How is *communication* between yourself and this child—how well can you exchange ideas or talk about things that really concern you?
13. In general, how *similar* are your views about life to those of this child?
14. How often do you *do things together* with this child?
15. Generally, how well do you and this child *get along together*?

SOURCE: V. L. Bengtson and K. D. Black. "Solidarity between Parents and Children: Four Perspectives on Theory Development." Paper presented to the Theory Development Workshop, National Council on Family Relations, Toronto, October 16, 1973.

V2.4.I.c

INTERACTION INDEX

V. L. Bengtson, 1973

II. Associational Solidarity
ACTIVITIES. We are interested in finding out what kinds of things people do with their families. (If one of the relatives we ask about in this section is deceased, just skip the question. If your answer is for a step-child, please write "step" at the beginning of that section.)
REPEAT FOR OTHER CHILDREN
WITH YOUR CHILD:
How often do you do the following?
(Put an "x" in the right box)

	Almost never	About once a year	Several times a year	Every other month or so	About once a year
1. Recreation outside the home (movies, picnics, swimming, trips, hunting, etc.)					
2. Brief visits for conversation					
3. Family gatherings like reunions or holiday dinners where a lot of family members get together					
4. Small family gatherings for special occasions like birthdays or anniversaries					
5. Talking over things that are important to you					
6. Religious activities of any kind					
7. Writing letters					
8. Telephoning each other					
9. Dinner together					
10. Gift exchange					
11. Your helping him out with chores or errands					
12. His helping you out with chores or errands					

13. Other (write in:_____

14. How many miles do you live from this
    child?_____

SOURCE: V. L. Bengtson and K. D. Black. "Solidarity between Parents and Children: Four Perspectives on Theory Development." Paper presented to the Theory Development Workshop, National Council on Family Relations, Toronto, October 16, 1973.

V2.4.I.d.

CROSS-ETHNIC BATTERY OF FAMILISM

V. L. Bengtson and R. Manuel, 1976

I. *Family Structure*

    36.   Do you *have* any children, your own or adopted?
           YES. . . . . SKIP TO Q36B . . . .
           NO . . . . .ASK A . . . .
        A.   Have you *ever* had any children?
           YES. . . . . SKIP TO Q37 . . . .
           NO . . . . .SKIP TO Q37. . . . .
        B.   How many? (LIVING CHILDREN)
           NUMBER OF CHILDREN:_____

    C.   How many are over 18?
          NUMBER OVER 18:
          NONE . . . . SKIP TO Q37 . . . .

37.   Have you raised any/other children?
      YES. . . . . ASK A. . . . .
      NO . . . . SKIP TO INST. *ABOVE* Q38 . . . .
      A.   How many are over 18?
          NUMBER OVER 18:
          NONE . . . . SKIP TO INST. *ABOVE* Q38 . . . .

II. *Associational Solidarity*

38-D. When did you last see any of your adult children who do not live with you? Was it:
      TODAY OR YESTERDAY . . . .
      WITHIN THE LAST WEEK . . . .
      WITHIN THE LAST MONTH . . . .
      WITHIN THE LAST YEAR, OR . . . .
      MORE THAN A YEAR AGO? . . . .
      ADULT CHILDREN LIVE WITH R . . . . SKIP TO Q37. . . . .

38-E. In general, do you see your adult child/children as often as you would like to, or would you like to see him/her/them more often?
      AS OFTEN AS WOULD LIKE TO . . . .
      SOME AS OFTEN, OTHERS NOT AT OFTEN. . . . .
      NOT AS OFTEN, WOULD LIKE TO SEE MORE OFTEN . . . .
      TOO OFTEN . . . .

V. *Norms, Expectations*

23-C. It usually doesn't work out too well for older people to live with their children and grandchildren.
      (1 = agree; 2 = disagree; 3 = depends/neither agree nor disagree; 8 = don't know/ no opionion.)

73-I. It is the obligation of grown children to take care of their older parents. (Same response categories.)

41.   If there came a time when you could no longer live alone, would you expect to live with your children?
      (yes = 1; no = 2; already living with children = 3.)

42.   If you ever found yourself without enough money, would you expect your family to help out? (yes = 1; no = 2.)

39-A. Would you prefer to live in the same neighborhood as your children, or at a greater distance? (1 = same neighborhood; 2 = greater distance.)

40.   Would you prefer to live with one of your children, or in a separate residence? (1 = with children; 2 = separate residence.)

SOURCE: V. L. Bengtson and R. Manuel. "Ethnicity and Family Patterns in Later Life: Effects of Race, Age, S.E.S. and Gender." Unpublished paper: Andrus Gerontology Center, 1976.

V2.4.I.e

FAMILY MUTUAL AID AND INTERACTION INDEX

M. H. Cantor, 1976; M. Mayer, 1976

I. *Family Structure*

34a. Now, I would like to know a few things about your family. How many children,

if any, have you *had* or *adopted in all?*
IF *HAVE HAD* OR *ADOPTED* CHILDREN, ASK Q.34b-c . . . .
IF *NONE*, SKIP TO Q.34c. . . . .

34b. How many are presently living?

34c. How many other children, if any, have you raised, or been solely responsible for?

	34a. Children Have Had or Adopted	34b. Children Living	34c. Children Raised
	42	43	44
1 child	___ 1	___ 1	___ 1
2 children	___ 2	___ 2	___ 2
3 children	___ 3	___ 3	___ 4
4-5 children	___ 4	___ 4	___ 4
6-7 children	___ 5	___ 5	___ 5
8-10 children	___ 6	___ 6	___ 6
11 or more children.	___ 7	___ 7	___ 7

II. *Associational Solidarity and Living Arrangements*

85a. Please give me the first names of all your living children.
IF OTHER CHILDREN RAISED (REFER TO Q. 84c), ASK: Now, give me the first names of other children you may have raised who are still living.
(LIST THE NAMES BELOW AS DESCRIBED IN YOUR INSTRUCTION SHEET—USE NEXT PAGE IF NECESSARY.)
FOR FIRST CHILD LISTED IN Q.85a, ASK Q85b-g, THEN ASK Q.85b-g, IN TURN, FOR EACH OF THE OTHER CHILDREN LISTED

85b. Is (*NAME*) a male or a female?

85c. How old is he/she?

85d. Where does (*NAME*) live? (PROBE FOR CATEGORIES LISTED BELOW—WITH RESPONDENT, IN SAME BUILDING, WITHIN WALKING DISTANCE, ETC.)

c. *Age*	46	52	58	64
Under 18 years	___1	___1	___1	___1
18-24 years	___2	___2	___2	___2
25-34 years	___3	___3	___3	___3
35-44 years	___4	___4	___4	___4
45-54 years	___5	___5	___5	___5
55 years or over.	___6	___6	___6	___6
d. *Where lives*	47	53	59	65
With respondent.	___1	___1	___1	___1
Same building as respondent.	___2	___2	___2	___2
Within walking distance	___3	___3	___3	___3
Within city limits	___4	___4	___4	___4
In same metropolitan area	___5	___5	___5	___5
Beyond metropolitan area	___6	___6	___6	___6
e. *Frequency of seeing*	48	54	60	66
Every day	___1	___1	___1	___1
Every week	___2	___2	___2	___2
Every month.	___3	___3	___3	___3
Several times a year.	___4	___4	___4	___4
Once a year or less	___5	___5	___5	___5
f. *Frequency of talking on phone*	49	55	61	67
Every day	___1	___1	___1	___1

f. *Frequency of talking on phone*   49   55   61   67
   Every week . . . . __2   __2   __2   __2
   Every month. . . . . __3   __3   __3   __3
   Several times a year. . . . . __4   __4   __4   __4
   Once a year or less . . . . __5   __5   __5   __5

III. *Affectional Solidarity*

  g. *Closeness*   50   56   62   68
   Very close . . . . __1   __1   __1   __1
   Fairly close . . . . __2   __2   __2   __2
   Not too close . . . . __3   __3   __3   __3
   Not close at all . . . . __4   __4   __4   __4

86a. Would you like to see your child/children   More often . . . . . .1⟩ASK Q.86b
     more often, about the same or *less often*   About the same . . .2⟩SKIP TO Q. 87a
     than you do now?   Less often . . . . . .3⟩

   b. What are the things that keep you from getting together more often? Anything else?

     _____
     _____ 25 __
     _____ 26 __

IV. *Exchanges of Assistance and Support*

32a. Does anyone else, other than   YES. . . . . .1 ASK Q.32b-c
     your wife/husband, contribute   NO . . . . .2 SKIP TO Q.50a
     to the cost of running this place?

   b. Who is that?   42
              Brother. . . . . ____1
              Sister . . . . ____ 2
              Parent . . . . ____ 3
              Child . . . . ____ 4
              Other relative . . . . ____ 5
              Friend . . . . ____6
              Other _____ (specify)
                                     43

   c. How much is contributed—   All . . . . ____ 1
     would you say, *all* of the cost,   More than half. . . . ____ 2
                                 SKIP TO Q.50a
     more than half, *about* half or   About half . . . . . . ____ 3
     less than half?   Less than half . . . . ____ 4

87a. As you know, parents and children sometimes help each other in different ways. Do you *ever help* your child/children in any of the following ways? (GO THROUGH LIST)

              FOR EACH ITEM CHECKED *YES* IN Q.87a, ASK Q. 87b

   b. On the average, do you do this very often, fairly often or only occasionally?

	Q.87a		Q.87b	Frequency	
	Ever Help		*Very*	*Fairly*	*Only*
	Yes	*No*	*Often*	*Often*	*Occasionally*
	27				
Help out when someone is ill	__ 1	__ 28	__1	__ 2	__ 3
Babysit for a while when parents are out.	__ 2	__ 29	__1	__ 2	__ 3
Give advice on running a home and bringing up your grandchildren.	__ 3	__ 30	__1	__ 2	__ 3
Shop or run errands.	__ 4	__ 31	__1	__ 2	__ 3

	Q.87a Ever Help Yes	No	Q.87b Very Often	Fairly Often	Frequency Only Occasionally
Give gifts.	__ 5	__ 32	__ 1	__ 2	__ 3
Help your child/children out with money	__ 6	__ 33	__ 1	__ 2	__ 3
Fix things around their/his/ her house	__ 7	__ 34	__ 1	__ 2	__ 3
Give advice on jobs and business matters	__ 8	__ 35	__ 1	__ 2	__ 3
Help them/him/her make a decision on a big purchase, such as a car	__ 9	__ 36	__ 1	__ 2	__ 3
Keep house for them/him/her	__ 0	__ 37	__ 1	__ 2	__ 3

88a. Now, I would like to know if your child/children *ever helps/help* you in any of the following ways. (GO THROUGH LIST)
FOR EACH ITEM CHECKED *YES* IN Q.88a, ASK Q.88b

b. On the average, does he/she (do they) do this *very* often, *fairly* often or *only occasionally*?

	Q.88a Ever Help Yes	No	Q.88b Very Often	Fairly Often	Frequency Only Occasionally
Help you when you are ill (or when your wife/husband is ill) . . . . . [38]	__ 1	__ 39	__ 1	__ 2	__ 3
Give you advice on money matters . . .	__ 2	__ 40	__ 1	__ 2	__ 3
Help you make a decision on a big purchase	__ 3	__ 41	__ 1	__ 2	__ 3
Shop or run errands for you	__ 4	__ 42	__ 1	__ 2	__ 3
Give you gifts	__ 5	__ 43	__ 1	__ 2	__ 3
Help fix things around the house	__ 6	__ 44	__ 1	__ 2	__ 3
Keep house for you.	__ 7	__ 45	__ 1	__ 2	__ 3
Prepare meals for you, but not keep house	__ 8	__ 46	__ 1	__ 2	__ 3
Take you away during the summer . . .	__ 9	__ 47	__ 1	__ 2	__ 3
Help you out with money	__ 0	__ 48	__ 1	__ 2	__ 3
Drive you places, such as the doctor, shopping, church	__ 11	__ 49	__ 1	__ 2	__ 3

100. From time to time, all of us are faced with situations where we might need help. I will read some of these situations to you. For each one, please tell me who, if anyone, you would be most likely to turn to if you were in that situation.

Let's start with an instance where (*READ FIRST SITUATION*—who, if anyone, would you turn to or call? (CONTINUE THROUGH LIST. IF RESPONDENT SAYS WIFE/HUSBAND, ASK) Suppose your wife/husband were not available, who would you turn to?

	No One	My self	Child	Other Relative	Friend	Neighbor	Social Agency	Other (Specify)
A. You suddenly feel sick or dizzy . .10		__ 1	__ 2	__ 3	__ 4	__ 5	__ 6	__ 7 __
B. You want to talk with someone about a problem concerning your child or someone else in your family 11		__ 1	__ 2	__ 3	__ 4	__ 5	__ 6	__ 7 __

	No One	My self	Child	Other Relative	Friend	Neigh-bor	Social Agency	Other (Specify)
C. You need to borrow a few dollars until your next check comes . 12	__1	__2	__3	__4	__5	__6	__7	____
D. You feel lonely and want to talk . . . 13	__1	__2	__3	__4	__5	__6	__7	____
E. You need a new light bulb in the ceiling 14	__1	__2	__3	__4	__5	__6	__7	____
F. You need someone to help you get to the doctor's . . . 15	__1	__2	__3	__4	__5	__6	__7	____
G. You find you do not have enough money to cover a very big medical bill 16	__1	__2	__3	__4	__5	__6	__7	____
H. You are in the hospital and need someone to look after your apartment 17	__1	__2	__3	__4	__5	__6	__7	____
I. You need someone to help you fill out a form 18	__1	__2	__3	__4	__5	__6	__7	____
J. You have an accident and need someone in each day to bathe and help you take your medicine 19	__1	__2	__3	__4	__5	__6	__7	____

SOURCE: M. H. Cantor. "The Configuration and Intensity of the Informal Support System in a New York City Elderly Population." Paper presented at the 29th Annual Meeting of the Gerontological Society, New York, October 13-17, 1976.

V2.4.I.f

FAMILISM INDEX

M. H. Cantor, 1976; L. Wilker, 1976

FACTOR LOADINGS ON VARIMAX ROTATED FACTORS OF
FAMILISM ITEMS IN NEW YORK CITY INNER CITY STUDY
(RESPONDENTS WITH ONE OR MORE CHILDREN, N = 997)

HAND RESPONDENT CARD E

Here are some statements that people make about relatives and friends. As I read each statement, I'd like you to tell me if you *agree* or *disagree* with it. (Go through list.)

	FACTOR			
	1	2	3	h^2
A. It is usually nice for a young married couple to live near their parents	.70	.08	.25	.56

| | FACTOR | | | |
	_1_	_2_	_3_	_b^2_
B. If you have to borrow money it's better to do it from a relative than a bank	_.31_	.19	_.37_	.27
C. It is good for a young mother to have her own mother close by to help her	_.74_	.18	.06	.58
D. It is humiliating for parents to be supported by children in later life*	.02	.21	.28	.12
E. Parents are entitled to some return for the sacrifices they have made for their children	.13	_.76_	.15	.61
F. One usually has more in common with relatives than with friends	.22	.15	_.46_	.28
G. Friends and neighbors are frequently more help to an older person than his own family*	.05	−.01	_.45_	.21
H. A family should be willing to sacrifice some of the things they want for their children in order to help support their aged parents	.14	_.53_	.07	.30

NOTE: Factor loadings of .3 or greater are italicized.
*The disagree response was given the highest score.

SOURCE: M. H. Cantor. "The Configuration and Intensity of the Informal Support System in a New York City Elderly Population." Paper presented to the 29th Annual Meeting of the Gerontological Society, New York, October 13-17, 1976.

V2.4.I.g

CHILDREN'S ATTITUDES TOWARD SUPPORTING AGED PARENTS

R. M. Dinkel, 1944

DIRECTIONS

Please read carefully

1. You are requested to check ($\sqrt{}$) the statements with which you agree. Leave other spaces blank.
2. Let your own way of thinking and feeling guide you. Opinions differ widely and your own view is as good as that of anybody else.
3. In all statements, the parent is to be considered as aged and as in need of help.

STATEMENTS

1. If aged parents are a nuisance in the home, children should refuse to take them in. . ( )
2. Children should not be made to think there is any obligation to support aged parents. . . . . ( )
3. Every family should be entitled to be entirely free from the care of aged parents . . ( )
4. It is only proper that children should place the happiness of an aged parent before their own. . . . . ( )
5. Children should overlook the trouble that aged parents might cause in the home. . . ( )
6. Aged parents who interfere with family affairs should be put out of your home . . . ( )
7. Aged parents should understand they have to stand on their own feet without help from children . . . . ( )

8. Children should not take care of aged parents if it makes for squabbling and turmoil all the time. . . . . ( )
9. Aged parents who keep getting in the way should not be given a home by their children. . . . . ( )
10. We should look to children to support aged parents . . . . ( )
11. The duty of caring for aged parents should be taught each child . . . . ( )
12. Children should give a home even to aged parents who interfere a lot in family affairs ( )
13. Children should put up with any inconvenience in their family life in order to help aged parents . . . . ( )
14. No matter how crabby, critical, and interfering aged parents are, children should give them a home. . . . . ( )
15. It should be considered highly immoral for children to refuse to help aged parents . ( )
16. Children should not give a home to aged parents who are quarrelsome. . . . . ( )
17. If aged parents haven't learned you have your own life to live, they should not be given a home. . . . . ( )
18. If aged parents are unpleasant, children should not give them a home . . . . ( )
19. Children should be willing to give a home to an aged parent who is an extremely jealous busybody . . . . ( )
20. Children should not mind crowding their home in order to help aged parents. . . . . ( )

SOURCE: R. M. Dinkel. "Attitudes of Children toward Supporting Aged Parents." *American Sociological Review*, 1944, 9: 370-79.

V2.4.I.h

EXCHANGES BETWEEN GENERATIONS INDEX

R. Hill, N. Foote, J. Aldous, R. Carlson, and R. MacDonald, 1970

II. *Associational Solidarity*
   3. Social Activities and Rituals
      Instructions: Use the code below to indicate on the chart with whom the family Always, Almost Always and Sometimes does these activities.
      Code:

I	= Immediate family (wife, husband, and resident children)	HP	= Husband's parents
		HGP	= Husband's grandparents
H-W	= Husband and wife only	HS or HB	= Husband's sister(s) or brother(s)
MC	= Married children	F or N	= Friends, neighbors (other than fellow club members)
MGC	= Married grandchildren		
WP	= Wife's parents	CM	= Club or organiza-members
WGP	= Wife's grandparents		
WS or	= Wife's sister(s) or	RO	= Cousins, aunts and uncles and other relatives (specify which of these
WB	= Wife's brother(s)		

Note I — If one member only of the family engages in an activity with a certain person, indicate this separately by circling the code letter and placing this alongside the code letter(s) of whomever the family member does this activity with; e.g., if the husband *Always goes bowling* with his brother and the wife *Sometimes goes bowling with fellow P.T.A. members* then you would check item (f) as below:

	Always	Almost Always	Sometimes
(f) Sports	(H) HB		(W) CM

Note II — For *Special Holidays* (item C) and *Recreation* (item H), *circle* the one activity (or two at the most) considered by the family to be the most important single holidays for their family or the most usual type of recreation.

Note III — If the family alternates between grandparents on some holidays or anniversaries; e.g., Christmas one year with the wife's parents, one year with the husband's parents, check both under "Sometimes."

Introduction: "On this page below we have a list of common activities and special events in which many families participate. I will ask you, for each activity, with whom you participate — then ask you whether you *Always* participate with those you mention or is it only *Almost Always*, or only *Sometimes*?

"Let's begin with birthdays. How about your birthday (or your husband's) — with whom do you spend your birthday?"

Activities	With Whom Do You Participate in These Activities		
	Always (Weight 5)	Almost Always (Weight 3)	Sometimes (Weight 1)
(a) Birthdays: Your own and your husband's Your children's Your parents'			
(b) Mother's Day			
(c) Special Holidays (July 4, Thanksgiving, New Year's, Easter, etc.) (Circle the most important one)			
(d) Anniversaries, weddings: Your own Your parents' Your children's			
(e) Vacation trips			
(f) Sports (bowling, golf, fishing, ball games, etc.)			
(g) Picnics, drives			
(h) Recreation (movies, dancing, bingo, card games, etc.) (Circle usual type of recreation)			
(i) Religious observances (church, synagogue, etc.)			
(j) Dining out			
(k) Club or organization activities			

IV. *Exchanges of Assistance and Support*

    1. Introduction

        "We're going to discuss ways in which people help one another. Some do it financially; some by sharing goods; some by lending a hand in providing services; some by sharing of their ideas, knowledge and experience. We know some families only help their family members; that is, children, parents, and grandparents. Some families only help others outside, such as friends, neighbors, underprivileged people, and so forth. Some families help each other only by money, loans, gifts, and the like. Some don't believe in this and only give goods or provide services.

"*When families want help*, they have their preferences, too. Some families *never* go outside their immediate families, for professional advice or counseling, to agencies such as County Welfare Departments, Family Service Agencies or Catholic Charities. And some families *never* discuss their own troubles with other family relatives and in-laws but instead go to friends, neighbors, doctors, ministers or social agencies for help with their personal problems.

"First I'm going to ask about the people and organizations you and your husband have helped in the past year. Then I'll ask the situation or reason that prompted you to give this help and whether or not you expect some return for the help you gave.

"Let's begin with financial or money help. In the past year, to whom have you given or loaned money?"

A. Financial Help Given   Total Amount Given Last Year to All Sources, \$ . . . . . .

Financial Help To	Amount,\$	Circumstances * (What was the need?)	Conditions* (See Conditions code** below.)

* Code for Circumstances which Prompted Help or Giving

A. Children
  1. Birth of child
  2. Special occasion, such as anniversary or Christmas
  3. Improvement of grades
  4. Child-care problems
  5. Child-teacher problems
  6. Child-parent problems
  7. Improvement of play space
  8. Improvement of play equipment
  9. Special schooling
  10.Parent replacement

B. Couples
  1. Special occasion
  2. Education and/or rehabilitation
  3. In-laws
  4. Money
  5. Drinking/gambling
  6. Infidelity
  7. Sexual relations
  8. Peer group problems—friends, neighbors
  9. Old age

C. Disasters
  Major Wage Earner
  1. Death
  2. Incapacity/disability
  3. Loss of employment
  4. Insufficient income
  5. Illness
  Spouse
  6. Death
  7. Incapacity/disability
  8. Loss of employment
  9. Illness
  General Loss or Failure
  10. Fire or flood
  11. Major appliance
  12. Major equipment of business
  13. Replacement—wear and tear
D. Raise Scale of Living
E. Living Costs—General Assistance

Code	Finances	Goods	Lend-a-Hand Services	Share the Brain Knowledge

** Code for Types of Conditions Set on Giving or Helping

1	Gift	Gift	Gives or receives total capacity to do the job— other take over job entirely.	Assumption of problem and solution—others take over problem entirely.

Code	Finances	Goods	Lend-a-Hand Services	Share the Brain Knowledge

** Code for Types of Conditions Set on Giving or Helping

Code	Finances	Goods	Lend-a-Hand Services	Share the Brain Knowledge
2	Loan—Not expected or intended repayment	Loan—Not expected to repay or return.	Helps out—Lends a hand and expects no repayment or return	Seeks or gives constant information—"Tell me what to do" or "I'll tell you what to do."
3	Loan—-Expects return or to return services.	Loan—Expects replacement or to replace with other items of less value.	Expect other or intend to reciprocate in own way (less).	Swaps information only, shares experiences and problems. Sympathize with one another.
4	Loan—Expects or intends to return. No time limit.	Return as is when finished using.	Reciprocate—Expect or intend to repay in same way sometime.	Good listener—Seeks or is a broad shoulder to cry on. Available when needed and know would use other similarly.
5	Loan—Expects or intends return. Stated time.	Return and replace if worn, fix up.	Reciprocate—Expect or intend equivalent service at or within specified time (with maximum skills).	Seek and use specific information or counsel. Limited time counseling if counseling is accepted. Or refers or helps to go to more appropriate source for help.
6	Loan and expect or intend return with interest.	Replace with a new one.	Pay or reciprocity and additional service.	Seeks or gives support, counseling—but helps other person assume total problem for self.

B. Goods Given Last Year
   "Now let's think of the goods you gave or loaned to people or organizations in the past year"

Goods Given To	Type of Article	Circumstances (What was the need?)	Conditions (Gift, loan, exchange, expect return?

C. Services Given Last Year
   "Now how about services given to others in the past year, such as help in child care or babysitting, nursing, housework, redecorating, helping your club, church or some welfare agency, etc.?"

Services Given To	Type	Circumstances (What was the need?)	Conditions (Gift, exchange, etc.)

D. Giving Knowledge, Sharing Experiences, Ideas, Counseling
   "Now let's talk about whether or not you or your husband helped others last year by sharing with them the knowledge you have gained from experience. Have you helped others by giving information or counseling or by being a good listener when others had family or personal problems, school, money or business problems?"

Knowledge Help Given to Whom		Circumstances (What was the need or problem?)	Conditions (How did you help?) (Help decide; shared problem, advice; listen?)

Help Received — Introduction

"We've talked about all the ways in which you and your immediate family helped others last year. Now let's talk about the ways in which you received help from others. This time I would like to know from what people and organizations you received the kinds of help we've just discussed and the circumstances or reasons for receiving their help.

"Let's begin with financial or money help — in the past year from what people or organizations have you received or borrowed money?"

E. Financial Help Received   Total Amount Received from All Sources Last Year, $ . .

Financial Help From	Amount, $	Circumstances (What was the need?)	Conditions (Gift, loan, exchange, etc.)

F. Goods Received Last Year
"Now let's think of the goods you were given or had loaned to you from people or organizations in the past year."

Goods Received From	Type of Article	Circumstances (What was the need?)	Conditions (Gift, loan, exchange, expect return?)

G. Services Received Last Year
"Now how about services received from others in the past year, such as help in child care or babysitting, nursing, housework, redecorating, help from your club, church or some welfare agency, etc.?"

Services Received From	Type	Circumstances (What was the need?)	Conditions (Gift, exchange, etc.)

H. Receiving Knowledge, Sharing Experience, Ideas, Counseling
"Now let's talk about whether or not you or your husband received help from others last year by sharing with them the knowledge they had gained from experience. Have you been helped by others by getting information or counseling or by seeking a good listener when you had family or personal problems, school, money or business problems?"

Knowledge, Help (Received from whom?)	Circumstances (What was the need or problem?)	Conditions (How were you helped?) (Helped decide; shared problem, advice; listening?)

2. For the family and personal problems you met or solved during the past year or are presently working on, to whom did you go for advice and counseling?

. . . . Doctor
. . . . Lawyer
. . . . School Nurse
. . . . Social Worker
. . . . Religious Leader
. . . . None of These
. . . . No family or personal problems last year?
        (Probe: If you did have, to whom would you have gone?)

Comments:

SOURCE: R. Hill, N. Foote, J. Aldous, R. Carlson, and R. MacDonald. *Family Development in Three Generations.* Cambridge, Mass.: Schenkman, 1970, pp. 400-407.

FAMILY STRUCTURE AND CONTACT BATTERY

H. Z. Lopata, 1973

I. *Family Structure*

14. How many children do you have?. . . . .

(IF ANY, ASK 14 A-G FOR EACH, IF NONE, SKIP TO Q.15)

	A.	B.	C.	D.
	What is the name of your (oldest) child? And the next oldest? And the next?	Code sex of each person mentioned. (ASK IF NOT OBVIOUS.)	What is (his/her) age?	(IF 16 YEARS OR OLDER) What is (his/her) marital status?

Person No.		M F	Married	Separated	Divorced	Widowed	Never Married
01		1 2	1	2	3	4	5
02		1 2	1	2	3	4	5
03		1 2	1	2	3	4	5
04		1 2	1	2	3	4	5
05		1 2	1	2	3	4	5
06		1 2	1	2	3	4	5
07		1 2	1	2	3	4	5
08		1 2	1	2	3	4	5

II. *Associational Solidarity*

E.	F.
Does (he/she live in the neighborhood? IF YES, ASK (1). IF NO, ASK (2) AND (3).	ASK UNLESS SAME DU OR SAME BUILDING.
Where does (he/she) live—in the same DU, same block, or somewhere else in the neighborhood? (GO TO F.)	How long does it take to get to (his/her house—an hour or less, over an hour or over a day?	What is your usual mode of transportation? Do you usually go by car, by local bus or "L", by Greyhound bus or train, or by airplane?	How often do you see (child)—almost daily, every week or so, about every month, a few times a year or less often than that?

Same DU	Same Building, Other DU	Same Block	Somewhere Else in the Neighborhood	An Hour or Less	Over an Hour	Over One Day	Car	Local Bus or "L"	Greyhound or Train	Airplane	Almost Daily	Every Week or So	About Every Month	A Few Times a Year	Less Often Than That
1	2	3	4	5	6	7	1	2	3	4	5	6	7	8	9
1	2	3	4	5	6	7	1	2	3	4	5	6	7	8	9

Same DU	Same Building, Other DU	Same Block	Somewhere Else in the Neighborhood	An Hour or Less	Over an Hour	Over One Day	Car	Local Bus or "L"	Greyhound or Train	Airplane	Almost Daily	Every Week or So	About Every Month	A Few Times a Year	Less Often Than That
1	2	3	4	5	6	7	1	2	3	4	5	6	7	8	9
1	2	3	4	5	6	7	1	2	3	4	5	6	7	8	9
1	2	3	4	5	6	7	1	2	3	4	5	6	7	8	9
1	2	3	4	5	6	7	1	2	3	4	5	6	7	8	9
1	2	3	4	5	6	7	1	2	3	4	5	6	7	8	9
1	2	3	4	5	6	7	1	2	3	4	5	6	7	8	9

14.G. How many times, altogether, would you say you talk on the telephone to your children within a week?
ASK EVERYONE

21.A. Who is living here with you at the present time? (Anyone else?) LIST IN COLUMN BELOW. IF NO ONE, INDICATE AND GO TO Q. 22.

ASK FOR EACH PERSON LISTED IN A.

How is (person) related to you?   How old is (person)?

UNLESS LIVES ALONE

B. Whose home is this?

22. Have you ever lived with any (other) of your children for longer than a month?
Yes . . . . .(ASK A & B) 1   No 2
IF YES:
A. How long was the longest time?. . . . .
B. What factors influenced you to move to another place after living there?

29. What is the total number of relatives who live in the neighborhood?
A. Who is that/are they? CIRCLE ALL THAT APPLY.
Children 1   Siblings. . . 2   Others (SPECIFY)

IV.*Exchanges of Assistance and Support*
ASK Q.19 IF ANY CHILDREN.
INTERVIEWER INSTRUCTION: USE THE PERSON NUMBER ASSIGNED TO EACH CHILD IN QUESTION 14.

19. We realize that individual circumstances alter how much help children can be to their widowed mothers—some are able to do more than others for one reason or another. We'd like to know something about the help received from your (child/children) in the following areas of your life.
(FOR ONLY CHILD, USE SECTION A—FOR MORE THAN ONE CHILD, USE SECTION B.)

A.	B.
FOR ONLY CHILD	IF MORE THAN ONE CHILD
Has you child helped you much or little in the following areas of life? (ASK (1)-(9))	Which of your children has helped you the most, and which has helped you the least in the following areas of life? (ASK (1)-(9))

		Much	Little	Does Not Apply	The Most ENTER PERSON#	The Least ENTER PERSON#	Can't Decide	Does Not Apply
(1)	During your husband's last illness	1	2	3			4	5
(2)	During the funeral	1	2	3			4	5
(3)	With finances	1	2	3			4	5
(4)	By being close to you	1	2	3			4	5
(5)	Emotionally, when you are blue	1	2	3			4	5
(6)	By giving advice	1	2	3			4	5
(7)	By performing services	1	2	3			4	5
(8)	By inviting you to (his/her) home	1	2	3			4	5
(9)	By coming to see you	1	2	3			4	5

25. During the past year, have you stayed overnight in anyone's home (aside from people in this household)—someone like children, brothers or sisters, other relatives or friends?

Yes . . . . (ASK A & B) 1   No 2

IF YES:

A. Who was that? CIRCLE ALL THAT APPLY

Children 5   Friends 8

Siblings 6   Other 9

Other relatives 7

B. Altogether, how many nights did you stay?

26. And during the past year, did anyone come to visit you for overnight, or longer?

Yes . . . . (ASK A & B) 1   No 2

IF YES:

A. Who was that (CIRCLE ALL THAT APPLY)

Children 5   Friends 8

Siblings 6   Other 9

B. Altogether, how many nights did (he/she/they) stay?

SOURCE: H.Z. Lopata. *Widowhood in an American City*. Cambridge, Mass.: Schenkman, 1973; pp. 281-82, 286-89.

V. *Norms Regarding Parent-Child Relations (see Chapter 3, Instrument V2.3.III.c)*

V2.4.I.j

SOCIAL AND FAMILY CONTACT SCALE

National Council on the Aging, 1975; 1976

I. *Family Structure*

12a. Do you have any living (READ LIST), or not? (IF YES) How many living (*item*) do you have? (RECORD BELOW FOR EACH ITEM ON LIST)

	12a					
	Don't Have	One	Two	Three	Four	Five or More
1. Children	___	___	___	___	___	___
2. Brothers or sisters	___	___	___	___	___	___
3. Parents	___	___	___	___	___	___

	Don't Have	One	Two	Three	Four	Five or More
4. Close friends						
5. Grandparents/ grandchildren						

II. *Associational Solidarity*

12b. (ASK FOR EACH "HAVE" IN 12a) When did you last see (any of) your (*item*) — within the last day or two, within the last week or two, a month ago, two to three months ago, or longer ago than that?
(RECORD BELOW FOR EACH APPLICABLE ITEM)

	12b						
	Within Last Day or Two	Within Last Week or Two	A Month Ago	2 - 3 Months Ago	Longer Than That	"Live" with Them (vol.)	Not Sure
1. Children							
2. Brothers or sisters							
3. Parents							
4. Close friends							
5. Grandparents/ Grandchildren							

SOURCE: Reproduced with permission from *Codebook for "The Myth and Reality of Aging,"* a survey conducted by Louis Harris and Associates for the National Council on the Aging; prepared by the Duke University Center for the Study of Aging and Human Development under a grant from the Edna M. Clark Foundation, 1976.

V2.4.I.k

EXCHANGES OF SUPPORT AND ASSISTANCE INDEX

National Council on the Aging, 1975; 1976

IV. Exchanges of Support and Assistance

13a. (ASK IF PARENT(S) "OVER 65" IN 12c, OR GRANDPARENT(S) "OVER 65" IN 12d—OTHER SKIP TO 14a) As you know, older parents/grandparents often help their children/grandchildren in different ways. Do your parents/grandparents ever help you in any of the following ways? (IF YOU HAVE BOTH PARENTS OVER 65 AND GRANDPARENTS OVER 65, ASK:) Do either your parent(s) or grandparent(s) ever help you in any of the following ways? (READ LIST AND RECORD BELOW FOR EACH ITEM)

13a. (ASK IF HAVE "CHILDREN" IN 12a, ITEM # 1 OR "GRANDCHILDREN" IN 12a, ITEM # 5—OTHERS SKIP TO 14a) As you know, parents often help children/grandchildren in different ways. Do you ever help your children/grandchildren in any of the following ways? (READ LIST AND RECORD BELOW FOR EACH ITEM) (IF HAVE BOTH CHILDREN AND GRANDCHILDREN) Do you ever help either your children or grandchildren in any of the following ways?

	Do	Don't Do	No Need/Not Applicable (vol.)	Not Sure
1. Help out when someone is ill				
2. Take care of small children				

	Do	Don't Do	No Need/Not Applicable (vol.)	Not Sure
3. Give advice on running a home	___	___	___	___
4. Give advice on bringing up children	___	___	___	___
5. Shop or run errands.	___	___	___	___
6. Give you/them gifts.	___	___	___	___
7. Help out with money.	___	___	___	___
8. Fix things around your/their house or keep house for you/them . .	___	___	___	___
9. Give advice on jobs or business matters.	___	___	___	___
10. Give general advice on how to deal with some of life's problems.	___	___	___	___
11. Take grandchildren, nieces or nephews into their/your home to live with them/you	___	___	___	___

13b. Do you ever help your parents/grandparents in any of the following ways? (READ LIST AND RECORD BELOW FOR EACH ITEM) (IF YOU HAVE BOTH, ASK:) Do you ever help either your parents or grandparents in any of the following ways?

13b. Do your children/grandchildren ever help you in any of the following ways? (READ LIST AND RECORD BELOW FOR EACH ITEM) (IF HAVE BOTH) Do either your children or grandchildren ever help you in any of the following ways?

	Do	Don't Do	No Need/Not Applicable (vol.)	Not Sure
1. Help out when someone is ill	___	___	___	___
2. Give advice on money matters.	___	___	___	___
3. Shop or run errands for them	___	___	___	___
4. Give them/you gifts.	___	___	___	___
5. Help fix things around the house or keep house for them/you	___	___	___	___
6. Help out with money.	___	___	___	___
7. Take them/you places, such as the doctor, shopping, church.	___	___	___	___
8. Give advice on running their/your home	___	___	___	___
9. Give advice on job or business matters.	___	___	___	___
10. Give general advice on how to deal with some of life's problems.	___	___	___	___

SOURCE: Reproduced with permission from the *Codebook for "The Myth and Reality of Aging,"* a survey conducted by Louis Harris and Associates for the National Council on the Aging; prepared by the Duke University Center for the Study of Aging and Human Development under a grant from the Edna M. Clark Foundation, 1976.

V2.3.I.l

EMOTIONAL DEPENDENCE ON CHILDREN SCALE

I. Rosow, 1967

Emotional Dependency Scale

The Guttman scale is as follows:

1. All or most children have kept in close touch (with me) since they left home (89% reported "yes").
2. My children are very devoted and do whatever they can for me (66%).
3. I enjoy seeing my children more than anything else (39%).
4. All children should take parents along when they go out with *their own* friends to a movie, restaurant, or picnic (13%).

These responses (*) are from the following larger set of questions:

10. *How many of your children have always kept in close touch with you since they left home — all of them, some of them, or none of them?*
   *5. All or most.
    6. Some.
    7. None.
    8. NA.

17. *Which of these things do you think all children should do when their parents are getting older?* READ:
    1. See them often. Or, if they live out of town, keep in close contact.
    2. Take care of them when they get sick, even if it is not convenient.
   *3. Take parents along when they go out with their *own* friends to a movie, restaurant or picnic.
    4. Live near enough so that parents can see them (and the grandchildren) whenever they like, even it it means *giving up a better job* somewhere else.
    5. Help them with money *whenever* they need it, even if the children *cannot* spare much.
    6. Give parents a place to live if they need it, even if children have to take parents *into their own home.*
    7. None of these.
    8. NA.

18. *What one of these statements fits you best?* READ:
   *1. I enjoy seeing my children more than anything else.
    2. I like to see my children whenever I can.
    3. Visits with my children can be a strain.
    4. DK/NA.

19. *Which one of these statements describes your children best?* READ:
   *5. My children are very devoted and do whatever they can for me.
    6. My children think about me, but their own affairs are more important to them than mine.
    7. My children don't think about me much or feel very close to me.
    8. DK/NA.

---

*Guttman scale items.

SOURCE: I. Rosow. *Social Integration of the Aged.* New York: Free Press, 1967, p. 201. Additional information provided by personal communication with Rosow, 1978.

V2.4.I.m

FAMILY STRUCTURE AND CONTACT BATTERY

E. Shanas, P. Townsend, D. Wedderburn, H. Friis, P. Milhøj, and J. Stehouwer, 1968-1975

I. *Family Structure*

B. *IF EVER MARRIED:* Now I'd like to ask some questions about your family. Do you have any living children (including step-children, adopted children, and foster children)?

> Yes, living children . . . . . .
> No, none (SKIP TO Q.56) . . .

C. *IF ANY LIVING CHILDREN:* How many of these are sons and how many are daughters?

> _____ sons
> _____ daughters

50. Tell me about your children . . . .

D. *ASK ALL:* Do you and (CHILD) live together?

| Yes (ASK E) | Yes (ASK E) | Yes (ASK E) |
| No (ASK F & G) | No (ASK F & G) | No (ASK F & G) |

E.[1] *IF YES, LIVE TOGETHER:* How long have you lived together?

E1. *IF NOT CLEAR:* About how long ago was that— how many months or years?

E2. *IF NOT CLEAR:* Any special reason you started living together at that time?

IF NOT IN SAME HHD:

F. How long would it take for (him) (her) to get here from where (he)(she) lives lives (by the usual way)?

10 min or less . . 1	10 min or less . . 1	10 min or less. . 1
11-30 minutes . . 2	11-30 minutes . . 2	11-30 min. . . . 2
31-60 minutes . . 3	31-60 minutes . . 3	31-60 min. . . . 3
More than an hour, less than a day . . . 4	More than an hour, less than a day . . 4	More than an hour, less than a day. . 4
One day or longer. . . . 5	One day or longer. . . 5	One day or longer. . . 5

II. *Associational Solidarity*

Tell me about your children . . . .

G. When did you last see (him)(her)? (Either here or at his/her home?)

> Today or yesterday 1
> 2-7 days 2
> 8-30 days. 3
> During last year,
>   more than 30 days. 4
> More than a year 5

51. *THIS QUESTION ONLY FOR PERSONS WITH CHILDREN LIVING OUTSIDE THE HOUSEHOLD:*

A. (Apart from the child(ren) you live with) Have you visited overnght at the home of (any of) your other child(ren) during the past 12 months?

> Yes, have visited. . . . .
> No, have not visited. . . . .
> DNA. No children or only children
>   in household . . . .

B. (Have any/either of your other children) (Has your other son/daughter) stayed overnight with you during the past 12 months?

> Yes, have stayed. . . . .
> No, have not stayed. . . . .
> DNA. No children or only children
>   in household. . . . .

IV. *Exchanges of Assistance and Support*
   52. *ASK ALL:*
      A. People help their children in many different ways. It could be just little things you do for them, it could be money, or it could be other kinds of help. Are you able to do *anything* to help your child(ren) in any way—even small things?

      Yes . . . .
      Yes, but they wouldn't let me . . . .
      I would if they needed it . . . .
      No, can't help . . . .

      B. IF YES (CODE 1 ONLY): How about during the last month—are there any things you did do to help your child(ren)? (Anything else?) DO *NOT* READ CODES. RECORD *VERBATIM* AND THEN CRICLE ALL CODES THAT APPLY.

      Nothing during last month . . . .
      Grandchildren lived with me . . . .
      Helped care for grandchildren . . . .
      Helped out when someone was ill . . . .
      Gave money or money gifts . . . .
      Gave other gifts (clothing, food, etc.) . . . . .
      Fixed things around child's house
      (home repairs, gardening, etc.) . . . .
      Housekeeping, housework, mending, sewing,
      cooking, laundry, etc. . . . .
      Other (SPECIFY): . . . .
      . . . .

   (Do your children) (Does your son/daughter) help you in any way, even with small things?

      Yes, they help 1
      They would if necessary . . . 2   *SKIP*
      No, they don't help 3   *TO*
      No, I won't let them help . . . 4   *Q.54*

      B. *IF YES (CODE 1 ONLY):* During the last month, what sorts of things did your child(ren) do to help you? (Anything else?) DO *NOT* READ CODES. RECORD *VERBATIM* AND CIRCLE ALL CODES THAT APPLY.

      Nothing during the last month . . . .
      Helped out when I was ill . . . .
      Helped out when my husband/wife was ill . . .
      Personal care (gave me permanent, washed
      my hair, etc.) . . . .
      Gave money or money gifts . . . .
      Gave other gifts (clothing, food, etc.) . . . . .
      Took me or sent me on holidays, vacation,
      excursions, etc. . . . .
      Provided transportation (drove me to doctor,
      grocery, sent taxi, etc.) . . . .
      Fixed things around house (home repairs,
      gardening, etc.) . . . .
      Housekeeping, housework, mending, sewing,
      cooking, laundry, etc. . . . .
      Other (SPECIFY): . . . .
      . . . .

54. A. In the last 12 months have (any/either of) your child(ren) paid any medical, dental, nursing or hospital bills for you?

Yes . . . .

No (SKIP TO Q.55). . . . .

    B. *IF YES:* About how much did these bills amount to?

About $ _____

55. In the last 12 months (have(any)(either) of your children)(has your child) given you—

    A. A regular money allowance, or paid your rent regularly or paid any other bills for you regularly?

Yes . . . .

No . . . .

    B.[1] (In addition to that) Did he/she/they give you occasional money gifts or pay the rent once in awhile?

Yes . . . .

No . . . .

V. *Norms Regarding Parent-Child Relations*

Here's a list of things some people believe. Would you tell me whether you agree or disagree with each statement? (Just give me your opinion!)

    D. Most families like to have older people around . . . .

    G. Children don't care anything about their parents except for what they get out of them . . . .

1. These items were added for the 1975 survey.

SOURCE: E. Shanas, personal communication, 1976.

V2.4.I.n

FAMILY STRUCTURE AND INTERACTION BATTERY

G. F. Streib and C. J. Schneider, 1971

I. *Family Structure*

    5. a) How many living children do you have? (WRITE THE NUMBER IN THE BLANK)

        I have_____ living children. IF NO CHILDREN, GO TO QUESTION 6.

NOW WE WOULD LIKE TO ASK YOU SOME QUESTIONS ABOUT YOUR LIFE AT PRESENT

    2. How many other people live with you in the same house or apartment?

        1__I live alone

        2__I live with my wife (or husband)

        3__Someone else lives with me also: How many others? _____

        (CHECK WHO LIVES WITH YOU—CHECK ALL THAT APPLY)

        4__Child (or children) without a family of their own live with me

        5__Child (or children) and their family live with me

        6__Grandchild (or grandchildren) live with me

        7__Other relatives—such as parents, brothers, sisters, uncles, cousins, mother-in-law, and the like

        8__Other people who are not relatives live with me

II. *Associational Solidarity*

As people grow older they sometimes see less of their relatives, although this is not always the case. We are interested in knowing how often you are in touch with your relatives.

    1. On this question, just go down the list and check how often you *see SOME* of the following relatives: (PUT A CHECK IN FRONT OF EITHER "OFTEN" OR "SOMETIMES" OR "HARDLY EVER OR NEVER" FOR EACH ITEM IN THE LIST)

How often do you see:

	(1)	(2)	(3)	(4)
Some of your children	__OFTEN	__SOMTIMES	__ HARDLY EVER OR NEVER	
Some of your brothers	__ OFTEN	__ SOMETIMES	__ HARDLY EVER OR NEVER	
Some of your sisters	__ OFTEN	__ SOMETIMES	__ HARDLY EVER OR NEVER	
Some of your grand-children		__ OFTEN __ SOMETIMES	__ HARDLY EVER OR NEVER	
Some of your nieces	__OFTEN	__ SOMETIMES	__HARDLY EVER OR NEVER	
Some of your nephews	__OFTEN	__ SOMETIMES	__HARDLY EVER OR NEVER	
Some of your cousins	__OFTEN	__ SOMETIMES	__HARDLY EVER OR NEVER	

2. ON THIS QUESTION, CHECK ONLY ONE ANSWER. How many of your children live close enough so that you can see them whenever you want to?

1__ I do not have any living children
2__ All of my children live close enough for me to see them whenever I want to
3__ Some of my children live close enough for me to see them whenever I want to
4__ None of my children live close enough for me to see them whenever I want to

3. Do you have any children whom you do *not* see often?
(CHECK ONLY ONE)

6__ I do not have any living children
7__ I see all of my children often
8__ A few of my children I do *not* see often
9__ Most of my children I do *not* see often
0__ I do *not* see *any* of my children often
X__ Some I see often, some I do not

1. On this question, just go down the list and check how often you *write SOME* of your relatives: (PUT A CHECK IN FRONT OF EITHER "OFTEN" OR "SOMETIMES" OR "HARDLY EVER OR NEVER" FOR EACH ITEM IN THE LIST)

How often do you write to:

	(9)	(0)	(X)	(Y)
Some of your children	__OFTEN	__ SOMETIMES	__ HARDLY EVER OR NEVER	
Some of your brothers	__ OFTEN	__ SOMETIMES	__ HARDLY EVER OR NEVER	
Some of your sisters	__ OFTEN	__ SOMETIMES	__ HARDLY EVER OR NEVER	
Some of your grand-children		__ OFTEN __ SOMETIMES	__ HARDLY EVER OR NEVER	
Some of your nieces	__ OFTEN	__ SOMETIMES	__ HARDLY EVER OR NEVER	
Some of your nephews	__OFTEN	__ SOMETIMES	__ HARDLY EVER OR NEVER	
Some of your cousins	__ OFTEN	__ SOMETIMES	__HARDLY EVER OR NEVER	

2. ON THIS QUESTION, CHECK AS MANY ANSWERS AS APPLY TO YOU. Do your family and relatives, either yours or your wife's, ever have any *large* family gatherings, when a lot of you get together at one time?

1__ We have no such large family gatherings
2__ We have such gatherings on national holidays such as Thanksgiving and Labor Day
3__ We have such gatherings on religious holidays such as Christmas and Easter
4__ We also have such gathers on other occasions. When? _____

3. How much do you enjoy these large family get-togethers?
(CHECK ONLY ONE)

6__ We do not have such get-togethers
7__ I enjoy them a great deal
8__ I enjoy them somewhat
9__ I enjoy them very little

    0__I do not enjoy them at all

2. How often does your immediate family get together for a meal? (CHECK ONLY ONE)

    1__My immediate family never has such get-togethers

    2__We often get together

    3__We sometimes get together

    4__We seldom get together

3. How much do you enjoy these *immediate* family get-togethers (CHECK ONLY ONE)

    6__My immediate family does not have such get-togethers

    7__I enjoy them a great deal

    8__I enjoy them somewhat

    9__I enjoy them very little

    0__I do not enjoy them at all

11. How well do you get along with your family? (CHECK ONE)

    1__We get along very well

    2__We get along fairly well

    3__We get along poorly

    4__We get along very poorly

12. How often do you worry about your family? (CHECK ONE)

    1__Often

    2__Sometimes

    3__Hardly ever

3. Have your children kept in close contact with you since leaving home? (CHECK ONLY ONE)

    1__I do not have any children

    2__My children have not left home

    3__All of my children have kept in close contact with me

    4__Some of my children have kept in close contact with me

    5__None of my children have kept in close contact with me

4. Have your children who have families of their own kept in close contact with you? (CHECK ONLY ONE)

    7__I do not have any children

    8__None of my children have families of their own

    9__All have kept in close contact with me

    0__Some have kept in close contact with me

    X__None have kept in close contact with me

5. On this question, just go down the list and check how often you *telephone SOME* of your relatives: (PUT A CHECK IN FRONT OF EITHER "OFTEN" OR "SOMETIMES" OR "HARDLY EVER OR NEVER" FOR EACH ITEM IN THE LIST)

How often do you telephone:

	(5)	(6)	(7)	(8)
Some of your children	__ OFTEN	__SOMETIMES	__HARDLY EVER OR NEVER	
Some of your brothers	__ OFTEN	__ SOMETIMES	__HARDLY EVER OR NEVER	
Some of your sisters	__ OFTEN	__ SOMETIMES	__HARDLY EVER OR NEVER	
Some of your grand-children	__ OFTEN	__SOMETIMES	__HARDLY EVER OR NEVER	
Some of your nieces	__ OFTEN	__SOMETIMES	__HARDLY EVER OR NEVER	
Some of your nephews	__ OFTEN	__SOMETIMES	__HARDLY EVER OR NEVER	
Some of your cousins	__ OFTEN	__SOMETIMES	__HARDLY EVER OR NEVER	

III. *Affectional Solidarity*

   3. Would you say that you and your children form a close family group? CHECK ONLY ONE)

      1__I do not have any children

      2__We are very close

      3__We are somewhat close

      4__We are not a close family group

  2. ON THIS QUESTION, CHECK ONLY ONE ANSWER. The way life is today my children have less respect for me than they should.

      1__ I do not have any children

      2__ I agree: they do have less respect than they should

      3__ I disagree: they respect me as much as they should

  4. How much would you like to be in touch with your children more than you are these days? (CHECK ONLY ONE)

      7__ I do not have any living children

      8__ I would like to be in touch with them a *good deal* more

      9__ I would like to be in touch with them *somewhat* more

      0__ I would *not* like to be in touch with them any more than I am

  3. Would you say that your children have been more successful in earning a living and getting ahead in life than you have been? (CHECK ONLY ONE)

      1__ I do not have any children

      2__ All of my children have been more successful

      3__ Most of my children have been more successful

      4__ Some of my children have been more successful

      5__ None of my children have been more successful

  1. Would you say that, for the most part, you have not worried about your grown-up children's affairs? (CHECK ONLY ONE)

      1__ I do not have any children

      2__ I have not worried

      3__ I have worried

      4__ Undecided

  2. Would you say that, for the most part, your children have not mixed in your affairs? (CHECK ONLY ONE)

      6__I do not have any children

      7__ My children have mixed in my affairs

      8__ My children have not mixed in my affairs

      9__ Undecided

  3. Most parents try to treat all their children alike. However, it is a very human experience to feel closer to some children than to others. Would you say that you feel closer to some of your children than to others? (CHECK ONLY ONE)

      1__I do not have any children

      2__I have only one child

      3__ I feel closer to one of my sons. Why? _____

      4__ I feel closer to one of my daughters. Why? _____

      5__ I feel closer to some of my children. Why? _____

      6__ I feel about the same towards all of my children

  4. Is there a tendency for some members of your family to keep their plans and problems to themselves, or are all personal matters discussed freely within the family? (CHECK ONLY ONE)

      1__ All personal matters are discussed freely with family members

      2__ Some personal matters are discussed with family members

3__Hardly any personal matters are discussed with family members

4__Personal matters are never discussed with other family members

5. How often do the members of your family criticize each other? (CHECK ONLY ONE)

1__We often criticize each other

2__We sometimes criticize each other

3__We seldom criticize each other

4__We never criticize each other

IV. *Exchanges of Assistance and Support*

5. Have some of your children been more successful than others in earning a living and getting ahead in life? (CHECK ONLY ONE)

1__ I do not have any children

2__I have only one child

3__One of my children has been more successful than the others

4__Some of my children have been more successful

5__ All of my children have been equally successful

6. How willing are your children to make sacrifices for you? (CHECK ONLY ONE)

6__I do not have any children

7__My children are very willing to make sacrifices for me

8__My children are somewhat willing to make sacrifices for me

9__My children are not willing to make sacrifices for me

7. Are any of your children more willing than the others to make sacrifices for you? (CHECK ONLY ONE)

1__I do not have any children

2__I have only one child

3__Yes, one child is more willing than the others to make sacrifices for me

4__Yes, some of my children are more willing than the others

5__They are all equally willing to make sacrifices

2. How many of your children have offered you financial help? (CHECK ONLY ONE)

1__ I do not have any children

2__All of them have offered financial help

3__Some of them have offered financial help

4__None of them have ever offered help

5__ I have never needed financial help

3. How often have you asked your children to give you financial help? (CHECK ONLY ONE)

7__I do not have any children

8__I have often asked for financial help

9__I have sometimes asked for financial help

0__I have never asked for financial help

X__I have never needed financial help

4. Here are a list of ways in which children may help their parents. (JUST GO DOWN THE LIST AND CHECK THE THINGS THAT YOUR CHILDREN DO FOR YOU)

1__I do not have any children

2__ Take care of parents when they are ill

3__Give advice on business or money matters

4__Visit parents frequently

5__Write parents often

6__Ask parents to visit them often

7__ Live close to their parents

8__ Give financial help
9__Provide a home for their parents
0__None of the above

5. Here are a list of ways in which parents may help their children. How many do you do for your children? (JUST GO DOWN THE LIST AND CHECK THE THINGS THAT YOU DO FOR YOUR CHILDREN)
    1__ I do not have any children
    2__Take care of children or their family when someone is ill
    3__Give advice on business or money matters
    4__Visit children frequently
    5__Write children often
    6__ Ask children to visit often
    7__ Live close to children
    8__ Give financial help
    9__ Provide a home for grown-up children
    0__ Baby-sitting and child care
    X__ None of the above

1. How much have you helped your grown-up children in their personal affairs? (CHECK ONLY ONE)
    1__ I do not have any children
    2__ I have helped my children a great deal
    3__ I have helped my children somewhat
    4__ I have helped my children a little
    5__ I have not helped my children at all

2. How much have your children helped you in your personal affairs? (CHECK ONLY ONE)
    1__ I do not have any children
    2__ My children have helped me a great deal
    3__ My children have helped me somewhat
    4__ My children have helped me a little
    5__ My children have not helped me at all

V. *Norms Regarding Parent-Child Relations*

1. How much should children be concerned with their parents' affairs? (CHECK ONLY ONE)
    6__They should not be concerned at all
    7__They should be concerned a little
    8__They should be concerned some
    9__They should be concerned a great deal

2. Here are some statements that people answer in different ways. Read each one carefully and decide whether you tend to agree or disagree with it. If you tend to agree with the statement, check *AGREE*. If you tend to disagree, check *DISAGREE*. Be sure to check something for each one.

	If You Agree (1)	If You Disagree (2)	(3)	(4)
When children are trying to make their own way in the world they should not have to help support their parents	__ AGREE	__ DISAGREE	__UNDECIDED	

	If You Agree (1)	If You Disagree (2)	(3)	(4)
When children have a job and are settled they should help out if their parents need it	__ AGREE	__DISAGREE	__UNDECIDED	
Even when children have families of their own they should help out if their parents need it	__ AGREE	__ DISAGREE	__UNDECIDED	
Children who move up in the world tend to neglect their parents	__ AGREE	__ DISAGREE	__ UNDECIDED	
When parents get older their children should help support them	__AGREE	__ DISAGREE	__ UNDECIDED	
After children have left home they should keep in close contact with their parents	__ AGREE	__DISAGREE	__UNDECIDED	
Even when children have families of their own they should keep in close contact with their parents	__ AGREE	__ DISAGREE	__UNDECIDED	
No one is going to care much what happens to you, when you get right down to it	__ AGREE	__DISAGREE	__UNDECIDED	

4. How much should parents be concerned with their grown-up children's affairs? (CHECK ONLY ONE)

1__They should not be concerned at all
2__They should be concerned a little
3__They should be concerned some
4__They should be concerned a great deal

1. Here are some statements that people answer in different ways. Reach each one carefully and decide whether you tend to agree or disagree with it. If you tend to agree with the statement, check *AGREE*. If you tend to disagree, check *DISAGREE*. *Be sure to check something for each one.*

	If You Agree (1)	If You Disagree (2)	(3)	(4)
Parents are the ones who suffer most when children move away	__AGREE	__ DISAGREE	__ UNDECIDED	
Children who move far away are not being fair to their parents	__AGREE	__ DISAGREE	__UNDECIDED	
When children move away they get different ideas and lose respect for their parents	__ AGREE	__DISAGREE	__ UNDECIDED	

	If You Agree (1)	If You Disagree (2)	(3)	(4)
When children move too far away family ties become broken	__ AGREE	__ DISAGREE	__ UNDECIDED	
When children move far away they tend to neglect financial responsibilities to their parents	__ AGREE	__ DISAGREE	__UNDECIDED	
When your children go out on their own you have to turn to your brothers and sisters if you are going to have any family ties	__ AGREE	__DISAGREE	__ UNDECIDED	
Children should not allow getting ahead in the world to interfere with their responsibilities to their parents	__ AGREE	__ DISAGREE	__ UNDECIDED	
Getting ahead in the world can be a bad thing if it keeps your family from being close	__ AGREE	__ DISAGREE	__ UNDECIDED	
Children should not allow better financial opportunities elsewhere to take them away from their parents	__ AGREE	__DISAGREE	__UNDECIDED	

BE SURE YOU CHECKED SOMETING FOR EVERY ITEM

3. If parents need financial assistance, how much should children be expected to help? (CHECK ONLY ONE)
    1__They should be expected to help a great deal
    2__They should be expected to help some
    3__They should be expected to help a little
    4__They should not be expected to help

4. What do you think is the most important thing for children to consider when choosing their life work? (CHECK ONLY ONE)
    0__Getting a job that keeps them near their family
    X__Getting ahead in life no matter where it takes them

1. (ON THIS QUESTION, CHECK AS MANY ANSWERS AS YOU THINK SHOULD BE INCLUDED) When children grow up they should:
    1__Help their parents
    2__Visit their parents frequently
    3__Write their parents often
    4__Ask their parents to visit them often
    5__Live close to their parents
    6__Take care of their parents when they are ill
    7__None of the above are important

5. ON THIS QUESTION, CHECK ONLY ONE ANSWER. Some people think that the major responsibility children have to their parents is financial; others feel that ties of affection are more important. How do you feel?

      1__ I feel that financial help from children is more important than ties of affection
      2__ I feel that ties of affection are more important than financial help
      3__ I feel that they are equally important

6. If you had a son or daughter graduating from high school would you prefer that he or she go on to college, or would you prefer that he or she take a good job? (CHECK ONLY ONE)

      0__ I would prefer my children to go on to college
      X__ I would prefer my children to take a good job

1. Here are some statements that people answer in different ways. Read each one carefully and decide whether you tend to agree or disagree with it. If you tend to agree with the statement, check *AGREE*. If you tend to disagree, check *DISAGREE*. *Be sure to check something for each one.*

      1__ I feel that financial help from children is more important than ties of affection
      2__ I feel that ties of affection are more important than financial help
      3__ I feel that they are equally important

1. ON THIS QUESTION CHECK AS MANY ANSWERS AS YOU THINK SHOULD BE INCLUDED. When children grow up, they should:

      1__ Take care of parents when they are ill
      2__ Give advice on business or money matters
      3__ Visit parents frequently
      4__ Write parents often
      5__ Ask parents to visit them often
      6__ Live close to their parents
      7__ Give parents financial help
      8__ Provide a home for their parents
      9__ None of the above

SOURCE: G. F. Streib and C. J. Schneider. *Retirement in American Society*, Appendix II. Ithaca, N.Y.: Cornell University Press, 1971. Copyright by Cornell University. Used by permission of publisher and author.

V2.4.I.o

MARRIED OFFSPRING-PARENT ADJUSTMENT CHECKLIST

S. Stryker, 1955

1. I love him very much
2. I rarely call on him for help
3. I find myself imitating him often
4. He often nags me
5. No love lost between us
6. Confide in him often
7. He does many things I would not do
8. Never any tension between us
9. Very fond of him
10. Seems to be a wall between us
11. I understand his moods
12. He criticizes me when I don't deserve it
13. Don't have the warm feeling for him that I do for others
14. Can always turn to him when I have a problem
15. Wouldn't particularly care to be like him

16. We rarely argue or fight
17. Have strong feelings of affection for him
18. We go our own ways
19. Believe in him completely
20. Sometimes I get angry with him
21. Can't really say I'm overly fond of him
22. Keep no secrets from him
23. We don't think alike
24. Never annoys me by what he says
25. Being with him gives me a warm feeling
26. Have grown away from him
27. Would like to be more like him if I could
28. Often feel upset after I'm with him
29. Love is too strong a word for our relationship
30. We're as close as any pair can be
31. I often disapprove of what he does
32. He never nags me
33. Can't help feeling sentimental about him
34. I can't always tell him what I think
35. He serves as a model for me
36. He's too curious about what I do
37. Have little feeling for him, one way or the other
38. Never have to worry about what I say to him
39. We have little in common
40. He rarely finds fault with what I do

Items 1, 5, 9, 13, 17, 21, 25, 29, 33, 37 are the affection items.
The intimacy items are 2, 6, 10, 14, 18, 22, 26, 30, 34, 38.
Sympathy items are 3, 7, 11, 15, 19, 23, 27, 31, 35, 39.
(Sympathy was defined in the sense of "ego-involvement.")
Items 4, 8, 12, 16, 20, 24, 28, 32, 36, 40 are the tension items.

SOURCE: S. Stryker. "Attitude Ascription in Adult Married Offspring-Parent Relationships: A Study of Implications of the Social Psychological Theory of G. H. Mead." Ph.D. dissertation, University of Minnesota, 1955.

V2.4.I.p

DEPENDENCE CHECKLIST

S. Stryker, 1955

1. I win our arguments most of the time
2. I always do as he says
3. He's pretty much of a follower, rather than a leader
4. I rely on him a lot
5. Asks my advice more than I ask his
6. I think of him as a leader
7. If we differ, I can generally convince him that I'm right
8. He makes the decisions in things we're both involved in
9. He relies on me more than I do on him
10. I find that I often call on him to help me make my decisions

These items, incidently, were interspersed among the adjustment index when used.

SOURCE: S. Stryker. "Attitude Ascription in Adult Married Offspring-Parent Relationships: A Study of Implications of the Social Psychological Theory of G. H. Mead." Ph.D. dissertation, University of Minnesota, 1955.

V2.4.I.q

INTERGENERATIONAL FAMILY CONTINUITY RATING SCALE

M. B. Sussman, 1960

This instrument is not available at this time.

Chapter 5

Kinship Relations

Charles H. Mindel

For elderly individuals the nature and quality of their relationships with kin are a crucial aspect of life. Assessing how well an elderly individual is integrated into his or her family and kinship system is essential to gaining an understanding of the quality of life and the well-being of that elderly person. The study of kinship relations (i.e., the investigation of the nature and organization of the relationships of individuals to their socially defined relatives) has a fairly long history in American sociology and an even longer one in anthropology. In American sociology, this field of interest has long been considered a subspecialty within the field of family sociology. It has, however, overlapped at many points with social gerontology. Researchers in both family sociology and social gerontology have been concerned with the nature of relationships between parents and children; this interest has given rise to studies of the visiting patterns and the support systems that exist among various kin members that attempt to demonstrate the existence and persistence of kinship systems.

In reviews of the literature in the area of kinship relations, in particular as they are related to studies of the aged, it is possible to divide the field into three broad areas. First is the area that might be called kinship structure. Within this broad category are numbers of studies that have estimated how many kin an individual has, how often the individual is in contact with those kin, and/or how geographically close those kin are to the individual. This area is a crucial one for analyzing the nature of family relations in a society. An estimation of these factors in some way is a sine qua non for understanding everything about kinship relations. As a result, numerous studies have attempted to provide such estimates.

Kinship studies can also be categorized as investigations of kinship solidarity, another area in which much concern has been shown. Aside from counting the number of kin that an individual is in contact with or has available, there has been concern with the level of integration or the nature of the ties that are maintained with relatives. For example, Bardis (1959) defined *familism* as incorporating strong in-group feelings, an emphasis on family goals, common property, and a desire to perpetuate the family. Researchers have often sought to arrange types of families along some continuum from extended family orientation to nuclear family orientation. Unlike measures developed to account for kinship structure, measures of kinship solidarity and extended familism have most often been attitudinal in design.

The third and last area of kinship research is more diffuse and less easily defined than the other areas. It might be called studies on kinship norms and on relations among older persons and their families. Measures that have fallen into this category have often involved the question of conflict among family members. Kerckhoff (1966) and Mindel (1977), for example, developed measures that pursue the problems of potential conflict in the family.

Although there has frequently been an overlap between research on kinship as a family sociology specialty and research on kinship as an aspect of gerontology, it is clear from a review of the research literature that most studies on kinship relations have not used the elderly person as the primary focus. An overwhelming majority of the studies of kinship relations have been done on younger populations. This is not to say that these studies have not been concerned with the elderly; it is only that information concerning relationships with the elderly members of the family has been provided by the younger generations. All of the research instruments discussed in this chapter are applicable, with either no change or only slight modifications, to an elderly population. Thus, in spite of the historical orientation of kinship studies toward younger respondents, the research instruments that have been developed can easily be applied to an elderly population. It must be noted, however, that reliability analyses of the measures that have been done on younger populations may not be applicable when the measures are used on older populations. New reliability analyses should be conducted and reported.

Instruments Reviewed

In the following pages, 23 research instruments, categorized into the three areas just discussed, are reviewed. It appears from an evaluation of this relatively large number of research instruments that the concerns of reliability and validity are not often dealt with in the published literature. For some of the research instruments, the problem of validity and reliability was not severe because the goals of the research were often simple. Frequently, however, the indexes and scales that are examined lack validation and estimates of their reliability. It is hoped that through the use of this material by future researchers these instruments can be validated and tested for reliability. (See Table 5.1.)

Measures of Kinship Structure

Several of the scales on kinship structure are concerned with similar matters, mainly, the frequency of interaction with kin. Swarzweller and Seggar's Kinship Involvement index, Cumming and Henry's Frequency of Interaction with Relatives Scale, Bultena's Familial Interaction Index, and Berardo's Kin Interaction index are all very similar in that they try to develop a single score that indicates the average frequency of visiting with kin. Berardo's Kin Interaction index is useful in inventories of kin, that is, when the researcher is interested in the frequency of interaction with a particular relative or set of relatives. Swarzweller and Seggar's Kinship Involvement index defines the kin to be used in the calculation as those who live within a 50-mile radius of the subject's place of residence. For this measure, the frequency of visits is converted to a yearly basis. The sum total of visits among kin divided by the total number of close kin families in the area yields an average visiting frequency. Bultena's Familial Interaction Index and Cumming and Henry's Frequency of Interaction with Relatives scale are very closely related. Both take a specified group of kin and convert their frequency of interaction into a weighted score. On the Cumming and Henry scale, the weights correspond to the number of days per month that a relative is seen by the subject. Bultena, in his modification of the Cumming and Henry measure, gave less weight to daily interaction and more weight to less frequent visiting.

The Patrilineage Integration Index (Hutter, 1970) is a somewhat similar measure of kinship interaction. It differs from the others in that, in addition to a frequency score, an enjoyment score is calculated to measure the quality of the interaction among kin. Unfortunately, it seems that little work was done on establishing the validity of this measure.

Aldous and Straus's (1966) Kinship Integration and Network Connectedness index is a measure that moves one step beyond a simple measure of interaction among kin. It attempts to measure the proportion of an individual's social life that involves relatives by calculating the ratio of relatives to nonrelatives with whom an individual regularly interacts. This measure also suffers from a lack of testing with respect to its reliability and validity.

Sweetser's (1970) Sibling Communication Scale constitutes another attempt to measure the quality of interaction with kin as well as the frequency of interaction. Interaction on this scale is defined as more than face-to-face interaction. Sweetser's scale also has the added value of having some formal validation. Her sample, however, consisted of Norwegian married couples; further validation probably should be done on American couples as well.

The last measure in this category of research instruments is the one developed by Winch, Greer, and Blumbers (1967). In fact, this measure is not a single measure at all but actually four different measures of what Winch called "extended familism." In spite of the fact that the measure is called Extended Familism (and so it might be more properly categorized with measures of kinship solidarity), this measure is included under measures of kinship structure because three of its four dimensions concern structural aspects of kinship (the fourth deals with mutual aid and support). This measure, or set of measures, is not a scale but a rather reliable measure of kinship presence. In one measure, they encompass most of the important dimensions of kinship. The investigators provided no validity checks, but they assumed that the measures are accurate reflections of the important dimensions underlying extended familism. The primary difficulty with this measure is its lack of a qualitative measure of familism, which is perhaps incorporated into Hutter's Patrilineage Integration Index.

Measures of Kinship Solidarity and Extended Familism

In the second category of instruments are the measures of kinship solidarity and extended familism. The nine research instruments that fall into this category are all basically attitudinal measures; that is, they all attempt to tap certain feelings about the importance of family and kin in an individual's life. Seven of the instruments either are scales or are scalelike in construction. One instrument is a single-item measure, and one is a battery of attitudinal items used in the accumulation of a kinship inventory. The most adequate in terms of tested reliability and validity are the Familism Scale by Bardis (1959), the

Kinship Orientation scale by Rogers and Sebald (1955; 1962), and (to a lesser extent) the Extended Family Orientation scale developed by Litwak (1960) and subsequently used by Stuckert (1963).

Bardis's (1959) Familism Scale does not concern itself solely with extended familism but with familism in general, namely, with strong in-group feelings, emphasis on family goals, common property, and desire to perpetuate the family. It also has a strong international flavor, which does not always seem especially appropriate for use with American populations.

Rogers and Sebald's (1962) Kinship Orientation scale attempts to break down the concept of familism into two components: family integration and kinship orientation. The measures that they developed to measure these two components support their view that familism can be divided into these orthogonal dimensions.

Reiss (1962) developed a single-item measure ("If you had it within your power to have your relatives reside where you wanted, which would you set up as the most ideal arrangement?"). This question is followed by a set of choices of different geographical distances ranging from living in a distant city to living in the same neighborhood. This measure is included with the familism measures primarily because of its attitudinal nature, which is unlike the primarily demographic nature of the measures in the first group of research instruments. Though interitem reliability is not relevant for this measure, it certainly should be asked whether or not using a single item concerning the residence of relatives is the most reliable and valid method of examining the nature of familism.

Farber (1971) developed an attitudinal instrument consisting of 12 items that tapped the relationships of individuals with their relatives. A factor analysis indicated that these 12 items formed a general factor probably best identified by the single item concerning how close an individual feels to a particular relative. Farber himself chose to use that single item in his analysis, rather than all 12 items, but the different questions do tap different aspects of relationships with kin and would probably be a useful instrument in understanding kinship relations.

Kerckhoff (1965) attempted to examine the relationships among normative aspects of extended family relationships by using the Mutual Aid and Affection Index and the behavioral aspects of extended family relationships by using the Mutual Support Index. Both of these measures are quite interesting conceptually, although Kerckhoff did not provide any information on formal tests of reliability or validity. However, he did make a considerable effort to provide a theoretical justification for the types of items that are included in the scale.

Measures of Kinship Norms and the Quality of Relationships

The third and last set of research instruments covers the area of kinship norms and the quality of relationships. These instruments are concerned less with the support systems and visiting patterns of the elderly and more with the nature of the relationships among various family members. Six research instruments in this category are reviewed.

With his measure Reasons for Keeping in Touch with Parents, Adams (1968) attempted to investigate the obligatory nature of kinship relations. This four-item index attempts to measure the reasons why individuals maintain contact with their kin.

Robertson and Wood's (1970) Meaning of Grandparenthood scale and Robertson's (1976) Significance of Grandparents scale do not appear to have been tested with respect to their reliability and validity. The subject, however, is an important one, and these instruments seem to offer many suggestions for studies in this area.

The Index of Perceived Conflict developed by Kerckhoff (1966) consists of a six-item set of statements concerning the potential for problems in the relationships between children and their parents. This scale is quite usable on an elderly population. Although Kerckhoff provided no tests of reliability for this scale, he did demonstrate a certain amount of validity for it in that it was moderately correlated with three other closely related measures. Questions concerning the internal consistency and homogeneity of the items still remain.

Stuckert's (1963) Extended Family as a Reference Group scale is a five-item Guttman scale. It could be a useful measure for an important and relatively unrecognized area of family influence, namely, kin as a reference group.

Mindel's (1977) Attitudes toward Multigenerational Households scale provides a measure useful for a specific concern with multigenerational families. It was tested on an elderly population as well as on a younger population, and it deals with attitudes toward living in multigenerational households, a relatively unstudied area in family relations.

Summary

In an examination of the literature on kinship relations and aging, several points clearly emerge concerning the adequacy of current measurement techniques. Specifically, researchers have been lax in their willingness to test their measures for reliability and validity and to report their conclusions. Some measures—those that are not summative scales, for example—do not lend themselves to reliability tests of internal consistency, but they can be tested by test-retest and interrater reliability techniques. Perhaps even more important is the lack of validity testing. Various methods exist—factor analysis, correlation to a criterion, for example—but generally these remain unused. Decisions on the use of a particular instrument should not be made solely on the basis of face or content validity. The validity of many measures often suffers because of the researchers' poor explication of the conceptual basis for the construct. A clearer theoretical justification of the measures would be a major step toward improving measurement techniques. In far too many works, authors and editors fail to include complete descriptions of the scales and indexes or they do not indicate their sources and where they can be located. More careful documentation of measures would be an important contribution to reducing the proliferation of untested and redundant instrumentation. What we need is refinement of existing measures rather than new measures.

TABLE 5-1
Instruments Reviewed in Chapter 5

Instrument	Author(s)	Code Number
I. Kinship Structure		
a. Kinship Involvement	Swarzweller and Seggar (1967)	No special material
b. Patrilineage Integration Index	Hutter (1970)	Single-item indicator
c. Kinship Integration and Network Connectedness	Aldous and Straus (1966)	Singe-item indicator
d. Sibling Communication Scale	Sweetser (1970)	Reproduced in abstract
e. Frequency of Interaction with Relatives Scale	Cumming and Henry (1961)	Single-item indicator
f. Familial Interaction Index	Bultena (1969)	Single-item indicator
g. Kin Interaction	Berardo (1966)	Single-item indicator
h. Extended Familism	Winch, Greer, and Blumberg (1967)	Reproduced in abstract
II. Kinship Solidarity and Extended Familism		
a. Measure of Kinship Orientation	Farber (1971)	V2.5.II.a

TABLE 5-1—*Continued*

Instrument	Author(s)	Code Number
b. Kinship Orientation	Rogers and Sebald (1955; 1962)	V2.5.II.b
c. Familism Index	Mapstone (1970)	V2.5.II.c
d. Familism Scale	Bardis (1959)	V2.5.II.d
e. Preferred Location of Residence of Kin	Reiss (1962)	Single-item indicator
f. Extended Family Orientation	Litwak (1960)	V2.5.II.f
g. Participation in the Extended Family	Key (1961)	V2.5.II.g
h. Mutual Aid and Affection Index	Kerckhoff (1965)	V2.5.II.h
i. Mutual Support Index	Kerckhoff (1965)	V2.5.II.i
III. Kinship Norms and the Quality of Relationships		
a. Reasons for Keeping in Touch with Parents	Adams (1968)	V2.5.III.a
b. Meaning of Grandparenthood	Robertson and Wood (1970)	V2.5.III.b
c. Index of Perceived Conflict	Kerckhoff (1966)	V2.5.III.c
d. Significance of Grandparents	Robertson (1976)	V2.5.III.d
e. Extended Family as a Reference Group	Stuckert (1963)	V2.5.III.e
f. Attitudes toward Multi-generational Households	Mindel (1977)	V2.5.III.f

REFERENCES

Adams, B. N. *Kinship in an Urban Setting*. Chicago: Markham, 1968.

Aldous, J., and M. A. Straus. "Social Networks and Conjugal Roles: A Test of Bott's Hypothesis." *Social Forces*, 1966, 44: 576-80.

Bardis, P. D. "A Familism Scale." *Marriage and Family Living*, 1959, 21: 340-41.

Berardo, F. "Kinship Interaction in Migrant Adaptation in an Aerospace Related Community." *Journal of Marriage and the Family*, 1966, 28: 296-304.

Bultena, G. L. "Rural-Urban Differences in the Familial Interaction of the Aged." *Rural Sociology*, 1969, 34: 5-15.

Cumming, E., and W. E. Henry. *Growing Old*. New York: Basic Books, 1961.

Farber, B. *Kinship and Class: A Midwestern Study*. New York: Basic Books, 1971.

Hutter, M. "Transformation of Identity, Social Mobility, and Kinship Solidarity." *Journal of Marriage and the Family*, 1970, 32: 133-37.

Kerckhoff, A. C. "Nuclear and Extended Family Relationships: A Normative and Behavioral Analysis." In *Social Structure and the Family: Generational Relations*, E. Shanas and G. F. Streib (eds.), pp. 93-112. Englewood Cliffs, N.J.: Prentice-Hall, 1965.

Kerckhoff, A. C. "Norm Value Clusters and the 'Strain toward Consistency' among Older Married Couples." In *Social Aspects of Aging*, I. H. Simpson and J. C. McKinney (eds.), pp. 138-59. Durham, N.C.: Duke University Press, 1966.

Key, W. H. "Rural-Urban Differences and the Family." *Sociological Quarterly*, 1961, 2: 49-56.

Litwak, E. "Occupational Mobility and Extended Family Cohesion." *American Sociological Review*, 1960, 25: 9-21.

Mapstone, J. R. "Familistic Determinants of Property Acquisition." *Journal of Marriage and the Family*, 1970, 32: 143-50.

Mindel, C. H. "A Multiple Regression Approach to Satisfaction in Multigenerational Households." Paper presented to the 30th Annual Meeting of the Gerontological Society, San Francisco, November 18-22, 1977.

Reiss, P. J. "The Extended Kinship System: Correlates of and Attitudes on Frequency of Interaction." *Marriage and Family Living,* 1962, 24: 333-39.

Robertson, J. "Significance of Grandparents: Perceptions of Young Adult Grandchildren." *The Gerontologist*, 1976, 16: 137-40.

Robertson, J., and V. Wood. "Grandparenthood: A Study of Role Conceptions." Paper presented to the 23rd Annual Meeting of the Gerontological Society, Toronto, October 22-24, 1970.

_____. "Grandparenthood: A Study of Role Conceptions of Grandmothers." Ph.D. dissertation, University of Minnesota, 1971.

Rogers, E. M., and H. Sebald. "Familism, Family Integration and Kinship Orientation." *Marriage and Family Living*, 1962, 24: 25-30.

Stuckert, R. "Occupational Mobility and Family Relationships." *Social Forces*, 1963, 41: 301-7.

Swarzweller, H. K., and J. F. Seggar. "Kinship Involvement: A Factor in the Adjustment of Rural Migrants." *Journal of Marriage and the Family*, 1967, 29: 662-71.

Sweetser, D. A. "The Structure of Sibling Relationships." *American Journal of Sociology*, 1970, 76: 17-58.

Wilkening, E. A. *Adoption of Farm Practices as Related to Family Factors.* Madison: University of Wisconsin Agricultural Experiment Station, Bulletin 183, 1953.

Winch, R. "Some Observations on Extended Familism in the U. S." In *Selected Studies in Marriage and the Family*, R. F. Winch and L. W. Goodman (eds.), pp. 127-38. New York: Holt, Rinehart and Winston, 1968.

Winch, R., and S. Greer. "Urbanism, Ethnicity, and Extended Familism." *Journal of Marriage and the Family*, 1968, 30: 40-45.

Winch, R., S. Greer, and R. C. Blumberg."Ethnicity and Extended Familism in an Upper-Middle Class Suburb." *American Sociological Review*, 1967, 32: 265-72.

Wood, V., and J. Robertson. *A Study of Grandparenthood*. Madison: Institute of Gerontology at the University of Wisconsin, 1971.

Abstracts

KINSHIP INVOLVEMENT

H. K. Swarzweller and J. F. Seggar, 1967

Definition of Concept

The degree of an individual's interaction with nearby kin is assessed.

Description of Instrument

Subjects are asked to list all of their close relatives who live outside their household, including parents, parents-in-law, siblings, siblings-in-law, and adult children. Then, information on the frequency of exchanging visits and the residential location of each family unit is obtained. The *effective kinship group* is defined as kin families within a 50-mile radius of the subject's place of residence.

Method of Administration

The measure is administered as an interview schedule.

Development and Subsequent Use

This measure was developed as part of a study of the migration of families from rural to urban regions. It is part of the large literature on the viability and usefulness of kin relationships in modern society.

Sample

This particular measure has been used only by Swarzweller, Brown, and Mangalam (1971) on a sample of 161 white men and women of various ages from the Appalachian region of the United States.

Scoring, Scale Norms, and Distribution

The frequency of visits is converted to a yearly basis. The sum total of visits among relatives divided by the total number of close kin families in the area yields an average visiting frequency. For migrants this kinship involvement measure is interpreted as an indicator of the degree of interaction maintained with kinsfolk in the area of destination and, indirectly, of the strength of familial bonds within the kinship circle. The score is dichotomized at about the median point, so that migrants included in the high category are those who visit with close kin on an average of more than once a week.

Formal Tests of Reliability

Cross-checking of the information on location and visiting frequency was done. "Since the residence locations of all persons in the population were known by the researchers, interview data could be and were subjected to rigorous reliability checks" (Swarzweller and Seggar, 1967).

Formal Tests of Validity

The researchers pointed out that "the simple fact of 'seeing' kinsfolk—in many ways, a reinforcement ritual—is a valid indication that some degree of familistic sentiment or cohesion, some form of attachment to extended family group exists" (Swarzweller and Seggar, 1967). They also pointed out that the duration, intensity, and content of the interaction were not taken into account.

Usability on Older Populations

Though the instrument was developed on younger populations, it appears to be usable on older populations as well.

General Comments and Recommendations

This measure is one of many measures developed to tap interaction with kin. It is a good measure because it provides a summary source based on information on individual kin rather than merely a summary of "how often do you visit your kin?"

References

Swarzweller, H. K., J. S. Brown, and J. J. Mangalam. *Mountain Families in Transition*. University Park, Pa.: Pennsylvania State University Press, 1971.

Swarzweller, H. K., and J. F. Seggar. "Kinship Involvement: a Factor in the Adjustment of Rural Migrants." *Journal of Marriage and the Family*, 1967, 29:622-71.

Instrument

See the description of the instrument given above.

PATRILINEAGE INTEGRATION INDEX

M. Hutter, 1970

Definition of Concept

Integration into a patrilineal and/or matrilineal kin group is examined.

Description of Instrument

The Patrilineage Integration Index takes into account both the frequency of interaction with an individual's father's kin and the individual's enjoyment of each interaction.

Method of Administration

The index is administered by questionnaire, but it can also be used in an interview schedule.

Development and Subsequent Use

The index has been used in cross-cultural research on the family, e.g., Hutter's (1970) comparison of Japanese and Western family structure.

Sample

This index was developed cross-culturally. A sample of 75 students in the United States and 56 in Japan was used in the study.

Scoring, Scale Norms, and Distribution

The index is obtained by first adding the number of times that the respondent visited the father's brothers, sisters, and parents. The question used to obtain this information is: "When you last lived at home, how many times did you see . . . ?" (0 scored for never; 1 for less than once in three years; 2 for every two or three years; 5 for four or eight times a year; 6 for once or twice a month; 7 for three or more times a month). The scores for each brother, sister, and parents are summed. For each enjoyment score, the respondent is asked to indicate for each of his father's brothers, sisters, and parents an answer to the question: "How much did you like . . . ?" (0 scored for dislike a great deal; 1 for dislike considerably; 2 for dislike somewhat; 3 for dislike a little; 4 for like a little; 5 for like somewhat; 6 for like considerably; 7 for like extremely well). Finally, the Patrilineage Integration Index is computed by multiplying the sum of the visiting scores by the sum of the liking scores. The rationale behind this scoring system is that the concept of integration implies that there is interaction and that the interaction has positive value to the persons involved.

Formal Tests of Validity

The index's face validity is based on the rationale that integration implies that there is interaction and that this interaction has positive value for the persons involved.

Usability on Older Populations

The instrument could be usable if the wording of the questions were changed somewhat.

General Comments and Recommendations

The validity of this scale rests on the untested assumption that family integration implies interaction. It would be useful to develop some indications of its relationship to other measures in order to provide criterion or convergent validity.

Reference

Hutter, M. "Transformation of Identity, Social Mobility, and Kinship Solidarity." *Journal of Marriage and the Family*, 1970, 32: 133-37.

Instrument

See the scoring, scale norms, and distribution described above.

KINSHIP INTEGRATION AND NETWORK CONNECTEDNESS

J. Aldous and M. A. Straus, 1966

Definition of Concept

(1) Kinship integration is measured by the proportion of an individual's social life that involves relatives. (2) Network connectedness is measured by the extent to which an individual's friends are friends of each other.

Description of Instrument

Respondents are asked to give the first names of the eight people they "most often visit socially" and to indicate whether each of these people is their spouses' kin. Respondents are then asked to indicate for each person on the list how many of the other seven that person visits socially. The Kinship Integration Index (Aldous and Straus, 1966) is the number (ranging from 0 to 8) of those listed who are relatives. Separate scores can be computed for consanguineal and affinial kin integration. The Network Connectedness Index (Aldous and Straus, 1966) is the sum of the number of others on the list whom each respondent visits, divided by 7.

Method of Administration

The indexes are administered in interview schedules or questionnaires.

Development and Subsequent Use

The indexes were developed as tests of Bott's (1957) hypothesis on social networks and conjugal roles.

Sample

This measure was developed in a study of 391 women who were of blue- or white-collar socioeconomic status.

Usability on Older Populations

The indexes can be used on older populations

General Comments and Recommendations

These indexes appear to have a certain level of face validity and are easy to use. They probably should not be used as general measures of kinship interaction because of the restriction on the number of kin that can be mentioned.

References

Aldous, J., and M. A. Straus. "Social Networks and Conjugal Roles: A Test of Bott's Hypothesis." *Social Forces*, 1966, 44: 576-80.
Bott, E. *Family and Social Network*. London: Tavistock, 1957.

Instrument

See the description of the instrument given above.

SIBLING COMMUNICATION SCALE

D. A. Sweetser, 1970

Definition of Concept

The frequency of interaction between adult siblings is measured.

Description of Instrument

A communication scale is constructed from three items: (1) whether or not the respondent reported that he or she and the sibling visited each other without special invitations; (2) whether or not they had seen and talked with each other during the last month; and (3) whether or not they had talked on the phone during the last month. Scores range from 0 to 3 according to the number of items receiving an affirmative response.

Development and Subsequent Use

The study by Sweetser (1970) examined the nature of sibling relationships. It was concerned with the (presumed) greater involvement of females in ties with relatives.

Sample

Sweetser interviewed 200 Norwegian married couples. The median age for husbands was 45; for wives, 25.

Formal Tests of Validity

Face Validity: Sweetser felt that the items had a strong underlying unidimensional component and that they pertained to an aspect of interaction that is not a priori a sex-specialized task, as are such things as babysitting.

Convergent Validity: 92% of respondent-sibling relationships with a 0 score on communication were marked by the absence of any affirmative answers to other sibling contact items. This figure declined to 49% for those with a score of 3 on communication.

Usability on Older Populations

The scale seems to be usable on an older population.

Sensitivity to Age Differences

Aspects of communication assumed in this scale include physical mobility, a potential problem with extremely old respondents.

General Comments and Recommendations

The scale is a brief measure of sibling interaction that could be quite useful in a study of elderly populations. Sweetser demonstrated some validity for the scale, although correlational evidence is lacking. No reliability data are provided.

Reference

Sweetser, D. A. "The Structure of Sibling Relationships." *American Journal of Sociology*, 1970, 76: 17-58.

Instrument

See the description of the instrument given above.

FREQUENCY OF INTERACTION WITH RELATIVES SCALE

E. Cumming and W. Henry, 1961

Definition of Concept

The frequency of interaction with relatives is examined.

Description of Instrument

This measure reflects the number of days in a month that a relative is seen by the respondent.

Method of Administration

The scale is administered as an interview schedule.

Development and Subsequent Use

This scale was actually part of a "lifespace measure" used by Cumming and Henry (1961) to test their theory of disengagement. The lifespace measure itself consisted of six elements, with the relatives scale being but one element.

Sample

Cumming and Henry (1961) studied 107 white males and 104 white females aged 50 to 75 and from the working and middle classes of Kansas City. Of these middle-aged and elderly individuals, 8% were never married, 20% were widowed, and 72% were married. All were free of chronic illness.

Scoring, Scale Norms, and Distribution

For each relative mentioned by the respondent as being "close," the frequency of interaction is scored as follows: if seen every day, score 30; if seen once a week, score 4; if seen a few times a month, score 3; if seen once a month, score 1; and if seen anything less, score 0.

Usability on Older Populations

This measure was developed on, and used with, an older population.

General Comments and Recommendations

This index is one of many that measure the frequency of interaction with kin. The score values reflect the number of days a relative is seen per month. Bultena (1969) modified this method to give greater weight to weekly and monthly contact, arguing that, qualitatively, daily contact should not be weighed so highly. In light of the fact that Bultena provided no empirical justification or strong theoretical backing for his set of weights, the Cumming and Henry measure has a more solid behavioral foundation, since it makes fewer assumptions about the imputed quality of interaction frequency.

References

Bultena, G. L. "Rural-Urban Differences in the Familial Interaction of the Aged." *Rural Sociology*, 1969, 34: 5-15.

Cumming, E., and W. Henry. *Growing Old*. New York: Basic Books, 1961.

Instrument

See the scoring, scale norms, and distribution described above.

FAMILIAL INTERACTION INDEX

G. L. Bultena, 1969

Definition of Concept

The frequency of face-to-face familial interaction is assessed.

Description of Instrument

The frequency with which respondents see each of their adult children and their siblings is ascertained. A cumulative score that provides a measure of the overall degree of personal contact between the respondents and their children and siblings is obtained.

Method of Administration

The index is part of an interview schedule.

Development and Subsequent Use

The study (Bultena, 1969) was an investigation of rural-urban differences in familial interaction. Bultena regarded the measure as an improvement over the Cumming and Henry (1961) measure, which weighs the degree of interaction at different levels.

Sample

This measure was used on a sample of 507 older (64 and over) persons residing in four rural communities and one urban community in Wisconsin (374 respondents were rural, and 133 were urban).

Scoring, Scale Norms, and Distribution

The index is scored in the following way: 25 points for each child or sibling seen daily; 19 points for each child or sibling seen several times a week; 16 points for each child or sibling seen once a week; 9 points for each child or sibling seen several times a month; 7 points for each child or sibling seen once a month; 4 points for each child or sibling seen several times a year; 2 points for each child or sibling seen once a year; and 1 point for each child or sibling seen less than once a year. The points are summed to obtain the interaction score. Median score for the rural sample was 19 and for the urban, 20.

Usability on Older Populations

This index was devised for use on an elderly population.

General Comments and Recommendations

Bultena developed a means of measuring interaction with children and siblings for an elderly population. He provided a rationale for departing from the method used by Cumming and Henry (1961) in that he gave greater weight to weekly and monthly contact vis-à-vis daily contact. Neither technique appears to have sound empirical justification, and both have only limited theoretical backing. The scale does provide a useful summary measure of familial interaction, one of the few measures on this subject devised specifically for an elderly population.

References

Bultena, G. L. "Rural-Urban Differences in the Familial Interaction of the Aged." *Rural Sociology*, 1969, 34: 5-15.

Cumming, E., and W. Henry. *Growing Old*. New York: Basic Books, 1961.

Instrument

See the scoring, scale norms, and distribution described above.

KIN INTERACTION

F. Berardo, 1966

Definition of Concept

The frequency of interaction with selected relatives is assessed.

Description of Instrument

In this single-item measure respondents are asked, "How often, on the average, do you see your _____ (relative) _____ who lives in (outside) Florida (or whatever state the study is being done in)?" Response categories range from every day to less often than every three years.

Method of Administration

The measure is part of an interview schedule, but it could be used in a questionnaire.

Development and Subsequent Use

This is one of many studies on the effects of industrialization and social and geographical mobility on kinship relations.

Sample

This study was based on 1,093 (821 female and 272 male) married, middle-class individuals under the age of 40 who lived in Florida.

Usability on Older Populations

The instrument is usable on an older population for determining the extent of kin interaction.

General Comments and Recommendations

This is one of many similar instruments measuring a basic component of kinship relations. It is a more complete measure than some in that it inventories all the kin. Other measures are much less time-consuming but also less accurate, and they measure the extent of interaction with categories of kin taken as a whole. Kin inventories on interaction and other facts take enormous amounts of time, but the information obtained is invaluable. The shorter version (i.e., using categories of kin) is probably used more often, and the results are obtained more quickly and cheaply. The main reliability problem lies in requiring respondents to summarize the frequency of interaction in retrospect. Kin inventories of this nature are perhaps the most valid way of summarizing kinship interaction.

Reference

Berardo, F. "Kinship Interaction in Migrant Adaptation in an Aerospace Related Community." *Journal of Marriage and the Family*, 1966, 28: 296-304.

Instrument

See the description of the instrument given above.

EXTENDED FAMILISM

R. Winch, S. Greer and R. C. Blumberg, 1967

Definition of Concept

This is a multidimensional approach to extended familism—relationships with kin.

Description of Instrument

Extended Familism is not a scale but a comprehensive measure of four dimensions of the concept: (1) extensity of presence (availability of kin), (2) intensity of presence (presence of intimate kin), (3) interaction (contact with kin), and (4) functionality (mutual aid). (1) Extensity of presence—number of households of kin in the community (none = 0; some = 1-8; high = 9+). (2) Intensity of presence—degree of kin present in the community (none = no kin in the community; high = both respondent and spouse have households of nuclear kin of orientation and extended kin in community; some = presence of kin but not satisfying the conditions of the high category). (3) Interaction—number of categories of households of kin with which some member of the respondent's household has been in contact (face to face, by phone, or by mail) at least monthly (none = 0; some = 1-3; high = 4+). (4) Functionality—number of categories of service either given and/or received from kinsfolk (some = 1-2; high = 3+).

The investigators did not report the categories of households of kin, the categories of interaction, or the categories of service (in functionality).

Method of Administration

The measure is part of an interview, but it could be used in a questionnaire.

Development and Subsequent Use

It was developed to measure differences in extended familism among geographical, religious, and ethnic groups.

Sample

The original data were gathered from 513 individuals representing a cross section of the population in Wisconsin and the Chicago metropolitan area (Winch, Greer, and Blumberg, 1967).

Usability on Older Populations

The instrument was used on a statewide probability sample, but it could be used on an exclusively older population if the intensity of the presence measure were modified to include kin in family of procreation.

General Comments and Recommendations

This is one of the few attempts at making a comprehensive measurement of extended familism, i.e., one that examines the availability of kin, the presence of important kin, and interaction and mutual aid. Thus, it has much to commend it. Interaction is measured somewhat differently than in other studies; i.e., Winch measures it in terms of the "number of households of kin with which some members are in contact" (face to face, by phone or mail) monthly. Usually, interaction is measured by asking how often a kin member or a category of kin is seen, with the range being an ordinal measurement of time. There is some question about the validity of these measures, since, apparently, no attempts have been made to validate the measures.

References

Mindel, C. H. "Extended Kinship Relations among Urban Mexican Americans, Anglos and Blacks." *Hispanic Journal of Behavioral Science*, 1980, 2: 21-34.
Winch, R. "Some Observations on Extended Familism in the U.S." In *Selected Studies in Marriage and the Family*, R. F. Winch and L. W. Goodman (eds.), pp. 127-38. New York: Holt, Rinehart and Winston, 1968.
Winch, R., and S. Greer. "Urbanism, Ethnicity, and Extended Familism." *Journal of Marriage and the Family*, 1968, 30: 40-45.
Winch, R., S. Greer, and R. C. Blumberg. "Ethnicity and Extended Familism in an Upper-Middle Class Suburb." *American Sociological Review*, 1967, 32: 265-72.

Instrument

See the description of the instrument given above.

MEASURE OF KINSHIP ORIENTATION

B. Farber, 1971

Definition of Concept

Orientation and intimacy with kin are measured.

Description of Instrument

The instrument consists of 12 statements about different kinds of relationships with individual kinsfolk. Responses are scroed on a Likert-type scale. This measure is useful for accumulating information on a large number of individual relatives.

Method of Administration

The instrument is part of an interview schedule, but it could be used in a questionnaire.

Sample

Farber (1971) used this instrument on a sample of 395 husbands and wives (each with a child enrolled in a preschool program) from central Illinois. The respondents ranged in age from 20 to 50 (with the median age between 30 and 35 for both men and women). There were no elderly respondents.

Scoring, Scale Norms, and Distribution

This unscored battery was factor analyzed to yield the vector of coefficients shown in Table 5-2.

TABLE 5-2
Vector of Coefficients for the Measure of Kinship Orientation

Item	Factor Loading
1. Invite to Weddings	.74
2. Respect Advice	.84
3. Try to Avoid Him	−.82
4. Count on Help	.81
5. Would Help	−.77
6. Feel Close	.86
7. What He Thinks	.83
8. Sets Example	−.66
9. Tell Problems	.75
10. Get Along	−.68
11. Free to Joke	.73
12. Important Part	.67

SOURCE: B. Farber. *Kinship and Class: A Midwestern Study,* p. 35. New York: Basic Books, 1971.

Formal Tests of Validity

Factor analysis produced a single factor that explained 58.7% of the total variance, for construct validity.

Usability on Older Populations

This measure is useful on any sample in which a broad measure of orientation toward individual kinsfolk is sought.

Scale Development Statistics

Factor analysis indicated one factor with the item "Feel close to him/her—Do not feel close to him/her" loading highest (.86). (See Table 5-2.)

General Comments and Recommendations

This battery of items, though it was not used by Farber as a cumulative or summative scale, does form one factor and could probably be used as a scale. Farber chose to use the item indicator of the whole dimension. This set of items is useful for investigating feelings toward particular individuals, rather than groups of kin.

Reference

Farber, B. *Kinship and Class: A Midwestern Study.* New York: Basic Books, 1971.

Instrument

See Instrument V2.5.II.a.

KINSHIP ORIENTATION

E. M. Rogers and H. Sebald, 1962

Definition of Concept

Kinship orientation is defined as the degree to which an individual fulfils the role expectations of his or her kinship reference group.

Description of Instrument

The measure consists of seven items in which item-response categories are not specified.

Method of Administration

The measure is part of an interview schedule, but it could be used in a questionnaire.

Development and Subsequent Use

Rogers and Sebald were attempting to divide the familism concept into family integration and kinship orientation. *Family integration* is defined as the degree to which a family member is oriented toward optimizing rewards and satisfactions for other family members; *kinship orientation* is concerned with fulfillment of the role expectations of the kinship group.

Sample

This scale was developed on a sample of 148 white farm operators—men and women—in rural Iowa (Rogers and Sebald, 1962).

Formal Tests of Reliability

Split-half reliability was .50, and item-total correlations ranged from .36 to .79 (Rogers and Sebald, 1962).

Formal Tests of Validity

The differentiation of family integration and kinship orientation that the investigators found ($r = -.10$) has been supported by other researchers (Litwak, 1960, and Bardis, 1959). Rogers and Sebald attempted to provide construct validity by relating the items to the underlying theoretical construct.

Usability on Older Populations

The scale is usable on both older and younger populations.

General Coments and Recommendations

The split-half reliability (.50) of this measure is not especially high. However, the scale does appear to top a distinct dimension of familism independent of family integration; this adds to validity of the scale. The construct validity of the scale rests on the assumption that an individual's orientation toward his or her kin is reflected in behavior (such as visiting, helping, etc.). This assumption has not been tested by correlational validation. Rogers and Sebald did not provide information on the scale's response categories or scoring procedures.

References

Havens, A. E. "Alienation and Community Integration in a Suburban Community." M.A. thesis, Ohio State University, 1960.

Rogers, E.M. "A Conceptual Variables Analysis of Technological Change." Ph.D. dissertation, Iowa State University, 1957.

Rogers, E. M., and H. Sebald. "Familism, Family Integration, and Kinship Orientation." *Marriage and Family Living*, 1962, 24: 25-30.

Sebald, H., and W. H. Andrews. "Family Integration and Related Factors in a Rural Fringe Population." *Marriage and Family Living*, 1962, 24: 347-51.

Instrument

See Instrument V2.5.II.b.

FAMILISM INDEX

J. R. Mapstone, 1970

Definition of Concept

The individual's commitment to a familistic behavior pattern is assessed. Mapstone used Burgess's description of familism as the theoretical construct.

Description of Instrument

The index is made up of 11 attitude and behavior questions. Responses that contributed to the creation, the continuity, and the maintenance of an integrated and solidary family system were coded as familistic.

Method of Administration

The index is administered in an interview, but it could be used in a questionnaire.

Development and Subsequent Use

The measure was used in a study of the influence of family ties on the acquisition of property (Mapstone, 1970).

Sample

This study (Mapstone, 1970) was done on 54 Australian, adult male farm workers of Greek and British origin.

Scoring, Scale Norms, and Distribution

Familistic responses to the items received a score of 1; nonfamilistic responses were scored as 0. Mapstone summed the scores and divided the sample at median into high and low familism groups.

Usability on Older Populations

The index could be used on an elderly population.

General Comments and Recommendations

This scale has some interesting items, but it does not seem to have been tested for reliability or validity. Mapstone apparently assumed its face validity.

Reference

Mapstone, J. R. "Familistic Determinants of Property Acquisition." *Journal of Marriage and the Family*, 1970, 32: 143-50.

Instrument

See Instrument V2.5.II.c.

FAMILISM SCALE

P. D. Bardis, 1959a; 1959b; 1959c; 1959d

Definition of Concept

Familistic role prescriptions are examined.

Description of Instrument

The measure is made up of 16 scaled intensity-of-agreement attitude questions ranging from strongly agree to strongly disagree.

Method of Administration

The scale is a questionnaire.

Development and Subsequent Use

Bardis's studies (1959a; 1959b; 1959c; 1959d) attempted to examine the ideal typical familism (viz., strong in-group feelings, the emphasis on family goals, common property, and desire to perpetuate the family).

Sample

This measure was used on 100 male and female college students in Michigan (Bardis, 1959a).

Scoring, Scale Norms, and Distribution

The scores on each item range from 0 (strongly disagree) to 4 (strongly agree). A high score indicates ideal typical familism (Bardis, 1959a).

Formal Tests of Reliability

The 30-day test-retest reliability was .904 on a sample of 37 Michigan college students. The Spearman-Brown split-half correlation for this sample was .77; two other samples of Michigan college students produced split-half coefficients of .84 and .81 (Bardis, 1959a; 1959b; 1959c).

Formal Tests of Validity

The scale was translated into Greek and administered to 37 male and female students in a familistic community. Their mean score of 46.95 (theoretical range 0 to 64) was compared with a mean score of 30.56 from 37 students in an industrial city in Michigan. The difference was significant at the .01 level ($t = 11.15$; $df = 71$). Similar comparisons of the Greek sample with two other American samples, 37 Methodist students attending a Michigan college and 30 Mennonites attending a Mennonite college, also showed significant differences at the .01 level (Bardis, 1959b).

Usability on Older Populations

This scale has only been tested on college students, but it certainly is relevant for use on older populations.

General Comments and Recommendations

This scale has been shown to be reliable and valid to a degree, although it has not been tested on older populations. An examination of its reliability on older populations is needed.

References

Bardis, P. D. "Attitudes toward the Family among College Students and Their Parents." *Sociology and Social Research*, 1959a, 43: 352-58.

————. "A Comparative Study of Familism." *Rural Sociology*, 1959b, 24: 362-71.

————. "A Familism Scale." *Marriage and Family Living*, 1959c, 21: 340-41.

————. "Influence of a Functional Marriage Course on Attitudes toward Familism." *Journal of Educational Sociology*, 1959d, 32: 232-39.

Blair, M. J. "An Evaluation of the Bardis Familism Scale." *Journal of Marriage and the Family*, 1972, 34: 265-68.

Geersten, H. R., and R. M. Gray. "Familistic Orientation and Inclination toward Adopting the Sick Role." *Journal of Marriage and the Family*, 1970, 32: 638-46.

Kassees, A. S. "Cross-cultural Comparative Familism of a Christian Arab People." *Journal of Marriage and the Family*, 1972, 34: 538-44.

Larsen, K. S. "Premarital Sex Attitudes: A Scale and Some Validity Findings." *Journal of Social Psychology*, 1973, 20: 339-40.

Shaw, M. E., and J. M. Wright. *Scales for the Measurement of Attitudes*. New York: McGraw-Hill, 1967.

Instrument

See Instrument V2.5.II.d.

PREFERRED LOCATION OF RESIDENCE OF KIN

P. J. Reiss, 1962

Definition of Concept

Attitudes of the desired physical proximity of kin are examined.

Description of Instrument

This is a single-item measure: "If you had it within your power to have your relatives reside where you wanted, which would you set up as the most ideal arrangement? (a) Distant city; (b) Nearby city; (c) Same metro area; (d) Same neighborhood" (Reiss, 1962).

Method of Administration

The item is part of an interview schedule, but a questionnaire could also be used.

Development and Subsequent Use

The item was developed as part of an investigation of the correlates of, and frequency of, interaction with extended kin.

Sample

This study was done on 161 white middle-class family members (69 males and 92 females) from the Boston area; 30% were Irish ethnics (Reiss, 1962).

Usability on Older Populations

The measure could be used on older populations.

General Comments and Recommendations

It might be useful to test the utility of this single-item indicator as a valid measure of kinship solidarity by correlating the score with some of the other measures discussed elsewhere in this chapter. Its simplicity, if the measure is valid, could save much time and expense.

Reference

Reiss, P. J. "The Extended Kinship System: Correlates of and Attitudes on Frequency of Interaction." *Marriage and Family Living*, 1962, 24: 333-39.

Instrument

See the description of the instrument given above.

EXTENDED FAMILY ORIENTATION

E. Litwak, 1960a; 1960b

Definition of Concept

Extended family orientation is defined as the extent to which an individual identifies with his or her extended family.

Description of Instrument

The instrument is a four-item Guttman scale.

Method of Administration

It is administered by questionnaire or interview.

Development and Subsequent Use

The scale was developed in a secondary analysis of data. The context was an examination of the impact of occupational mobility on extended family orientations. The results of the study led to Litwak's development of the concept of the modified extended family (Litwak 1960a; 1960b).

Sample

Litwak (1960a; 1960b) studied 920 white, middle-class, married women from Buffalo, N.Y. They were between young and middle-aged, all with children 19 years old or younger.

Scoring, Scale Norms, and Distribution

Although it was not explicitly stated by Litwak, apparently responses to the questions are along a Likert-type set of categories ranging from very strongly agree to very strongly disagree. Cutoff points for the Guttman-scale dichotomy are at the very-strong-agreement points. Very strong agreement with the first three items indicates extended-family orientations, agreement with the first two indicates nuclear-family orientations, and not agreeing very strongly with any of the items indicates no family orientation. A majority of the respondents indicated a nuclear-family orientation (Litwak, 1960a; 1960b).

Formal Tests of Reliability

Litwak reported that the responses formed a Guttman scale. Stuckert (1963) in a later use of the same scale found a coefficient of reproducibility of .90.

Formal Tests of Validity

Litwak, and later Stuckert (1963), did not address directly the question of validity. Stuckert provided a theoretical statement that might be construed as an attempt at construct validity.

Usability on Older Populations

Like many measures of kin relations, this measure asks about older individuals rather than questioning them directly.

General Comments and Recommendations

This four-item Guttman scale attempts to measure extended/nuclear/nonfamily orientation. With little validity analysis to back it up, this complex issue appears to be inadequately captured by this measure.

References

Litwak, E. "Occupational Mobility and Extended Family Cohesion." *American Sociological Review*, 1960a, 25: 9-21.

———. "Geographical Mobility and Extended Family Cohesion." *American Sociological Review*, 1960b, 25: 22-24.

Stuckert, R. "Occupational Mobility and Family Relationships." *Social Forces*, 1963, 41: 301-7.

Instrument

See Instrument V2.5.II.f.

PARTICIPATION IN THE EXTENDED FAMILY

W. H. Key, 1961

Definition of Concept

Participation in extended-family activities is assessed.

Description of Instrument

The five-item Guttman scale differentiates high and low participation.

Method of Administration

The scale is part of an interview schedule, but it could be administered in a questionnaire.

Development and Subsequent Use

This study is one of many similar studies of American kinship. Like Bultena's measure, it examines rural-urban differences in kinship relations and, also like Bultena's measure, it identifies no substantial differences between rural and urban kinship relations.

Sample

This measure was derived from a sample of 357 males and females in the Midwest, which made up a cross section of individuals with respect to age, sex, race, and education (Key, 1961).

Scoring, Scale Norms, and Distribution

The scoring weights are printed with the items on the instrument. Item scores are summed across the five questions. (See Table 5-3.)

TABLE 5-3
Scale Distribution

Population Groups	Total $\overline{X}$	Male $\overline{X}$	Female $\overline{X}$
Rural	6.22	6.10	6.40
Village	5.19	5.20	5.19
Small urban	5.50	6.40	5.04
Medium-sized city	5.92	6.00	5.91
Metropolitan	5.87	7.00	5.25

SOURCE: W. H. Key. "Rural-Urban Differences and the Family." *Sociological Quarterly*, 1961, 2: 49-56. Reprinted by permission of author and publisher.

Formal Tests of Reliability

The coefficient of reproducibility was .95 (Key, 1961).

Usability on Older Populations

This scale is usable on older populations.

General Comments and Recommendations

This is a reliable measure of an important aspect of kinship relations—participation. It constitutes a useful addition to the common question "How frequently do you see your relatives?"

Reference

Key, W. H. "Rural-Urban Differences and the Family." *Sociological Quarterly*, 1961, 2: 49-56.

Instrument

See Instrument V2.5.II.g.

MUTUAL AID AND AFFECTION INDEX

A. C. Kerckhoff, 1965

Definition of Concept

Extended- versus nuclear-family norms regarding aid giving between parents and children are examined.

Description of Instrument

This scale consists of two components: a 10-item Likert scale (mutual aid and affection scale) and a single-item propinquity measure ("Married children should live close to their parents") (Kerckhoff, 1965).

Method of Administration

The scale is part of an interview schedule; it could also be used in a questionnaire. The items should take no more than 10 minutes to complete.

Development and Subsequent Use

This scale, along with others, was developed to examine the relationship between normative and behavioral aspects of extended family relationships (Kerckhoff, 1965).

Sample

The index was derived from a study of aged residents of the Piedmont region of North Carolina. The cross-sectional sample consisted of 201 married couples with a married child or a child at least 25 years old. Spouses were interviewed simultaneously but separately (Kerckhoff, 1965).

Scoring, Scale Norms, and Distribution

A respondent agreeing with at least 7 of the 10 mutual-aid items and the propinquity item is classified as having extended-family norms. A respondent agreeing with 7 or more of the 10 items but disagreeing with the propinquity item is classified as having modified extended-family norms. A respondent agreeing with 6 or fewer of the items and disagreeing with the propinquity item possesses nuclear-family norms. The remaining response combination is classified as missing data. Responses are made to a five-point Likert-type format. In the original sample, extended-family norms were held by 62 husbands and 40 wives. Modified extended-family norms were held by 92 husbands and 116 wives. Nuclear-family norms were held by 45 husbands and 39 wives (Kerckhoff, 1965, p. 100).

Formal Tests of Validity

Though he reported no formal tests of validity, Kerckhoff did report a husband-wife correlation of .141 when the typology was treated as a three-point Guttman scale (1966a, p. 147).

Usability on Older Populations

This scale is usable on both younger and older populations.

Sensitivity to Age Differences

This scale differentiates older people from younger people, but it makes no distinctions within the older group.

General Comments and Recommendations

This measure measures quite directly attitudes toward supporting children and aged parents (and it is appropriate for use on elderly populations). Its major weakness is the lack of support in terms of reliability or validity for using scale scores to classify individuals into extended-, modified extended-, or nuclear-family norms. The instrument depends on the assumption that the extension of family structure can be measured on a normative level by examining statements about the relations between two vertically related groups (i.e., generations); thus, it ignores other possible salient relatives.

NOTE: This abstract combines information provided by Mindel and Bengtson and Schrader. (See also their chapter in this volume.)

References

Johnson, C. M., and A. C. Kerckhoff. "Family Norms, Social Position, and the Value of Change." *Social Forces*, 1964, 43: 149-56.

Kerckhoff, A. C. "Nuclear and Extended Family Relationships: A Normative and Behavioral Analysis." In *Social Structure and the Family: Generational Relations*, E. Shanas and G. F. Streib (eds.), pp. 93-112. Englewood Cliffs, N. J.: Prentice-Hall, 1965.

————. "Norm-Value Clusters and the 'Strain toward Consistency' among Older Married Couples." In *Social Aspects of Aging*. I. H. Simpson and J. C. McKinney (eds.), pp. 138-59. Durham, N.C.: Duke University Press, 1966a.

————. "Family Patterns and Morale in Retirement." In *Social Aspects of Aging*, I. H. Simpson and J. C. McKinney (eds.), pp. 173-92. Durham, N.C.: Duke University Press, 1966b.

Instrument

See Instrument V2.5.II.h.

MUTUAL SUPPORT INDEX

A. C. Kerckhoff, 1965

Definition of Concept

This behavioral index of extended-family relations is used in conjunction with the normative Mutual Aid and Affection Index.

Description of Instrument

This six-item set of questions concerns children's provided support of parents during time of need; also included is a single item on propinquity. Together, these items define a behavioral typology of intergenerational family structure: (1) extended family, (2) modified extended families, (3) nuclear families, and (4) individuated families.

Method of Administration

Husbands and wives were interviewed simultaneously but separately in the original study (Kerckhoff, 1965). No special skills are needed for administering the measure, and the instrument probably could be used in a questionnaire form.

Development and Subsequent Use

This scale, along with several others, was developed to examine the relationship between the normative and behavioral aspects of extended-family relationships.

The general hypothesis guiding the research was that the family context of both members of an older couple would make a difference in their level of morale.

Sample

This scale was derived from a study of the aged people living in the Piedmont region of North Carolina. The cross-sectional sample consisted of 201 married couples with a married child or a child at least 25 years old (Kerckhoff 1965; 1966).

Scoring, Scale Norms, and Distribution

For each question: a score of 1 is given when there has not been a need for the type of assistance described; when the need described has been present and has been met, a score of 2 is given; when the need described has been present and has not been met, a score of zero is

NOTE: This abstract combines information provided by Mindel and Bengtson and Schrader. (See their chapter in this volume.)

given. Propinquity is measured by averaging the distance of a couple's children from the parental home. High propinquity (i.e., children close by) and high support scores indicate the extended type; low propinquity (i.e., children distant) and high support scores indicate the modified type; high propinquity and low mutual-support scores indicate an individuated family type; and low propinquity and low support scores indicate the nuclear type. In the original study, distribution of the couples by behavioral typology was as follows: 59, extended; 33, modified extended; 50, nuclear; and 51, individuated (Kerckhoff, 1965; p. 102).

Usability on Older Populations

The measure is usable on middle-aged and older populations.

Sensitivity to Age Differences

The measure is not sensitive to gradations in old age; however, this may not be necessary.

General Comments and Recommendations

This scale appears to be a good measure of the behavioral manifestations of extended-family support. It would be very useful in studies of the support systems of the elderly. Unlike the attitudinal scale developed by Kerckhoff, this measure does not have to meet the criteria of internal consistency. However, the reliability problems of using retrospection as a method to ascertain frequencies of behavior in the past can be difficult to handle. The measure appears to have considerable content validity, although tests would be useful. The cutoff points for low and high scores are arbitrary as stated by Kerckhoff.

References

Kerckhoff, A. C. "Nuclear and Extended Family Relationships: A Normative and Behavioral Analysis." In *Social Structure and the Family: Generational Relations*, E. Shanas and G. F. Streib (eds.), pp. 93-112. Englewood Cliffs, N.J.: Prentice-Hall, 1965.

Kerckhoff, A. C. "Family Patterns and Morale in Retirement." In *Social Aspects of Aging*, H. Simpson and J. C. McKinney (eds.), pp. 173-92. Durham, N.C.: Duke University Press, 1966.

Instrument

See Instrument V2.5.II.i.

REASONS FOR KEEPING IN TOUCH WITH PARENTS

B. N. Adams, 1968

Definition of Concept

The reasons why individuals keep in touch with their parents are investigated in this measure of the obligatory aspects of kinship relations.

Description of Instrument

The measure examines the importance of four reasons for maintaining contact with parents; the reasons are not compiled in a scale or an index. The Likert-type format is scored 1 for very important; 2 for somewhat important; and 3 for unimportant.

Method of Administration

The instrument is administered as an interview or a questionnaire.

Development and Subsequent Use

This measure was developed to test the obligatory aspect of kinship relations. The measure examines general obligations to keep in touch, reciprocal obligations to help family members, and the nonobligatory affectional aspect of kinship relations.

Sample

Adams (1968) studied 799 (467 females, 332 males) white individuals from Greensboro, N.C., who had been married only once and for 29 years or less. The median age was 34.5 years for males and 32.3 years for females.

Usability on Older Populations

This measure is most useful with younger respondents, who describe their contact with their elderly parents. The questions could be changed from asking about parents to asking about children, thus making it usable on older populations. (Adams [1968] used it at another point on siblings in the same work.)

General Comments and Recommendations

Adams was exploring theoretically the obligatory aspects of contact with kin. The items seem to have face validity. Adams (1968) acknowledged that verbally expressing underlying motives is, to some degree, suspect, but he felt that respondents showed little hesitation about expressing low feelings of closeness or obligation as a reason for keeping in touch. It is a good measure for examining the reasons for contact with parents and other relatives. Its main problem is that it may not constitute a complete list of reasons for keeping in touch, although its stated purpose is only to examine the obligatory aspects of contact.

Reference

Adams, B. N. *Kinship in an Urban Setting*. Chicago: Markham, 1968.

Instrument

See Instrument V2.5.III.a.

MEANING OF GRANDPARENTHOOD

J. Robertson and V. Wood, 1970

Definition of Concept

The meaning of grandparenthood is examined.

Description of Instrument

The measure is made up of 29 Likert-scaled statements with which the respondent strongly agrees, agrees, disagrees, or strongly disagrees.

Method of Administration

The measure is used in an interview, but it could be used in a questionnaire as well.

Development and Subsequent Use

The measure used originally was used in a study of grandparenthood (Robertson and Wood, 1970; 1971).

Sample

An area probability sample of a predominantly working-class area of Madison, Wis., yielded a sample of 257 grandparents (125 females and 132 males). The grandparents could neither reside with their children nor serve as surrogate parents for their grandchildren and retain eligibility for the study. The average age of the participants was approximately 65 years. For further information on sample characteristics, see Wood and Robertson (1976).

Scoring, Scale Norms, and Distribution

Factor analysis of the items indicated two dimensions. Conception of the grandparental role in normative terms formed the first factor, and items tapping the personal meaning of the role formed the second factor. A more detailed description of these procedures is available from Robertson and in Robertson (1971) and Robertson and Wood (1970; 1973).

The two dimensions were dichotomized at their median scores and cross-tabulated to develop a typology. Respondents who scored high on both dimensions ($N = 77$) were the apportioned type; those who scored low on both dimensions ($N = 70$) were the remote type; those who scored high on the social/normative dimension and low on the personal dimension ($N = 67$) were the symbolic type; and those who scored low on the social/normative dimension but high on the personal dimension ($N = 43$) were the individualized type (Wood and Robertson, 1976).

Formal Tests of Validity

The two dimensions emerged in a factor analysis. Further information on the measure's validity is not available.

Usability on Older Populations

This scale was designed for use on a sample of grandparents and is useful only on grandparents.

Sensitivity to Age Differences

The scale does not appear to distinguish between older and younger grandparents.

General Comments and Recommendations

This scale is included in this chapter in spite of the fact that there appears to be little information on its accuracy because of the dearth of measures in this area. Extreme care should be used in employing this instrument, and certainly pretesting is advisable.

References

Robertson, J. "Grandparenthood: A Study of Role Conceptions of Grandmothers." Ph.D. dissertation, University of Wisconsin, 1971.

Robertson, J., and V. Wood. "Grandparenthood: A Study of Role Conceptions." Paper presented to the 23rd Annual Meeting of the Gerontological Society, Toronto, October 22-24, 1970.

————. "Grandparenthood: A Theoretical Perspective." Madison: University of Wisconsin, Faye McBeath Institute on Gerontology, 1973.

Wood, V., and J. Robertson. "The Significance of Grandparenthood." In *Time, Roles, and Self in Old Age*, J. Gubrium (ed.), pp. 278-304. New York: Human Sciences Press, l976.

Instrument

See Instrument V2.5.III.b.

INDEX OF PERCEIVED CONFLICT

A. C. Kerckhoff, 1966

Definition of Concept

The degree of conflict the older person perceives and feels regarding family cohesion and the geographic and social mobility of his or her children is assessed.

Description of Instrument

This measure consists of six Likert-scaled items.

Method of Administration

The instrument is administered as an interview schedule or a questionnaire.

Sample

This measure was used in a study of 201 elderly couples (including those in which the husband had retired or was within five years of retirement) in the Piedmont region of North Carolina.

Scoring, Scale Norms, and Distribution

Scoring is on a Likert-type format ranging from 1 (strongly agree) to 5 (strongly disagree). The items are summed to produce the Index of Perceived Conflict.

Formal Tests of Validity

Face Validity: Kerckhoff (1966, p. 145) stated that "all of these items ask: 'Can adult children be mobile without disrupting a satisfying parent-child relationship?'"

Convergent Validity: This measure was moderately correlated with three other closely related measures.

Usability on Older Populations

The index was used originally on an older population.

General Comments and Recommendations

As Kerckhoff (1966) put it, these items all ask "Can adult children be mobile without disrupting a satisfying parent-child relationship?" It is unfortunate that there was no test for reliability because this scale does tap an important area of parent-child relations. The convergent validity of the scale (scale scores were clustered with several other interrelated measures) probably justifies its use as a reasonably adequate measure.

Reference

Kerckhoff, A. C. "Norm Value Clusters and the 'Strain toward Consistency' among Older Married Couples." In *Social Aspects of Aging*, I. H. Simpson and J. C. McKinney (eds.), pp. 138-59. Durham, N.C.: Duke University Press, 1966.

Instrument

See Instrument V2.5.III.c.

SIGNIFICANCE OF GRANDPARENTS

J. Robertson, 1976

Definition of Concept

The items tap the attitudes and expectations of young adult grandchildren toward their grandparents and their conceptions of the ideal grandparent.

Description of Instrument

This is a battery of items (number unknown) with Likert-type response categories. Scale development procedures were not discussed by Robertson (1976). Items cover both the respondents' attitudes toward grandparents and their conceptions of the characteristics of an ideal grandparent.

Method of Administration

The measure is administered to groups. No time requirements or special instructions are given.

Development and Subsequent Use

The items were developed in a study of views on grandparents that also assessed the respondents' perceptions of appropriate/expected grandparent behavior, responsibility toward grandparents, and the perceived influence of the respondents' parents on attitudes toward grandparents.

Sample

The sample population was an available group of 86 young (18-26 years old) adult grandchildren — 83% single, 66% women, 56% from stable blue-collar backgrounds.

Scoring, Scale Norms, and Distribution

Individual item responses are given by Robertson (1976) for selected items.

General Comments and Recommendations

The measure's focus on a specific role relationship appears to be useful. It can be contrasted with the respondents' descriptions of "ideal" grandparents. Further testing and refinement of the scale are needed.

Reference

Robertson, J. F. "Significance of Grandparents: Perceptions of Young Adult Grandchildren." *The Gerontologist*, 1976; 16-137-46.

Instrument

See Instrument V2.5.III.d.

EXTENDED FAMILY AS A REFERENCE GROUP

R. Stuckert, 1963

Definition of Concept

The instrument examines the extended family as a reference group and concern for the unity of the extended family.

Description of Instrument

Five statements form a Guttman scale.

Method of Administration

The measure is administered as an interview, but it could also be used as a questionnaire.

Development and Subsequent Use

This scale formed part of the extensive literature of the 1950s and 1960s that examined the effects of modern industrialized society on kinship relationships, in this case, the phenomenon of occupational mobility. Findings on the effects of mobility on extended-family unity remain somewhat contradictory, with some scholars finding attenuation of family unity and others (such as Litwak) finding continuing strength.

Sample

This measure was used on a sample of 275 white married couples in Milwaukee, Wis. The range in age was not specified, but the median age was 35 for males and 31 for females.

Scoring, Scale Norms, and Distribution

Affirmative responses to the first two questions indicated the use of the extended family as a reference group. Affirmative responses to all five questions indicate a concern with the extended family unity. Responses are either yes or no.

Formal Tests of Reliability

The coefficient of reproducibility was .93.

Usability on Older Populations

The measure is usable on younger populations for examinations of feelings toward older people.

General Comments and Recommendations

This scale probably measures extended-family unity better than the extended family as a reference group. Stuckert made only minor attempts at establishing the validity of the measure, and they are not entirely convincing. The researcher did not supply the series of questions about common family problems mentioned in his instructions for the instrument. The questions in the scale are somewhat ambiguous. Despite these drawbacks, this scale is one of few—if not the only—measures that look at a reference group as a dimension of kinship relations.

Reference

Stuckert, R. "Occupational Mobility in Family Relationships" *Social Forces*, 1963, 41:301-7.

Instrument

See Instrument V2.5.III.e.

ATTITUDES TOWARD MULTIGENERATIONAL HOUSEHOLDS

C. H. Mindel, 1977

Definition of Concept

Attitudes toward living with parents or adult children are assessed.

Description of Instrument

The measure is an eight-item Likert-type scale.

Method of Administration

It is administered in an interview schedule, but it could be used in a questionnaire as well.

Development and Subsequent Use

The scale was developed and used in a study of individuals living in multigenerational family households.

Sample

A sample of 62 persons aged 60 to 97 was collected. The respondents were mostly female, Caucasian, unmarried people with moderate to poor health (Mindel, 1977).

Scoring, Scale Norms, and Distribution

Each item has a unit weight. Scoring is on a five-point Likert-type scale from 1 (strongly disagree) to 5 (strongly agree).

Formal Tests of Reliability

The Cronbach alpha was .85.

Formal Tests of Validity

Criterion Validity: The scale correlates with the question "Do you think it is a good idea for elderly to live with their adult children?" ($r = .33: p < .004$).

Construct Validity: See Table 5-4.

Usability on Older Populations

This scale was used on both elderly people and their children.

Sensitivity to Age Differences

The same scale was used on both a younger and an older population. Comparison of the responses of the two subpopulations indicated different perceptions of this living arrangement. The scale is sensitive to generational differences (Mindel, 1977).

Scale Development Statistics

The scale produced a single factor that explained 67% of the item variance. See Table 5-4.

TABLE 5-4
Item Analysis for Attitude Scale

Item	Mean	SD	Factor Loading	Item-Total Correlation
1	3.51	1.04	.67	.61
2	3.49	.97	.75	.70
3	3.92	.88	.60	.54
4	2.93	1.31	.46	.40
5	3.54	.99	.74	.64
6	3.54	.90	.88	.78
7	3.46	1.18	.60	.54
8	3.31	1.00	.71	.67

SOURCE: Mindel, 1977.

General Comments and Recommendations

This scale can be used on both elderly and younger populations. When used on a younger population, the reliability of the scale is lower (.78) and a second factor emerges.

Reference

Mindel, C. H. "A Multiple Regression Approach to Satisfaction in Multigenerational Households." Paper presented to the 30th Annual Meeting of the Gerontological Society, San Francisco, November 18-22, 1977.

Instrument

See Instrument V2.5.III.f.

Instruments

V2.5.I.a

KINSHIP INVOLVEMENT

H. K. Swarzweller and J. F. Seggar, 1967

See the description of the instrument in the abstract.

V2.5.I.b

PATRILINEAGE INTEGRATION INDEX

M. Hutter, 1970

See the scoring, scale norms, and distribution described in the abstract.

V2.5.I.c

KINSHIP INTEGRATION AND NETWORK CONNECTEDNESS

J. Aldous and M. A. Straus, 1966

See the description of the instrument in the abstract.

V2.5.I.d

SIBLING COMMUNICATION SCALE

D. A. Sweetser, 1970

See the description of the instrument in the abstract.

V2.5.I.e

FREQUENCY OF INTERACTION WITH RELATIVES SCALE

E. Cumming and W. Henry, 1961

See the scoring, scale norms, and distribution in the abstract.

V2.5.I.f

FAMILIAL INTERACTION INDEX

G. L. Bultena, 1969

See the scoring, scale norms, and distribution in the abstract.

V2.5.I.g

KIN INTERACTION

F. Berardo, 1966

See the description of the instrument in the abstract.

V2.5.I.h

EXTENDED FAMILISM

R. Winch, S. Greer, and R. C. Blumberg, 1967

See the description of the instrument in the abstract.

V2.5.II.a

MEASURE OF KINSHIP ORIENTATION

B. Farber, 1971

NAME OF RELATIVE _____ Relative _____

Relationship _____

	Definitely	More Often Than Not		More Often Than Not		Definitely	
			Not Sure				
	Usually		(50-50)			Usually	

1. Would invite him to weddings, christenings, etc.   (1) (2) (3) (4) (5) (6) (7)   Would not invite him to weddings, etc.

2. Respect his advice   — — — — — — —   Did not care for his advice

3. Try to avoid him   — — — — — — —   Try to see him as often as I can

4. Can count on his help if I need it   — — — — — — —   He would avoid helping me

5. Would not help him if he asked   — — — — — — —   Would go out of my way to help him

6. Feel close to him   — — — — — — —   Do not feel close to him

7. What he thinks of me is important to me   — — — — — — —   I don't care what he thinks of me

8. Does not set a good example for children   — — — — — — —   Sets a good example for children

9. Would tell him my problems   — — — — — — —   Would not tell him my problems

10. Do not get along with him   — — — — — — —   Get along with him

11. Feel free to joke or have fun with him   — — — — — — —   Do not feel free — but feel inhibited, self-conscious with him

12. Has played an important part in my life   — — — — — — —   Has not played an important part in my life

SOURCE: B. Farber. *Kinship and Class: A Midwestern Study.* New York: Basic Books, 1971, p. 35. Reprinted by permission of author and publisher.

V2.5.II.b

KINSHIP ORIENTATION

E. M. Rogers and H. Sebald, 1955; 1962

1. Attend community events with relatives* rather than with others.
2. Attend events outside community with relatives rather than others.
3. More informal participation with relatives than with others.
4. Exchange work more with relatives than with others.
5. If renter, related to landlord.
6. Individual associates more with relatives than with non-relatives.
7. Individual discusses matter more with relatives than with non-relatives.

*The "relatives" specified in these items are members of the extended family. The respondents were informed as to the intended meaning of "relatives" in these scale items.

SOURCE: E. M. Rogers and H. Sebald. "Familism, Family Integration, and Kinship Orientation." *Marriage and Family Living*, 1962, 24:25-30. Reprinted by permission of the authors and the National Council on Family Relations.

V2.5.II.c

FAMILISM INDEX

J. R. Mapstone, 1970

(1) Do you think children under 16 years of age should be paid for the work they do in the family?

(2) Do you think that children under 21 years of age — living at home — should give all their pay to their parents?

(3) Who should be expected to look after elderly parents, the government or the children?

(4) Do you think that children under 21 years of age — living at home — should give all their pay to their parents?

(5) If your father and mother disapproved of the girl you wanted to marry would you marry anyway?

(6) Should married children live with their parents?

(7) Do you think a person should marry someone with a different religion?

(This and the next question tap the intense religious and nationalistic feelings of the Orthodox settlers from the Balkans with the realization that familism influences the continuation of both patterns.)

(8) Do you think a person should marry someone with a different nationality?

(9) If you had a son, would you make him a partner in your firm?

(10) Would you like your son to continue in the same work you are doing?

(11) If you had two sons and one daughter would the daughter get any land? As much as a son?

(This last question refers to the patrilineal pattern characteristic of the integrated extended Balkan families.)

SOURCE: J. R. Mapstone. "Familistic Determinants of Property Acquisition." *Journal of Marriage and the Family*, 1970, 32:143-50. Reprinted by permission of the author and the National Council on Family Relations.

V2.5.II.d

FAMILISM SCALE

P. D. Bardis, 1959

Below is a list of issues concerning the family in general, not your own. Please read all statements very carefully and respond to all of them on the basis of your own true beliefs without consulting any other persons. Do this by reading each statement and then writing, in the space provided at its left, only the following numbers, 0, 1, 2, 3, 4. The meaning of each of these figures is:

> 0: Strongly disagree
> 1: Disagree
> 2: Undecided
> 3: Agree
> 4: Strongly agree

(For research purposes, you must consider all statements as they are, without modifying any of them in any way.)

_____ 1. A person should always support his uncles or aunts if they are in need.

_____ 2. Children below 18 should give almost all their earnings to their parents.

_____ 3. The family should consult close relatives (uncles, aunts, first cousins) concerning its important decisions.

_____ 4. Children below 18 should almost always obey their older brothers and sisters.

_____ 5. A person should always consider the needs of his family as a whole more important than his own.

_____ 6. At least one married child should be expected to live in the parental home.

_____ 7. A person should always be expected to defend his family against outsiders at the expense of his own personal safety.

_____ 8. The family should have the right to control the behavior of each of its members completely.

_____ 9. A person should always support his parents-in-law if they are in need.

_____ 10. A person should always avoid every action of which his family disapproves.

_____ 11. A person should always share his home with his uncles, aunts, or first cousins if they are in need.

_____ 12. A person should always be completely loyal to his family.

_____ 13. The members of a family should be expected to hold the same political, ethical, and religious beliefs.

_____ 14. Children below 18 should always obey their parents.

_____ 15. A person should always help his parents with the support of his younger brothers and sisters if necessary.

_____ 16. A person should always share his home with his parents-in-law if they are in need.

SOURCE: P. D. Bardis. "A Familism Scale." _Marriage and Family Living_, 1959, 21:340-41. Reprinted by permission of the author and the National Council on Family Relations.

V2.5.II.e

PREFERRED LOCATION OF RESIDENCE OF KIN

P. J. Reiss, 1962

See the description of the instrument in the abstract.

V2.5.II.f

EXTENDED FAMILY ORIENTATION

E. Litwak, 1960

Respondents were asked to what degree they agreed with the following statements:

1. Generally, I like the whole family (husband, wife, and children) to spend evenings together.
2. I want a house where family members can spend time together.
3. I want a location which would make it easy for relatives to get together.
4. I want a house with enough room for our parents to feel free to move in.

SOURCE: E. Litwak. "Occupational Mobility and Extended Family Cohesion." *American Sociological Review*, 1960, 25:16. For nonprofit use only.

V2.5.II.g

PARTICIPATION IN THE EXTENDED FAMILY

W. H. Key, 1961

1. How often do you visit in the homes of relatives whether here or elsewhere?
   At least once a month   2
   At least once a year but less than once a month   1
   Less often than once a year   0
2. How often do you engage in activities with relatives outside your homes?
   At least once a month   1
   Less often than once a month   0
3. How often do you borrow things from or lend things to relatives?
   At least once a week   3
   At least once a month but less than once a week   2
   At least once a year but less than once a month   1
   Less often than once a year   0
4. How often do you do favors other than lending for relatives?
   At least once a week   3
   At least once a month but less than once a week   2
   At least once a year but less than once a month   1
   Less often than once a year   0
5. Do you visit more with friends or relatives?
   As much or more with relatives   1
   More with friends   0

SOURCE: W. H. Key. "Rural-Urban Differences and the Family." *Sociological Quarterly*, 1961, 2:49-56. Reprinted by permission of author and publisher.

V2.5.II.h

MUTUAL AID AND AFFECTION INDEX

A. C. Kerckhoff, 1965

At the normative level of analysis the criterion of propinquity was measured by agreement or disagreement with the following statement "married children should live close to their parents."

1. Children should take care of their parents, in whatever way necessary, when they are sick.

2. The older couple should take care of their children, in whatever way necessary, when they are sick.
3. The children should give their parents financial help.
4. The older couple should give their children financial help.
5. If the children live nearby after they grow up, they should visit their parents at least once a week.
6. If children live nearby after they grow up, their parents should visit them at least once a week.
7. Children who live at a distance should write to their parents at least once a week.
8. Parents should write to their children who live at a distance at least once a week.
9. The children should feel responsible for their parents.
10. The older couple should feel responsible for their children.

SOURCE: A. C. Kerckhoff. "Nuclear and Extended Family Relationships: A Normative and Behavioral Analysis." In *Social Structure and the Family: Generational Relations*, E. Shanas and G. F. Streib (eds.). pp. 99-100. Englewood Cliffs, N.J. Prentice-Hall, 1965. Reprinted by permission of the author and publisher.

V2.5.II.i

MUTUAL SUPPORT INDEX

A. C. Kerckhoff, 1965

1. Have any of your children helped out when either of you were sick?
2. Have any of your children given advice on business or money matters?
3. Have you helped your children in any way when someone was sick in their family?
4. Have you given any of your children advice on business or money matters?
5. Have any of your children ever offered you financial assistance?
6. How willing would you say your children are to make sacrifices for you?

SOURCE: A. C. Kerckhoff. "Nuclear and Extended Family Relationships: A Normative and Behavioral Analysis." In *Social Structure and the Family: Generational Relations*, E. Shanas and G. F. Streib (eds.). p. 101. Englewood Cliffs, N.J.: Prentice-Hall, 1965. Reprinted by permission of author and publisher.

V2.5.III.a

REASONS FOR KEEPING IN TOUCH WITH PARENTS

B. N. Adams, 1968

Now I want us to look a little deeper into your relations with your parent(s), to see if we can get at *why* you keep in touch. There are several reasons people might give for keeping in touch with their parents. As I read each of the following reasons, tell me if it is very important, somewhat important, or unimportant, in your relation with your parents.

		Very Impt.	Some. Impt.	Unimpt.
A67.	First, you feel you ought to, or have an obligation to keep in touch.	1. ____	2. ____	3. ____
A68.	You need their help in some way.	1. ____	2. ____	3. ____
A69.	They need your help in some way.	1. ____	2. ____	3. ____
A70.	You simply enjoy being in touch.	1. ____	2. ____	3. ____

SOURCE: B. N. Adams. *Kinship in an Urban Setting*, pp. 200-201. Chicago: Markham, 1968. Reprinted by permission of author and publisher.

V2.5.III.b

MEANING OF GRANDPARENTHOOD

J. Robertson and V. Wood, 1970

Now, I'm going to read several statements which grandparents might make as they think of the meaning of grandparenthood to them. For each statement I read would you please tell me how much you agree or disagree with it by using one of the answers on this card. (SHOW CARD 3)

There are no right or wrong answers to any statement. We are simply interested in which of the five responses on the card you feel best describes your reaction to the statement.

CARD 3

1. Strongly agree   2. Agree   3. Agree and disagree   4. Disagree   5. Strongly disagree

25. One of the most important things about having grandchildren is that they provide me with a way to see my blood line carried on for another generation. _____(#)
26. The greatest happiness is found in a family where all members work together as a group. _____(#)
27. Going to visit a friend for Christmas is more enjoyable than having Christmas with one's family. _____ (#)
28. One of the most important things I want from my grandchildren is for them to "respect their elders". _____ (#)
29. I would tell my grandchildren to always remember that love and companionship are more important to a successful marriage than money. _____ (#)
30. Life would be very lonely for me without my grandchildren. _____(#)
31. I feel I should do what is morally right to set a good example for my grandchildren. _____(#)
32. I feel that my grandchildren should be encouraged to choose their own occupation regardless of whether their parents agree or disagree with their choice. _____ (#)
33. I think I should be able to give my grandchildren whatever I can and not be worried about spoiling them. _____(#)
34. The most important thing about having grandchildren for me is that they make me feel young again. _____(#)
35. One of the most important things about having grandchildren for me is that they have brought a deep sense of emotional satisfaction to my life. _____(#)
36. If one of my grandchildren had the opportunity to take a pleasure trip around the world, I think he should take the trip first and see life while he is still young, and worry about going to college and getting a job later. _____ (#)
37. What my grandchildren do is important to me because it affects my family's reputation. _____(#)
38. As I look at my grandchildren, I can't help but feel I have accomplished something in bringing up my children. _____(#)
39. The most important thing I expect from my grandchildren is respect. _____(#)
40. I feel very close to my grandchildren. _____(#)
41. I have a life of my own and don't have much time to get involved in my grandchildren's lives. _____ (#)
42. I feel my grandchildren should give more consideration to me than to their friends if the need arises. _____ (#)
43. Religious beliefs are important sources of strength to me. _____ (#)

44. I don't care if my grandchildren think of me more as a friend or companion than as an adult they respect. _____(#)
45. Family background is an important consideration in marriage. _____(#)
46. As I get older, grandparenthood provides me with one of the most enjoyable ways to occupy my life. _____(#)
47. It would have been an unhappy life for me if I didn't have grandchildren. _____(#)
48. Being a grandparent makes me feel old. _____(#)
49. Grandparents and grandchildren should treat each other as equals. _____(#)
50. When times are rough, my grandchildren give me something to think about. _____(#)
51. Grandparenthood is not all that important to me now—maybe later. _____(#)
52. I'm so busy with my own interests, I don't have time to become involved in my grandchildren's lives. _____(#)
53. If the need arises, grandparents should always feel free to discipline their grandchildren. _____(#)

SOURCE: J. Robertson, "Grandparenthood: A Study of Role Conceptions of Grandmothers." Ph.D. dissertation, University of Wisconsin, 1971.

V2.5.III.c

INDEX OF PERCEIVED CONFLICT

A. C. Kerckhoff, 1966

1. In choosing their life work, it is most important that children consider getting ahead in life no matter how far from home this may take them.
2. Children who move far away are not being fair to their parents.
3. When children move far away, family ties become broken.
4. When children move away they get different ideas and lose respect for their parents.
5. Children who move up in the world tend to neglect their parents.
6. Getting ahead in the world can be a bad thing if it keeps your family from being close.

SOURCE: A. C. Kerckhoff. "Norm Value Clusters and the 'Strain toward Consistency' among Older Married Couples." In *Social Aspects of Aging*, I. H. Simpson and J. C. McKinney (eds.). pp. 144-45. Durham N.C.: Duke University Press, 1966. Reprinted by permission of author and publisher.

V2.5.III.d

SIGNIFICANCE OF GRANDPARENTS

J. Robertson, 1976

1. A child would miss much if there were no grandparents when he was growing up.
2. Grandparents are not too old-fashioned or out of touch to be able to help their grandchildren.
3. A good grandparent does not spoil grandchildren.
4. Grandparents have much influence on grandchildren.
5. Grandparents would rather spend time with their friends of their own age than with their grandchildren.
6. Teenagers do not feel that grandparents are a bore.
7. Grandparents should be more like a friend than a respected elder.
8. Grandparents should discipline grandchildren.

9. Grandparents don't usually have much influence on their grandchildren.

SOURCE: J. Robertson. "Significance of Grandparents: Perceptions of Young Adult Grandchildren." *The Gerontologist*, 1976, 16:137-46. Reprinted by permission of author and publisher.

V2.5.III.e

EXTENDED FAMILY AS REFERENCE GROUP

R. Stuckert, 1963

All respondents are asked a series of questions about common family problems such as furnishing their homes, raising their children, and disagreements with relatives and friends. They are then asked the following questions about these problems (response is "yes" or "no"):

1. Would thinking about how your parents (relatives) might handle a problem like this help you or hinder you in deciding what to do?
2. Have you gotten any ideas about matters such as this from you parents (relatives) recently?
3. If your parents (relatives) strongly disagreed with you on this matter would you be concerned about it?
4. Would you talk over your differences with them?
5. Would you reconsider your ideas or feelings about this matter?

SOURCE: R. Stuckert. "Occupational Mobility and Family Relationships." *Social Forces*, 1963, 41:301-7. Reprinted by permission of author and publisher.

V2.5.III.f

ATTITUDES TOWARD MULTIGENERATIONAL HOUSEHOLDS

C. H. Mindel, 1977

We want to ask a few general questions about family life. These are about any family, *not* just yours in particular. There are no right or wrong answers, just answer how you feel. Please answer whether you:

1 Strongly Agree
2 Agree
3 Not Sure
4 Disagree
5 Strongly Disagree

with these statements.

1. If children have enough room in their homes it is only proper for them to ask their elderly relative to live with them.
2. If children are financially able it is only proper for them to ask their elderly relative to live with them.
3. People should help their elderly relative just as a matter of course, as part of family living.
4. The help people give their elderly relatives should be considered a *repayment* to them for the things they did for you earlier in life.
5. People who cannot live independently should live with their children rather than live in a *nursing home*.
6. People who cannot live independently should live with their children rather than live in a *boarding home* (i.e., a residence where room and board is provided).

7. When children have become adults it is still nice to have them live at home with the parents.
8. When parents get older and need help they should be asked to move in with their married children.

SOURCE: C. H. Mindel. "A Multiple Regression Approach to Satisfaction in Multigenerational Households." Paper presented to the 30th Annual Meeting of the Gerontological Society, San Francisco, November 18-22, 1977.

Chapter 6

Work and Retirement

Edward A. Powers

One of the more extensive areas of research in social gerontology is that of work and retirement. Walther (1976) recently identified almost 200 studies funded by the federal government during the 10-year period between 1965 and 1976, and the research continues at a phenomenal rate. The range of concerns is extensive: social insurance and public assistance, social and financial policy, employment and earning patterns, work performance, pensions and personnel policies, reeducation and rehabilitation, pre- and postretirement education, and attitudes and adjustment to work and retirement. (For a review of some of this literature, see Donahue, Orbach, and Pollak, 1960; Friedmann and Orbach, 1974; Sheppard, 1976; and Walther, 1976.) Since much of the work is descriptive, there has been little need for scales or indexes. The potential for scale development, for the most part, has been in the areas of attitudes toward work and retirement, and pre- and postretirement education.

In research on work and retirement, systematic instrument development has been poor. Researchers tend to use single-item indicators, borrowing rather freely from each other and rewording questions to fit their specific needs. In fact, a variation of the same question can be identified in a number of studies, although the item seldom is worded the same. For example, Parnes and Nestel (1974), Kerckhoff (1964), Glamser (1976), and Thompson (1956) each have used a variation of a question concerning whether individuals look forward to retirement. A question on whether individuals would continue working even if they had a sufficient outside income has been used as a single-item indicator by Morse and Weiss (1955), Bauder and Doerflinger (no date), Crook and Heinstein (1958), and Powers and Goudy (1971), and it has been used as part of a scale or an index by Miljus (1970), Simpson, Back, and McKinney (1966), and Parnes and Nestel (1974). Many similar examples could be cited. The point is that, because there has been little attention paid to exact replication, the comparison of findings is questionable.

The scales that do exist are, for the most part, poorly developed and/or tested. Researchers delete items, not because that has been suggested by psychometric testing, but because it is their personal preference.

There is another body of research, however, that is related to work and retirement. In the fields of personnel and guidance, and work and occupations there has been research on job satisfaction, occupational roles, leadership, and vocational interests. (See Carroll, 1973; and Robinson, Athanasion, and Head, 1969, for a review of the instruments.) In these areas psychometric testing and replication have received careful attention, although the factor of age seldom has been important in scale construction, at least for individuals over 55 years old. Thus, in two parallel bodies of knowledge, there are few well-substantiated instruments that measure the attitudes toward work and retirement of older individuals.

Major Research Concerns

Adjustment to Retirement

Many researchers tried to identify the consequences of retirement. (See, for example, Carp, 1972; Eisdorfer, 1972; Friedmann and Orbach, 1974; Livson, 1962; Riley and Foner, 1968; Shanas, 1972; Sheldon, McEwan, and Ryser, 1975; Streib and Schneider, 1971; and Thompson and Streib, 1958.) Yet, only at the most general level is there much agreement as to what factors are affected by retirement. Among those typically listed are level of living, social roles, levels of social interaction, attitude toward the loss of work and retirement, and self-perceptions and outlooks on life. Some have argued that health also is affected by retirement, but this conclusion is questionable (Friedmann and Orbach, 1974; Riley and Foner, 1968).

How adjustment to retirement should be measured is even more debatable. Researchers have devised numerous measures that depend on factors of adjustment thought to be important. The operationalization of these factors reflects the differences in conceptualization; hence, comparability is low. Measures of adjustment usually consist of a combination of single-item indicators and, occasionally, scales.

Only recently has there been attention to whether dimensions of retirement adjustment are correlated (Sheldon, McEwan, and Ryser, 1975).

Feelings and Attitudes about Work or Retirement

Most of the instruments reviewed in this chapter were designed to measure a specific attitude or behavior. Research, for the most part, has been limited to how preretirement-age persons evaluate work or retirement.

Instruments Reviewed

It would not be possible to divide the instruments reviewed here into work scales and retirement scales. Some contain items on both work and retirement. Others have been reworded to apply to either topic. The instruments in this chapter, therefore, are listed in order of overall merit, reflecting not only psychometric testing but potential usefulness as well. Two single-item indicators are included last. (See Table 6-1).

TABLE 6-1
Measures Reviewed in Chapter 6

	Instrument	Author(s)	Code Number
a.	Internal-External Control Scale	Andrisani and Nestel (1974)	V2.6.I.a
b.	Retirement Descriptive Index	Smith, Kendall, and Hulin (1969)	Copyrighted
c.	Preretirement Scale	Boyack and Tiberi (1975)	V2.6.I.c
d.	Satisfaction with Retirement Scale	Thompson and Streib (1958)	V2.6.I.d
e.	Index of Job Satisfaction	Quinn and Shepard (1974)	V2.6.I.e
f.	Attitudes toward the Employment of Older People	Kirchner, Lindbom, and Paterson (1952)	V2.6.I.f
g.	Attitude toward Retirement	Thompson (1956)	V2.6.I.g
h.	Work Commitment	Simpson, Back, and McKinney (1966)	V2.6.I.h
i.	Avoid Retirement Scale	Goudy, Powers, and Keith (1975)	V2.6.I.i
j.	Propensity to Retire	Miljus (1970)	V2.6.I.j
k.	Resistance to Retirement Scale	Greene et al. (1969)	V2.6.I.k
l.	Job Satisfaction Scale	Goudy, Powers, and Keith (1975)	V2.6.I.l
m.	Commitment to Work	Westoff et al. (1961)	V2.6.I.m
n.	Attitude toward Retirement	Glamser (1976)	V2.6.I.n
o.	Index of Work Commitment	Parnes and Nestel (1974)	V2.6.I.o
p.	Index of Involvment with Retirement	Barfield and Morgan (1969)	V2.6.I.p
q.	Attitude toward Retirement Index	Parnes and Nestel (1974)	V2.6.I.q
r.	Meaning of Work I	Friedmann and Havighurst (1954)	Single-item indicator
s.	Meaning of Work II	Morse and Weiss (1955)	Single-item indicator

The Internal-External Control Scale has been a common research tool, although it usually has been employed with adolescent or ethnic samples. Only recently has research on external-internal control been performed with older samples. Andrisani and Nestel (1974) used an abbreviated Internal-External Control Scale consisting of the Rotter (1966) items that were appropriate for an adult sample, including several work-oriented items. The abbreviated Andrisani and Nestel scale is reliable, and it correlates well with the original instrument. (See Chapter 4 of Volume 1 for a discussion of internal-external control scales.)

The Retirement Descriptive Index developed by Smith, Kendall, and Hulin (1969) is a well-tested instrument. The RDI taps four dimensions of retirement: activities, finances, people, and health. It has been tested with a sizable national sample of both men and women, although only in industrial settings. The length of the instrument and its method of administration require a major time commitment, and, therefore, the scale will not be useful in some research. The instrument is a fairly comprehensive measure of the dimensions of retirement. Additional testing is necessary, but the scale is promising.

One of the more extensively tested instruments in work and retirement is Boyack and Tiberi's (1975) Preretirement Scale. The scale was systematically developed, and it taps a number of different preretirement attitudes and behaviors. Using the scale, however, requires a sizable time investment. The instrument was developed with a nonrepresentative sample.

Thompson and Streib's four-item Satisfaction with Retirement Scale (1958) has been used a number of times, and so it exists in three different versions. It measures one aspect of retirement—reactions to the loss of the job. Simpson, Back, and McKinney (1966) labeled the scale Job Deprivation, which seems a better description of the items. The scale was developed with a large national sample.

The Quinn and Shepard Index of Job Satisfaction (1974) is one of the few scales to be developed on a general sample of workers and with norms for older individuals. The instrument differentiates between age-groups. The sections of the scale tap both global and specific dimensions of job satisfaction. Major drawbacks of the index are the method of administration and the time investment it requires. The instrument involves a card sort that is inappropriate for self-administration. Each card sort requires approximately 5 minutes. The instrument does provide comprehensive coverage of many dimensions of job satisfaction.

Attitudes toward the Employment of Older People (Kirchner, Lindbom, and Paterson, 1952) is a scale about older individuals that has been used with a number of samples covering a wide age range, including an aged subsample. The scale is clear, well written, and easy to administer.

Although quite old and not widely used of late, the Attitude toward Work subscale of the Attitude Inventory (Cavan et al., 1949) was rigorously developed. The instrument consists of seven simple and clear items tapping various aspects of work. Given the history of the instrument and the individuals associated with its development, it should not be surprising that several of the items appear on general life-satisfaction scales. (See Chapter 5 of Volume 1.) The instrument was developed with a large national sample of both men and women, although the sample was biased toward middle-class, college-town individuals. The scale takes little time and is easy to administer. It requires careful retesting for reliability and validity, but it can be a useful instrument. (The entire Attitude Inventory is reviewed in Chapter 5 of Volume 1.)

Thompson's Attitude toward Retirement (1956) has been used with a number of samples, some very large. The scale is a short, well-written set of items that measures reluctance to retire. Fillenbaum (1971) suggested that one of the items is more a measure of job mobility than interest in work.

Simpson, Back, and McKinney's Work Commitment scale (1966) was developed with a limited sample and has received little psychometric testing. There is not a great deal upon which to judge the instrument, but it is a well-written, comprehensive set of items. The instrument's ability to distinguish between occupational categories should be explored in greater detail. The scale could provide good coverage of work commitment with very few items.

Through factor analysis the Avoid Retirement Scale (Goudy, Powers, and Keith, 1975) was developed with a sizable but nonrepresentative sample. The scale consists of items that measure feelings about the negative aspects of retirement. Further development is needed.

The items in Miljus's (1970) Propensity to Retire index appear to be a good measure of how desirable retirement may be, although the index has had little psychometric testing. The index differentiates between age and occupational categories.

Greene and associates (1967) developed the Resistance to Retirement Scale in order to tap two dimensions of retirement—how involved and also how bored an individual expects to be during retirement. This short, self-administered scale is appropriate when research is limited to these two areas.

The Job Satisfaction Scale developed by Goudy, Powers, and Keith, (1975) consists of frequently used measures of evaluations of an individual's job. For this reason, the scale may be of interest, but it needs psychometric testing.

The Commitment to Work scale (Westoff et al., 1961) was developed for use with other age-groups but more recently has been employed with an older sample (Glamser, 1976). In both cases, it was considered a measure of commitment to work. The items are scaled, but they are general and, at times, only indirectly related to work. In fact, the instrument seems to measure the extent to which work provides an individual satisfaction more than an individual's commitment to work. Further development is needed. The scale cannot be recommended as a measure of work commitment.

According to Glamser (1976), items in the Attitude toward Retirement scale were drawn from a number of sources. Questions are equally divided between personal and more general reactions to retirement. One item, however, seems to be a more appropriate measure of commitment to work than attitude toward retirement. Other items tap overall judgment of retirement instead of reactions to specific dimensions. The instrument is short and easy to administer.

There has been little psychometric testing of the Index of Work Commitment developed by Parnes and Nestel (1974). The index seems as much a test of the meaning of work as of work commitment.

There is little at this time to recommend the Index of Involvement with Retirement by Barfield and Morgan (1969). Although developed with a large national sample, it has received little psychometric testing. The scale measures components of the social environment that may have little to do with feelings about retirement. Why, for example, would having a hobby appropriate for retirement be a measure of involvement with retirement?

The Parnes and Nestel's (1974) Attitude toward Retirement Index was developed with a large national sample. Each item seems to tap a different aspect of retirement but is likely to be related only indirectly to retirement as "a reasonably happy state."

A frequent measure of the meaning of work is an item concerning having enough money to quit work. For this reason, it is perhaps unwise to identify the question with Morse and Weiss (1955). This item taps the extent to which dimensions of the job, other than finances, are sufficient to prevent an individual from ceasing work when the opportunity arises. Friedmann and Havighurst's (1954) single-item measure of the meaning of work is concerned with the satisfaction, if any, received from a job. Since the two items address different aspects of the meaning of work, it is difficult to recommend one over the other, although the Friedmann and Havighurst's item has been used with cross-national samples.

Recommendations

There are three main directions for the future development of scales that assess aspects of work and retirement. First, additional psychometric testing is urgently needed since very few scales have been carefully examined. Reliability and validity seldom have been established. This could be accomplished if researchers would stop revising each other's work. Norms for various samples, especially for women, are needed. Second, the existing scales in personnel, work, and occupations (which for the most part have received more extensive psychometric development) should be employed with older samples. It is likely that some information on older subjects already exists since many instruments were developed with general samples of the labor force. Norms for aged subsamples need to be derived from these studies. Finally, the measurement of "adjustment to retirement" needs to be improved. There seems to be little agreement about retirement adjustment beyond an acknowledgment that both structural and social psychological factors must be measured. Perhaps it is unreasonable to assume that various aspects of adjustment to retirement should intercorrelate, but this should be attempted, at least.

REFERENCES

Andrisani, P., and G. Nestel. "Internal-External Control and Labor Market Experience." In *The Preretirement Years* (vol. 4), H. Parnes, A. Adams, P. Andrisani, A. Kohen, and G. Nestel (eds.), pp. 197-235. Columbus, Ohio: Center for Human Resource Research, 1974.

Atchley, R. "Respondents vs. Refusers in an Interview Study of Retired Women: An Analysis of Selected Characteristics." *Journal of Gerontology*, 1969, 24:44-47.

Barfield, R. E., and J. Morgan. *Early Retirement*. Ann Arbor, Mich.: Institute for Social Research, University of Michigan, 1969.

Bauder, W., and J. Doerflinger. *Patterns of Withdrawal from Occupational Roles among Older Men*. Ames, Iowa: Cooperative Research and Demonstration Grants Program, Iowa State University, no date.

Boyack, V.L., and D. M. Tiberi. "A Study of Preretirement Education." Paper presented to the 28th Annual Meeting of the Gerontological Society, Louisville, October 26-30, 1975.

Carp, F. M. *Retirement*. New York: Behaviorial Publications, 1972.

Carroll, B. *Job Satisfaction*. Ithaca, N.Y.: School of Industrial and Labor Relations, Cornell University, 1973.

Cavan, R. S., E. W. Burgess, R., J. Havighurst, and H. Goldhammer. *Personal Adjustment in Old Age*. Chicago: Science Research Associates, 1949.

Crook, G. H., and M. Heinstein. *The Older Worker in Industry*. Berkeley, California: Institute of Industrial Relations, University of California, 1958.

Donahue, W., H. L. Orbach, and O. Pollak. "Retirement: The Emerging Social Pattern." In *Handbook of Social Gerontology*, C. Tibbitts (ed.), pp. 330-406. Chicago: University of Chicago Press, 1960.

Eisdorfer, C. "Adaptation to Loss of Work." In *Retirement*, F. M. Carp (ed.), pp. 245-66. New York: Behavioral Publications, 1972.

Fillenbaum, G. "On the Relation between Attitude to Work and Attitude to Retirement." *Journal of Gerontology*, 1971, 26:244-48.

Friedmann, E. A., and R. J. Havighurst. *The Meaning of Work and Retirement*. Chicago: University of Chicago Press, 1954.

Friedmann, E. A., and H. L. Orbach. "Adjustment to Retirement." In *American Handbook of Psychiatry*, S. Arieti (ed.), pp. 609-45. New York: Basic Books, 1974.

Glamser, F. D. "Determinants of a Positive Attitude toward Retirement." *Journal of Gerontology*, 1976, 31: pp. 104-7.

Goudy, W. J., E. A. Powers, and P. Keith. "Work and Retirement: A Test of Attitudinal Relationships." *Journal of Gerontology*, 1975, 30: pp. 193-98.

Greene, M. R., C. H. Pyron, V. V. Manion, and H. Winklevoss. *Preretirement Counseling: Retirement Adjustment and the Older Employee*. Eugene, Ore.: School of Management and Business, University of Oregon, 1969.

Hunt, P., D. Schupp, and S. Cobb. *An Automated Self Report Technique*. Ann Arbor, Mich.: Institute for Social Research, University of Michigan, 1966.

Hunter, W. W. *Pre-Retirement Education for Hourly-Rated Workers*. Ann Arbor, Mich.: University of Michigan, Division of Gerontology, 1968.

Jaffe, A. J. "Retirement: A Cloudy Future." *Industrial Gerontologist*, 1972, special issue:1-90.

Keahey, S. "The Relationship of Self-actualization and Adjustment in Retirement and the Implications for Curriculum Development in Adult Education." Ph.D. dissertation, Texas A. & M. University, 1973.

Kerckhoff, A. C. "Husband-Wife Expectations and Reactions to Retirement." *Journal of Gerontology*, 1964, 19:510-16.

Kirchner, W. K., T. Lindbom, and D. Paterson. "Attitude toward the Employment of Older People." *Journal of Applied Psychology*, 1952, 36:154-56.

Livson, F. "Adjustment to Retirement." In *Aging and Personality*, S. Reichard, F. Livson, and P. G. Petersen (eds.), pp. 71-92. New York: John Wiley and Sons, 1962.

Miljus, R. "The Propensity to Retire." In *The Preretirement Years* (vol. 1). B. Fleisher, R. Miljus, and R. Spitz (eds.), pp. 169-202. Washington, D.C.: U.S. Department of Labor, 1970.

Morse, N. C., and R. S. Weiss. "The Function and Meaning of Work and the Job." *American Sociological Review*, 1955, 20:191-98.

National Council on the Aging. *The Myth and Reality of Aging in America*. Washington, D.C.: National Council on the Aging, 1975.

Palmore, E. (ed.). *Normal Aging*. Durham, N.C.: Duke University Press, 1970.

Parnes, H., and G. Nestel. In *The Preretirement Years* (vol. 4), H. Parnes, A. Adams, P. Andrisani, A. Kohen, and G. Nestel (eds.), pp. 153-96. Columbus, Ohio: Center for Human Resource Research, 1974.

Powers, E. A., and W. J. Goudy. "Examination of the Meaning of Work to Older Workers." *International Journal of Aging and Human Development*, 1971, 2: 38-45.

Quinn, R. P., and L. J. Shepard. *The 1972-1973 Quality of Employment Survey*. Ann Arbor, Mich.: Institute for Social Research, University of Michigan, 1974.

Riley, M. W., and A. Foner. *Aging and Society* (vol. 1). New York: Russell Sage Foundation, 1968.

Robinson, J., R. Athanasion, and K. B. Head. *Measures of Occupational Characteristics*. Ann Arbor, Mich.: Institution for Social Research, University of Michigan, 1969.

Rotter, J. "Generalized Expenctancies for Internal vs. External Control of Reinforcement." *Psychological Monographs*, 1966, number 609.

Shanas, E. *The Health of Older People: A Social Survey*, Cambridge, Mass.: Harvard University Press, 1962.

Shanas, E. "Adjustment to Retirement: Substitution or Accommodation?" In *Retirement*, F. M. Carp (ed.), pp. 219-44. New York: Behavioral Publications, 1972.

Shanas, E., P. Townsend, D. Wedderburn, H. Friis, P. Milhoj, and J. Stehouwer. *Old People in Three Industrial Societies*. New York: Atherton Press, 1968.

Sheldon, A., P. J. McEwan, and C. P. Ryser. *Retirement Patterns and Predictions*. Rockville, Md: National Institute of Mental Health, 1975.

Sheppard, H. "Work and Retirement." In *Handbook of Aging and the Social Sciences*, R. Binstock and E. Shanas (eds.), pp. 286-309. New York: Van Nostrand Reinhold, 1976.

Simpson, I. H., K. W. Back, and J. C. McKinney. "Attributes of Work, Involvement in Society, and Self-Evaluation in Retirement." In *Social Aspects of Aging*, I. H. Simpson and J. C. McKinney (eds.), pp. 45-54. Durham, N.C.: Duke University Press, 1966.

Smith, P. C., L. M. Kendall, and C. L. Hulin. *The Measurement of Satisfaction in Work and Retirement*. Skokie, Ill.: Rand McNally, 1969.

Streib, G. F., and C. J. Schneider. *Retirement in American Society*. Ithaca, N.Y.: Cornell University Press, 1971.

Thompson, W. E. "The Impact of Retirement." Ph.D. dissertation, Cornell University, 1956.

Thompson, W. E., and G. F. Streib. "Situational Determinants: Health and Economic Deprivation in Retirement." *Journal of Social Issues*, 1958, 14 (5):25-34.

Walther, R. "Education, Employment, Income and Retirement." In *A Comprehensive Inventory and Analysis of Federally Supported Research in Aging, 1966-1975*, Documentation Associates (eds.), pp. 225-64. Los Angeles, Calif. Documentation Associates Information Services, 1976.

Westoff, C., R. Potter, P. Nagi, and E. Mishler. *Family Growth in Metropolitan America*. Princeton, N.J.: Princeton University Press, 1961.

Abstracts

INTERNAL-EXTERNAL CONTROL SCALE

P. Andrisani and G. Nestel, 1974

Definition of Variable or Concept

The variable is the "degree to which an individual perceives success as being contingent upon initiative" (Adrisani and Nestel, 1974, p. 198).

Description of Instrument

The scale is an 11-item abbreviated version of Rotter's (1966) Internal-External Control Scale. The abbreviated scale includes only the items from the 23-item Rotter scale that appear to be related to work and are oriented toward adults.

Method of Administration

The scale may be used with either questionnaires or interviews. No special skill is needed to administer it.

Context of Development

One major concern in research has been the extent to which personal initiative results in individual success, a basic assumption of the American work ethic. Rotter (1966) developed his Internal-External Control Scale during work with an adolescent sample. Most of the concern in this area has been for the work orientation of young people or for establishing racial and ethnic differences. Only recently has there been attention to the role of internal-external control in the dynamics of the work experience. One concern of the National Longitudinal Survey (1974) was for the "active-mastery" approach to life of middle-aged men. An abbreviated Internal-External Control Scale that contained only adult-oriented and work-oriented items was developed with a sample of 56 technical-school students.

Sample

The scale was used in the 1969 National Longitudinal Survey sample of men 48 to 62 years of age. The benchmark study in 1966 consisted of 5,020 employed men between the ages of 45 and 59. The study utilized a multistage probability sample in 235 sample areas comprising 485 counties and cities representing every state and the District of Columbia. By the time of the 1971 interviews, the sample had experienced a 17% attrition, but the 1966 and 1971 samples were similar.

Scoring, Scale Norms, and Distribution

Scores are summed, with a range of 11 to 44. The abbreviated scale is one of the few internal-external scales to be used with an older sample.

The format of the 11 items is elaborated. Respondents are asked to indicate how closely the forced choice responses represent their opinions. Thus, four response options, not two, are possible on each item: 1 for the internal response "much closer"; 2 for the internal response "slightly closer"; 3 for the external response "slightly closer"; and "4" for the external response "much closer." See Table 6-2.

TABLE 6-2
Racial Distribution of Responses

Scores	Whites	Blacks
11-14	8.6%	3.4%
15-18	19.8%	10.6%
19-22	25.0%	17.2%
23-26	24.3%	29.3%
27-30	14.1%	24.2%
31-36	7.0%	13.1%
37-44	1.2%	2.2%

SOURCE: P. Andrisani and G. Nestel. "Internal-External Control and Labor Market Experience." In *The Preretirement Years* (vol. 2), H. Parnes, A. Adams, P. Andrisani, A. Kohen, and G. Nestel (eds.), p. 217. Columbus, Ohio: Center for Human Resource Research, 1974. Reprinted by permission.

Formal Tests of Reliability

On the 1969 sample of men, the internal consistency reliability estimate was .749. However, over a 2-year period, 1969-1971, the test-retest correlation between scores was only .55 for whites and .35 for blacks.

Formal Tests of Validity

The correlation between Rotter's scale and the abbreviated scale is .71. An item analysis of the 11-item scale resulted in item-total (minus item) correlations ranging from .192 to .420 in 1969, and .193 to .455 in 1971 (Andrisani and Nestel, 1974, p. 227).

Usability on Older Populations

As revised, it is a good scale for use with older samples.

General Comments

Internal-external control has been a common research topic, but usually it has been used with younger samples. Andrisani and Nestel's revision makes the scale appropriate for older samples.

References

Andrisani, P., and G. Nestel. "Internal-External Control and Labor Market Experience." In *The Preretirement Years* (vol. 4), H. Parnes, A. Adams, A. Andrisani, A. Kohen, and G. Nestel (eds.), pp. 197-235. Columbus, Ohio: Center for Human Resource Research, 1974.

Rotter, J. "Generalized Expectancies for Internal vs. External Control of Reinforcement." *Psychological Monographs*, 1966, number 609.

Instrument

See Instrument V2.6.I.a.

RETIREMENT DESCRIPTIVE INDEX (RDI)

P. C. Smith, L. M. Kendall, and C. L. Hulin, 1969

Definition of Variable or Concept

Feelings or affective responses to various facets of retirement are assessed.

Description of Instrument

The RDI measures the satisfaction of retirees in four areas: activities and work, financial situation, health, and people. Twelve factors were identified and collapsed into these four subscales.

Method of Administration

This index is usually administered in a questionnaire format. Each of the four subscales is presented on a separate page.

Context of Development

The investigators (Smith, Kendall, and Hulin, 1969) felt that the method of scale construction used to produce their Job Descriptive Index could be used to develop measures of retirement satisfaction as well. The RDI has been used with a rural-urban and black-white sample in Texas (Keahey, 1973).

Sample

The sample consisted of 600 male and 240 female retirees from 21 different plants in 16 different standard metropolitan statistical areas in the United States.

Scoring, Scale Norms, and Distribution

The items are scored in the following way, with a score assigned to each subscale: yes to a positive item, 3; no to a negative item, 3; ? to any item, 1; yes to a negative item, 0; and no to a positive item, 0.

Subscale median scores for males and females are as follows: activities and work, males 39, females 39; financial situation, males 32, females 29; people, males 44, females 44; and health, males 34, females 36. Additional data are available in Smith, Kendall, and Hulin, (1969).

Formal Tests of Validity

Correlations among the four dimensions for males ranged from .19 to .43.

Usability on Older Populations

It appears to be a good scale for retired persons.

Sensitivity to Age Differences

Overall, there were lower satisfaction scores among older retirees of both sexes. (See Smith, Kendall, and Hulin, 1969, for normative RDI scores for each subscale by age and sex.)

General Comments

Little research has been conducted with the RDI, and little is known about its measurement properties.

References

Smith, P. M., L. M. Kendall, and C. L. Hulin. *The Measurement of Satisfaction in Work and Retirement*. Skokie, Ill.: Rand McNally, 1969.

Keahey, S. "The Relationship of Self-actualization and Adjustment in Retirement and the Implications for Curriculum Development in Adult Education." Ph.D. dissertation, Texas A. & M. University, 1973.

Instrument

This copyrighted instrument is available from the Test Research Fund, Department of Psychology, Bowling Green State University, Bowling Green, Ohio 43403.

PRERETIREMENT SCALE

V. L. Boyack and D. M. Tiberi, 1975

Definition of Variable or Concept

This preretirement questionnaire measures attitudes, information, and behavior related to aging, retirement, and preretirement planning.

Description of Instrument

This is a factor-analyzed scale with 17 subscales. Seven of the subscales are attitudinal (retirement in general, resistance to retirement, preretirement optimism, functional worth and capability in retired persons, preretirement pessimism, perceived zest in retirement, and vulnerability to depression in retirement), five are informational (personal adjustment issues, health-care issues, economic planning, health-maintenance issues, and social relationships), and five are behavioral (life planning, volunteer/community activities, financial planning, health maintenance, and intimate relationships).

Method of Administration

The questionnaire requires approximately 30 minutes to complete. It has been used in group settings, but it could be altered to an interview format.

Context of Development

The measure was developed by the investigators to tap preretirement attitudes, knowledge, and behavior.

Sample

The scale was developed with 295 men and women (44% male and 56% female) between the ages of 45 and 72 (mean 58 years). The racial and marital status of the sample was fairly representative, but respondents had higher education and income levels than would be anticipated (30% were college graduates and only 29% had less than $15,000 income annually).

Scoring, Scale Norms, and Distribution

To develop the scales, two methods can be used: (1) each item score, within a factor, can be multiplied by its loading and summed; or (2) factor analysis can be performed on all items comprising each of the global variables: attitudes, information, and behavior. Each item, across factors within each global variable, then is multiplied by its factor loading and summed. The first method is the more convenient procedure, but the second method enhances discriminant validity. The scale measures reported are based on the second method. Factor loadings are presented with the instrument.

Formal Tests of Validity

Correlations among the subscales are listed in Table 6-3.

TABLE 6-3
Interscale Correlations for the Seven Attitudinal Subscales

Attitudes	1	2	3	4	5	6	7
1		−.35	.86	.85	−.86	.81	−.54
2			−.35	−.34	.48	−.49	.72
3				.80	−.79	.83	−.59
4					−.82	.84	−.60
5						−.88	.58
6							−.64
7							

(1) Positive attitude toward retirement in general.
(2) Attitude toward resistance to retirement in general.
(3) Attitude toward preretirement optimism.
(4) Attitude toward functional work and capability in retired persons.
(5) Attitude toward preretirement pessimism.
(6) Attitude toward perceived zest in retirement.
(7) Vulnerability to depression in retirement.

SOURCE: V. L. Boyack and D. M. Tiberi. "A Study of Preretirement Education." Paper presented to the 28th Annual Meeting of the Gerontological Society, Louisville, October 26-30, 1975. Reprinted by permission of the Ethel Percy Andrus Gerontology Center.

Selected information and behavior interscale correlations (Boyack and Tiberi, 1975): information about personal adjustment issues *with* behavior related to life planning ($r = .33$); information about health-care issues *with* behavior related to financial planning ($r = .43$); information about economic-planning issues *with* behavior related to financial planning ($r = .50$); information about health-maintenance issues *with* behavior related to health maintenance ($r = .41$); and information about social relationships *with* behavior related to intimate relationships ($r = .27$).

Usability on Older Populations

The scale is useful with preretirement-age samples.

General Comments and Recommendations

This scale takes a great deal of time to administer. If one can afford the time, many facets of preretirement attitudes and behavior may be tapped with a well-constructed instrument. The scale needs to be tested with a more representative sample.

Reference

Boyack, V. L., and D. M. Tiberi. "A Study of Preretirement Education." Paper presented to the 28th Annual Meeting of the Gerontological Society, Louisville, October 26-30, 1975.

Instrument

See Instrument V2.6.I.c.

SATISFACTION WITH RETIREMENT SCALE

W. E. Thompson and G. F. Streib, 1958

Definition of Variable or Concept

Postretirement satisfaction with retirement is examined.

Description of Instrument

This four-item Guttman-type scale measures what a person feels he or she would miss if he or she retired.

Method of Administration

The scale can be used in either a questionnaire or an interview, with closed- or open-ended response categories.

Context of Development

The scale was developed for the Cornell Study of Occupational Retirement (Thompson and Streib, 1958). Streib and Schneider (1971) utilized the scale for continued analysis of the same sample. In addition, they reworded the items and used the scale on a postretirement group for pre- and postretirement comparisons. Hunter (1968) employed the reworded scale in his study of preretirement education. Simpson, Back, and McKinney (1966) used the scale, labeling it Job Description. They restated the items as attitude statements with which respondents might agree or disagree (there were four response categories: strongly agree, agree, disagree, strongly disagree). Agreement with an item received 1 point, with a scale range of 0 through 4. Scores 0 through 2, which fell below or at the median, were grouped together as low job deprivation; scores 3 and 4 were grouped as high job deprivation. Atchley (1969) employed Simpson's version of the job commitment scale with a sample of retired women.

Sample

The sample reported in the 1958 article was first contacted in 1952-1953 and consisted of 1,260 gainfully employed men approximately 64 years of age. Streib and Schneider contacted respondents through industrial, state, county, and civil service systems; colleges and universities; and professional organizations. Respondents resided in the United States and were concentrated in industrial regions. The investigators acknowledged that the sample is not representative, but they felt that it included a variety of occupations and a range of skills, income levels, and job responsibilities (Thompson and Streib, 1958).

Scoring, Scale Norms, and Distribution

Respondents are dichotomized into satisfied and dissatisfied categories. A respondent is classified as satisfied only when he or she answers "hardly ever" or "never" to each of the four questions. (See Table 6-4.)

TABLE 6-4
Satisfaction with Retirement by Sex and Occupation

Occupation	Men[*]	Women[*]
Professional	37%	44%
Managerial, clerical	29%	34%
Skilled	31%	21%
Semiskilled	27%	19%
Unskilled	31%	37%

[*]Percentage scored satisfied in their year of retirement.

SOURCE: G. F. Streib and C. J. Schneider. *Retirement in American Society*. Ithaca, N.Y.: Cornell University Press, 1971, p. 132.

NOTE: See Streib and Schneider (1971) for cross-tabulations of the scale with other variables.

Formal Tests of Reliability

Reproducibility in 1954 (Thompson and Streib, 1958) was .97. Error ratio in 1954 was .40.

Usability on Older Populations

This is an appropriate scale for older individuals, either in their postretirement or preretirement years (if reworded).

Sensitivity to Age Differences

Simpson, Back, and McKinney (1966) found low correlations between age and retirement satisfaction ranging from .03 (for semiskilled workers) to .28 (for middle-stratum workers).

General Comments

This short, well-used scale seems to be testing only one aspect of retirement—reactions to the loss of a job.

References

Atchley, R. "Respondents vs. Refusers in an Interview Study of Retired Women: An Analysis of Selected Characteristics." *Journal of Gerontology*, 1969, 24: 44-47.

Hunter, W. W. *Pre-Retirement Education for Hourly-Rated Workers*, Ann Arbor, Mich.: University of Michigan, Division of Gerontology, 1968.

Simpson, I. H., K. W. Back, and J. C. McKinney. "Attributes of Work, Involvement in Society, and Self-evaluation in Retirement." In *Social Aspects of Aging*, I. H. Simpson and J. C. McKinney (eds.), pp. 45-54. Durham, N.C.: Duke University Press, 1966.

Streib, G. F., and C. J. Schneider. *Retirement in American Society*. Ithaca, N.Y.: Cornell University Press, 1971.

Thompson, W. E., and G. F. Streib. "Situational Determinants: Health and Economic Deprivation in Retirement." *Journal of Social Issues*, 1958, 14 (5): 25-34.

Instrument

See Instrument V2.6.I.d.

INDEX OF JOB SATISFACTION

R. P. Quinn and L. J. Shepard, 1974

Definition of Variable or Concept

The index assesses the favorable viewpoint of workers toward the work roles they occupy.

Description of Instrument

The index includes two equally weighted sections — 5 facet-free or global questions, and 33 facet-specific questions about six job dimensions (comfort, challenge, financial rewards, promotions, relations with co-workers, and resource adequacy).

Method of Administration

Both portions of the index are performed through a card-sort procedure. The facet-free card sort is introduced in the following manner (Quinn and Shepard, 1974, p. 53).

"The next question involves things a person may or may not look for in a job. Some of these things are on this set of cards. People differ a lot in terms of which of these things are more important to them. We'd like to know how important each of these things is to *you*. Please put each card *below* the (alternative) card which best reflects *how important* each thing is to *you*."

The instructions for the facet-fixed card sort are:

"Here are some cards that describe different aspects of a person's job. I'd like you to put each card *below* the (alternative) card which best reflects *how true* you feel each is of *your* job."

The four alternative cards for the card sort concerning the importance of certain job characteristics read: "It is very important to me to have a job where . . ."; "It is somewhat important to me to have a job where . . ."; "It is a little important to me to have a job where . . ."; and "It is not at all important to me to have a job where . . . ."

The four alternative cards for the job-satisfaction card sort read: "This is very true of my job"; "This is somewhat true of my job"; "This is a little true of my job"; and "This is not at all true of my job."

Workers are handed the set of statements and asked to sort them. No restriction is made on how many cards can be put in each pile. Once the worker has finished sorting his or her cards, the four piles are assembled by the interviewer and submitted for direct computer processing in accordance with a procedure developed by Hunt, Schupp, and Cobb (1966). The average time for administering each card sort is about 5 minutes.

Context of Development

The Index of Job Satisfaction was developed as part of the 1972-1973 Quality of Employment Survey (Quinn and Shepard, 1974). Items were selected from previous factor analytic studies of job satisfaction and from responses to open-ended questions about the attributes of an ideal occupation. Through a cluster analysis of two samples, the final index was developed.

Sample

Interviews were conducted with 1,496 employed persons 16 years of age or older and living in the United States. The sample was a national probability sample of dwellings.

Scoring, Scale Norms, and Distribution

The facet-free score is the arithmetic mean of the five questions; scores range from 1 to 5, a high score indicating high job satisfaction. The facet-specific score is the mean of the 33 questions; scores range from 1 to 4, a high score indicating high satisfaction.

Overall job satisfaction is computed by transforming the distributions of raw scores for facet-specific and facet-free job satisfaction into Z scores and taking a mean of the two resulting Z scores for each respondent. These scores are then multiplied by 100 to remove decimal points. The resulting scores are either positive or negative numbers, with higher scores indicating greater satisfaction.

TABLE 6-5
Overall, Facet-Free, and Facet-Specific Job Satisfaction, by Age

Age	Overall Job Satisfaction	Facet-Free Job Satisfaction	Facet-Specific Job Satisfaction
Under 21	−37	3.48	2.95
21-29	−24	3.49	3.07
30-44	14	3.95	3.21
45-54	10	3.92	3.20
55-64	16	3.95	3.24
65 or older *	67	4.57	3.44

* $N = 100$.

SOURCE: R. P. Quinn and L. J. Shephard. *The 1972-1973 Quality of Employment Survey*, p. 86. Ann Arbor, Mich.: Institute for Social Research, University of Michigan, 1974. Reprinted by permission.

NOTE: For additional information on the index, see Quinn and Shepard, 1974.

Formal Tests of Reliability
Internal consistencies of .88, .72, and .92 were noted for overall, facet-free, and facet-specific satisfaction, respectively.

Formal Tests of Validity
The facet-specific and facet-free scales correlate moderately ($r = .46$).

Usability on Older Populations
The index is appropriate for employed persons.

Sensitivity to Age Differences
As noted above, older workers exhibit greater general, facet-specific, and overall job satisfaction.

General Comments
The index is one of the most comprehensive measures of job satisfaction.

References
Hunt, P., D. Schupp, and S. Cobb. *An Automated Self Report Technique.* Ann Arbor, Mich.: Institute for Social Research, University of Michigan, 1966.

Instrument
See Instrument V2.6.I.e.

ATTITUDES TOWARD THE EMPLOYMENT OF OLDER PEOPLE
W. R. Kirchner, T. Lindbom, and D. Paterson, 1952

Definition of Variable or Concept
Attitudes toward the employment of older workers in business and industry are assessed.

Description of Instrument
The summated scale consists of 24 Likert-type attitude items concerning a range of older persons' job-related behaviors.

Method of Administration
The scale can be administered through either an interview or a questionnaire. No special administration skill is needed.

Context of Development

The investigators at the Industrial Relations Center (University of Minnesota) developed the attitude scale during their studies of older employees (Kirchner, Lindbom, and Paterson, 1952). Items reflecting opinions about older employees were gathered from the literature and administered to 42 college students and 38 business supervisors. A revised 27-item scale was administered to 46 employees and 16 supervisors and executives. A final form of the scale containing 24 items was developed with a much larger sample.

Sample

The final 24-item scale was developed with a sample of 1,460 men and women. The sample was diverse; including a general sample from Minnesota, a nationwide group of personnel people, and 200 psychologists, among others. The age range of the respondents was from 20 to over 60, with a sizable number (116) over 60 years of age (Kirchner, Lindbom, and Paterson, 1952).

Formal Tests of Reliability

Reliability was not computed for the aged subgroup of the sample. For the entire sample test-retest reliability ranged from .49 to .86 for the various subgroups, with an overall coefficient of .67. Split-half coefficients ranged from .60 to .92 for the various subgroups (Kirchner, Lindbom, and Paterson, 1952).

Scoring, Scale Norms, and Distribution

The scale is scored from 0 to 4 for a score range of 0 to 96, with 48 as the neutral point. A low score indicates a negative attitide toward older workers.

Sex, education, marital status, and years on the job are not related to scale scores. Age does appear to be related to scale scores, with an estimated coefficient for all of the nine subsamples of .55. The data are biased somewhat because some respondents with advanced psychological training refused to take a position on many of the items.

Usability on Older Populations

The scale appears to be usable with any age sample.

Sensitivity to Age Differences

As noted above, age is positively correlated with attitudes toward the employment of older persons.

General Comments and Recommendations

This scale was developed in a very thorough manner, but, unfortunately, it was not examined for validity. Additional work is needed, but it has great promise.

References

Kirchner, W. K. "Attitudes toward the employment of older persons." Ph.D. disserartation, University of Minnesota, 1954.
Kirchner, W. K., T. Lindbom, and D. Paterson. "Attitude toward the Employment of Older People." *Journal of Applied Psychology*, 1952, 36: 154-56.

Instrument

See Instrument V2.6.I.f.

ATTITUDE TOWARD RETIREMENT

W. E. Thompson, 1956

Definition of Variable or Concept

Preretirement willingness or reluctance to retire in both attitude and planning is assessed.

Description of Instrument

The three-item, Guttman-type scale examines an individual's preretirement feelings about work and retirement.

Method of Administration

The scale can be used in either questionnaires or interviews, with closed or open-ended response categories. No special skill is needed to administer the items.

Context of Development

The scale apparently was developed by the investigator to measure preretirement attitudes (Thompson, 1956). It was used in the work of Thompson and Streib (1958) and Streib and Schneider (1971). Fillenbaum (1971) used only two of the items because she felt the third item ("If it were up to you alone, would you continue working for your present employer?") reflected job mobility rather than interest in work.

Sample

The Thompson and Streib (1958) sample, when first contacted in 1952-1953, consisted of 1,260 gainfully employed men approximately 64 years old. The researchers contacted respondents through industrial, state, county, and civil service systems; colleges and universities; and professional organizations. The respondents resided in the United States and were concentrated in industrial regions. The investigators acknowledged the fact that the sample was not representative, but they felt that it included respresentatives of a variety of occupations and a range of skills, income levels, and job responsibilities.

Scoring, Scale Norms, and Distribution

The scale is scored through summation with unit weights of the positive responses. See Streib and Schneider (1971) for cross-tabulations of the scale by many variables.

Formal Tests of Reliability

Reproducibility in 1952 was .96. Error ratio in 1952 was .32 (Thompson, 1958).

Usability on Older Populations

This is an appropriate scale for use with samples of preretired persons.

Sensitivity to Age Differences

There is no indication the scale's sensitivity to age differences in the available literature.

General Comments and Recommendations

The scale has been used by several researchers with a variety of samples. It needs further testing but seems to be tapping general attitudes about retirement with very few items. Fillenbaum's reservations (1971) should be given careful consideration.

References

Fillenbaum, G. "On the Relation between Attitude to Work and Attitude to Retirement." *Journal of Gerontology*, 1971, 26: 244-48.

Streib, G. F., and C. J. Schneider. *Retirement in American Society*, Ithaca, N.Y.: Cornell University Press, 1971.

Thompson, W. E. "The Impact of Retirement." Ph.D. dissertation, Cornell University, 1956.

————. "Pre-Retirement Anticipation and Adjustment in Retirement," *Journal of Social Issues*, 1958, 14 (5): 35-45.

Thompson, W. E., and G. F. Streib. "Situational Determinants: Health and Economic Deprivation in Retirement." *Journal of Social Issues*, 1958, 14 (5): 25-34.

Instrument

See Instrument V2.6.I.g.

WORK COMMITMENT

I. H. Simpson, K. W. Back, and J. C. McKinney, 1966

Definition of Variable or Concept

The degree of an individual's intrinsic satisfaction from work is examined.

Description of Instrument

This scale is a five-item, dichotomously scored, Guttman-type scale that examines the individual's orientation toward the nature of work, the financial aspects of work, and the individual's cognizance of time while at work.

Method of Administration

The items may be used with either interviews or questionnaires. No special administration skill is needed.

Context of Development

The scale was developed as a measurement of one dimension of an individual's overall orientation toward work.

Sample

Questionnaires and interviews were administered to 304 retired workers and 161 workers within 5 years of retirement in the Piedmont region of North Carolina. All the respondents were white, longtime residents of the area. They were or had been employed by a tobacco company, a textile and/or chemical factory, an insurance company, or one of three universities, or they were selected from local membership lists of the American Bar Association, American Medical Association, and the executive directories of a local YMCA.

Scoring, Scale Norms, and Distribution

Scale scores range from 0 through 5 and are grouped into high and low categories; low scores, 0 through 2, fall at or below the median; and high scores, 3 through 5, are above the median. Of the upper-level white-collar occupational group, 65.1% of the retired and 57.6% of the preretired were highly committed to their work. Middle-level employees reported less commitment (35.7% of the retired and 40.6% of preretired), and semi-skilled employees reported the least commitment (24.7% of the retired and 29.4% of the preretired). Additional cross-tabulations are presented in Simpson, Back, and McKinney (1966).

Formal Tests of Reliability

The Guttman coefficient of reproducibility was .91.

Usability on older Populations

The scale seems to be usable with older samples.

Sensitivity to Age Differences

There are no sensitivities to age differences noted, although there is an indirect indication that retirees tend to exhibit lower commitment in middle-level and semiskilled occupations.

General Comments and Recommendations

This measure is a good scale of work commitment that distinguishes between occupational categories. It should be used further.

Reference

Simpson, I. H., K. W. Back, and J. C. McKinney. "Orientation toward Work and Retirement, and Self-evaluation in Retirement." In *Social Aspects of Aging*, I. H. Simpson and J. C. McKinney (eds.), pp. 75-89. Durham, N.C.: Duke University Press, 1966.

Instrument

See Instrument V2.6.I.h.

AVOID RETIREMENT SCALE

W. J. Goudy, E. A. Powers, and P. Keith, 1975

Definition of Variable or Concept

Negative judgments about retirement are investigated.

Description of Instrument

This four-item, Likert-type scale examines an individual's health, perceived proximity to death, and avoidance of retirement.

Method of Administration

It can be used with either questionnaires or interviews. No special administration skill is needed.

Context of Development

The investigators developed the scale through a factor analysis of a larger set of items, with a sample of nonmetropolitan males. The same individuals were reinterviewed on identical items 10 years later.

Sample

The scale was developed with a 1964 sample of 1,332 nonmetropolitan employed men aged 50 and older and living in a midwestern state. The respondents were from five occupational groups: self-employed professionals, salaried professionals, owner-merchants, factory workers, and farmers. The same individuals were reinterviewed 10 years later.

Scoring, Scale Norms, and Distribution

The scale is scored by summation with unit weights of the response options. This yields a scale ranging from 4 (negative judgment of retirement) to 20 (favorable judgment of retirement). In 1964, 2% of the respondents received scores of between 4 and 7, 32% scored between 8 and 11, 49% scored between 12 and 15, and 16% scored between 16 and 20.

Formal Tests of Reliability

The coefficient alpha in 1964 was .648. In 1974 for a fuller employed sample it was .681; for a partly retired sample, .640; and for a retired sample, .653.

Formal Tests of Validity

The Avoid Retirement Scale was weakly correlated with the respondents' willingness to accept an annuity (.10) and perceptions of other people's views of their job (−.13) (Goudy, Powers, and Keith, 1975).

Usability on Older Populations

The scale appears to be usable with an aged sample.

General Comments and Recommendations

The four-item scale taps general reactions to retirement. Before it can be used as an overall measure of retirement avoidance, it must be tested with female samples.

Reference

Goudy, W. J., E. A. Powers, and P. Keith. "Work and Retirement: A Test of Attitudinal Relationships." *Journal of Gerontology*, 1975, 30: 193-98.

Instrument

See Instrument V2.6.I.i.

PROPENSITY TO RETIRE

R. Miljus, 1970

Definition of Variable or Concept

Workers' attitudes concerning the desirability of retirement are assessed.

Description of Instrument

This index measures the desirability of retirement through four questions about preferred age of retirement, desire to continue work, reaction to job loss, and desire to work even with adequate resources.

Method of Administration

This index can be used in either a questionnaire or an interview. No special administration skill is needed.

Context of Development

The index was developed for use in the 1966 interviews in the National Longitudinal Survey studying the correlates of retirement attitudes.

Sample

The scale was developed with a probability sample consisting of 5,020 individuals representing the civilian noninstitutionalized population of males in the United States who (in 1966) were 45 to 59 years of age. The sample was drawn by the U.S. Bureau of the Census from 235 areas of the country.

Scoring, Scale Norms, and Distribution

Point values are assigned to responses to each question and the scores are summed; the highest values are assigned to responses that reflect a preference for a nonworking or retired role (Miljus, 1970, p. 181).

1. Preferred age of retirement:
   already retired—4 points
   under 65—3 points
   65—2 points
   66 or later; will always keep working—1 point
   don't know; no data—no points assigned, index cannot be computed

2. Whether will take another job following retirement from regular job:
   yes—no points
   no—2 points
   don't know; no data—no points assigned, index cannot be computed.

3. What the individual would do if he were to lose his job:
   retire—3 points
   any response which suggests not working—2 points
   look for work; become self-employed—1 point
   no answer; not ascertained—no points

4. Whether would continue to work even if were to receive enough money to live comfortably without working:
   no—3 points
   don't know; it depends—2 points
   yes—1 point
   no answer; not ascertained—no points

TABLE 6-6
Distribution of Scores by Age, Race, and Occupation

Type of Occupation and Age	Whites		Blacks	
	Average Score	High Propensity	Average Score	High Propensity
White-collar	5.3	27%	5.1	22%
45-49	5.2	25%	4.9	18%
50-54	5.3	26%	5.0	20%
55-59	5.6	32%	5.8	37%
Blue-collar	5.6	32%	5.3	26%
45-49	5.5	29%	5.4	25%
50-54	5.6	31%	5.2	30%
55-59	5.7	36%	5.3	22%
Service	5.6	35%	5.5	32%
45-49	5.6	29%	5.6	26%
50-54	5.7	39%	5.4	38%
55-59	5.5	37%	5.4	31%
Farm	4.6	15%	4.8	24%
45-49	4.6	15%	4.7	22%
50-54	4.6	18%	5.1	32%
55-59	4.7	10%	4.6	15%

SOURCE: R. Miljus. "The Propensity to Retire." In *The Preretirement Years* (vol. 1), H. Parnes, B. Fleisher, R. Miljus, and R. Spitz (eds.), p. 183. Washington, D.C.: U.S. Department of Labor, 1970. Reprinted by permission.

NOTE: For additional cross-tabulations, see Miljus, 1970.

Formal Tests of Validity

Although the investigators maintained that attitudes toward work are related to the propensity to retire, there is not much evidence presented to support this assertion.

Usability on Older Populations

The index is used with a preretirement sample.

Sensitivity to Age Differences

See Table 6-6.

General Comments

There has been little psychometric testing done on this scale, but it seems to have great potential. The scale apparently differentiates between occupational groups more than age-groups, although it is sensitive to both.

Reference

Miljus, R. "The Propensity to Retire." In *The Preretirement Years* (vol. 1), H. Parnes, B. Fleisher, R. Miljus, and R. Spitz (eds.), pp. 169-202. Washington, D.C.: U.S. Department of Labor, 1970.

Instrument

See Instrument V2.6.I.j.

RESISTANCE TO RETIREMENT SCALE

M. R. Greene, C. H. Pyron, V. V. Manion, and H. Winklevoss, 1969

Definition of Variable or Concept

The perceived difficulties and perceptions of retirement held by preretirement-age workers are assessed.

Description of Instrument

Six items with a four-point, Likert-type response set examine retirement planning, positive and negative reactions to retirement, and retirement activities.

Method of Administration

The scale can be used with either interviews or questionnaires. No special administration skill is needed.

Context of Development

The scale was developed for the investigators' study of preretirement counseling and retirement adjustment.

Sample

In the study, 230 active employees, aged 60 to 65, were interviewed about their views toward their impending retirement. The respondents were randomly selected (and stratified by skill level) from four medium to large (with 1,000 or more employees) companies in the western states.

Scoring, Scale Norms, and Distribution

Scores are summed. Respondents with scores in the top third are considered to exhibit high resistance to retirement (44.3%), respondents in the middle third are assigned an ordinal resistance rank of medium (23.9%), and respondents in the bottom third are classified as having low resistance (31.7%). (See Table 6-7.)

TABLE 6-7
Resistance to Retirement and Feelings about Retirement

	Resistance to Retirement Score			
	High Resistance	Medium Resistance	Low Resistance	Total %
Dislike retirement or reluctant	39.2%	21.8%	17.8%	28.3%
Look forward to retirement or can't wait to retire	60.8%	78.2%	82.2%	71.7%

SOURCE: M. R. Greene, C. H. Pyron, V.V. Manion, and H. Winkelvoss. *Preretirement Counseling: Retirement Adjustment and the Older Worker*, p. 77. Eugene, Ore.: University of Oregon, 1969. Reprinted by permission.

Formal Tests of Validity

The scale scores were significantly related to selected steroetypes of retirement items at the .001 level. To the investigators this suggested that resistance to retirement may be based on a negative or inaccurate view of retirement. (For a discussion of the association between resistance to retirement and other selected variables, see Green et al., 1969.)

Usability on Older Populations

The scale appears to be appropriate for older workers.

General Comments and Recommendations

A great deal more work should be done on this scale. It is a short, well-written set of items that has potential.

Reference

Greene, M. R., C. H. Pyron, V. V. Manion, and H. Winklevoss. *Preretirement Counseling: Retirement Adjustment and the Older Worker*. Eugene, Ore.: University of Oregon, 1969.

Instrument

See Instrument V2.6.I.k.

JOB SATISFACTION SCALE

W. J. Goudy, E. A. Powers, and P. Keith, 1975

Definition of Variable or Concept

An individual's positive evaluations of his or her line of work are assessed.

Description of Instrument

This four-item, factor-analyzed scale measures an individual's affective responses to his or her job, desire to continue in the same occupation, and his or her recommendation of the job to a friend.

Method of Administration

The scale can be used with either interviews or questionnaires. No special administration skill is needed.

Context of Development

The scale was part of a longitudinal study of work patterns in later life.

Sample

The scale was developed with a sample of 1,332 employed males 50 years of age and older and living in nonmetropolitian areas of a midwestern state. Five occupational groups were represented: self-employed professionals, salaried professionals, owner-merchants, factory workers, and farmers. All were reinterviewed 10 years later.

Scoring, Scale Norms, and Distribution

Responses to the first two items are on a Likert-type format. Because of the skewed distributions on these items, responses are bifurcated. Each item is scored 1 or 2; the lower the score, the lower the job satisfaction. (See Table 6-8.)

TABLE 6-8
Distribution of Scale Scores

Scale Score	Percentage of Total Respondents
4	10.8
5	14.5
6	26.7
7	27.5
8	20.6

SOURCE: E. A. Powers, personal communication, 1980.

Formal Tests of Reliability

Goudy, Powers, and Keith (1975) reported a Cronbach alpha of .60.

Usability on Older Populations

The scale appears to be appropriate for older workers.

General Comments

The items in this scale have been used in many studies as global measures of reactions to work.

Reference

Goudy, W. J., E. A. Powers, and P. Keith. "The Work-Satisfaction, Retirement-Attitude Typology: Profile Examination." *Experimental Aging Research*, 1975, 1:267-79.

Instrument

See Instrument V2.6.I.l.

COMMITMENT TO WORK

C. Westoff, R. Potter, P. Nagi, and E. Mishler, 1961

Definition of Variable or Concept

The degree to which individuals are committed to work and find continued satisfaction from employment is assessed.

Description of Instrument

This eight-item, summated scale measures an individual's regrets about work and work satisfaction.

Method of Administration

The scale can be used in either questionnaires or interviews. No special skills are needed to administer the scale.

Context of Development

The items are from the Westoff and associates (1961) study of completed family fertility. The scale then was used with an aged sample by Glamser (1976).

Sample

The Glamser (1976) sample was of workers in six glass-manufacturing plants in Pennsylvania. All male employees 60 years old and older were mailed a questionnaire; 70 responded (response rate 53%). The range of the occupations of the respondents was great, the mean level of education was 10 years, 60% of the respondents were hourly workers, and 40% were salaried employees.

Formal Tests of Reliability

The Cronbach's alpha coefficient for Glamser's (1976) aged sample was .82.

Usability on Older Populations

The scale appears to be appropriate for use with older workers.

General Comments and Recommendations

The scale needs further development. Although labeled Commitment to Work, it seems to be more concerned with the satisfaction in life provided by work.

References

Glamser, F. D. "Determinants of a Positive Attitude toward Retirement." *Journal of Gerontology*, 1976, 31:104-7.

Westoff, C., R. Potter, P. Nagi, and E. Mishler. *Family Growth in Metropolitan America.* Princeton, N.J.: Princeton University Press, 1961.

Instrument

See Instrument V2.6.I.m.

ATTITUDE TOWARD RETIREMENT

F. D. Glamser, 1976

Defnintion of Variable or Concept

The scale measures a "pre-retirement attitude toward retirement" (Glamser, 1976).

Description of Instrument

The five-item, Likert-type scale measures both positive and negative global feelings about retirement.

Method of Administration

The scale can be used with both interviews and questionnaires. No special administration skill is needed.

Sample

The sample was of workers in six glass-manufacturing plants in Pennsylvania. All male employees 60 years old and older were sent questionnaires; 70 responded (response rate 53%). The range of the occupations of the respondents was great, and the mean level of education was 10 years. Of the respondents 60% were hourly workers and 40% were salaried employees.

Scoring, Scale Norms, and Distribution

The scale has a range of possible scores from 5 to 25, with the higher scores indicating a more positive attitude toward retirement.

Formal Tests of Reliability

The Chronbach's alpha coefficient was .77.

Usability on Older Populations

The scale appears to be appropriate only for use with currently employed workers.

General Comments and Recommendations

The scale needs further development. There is no justification for the items included in the scale. In fact, the last item would be just as appropriate for a commitment-to-work scale as an attitude-toward-retirement scale.

Reference

Glamser, F. D. "Determinants of a Positive Attitude toward Retirement." *Journal of Gerontology*, 1976, 31:104-7.

Instrument

See Instrument V.2.6.I.n.

INDEX OF WORK COMMITMENT

H. Parnes and G. Nestel, 1974

Definition of Variable or Concept

The extent of preretirement attachment to the work role is assessed.

Description of Instrument

This is a two-item index. The first item asks whether an individual would continue to work even if he or she had enough money to live comfortably, and the second asks what the individual would do if he or she were permanently laid off from his or her current job.

Method of Administration

The index can be used with either interviews or questionnaires. No special administration skill is needed.

Context of Development

The index was designed by Parnes and Nestel. The first item (whether the respondent would continue to work even if he or she had enough money to live comfortably) is a variation of an item used by other investigators as a measure of the meaning of work. The second (what if the respondent lost his or her job) is similar to a question on the Social Security Administration's Longitudinal Work History Study.

Sample

The index was developed with a subsample of the National Longitudinal Survey (Parnes and Nestel, 1974). The age-group used in the subsample included approximately half of the 1966 national sample of 5,020 employed men between the ages of 45 and 59. The study utilized a multistage probability sample in 235 sample areas made up of 485 counties and cities representing every state and the District of Columbia.

Scoring, Scale Norms, and Distribution

When a respondent would continue to work and seek employment (56.4%), he or she is classified as having a high work commitment; when he or she would continue to work *or* seek employment (6.5%), he or she has a medium work commitment; and the individual has a low work commitment when he or she would quit work and not seek employment (18.0%). Responses were not obtained from 19.1% of the respondents.

Formal Tests of Validity

Among persons with high job commitment, 36% planned to retire before age 65, compared with 47% of those with low commitment (F ratio 8.96, significant at the .01 level). The Work Commitment Index was associated with expected early retirement.

Usability on Older Populations

The index appears to be appropriate for a preretirement-age population.

General Comments and Recommendations

There should be a great deal more work done on the index before it could be used with confidence.

Reference

Parnes, H., and G. Nestel. "Early Retirement." In *The Preretirement Years* (vol. 4), H. Parnes, A. Adams, P. Andrisani, A. Kohen, and G. Nestel (eds.), pp. 153-96. Columbus, Ohio: Center for Human Resource Research, 1974.

Instrument

See Instrument V2.6.I.o.

INDEX OF INVOLVEMENT WITH RETIREMENT
R. E. Barfield and J. Morgan, 1969

Definition of Variable or Concept

Preretirement behavior or experience with retirement is assessed.

Description of Instrument

This four-item index with a yes-no response category measures an individual's orientation toward retirement from his or her network, retirement hobbies, and expected age of retirement.

Method of Administration

The index is appropriate for use with either questionnaires or interviews. No special skills or requirements are needed to administer the index.

Context of Development

Barfield and Morgan (1969) wanted a multivariable alternative to the question "When will you retire?" for greater reliability and variance. Jaffe (1972) used the fourth item on the index as a single indicator of the respondent's attitude toward retirement, and the first item appears in the Social Security Administration's Longitudinal Work History Study.

Sample

A multistage area probability sample of 1,652 labor-force participants between the ages of 35 and 59 and residing in American private households (excluding Alaska and Hawaii) was used by Barfield and Morgan (1969).

Scoring, Scale Norms, and Distribution

In scoring, 1 point is given for each yes response on the first three items, 1 point is added for planning to retire before age 65, and 1 more point is given for planning to retire before age 60. The scale range of 0 to 5 is multiplied by 20 to produce a scale of 0 to 100, with a mean score of 37 (Barfield and Morgan, 1969, p. 30).

Usability on Older Populations

Obviously, the scale was designed for preretirement-age persons. With this restriction, it appears to be usable with older populations.

Sensitivity to Age Differences

The involvement index is actually measuring something different from the single item "When will you retire?" Yet, it does seem to be a reasonable assessment of preretirement activity.

References

Barfield, R. E., and J. Morgan. *Early Retirement.* Ann Arbor, Mich.: Institute for Social Research, University of Michigan, 1969.

Jaffe, A. J. "Retirement: A Cloudy Future." *Industrial Gerontologist*, 1972, special issue: 1-90.

Instrument

See Instrument V2.6.I.p.

ATTITUDE TOWARD RETIREMENT INDEX

H. Parnes and G. Nestel (1974)

Definition of Variable or Concept

The extent to which individuals view "retirement as a reasonably happy state" is assessed.

Description of Instrument

This four-item index measures the respondent's attitudes and perceptions about retirement.

Method of Administration

The index can be used in either questionnaires or interviews. No special administration skill is needed.

Context of Development

The index was developed for the National Longitudinal Survey in an attempt to help explain variation among individuals during their early retirement years.

Sample

The index was developed with the 1971 National Longitudinal Survey sample of men 50 to 64 years old. The benchmark study in 1966 consisted of 5,020 employed men between the ages of 45 and 59. The study utilized a multistage probability sample in 235 sample areas made up of 485 counties and cities representing every state and the District of Columbia. The 1971 sample had experienced a 17% attrition, but in most cases the 1966 and 1971 samples were similar.

Scoring, Scale Norms, and Distribution

Each question is assigned a binary code. A value of 1 is assigned to the item when the response suggests a favorable attitude toward retirement; otherwise, the response is coded 0. The codes are then summed. A score of 4 (for positive responses to all four items) is classified as a positive attitude toward retirement, a score of 3 is classified as ambivalent, and a score of 2 or less is classified as negative.

The distribution of the index was as follows: positive, 6.5%; ambivalent, 12.7%; negative, 16.9%; and not ascertained, 63.9%.

Usability on Older Populations

The index is usable with older samples, but it also seems appropriate for a younger sample.

General Comments and Recommendations

There is little to recommend the index at this time. The items are interesting, but do they measure "retirement as a reasonably happy state?"

Reference

Parnes, H., and G. Nestel. "Early Retirement." In *The Preretirement Years* (vol. 4), H. Parnes, A. Adams, P. Andrisani, A. Kohen, and G. Nestel (eds.), pp. 153-96. Columbus, Ohio: Center for Human Resource Research, 1974.

Instrument

See Instrument V2.6.I.q.

MEANING OF WORK I

E. A. Friedmann and R. J. Havighurst, 1954

Definition of Variable or Concept

The item measures "the individual's recognition of the part the job has played in his life and the type of affective response he has made to it" (Friedmann and Havighurst, 1954, p. 6).

Description of Instrument

This single, open-ended item asks the respondent what he or she misses (or will miss) about his or her job upon retirement. The item is "What will (do) you miss about your job?"

Method of Administration

The item is appropriate for use in either questionnaires or interviews. No special administration skill is needed.

Context of Development

The item was used by Friedmann and Havighurst (1954) in their investigation of the meanings of work for five occupational groups. In 1955 Morse and Weiss included the item in their national study of the meaning of work. Shanas used the item in both national and cross-national studies (1962; 1968). The recent national study (NCOA, 1975) Louis Harris and Associates performed for the National Council on the Aging also contained a variation of the item.

Sample(s)

The item has been used with steelworkers—a sample of 128 white, male, unskilled and semiskilled workers, 55 years and older, who were or had been employed in one midwestern steel mill; coal miners—153 men between 50 and 76 years of age who were employed in four large mining companies in southern Illinois; salespeople—74 men and women between 55 and 70 years of age employed in a large metropolitan department store; skilled craftsmen—208 men 65 years of age or older who were then, or who had retired from, working at a Chicago local of a small craft union; physicians—39 members of the American Medical Association living in Cook County, Illinois, who were 65 years of age or older (Friedmann and Havighurst, 1954).

Scoring, Scale Norms, and Distribution

This single-item indicator is analyzed as the percentage distribution of various responses coded from the open-ended interview. Table 6-9 lists the distribution of responses according to occupation.

TABLE 6-9
Distribution of Scores by Occupation
(in percentages)

	Steelworkers (Unskilled and Semiskilled)	Coalminers	Skilled Craftsmen	Salespeople	Physicians
No meaning other than money	28	18	11	0	0
Routine	28	19	15	21	15
Self-respect	—	—	—	12	7
Prestige, respect of others	16	18	24	11	13
Association	15	19	20	20	19
Purposeful activity, self-expression, new experience	13	11	30	26	15
Service to others	*	†	*	10	32

*Not covered in the questionnaire or interview.
†"Work has given me a chance to be useful."

SOURCE: E. A. Friedmann and R. J. Havighurst. *The Meaning of Work and Retirement*, p. 173. Chicago: University of Chicago Press, 1954.

NOTE: For distributions for various occupations and nationalities, see Friedmann and Havighurst, 1954; and Shanas et al., 1968.

Usability on Older Populations

The item is appropriate for any age sample.

General Comments

This item is good for measuring what meaning, other than money, work may have in life.

References

Friedmann, E. A., and R. J. Havighurst. *The Meaning of Work and Retirement*. Chicago: University of Chicago Press, 1954.

Morse, N. C., and R. J. Weiss. "The Function and Meaning of Work and the Job." *American Sociological Review*, 1955, 20; 191-98.

National Council on the Aging. *The Myth and Reality of Aging in America*. Washington, D.C.: National Council on the Aging, 1975.

Shanas, E. *The Health of Older People: A Social Survey*. Cambridge, Mass.: Harvard University Press, 1962.

Shanas, E., P. Townsend, D. Wedderbrun, H. Friis, P. Milhoj, and J. Stehouwer. *Old People in Three Industrial Societies*. New York: Atherton Press, 1968.

Instrument

See the description of the instrument given above.

MEANING OF WORK II

N. C. Morse and R. S. Weiss, 1955

Definition of Variable or Concept

The function of work and the job is assessed.

Description of Instrument

This single, closed-ended item asks the respondent whether he or she would quit work if offered the chance: "If by some chance you inherited enough money to live comfortably, without working, do you think that you would work anyway or not" (Morse and Weiss, 1955 [item may be used only for nonprofit purposes]). Frequently, the follow-up question "Why do you feel you would continue (quit) work?" is asked.

Method of Administration

The question can be used with both questionnaires and interviews. No special administration skill is needed.

Context of Development

The item has been used by many investigators, although the working of the item varies greatly. The question has been used by Morse and Weiss (1955), Bauder and Doerflinger (no date), Powers and Goudy (1971), Glamser (1976), and Crook and Heinstein (1958) as a single item. Miljus (1970) used the item as part of his Propensity to Retire scale; Simpson,

Back, and McKinney (1966) used it as part of their Work Commitment scale; and Parnes and Nestel (1974) used it as part of their Index of Work Commitment.

Sample

A random sample of 401 employed men in the United States was used by Morse and Weiss (1955).

Scoring, Scale Norms, and Distribution

The distribution of responses differes among the studies. For example, 80% of the men in Morse and Weiss's (1955) national sample would have taken an annuity, but only 57% of the men in Powers and Goudy's work (1971) gave the same response. There has not been enough similarity in the samples of research on this topic to permit comparison. Powers and Goudy (1971) and Morris and Weiss (1955) differed in the time of their research, the rural-urban nature of their samples, and the wording of the question. The distribution may be sample specific.

Usability on Older Populations

The item is appropriate for any age sample.

Sensitivity to Age Differences

In general, as age increases, the percentage of those who would continue to work decreases (Morse and Weiss, 1955); however, males of postretirement age express an *increased* desire to continue work (Morse and Weiss, 1955; Powers and Goudy, 1971).

General Comments and Recommendations

This is one of the most frequently used single-item indicators in the literature. There should be more consistency in item wording among the studies so that results can be compared.

References

Bauder, W., and J. Doerflinger. *Patterns of Withdrawal from Occupational Roles among Older Men*. Ames, Iowa: Cooperative Research and Demonstration Grants Program, no date.

Crook, G. H., and M. Heinstein. *The Older Worker in Industry*. Berkeley, Calif.: Institute of Industrial Relations, University of California, 1958.

Glamser, F. D. "Determinants of a Positive Attitude toward Retirement." *Journal of Gerontology*, 1976, 31:104-7.

Miljus, R. "The Propensity to Retire." In *The Preretirement Years* (vol. 1), H. Parnes, B. Fleisher, R. Miljus, and R. Spitz (eds.), pp. 169-202. Washington, D.C.: U. S. Department of Labor, 1970.

Morse, N. C., and R. J. Weiss. "The Function and Meaning of Work and the Job." *American Sociological Review*, 1955, 20: 191-98.

Parnes, H., and G. Nestel. "Early Retirement." In *The Pretirement Years* (vol. 2), H. Parnes, A. Adams, P. Andrisani, A. Kohen, and G. Nestel (eds.), pp. 153-96. Columbus, Ohio: Center for Human Resource Research, 1974.

Powers, E. A., and W. J. Goudy. "Examination of the Meaning of Work to Older Workers." *International Journal of Aging and Human Development*, 1971, 2:38-45.

Simpson, I. H., K. Back, and J. McKinney. "Orientation toward Work and Retirement and Self-evaluation in Retirement." In *Social Aspects of Aging*, I. H. Simpson and J. C. McKinney (eds.), pp. 75-89. N.C.: Duke University Press, 1966.

Instrument

See Instrument V2.6.I.s.

Instruments

V2.6.I.a.

INTERNAL-EXTERNAL CONTROL SCALE

P. Andrisani and G. Nestel, 1974

We would like to find out whether people's outlook on life has any effect on the kind of jobs they have, the way they look for work, how much they work, and matters of that kind. On each of these cards is a pair of statements, numbered 1 or 2. For each pair, please select ONE statement which is closer to your opinion. In addition, tell me whether the statement you select is MUCH CLOSER to your opinion or SLIGHTLY CLOSER.

In some cases you may find that you believe both statements, in other cases you may believe neither one. Even when you feel this way about a pair of statements, select the one statement which is more nearly true in your opinion.

Try to consider each pair of statements separately when making your choices — do not be influenced by your previous choices.

a. 1 ___ Many of the unhappy things in people's lives are partly due to bad luck.

2 ___ People's misfortunes result from the mistakes they make.

Is this statement much closer or slightly closer to your opinion?

8 ___ Much   9 ___ Slightly

b. 1 ___ In the long run, people get the respect they deserve in this world.

2 ___ Unfortunately, an individual's worth often passes unrecognized no matter how hard he tries.

Is this statement much closer or slightly closer to your opinion?

8 ___ Much   9 ___ Slightly

c. 1 ___ Without the right breaks, one cannot be an effective leader.

2 ___ Capable people who fail to become leaders have not taken advantage of their opportunities.

Is this statement much closer or slightly closer to your opinion?

8 ___ Much   9 ___ Slightly

d. 1 ___ Becoming a success is a matter of hard work; luck has little to do with it.

2 ___ Getting a good job depends mainly on being in the right place at the right time.

Is this statement much closer or slightly closer to your opinion?

8 ___ Much   9 ___ Slightly

e. 1 ___ What happens to me is my own doing.

2 ___ Sometimes I feel that I don't have enough control over the direction my life is taking.

Is this statement much closer or slightly
closer to your opinion?

8 ___ Much   9 ___ Slightly

f. 1 ___ When I make plans, I am almost   2 ___ It is not always wise to plan too far
certain that I can make them work.   ahead, because many things turn
out to be a matter of good or bad
fortune anyhow.

Is this statement much closer or slightly
closer to your opinion?

8 ___ Much   9 ___ Slightly

g. 1 ___ In my case, getting what I want has   2 ___ Many times we might just as well
little or nothing to do with luck.   decide what to do by flipping a coin.

Is this statement much closer or slightly
closer to your opinion?

8 ___ Much   9 ___ Slightly

h. 1 ___ Who gets to be boss often depends   2 ___ Getting people to do the right thing
on who was lucky enough to be in   depends upon ability; luck has little
the right place first.   or nothing to do with it.

Is this statement much closer or slightly
closer to your opinion?

8 ___ Much   9 ___ Slightly

i. 1 ___ Most people don't realize the extent   2 ___ There is really no such thing as
to which their lives are controlled by   "luck".
accidental happenings.

Is this statement much closer or slightly
closer to your opinion?

8 ___ Much   9 ___ Slightly

j. 1 ___ In the long run, the bad things that   2 ___ Most misfortunes are the result of
happen to us are balanced out by   lack of ability, ignorance, laziness,
the good ones.   or all three.

Is this statement much closer or slightly
closer to your opinion?

8 ___ Much   9 ___ Slightly

k. 1 ___ Many times I feel that I have little   2 ___ It is impossible for me to believe
influence over the things that happen   that chance or luck plays an im-
to me.   portant role in my life.

Is this statement much closer or slightly
closer to your opinion?

8 ___ Much   9 ___ Slightly

SOURCE: P. Andrisani and G. Nestel. "Internal-External Control and Labor Market Experience." In *The Preretirement Years* (vol. 4), H. Parnes, A. Adams, P. Andrisani, A. Kohen, and G. Nestel (eds.), pp. 197-235. Columbus, Ohio: Center for Human Resource Research, 1974.

V2.6.I.b

RETIREMENT DESCRIPTIVE INDEX

P. C. Smith, L. M. Kendall, and C. L. Hulin, 1969

This copyrighted instrument is available from the Test Research Fund, Department of Psychology, Bowling Green State University, Bowling Green, Ohio 43403.

V2.6.I.c

PRERETIREMENT SCALE

V. L. Boyack and D. M. Tiberi, 1975

ATTITUDES

1) positive attitude toward retirement in general

I-R Categories	Loading
Semantic differential	
"My Retirement"	
Good/Bad	−.798
Rough/Smooth	.695
Active/Passive	−.626
Empty/Full	.723
Happy/Miserable	−.806
Worthless/Valuable	.783
Planned/Unplanned	−.627
Uncomfortable/Comfortable	.726
Fair/Unfair	−.666
Dull/Interesting	.800
Rewarding/Painful	−.827
Boring/Exciting	.743

2) attitude toward resistance to retirement

Likert Scale
1. Strongly agree
2. Agree
3. Undecided
4. Disagree
5. Strongly disagree

Much of a retired person's life is boring and monotonous	.602
Idle hands are the devil's playthings	.290
Older people can learn new things just as well as younger people	−.408
I expect retirement to be the best years of my life	−.215

3) attitude toward preretirement optimism

1. Very much like me
2. Generally like me
3. Undecided
4. Generally not like me
5. Not like me at all

Lately I have been feeling useless	.543
I need somebody to push me in order to accomplish the things I want	.465

I-R Categories	Loading
The thought of growing old scares me	.498
When I think of retirement I get depressed	.469

4) attitude toward preretirement pessimism

I am looking forward to my retirement	.558
I feel that things are getting better as I grow older	.456
I expect retirement to be the best years of my life	.403

5) attitude toward functional worth and capability in retired persons

1. Strongly agree
2. Agree
3. Undecided
4. Disagree
5. Strongly disagree

Older people shouldn't exercise when they don't have to	.386
Sex is something that retired people are generally not interested in	.548
The basic needs of older people are different from those of younger people	.275
Retirement means not doing much of anything	.503
The more education a person has the better they can plan for their retirement	−.241

6) attitude toward perceived zest in retirement

Retired people are generally more lonely than nonretired people	.533
In general a person's health typically gets worse after they retire	.481
Retired people have plenty to do	.438
Most older people prefer not to get involved in community affairs	.319

7) vulnerability to depression in retirement

Older people are valuable because of their experiences	.742
Older people are just as useful to society as younger people	.433

INFORMATION

1. No knowledge
2. A little knowledge
3. Some knowledge
4. Knowledgeable
5. Very Knowledgeable

1) information about personal adjustment issues

How to deal with loneliness	.716
How to become a better and more interesting person	.661
How to plan my leisure time	.657
How to develop good relationships between older and younger generations	.614
How to deal with boredom	.747
How attitudes toward the aged are changing	.432
How to be more sensitive and aware of my changing needs and feelings	.570
Changes to expect in my personal life when I retire	.496

2) information about health care issues

The difference between Medi-Care medical and Medi-Care hospital insurance	.770
What services my Medi-Care medical insurance will pay for	.849
What services my Medi-Care hospital insurance will pay for	.852
The difference between Medi-Care and Medi-Caid	.700

3) information about economic planning

I-R Categories	*Loading*
The consequences of not making a will	.411
Employment opportunities for the retired	.401
How much money I can earn in retirement without losing any Social Security benefits	.548
How to estimate the amount of Social Security I will receive	.680
Where to find help in coping with problems I may face in my later years	.421
The changes to expect in my personal income upon retirement	.641
How to figure my net worth upon retirement	.767

4) information about health maintenance issues

The effects of exercise upon older people	.482
The kinds of foods older people should eat	.529
The sexual needs of my spouse as he/she grows older	.694
Health problems which aging people commonly have	.510
My own changing sexual needs as I grow older	.652

5) information pertaining to social relationships

The problems associated with being widowed	.585
Changes to expect in my marriage when I retire	.721
What to expect if I decide to live with my children	.475

BEHAVIOR

Check list
1. No
2. Yes

1) behavior related to life planning

"Have you sought help in planning your retirement?"
"IF YES, in what areas, and from whom?"

-Financial planning	.806
-Health insurance	.701
-Legal affairs	.832
Accountant	.602
-Lawyer	.788
-Spouse	.554

2) behavior related to volunteer/community activities

"Do you participate in any community or other non-work related organizations?"
"IF YES, how many?"

Number of organizations participate in	.769
"How active are you in the organizations in which you participate?"	.825

1. Not applicable
2. Not very active
3. Somewhat active
4. Active
5. Very active

"How many hours per week do you spend participating in volunteer/community activities?"	.768

1. None
2. 1-2
3. 3-4

I-R Categories   *Loading*

    4. 5-9
    5. 10-20
    6. 20 or more

3) behavior related to financial planning

    1. No
    2. Yes

"Have you done any of the following?"
-Obtained information that will help you plan for retirement housing   .432
-Read books on preretirement planning   .139
-Experimented with living on a retirement budget   .305
-Figured out your net worth   .645
-Estimated the amount of Social Security you will receive in retirement   .639

4) behavior related to health maintenance

"Have you recently changed the kind and/or amount of food you eat?"
"IF YES, for what reason(s)?"
-Cost of food   .502
-Trying to lose weight   .594
-Doctor's orders   .606
-Better for my health   .530
"How often do you exercise?"   .257

    1. I do not exercise
    2. About once a month
    3. About once a week
    4. Several times a week
    5. Every day

5) behavior related to intimate relationships

"How close do you feel towards your spouse, or if not married,
a friend with whom you are intimate?"   .150
    1. Not very close
    2. We have always been close, but recently seem to be drifting apart
    3. We are very close
    4. We have always been close, but recently seem to be growing closer

"Has there been any change in your relationship with your
spouse (or partner) in terms of your sex life?"   .117
    1. No change, we have never had a good sex life
    2. Recently our sex life has become worse
    3. Recently our sex life has become better
    4. No change, we have always had a good sex life

"How often do you and your spouse (or partner)
spend time alone with each other?"   .598
    1. Hardly ever
    2. About once a month
    3. A few times a month
    4. About once a week
    5. A few times a week
    6. About once a day

I-R Categories   *Loading*

    7. A few times every day

    8. Many times every day

"About how often do you and your spouse (or partner) participate
in social and/or leisure activities (such as playing tennis, going to the
movies, bowling, dancing, parties, etc.)?"   .539

    1. Hardly ever

    2. A couple times a month

    3. About once a week

    4. A few times a week

SOURCE: V. L. Boyack and D. M. Tiberi. "A Study of Preretirement Education." Paper
presented to the 28th Annual Meeting of the Gerontological Society, Louisville, October 26-
30, 1975. Reprinted by permission of the Ethel Percy Andrus Gerontology Center.

V2.6.I.d

SATISFACTION WITH RETIREMENT SCALE

W. E. Thompson and G. F. Streib, 1958

	Never	Hardly Ever	Sometimes	Often
How often do you miss the feeling of doing a good job?				
How often do you feel that you want to go back to work?				
How often do you worry about not having a job?				
How ovten do you miss being with the other people at work?				

SOURCE: W. E. Thompson and G. F. Streib. "Situational Determinants: Health and Economic Deprivation in Retirement." *Journal of Social Issues*, 1958, 14:25-34.

V2.6.I.e

INDEX OF JOB SATISFACTION

R. P. Quinn and L. J. Shepard, 1974

Facet-free:

Question	*Response Category**
"All in all, how satisfied would you say your are with your job—very satisfied, somewhat satisfied, not too satisfied, or not at all satisfied?"	Very satisfied (5) Somewhat satisfied (3) Not too satisfied (1) Not at all satisfied (1)
"Before we talke about your present job, I'd like to get some idea of the kind of job you'd *most* like to have. If you were free to go into any type of job you wanted, what would your choice be?"	Worker would want the job he or she now has (5) Worker would want to retire and and not work at all (1) Worker would prefer some other job to the job he or she now has (1)

Question	Response Category*
"Knowing what you know now, if you had to decide all over again whether to take the job you now have, what would you decide? Would you decide without any hesitation to take the same job, would you have some second thoughts, or would you decide definitely not to take the same job?"	Decide without hesitation to take same job (5) Have some second thoughts (3) Decide definitely *not* to take the job (1)
"In general how well would you say that your job measures up to the sort of job you wanted when you took it? Would you say it is very much like the job you wanted, somewhat like the job you wanted, or not very much like the job you wanted?"	Very much like the job worker wanted (5) Somewhat like the job worker wanted (3) Not very much like the job worker wanted (1)
"If a good friend of yours told you (he/she) was interested in working in a job like yours for your employer, what would you tell (him/her)? Would you strongly recommend this job, would you have doubts about recommending it, or would you strongly advise (him/her) against this sort of job?"	Worker would strongly recommend it (5) Worker would have doubts about recommending it (3) Worker would advise friend against it (1)

*Numerical code values are listed in parentheses following response categories.

Facet-specific:

	Very Important (4)	Somewhat Important (3)	Not Too Important (2)	Not at All Important (1)

Factor I: Comfort

"I have enough time to get the job done."

"The hours are good."

"Travel to and from work is convenient."

"The physical surroundings are pleasant."

"I can forget about my personal problems."

"I am free from the conflicting demands that other people make of me."

"I am not asked to do excessive amounts of work."

Factor II: Challenge

"The work is interesting."

"I have an opportunity to develop my own special abilities."

"I can see the results of my work."

"I am given a chance to do the things I do best."

"I am given a lot of freedom to decide how I do my own work."

"The problems I am expected to solve are hard enough."

	Very Important (4)	Somewhat Important (3)	Not Too Important (2)	Not at All Important (1)

Factor III: Financial Rewards

"The pay is good."

"The job security is good."

"My fringe benefits are good."

Factor IV: Relations with Co-workers

"The people I work with are friendly."

"I am given a lot of chances to make friends."

"The people I work with take a personal interest in me."

Factor V: Resource Adequecy

"I have enough information to get the job done."

"I receive enough help and equipment to get the job done."

"I have enough authority to do my job."

"My supervisor is competent in doing (his/her) job."

"My responsibilities are clearly defined."

"The people I work with are competent in doing their job."

"My supervisor is very concerned about the welfare of those under (him/her)."

"My supervisor is successful in getting people to work together."

"My supervisor is helpful to me in getting my job done."

"The people I work with are helpful to me in getting my job done."

"My supervisor is friendly."

Factor VI: Promotion

"Promotions are handled fairly."

"The chances for promotion are good."

"My employer is concerned about giving everyone a chance to get ahead."

---

*SOURCE: R. P. Quinn and L. J. Shepard, *The 1972-73 Quality of Employment Survey*, pp. 54-56, 63-65. Ann Arbor, Mich.: Institute for Social Research, 1974.

V2.6.I.f

ATTITUDES TOWARD THE EMPLOYMENT OF OLDER PEOPLE

W. K. Kirchner, T. Lindbom, and D. Paterson, 1952

DIRECTIONS

On this page and the following pages you will find a number of statements.
1. Read each statement carefully.
2. Choose the word that *best* tells how you feel about each statement.
3. Put an "X" in the space following the word.
4. Do this for all statements.

Here is an example:

There has been too much snow in Minnesota this winter.
Strongly agree _____ Agree _X_ Undecided _____ Disagree _____ Strongly disagree _____

If you agree with this statement, you would place an "X" in the space following the word "Agree", as has been done in the sample.

There are no "right" or "wrong" answers. Just tell how you feel about each statement.
Your answers are secret.
Important: In these statements when we say "Older" we mean *Over 50*.

1. I think older employees have fewer accidents on the job.
   Strongly agree_____ Agree _____ Undecided _____ Disagree_____ Strongly disagree _____

2. Most companies are unfair to older employees.
   Strongly agree_____ Agree _____ Undecided _____ Disagree _____ Strongly disagree _____

3. Older employees are harder to train for jobs.
   Strongly disagree _____ Disagree _____ Undecided _____ Agree _____ Strongly agree _____

4. Older employees are absent more often than younger employees (under age 30).
   Strongly disagree_____ Disagree_____ Undecided _____ Agree _____ Strongly agree _____

5. Younger people (under age 30) act too smart nowadays.
   Strongly agree _____ Agree _____ Undecided_____ Disagree _____ Strongly disagree _____

6. Younger employees (under 30) usually have more serious accidents than older employees.
   Strongly disagree_____ Disagree _____ Undecided _____ Agree _____ Strongly agree _____

7. In a case where two people can do a job about the same, I'd pick the older person for the job.
   Strongly disagree _____ Disagree _____ Undecided _____ Agree _____ Strongly agree _____

8. I think that Social Security payments are too small.
   Strongly disagree _____ Disagree _____ Undecided _____ Agree _____ Strongly agree _____

9. Occupational diseases are more likely to occur among younger employees (those under age 30).
   Strongly agree_____ Agree _____ Undecided _____ Disagree _____ Strongly disagree _____

10. The older employees usually turn out work of higher quality.
    Strongly disagree _____ Disagree _____ Undecided _____ Agree _____ Strongly agree _____

11. I think older employees are more grouchy on the job.
    Strongly disagree _____ Disagree _____ Undecided _____ Agree _____ Strongly agree _____

12. I believe that older people cooperate more on the job.
    Strongly disagree _____ Disagree_____ Undecided _____ Agree _____ Strongly agree _____

13. Older people seem to be happier on the job.
    Strongly agree _____ Agree _____ Undecided _____ Disagree _____ Strongly disagree _____

14. I feel that older people are more dependable.

Strongly disagree ____ Disagree ____ Undecided ____ Agree ____ Strongly agree ____

15. Most older people cannot keep up with the speed needed in modern industry.
   Strongly agree ____ Agree ____ Undecided ____ Disagree ____ Strongly disagree ____

16. Supervisors find it hard to get older people to adopt new methods on the job.
   Strongly agree ____ Agree ____ Undecided ____ Disagree ____ Strongly disagree ____

17. Older people should get higher wages for their jobs.
   Strongly disagree ____ Disagree ____ Undecided ____ Agree ____ Strongly agree ____

18. You'll find that the employees who are most loyal to the company are the older employees.
   Strongly agree ____ Agree ____ Undecided ____ Disagree ____ Strongly disagree ____

19. Older people are too set in their ways—they don't want to change.
   Strongly agree ____ Agree ____ Undecided ____ Disagree ____ Strongly disagree ____

20. I think older employees have as much ability to learn new methods as other employees.
   Strongly disagree ____ Disagree ____ Undecided ____ Agree ____ Strongly agree ____

21. I think companies should train middle-aged employees (those aged 35-50) to handle many different jobs.
   Strongly disagree ____ Disagree ____ Undecided ____ Agree ____ Strongly agree ____

22. I think that older employees make better employees.
   Strongly disagree ____ Disagree ____ Undecided ____ Agree ____ Strongly agree ____

23. I think that most younger people are too radical in their ideas.
   Strongly disagree ____ Disagree ____ Undecided ____ Agree ____ Strongly agree ____

24. Pay should be based on length of service rather than on what a person does (how long a person has worked in a company should count more than the amount of work he turns out).
   Strongly disagree ____ Disagree ____ Undecided ____ Agree ____ Strongly agree ____

SOURCE: W. K. Kirchner, T. Lindbom, and D. Paterson. "Attitudes toward the Employment of Older People." *Journal of Applied Psychology*, 1952, 36:154-56.

V2.6.I.g

ATTITUDE TOWARD RETIREMENT

W. E. Thompson, 1956

"Some people say that retirement is good for a person, some say it is bad. In general, what do you think?" (Positive response: it is good for a person.)

"Do you mostly look forward to the time when you will stop working and retire or in general do you dislike the idea?" (Positive response: I look forward to it.)

"If it were up to you alone, would you continue working for your present company?" (Positive response: I would stop working.)

SOURCE: W. E. Thompson. "The Impact of Retirement." Ph.D. dissertation, Cornell University, 1956.

V2.6.I.h

WORK COMMITMENT
I. H. Simpson, K. W. Back, and J. C. McKinney, 1966

Items and scoring, arranged in order from low to high intrinsic work value:

"Even if I had an entirely different job, I would have liked to do the same kind of work I used to do sometimes, just for fun" (strongly agree, agree)

"If I had inherited a million dollars, I would still have wanted to keep on doing the work I did." (strongly agree, agree)

"I wouldn't have taken a better paying job if it had meant I would have had to do work different from what I did." (strongly agree, agree)

"Nobody would have done the kind of work I did, if he didn't have to." (strongly disagree)

"Toward the end of the day, it often seemed as if quitting time would never come." (strongly disagree)

SOURCE: I. H. Simpson, K. W. Back, and J. C. McKinney. "Orientations toward Work and Retirement and Self-evaluation in Retirement." In *Social Aspects of Aging*, I. H. Simpson and J. C. McKinney (eds.), p. 78, Durham, N.C.: Duke University Press, 1966.

V2.6.I.i

AVOID RETIREMENT SCALE

W. J. Goudy, E. A. Powers, and P. Keith, 1975

When a man retires, his health is apt to decline.
1, strongly agree; 2, agree; 3, neutral; 4, disagree; 5, strongly disagree

It is better not to think about retirement.
1, strongly agree; 2, agree; 3, neutral; 4, disagree; 5, strongly disagree

When a person retires, he has one foot in the grave.
1, strongly agree; 2, agree; 3, neutral; 4, disagree; 5, strongly disagree

Retirement is something to be avoided as long as possible.
1, strongly agree; 2, agree; 3, neutral; 4, disagree; 5, strongly disagree

SOURCE: W. J. Goudy, E. A. Powers, and P. Keith. "Work and Retirement; A Test of Attitudinal Relationships." *Journal of Gerontology*, 1975, 30: 193-98.

V2.6.I.j

PROPENSITY TO RETIRE

R. Miljus, 1970

Is there a compulsory retirement plan where you work; that is, do you have to stop working at your present job at a certain age?

At what age?

Would you work longer than that if you could?

Do you expect to retire before this age?

At what age do you expect to stop working at a (your) regular job?

Some men, when they stop working at a regular job, take another job. Other men decide not to work any more at all. Which of these do you think you will do?

If for some reason you were permently to lose your present job tomorrow, what would you do? If "other", specify here _____ .

If by some chance, you were to get enough money to live comfortably without working, do you think that you would work anyway?

SOURCE: R. Miljus. "The Propensity to Retire." In *The Preretirement Years* (vol. 1), H. Parnes, B. Fleisher, R. Miljus, and R. Spitz (eds.), pp. 169-202. Washington, D. C., U.S. Department of Labor, 1970.

V2.6.I.k

RESISTANCE TO RETIREMENT SCALE

M. R. Greene, C. H. Pyron, V. V. Manion, and H. Winklevoss, 1969

I have made many plans for things I'll be doing in retirement.
SD = 1   D = 2   A = 3   SA = 4

Much of a retired person's life is boring and monotonous.
SA = 1   A = 2   D = 3   SD = 4

Retirement will probably be the dreariest time of my life.
SA = 1   A = 2   D = 3   SD = 4

I expect some interesting and pleasant things to happen to me in retirement.
SD = 1   D = 2   A = 3   SA = 4

I expect retirement to be the best years of my life.
SD = 1   D = 2   A = 3   SA = 4

I'll probably find a hard time keeping busy in retirement.
SA = 1   A = 2   D = 3   SD = 4

SOURCE: M. R. Green, C. H. Pyron, V. V. Manion, and H. Winklevoss. *Preretirement Counseling: Retirement Adjustment and the Older Worker*, p. 312. Eugene, Ore.: University of Oregon, 1969. Reprinted by permission.

V2.6.I.l

JOB SATISFACTION SCALE

W. J. Goudy, E. A. Powers, and P. Keith, 1975

How well do you like your occupation?
1 - strongly dislike it, dislike it, indifferent, like it.
2 - enthusiastic about it.

How much of the time do you feel satisfied with this occupation?
2 - all of the time.
1 - a good deal of the time, about half of the time, occasionally, practically never.

If you had to do it over again, would you still choose your line of work?
1 - no
2 - yes

Would you recommend this work to a friend?
2 - yes
1 - no

SOURCE: W. J. Goudy, E. A. Powers, and P. Keith. "The Work-Satisfaction, Retirement-Attitude Typology: Profile Examination." *Experimental Aging Research*, 1975, 1:267-79.

V2.6.I.m

COMMITMENT TO WORK

C. Westoff, R. Potter, P. Nagi, and E. Mishler, 1961

"I would much rather relax around the house all day than go to work."
No (+)
Yes (−)

"My work is more satisfying to me than the time I spend around the house."
No (−)
Yes (+)

"If I inherited so much money that I didn't have to work, I would still continue to work at the same thing I am doing now."
No (−)
Yes (+)

"Some of my main interests and pleasures in life are connected with my work."
No (−)
Yes (+)

"I have sometimes regretted going into the kind of work I am now in."
No (+)
Yes (−)

"The work I do is one of the most satisfying parts of my life."
No (−)
Yes (+)

"I enjoy my spare-time activities much more than my work."
No (+)
Yes (−)

"To me, my work is just a way of making money."
No (+)
Yes (−)

SOURCE: C. Westoff, R. Potter, P. Nagi, and E. Mishler. *Family Growth in Metropolitan America*. Princeton, N.J.: Princeton University Press, 1961.

V2.6.I.n

ATTITUDE TOWARD RETIREMENT

F. D. Glamser, 1976

Response Categories	Strongly Agree	Agree	Uncertain	Disagree	Strongly Disagree
Retirement is mostly good for a person.	___	___	___	___	___
I think that things will go well for me in retirement.	___	___	___	___	___
It is not fair to make a person retire because of his age.	___	___	___	___	___
I am looking forward to the time off that retirement will bring.	___	___	___	___	___
If it were up to me alone, I would keep on working as long as possible.	___	___	___	___	___

SOURCE: F. D. Glamser. "Determinants of a Positive Attitude toward Retirement." *Journal of Gerontology*, 1976, 31: 104-7.

V2.6.I.o

INDEX OF WORK COMMITMENT

H. Parnes and G. Nestel, 1974

"If, by some chance, you were to get enough money to live comfortably without working, do you think that you would work anyway?"

_____ Yes

_____ No

_____ Undecided

"If for some reason you were permanently to lose your present job tomorrow, what would you do?"

_____ Retire

_____ Take another job I know about

_____ Go into business

_____ Look for work

_____ Other

SOURCE: H. Parnes and G. Nestel. "Early Retirement." In _The Preretirement Years_ (vol. 4), H. Parnes, A. Adams, P. Andrisani, A. Kohen, and G. Nestel (eds.), pp. 153-96. Columbus, Ohio: Center for Human Resource Research, 1974.

V2.6.I.p

INDEX OF INVOLVEMENT WITH RETIREMENT

R. E. Barfield and J. Morgan, 1969

"Have you talked about the question of when to retire with other people?"

"Do you know anyone who has retired early?"

"Do you have any hobbies you hope to spend more time on when you retire?"

"When do you think you will retire from the main work you are now doing—I mean at what age?"

SOURCE: R. E. Barfield and J. Morgan. _Early Retirement_, pp. 197-98, 204. Ann Arbor, Mich.: Institute for Social Research, University of Michigan, 1969.

V2.6.I.q

ATTITUDE TOWARD RETIREMENT INDEX

H. Parnes and G. Nestel, 1974

Respondent's attitude toward his retirement

_____ Look forward to it

_____ Bored

_____ Other

Respondent's perception of wife's attitude to his retirement

_____ Retire as soon as possible

_____ Keep working

_____ Do whatever I want

_____ Other

Respondent's perception of post-retirement experiences of retired friends

_____ Very happy

_____ Fairly happy
_____ Somewhat happy
_____ Very unhappy

Respondent's expectation of the age when most of his friends will retire

_____ 65
_____ Before 65
_____ After 65

SOURCE: H. Parnes and G. Nestel. "Early Retirement." In *The Preretirement Years* (vol. 4), H. Parnes, A. Adams, P. Andrisani, A. Kohen, and G. Nestel, (eds.), pp. 153-96. Columbus, Ohio: Center for Human Resource Research, 1974.

V2.6.I.r

MEANING OF WORK I

E. A. Friedmann and R. J. Havighurst, 1954

See the description of the instrument in the abstract.

V2.6.I.s

MEANING OF WORK II

N. C. Morse and R. S. Weiss, 1955

See the description of the instrument in the abstract.

Chapter 7

Socioeconomic Status and Poverty

Angela M. O'Rand

Although socioeconomic status is probably the most widely used variable across studies in social gerontology, its measurement and application have been inconsistent and, in some cases, perhaps inappropriate for the study of aging and aged populations. Critics of past uses and abuses of socioeconomic status in research have called for more valid measures of this variable for use with the aged that would capture the meaning of the concept (Bloom, 1972). And they have called for new approaches that would take into account the multidimensional aspects of socioeconomic status, i.e., income, wealth, occupational prestige, educational level, community reputation, perceived income adequacy, and subjective class identification (Streib, 1976), which probably vary in relative importance across age-groups and age cohorts (Riley, 1971). Still, despite the unrefined state of measurement of the socioeconomic status of the aged, this variable (however it is measured) persistently differentiates within and between age cohorts in various studies of behavior and attitudes.

A general review of the literature in gerontology including socioeconomic status shows that this variable is most often measured as income, occupational status, educational attainment, or some combined measure that includes at least two or all of these factors. More recent studies have added measures of economic welfare (such as net worth and estimates of in-kind and nonmoney transfers) as indicators of socioeconomic status, since these economic resources tend to be relatively more important among retired populations whose current income is reduced after retirement (Projector and Weiss, 1966). Occupational status is perhaps a carry-over from preretirement years or an obsolete claim to status (Streib, 1976). A retired person's educational level is a doubtful proxy for potential consumption levels, although it may be related to tastes and life-styles in retirement (Bloom, 1972). A brief review of the potentials and limitations of various measures of the socioeconomic status of the aged is presented next, followed by reviews of 12 measures of socioeconomic status and poverty.

Measures of Economic Welfare and Poverty

Measures of the economic welfare of the aged are usually based on estimates of current income or net worth or composite measures of both (Moon, 1977; Morgan et al., 1962; Schulz, 1968; 1976a; 1976b; Sirageldin, 1969, Taussig, 1973, Wentworth and Motley, 1970). Income (as current cash receipts from selected sources) and net worth (as all assets minus all debts) represent, respectively, the flow and the stock of the family's economic resources (Weisbrod and Hansen, 1968). Since a reduction in income usually follows retirement, the determination of an income level for a retired person or couple to maintain a "modest but adequate" standard of living has occupied government agencies and economic researchers (Lamale, 1965; U.S. Department of Health, Education, and Welfare, 1976). Several standards of adequacy have been developed, but two are most often used: the poverty thresholds originally established by the Social Security Administration (SSA) (Orshansky, 1965a; 1965b; 1966; 1968; 1969; U.S. Bureau of the Census, 1977a; 1977b) and the Bureau of Labor Statistics (BLS) budgets for retired couples (U.S. Bureau of Labor Statistics, 1968; 1970). Both standards are based on the estimated costs of required consumer items for families of varying composition and location. Since the difference between the two standards is considered to be negligible (see Schulz, 1968), only one standard is abstracted in this chapter, the SSA poverty thresholds. These standards consist of 124 thresholds that report minimally adequate income levels for individuals and families varying by age, sex, number of children under 18, and farm versus nonfarm residence, including special breakdowns for households with heads aged 65 and over.

The poverty thresholds were developed by the Social Security Administration as statistical yardsticks; they were never intended to evaluate individual families or persons as falling above or below the poverty line. However, with the proliferation of programs designed to aid the poor, and in the absence of other measures, they have often been used to determine individual eligibility and status. Studies of the income and poverty of the elderly refer to the poverty thresholds to determine relative and absolute levels of income adequacy

(Brotman, 1977; Chen, 1966; Miller and Winard, 1974; Rosenberg, 1967) for various samples of the elderly.

Current money income alone, however, may underestimate the actual economic well-being of the elderly (Moon, 1977; Projector and Weiss, 1966; 1969; Streib, 1976), since this age-group often benefits from the accumulation of assets over a lifetime, more leisure time, and relatively greater amounts of interhousehold and government transfers (e.g., family gifts, free transportation, Medicaid, and food stamps). As such, the economic welfare of the elderly is significantly influenced by money *and* nonmoney components, such as residing with relatives, imputed rent to home owners, home production (Morgan et al., 1962), and leisure time (Sirageldin, 1969; Taussig, 1973). Home ownership alone accounts for important differences in potential for discretionary spending in old age and retirement (Kent and Hirsch, 1971; Henretta and Campbell, 1978). Net-worth holdings paid out regularly over the life expectancy of the older family can add significantly to its annual current money income (Moon, 1976). For these reasons, several composite measures of net worth, income-net worth, and general economic welfare of the aged have been developed. Three of these measures have been selected for summary here: the measure of income-net worth developed by Weisbrod and Hansen (1968), Net Worth as an Aspect of Status by Henretta and Campbell (1978), and the Composite Measure of Economic Welfare of the Aged by Moon (1977). The third measure is probably the most comprehensive yet developed, since it attempts to take into account most money and nonmoney components of economic welfare.

The major limitation of these income and wealth measures is their reliance on self-reported data, which are notoriously susceptible to nonsampling error. (See Barlow, Brazer, and Morgan, 1966, on income; and Ferber, 1966, on assets and wealth.) The tendency to underreport or misreport this information, especially among higher-income groups, has been documented repeatedly. Efforts to cross-validate such data through records, etc., are recommended when they are possible. Similarly, the measure of home equity is susceptible to response errors since owner's estimates of home values may not coincide with professional appraisals (Kain and Quigley, 1973; Kish and Lansing, 1954; Robins and West, 1977).

Measures of Objective Social Status

Measures of objective social status rely heavily on occupational rankings, even among older or retired populations (Cumming and Henry,

1961; Shanas et al., 1968; Haug and Sussman, 1971; Coleman and Neugarten, 1971; Henretta and Campbell, 1976; Haug, 1977). The rationale for this dependence on occupational status as an index of social status or social class in old-age is multifaceted. First, past occupational attainment tends to be positively associated with income in old-age among all races (Shanas et al., 1968; Henretta and Campbell, 1976). Second, occupational status in association with educational attainment is believed to contribute to general life-style and consumption patterns throughout the life cycle (Cumming and Henry, 1961; Coleman and Neugarten, 1971; Hollingshead, 1965). And, third, occupational rankings or prestige scales are highly reliable indicators of general social standing or "desirability" that have held up across time (Hodge, Siegel, and Rossi, 1964; Siegel, 1971), across cultures (Inkeles and Rossi, 1956; Blau and Duncan, 1967; Treiman, 1977), and across age-groups (Gunn, 1964). The hardiness of the prestige measure suggests that occupational status may have the staying power to carry over into retirement, particularly among the higher ranks (Streib, 1976). Since no serious challenge to this rationale has emerged, this variable persists as the basis for most measures of the general social status of the elderly, despite their sex bias and the lack of direct evidence for their validity as indicators of status in retirement.

Six objective social status or class scales are reviewed in this chapter; two rely on occupational rankings alone (Occupational Status and Occupational Prestige Scales), and four are composite measures or indexes that include occupational status or prestige as one among several components consisting of education, income, neighborhood status, and housing quality (U.S. Census Socioeconomic Status, the Duncan [1961] Socioeconomic Index of Occupations, Hollingshead's [1965] two-factor index of social position, and the Kansas City Index of Urban Status). These examples are not exhaustive, but they illustrate the major approaches that have been or can be taken on older populations. Not all of these measures have been systematically applied to older or aged samples, (e.g., occupational prestige), but, since they often overlap (i.e., are components of each other) or can serve to validate each other, they are included here. Also, the measures are the most current, or the most readily updated, for study of contemporary populations.

Several measures have been excluded for practical reasons. The outdated Warner Index of Status Characteristics (Warner, Meeker, and Eells, 1949), for example, is excluded, although the Index of Urban Status (Coleman and Neugarten, 1971), a modification of the Warner index, is included. The Warner index is summarized in Bonjean, Hill, and McLemore (1967) and Miller (1977). Likewise, Cumming and Henry's (1961) three-factor (location of household, occupation, and education) index of present socioeconomic status is excluded because it was developed in the same study context as the Index of Urban Status and reflects a very similar modification of Warner's index. Furthermore, the cumbersome procedural details of community-based measures like those used by Coleman and Neugarten and Cumming and Henry require firsthand reading, since abstracts cannot portray their necessary operations fully enough.

When employing measures of occupational status, the user should be alerted to the special problems of coding occupations (Hauser and Featherman, 1977). Job titles, responsibilities, and duties and industry and class of work must be carefully evaluated before assigning occupational status. Detailed coding manuals (like Featherman, Sobel, and Dickens, 1975) should be referred to with care.

Measures of Subjective Class Identification

Class identification and class consciousness have been observed among elderly populations (Streib, 1976; Coleman and Neugarten, 1971; Rosenberg, 1970). Single- and multiple-item approaches to self-evaluations are combined in a summary of two measures of Subjective Class Identification. The single-item method (Centers, 1949; Kahl and Davis, 1955) and the multiple-indicator approach (Kluegel, Singleton, and Starnes, 1977) have been used primarily on younger populations; but, in combination with other (objective) indicators of socioeconomic status like income, occupation, and education, these might prove useful in the study of older populations.

The importance of combining subjective and objective indicators cannot be overemphasized. Studies of income in retirement, for example, show that perceived adequacy of income may often be inconsistent with objective determinations (Bultena et al., 1971; Streib and Schneider, 1971; Tissue, 1972). Similarly, objective class or status placements may not coincide with subjective evaluations and thus may not accurately portray life-styles. (See Table 7-1).

TABLE 7-1
Instruments Reviewed in Chapter 7

Instrument	Author(s)	Code Number
I. Economic Welfare and Poverty		
a. Current Money Income	U.S. Bureau of the Census (ongoing)	V2.7.I.a

TABLE 7-1 — *Continued*

Instrument	Author(s)	Code Number
b. Poverty Thresholds	U.S. Bureau of the Census (ongoing)	V2.7.I.b
c. Income-Net Worth Measure of Economic Position	Weisbrod and Hansen (1968)	V2.7.I.c
d. Net Worth as an Aspect of Status	Henretta and Campbell (1978)	V2.7.I.d
e. Composite Measure of Economic Welfare of the Aged	Moon (1976; 1977)	V2.7.I.e
II. Objective Social Status		
a. Occupational Status	U.S. Bureau of the Census (1960)	V2.7.II.a
b. U.S. Census Socioeconomic Status	U.S. Bureau of the Census (1963)	V2.7.II.b
c. Occupational Prestige Scales	North and Hatt (1947); Hodge, Siegel, and Rossi (1964), Treiman (1977)	Copyrighted
d. Socioeconomic Index of Occupations	Duncan (1961)	Copyrighted
e. Index of Social Status	Hollingshead (1965)	V2.7.II.e
f. Index of Urban Status	Coleman and Neugarten (1971)	V2.7.II.f
III. Subjective Class Identification		
a. Subjective Class Identification	Centers (1949); Kahl and Davis (1955); Kluegel, Singleton, and Starnes (1977)	Single-item indicator

Summary

The use of multiple measures of objective economic and social status along with subjective placements is ideal although usually impossible. The expense of survey research and the increasing reliance on secondary analyses of large data sets are major constraints on the development of new multidimensional measures. New measures are needed that take better account of women's occupational attainments (Bose, 1973), general household standing based on attainments of both heads of household (e.g., Rossi et al., 1974; Sampson and Rossi, 1975), and status-based social interaction patterns among the elderly, like those captured by Laumann's (e.g., 1965; 1966) measures of subjective social distance.

REFERENCES

Barlow, R., H. E. Brazer, and J. N. Morgan. *Economic Behavior of the Affluent*. Washington, D.C.: The Brookings Institute, 1966.

Blau, P. M., and O. D. Duncan. *The American Occupational Structure*. New York: John Wiley and Sons, 1967.

Bloom, M. "Measurement of the Socioeconomic Status of the Aged: New Thoughts on an Old Subject." *The Gerontologist*, 1972, 12(4):375-78.

Bonjean, C. M., R. H. Hill, and S. D. McLemore. *Sociological Measurement: An Inventory of Scales and Indices*. San Francisco: Chandler, 1967.

Bose, C. E. *Jobs and Gender: Sex and Occupational Prestige*. Baltimore: Johns Hopkins University, Center for Metropolitan Planning and Research, 1973.

Brotman, H. B. "Income and Poverty in the Older Population in 1975." *The Gerontologist*, 1977, 17:23-26.

Bultena, G. L., E. A. Powers, P. Falkman, and D. Frederick. *Life after 70 in Iowa*. Sociology Report, number 95. Ames, Iowa: Iowa State University, 1971.

Centers, R. *The Psychology of Social Classes*. Princeton, N.J.: Princeton University Press, 1949.

Chen, Y. P. "Economic Poverty: The Special Case of the Aged." *The Gerontologist*, 1966, 6 (1):39-45.

Coleman, R. P., and B. L. Neugarten. *Social Status in the City*. San Francisco: Jossey-Bass, 1971.

Cumming, E., and W. E. Henry. *Growing Old*. New York: Basic Books, 1961.

Duncan, O. D. "A Socioeconomic Index for All Occupations." In *Occupations and Social Status*, A. J. Reiss, Jr., O. D. Duncan, P. K. Hatt, and C. C. North (eds.), pp. 109-38. New York: Free Press, 1961.

Edwards, A. M. *Alphabetical Index of Occupations by Industries and Socio-Economic Groupings*. Washington, D.C.: U.S. Government Printing Office, 1937.

——————. *A Social-Economic Grouping of the Gainfully Employed Workers of the United States, 1930*. Washington, D.C.: U.S. Government Printing Office, 1938.

Featherman, D. L., M. Sobel, and D. Dickens. *A Manual for Coding Occupations and Industries into Detailed 1970 Categories and a Listing of 1970-Basis Duncan Socioeconomic and NORC Prestige Scores*. Working Paper number 75-1. Madison, Wis.: Center for Demography and Ecology, University of Wisconsin, 1975.

Ferber, R. "The Reliability of Consumer Reports of Financial Assets and Debts." *Studies in Consumer Savings*, number 6. Urbana, Ill.: Bureau of Economic and Business Research, University of Illinois, 1966.

Grad, S. *Income of the Population Aged 60 and Older, 1971*. HEW Publication number (SSA) 77-11851. Washington, D.C.: U.S. Government Printing Office, 1977.

Gunn, B. "Children's Conceptions of Occupational Prestige." *Personnel and Guidance Journal*, 1964, 42:558-63.

Haug, M. R. "Measurement in Social Stratification." *Annual Review of Sociology* (vol. 3). Palo Alto, Calif.: Annual Reviews, 1977.

Haug, M. R., and M. B. Sussman. "The Indiscriminate State of Social Class Measurement." *Social Forces*, 1971, 49:549-63.

Hauser, R. M., and D. L. Featherman. *The Process of Stratification: Trends and Analyses*. New York: Academic Press, 1977.

Henretta, J. C., and R. T. Campbell. "Status Attainment and Status Maintenance: A Study of Stratification in Old Age." *American Sociological Review*, 1976, 41:981-92.

——————. "Net Worth as an Aspect of Status." *American Journal of Sociology*, 1978, 83: 1204-23.

Hodge, R. W., P. M. Siegel, and P. H. Rossi. "Occupational Prestige in the United States, 1925-63." *American Journal of Sociology*, 1964, 70:286-302.

Hodge, R. W., and D. J. Treiman. Class Identification in the United States." *American Journal of Sociology*, 1968, 73:535-47.

Hollingshead, A. B. *Two-Factor Index of Social Position*. New Haven, Conn.: Yale University Press, 1965.

Hollingshead, A. B., and F. C. Redlich. *Social Class and Mental Illness*. New York: John Wiley and Sons, 1958.

Inkeles, A., and P. H. Rossi. "National Comparisons of Occupational Prestige." *American Journal of Sociology*, 1956, 61:329-39.

Kahl, J. A., and J. A. Davis. "A Comparison of Indexes of Socioeconomic Status." *American Sociological Review*, 1955, 20:317-25.

Kain, J. F., and J. M. Quigley. "Housing Market Discrimination, Home Ownerships and Savings Behavior." *American Economic Review*, 1973, 62:263-77.

Kent, D. P., and C. Hirsch. "Social and Economic Conditions of Negro and White Aged Residents of Urban Neighborhoods of Low Socio-Economic Status (vol. 1). Final Report Submitted to the Administration on Aging. University Park, Pa.: Pennsylvania State University, 1971.

Kish, L., and J. B. Lansing. "Response Error in Estimating the Value of Homes." *Journal of the American Statistical Association*, 1954, 49:520-38.

Kluegel, J. R., R. Singleton, Jr., and C. E. Starnes. "Subjective Class Identification: A Multiple Indicator Approach." *American Sociological Review*, 1977, 42:599-610.

Kreps, J. "The Economy and the Aged." In *Handbook of Aging and the Social Sciences*, R. H. Binstock and E. Shanas (eds.), pp. 272-85. New York: Van Nostrand Reinhold, 1976.

Lamale, H. H. "Poverty: The Work and the Reality." *Monthly Labor Review*, 1965, 83:822-35.

Laumann, E. O. "Subjective Social Distance and Urban Occupational Stratification." *American Journal of Sociology*, 1965, 71:26-36.

_____ . *Prestige and Association in an Urban Community: An Analysis of an Urban Stratification System*. Indianapolis: Bobbs-Merrill, 1966.

_____ . *Bonds of Pluralism: The Form and Substance of Urban Social Networks*. New York: John Wiley and Sons, 1973.

Laumann, E. O., and J. S. House. "Living Room Styles and Social Attributes: The Patterning of Material Artifacts in a Modern Urban Community." In *The Logic of Social Hierarchies*, E. O. Laumann, P. M. Siegel, and R. W. Hodge (eds.), pp. 189-203. Chicago: Markham, 1970.

Laumann, E. O., and R. Senter. "Subjective Social Distance, Occupational Stratification, and Forms of Status and Class Consciousness: A Cross-national Replication and Extension." *American Journal of Sociology*, 1976, 81:1304-38.

Miller, D. C. *Handbook of Research Design and Social Measurement* (3rd ed.). New York: Longman, Green and Company, 1977.

Miller, R., and A. I. Winard. "Trends and Composition of the Low-Income Population." In *Proceedings of the Social Statistics Section of the American Statistical Association*, pp. 200-209. Washington, D.C.: American Statistical Association, 1974.

Miller, S. M., and P. Roby. *The Future of Inequality*. New York: Basic Books, 1970.

Moon, M. "The Economic Welfare of the Aged and Income Security Programs." *Review of Income and Wealth*, 1976, 22:253-69.

_____ . *The Measurement of Economic Welfare: Its Application to the Aged Poor*. New York: Academic Press, 1977.

Moon, M., and E. Smolensky (eds.). *Improving Measures of Economic Well-being*. New York: Academic Press, 1977.

Morgan, J., M. David, W. Cohen, and H. Brazer. *Income and Welfare in the United States*. New York: McGraw-Hill, 1962.

North, C. C., and P. K. Hatt. "Jobs and Occupations: A Popular Evaluation." *Opinion News*, 1947, 9:3-13.

Orshansky, M. "Counting the Poor: Another Look at the Poverty Profile." *Social Security Bulletin*, 1965a, 28 (1):3-29.
——— . "Who's Who among the Poor: A Demographic View of Poverty." *Social Security Bulletin, 1965b, 28 (7):3-32.*
——— ."Recounting the Poor: A Five-Year Review." *Social Security Bulletin*, 1966, 29 (4):2-9.
——— . "The Shape of Poverty in 1966." *Social Security Bulletin*, 1968, 31 (3):3-32.
——— . "Perspectives on Poverty: How Poverty is Measured." *Monthly Labor Review*, 1969, 92 (2):244-83.
Parnes, H. S. "The Pre-retirement Years: A Longitidunal Study of the Labor Market Experience of Men." *Manpower Research Monograph*, number 15 (2 vols.). Washington, D.C.: U.S. Department of Labor, 1970.
——— . "The Pre-retirement Years: A Longitudinal Study of the Labor Market Experience of Men." *Manpower Research Monograph*, number 15 (vol. 3). Washington, D.C.: U.S. Department of Labor, 1973.
——— . "The National Longitudinal Surveys: New Vistas for Labor Market Research." *American Economic Review*, 1975, 65:244-49.
Projector, D. S., and G. S. Weiss. *Survey of Financial Characteristics of Consumers*. Washington, D.C.: Board of Governors of the Federal Reserve System, 1966.
——— . "Income-Net Worth Measures of Economic Welfare." *Social Security Bulletin*, 1969, 32 (11):14-17.
Reiss, A. J., Jr. *Occupations and Social Status*. New York: Free Press, 1961.
Riley, M. W. "Social Gerontology and the Age Stratification of Society." *The Gerontologist*, 1971, 11 (1, part 1):79-87.
Robins, P. K., and R. W. West. "Measurement Errors in the Estimation of Home Value." *Journal of the American Statistical Association*, 1977, 72:290-94.
Rosenberg, G. S. *Poverty, Aging and Social Isolation*. Washington, D.C.: Bureau of Social Science Research, 1967.
——— . *The Worker Grows Old*. San Francisco: Jossey-Bass, 1970.
Rossi, P. H., W. A. Sampson, C. E. Bose, G. Jasso, and J. Passel. "Measuring Household Social Standing." *Social Science Research*, 1974, 3:169-90.
Sampson, W. A., and P. H. Rossi. "Race and Family Social Standing." *American Sociological Review*, 1975, 40:201-14.
Schulz, J. H. *The Economic Status of the Retired Aged in 1980: Simulation Projections*. Social Security Administration, U.S. Department of Health, Education, and Welfare, Research Report number 24. Washington, D.C.: U.S. Government Printing Office, 1968.
——— . *The Economics of Aging*. Belmont, Calif.: Wadsworth, 1976a.
——— . "Income Distribution and the Aging." In *Handbook of Aging and the Social Sciences*, R. H. Binstock and E. Shanas (eds.), pp. 561-91. New York: Van Nostrand Reinhold, 1976b.
Shanas, E., P. Townsend, D. Wedderburn, H. Friis, P. Milhoj, and J. Stehouwer. *Old People in Three Industrial Societies*. New York: Atherton Press, 1968.
Siegel, P.M. "Prestige in the American Occupational Structure." Ph.D. dissertation, University of Chicago, 1971.
Siegel, P. M., R. W. Hodge, and P. H. Rossi. *Occupational Prestige in the United States*. New York: Academic Press, 1974.
Simmons, D. D. "Children's Ranking of Occupational Prestige." *Personnel and Guidance Journal*, 1962, 41:332-36.
Sirageldin, I. *Nonmarket Components of National Income*. Ann Arbor, Mich.: Survey Research Center, University of Michigan, 1969.
Streib, G. F. "Social Stratification and Aging." In *Handbook of Aging and the Social Sciences*,

R. H. Binstock and E. Shanas (eds.), pp. 160-85. New York: Van Nostrand Reinhold, 1976.

Streib, G. F., and C. J. Schneider. *Retirement in American Society: Impact and Process.* Ithaca, N.Y.: Cornell University Press, 1971.

Taussig, M. K. *Alternative Measures of the Distribution and Economic Welfare.* Princeton, N.J.,: Industrial Relations Section, Princeton University, 1973.

Tissue, T. "Old Age and the Perception of Poverty." *Sociology and Social Research*, 1972, 56:331-44.

Treiman, D. J. *Occupational Prestige in Comparative Perspective.* New York: Academic Press, 1977.

U.S. Bureau of the Census. *1960 Census of Population: Classified Index of Occupations and Industries.* Washington, D.C.: U.S. Government Printing Office, 1960.

_____. "Characteristics of the Population below the Poverty Level: 1975." *Current Population Reports.* Consumer Income Series P-60, number 106 (June). Washington, D.C.: U.S. Department of Commerce, U.S. Government Printing Office, 1977a.

_____. "Money Income and Poverty Status of Families and Persons in the United States: 1976 (Advance Report." *Current Population Reports.* Consumer Income Series P-60, number 107 (September). Washington, D.C.: U.S. Department of Commerce, U.S. Government Printing Office, 1977b.

U.S. Bureau of Labor Statistics. *Revised Equivalence Scale for Estimating Incomes on Budget Costs by Family Type.* Bulletin 1570-2. Washington, D.C.: U.S. Government Printing Office, 1968.

_____. *Three Budgets for a Retired Couple in Urban Areas of the United States, 1967-68.* Bulletin 1570-6. Washington, D.C.: U.S. Government Printing Office, 1970.

U.S. Department of Health, Education, and Welfare. *The Measure of Poverty: Report Prepared for the Congress by the Interagency Poverty Studies Task Force.* Technical papers I to XVIII. Washington, D.C.: Office of the Assistant Secretary for Planning and Evaluation, HEW, 1976.

Warner, W. L., M. Meeker, and K. Eells. *Social Class in America: A Manuel of Procedure for the Measurement of Social Status.* Chicago: Science Research Associates, 1949.

Watts, H. W. "The Iso-Prop Index: An Approach to the Determination of Differential Poverty Income Thresholds." *Journal of Human Resources*, 1967, 2:3-18.

Weisbrod, B. A., and W. L. Hansen. "An Income-Net Worth Approach to Measuring Economic Welfare." *American Economic Review*, 1968, 8:1315-29.

Wentworth, E. C., and D. K. Motley. *Resources after Retirement: A Study of Income, Assets and Living Arrangements of Social Security Beneficiaries, 1941-1962.* Social Security Administration, U.S. Department of Health, Education and Welfare, Research Report number 34. Washington, D.C.: U.S. Government Printing Office, 1970.

Abstracts

CURRENT MONEY INCOME

U.S. Bureau of the Census, 1976

Definition of Concept or Variable

Current money income usually consists of the sum of all income received (during the preceding year) by an aged unit (household, family) from selected sources.

Context of Development

The Social Security Administration has conducted periodic surveys of the economic status of beneficiaries since 1941. Three studies conducted in 1963, 1968, and 1972, in conjunction with the Current Populations Surveys of the U.S. Bureau of the Census, have surveyed representative national samples of both beneficiaries and nonbeneficiaries. The Grad (1977) report is from the 1972 Survey of the Status of the Elderly (STATEL). It reports the relative importance of different sources of income over time for persons of pre- and postretirement status.

Description of Instrument

The U.S. Bureau of the Census's definition of total money income is the sum of all income, before taxes, from the following sources: (1) earnings, including money wages or salary before deductions for taxes, bonds, insurance, pensions, etc., and net income from farm and nonfarm self-employment (gross cash receipts minus operating expenses); (2) retirement benefits, including Old Age, Survivors, Disability and Health Insurance (OASDHI) cash benefits, benefits under other public programs (for railroad workers; federal, state, and local government employees; and retired members of the armed forces), and private group pensions paid by a former employer or a union directly or through an insurance company; (3) veterans' benefits, including compensation for service-connected disability or death and pensions for nonservice-connected disability or death; (4) public assistance payments (excluding vendor medical payments); (5) income from assets in the form of interest (on bonds or savings), dividends from stock holdings or membership in associations and cooperatives, and net rental income from rental of houses, apartments, business buildings, and vacant lots or from rooms and boarders; (6) cash contributions from relatives or friends not living in the household; and (7) all other money income (except from relatives in the household), including unemployment insurance benefits, worker's compensation, private welfare or relief, and private annuities. Money receipts excluded from the income measure are money from the sale of property (real, stocks, bonds), unless respondent was engaged in the business of selling property; bank deposit withdrawals and loans; tax refunds; gifts; and lump-sum inheritances or insurance benefits. (Refer to series P-60 of the U.S. Bureau of the Census *Current Population Reports* for facsimile copies of the Current Population Survey [CPS] questions on income and other information. Sample CPS income questions are included in Instrument V2.7.I.a.)

Sample

The sample chosen here to illustrate procedures for collecting information on the current income of the elderly is the 1972 Survey of the Status of the Elderly (STATEL) derived from the March 1972 Current Population Survey sample of the U.S. Bureau of the Census matched with information from the Social Security Administration's Master Beneficiary Record (MBR). Persons who have not filed for social security benefits are not included in the MBR. STATEL extracted annual work and income information from the 1972 CPS for all individuals aged 60 and over and their spouses. The sample consisted of 14,724 aged units. The match rate for the final sample with the MBR was 81% for married couples and 74% for unmarried persons.

Formal Tests of Reliability and Validity

Nonsampling error from underreporting, misreporting, and nonresponse is a special problem in income surveys. The Bureau of the Census has developed procedures to impute work and income for missing data on sample cases (e.g., see Ono and Miller, 1969).

Norms and Distribution

The distribution of aged units by money-income class in 1971 is shown in Table 7-2 from Grad (1977), by marital status and sex. Married couples have a relative advantage in income. The sources of this income are as important as the income levels of the elderly. A regression analysis of these data shows that between 23% and 33% of the variation in the amount of total income is explained by four variables in order of importance: (1) earnings/social security (receipt of these sources is an indications of retirement status), (2) asset income (except for the unmarried on public assistance), (3) private pensions, and (4) government employee pensions. A breakdown of income sources by race reveals that public assistance replaces asset income in relative importance for the income of black elderly retirees (Grad, 1977, Table II, p. 29).

TABLE 7-2

Income Size: Percentage Distribution of Aged
Units 65 and Older, by Money Income Class, 1971

Income	All Units	Married Couples	Nonmarried Persons		
			Total	Men	Women
Number (in thousands)	15,637	6,300	9,336	2,023	7,313
Total percent	100	100	100	100	100
Less than $1,000	8	1	13	8	15
$1,000-$1,499	10	1	17	12	18
$1,500-$1,999	13	3	19	14	20
$2,000-$2,499	10	5	14	15	14
$2,500-$2,999	7	6	8	10	8
$3,000-$3,499	6	7	6	8	5
$3,500-$3,999	6	7	4	7	4
$4,000-$4,999	10	15	6	9	5
$5,000-$6,999	12	21	6	7	5
$7,000-$9,999	8	14	4	5	3
$10,000-$14,999	6	11	2	2	2
$15,000 and over	4	8	1	2	1
Median[1]	$3,071	$5,358	$2,049	$2,540	$1,935

1. Medians are calculated from an income distribution with a finer breakdown.

SOURCE: S. Grad. *Income of the Populations Aged 60 and Older, 1971.* HEW Publication number (SSA) 77-11851. Washington, D.C.: U.S. Government Printing Office, 1977, p. 21.

Usability on Older Populations

Income measures that account for all sources of income—and particularly earnings/social security, asset income, private pensions, supplemental security income (public assistance), and government employee pensions—are usable on older populations.

Sensitivity to Age Differences

Income distributions by age (reported by age in the P-60 series of *Current Population Reports*) show relatively greater dependence by younger groups on earnings alone. Lifetime income patterns show rising income until the ages between 45 and 54 and then a gradual decline until retirement, when a sharp decline occurs (Kreps, 1976).

General Comments and Recommendations

Current money income alone as a measure of socioeconomic status probably underestimates actual status or potential for consumption, especially within the white population. In-kind transfers complement current cash resources in retirement in important ways. Food stamps, Medicaid, public housing, health care, imputed rental value of owner-occupied homes, etc., all contribute to the economic well-being of elderly people. Asset holdings, or net worth, are equally significant.

References

Bixby, L. E. "Income of People Aged 65 and Older: Overview from 1968 Survey of the Aged." *Social Security Bulletin*, 1970, 33 (4):3-34.

Grad, S. *Income of the Population Aged 60 and Older, 1971*. HEW Publication number (SSA) 77-11851. Washington, D.C.: U.S. Government Printing Office, 1977.

Kreps, J. "The Economy and the Aged." In *Handbook of Aging and the Social Sciences*, R. H. Binstock and E. Shanas (eds.), pp. 272-85. New York: Van Nostrand Reinhold, 1976.

Ono, M., and H. P. Miller. "Income Nonresponses in the Current Population Survey." In *Proceedings of the Social Statistics Section of the American Statistical Association*, pp. 277-88. Washington, D.C.: American Statistical Association, 1969.

Spiers, E. F., J. Coder, and M. Ono. "Characteristics of Income Nonrespondents in the Current Population Survey." In *Proceedings of the Social Statistics Section of the American Statistical Association*, pp. 369-74. Washington, D.C.: American Statistical Association, 1971.

U.S. Bureau of the Census. "Money Income and Poverty Status of Families and Persons in the United States: 1976 (Advance Report)." *Current Population Reports*. Consumer Income Series P-60, number 107 (September). Washington, D.C.: U.S. Department of Commerce, U.S. Government Printing Office, 1976.

Instrument

See Instrument V2.7.I.a.

POVERTY THRESHOLDS

U.S. Bureau of the Census, 1978

Definition of Concept or Variable

Poverty thresholds define levels of income that divide families (households) of differing composition, place, and time into the poor and the near-poor. More specifically, the modified Orshansky (1965a; 1969) thresholds vary by (1) family size and composition and (2) sex and age of family head and are adjusted for (3) annual changes in the Consumer Price Index (CPI) and (4) differences between farm and nonfarm residence.

Context of Development

Poverty *is not measured* by an index, a scale, or a battery in the usual sense of these terms. The measure of poverty depends on the decisions of governmental agencies to draw the line at selected points in the income scale and establish what is believed to be an adequate income for a person or group of persons with respect to the income of others.

The definition of an adequate income was based initially on a food-income relationship defined in 1955 by the Department of Agriculture's economy food plan and adopted officially in 1961 by the Council of Economic Advisers. This plan set down the minimum money income that could support an average family (of four) purchase of a nutritionally adequate diet, or approximately one-third of family income. As such, the poverty level was set at three times the cost of the economy food plan. This meant that, for a nonfarm family of four or more persons in 1959, an annual income of $3,000 was defined as the poverty level, with the threshold for unrelated (not living with a family) individuals set at $1,500.

The definition was then modified by Orshansky (1965a), who represented the Social Security Administration. The Orshansky sliding scale had three components: (1) the economy food plan adjusted for smaller families and single persons, with higher multipliers that compensated for the relatively higher fixed expenses of smaller households; (2) the amount of income required for nonfood items, defined as twice the amount required for food (with higher multipliers for one- and two-person families); and (3) adjustments for the farm or nonfarm residence of family (based on the assessment that cash requirements for food of farm families could be reduced to 60% of nonfarm levels to allow for food produced and consumed in the farm home).

In 1969 a federal interagency committee modified the original Orshansky thresholds by introducing (1) Consumer Price Index adjustments for food and nonfood costs over time, (2) further refinements by sex and age of head of household, and (3) readjustments of farm-resident thresholds to 85% of nonfarm residents' current poverty thresholds (as of 1977). These thresholds are defined in terms of real (1963) dollars and are published annually on the basis of the income sample of the Current Population Survey.

Description of Instrument

Thresholds are set annually for 124 different kinds of families to define the "poor" whose household incomes fall below these levels and the "near-poor" whose household incomes fall within 125% of these levels. The thresholds are arranged in a four-dimensional matrix, with family size (ranging from one person to six or more persons) cross-classified by (1) presence and number of family members under 18 years old, (2) sex of family head, and (3) farm-nonfarm residence. Two-person families and unrelated individuals are further distinguished when the age of the head is under or over 65 years. Table 7-3 from the U.S. Bureau of Census (1978) displays the 124 thresholds based on these cross-classifications.

TABLE 7-3

Income Thresholds at the Poverty Level in 1976 by Sex of Head, Size of Family, and Number of Related Children under 18 Years Old, by Farm-Nonfarm Residence

Size of Family Unit	Number of Related Children under 18 Years Old						
	None	1	2	3	4	5	6 or more
NONFARM							
Male Head							
1 person (unrelated individual):							
Under 65 years	$ 3,069						
65 years and over	2,758						
2 persons:							
Head under 65 years	3,838	$ 4,300					
Head 65 years and over	3,446	4,300					
3 persons	4,468	4,613	$ 4,876				
4 persons	5,890	5,977	5,771	$6,063			
5 persons	7,109	7,194	6,964	6,788	$6,934		
6 persons	8,154	8,180	8,008	7,833	7,602	$7,718	
7 or more persons	10,268	10,357	10,153	9,979	9,749	9,399	$9,313

TABLE 7-3—*Continued*

Size of Family Unit	Number of Related Children under 18 Years Old						
	None	1	2	3	4	5	6 or more
Female Head							
1 person (unrelated individual):							
Under 65 years	$2,840						
65 years and over	2,722						
2 persons							
Head under 65 years	3,545	$ 3,871					
Head 65 years and over	3,403	3,871					
3 persons	4,324	4,119	$ 4,555				
4 persons	5,655	5,860	5,832	$5,771			
5 persons	6,788	6,993	6,964	6,906	$6,673		
6 persons	7,920	8,065	8,008	7,949	7,688	$7,455	
7 or more persons	9,950	10,096	10,066	9,979	9,719	9,516	$9,052
FARM							
Male Head							
1 person (unrelated individual):							
Under 65 years	$2,608						
65 years and over	2,344						
2 persons							
Head under 65 years	3,262	$ 3,653					
Head 65 years and over	2,929	3,653					
3 persons	3,798	3,921	$4,144				
4 persons	5,007	5,082	4,905	$5,153			
5 persons	6,043	6,116	5,918	5,770	$5,893		
6 persons	6,930	6,953	6,807	6,658	6,461	$6,560	
7 or more persons	8,730	8,804	8,632	8,483	8,287	7,990	$7,917
Female Head							
1 person (unrelated individual):							
Under 65 years	$2,414						
65 years and over	2,313						
2 persons							
Head under 65 years	3,014	$ 3,290					

TABLE 7-3—*Continued*

Size of Family Unit	Number of Related Children under 18 Years Old						
	None	1	2	3	4	5	6 or more
Female Head							
Head 65 years and over	2,893	3,290					
3 persons	3,673	3,501	$3,872				
4 persons	4,809	4,980	4,957	$4,905			
5 persons	5,770	5,944	5,918	5,869	$5,672		
6 persons	6,773	6,856	6,807	6,758	6,535	$6,337	
7 or more persons	8,456	8,583	8,557	8,483	8,262	8,088	$7,694

SOURCE: U.S. Bureau of the Census. "Characteristics of the Population Below the Poverty Level: 1975." *Current Populations Reports.* Consumer Income Series P-60, number 115 (July). Washington, D.C.: U.S. Department of Commerce, U.S. Government Printing Office, 1978, Table A-2, p. 206.

The measure of annual income (during the preceding year) in the Current Population Survey—on which the 124 thresholds are based—is drawn for each person 14 years old and older. The sources include money wages or salary; net income from nonfarm self-employment; net income, or estate or trust income; veterans' payments, unemployment compensation, curity income; public assistance or welfare; interest on savings or bonds; dividends, net rental income, or estate or trust income; veterans' payments, unemployment compensation, or workers' compensation; private pensions or annuities; military retirement or government employee pensions; alimony or child support; and other regular contributions or periodic income. Nonmoney income from transfers such as food stamps, health benefits, rent-free housing, free transportation, educational benefits, etc., is not included.

A shorter form of 36 weighted average thresholds is derived from the larger table and for most purposes is sufficient for determining the relative poverty levels of elderly persons. Instrument V2.7.I.b presents the current (1976) weighted average poverty thresholds for elderly persons, based on the March 1977 Current Population Survey (U.S. Bureau of the Census, 1978, p. 207).

Sample

The Current Population Survey is conducted annually in March by the Bureau of the Census. The March 1977 sample was drawn from 1970 census files covering all 50 states and the District of Columbia and supplemented by a sample of housing units in 24 states and the District of Columbia. The sample consisted of approximately 56,000 occupied households.

Formal Tests of Reliability

Since the poverty thresholds are based on income reports from a sample, the estimates reflect both sampling and nonsampling variability. Nonsampling variability in all surveys is difficult to determine. Income estimates based on self-reports are limited by underreporting, nonreporting, and misreporting. Year-to-year correlation coefficients for poverty estimates can be derived, however, and are reported for the CPS. These coefficients for persons and families of all racial and ethnic categories for 1974-1975, 1973-1974, 1972-1973, for example, all fall within the range of .30 to .45.

Formal Tests of Validity

No formal tests of validity apply. The poverty (income) thresholds are meant to be statistical yardsticks established for policymaking, not theoretical, purposes.

Norms and Distribution

Poverty rates for persons 65 years old and older, as well as for those of all ages in the general population, have steadily declined since 1959. But "unrelated" (single) elderly individuals of all race-sex breakdowns continue to have significantly higher poverty rates than older persons in families (U.S. Bureau of the Census, 1977, Table 3).

Usability on Older Populations

The thresholds are specifically adjusted for persons and families under and over age 65.

Sensitivity to Age Differences

Poverty rates published for the period 1969 through 1976 (U.S. Bureau of the Census, 1977) show that persons 65 years old and older have consistently higher poverty rates year by year than the total sample for all racial groups.

General Comments and Recommendations

It cannot be overemphasized that poverty thresholds are not theoretical constructs, but governmental yardsticks. Thresholds are not meant to be calculated independently by researchers, but used for reference and for purposes of comparison at an aggregate level. The thresholds are not sensitive to regional differences in income and consumer prices and, therefore, may need further adjustments for analyses of that kind.

References

Orshansky, M. "Counting the Poor: Another Look at the Poverty Profile." *Social Security Bulletin*, 1965a, 28 (1)3-29.

—————. "Who's Who among the Poor: A Demographic View of Poverty." *Social Security Bulletin*, 1965b, 28 (7):3-32.

—————. "Recounting the Poor: A Five-Year Review." *Social Security Bulletin*, 1966, 29 (4):2-19.

—————. "The Shape of Poverty in 1966." *Social Security Bulletin*, 1968, 31 (3):3-32.

—————. "Perspectives on Poverty 2: How Poverty Is Measured." *Monthly Labor Review*, 1969, 92 (2):244-83.

U.S. Bureau of the Census. "Characteristics of the Population below the Poverty Level: 1975." *Current Population Reports*. Consumer Income Series P-60, number 106 (June). Washington, D.C.: U.S. Department of Commerce, U.S. Government Printing Office, 1977.

—————. "Characteristics of the Population below the Poverty Level: 1976." *Current Population Reports*. Consumer Income Series p-60, number 115 (July). Washington, D.C.: U.S. Department of Commerce, U.S. Government Printing Office, 1978.

U.S. Department of Health, Education, and Welfare. *The Measure of Poverty: Report Prepared for the Congress by the Interagency Poverty Studies Task Force*. Technical papers I to XVIII. Washington, D.C.: Office of the Assistant Secretary for Planning and Evaluation, HEW 1976.

Instrument

See Instrument V2.7.I.b.

INCOME-NET WORTH MEASURE OF ECONOMIC POSITION

B. A. Weisbrod and W. L. Hansen, 1968

Definition of Concept or Variable

Economic position is defined as a summary measure composed of the current income and current net worth of a consumer unit. Net worth is defined as all assets less all debts.

Context of Development

A summary measure of economic welfare is proposed since families or individuals with the same current money income may differ widely in the amount of wealth held. As such, income is viewed as flow and net worth is viewed as stock, with the latter accumulated over a lifetime (Projector and Weiss, 1966; 1969; Weisbrod and Hansen, 1968).

Description of Instrument

The income-net worth measure of economic position is summarized as follows.

$Y_t^* = Y_t + NW_t \cdot A_n$, where

Y_t^* = economic position in period t,

Y_t = current annual income of the consumer unit, net of yield on net worth,

$NW_t \cdot A_n$ = annual lifetime annuity value of current net worth, where A_n is the value of an n year annuity whose present value is \$1,

$A_n = \dfrac{r}{1 - (1 + r) -N}$, with r representing the (interest) rate of return on assets, e.g., .04 or .10.

The size of the lifetime annuity was calculated by using 4% and 10% interest rates, alternatively, "to give a notion of the sensitivity of the results" (Weisbrod and Hansen, 1968, p. 1319). In estimates of joint life-expectancy values, family (male) heads were assumed to be 5 years older than their wives. Finally, it was assumed that full annuity would be received while both spouses were alive but that a surviving spouse would receive only two-thirds of the annuity during the remainder of his or her life.

Assets or wealth include the following: owned home, automobile, business or profession (farm and nonfarm), liquid assets, investment assets, and miscellaneous assets. Life-insurance investments and equities in annuities and retirement plans are not included on the data set used. Debts include debt secured by a home, debt by investment assets, personal debt, and debt on life-insurance policies.

Sample

The measure was applied to data from the Survey of Financial Characteristics of Consumers (SFCC) and the Current Population Survey for 1962. The SFCC provided data on families by age of head, income, and net worth (as defined above); the CPS data set was added since it provided larger sample size at the lower income levels. Thus, the SFCC net worth data were combined with CPS income data. The median value of total net worth of families by income class was assigned as equivalent in both sets.

Formal Tests of Reliability and Validity

No formal test or explicit treatment of either reliability or validity is offered. The estimates are meant to be illustrative of the approach taken and are regarded by the authors as incomplete and "somewhat rough" (Weisbrod and Hansen, 1968, p. 1319). Survey data on income and assets, even in a more complete form than is found in these data, tends to be especially vulnerable to nonsampling error. (See Ferber, 1966, for a thorough review of this problem.)

Norms and Distribution

The distributions observed in Table 7-4 indicate (1) the rise and subsequent decline of income over the life cycle, (2) an increasing ratio of net worth to income over the life cycle, and (3) the decreasing life expectancy over the life cycle. In Table 7-5 these distributions appear to persist for both low- and high-income groups.

TABLE 7-4
Median Income, Median Net Worth, and Life
Expectancy of Families, by Age of Family Head, 1962

Age of Family Head	(1) Median Income	(2) Median Net Worth	(3) Ratio (2) / (1)	(4) Family Life Expectancy (years)[1]
Under 35	$5,585	$ 759	0.14	49
35-54	6,918	7,664	1.11	34
55-64	6,219	13,210	2.12	21
65 and over	3,204	9,719	3.03	11
All	5,956	8,329	1.40	

1. "Family life expectancy" is weighted average of the life expectancies of husbands and wives at the mean age of the family head and on the assumption that wives are five years younger than their husbands. A weight of two-thirds is given to the additional years of life expectancy of the wife; this results from the assumption that widows will receive an annuity of two-thirds of the amount previously received by the combined husband and wife unit.

SOURCE: B. A. Weisbrod and W. L. Hansen. "An Income-Net Worth Approach to Measuring Economic Welfare." *American Economic Review*, 1968, 8:1322. Reprinted by permission of authors and publisher.

TABLE 7-5
Median Income and Median Net Worth of Families with Incomes of Less than
$3,000 per Year and of More than $10,000 per Year by Age of Family Head, 1962

Age of Family Head	Less than $3,000 per Year		
	Median Net Worth (NW)	Median Income (Y)	Ratio (NW/Y)
Under 35	$ 0	$1,782	0
35-54	385	1,760	0.22
55-65	5,625	1,646	3.42
65 and over	6,667	1,844	3.62
All	$2,250	$1,788	1.26

Age of Family Head	More than $10,000 per Year		
	Median Net Worth	Median Income	Ratio (NW/Y)
Under 35	$ 7,634	$12,969	0.59
35-54	20,349	13,449	1.51
55-64	35,524	12,420	2.86
65 and over	45,800	14,084	3.25
All	21,714	13,454	1.61

SOURCE: B. A. Weisbrod and W. L. Hansen. "An Income-Net Worth Approach to Measuring

Economic Welfare." *American Economic Review*, 1968, 8:1326. Reprinted by permission of authors and publisher.

Usability on Older Populations

The measure is usable on older populations.

Sensitivity to Age Differences

Since older persons tend to have higher ratios of net worth to current money income than younger persons, along with shorter life expectancies, their economic position appears to be most affected by net worth; i.e., they tend to be better-off than what is shown by their current income alone. The economic position of younger persons, by contrast, is less affected by net worth, especially among those in the low-income ($3,000 per year) class. (See Table 7-5.)

General Comments and Recommendations

The approach has been adopted and improved upon by other researchers, including Moon, whose composite measure of economic welfare is summarized elsewhere in this chapter.

References

Ferber, R. "The Reliability of Consumer Reports of Financial Assets and Debts." *Studies in Consumer Savings*, number 6. Urbana, Ill.: Bureau of Economic and Business Research, University of Illinois, 1966.

Projector, D. S., and G. S. Weiss. *Survey of Financial Characteristics of Consumers*. Washington, D.C.: Board of Governors of the Federal Researve System, 1966.

——————. "Income-Net Worth Measures of Economic Welfare." *Social Security Bulletin*, 1969, 32 (11):14-17.

Weisbrod, B. A., and W. L. Hansen. "An Income-Net Worth Approach to Measuring Economic Welfare." *American Economic Review*, 1968, 8:1315-29.

Instrument

See the description of the instrument given above.

NET WORTH AS AN ASPECT OF STATUS

J. C. Henretta and R. T. Campbell, 1978

Definition of Concept or Variable

Net worth, or assets minus debts, is viewed as an important aspect of the status of the elderly, whether status is defined as life chances, life-styles, or potential level of consumption.

Context of Development

The measures of status that depend on education, income, and/or occupational attainment become less appropriate for older samples. Instead, the socioeconomic status of older groups is seen to be determined increasingly by considerations of wealth or net worth. The standard of living of retirees, who usually experience large reductions in current income, is maintained by cash (other than income) and in-kind transfers and by accumulated assets (Weisbrod and Hansen, 1968; Moon, 1977). Home ownership alone, as only one component of assets held, contributes significantly to the stock of resources available to older groups and individuals for consumption purposes.

Description of Instrument

The basic measure of net worth presented is:

net worth = home equity + liquid savings + business assets + other real estate − other debt, where home equity = estimate of value of home – present value of mortgage,

liquid savings = savings account balance + estimate of value of stocks and bonds + value of savings bonds + other bank deposits or investments, and

business assets and other real estate assets are the net of the debt applicable to them.

The measure excludes equity in a pension or other forced savings such as life insurance.

Sample

The measure is applied primarily to data from the National Longitudinal Surveys of Labor Force Participation in 1971 with the sample of male respondents that fell within the age range of 50 to 64 years. The design and characteristics of all waves of these surveys are described in Parnes (1970; 1973; 1975).

Formal Tests of Reliability and Validity

No formal tests are reported. The investigators do warn of the tendency for underreporting of asset holdings (Ferber, 1966) and income (Barlow, Brazer, and Morgan, 1966), which result in the possible downward bias of estimates. The lack of inclusion of equity in a pension and forced savings in the measure of net worth may further bias the estimates downward.

Norms and Distribution

The relationship of net worth to selected status-attainment variables is reported in five states in Table 7-6, with unstandardized and standardized regression coefficients (Henretta and Campbell, 1978, p. 1212). The natural logarithm of net worth (Ln Net Worth) was taken to adjust for the nonlinearity of the relationship between net worth and social standing. Education was represented in the model as a series of contrasts with high school graduates (dummy variables) to deal with the effects of nonlinearity and interactions. The occupational status of the respondent and his or her father was measure by using the Duncan Socioeconomic Index. Age, family earnings, occupational status, and marital status have significant effects on net worth, thus providing support for the construct validity of net worth as an aspect of status.

TABLE 7-6
Reduced and Full Form Equations for Ln Net Worth
(White, Nonfarm Males, Aged 50-64, 1971)

	Dependent Variable: Ln Net Worth[1]				
	1	2	3	4	5
1. Father's Education	.065	−.007	−.013	−.012	−.022
	(.020)	(.019)	(.018)	(.018)	(.018)
2. Father's SEI	.018	.007	.003	.003	.001
	(.003)	(.003)	(.003)	(.003)	(.003)
3. R's AGE	.001	.027	.018	.020	.031
	(.014)	(.014)	(.013)	(.014)	(.013)
4. 0-4 years EDUC[2]		−.3.95	−2.94	−2.84	−2.60
		(.316)	(.307)	(.310)	(.302)
5. 5-8 years		−1.22	−.751	−.727	−.647
		(.166)	(.163)	(.163)	(.159)
6. 9-12 years		−.470	−.293	−.284	−2.80
		(.176)	(.169)	(.168)	(.164)
7. 13-15 years		.600	.338	.363	.071
		(.234)	(.223)	(.223)	(.218)

TABLE 7-6—*Continued*

		Dependent Variable: Ln Net Worth[1]			
	1	2	3	4	5
8. 16 years		.654 (.288)	−.088 (.283)	−.094 (.283)	−.452 (.277)
9. 17+ years		.484 (.295)	−.181 (.290)	−.190 (.290)	−.559 (.284)
10. R's SEI			.026 (.002)	.026 (.002)	.015 (.002)
11. Divorce[3]			−2.96 (.326)	−2.93 (.326)	−2.75 (.318)
12. Other Marital Status			−1.87 (.222)	−1.83 (.223)	−1.47 (.219)
13. Household Size			−.156 (.042)	−.157 (.042)	−.169 (.041)
14. Pension				.241 (.116)	.112 (.114)
15. Earnings[4] ($1,000)					.12 (.01)
Intercept	8.05	8.04	8.20	7.93	6.89
R^2	.033	.124	.219	.221	.264

	Standardized Coefficients[5]				
	1	2	3	4	5
Father's Education	.076	.008	−.015	−.014	−.025
Father's SEI	.137	.053	.023	.024	.006
R's Age	.001	.040	.027	.030	.045
R's SEI			.219	.216	.127
Household Size			−.077	−.164	−.084
Earnings					.259

1. Standard errors (not corrected for sampling efficiency) in parentheses, N = 2,125.
2. Each education category is a contrast with high school graduate.
3. Each marital status category is a contrast with married, spouse present.
4. Increment of $1,000.
5. Standardized coefficients are not reported for dummy variables for reasons reported in footnote 10 to the text.

SOURCE: J. C. Henretta and R. T. Campbell. "Net Worth as an Aspect of Status." *American Journal of Sociology*, 1978, 83:1212. Reprinted by permission of authors and publisher, the University of Chicago Press.

Usability on Older Populations

The measure was developed using the explicit rationale that wealth is a major aspect of status at the end of the life cycle.

Sensitivity to Age Differences

The sample in this study was limited to males 50 to 65 years old, but other studies (e.g., Weisbrod and Hansen, 1968; Projector and Weiss, 1969) have reported age differences in net worth that include younger and older samples. (See the abstract in this chapter for the Income-Net Worth Measure of Economic Position.)

General Comments and Recommendations

This measure is an important breakthrough in the sociological literature on the status of the elderly, but it is still undergoing refinement. As a simple summary measure without unit weighting, it is still not sensitive enough to the relative contributions of different sources of net worth (such as home equity) to consumption patterns.

References

Barlow, R., H.E. Brazer, and J. N. Morgan. *Economic Behavior of the Affluent*. Washington, D.C.: The Brookings Institute, 1966.

Ferber, R. "The Reliability of Consumer Reports of Financial Assets and Debts." *Studies in Consumer Savings*, number 6. Urbana, Ill.: Bureau of Economic and Business Research, University of Illinois, 1966.

Henretta, J.C., and R. T. Campbell. "Net Worth as an Aspect of Status." *American Journal of Sociology*, 1978, 83:1204-23.

Moon, M. *The Measurement of Economic Welfare: Its Application to the Aged Poor*. New York: Academic Press, 1977.

Parnes, H. S. "The Pre-retirement Years: A Longitudinal Study of the Labor Market Experience of Men." *Manpower Research Monograph*, number 15 (2 vols.). Washington, D.C.: U.S. Department of Labor, 1970.

————. "The Pre-retirement Years: A Longitudinal Study of the Labor Market Experience of Men." *Manpower Research Monograph*, number 15 (vol. 3). Washington, D.C.: U.S. Department of Labor, 1973.

————. "The National Longitudinal Surveys: New Vistas for Labor Market Research." *American Economic Review*, 1975, 65:244-49.

Projector, D. S., and G. S. Weiss. "Income-Net Worth Measures of Economic Welfare." *Social Security Bulletin*, 1969, 32 (11): 14-17.

Weisbrod, B. A., and W. L. Hansen. "An Income-Net Worth Approach to Measuring Economic Welfare." *American Economic Review*, 1968, 8:1315-29.

Instrument

See the description of the instrument given above.

COMPOSITE MEASURE OF ECONOMIC WELFARE OF THE AGED

M. Moon, 1976; 1977

Definition of Concept or Variable

Economic welfare is defined as a multidimensional concept that takes into account both money and nonmoney aspects of the income and wealth (assets) of aged individuals and families. Specifically, measured components of the economic welfare of the aged include adjusted earnings, private pensions, shares of total family net worth, and adjusted intrafamily transfers.

Context of Development

This measure is a direct response to the need for an appropriate measure of the economic status of the elderly—and one that is more comprehensive than the income-net worth approach of Weisbrod and Hansen (reviewed elsewhere in this chapter). The idea of economic welfare is based on the life-cycle hypothesis of saving and requires a systematic account of yearly levels of potential consumption among aged families. Moon (1976; 1977) developed the measure in the tradition of a series of important studies on the distribution of economic welfare (cf. Morgan et al., 1962; Sirageldin, 1969; Taussig, 1973). In this tradition, current income alone is viewed as wholly insufficient as a measure of economic welfare, and especially in the case of the aged, who are relatively more dependent on the return of assets and resources other than current income from wages, etc.

Description of Instrument

The measure is expressed in a standard utility function framework. The estimated measure of economic welfare (W_t^*) for an aged family is:

$$W_t^* = (Y_t^* - S_t^*) \lambda, \text{ where,}$$

Y_t^* = current nonproperty resources, or estimated current family income, available for consumption in period t,

S_t^* = share of net worth allocated over period t,

λ = adjustment for family composition.

The precise estimation procedures for each of these components are complex, so the user is advised to refer to Moon (1977, Chapter 3) with care. However, a brief summary of these procedures can be presented here.

Y_t^* or estimated current family income includes the following observations over period t:

$$Y_t^* = Y_t^e + O_t + G_t^c + G_t^{k*} - T_t^* + I_t, \text{ where}$$

Y_t^e = earned income.

O_t = other income, not captured in earnings, property income, or cash transfers,

G_t^c = government cash transfers,

G_t^{k*} = estimated government in-kind transfers: Medicare, Medicaid, public housing,

T_t^* = estimated tax liability from federal income, payroll, and property taxes,

I_t = intrafamily transfers (both positive and negative).

S_t^* is the retired worker's share of the estimated net worth or stock of wealth of a family. Net worth includes all assets minus debts in the family, including adjusted home equity. S_t^* converts net worth into a flow across the family's estimated life expectancy. The standard annuity formula below thus reflects the rate of return on assets and the expected lifetime of the family's members.

$$S_t^* = A \left(\frac{r}{1 - (1 + r)^{-N}} \right), \text{ where}$$

S_t^* = annual estimated share of net worth,

A = net worth at the beginning of period t,

r = real rate of return (interest) on assets,

N = life expectancy in years from period t

(a composite figure based on *the average of* the life-expectancy estimates for each family member varied by the age and sex of individuals).

Finally, λ is an adjustment for family size and can be expressed as a "welfare ratio" (i.e., where actual family resources are divided by a standardized set of budget needs determined by the size and composition of the family, with a value of 1 indicating that family resources just coincide with needs, *or* in "equivalency units" expressed in dollar terms that convert measured resources into the number of dollars necessary for a standardized family or aged couple to reach a comparable level of economic welfare). The equivalency measure F_i for the ith family's welfare (W_i) is:

$F_i = W_i(p_i/\bar{p})$, where

$\bar{p}$ = poverty threhold for some family unit,

p_i = poverty threshold for the ith family.

(See abstract in this chapter on Poverty Thresholds.)

The measure of economic welfare (W_t^*) excludes the value of nonmarket productive activities, leisure time, some direct governmental expenditures, and some in-kind transfers and taxes.

Sample

The measure was applied by Moon (1976; 1977) to data drawn from a subsample of 7,000 persons aged 65 and over (in over 6,100 families with at least one member aged 65 or older) of the 1967 Survey of Economic Opportunity (SEO). The Bureau of the Census conducted the survey in 1966 and 1967 for the years 1965 and 1966. This data set contains detailed information on assets and family income divided by source. Table 4.2 in Moon (1977) documents the average values for this sample for the measured compenents of economic welfare.

Formal Tests of Reliability

The reliability problems in surveys of income and wealth are related to sampling and nonsampling errors. In the case of Bureau of the Census surveys, the problem is essentially one of coping with nonsampling error associated with nonresponse, underreporting, or misreporting. These errors in survey data appear to account for, more than any other source of disturbance, the underestimation of aggregate values (Ferber, 1966). Since the Survey of Economic Opportunity was conducted only once, more formal measures of reliability are not available.

Formal Tests of Validity, and Norms and Distribution

The validity of a measure of the economic welfare of the aged is indicated by its value in discriminating the potential for consumption within the aging population better than would be possible with the estimates of current income alone. A conspicuous tendency revealed in Table 4.4 from Moon (1977, p. 68) is that current income alone overestimates actual "poverty" incidence among potential consumption groups classified by dollar values. For example, while approximately 40% of the sample falls below $2,000 when current income alone is measured, only 14% of the sample falls below this level using the final measure of economic welfare. The life-cycle measure of economic welfare appears to overcome the age bias of current income estimates. Table 4.10 (Moon, 1977, p. 75) shows ratio values of mean economic welfare to mean current income by selected demographic characteristics. Among the norms reported are (1) the increasing ratio of welfare level to income by age-group, (2) the higher ratio values for retired as opposed to working elderly, and (3) the relatively higher ratio value for female-headed households.

Usability on Older Populations

The measure was developed specifically for use on older populations.

Sensitivity to Age Differences

Moon (1977) tentatively applied the measure to younger respondents in the SEO subsample of families but found that determining the appropriate share of net worth poses considerable problems. Still, others have documented the relatively greater importance of net worth as an aspect of the status of the elderly. (See the abstracts in this chapter on income-net worth and net worth.)

General Comments and Recommendations

The reader is advised to consult Moon (1977) for more detailed guidelines for these calculations.

References

Ferber, R. "The Reliability of Consumer Reports of Financial Assets and Debts." *Studies in Consumer Savings*, number 6. Urbana, Ill.: Bureau of Economic and Business Research, University of Illinois, 1966.

Moon, M. "The Economic Welfare of the Aged and Income Security Programs." *Review of Income and Wealth*, 1976, 22:253-69.

_____. *The Measurement of Economic Welfare: Its Application to the Aged Poor*. New York: Academic Press, 1977.

Morgan, J., M. David, W. Cohen, and H. Brazen. *Income and Welfare in the United States*. New York: McGraw-Hill, 1962.

Sirageldin, I. *Nonmarket Components of National Income*. Ann Arbor, Mich.: Survey Research Center, University of Michigan, 1969.

Taussig, M. K. *Alternative Measures of the Distribution of Economic Welfare*. Princeton: N.J.: Industrial Relations Section, Princeton University, 1973.

Instrument

See the description of the instrument given above.

OCCUPATIONAL STATUS

U.S. Bureau of the Census, 1960

Definition of Context or Variable

Occupation is viewed as an index of social class when occupations are group into four broad categories: white-collar workers, blue-collar workers, service workers, and agricultural workers.

Context of Development

Occupational status as an index of social class has proved useful in cross-national analyses (Shanas et al., 1968; Gross, 1959; Lipset and Bendix, 1959), even when broad categories were used. Edwards's (1937; 1938) six-level scale has been the basis for such occupational groupings. Shanas and associates' (1968) cross-national study of old people in three industrial societies applies the Edwards-census groupings to a study of the preretirement occupational status of the elderly as an indicator of social class.

Description of Instrument

Men and single women were classified in Shanas and associates (1968) by their own jobs; married women and widows, by the occupations of their husbands. Four broad categories of occupation were regrouped from the Edwards-census scale into white-collar workers, blue-collar workers, service workers, and agricultural workers as follows:

Regrouped Shanas et al. Categories	Original Edwards-Census Categories
White-collar	Professionals, technical workers, managers, officials and proprietors (except farm), clerical and sales workers
Blue-collar	Craftsmen, foremen, operatives, and laborers (except farm)
Service	Private household workers and other service workers

Regrouped Shanas et al. Categories	Original Edwards-Census Categories
Agricultural	Farm owners, managers, laborers, and fore-men

White-collar workers are considered comparable to "middle-class"; blue-collar and service workers, comparable to "working-class." The agricultural category was acknowledged by Shanas and associates (1968) as the most ambiguous of the four, but it does serve to differentiate older persons in three countries.

Sample

The sample drawn in the United States, Britain (England, Wales, and Scotland), and Denmark was a stratified, multistage probability sample of men and women 65 years old and older and living in private households. There were approximately 2,500 respondents from each country.

Distribution

Occupational status was found to be associated, by and large, with the financial position (income) of the elderly in all three countries, although important discrepancies were observed. Whereas between 20% and 30% of white-collar individuals were located in the highest income groups, as many as 20% of the individuals in this class were in the lowest income group. The agricultural class tended to be overwhelmingly located in the highest income group.

Usability on Older Populations

Occupational status can be used on older populations that consist of both retired and working groups.

General Comments and Recommendations

Reliance on general occupational groupings tends to be the most feasible approach for cross-national comparisons, but it is an inefficient measure of economic status. This measure should be used in conjunction with other economic variables, e.g., income, assets, etc.

References

Edwards, A. M. *Alphabetical Index of Occupations by Industries and Socio-Economic Group-ings*. Washington, D.C.: U.S. Government Printing Office, 1937.

_____. *A Social-Economic Grouping of the Gainfully Employed Workers of the United States, 1930*. Washington, D.C.: U.S. Government Printing Office, 1938.

Gross, E. "The Occupational Variable as a Research Category." *American Sociological Review*, 1959, 24:640-49.

Lipset, S. M., and R. Bendix. *Social Mobility in Industrial Society*. Berkeley, Calif.: University of California Press, 1959.

Shanas, E., P. Townsend, D. Wedderburn, H. Friis, P. Milhoj, and J. Stehouwer. *Old People in Three Industrial Societies*. New York: Atherton Press, 1968.

U.S. Bureau of the Census. *1960 Census of Population: Classified Index of Occupations and Industries*. Washington, D.C.: U.S. Government Printing Office, 1960.

Instrument

See the description of the instrument given above.

U.S. CENSUS SOCIOECONOMIC STATUS

A. M. Edwards, 1937; 1938; U.S. Bureau of the Census, 1963

Definition of Concept or Variable

Socioeconomic status has three components: occupation, education, and income.

Context of Development

Edwards (1937; 1938) developed a hierarchy of the socioeconomic grouping of occupations as a rough approximation of prestige and socioeconomic status as early as 1917. Although he did not measure prestige as such, he did demonstrate that levels of education and income increased, with few exceptions, from the unskilled to the professional groupings. The U.S. Bureau of the Census revised the Edwards scale in 1960 and included more-detailed occupational breakdowns.

Description of Instrument

Socioeconomic status (SES) scores are simple average scores for family income and the occupation and education of the family's "chief income recipient" that range from 0 to 100. Median scores for income and education are combined with occupational ranking as follows:

$$SES = \frac{Occupation + education + income}{3},$$

where major occupational groups are scored as follows:

Occupational Grouping	Socioeconomic Status Score
Professional, technical, and kindred workers	90
Managers, officials, and proprietors (except farm)	81
Clerical, sales, and kindred workers	71
Craftsmen, foremen, and kindred workers	58
Operatives and kindred workers	45
Service workers, including private household	34
Laborers (except farm and mine)	20
Farm laborers and foremen	06

educational scores are grouped by years completed, as follows:

Score	Category	
98	College:	5 or more years
93		4
89		3
86		2
83		1
67	High School:	4
49		3
42		2
34		1
23	Elementary:	8
13		7
08		5 and 6
04		3 and 4
02		1 and 2
01	None	

and income groups are classified and scored as follows:

Score	Category	Score	Category
100	$25,000 or more	49	$5,000 to $5,499
98	$15,000 to $24,999	41	$4,500 to $4,999
94	$10,000 to $14,999	34	$4,000 to $4,499
89	$ 9,500 to $ 9,999	27	$3,500 to $3,999
87	$ 9,000 to $ 9,499	21	$3,000 to $3,499
84	$ 8,500 to $ 8,999	17	$2,500 to $2,999
81	$ 8,000 to $ 8,499	12	$2,000 to $2,499
78	$ 7,500 to $ 7,999	08	$1,500 to $1,999
74	$ 7,000 to $ 7,499	05	$1,000 to $1,499
69	$ 6,500 to $ 6,999	03	$ 500 to $ 999
63	$ 6,000 to $ 6,499	01	Loss, none, or less than $500
57	$ 5,500 to $ 5,999		

Income consists of the total family income during the preceding year from salary-wages, self-employment, and other income (e.g., pensions, net, rent, public assistance) from all family members. Not included as income are money received from the sale of property, value or in-kind income, bank deposits, loans, tax refunds, gifts, and lump-sum inheritances or insurance payments. Detailed occupational scores were published by the U.S. Bureau of the Census (1963, Appendix 1, pp. 9-12).

Sample

The scale was applied to the 5% sample of the 1960 census.

Formal Tests of Reliability and Validity

This scale correlates highly (Pearsonian $r = .97$) with the Duncan socioeconomic index (which incorporates prestige ratings). This scale, like all occupational scales, is affected by the special problems of reliability associated with coding occupations. (See the abstract on Duncan's instrument in this chapter for a discussion of coding occupations.)

Sensitivity to Age Differences

Median socioeconomic-status scores increase between ages 14 and 44 and then decline between ages 45 and 64 and over for the white population; for blacks, the decline appears to begin earlier, at age 35 (U.S. Bureau of the Census, 1967).

General Comments and Recommendations

The census SES and Duncan's SEI are similar indexes based primarily on occupational evaluations. Mostly for this reason, these scales tend to lack face validity for the study of retired populations, though much work still needs to be done in this area.

References

Edwards, A. M. *Alphabetical Index of Occupations by Industries and Socio-Economic Groupings.* Washington, D.C.: U.S. Government Printing Office, 1937.

_____. *A Social-Economic Grouping of the Gainfully Employed Workers of the United States, 1930.* Washington, D.C.: U.S. Government Printing Office, 1938.

U.S. Bureau of the Census. *1960 Census of Population: Classified Index of Occupations and Industries.* Washington, D.C.: U.S. Government Printing Office, 1960.

_____. *Methodology and Score of Socioeconomic Status.* Working Paper number 15. Washington, D.C.: U.S. Government Printing Office, 1963.

_____. *U.S. Census of Population, 1960.* Socioeconomic Status, Final Report PC (2)-5C. Washington, D.C.: U.S. Government Printing Office, 1967.

Instrument

See the description of the instrument given above.

OCCUPATIONAL PRESTIGE SCALES

C. C. North and P. K. Hatt, 1947; R. W. Hodge, P. M. Siegel, and P. H. Rossi, 1964; D. J. Treiman, 1977

Definition of Concept or Variable

Occupational prestige is the evaluation, using representative judgments, of the relative "standing" or "desirability" of an occupation.

Context of Development

C. C. North and P. K. Hatt, in cooperation with the National Opinion Research Center (NORC), conducted a national survey study in 1947 that solicited ratings by respondents of the "standings" of each of 90 occupations. The NORC scale of standings (prestige) was replicated in 1963 on a comparable national sample by Hodge, Siegel, and Rossi (1964). Most recently, Treiman (1977) developed a Standard International Occupational Prestige Scale, following the rationale that a generic, worldwide occupational prestige hierarchy exists.

Description of Instrument

The 1947 and 1963 surveys asked respondents to rate the same list of approximately 90 occupations by using the following six-value scale: (1) excellent standing (score 100), (2) good standing (score 80), (3) average standing (score 60), (4) somewhat below average (score 40), and (5) poor standing (score 20), with an additional "don't know" category included. After "don't know" responses were excluded, a mean score for each occupation was calculated, producing a range of scores in 1947 from 33 (shoe shiner) to 96 (U.S. Supreme Court justice) and in 1963 from 34 (shoe shiner) to 94 (U.S. Supreme Court justice). The 1947 and 1963 prestige ratings are available in Hodge, Siegel, and Rossi (1964, Table 1).

Since 1963, Siegel has calculated prestige scores for the complete census listing of occupational titles with the current listings based on 1970 census titles (see Siegel, 1971; and Featherman, Sobel, and Dickens, 1975). These updated prestige scores are available in Hauser and Featherman (1977, pp. 320-29).

Finally, Treiman (1977) developed a standardized international prestige scale using all available data on occupational prestige from approximately 55 countries (scores for all occupational titles were not available from every country, but the average title has approximately seven ratings).

Scores on Treiman's standard scale are converted to a standard metric (i.e., U.S. metric) by equating the mean and the standard deviation of all occupations rated in common in the United States and the given foreign country. The standard metric score X'_{ij} for occupation i in country j is computed as follows:

$$X'_{ij} = \frac{s_{u_j}}{s_{j_u}} (X_{ij} - \bar{X}_{j_u}) = \bar{X}_{u_j} \text{ where}$$

X'_{ij} = the transformed prestige score for occupation i rated in country j,

s_{u_j} = the standard deviation of the U.S. scores for occupations rated in both the United States and country j,

s_{j_u} = the standard deviation of the country j scores for occupations rated in both the United states and country j,

X_{ij} = the original metric prestige score for occupation i rated in country j,

$\bar{X}_{j_u}$ = the mean of the country j scores for occupations rated in both country j and the United States,

$\bar{X}_{u_j}$ = the mean of the U.S. scores for occupations rated in both country j and the United States.

A standard metric with a range of approximately 0 to 100 is produced by this procedure for 509 occupations and aggregated categories of occupations (categories are major groups, minor groups, and unit groups).

Sample(s)

The 1947 survey was drawn from a national sample of 2,920 U.S. youths and adults; the 1963 study included a national sample of 651 youths and adults. Treiman's scale is based on international data from a wide variety of samples.

Formal Tests of Reliability and Validity

Occupational prestige ratings have held up consistently across time (Hodge, Siegel, and Rossi, 1964) and across countries (Inkeles and Rossi, 1956; Hodge, Treiman, and Rossi, 1966; Treiman, 1977), lending support to the notion of an occupational prestige hierarchy as a major structural component of industrialized and industrializing societies. Hodge, Siegel, and Rossi reported a correlation of .99 between 1947 and 1963 ratings, and Treiman (1977) reported an average intercountry ($N = 55$) prestige correlation of .88. Major occupational group scores for three prestige-based scales indicate the relative persistence of ratings. Hauser and Featherman (1977, p. 17fn) provided evidence for the relative persistence of prestige ratings for the Duncan, Siegal, and Treiman scales for major occupational groups. Interscale correlations for the Duncan, Siegel, and Treiman scales were computed in a sample of currently employed (farm and nonfarm) U.S. men aged 20 to 64 in 1962. (The OCG sample is described in the abstract on Duncan's socioeconomic index.) The correlations are Duncan-Siegel, .90; Duncan-Treiman, .84; and Siegel-Treiman, .93. (See Treiman, 1977.)

Systematic differences in the evaluations of occupations by different subgroups do not appear, indicating a relative homogeneity of ratings. The correlations of the mean prestige ratings of 200 occupations made by respondents (raters), broken down into nine major occupation groups in 1964 by Hodge, Siegel, and Rossi (1964), fall only as low as .90 (between farmers and professionals), with the average intergroup correlation .96.

Usability on Older Populations

Weighted prestige ratings incorporated into Duncan's socioeconomic index have been applied to an older population of males sampled in the 1963 OCG ($N = 3,125$, ages 55 to 64) and in the 1973, 1974, and 1975 NORC General Social Survey ($N = 209$, ages 66 to 77) samples by Henretta and Campbell (1976). In the NORC survey, retired persons reported on the occupations they "normally did."

General Comments and Recommendations

Occupation-based social-status scales for the elderly lack face validity, though a case could be made that occupational "standing" carries over into retirement and serves as a basis for "status maintenance."

References

Featherman, D. L., M. Sobel, and D. Dickens. *A Manual for Coding Occupations and Industries into Detailed 1970 Categories and a Listing of 1970-Basis Duncan Socioeconomic and NORC Prestige Scores.* Working Paper number 75-1. Madison, Wis.: Center for Demography and Ecology, University of Wisconsin, 1975.

Hauser, R. M., and D. L. Featherman. *The Process of Stratification: Trends and Analyses.* New York: Academic Press, 1977.

Henretta, J. C., and R. T. Campbell. "Status Attainment and Status Maintenance: A Study of Stratification in Old Age." *American Sociological Review*, 1976, 41: 981-92.

Hodge, R. W., P. M. Siegel, and P. H. Rossi. "Occupational Prestige in the United States, 1925-1963." *American Journal of Sociology*, 1964, 70: 286-302.

Hodge, R. W., D. J. Treiman, and P. H. Rossi. "A Comparative Analysis of Occupational Prestige." In *Class, Status and Power* (2nd ed.), R. Bendix and S. M. Lipset (eds.), pp. 309-21. New York: Free Press, 1966.

Inkeles, A., and P. H. Rossi. "National Comparison of Occupational Prestige." *American Journal of Sociology*, 1956, 61:329-39.

North, C. C., and P. K. Hatt. "Jobs and Occupations: A Popular Evaluation." *Opinion News*, 1947, 9:3-13.

Reiss, A. J., Jr. *Occupations and Social Status.* New York: Free Press, 1961.

Siegel, P. M. "Prestige in the American Occupational Structure." Ph.D. dissertation, University of Chicago, 1971.

Treiman, D. J. *Occupational Prestige in Comparative Perspective.* New York: Academic Press, 1977.

Instrument

Treiman's scale is copyrighted; measures for several countries are available in his book (1977, pp. 235-493).

SOCIOECONOMIC INDEX OF OCCUPATIONS (SEI)

O.D. Duncan, 1961

Definition of Concept or Variable

The Socioeconomic Index (SEI) of Occupations relates the occupational prestige, education, and income of individuals (males) employed in all occupations referenced by the U.S. Bureau of the Census in the *Alphabetical Index of Occupations and Industries.*

Context of Development

The SEI was originally developed to overcome the chief limitation of the NORC scale at the time, i.e., that it encompassed only those (90) occupations engaged in by less than half of the work force. The 1950 census of population's detailed classification of 446 occupations was used to construct an index that would take into account the educational, income, and age distributions of members of different occupations.

Description of Instrument

Each occupation was assigned (1) an education weight (X_2) based on the percentage in the occupation who had completed high school and (2) an income weight (X_3) based on the percentage of those in the occupation reporting earnings of $3,500 or more that year. The education and income values were adjusted to account for varying age distributions in the occupations. Then, NORC prestige scores (X_1) for 45 occupations from the NORC list that were determined to be equivalent to census titles were compared to occupational status scores on the adjusted education and income variables using multiple correlation-regression. The regression equation expressing this estimate of a socioeconomic index is $X_1 = 0.59 X_2 + 0.55 X_3 - 6.0$ (Duncan, 1961, p. 124). Scores range from 0 to 100. Since 1961, the occupational ratings have been updated. (See the abstract on Occupational Prestige Scales in this chapter for further discussion of this topic.)

The measure (coding) of occupation is crucial to this index. Proper classification of an individual's occupational status requires detailed information on the kind of work (e.g., college teacher), the types of activities and responsibilities in the job (e.g., classroom teaching), the kind of business or industry in which the job is located (e.g., state university), and the class of the worker (e.g., working for the state government for a salary). (See Featherman and Hauser, 1973; Hauser and Featherman, 1977, Chapter 2; and McTavish, 1964, for extensive details on collecting and classifying information on occupations.)

Educational attainment is enumerated as years of formal schooling; income is based on earnings in the occupation.

Sample(s)

The 1950 census of population formed the basis for the development of the SEI. The scale has been extensively applied to data from the Occupational Changes in a Generation (OCG) surveys taken in 1963 and 1973 as supplements to the Current Population Survey of the U.S. Bureau of the Census. Both samples consisted of civilian males aged 20 to 64 in the noninstitutionalized population; the 1973 OCG data has had only preliminary analyses reported. (See Blau and Duncan, 1967; and Hauser and Featherman, 1977, for details on both OCG samples.)

Usability on Older Populations

The SEI has been studied for persons aged 55 to 64 in the 1962 OCG ($N = 3{,}125$) and for persons 66 to 77 in the NORC general surveys of 1973, 1974, and 1975 ($N = 209$) by Henretta and Campbell (1976), who studied the relationship between pre- and postretirement status. (The NORC reported the occupations "normally done" by the retired.)

Formal Tests of Reliability and Validity

The two predictors—education and income—produced on multiple correlation (R_1 $(_{23})$ = .91) were reported by Duncan (1961); a strong approximation of "prestige" was suggested by these indicators. Interscale correlations of the 1970 SEI with occupational prestige (Siegel, 1971) for U.S. males currently employed ($r = .90$) and for Australian males currently employed ($r = .86$) are very strong as well. (The Australian data came from the 1965 mobility survey of adult male workers conducted by Australian National University under the direction of S. Broom and F. L. Jones.) This index is similar to the census SES as reflected in the Pearsonian r of .97 between the two scales. Finally, Henretta and Campbell (1976) showed for an older sample that the SEI is significantly, although not strongly, associated with education ($r = .54$) and income ($r = .38$).

These survey data are vulnerable to the nonsampling errors outlined earlier in sections of this chapter on income and occupational data.

Sensitivity to Age Differences

No systematic analysis of the SEI across age-groups has been reported, though some attention has been devoted to occupational distribution alone by age. Preliminary findings suggest, however, that the SEI may be a less efficient indicator of status for older groups close to and in retirement. (Refer to age differences reported for census SES scale in this chapter as a proxy for SEI data on age-groups.)

General Comments and Recommendations

This scale is similar to the census SES scale (abstracted elsewhere in this chapter). Furthermore, scale scores for major occupational groups can, in some cases, be applied to specific occupations falling into these groups, since it has been reported (Hauser and Featherman, 1977, pp. 17-20) that scores based on major occupational groups affect correlations very little compared to more detailed occupational scores. Since these scales are based largely on male occupational locations, they have limited utility for the study of retired populations and women.

References

Blau, P. M., and O. D. Duncan. *The American Occupational Structure*. New York: John Wiley and Sons, 1967.

Duncan, O. D. "A Socioeconomic Index for All Occupations." In *Occupations and Social*

Status, A. J. Reiss, O. D. Duncan, P. K. Hatt, and C. C. North (eds.), pp. 109-38. New York: Free Press, 1961.

Featherman, D.L., and R. M. Hauser. "On Measurement of Occupation in Social Surveys." *Sociological Methods and Research*, 1973, 2:239-51.

Featherman, D. L., M. Sobel, and D. Dickens. *A Manual for Coding Occupations and Industries in Detailed 1970 Categories and a Listing of 1970-Basis Duncan Socioeconomic and NORC Prestige Scores*. Working Paper number 75-1. Madison, Wis.: Center for Demography and Ecology , University of Wisconsin, 1975.

Hauser, R. M., and D. L. Featherman. *The Process of Stratification: Trends and Analyses*. New York: Academic Press, 1977.

Henretta, J. C., and R. T. Campbell. "Status Attainment and Status Maintenance: A Study of Stratification in Old Age." *American Sociological Review*, 1976, 41:981-92.

McTavish, D. G. "A Method for More Reliable Coding of Detailed Occupations into Duncan's Socioeconomic Categories." *American Sociological Review*, 1964, 29:402-6.

Siegel, P. M. "Prestige in the American Occupational Structure." Ph.D. dissertation, University of Chicago, 1971.

Instrument

This copyrighted measure is available in Hauser and Featherman, 1977, pp. 320-29.

INDEX OF SOCIAL STATUS
A. B. Hollingshead, 1965; 1971; 1975

Definition of Concept or Variable

The relative position of individuals and familes in the class structure is defined by the educational and occupational attainment of household heads.

Context of Development

The original Index of Social Position was developed to measure the relationship of social class to mental illness and other behavioral patterns in New Haven, Conn. It has two-, three-, and four-factor forms. The two-factor form is based on education and occupation. The three-factor form consists of residential, occupational, and educational components, with the residential scale specifically applicable to New Haven, Conn., during the 1950s. The educational and occupational scales, on the other hand, have broader applicability and have been combined widely since the 1950s as a two-factor index. The occupational component of the two-factor form was originally intended as a modification and improvement of the Edwards scale, which did not distinguish among professions and businesses of varying size and worth.

The four-factor form (Hollingshead, 1975) drops the residential component and adds gender and marital status in an attempt to incorporate the changing patterns of labor-force participation in American society. Though the two-factor form has been most widely used, the four-factor Index of Social Status is reviewed here.

Description of Instrument

Scores for the two-factor index are derived as the sum of the occupational factor weighted by 7 and the educational factor weighted by 4. The summed weighted scores range from 11 to 77 and can be broken down into five social classes: (1) scores of 11 to 17, (2) scores of 18 to 31, (3) scores of 32 to 47, (4) scores of 48 to 63, and (5) scores of 64 to 77.

The four-factor index incorporates information on gender and marital status in addition to occupation and education. If the respondent is married and living with his or her spouse, but only one of the spouses (either male or female) is employed, social position is based on the employed member's education and occupation. If both spouses are employed, educational and occupational scores for both spouses are summed and divided by 2. For never-married heads of household, the education and occupation of the head is used. Divorced persons who are employed full-time are assigned status scores on the basis of their education and occupation, but a divorced or separated person who is receiving support payments and is not gainfully employed is assigned status scores based on the education and occupation of the supporting spouse. Widows or widowers who are not gainfully employed and are living on the income of the deceased spouse's estate are assigned status scores based on the education and occupation of the deceased spouse. Retired persons/families have status scores based on their last occupation and education. The factor of marital status is handled similarly.

The educational scale consists of scores 1 to 7 as follows: 7 for holding a professional degree (M.A., M.S., M.E., M.D., Ph.D, L.L.B., etc.); 6 for holding a 4-year college degree (A.B., B.S., B.M.); 5 for having had 1 to 3 years college (including business schools); 4 for being a high school graduate; 3 for having completed 10 or 11 years of school; 2 for having completed 7 to 9 years of school; and 1 for completing less than 7 years of school.

The occupational scale consists of scores of 1 to 9 as follows: 9 for higher executives, proprietors of large businesses, and major professionals; 8 for administrators, lesser professionals, and proprietors of medium-sized businesses; 7 for smaller business owners, farm owners, managers, and minor professionals; 6 for technicians, semiprofessionals, and small-business owners; 5 for clerical and sales workers and small-farm and small-business owners; 4 for smaller business owners, skilled manual workers, craftspeople, and tenant farmers; 3 for machine operators and semiskilled workers; 2 for unskilled workers; and 1 for farm laborers and menial serivce workers.

(A detailed breakdown of 1970 census occupational codes is included in Instrument V2.7.II.e.)

The status score of an *individual* is derived by weighting occupation by 5 and education by 3 and summing these products. If more than one employed head of household is present, status scores for each individual are created. These are summed and divided by the number of household heads.

Sample

The original study focused on psychiatric patients living in the New Haven, Conn., area.

Formal Tests of Reliability and Validity

Hollingshead and Redlich (1958) reported the correlation of subjective evaluations of class with the two-factor index to be .91. Furthermore, they found significant variations in mental illness by social classes. This index has been used widely by researchers and is described in other measurement handbooks as among the most reliable intercommunity measures of the social position of adults (see Miller, 1977; and Bonjean, Hill, and McLemore, 1967).

The Pearson correlation between the four-factor index and Siegel prestige scores is .927.

Usability on Older Populations

The two-factor Index of Social Position has been applied to samples of persons 65 and older and found to vary consistently with such variables as life satisfaction and patterns of voluntary participation (see Cutler, 1973; and Bull and Aucoin, 1975).

General Comments and Recommendations

This measure is based on the assumption that levels of education and occupation can reflect a life-style (e.g., patterns of living, tastes, etc.), that survives throughout the life cycle and is passed from generation to generation. It should not be treated as a measure of economic sufficiency in retirement, although it may correlate with income and/or wealth in old-age. Dollar values in the occupational scale are out-of-date and need to be revised for use in future studies.

References

Bonjean, C. M., R. H. Hill, and S. D. McLemore. *Sociological Measurement: An Inventory of Scales and Indices*. San Francisco: Chandler, 1967.

Bull, C. N., and J. B. Aucoin. "Voluntary Association Participation and Life Satisfaction: A Replication Note." *Journal of Gerontology*, 1975, 30:73-76.

Cutler, S. J. "Voluntary Association Participation and Life Satisfaction: A Cautionary Research Note." *Journal of Gerontology*, 1973, 28:96-100.

Hollingshead, A. B. *Two-Factor Index of Social Position*. New Haven, Conn.: Yale University Press, 1965.

_____. "Commentary on the Indiscriminate State of Social Class Measurement." *Social Forces*, 1971, 49:563-67.

_____. "Four-Factor Index of Social Status," Unpublished working paper, Department of Sociology, Yale University, 1975.

Hollingshead, A. B., and F. C. Redlich. *Social Class and Mental Illness*. New York: John Wiley and Sons, 1958.

Miller, D. C. *Handbook of Research Design and Social Measurement* (3rd ed.). New York: Longman, Green and Company, 1977.

Instrument

See Instrument V2.7.II.e.

INDEX OF URBAN STATUS (IUS)

R. P. Coleman and B. L. Neugarten, 1971

Definition of Concept or Variable

The Index of Urban Status is an estimate of the social class standing of an urban family based on the average score from a multidimensional profile of social status. The multidimensional profile consists of scale (subjective) evaluations of eight aspects of urban family social status: (1) occupation of male head of household, (2) occupation of female head of household or employed wife, (3) neighborhood of residence, (4) quality of housing, (5) education of male head, (6) education of female head or wife, (7) church affiliation, and (8) community associations (including ethnic identity).

Context of Development

The IUS was developed as part of the Kansas City Study of Adult Life carried out between 1952 and 1962. The study sought to examine middle-age and aging in the urban context by adapting the methods of earlier studies of smaller communities (particularly the evaluated-participation techniques of Warner, Meeker, and Eells, 1949). The IUS is a revision of the Index of Kansas City Status (based on status evaluations made by Kansas Citians) that aspires to be applicable to a wide range of urban contexts.

Description of Instrument

A family's urban status is the average of eight scores, each based on the same seven-point rating scale. On any dimension, a score of 1 is predictive of upper-class status; a score of 2 is predictive of upper-middle-core (or upper-middle-elite) status; a score of 3 is almost equally predictive of either upper-middle-marginal or lower-middle-elite status; a score of 4 is predictive of lower-middle-core or possibly lower-middle-marginal status; a score of 5 is almost equally predictive of working-class status, at the core level or possibly the elite; a score of 6 is almost equally predictive of working-class status at the lower-marginal or lower-class status; a score of 7 is predictive of lower-class status at its lowest level.

The average of the eight scores from the profile places the family into one of the five social classes listed below.

Average IUS Score	Estimated Social Class
1.00-1.50	Upper class
1.51-3.00	Upper-middle class
3.01-4.49	Lower-middle class
4.50-5.99	Working class
6.00-7.00	Lower class

Abbreviated versions of the IUS using fewer than eight dimensions with special weightings (based on regression coefficients) can be found in a manual of detailed instructions for use of the IUS from Coleman.

Instrument V2.7.II.f supplies summaries or abbreviated versions of six of the eight scales from which the composite social-class estimate is derived: the neighborhood status scale, the quality of housing scale, the educational status scales, and the religious affiliation scale. The occupational status scale is too extensive to be reproduced here. The complicated protocol for scoring the associations scale is available in the IUS manual of instructions, which gives full information on all the scales.

Occupational Status Scale: The distinctive feature of this scale is that salary (or wages), rather than title, is treated as the primary gauge of status among males and that clientele served, rather than income, is the major consideration for according status to women. The salary-wage levels, of course, apply to occupations in Kansas City (or a similar city) of the mid-1950s.

Neighborhood Status Scale: The scale assumes a relative homogeneity of neighborhoods in which there is little variation block by block. Three sources of information were used in Kansas City: reputational data on neighborhoods and suburbs drawn from interviews, consultations with real estate specialists, and census data on housing values at the tract level.

Housing Quality Scale: This scale is based on researchers' estimates of home value and/or rents according to guidelines drawn from real estate experts. Details regarding size, condition, number of rooms, persons per room, etc., are not included in the scale development.

Educational Status Scales: The educational status scales combine several factors: time of attendance at college, sex, prestige of college attended, years of college completed, and collegiate social affiliations. The first factor, time of attending at college, is an attempt to control for different patterns of school attendance among successive age cohorts. The factors are combined into educational platform ratings. Abbreviated versions of two educational scales — class platform ratings and a simpler scale of period and length of attendance — are included with the instrument.

Reglious Affiliation Scale: Religious affiliation is referred to as "a status asset or handicap, not as a basic component of class position" (Coleman and Neugarten, 1971, p. 101). Unlike other measures of religious affiliation, this one focuses on reputational evaluations of the social makeup of the congregation, not on a denominational ranking.

Associations Scale: This scale combines estimates of ethnic status, social standing of formal associations (clubs, etc.), and status ranking of clique memberships.

Sample

Data were drawn from two subsamples of persons 40 to 69 years old from a master sample of noninstitutionalized persons residing in 2,300 Kansas City households in 1953, and a third subsample of a similar master sample in 1954. Interviews were completed on a total of 462 family units, representing an 80% response rate.

Formal Tests of Reliability and Validity

Objective placements (averaged scores) from the eight-factor scale yielded a 91% agreement with subjective evaluations of social-class placment. The relative efficiency of the eight-factor measure by selected class was 94% agreement of working-class families; 92% of lower-middle-class families; and 89% of the upper-middle-class families. For the upper-class groups, however, there was a greater discrepancy: for the upper class there was only 47% agreement and for the upper-middle class only 53%.

Norms and Distribution

The Kansas City social-class distribution generated by the urban index is shown in Table 7-7 (from Coleman and Neugarten, 1971, p. 59). A 13-tier hierarchy is diplayed by race, with the three middle classes broken down into elite, core, and marginal subclasses and the upper and lower classes each broken down into two subclasses. The distributions by race show the typical skewed distribution for blacks, placing this group largely in the working and lower classes.

TABLE 7-7
Kansas City Status Structure (for Persons Aged 40 to 69)

	Total Percentage	Whites Percentage	Negroes Percentage
Upper Class:			
Capital S Society	0.4	0.5	0.0
Non-Capital S upper class	1.4	1.6	0.1
Upper-Middle Class:			
Upper-middle-elite	1.3	1.5	0.2
Upper-middle-core	5.3	6.0	0.8
Lower-middle-marginals	5.0	5.6	1.2
Lower-Middle-Class:			
Lower-middle-elite	5.8	6.4	1.3
Lower-middle-core	17.2	19.0	4.1
Lower-middle-marginals	10.3	11.2	3.8
Working Class:			
Working-class-elite	5.0	5.2	2.7
Working-class-core	25.5	26.2	20.0
Working-class-marginals	9.7	8.6	18.1
Lower Class:			
Lower class but not quite the lowest	6.4	4.1	22.3
"Slumdwellers" and other			
"disreputables"	6.7	4.1	25.4

NOTE: Estimated percentages have been projected to the 2,300-household master sample described in Appendix B and from that sample to the total metropolitan population in the age-group.
SOURCE: R. P. Coleman and B. L. Neugarten. *Social Status in the City*. San Francisco: Jossey-Bass, 1971, p. 59. Reprinted by permission of authors and publisher.

Usability on Older Populations

The measure was applied to a late-middle-aged and aged subsample.

Sensitivity to Age Differences

The relationship between age and social class measured by the IUS has been briefly discussed by Coleman and Neugarten (1971, pp. 152-53) but not systematically portrayed. The suggested relationship is that age is positively related to social class since careers tend to reflect upward trends, at varying rates, in income, occupational status, and associational patterns.

General Comments and Recommendations

Like any community-based measure, the IUS must be adapted to the varying makeups of different urban contexts at different points in time. Such an approach should probably be restricted to communities of moderate to small size, since the evaluations required for the eight factors are many and complex.

References

Coleman, R. P., and B. L. Neugarten. *Social Status in the City*. San Francisco: Jossey-Bass, 1971.

Warner, W. L., M. Meeker, and K. Eells. *Social Class in America: A Manual of Procedure for the Measurement of Social Status*. Chicago: Science Research Associates, 1949.

Instrument

See Instrument V2.7.II.f.

SUBJECTIVE CLASS IDENTIFICATION

R. Centers, 1949; J. A. Kahl and J. A. Davis, 1955;
J. R. Kluegel, R. Singleton, Jr., and C. E. Starnes, 1977

Definition of Concept or Variable

The individual's perception of his or her own position in a class or status hierarchy is assessed by this measure.

Context of Development

Centers (1949) conducted the initial studies of class self-identification, or class consciousness, as a unidimensional construct, using a single item as a measure. Centers simply and directly asked a respondent to identify himself or herself as upper, middle, working, or lower class. Kahl and Davis (1955) later refined the procedure by adding a series of systematic probes for purposes of validating the single-, closed-item approach. Most studies subsequently have adopted the single-item approach (see Hodge and Treiman, 1968; and Jackman and Jackman, 1973). In response to this tendency, Kluegel, Singleton, and Starnes (1977) developed a multiple-indicator measure of class identification to (1) test the assumption of unidimensionality and (2) determine the validity and reliability of the standard single-item approach.

Description of Instrument

The Kahl and Davis's (1955) unidimensional measure was presented as follows (pp. 323-24):

There has been a lot of talk recently about social classes in the United States. I wonder what you think about this. What social classes do you think there are in this part of the country?

What social class do you think you are in?

What puts you in that class?

Which class is next below yours in social standing?

In what ways are people in that class different from people in your class?

If you were asked to use one of these four names for your social class, which would you say you belonged in: the middle class, the lower class, the working class, or the upper class? If Middle: Would you say you were in the upper-middle or lower-middle? (If no discrimination, answer was coded middle.)

SOURCE: J. A. Kahl and J. A. Davis. "A Comparison of Indexes of Socioeconomic Status." *American Sociological Review*, 1955, 20:323-24. Reprinted by permission of authors and publisher.

Responses were then classified as: upper, upper-middle, undifferentiated middle, lower-middle, working, and lower class.

The multidimensional approach taken by Kluegel, Singleton, and Starnes (1977) is based on five subjective class indicators: general class identification, occupation, income, way of life, and influence. Respondents were asked to place themselves in one of four ranked categories—lower, working, middle, or upper class—on each of the five dimensions; that is, they were asked which social class they were "most like" in general in their occupation, income, way of life, and influence. The five dimensions are treated as multiple indicators of an unobservable, latent variable referred to as true subjective class identification, following the maximum likelihood estimating procedures developed by Jöreskog (1970).

Sample

The single-item measure was used in the 1964 NORC survey of 651 youths and adults reported on by Hodge and Treiman (1968). The multiple-item measures were applied by Kluegel, Singleton, and Starnes (1977) to data from the 1969 Gary Area Project of the Institute for Social Research at Indiana University; 800 adults (432 whites and 368 blacks) were interviewed.

Norms and Distribution

Hodge and Treiman (1968) reported a significant decline between 1945 and 1964 in the number of respondents who considered themselves working-class, slightly over half in 1945 down to approximately one-third in 1964; 40% in 1945 and 44% in 1964 placed themselves in the middle class. No age distributions were reported.

Formal Tests of Reliability and Validity

On purpose of the multiple-indicator approach of Kluegel, Singleton, and Starnes (1977) was to determine the validity and reliability of the single-item measure by using maximum likelihood estimates. They suggested that, although the standard class identification item holds up, the multiple-indicator measure is somewhat more efficient. The regression of the single item on three objective class measures (education, occupational status, and family income) produces an R^2 of .079 for blacks and .138 for whites. The latent subjective class variable, on the other hand, results in an R^2 of .174 for blacks and .189 for whites.

Usability on Older Populations

Studies of class consciousness (conceptions of the class system) among older samples by Coleman and Neugarten (1971) and Rosenberg (1970) have suggested that subjective identification patterns can be observed among older samples.

Sensitivity to Age Differences

No systematic study of class identification by age to detect patterned differences has been reported.

General Comments and Recommendations

Although this measure in either single or multiple form has not been studied systematically on older samples, it appears to have some utility for future research, especially if it is used in conjunction with other objective measures of status. Questions would have to be adapted to retired populations on the occupational indicator. Either form of subjective indicator is a very weak function of objective indicators such as education, occupation, and income.

References

Centers, R. *The Psychology of Social Classes*. Princeton, N.J.: Princeton University Press, 1949.

Coleman, R. P., and B. L. Neugarten. *Social Status in the City*. San Francisco: Jossey-Bass, 1971.

Hodge, R. W., and D. J. Treiman. "Class Identification in the United States." *American Journal of Sociology*, 1968, 73:535-47.

Jackman, M. R., and R. W. Jackman. "An Interpretation of the Relation between Objective and Subjective Social Status." *American Sociological Review*, 1973, 38:569-82.

Jöreskog, K. G. "A General Method for Analysis of Covariance Structures." *Biometrika*, 1970, 57:239-51.

Kahl, J. A., and J. A. Davis. "A Comparison of Indexes of Socioeconomic Status." *American Sociological Review*, 1955, 20:317-25.

Kluegel, J. R., R. Singleton, Jr., and C. E. Starnes. "Subjective Class Identification: A Multiple Indicator Approach." *American Sociological Review*, 1977, 42:599-610.

Rosenberg, G. S. *The Worker Grows Old*. San Francisco: Jossey-Bass, 1970.

Instrument

See the description of the instrument given above.

Instruments

V2.7.I.a

CURRENT MONEY INCOME

FACSIMILE QUESTIONS FROM CURRENT POPULATION SURVEY

U.S. Bureau of the Census, 1977

1. Last year did . . . receive any money:

    a. In wages or salary?

    Yes_____ No_____

    How much did . . . receive before any deductions?

    b. In income from his own nonfarm business, partnership or professional practice?

    Yes_____ No_____

    How much did . . . receive *after expenses?*

    c. In income from his own farm?

    Yes_____ No_____

    How much did . . . receive *after expenses?*

2a. Last year did . . . receive from the Government any money from:

Social Security checks?

Yes____   No____

Railroad Retirement checks?

Yes____   No____

How much did . . . receive in Social Security or Railroad Retirement checks?

2b. Last year did . . . receive:

Any Supplemental Security Income checks from the U.S. Government?

Yes____   No____

Any Supplemental Security checks from the state or local government?

Yes____   No____

How much did . . . recieve in Supplementary Security Income checks altogether?

3.   Last year did . . . receive any money from:

a. Public assistance or welfare from the state or local welfare office?

Yes____   No____

Was it:

Aid to families with dependent children?
Other assistance?

How much did . . . receive?

b. Interest on savings accounts, bonds, etc.?

Yes____   No____

How much did . . . receive?

c. Dividends?

Yes____   No____

Net rental income or royalties?

Yes____   No____

Estates or trusts?

Yes____   No____

How much did . . . receive from . . .?

d. Veteran's payments excluding military retirement?

Yes____   No____

Unemployment compensation?

Yes____   No____

Workmen's compensation?

Yes____   No____

How much did . . . receive from . . .?

e. Private pensions or annuities?

Yes____   No____

Military retirement?

Yes____   No____

Other federal government employee pensions?

Yes____   No____

State or local government employee pensions?

Yes ____   No ____

How much did . . . receive from . . .?

f. Alimony or child support?

Yes ____   No ____

Other regular contributions from persons not living in the household?

Yes ____   No ____

Anything else? (Specify in notes)

Yes ____   No ____

How much did . . . receive from . . .?

SOURCE: U.S. Bureau of the Census. "Characteristics of the Population Below the Poverty Level: 1975." *Current Population Reports.* Consumer Income Series P-60, No. 106 (June). Washington, D.C.: U.S. Department of Commerce, U.S. Government Printing Office, 1977, p. 226.

V2.7.I.b

POVERTY THRESHOLDS

U.S. Bureau of the Census, 1978

WEIGHTED AVERAGE THRESHOLDS—POVERTY CUTOFFS IN 1976, BY SIZE OF FAMILY AND SEX OF HEAD, BY FARM-NONFARM RESIDENCE

| | Nonfarm | | |
Size of Family Unit	Total (Dollars)	Male Head[1] (Dollars)	Female Head[1] (Dollars)
1 Person (unrelated individual)	2,884	3,016	2,788
14 to 64 years	2,959	3,069	2,840
65 years and over	2,730	2,758	2,722
2 Persons	3,711	3,721	3,660
Head 14 to 64 years	3,826	3,846	3,733
Head 65 years and over	3,445	3,447	3,428
3 Persons	4,540	4,565	4,414
4 Persons	5,815	5,818	5,790
5 Persons	6,876	6,884	6,799
6 Persons	7,760	7,766	7,709
7 Persons or more	9,588	9,622	9,375
1 Person (unrelated individual)	2,438	2,532	2,348
14 to 64 years	2,542	2,608	2,413
65 years and over	2,322	2,344	2,313
2 Persons	3,128	3,133	3,033
Head 14 to 64 years	3,267	3,271	3,159
Head 65 years and over	2,928	2,928	2,922
3 Persons	3,858	3,864	3,734
4 Persons	4,950	4,953	4,840
5 Persons	5,870	5,871	5,847

WEIGHTED AVERAGE THRESHOLDS—POVERTY CUTOFFS IN 1976, BY SIZE OF
FAMILY AND SEX OF HEAD, BY FARM-NONFARM RESIDENCE—*Continued*

| | | Nonfarm | |
Size of Family Unit	Total (Dollars)	Male Head[1] (Dollars)	Female Head[1] (Dollars)
6 Persons	6,585	6,584	6,607
7 Persons or more	8,072	8,068	8,428

1. For one person (i.e., unrelated individual), sex of the individual.

SOURCE: U.S. Bureau of the Census. "Characteristics of the Population Below the Poverty Level: 1976." *Current Population Reports.* Consumer Income Series P-60, number 115 (July). Washington, D.C.: U.S. Department of Commerce, U.S. Government Printing Office, 1978, Table A-3, p. 207.

PERSONS 65 YEARS AND OVER BELOW THE POVERTY
LEVEL BY SEX 1959, AND 1966 TO 1975

| Year | Total | Poverty Rate in Families | | | | |
		Total	Head	Wives	Other Family Members	Unrelated Individuals
ALL RACES						
ALL PERSONS						
1975	15.3	8.0	8.9	8.2	4.3	31.0
1974[r]	14.6	7.6	8.5	7.3	4.4	30.3
1974	15.7	8.5	9.5	8.3	5.0	31.8
1973	16.3	9.4	10.5	8.4	7.0	32.0
1972	18.6	10.4	11.6	9.7	7.3	37.1
1971	21.6	12.4	14.2	11.8	7.5	42.3
1970	24.5	14.7	16.3	15.4	8.6	47.1
1969	25.3	16.0	17.5	17.2	10.0	47.3
1968	25.0	15.4	17.0	15.8	10.7	48.8
1967	29.5	19.7	21.5	21.4	11.9	55.2
1966[r]	28.5	19.2	20.9	22.0	10.7	53.8
1959[1]	35.2	26.9	29.1	30.5	17.4	61.9
MALE						
1975	11.4	8.1	8.3	—	4.5	27.8
1974[r]	10.8	7.8	7.9	—	5.4	25.8
1974	11.8	8.8	8.9	—	7.9	26.8
1973	12.4	9.4	9.5	—	8.0	27.1
1972	13.1	10.4	10.7	—	6.7	26.3
1971	15.6	12.2	12.8	—	3.8	32.6
1970	19.0	14.9	15.6	—	6.6	38.9
1969	20.2	16.0	16.4	—	12.3	39.8
1968	20.3	15.7	15.9	—	13.3	43.4

PERSONS 65 YEARS AND OVER BELOW THE POVERTY
LEVEL BY SEX 1959, AND 1966 TO 1975 — *Continued*

| Year | Total | Poverty Rate in Families | | | Other Family | Unrelated |
		Total	Head	Wives	Members	Individuals
1967	23.7	19.5	20.6	—	9.0	44.8
1966[r]	23.8	19.7	20.9	—	9.8	44.5
1959[1]	(NA)	(NA)	29.1	—	(NA)	59.0
FEMALE						
1975	18.1	8.0	12.7	8.2	4.1	31.9
1974[r]	17.3	7.4	12.3	7.3	4.2	31.6
1974	18.3	8.2	13.0	8.3	4.5	33.2
1973	19.0	9.3	16.8	8.4	6.7	33.5
1972	22.4	10.3	16.5	9.7	7.5	40.4
1971	25.8	12.6	23.0	11.8	8.4	45.1
1970	28.5	14.5	19.9	15.4	9.4	49.7
1969	29.2	16.1	23.6	17.2	9.1	49.9
1968	28.5	15.2	22.3	15.8	9.8	50.6
1967	33.9	19.8	25.8	21.4	12.9	59.5
1966[r]	32.2	18.6	20.4	22.0	11.1	57.0
1959[1]	(NA)	(NA)	28.8	30.5	(NA)	63.3

[r]Based on revised methodology. See section entitled "Revised 1974 Money Income and Poverty Statistics" for details on 1974 and section entitled "Nonresponses and Allocations" for details on 1966.

1. Based on 1-in-1000 sample of 1960 Census.

SOURCE: U.S. Bureau of the Census. "Characteristics of the Population Below the Poverty Level: 1975." *Current Populations Reports.* Consumer Income Series P-60, No. 106 (June). Washington, D.C.: U.S. Department of Commerce, U.S. Government Printing Office, 1977, Table 3, p. 21.

V2.7.I.c

INCOME-NET WORTH MEASURE OF ECONOMIC POSITION

B. A. Weisbrod and W. L. Hansen, 1968

See the description of the instrument in the abstract.

V2.7.I.d.

NET WORTH AS AN ASPECT OF STATUS

J. C. Henretta and R. T. Campbell, 1978

See the description of the instrument in the abstract.

V2.7.I.e

COMPOSITE MEASURE OF ECONOMIC WELFARE OF THE AGED
M. Moon, 1976; 1977

See the description of the instrument in the abstract.

V2.7.II.a

OCCUPATIONAL STATUS
U.S. Bureau of the Census, 1960

See the description of the instrument in the abstract.

V2.7.II.b

U.S. CENSUS SOCIOECONOMIC STATUS
A. M. Edwards, 1937; 1938; U.S. Bureau of the Census, 1963

See the description of the instrument in the abstract.

V2.7.II.c

OCCUPATIONAL PRESTIGE SCALES
C. C. North and P. K. Hatt, 1947; R. W. Hodge, P. M. Siegel, and P. H. Rossi, 1964; D. J. Treiman, 1977

Treiman's scale is copyrighted; measures for several countries are available in his book (1977, pp. 235-493).

V2.7.II.d

SOCIOECONOMIC INDEX OF OCCUPATIONS
O. D. Duncan, 1961

This copyrighted measure is available in Hauser and Featherman, 1977, pp. 320-29.

V2.7.II.e

INDEX OF SOCIAL STATUS
A. B. Hollingshead, 1965; 1971; 1975

Four Factor Version: Occupational Scale

Score 9   Higher Executives, Proprietors of Large Businesses, and Major Professionals

    a. *Higher executives*: chairpersons, presidents, vice-presidents, assistant vice-presidents, secretaries, treasurers;

    b. *Commissioned officers in the military*: majors, lieutenant commanders, and above, or equivalent;

    c. *Government officials, federal, state, and local*: members of the United States Congress, members of the state legislature, governors, state officials, mayors, city managers;

d. *Proprietors of businesses valued at $250,000 and more;*[14]

e. *Owners of farms valued at $250,000 and more;*

f. *Major professionals* (census code list).

Occupational title	Census code
Actuaries	034
Aeronautical engineers	006
Architects	002
Astronautical engineers	006
Astronomers	053
Atmospheric scientists	043
Bank officers	202
Biologic scientists	044
Chemical engineers	010
Chemists	045
Civil Engineers	010
Dentists	062
Economists	091
Electrical/electronic engineers	012
Engineers, not elsewhere classified[15]	023
Financial managers	202
Geologists	051
Health administrators	212
Judges	030
Lawyers	031
Life scientists, n.e.c.	054
Marine scientists	052
Materials engineers	015
Mathematicians	035
Mechanical engineers	014
Metallurgical engineers	015
Mining engineers	020
Optometrists	063
Petroleum engineers	021
Physical scientists, n.e.c.	054
Physicians	065
Physicists	053
Political scientists	092
Psychologists	093
Social scientists, n.e.c.	096
Sociologists	094
Space scientists	043
Teachers, college/university, including coaches	102-140
Urban and regional planners	095
Veterinarians	072

Score 8   Administrators, Lesser Professionals, Proprietors of Medium-Sized Businesses

a. *Administrative officers in large concerns*: district managers, executive assistants, personnel managers, production managers;

b. *Proprietors of businesses valued between $100,000 and $250,000;*

c. *Owners and operators of farms valued between $100,000 and $250,000;*

d. *Commissioned officers in the military*; lieutenants, captains, lieutenants, s.g. and j. g., or equivalent;

e. *Lesser professionals* (census code list).

Occupational title	Census code
Accountants	001
Administrators, college	235
Administrators, elementary/secondary school	240
Administrators, public administration, n.e.c.	222
Archivists	033
Assessors, local public administration	201
Authors	181
Chiropractors	061
Clergymen	086
Computer specialists, n.e.c.	005
Computer systems analysts	004
Controllers, local public administration	201
Curators	033
Editors	184
Farm management advisors	024
Industrial engineers	013
Labor relations workers	056
Librarians	032
Musicians/composers	185
Nurses, registered	075
Officials, public administration, n.e.c.	222
Personnel workers	056
Pharmacists	064
Pilots, airplane	163
Podiatrists	071
Sales engineers	022
Statisticians	036
Teachers, secondary school	144
Treasurers, local public administration, n.e.c.	201

Score 7   Smaller Business Owners, Farm Owners, Managers, Minor Professionals

a. *Owners of smaller businesses valued at $75,000 to $100,000;*

b. *Farm owners/operators with farms valued at $75,000 to $100,000;*

c. *Managers* (census code list);

d. *Minor professionals* (census code list);

e. *Entertainers and artists.*

Occupational title	Census code
Actors	175
Agricultural scientists	042
Announcers, radio/television	193
Appraisers, real estate	363
Artists	194
Buyers, wholesale/retail trade	205
Computer programmers	003
Credit persons	210
Designers	183

Occupational title	Census code
Entertainers, n.e.c.	194
Funeral directors	211
Health practitioners, n.e.c.	073
Insurance adjusters, examiners, investigators	326
Insurance agents, brokers, underwriters	265
Managers, administration, n.e.c.	245
Managers, residential building	216
Managers, office, n.e.c.	220
Officers, lodges, societies, unions	223
Officers/pilots, pursers, shipping	221
Operations/systems researchers/analysts	055
Painters	190
Postmasters, mail supervisors	224
Public relations persons	192
Publicity writers	192
Purchasing agents, buyers, n.e.c.	225
Real estate brokers/agents	270
Reporters	184
Sales managers, except retail trade	233
Sales representatives, manufacturing industries	281
Sculptors	190
Social workers	100
Stock/bond salesmen	271
Surveyors	161
Teachers, except college/university/secondary school	141-143
Teachers, except college/university, n.e.c.	145
Vocational/educational counsellors	174
Writers, n.e.c.	194

Score 6   Technicians, Semiprofessionals, Small Business Owners

a. *Technicians* (census code list);
b. *Semiprofessionals*; army, m/sgt., navy, c.p.o., clergymen (not professionally trained), interpreters (court);
c. *Owners of businesses valued at $50,000 to $75,000;*
d. *Farm owners/operators with farms valued at $50,000 to $75,000.*

Occupational title	Census code
Administrators, except farm—allocated	246
Advertising agents/salesmen	260
Air traffic controllers	164
Athletes/kindred workers	180
Buyers, farm products	203
Computer/peripheral equipment operators	343
Conservationists	025
Dental hygienists	081
Dental laboratory technicians	426
Department heads, retail trade	231
Dietitians	074
Draftsmen	152
Embalmers	165
Flight engineers	170

Occupational title	Census code
Foremen, n.e.c.	441
Foresters	025
Home management advisors	026
Inspectors, construction, public administration	213
Inspectors, except construction, public administration	215
Managers, except farm—allocated	246
Opticians, lens grinders/polishers	506
Payroll/timekeeping clerks	360
Photographers	191
Professional, technical, kindred workers—allocated	196
Religious workers, n.e.c.	090
Research workers, not specified	195
Sales managers, retail trade	231
Sales representatives, wholesale trade	282
Secretaries, legal	370
Secretaries, medical	371
Secretaries, n.e.c.	372
Sheriffs/bailiffs	965
Shippers, farm products	203
Stenographers	376
Teacher aides, except school monitors	382
Technicians	150-162
Technologists	080-083
Therapists	076
Tool programmers, numerical control	172

Score 5   Clerical and Sales Workers, Small Farm and Business Owners

a. *Clerical workers* (census code list);
b. *Sales workers* (census code list);
c. *Owners of small business valued at $25,000 to $50,000*;
d. *Owners of small farms valued at $25,000 to $50,000*.

Occupational title	Census code
Auctioneers	261
Bank tellers	301
Billing clerks	303
Bookkeepers	305
Bookkeeping/billing machine operators	341
Calculating machine operators	242
Cashiers	310
Clerical assistants, social welfare	311
Clerical workers, miscellaneous	394
Clerical/kindred workers	396
Clerical supervisors, n.e.c.	312
Clerks, statistical	375
Collectors, bill/account	313

Occupational title	Census code
Dental assistants	921
Estimators, n.e.c.	321
Health trainees	923
Investigators	321
Key punch operators	345
Library assistants/attendants	330
Recreation workers	101
Tabulating machine operators	350
Telegraph operators	384
Telephone operators	385
Therapy assistants	084
Typists	391

Score 4   Smaller Business Owners, Skilled Manual Workers, Craftsmen, and Tenant Farmers

a. *Owners of small businesses and farms valued at less than $25,000;*
b. *Tenant farmers owning farm machinery and livestock;*
c. *Skilled manual workers and craftsmen* (census code list);
d. *Noncommissioned officers in the military* below the rank of master sergeant and C.P.O.

Occupational title	Census code
Airline cabin attendants	931
Automobile accessoreis installers	401
Bakers	402
Blacksmiths	403
Boilermakers	404
Bookbinders	405
Brakemen, railroad	712
Brickmasons/stonemasons	410
Brickmason/stonemason apprentices	411
Cabinetmakers	413
Carpenters	415
Carpenter apprentices	416
Carpet installers	420
Cement/concrete finishers	421
Checkers/examiners/inspectors, manufacturing	610
Clerks, shipping/receiving	374
Compositors/typesetters	422
Conductors, railroad	226
Constables	963
Counter clerks, except food	314
Decorators/window dressers	425
Demonstrators	262
Detectives	964
Dispatchers/starters, vehicles	315
Drillers, earth	614
Dry wall installers/lathers	615
Duplicating machine operators, n.e.c.	344

Occupational Title	Census code
Electricians	430
Electrician apprentices	431
Electric power lineman/cablemen	433
Electrotypers	434
Engineers, locomotive	455
Engineers, stationary	545
Engravers, except photoengravers	435
Enumerators	320
Expediters	323
Firemen, fire protection	961
Firemen, locomotive	456
Floor layers	440
Foremen, farm	821
Forgemen/hammermen	442
Furriers	444
Glaziers	445
Heat treaters/annealers/temperers	446
Heaters, metal	626
Housekeepers, except private household	950
Inspectors, n.e.c.	452
Inspectors/scalers/graders, log and lumber	450
Interviewers	331
Jewelers/watchmakers	453
Job and diesetters, metal	454
Lithographers	515
Loom fixers	483
Machinists	461
Machinist apprentices	462
Mail carriers, post office	331
Mail handlers, except post office	332
Managers, bar/restaurant/cafeteria	230
Marshals, law enforcement	963
Mechanics	470-495
Meter readers	334
Millers, grain/flour/feed	501
Millwrights	355
Molders, metal	503
Molder apprentices	504
Office machine operators, n.e.c.	514
Patternmakers/modelmakers	522
Photoengravers	515
Plasterers	520
Plasterer apprentices	521
Plumbers/pipefitters	522
Plumber/pipefitter apprentices	523
Power station operators	525
Postal clerks	361

Occupational title	Census code
Practical nurses	926
Piano/organ tuners/repairmen	516
Pressmen, plate printers, printing trade	530
Pressmen apprentices	531
Projectionists, motion picture	505
Printing trade apprentices, except pressmen	423
Proofreaders	362
Radio operators	171
Receptionists	364
Repairmen	471-486
Rollers/finishers, metal	533
Sheetmetal workers	533
Sheetmetal worker apprentices	536
Stereotypers	434
Stock clerks/storekeepers	381
Stone cutters/carvers	546
Structural metal workers	550
Superintendents, building	216
Switchmen, railroad	713
Tailors	551
Telephone linemen/splicers	552
Telephone installers/repairmen	554
Ticket/station/express agents	390
Tile setters	560
Tool and diemakers	561
Tool and diemaker apprentices	562
Weighers	392
Welders/flame cutters	680

Score 3   Machine Operators and Semiskilled Workers (census code list)

Occupational title	Census code
Animal caretakers	740
Asbestos/insulation workers	601
Assemblers	602
Barbers	935
Blasters/powdermen	603
Boardinghouse/lodginghouse keepers	940
Boatmen/canalmen	701
Bottling operatives	604
Bulldozer operators	412
Bus drivers	703
Canning operatives	604
Carding, lapping, combing operatives	670
Chauffeurs	714
Child care workers, except private household	942
Conductors/motormen, urban rail transit	704

Occupational title	Census code
Cranemen/derrickmen/hoistmen	424
Cutting operatives	612
Deliverymen	704
Dressmakers/seamstresses, except factory	613
Drill press operatives	650
Dyers	620
Excavating/grading/road machine operators, except bulldozer	436
Farm services laborers, self-employed	824
File clerks	325
Filers/polishers/sanders/buffers	621
Fishermen/oystermen	752
Forklift/tow motor operatives	706
Furnacemen/smelters/pourers	622
Furniture/wood finishers	443
Graders/sorters/manufacturing	623
Grinding machine operatives	651
Guards/watchmen	962
Hairdressers/cosmetologists	944
Health aides, except nursing	922
Housekeepers, private household	982
Knitters/loopers/toppers	671
Lathe/milling machine operatives	652
Machine operatives, miscellaneous specified	690
Machine operatives, n.e.c.	692
Meat cutters/butchers, except manufacturing	631
Meat cutters, butchers, manufacturing	633
Metal platers	635
Midwives (lay)	924
Milliners	640
Mine operatives	640
Mixing operatives	710
Motormen, mine/factory/logging camp, etc.	710
Nursing aides/attendants	925
Oilers/greasers, except auto	642
Operatives, miscellaneous	694
Operatives, not specified	695
Operatives, except transport—allocated	696
Orderlies	925
Painters, construction/maintenance	510
Painter apprentices	511
Painters, manufactured articles	644
Paperhangers	512
Photographic process workers	645
Precision machine operatives, n.e.c.	653
Pressers/ironers, clothing	611
Punch/stamping press operatives	656
Riverters/fasteners	660

Occupational title	Census code
Roofers/slaters	534
Routemen	705
Sailors/deckhands	661
Sawyers	662
Service workers, except private household — allocated	976
Sewers/stichers	663
Shoemaking machine operatives	664
Shoe repairmen	542
Sign painters/letterers	543
Spinners/twisters/winders	672
Solderers	665
Stationary firemen	666
Surveying, chainmen/rodmen/axmen	605
Taxicab drivers	714
Textile operatives, n.e.c.	674
Transport equipment operatives — allocated	726
Truck drivers	715
Upholsterers	563
Weavers	673
Welfare service aides	954
Enlisted members of the armed services (other than noncommissioned officers)	—

Score 2   Unskilled Workers (census code list)

Occupational title	Census code
Bartenders	910
Busboys	911
Carpenters' helpers	750
Child care workers, private household	980
Construction laborers, except carpenters' helpers	751
Cooks, private household	981
Cooks, except private household	912
Crossing guards/bridge tenders	960
Elevator operators	943
Food service, n.e.c., except private household	916
Freight/materials handlers	753
Garage workers/gas station attendants	623
Garbage collectors	754
Gardeners/groundskeepers, except farm	755
Huscksters/peddlars	264
Laborers, except farm — allocated	796
Laborers, miscellaneous	780
Laborers, not specified	785
Laundry/drycleaning operatives, n.e.c.	630
Lumbermen/raftsmen/woodchoppers	761
Meat wrappers, retail trade	634
Messengers	333

Occupational title	Census code
Office boys	333
Packers/wrappers, n.e.c.	643
Parking attendants	711
School monitors	952
Waiters	915
Warehousemen, n.e.c.	770

Score 1   Farm Laborers/Mental Service Workers (census cod list)

Occupational title	Census code
Attendants, personal service, n.e.c.	933
Attendants, recreation/amusemen	932
Baggage porters/bellhops	934
Bootblacks	941
Chambermaids, maids, except private household	901
Cleaners, charwomen	902
Dishwashers	913
Farm laborers, wage workers	931
Farm laborers/farm foremen/kindred workers — allocated	846
Janitors/sextons	903
Laundresses, private household	983
Maids/servants, private household	984
Newsboys	266
Personal service apprentices	945
Private household workers — allocated	986
Produce graders/sorters, except factory/farm	625
Stockhandlers	762
Teamsters	763
Vehicle washers/equipment cleaners	764
Ushers, recreation/amusement	953

Dependent upon welfare — no regular occupation	—

SOURCE: A. B. Hollingshead. "Four-Factor Index of Social Status." Unpublished working paper, Department of Sociology, Yale University, 1975. Reprinted by permission.

V2.7.II.f

INDEX OF URBAN STATUS

R. P. Coleman and B. L. Neugarten, 1971

NEIGHBORHOOD STATUS SCALE

1   indicates neighborhoods, special blocks, or apartment complexes reputed to be where the city's social, professional, and executive elite live, and where a majority or at least 40 per cent of the houses or apartments are of the mansion or top luxury class as rated by the IUS Housing Quality scale.

2   indicates neighborhoods, special blocks, or apartment buildings which, in public opinion, are appropriate residential locations for prosperous managerial and professional families. The public impression should be that a majority of the residents are firmly established at a fairly high occupational and social status level.

3   indicates neighborhoods, special areas, or apartment buildings which are considered above

average in desirability either because they are: favored by aspiring young college-educated professional and managerial families, not so highly regarded as in former years but still occupied by many older high status families, or aspired to by the most socially sensitive white-collar and semiprofessional families.

4   indicates neighborhoods which are basically white-collar and/or middle class in the public eye, but do not merit a higher rank than this within the middle class world. Some of these neighborhoods may contain more blue-collar than white-collar workers, but if so, these will be blue-collar families who are thought to be aspiring to higher status, as distinguished from those who accept a definition of themselves as prosperous but not socially minded working class people.

5   indicates neighborhoods which are blue-collar or ordinary working class in the public eye but not substandard or markedly below average in desirability or appearance. The quality of housing may appear to be almost as good as in some neighborhoods given a 4 rating, but they will be given this lower rating because, in the opinion of the city's white-collar residents, these neighborhoods are on the wrong side of town, or in an undesirable school district.

6   indicates areas which are widely considered substandard in housing, or undesirable by virtue of proximity to industry, commerce, railroad tracks, or slums, or where more than half of the housing rates no better than a 6 on the IUS Housing Quality scale.

7   indicates neighborhoods viewed as "the worst in the city" in appearance and reputation, where the majority of housing units are rated as slums or which public opinion has condemned as inhabited by bad people, reliefers, or the poor of a widely disapproved ethnic group.

SOURCE: R. P. Coleman and B. L. Neugarten. *Social Status in the City*. San Francisco: Jossey-Bass, 1971, pp. 91-92. Reprinted by permission of authors and publisher.

QUALITY OF HOUSING SCALE

1   indicates housing associated with corporation presidents and other rich people—typically only 1 per cent of a city's housing.

2   indicates housing associated with the full-fledged manager level of businessesman—typically 5 per cent to 7 per cent of a city's housing.

3   indicates housing associated with better paid white-collar workers—typically 12 per cent to 15 per cent of a city's housing.

4   indicates housing associated with average white-collar workers and better paid blue-collar workers—typically 24 per cent to 27 per cent of a city's housing.

5   indicates housing associated with average blue-collar workers, but somewhat below average in desirability for modern, prosperous American families—about 28 per cent to 30 per cent of a city's housing in the 1950s and 1960s.

6   indicates substandard housing associated with families who are struggling to make ends meet—18 per cent or 20 per cent of a city's housing.

7   indicates housing derogated as slums and shacks, barely fit for human habitation, plus public housing projects for low-income people—7 per cent to 10 per cent of a city's housing.

SOURCE: R. P. Coleman and B. L. Neugarten. *Social Status in the City*. San Francisco: Jossey-Bass, 1971, pp. 95-96. Reprinted by permission of authors and publisher.

EDUCATIONAL STATUS—1: PLATFORM RATINGS

1   indicates an upper class platform rating, given to men with a socially prestigious college background—Harvard, Yale, Princeton, Williams or similar colleges of extremely high social status in previous eras; men who may not have attended so highly honored an undergraduate school but who earned law degrees at schools such as Harvard or Columbia or medical degrees at Pennsylvania and Johns Hopkins; and men who attended a semiprestigious college and while there joined one of the nationally elite fraternities such as Beta

Theta Pi or Phi Gamma Delta. This same rating is given to women who were educated at a four-year woman's college such as Vassar, Smith, or Bryn Mawr, or at an exclusive finishing school (Briarcliff Junior College, for example); also women who attended one of the semiprestigious private schools such as Northwestern or Duke and while there became affiliated with one of the nationally elite soroities such as Kappa Alpha Theta, Kappa Kappa Gamma, or Pi Beta Phi.

2   indicates an upper-middle platform rating, given to all men with professional degrees in law, medicine, dentistry, or architecture, which require typically more than four years of college attendance, or to men with master's degrees in an academic discipline; also all graduates of colleges in the same level of prestige as Beloit, Colgate, DePauw, Holy Cross, Massachusetts Institute of Technology, Notre Dame, Reed, Tulane, Vanderbilt, or Wooster —irrespective of era; men born before 1919 but who graduated from state universities on the prestige level of University of Arkansas or Pennsylvania State University or Purdue or private colleges of approximately similar social rank (Baylor, University of Cincinnati, Texas Christian). This same rating is given to women graduates of the same schools, with the same degrees, and at the same era; it is also given to those who attended college without graduating but who joined one or another of the more socially prominent sororities (Delta Delta Delta, Delta Gamma, and Gamma Phi Beta are examples).

3   indicates a middle-middle platform, given to graduates of all the lesser, private colleges, municipal universities, and teachers' colleges, irrespective of era; among older men and women it is given to those who attended colleges of medium status but did not graduate; among the youngest people it is given to those who graduated from the typical state university or one of the medium-status private colleges without membership in a socially significant fraternity or sorority. For men born before 1890 this rating can be applied even to graduates of business colleges or special technical schools, and for both men and women it is often granted in recognition of attendance at a recognized music school or art institute.

4   indicates an average lower-middle platform, given to men born after 1920 if they attended a municipal-type college, a teachers' college (or college formerly of this type transformed into a state university after World War II in the education boom of the 1950s), or lowly regarded private college without graduating—even up to three years of attendance; just one or two years of college at such schools also grants a 4 rating for men born between 1900 and 1919; and more recently, for men and women born in 1940 or after, this is the rating even for those who attended the recognized state universities and high-average private schools without graduating or without affiliating with one of the more prestigious of fraternities or sororities.

SOURCE: R. P. Coleman and B. L. Neugarten. *Social Status in the City*. San Francisco: Jossey-Bass, 1971, pp. 100-101. Reprinted by permission of authors and publisher.

IUS EDUCATION SCALES (ABBREVIATED VERSION),
MEN ONLY
(Collegiate Years Completed)

Birth Years	All Advanced Degrees	B.A. or B.S.	Three Years	Two Years	One Year	Post-H.S. Commercial or Technical Institute
1945-49	2	3	4	4	4	5
1940-44	2	3	4	4	4	4

IUS EDUCATION SCALES (ABBREVIATED VERSION),
MEN ONLY — *Continued*
(Collegiate Years Completed)

Birth Years	All Advanced Degrees	B.A. or B.S.	Three Years	Two Years	One Year	Post-H.S. Commercial or Technical Institute
1935-39	2	3	4	4	4	4
1930-34	2	3	4	4	4	4
1925-29	2	3	3	4	4	4
1920-24	2	3	3	4	4	4
1915-19	2	2	3	3	3	4
1910-14	2	2	3	3	3	4
1905-09	2	2	3	3	3	4
1900-04	2	2	3	3	3	4
1895-99	2	2	3	3	3	4
1890-94	2	2	3	3	3	4
1885-89	2	2	3	3	3	4
1880-84	2	2	3	3	3	3
1875-79	2	2	3	3	3	3
Pre-1875	2	2	3	3	3	3

IUS EDUCATION SCALES (ABBREVIATED VERSION),
WOMEN ONLY
(Collegiate Years Completed)

Birth Years	All Advanced Degrees	B.A. or B.S.	Three Years	Two Years	One Year	Post-H.S. Commercial or Technical Institute
1945-49	2	3	3	4	4	5
1940-44	2	3	3	4	4	4
1935-39	2	3	3	3	4	4
1930-34	2	3	3	3	4	4
1925-29	2	3	3	3	3	4
1920-24	2	3	3	3	3	4
1915-19	2	2	3	3	3	4
1910-14	2	2	3	3	3	4
1905-09	2	2	3	3	3	4
1900-04	2	2	3	3	3	4
1895-99	2	2	2	3	3	4
1890-94	2	2	2	3	3	4
1885-89	2	2	2	3	3	4
1880-84	2	2	2	3	3	4
1875-79	2	2	2	3	3	4
Pre-1875	2	2	2	3	3	4

IUS EDUCATION SCALES (ABBREVIATED VERSION),
MEN AND WOMEN
(Secondary Years Completed)

Birth Years	12th Grade	11th Grade	10th Grade	9th Grade
1945-49	5	6	6	6
1940-44	5	6	6	6
1935-39	5	5	6	6
1930-34	5	5	6	6
1925-29	5	5	5	6
1920-24	5	5	5	6
1915-19	4	5	5	5
1910-14	4	5	5	5
1905-09	4	5	5	5
1900-04	4	4	5	5
1895-99	4	4	4	5
1890-94	4	4	4	4
1885-89	4	4	4	4
1880-84	4	4	4	4
1875-79	4	4	4	4
Pre-1875	4	4	4	4

IUS EDUCATION SCALES (ABBREVIATED VERSION),
MEN AND WOMEN
(Grades of Elementary Schooling Completed)

Birth Years	8th Grade	7th Grade	6th Grade	5th Grade	4th Grade	3rd Grade	2nd Grade	1st Grade	No Schooling
1945-49	7	7	7	7	7	7	7	7	7
1940-44	7	7	7	7	7	7	7	7	7
1935-39	7	7	7	7	7	7	7	7	7
1930-34	6	7	7	7	7	7	7	7	7
1925-29	6	7	7	7	7	7	7	7	7
1920-24	6	6	7	7	7	7	7	7	7
1915-19	6	6	7	7	7	7	7	7	7
1910-14	6	6	6	7	7	7	7	7	7
1905-09	5	6	6	7	7	7	7	7	7
1900-04	5	6	6	6	7	7	7	7	7
1895-99	5	6	6	6	7	7	7	7	7
1890-94	5	5	6	6	6	7	7	7	7
1885-89	5	5	6	6	6	7	7	7	7
1880-84	5	5	6	6	6	7	7	7	7
1875-79	5	5	6	6	6	7	7	7	7
Pre-1875	5	5	6	6	6	6	7	7	7

SOURCE: R. P. Coleman and B. L. Neugarten. *Social Status in the City*. San Francisco: Jossey-Bass, 1971, Table 5, pp. 102-3. Reprinted by permission of authors and publisher.

RELIGIOUS AFFILIATION SCALE

1 indicates churches which in public reputation are society-oriented in membership and appeal.

2 indicates churches of the metropolitan prestige type, which are reputed to draw their leadership mainly from the managerial, executive, and professional strata, and thus are considered very desirable churches to attend. Also included are smaller churches of reputable denominations which serve a primarily upper management or country-club neighborhood.

3 indicates churches reputed to draw their membership from the middle echelons of the white-collar and semiprofessional world, that are of reputable denomination and generally regarded as above average in social status but not particularly prestigeful.

4 indicates churches reputed to draw their congregants mainly from white-collar neighborhoods and to be affiliated with one of the accepted mainstream denominations.

5 indicates churches reputed to draw their congregants mainly from average working class neighborhoods and thought to be composed dominantly of blue-collar people. Also included are churches of off-brand denominations located in middle class sections of the city and assumed to attract some white-collar people.

6 indicates churches of mainstream denomination which draw heavily from lower-level neighborhoods or churches of off-brand denominations which by virture of their location and/or their reputation are assumed to draw their membership mainly from average working class neighborhoods but not from substandard areas.

7 indicates churches in slum neighborhoods or of the "store front" and revivalist type which are the targets of scorn from solidly-established working class people as well as from those higher up.

SOURCE: R. P. Coleman and B. L. Neugarten. *Social Status in the City.* San Francisco: Jossey-Bass, 1971, p. 105. Reprinted by permission of authors and publisher.

V2.7.III.a

SUBJECTIVE CLASS IDENTIFICATION

R. Centers, 1949; J. A. Kahl and J. A. Davis, 1955; J. R. Kluegel, R. Singleton, Jr., and C. E. Starnes, 1977

See the description of the instrument in the abstract.

Chapter 8

Religiosity

Barbara Pittard Payne

One of the stereotypes about the elderly is that they are more religious than others in the population and that people turn to religion as they age (Orbach, 1961). The historical basis for this stereotype can be traced to Starbuck, the pioneer in the psychology of religion, who reported in 1911 that religious faith and belief in God grow in importance as the years advance (Payne, 1980). Yet, research on this stereotype is limited. In fact, religion and aging as an area of theoretical and empirical research in social gerontology is so underresearched that Heenan (1968) described it as the "empirical lacunae." Although Riley and Foner (1968) and Johnson (1963) did identify and review substantial research, they concluded that data on the religious role contribute less to an understanding of the aging process than data on other social roles. Further evidence of the "empirical lacunae" is that the latest work reporting social science research in aging, *The Handbook on Aging and the Social Sciences* (Binstock and Shanas, 1976), does not include a chapter on religion as the *Handbook of Social Gerontology* (Tibbitts, 1960) did.

The measures used for studies of religion and aging between 1948 and 1976 that are reviewed for this chapter reflect a theoretical absorption with disengagement theory and its counterpart, activity theory. Consequently, changes in religious participation and practice are interpreted as "normal" disengagement rather than differences in type of participation as a process of role change and reconstruction occurring during old-age. During this same period, social scientists who were developing more precise measures of religious behavior (Glock and Stark, 1966; King, 1967; Hoge, 1972) and those who were interested in the "new religions" of the 1960s (Payne-Pittard, 1980) showed little interest in, or sensitivity to, age differences in religiosity. The work of these researchers reflects a structure-functional theoretical base that focuses attention on institutional forms of commitment. Religiosity is measured by adherence to institutional (orthodox) beliefs and practices. However, the emergence of the new religions during the 1960s forced renewed attention to age and religious behavior and to methods appropriate to this area of inquiry. These religions were part of the youth culture and reflected the influence of Eastern religions. Researchers using survey research found it more difficult to apply their traditional methods to these phenomena. Furthermore, many of their methodological difficulties rested on theoretical inadequacies. There are intimations of theoretical developments that take more seriously the nonassociational qualities in the development of religious consciousness. These include a renewed emphasis on symbolic meanings (Bellah, 1976; Glock and Bellah, 1976) and transcendence (Brewer, 1974; 1978). This development allows for increasing participation in the symbolic dimension of religion while withdrawing from the associational forms.

The instruments included in this chapter represent a wide range of methodological sophistication. Some need additional refinement and testing, and others have proven reliability and validity but are 30 years old (Cavan et al., 1949).

The topics most commonly investigated can be classified into three main categories: (1) organizational participation; (2) religiosity, including privatized religious behavior; and (3) religious activities, practices, and personal adjustment. The sections under which the nine research measures reviewed in this chapter are arranged follow this general classification.

Measures of Organizational Participation

One of the standard measures of religious behavior is the frequency of church attendance. The objective intervals most frequently used form a five-point scale from once a week, twice a month, once a month, a few times a year, to never (Fichter, 1952; Albrecht, 1958; Orbach, 1961). The Gallup poll method (e.g., "Did you yourself happen to attend a church or synagogue in the last seven days?") limits the period of recall, requires no judgment about frequency and, as Argyle (1959) argued, leaves much less room for distortion than simply asking how often a person attends.

Many of the participation studies are secondary analyses of data from major studies, such as the Detroit Area Study (Orbach, 1961) and the Gallup Poll Surveys (Alston, Peek, and Wingrove, 1972). Wingrove and Alston (1974) developed a method of cohort analysis appropriate for use with the Gallup poll data on church attendance from 1939 to 1969. They argued that the use of separate surveys for cohort analysis avoids the cost and problems of maintaining a 30-year-long study and that, unlike the retrospective method, uses reponses based on current attitudes and behavior. In addition to the problems of recall, they point out that the tendency of people to idealize their past religious behavior could introduce biases that would support the disengagement theory (Alston, Peek, and Wingrove, 1972).

Bahr (1973) developed retrospective measures of affiliation and partiticipation that probe respondents until all episodes of regular attendance and the associated durations are specified. Obviously, the frequency measures represent efforts to develop objective, observable measures of religious behavior. These measures rely heavily on the common assumption that people are aware of the frequency of their participation and that they tend to be fairly honest in reporting such objective data about themselves. Bahr reported that discrepancy rates for items on "lifetime identification" such as religious preference ranged from 6% to 12% in his sample, compared to the discrepancy rates of 20% to 40% that are common for retrospective items (Bahr, 1973). The retrospective method used with older adults suggests a way gerontologists may operationalize the life-review concept.

Age is a major intervening variable in studies of religious participation. For adults over 65 there is a tendency to collapse age categories. Such a procedure not only obscures differences in the young old, old, and old old (Neugarten, 1968) but depends exclusively on age as defined arbitrarily by societal and legal definitions of retirement age and eligibility for social benefits. Gerontologists have long maintained that age is not a unidimensional measure determined by chronological age alone but that individuals age at different rates physically, biologically, psychologically, and socially. An exception to this focus on chronological age is Bell's (1971) research using family life stages as a determinant of organizational participation. Although he used a biased sample (Methodist) and research instrument, Bell provided a model adaptable to more universal measures.

Problems of Reliability and Validity

Since the researchers determine the operational definition of low and high frequency of participation as a measure of religiosity, little uniformity and hence comparability is found in the research literature. Although measures of religious attendance may yield reliable estimates of attendance, the validity of these as measures of religiosity or religious commitment may be questionable, insofar as no data are elicited about how members *feel* about their attendance. Participation may reflect a social habit, an effect of family and/or peer pressure, or a desire to increase the number of business or political contacts. As a result, valuable information pertaining to the *context* of participation is lost when the research focuses only on participation rates.

Most participation measures examine only formal church participation to the exclusion of other formal, informal, and everyday religious practices (e.g., prayer and Bible study groups, prayer and meditation, community services, decision making, and coping with daily crises and life situations). Furthermore, simple frequency measures do not account for the reasons for attendance or nonattendance, and so they may be less sensitive to changes in the variables that explain the social participation of the elderly (i.e., health, economic status, and family situation).

The objective measures of church attendance and chronological age are necessary unitary measures. However, they are not sufficient measures of religiosity, change in religious behavior, or aging. The participation must be supplemented by subjective evaluations and other social-psychological constructs in order to assess more completely the role of religious institutions and behaviors for the lives of older persons.

Investigators interested in the religious participation of older members can find several useful measures (D. O. Moberg, 1965; Cook, 1971); especially useful for those interested in the roles and attitudes of the clergy are Longino and Kitson (1976) and R. Moberg (1969).

Measures of Religiosity and Religious Commitment

Fichter's (1952) research developing a typology of church members and explicating the multidimensional nature of religious participation and commitment was the pioneer work in this area. Glock (1964) and Glock and Stark (1966) developed the first religious commitment scales based on dimensions of commitment. During the 1960s other scales testing or adapting these scales were constructed and factor analyzed (Fukuyama, 1961; King and Hunt, 1972; Pittard, 1966). The religiosity instruments selected for this chapter are those that have been specifically used with older populations. The other commitment and religiosity scales cited are to be found in Robinson and Shaver (1973).

The researchers developing these religiosity measures are more likely to report formal reliability and validity tests. Though these measures have been used in a wide range of studies as dependent variables, the various multidimensional measures were not explicitly constructed to measure aging and religious commitment. They have, however, been used with samples that included respondents 65 years of age and older.

In 1968 Stark raised the question of the relationship of age and faith and analyzed commitment data from the American Piety Study to determine whether people become more religious as they age. Among the three-dimensional measures—orthodoxy, ritual involvement, and private devotionalism—private devotionalism was found to be the primary outlet provided by religion for the anxieties and deprivations of old-age. The increasing piety of the elderly is manifested in the reported frequency of praying. From an examination of the items used to measure the dimensions it is evident that the social expression of religious commitment in a nonassociational context, such as sharing and discussing one's faith, has been neglected.

Some of the items in these scales reflect the social period in which they were constructed and are now less valid for measuring the dimension. As a result, items on "social drinking" and "blue laws" are included in the Pittard (1963) scale even though these are not the social or religious issues they were in the 1960s.

Gerontological researchers who rely on measures constructed for different populations or behaviors fail to take into account the period effects influencing the original construction of the scales and the social changes that have occurred since the instruments were developed. Moreover, they fail to recognize the uniqueness of adult life after age 65 or patterns of religious experience and practice emerging in the subculture of the aged.

Most of the religiosity measures reviewed here and those reviewed by Robinson and Shaver (1973) are Christian and church oriented. An exception useful to investigators interested in Jewish commitment (or religiosity) measures are the scales developed by Himmelfarb (1975).

Hoge's (1972) Intrinsic Religious Motivation Scale markes a departure from reliance on cognitive style and church participation as predictors of religious behavior. Kivett, Watson, and Bush (1977) found religious motivation to be a strong predictor of perceived control over the environment. Investigators of environmental control and adjustment in old-age will find this scale to be a reliable, valid, and easily administered measure.

Measures of Attitudes, Activities, and Adjustment in Old Age

The most frequently used measure of religion and aging was constructed by Cavan and associates in 1949. It was specifically developed to measure the social adjustment of older adults. In its full or modified form, it has been and is still used more than any other measure of religiosity and aging (Havighurst and Albrecht, 1953; D. O. Moberg, 1951; 1965; Hunter and Maurice, 1953). It was included in the Duke Longitudinal Study of normal aging (Blazer and Palmore, 1976). The structure, reliability, and validity of this measure suggest that researchers can continue to use it with confidence.

However, it has been almost 30 years since these measures were constructed. "Being old" and "adjustment to old age" are different for the present cohort of older adults than they were to those of 30 years ago. The items in the activities inventory need to be retested, and additional items need to be constructed that reflect the new religious activities open to the elderly, such as volunteering in church-based senior centers and providing services for their own age-group. The attitudes scale should also be subject to further analysis, and additional attitudinal items should be developed to reflect the importance and value of non-church oriented religious experiences and activities (Blazer and Palmore, 1976). The Attitude Inventory (Instrument V1.5.I.g) and Activity Inventory (Instrument V2.2.II.e) have been reviewed in other chapters in *Research Instruments in Social Gerontology*. Table 8-1 lists the measures reviewed in this chapter.

Conclusion

One of the values of this chapter will stem from the response of investigators whose work I have omitted. Efforts to locate the research have included the usual types of search, but it was inevitable that some significant new research would be missed.

As I reviewed the measures included here, it became increasingly evident that there are a limited number of reliable and valid measures of religious behavior and aging and that these assess a limited range of religious behavior. Even fewer measures of the unique religious behaviors of older people have been designed. More important, even the valid and reliable measures lack adequate theoretical foundations and, therefore, continue to substantiate Riley and Foner's (1968) opinion that data on the religious role contribute little to an understanding of the aging process. Too much effort and trust have been invested in attendance and activities as indications of religious role behavior. Researchers need to go beyond crude counting and develop more refined measures rooted in theoretical concepts.

Crucial, then, to this area of gerontological research are the development of the theoretical bases for measure of religiosity and the appli-

TABLE 8-1
Instruments Reviewed in Chapter 8

Instrument	Author(s)	Code Number
a. Religiosity	Orbach (1961)	V2.8.I.a
b. Instrinsic Religious Motivation Scale	Hoge (1972)	V2.8.I.b
c. Religious Disaffiliation	Bahr and Caplow (1973)	V2.8.I.c
d. Social Integration of the Aged in Churches	Moberg (1965)	V2.8.I.d
e. Religious Commitment	Glock and Stark (1966); Stark (1968)	V2.8.I.e
f. Religious Commitment	Pittard (1963)	V2.8.I.f
g. Dimensions of Religion	King (1967); King and Hunt (1969; 1972; 1975)	V2.8.I.g
h. Measures of Religious Involvement	Himmelfarb (1975)	V2.8.I.h
i. Attitudes toward the Church and Religion	Bell (1971)	V.2.8.I.i

cation of these measures to large, representative samples of older adults. There is also a need for the development of theories and methods for studying the role of religion in the symbolic lives of older people. Perhaps then the relationship of age to the attitudinal and behavioral components of religiosity will be fully explicated.

REFERENCES

Albrecht, R. "The Meaning of Religion to the Older Person." In *Organized Religion and the Older Person*, D. L. Scudder (ed.), pp. 53-70. Gainesville, Fla.: University of Florida Press, 1958.

Alston, J. P., C. W. Peek, and C. R. Wingrove. "Religiosity and Black Militants: A Reappraisal." *Journal for the Scientific Study of Religion*, 1972, 11:252-69.

Argyle, M. *Religious Behavior*. New York: Free Press, 1959.

Atchley, R. *Social Forces in Late Life*. Belmont, Calif.: Wadsworth, 1977.

Bahr, H. M. "Aging and Religious Disaffiliation." *Social Forces*, 1970, 49:59-71.

Bahr, H. M., and T. Caplow. *Old Men Drunk and Sober*. New York: New York University Press, 1973.

Bell, B. D. "Church Participation and the Family Life Cycle." *Review of Religious Research*, 1971, 13 (1):57-64.

Bellah, R. N. "New Religious Consciousness and the Crisis in Modernity." In *The New Religious Consciousness*, C. Y. Glock and R. N. Bellah, (eds.), pp. 333-52. Berkeley, Calif.: University of California Press, 1976.

Binstock, R. H., and E. Shanas (eds.). *Handbook of Aging and the Social Sciences*. New York: Van Nostrand Reinhold, 1976.

Blazer, D., and E. Palmore. "Religion and Aging in a Longitudinal Panel." *The Gerontologist*, 1976, 16:82-85.

Busse, E. W., and E. Pfeiffer (eds.). *Behavior and Adaptation in Late Life*. Boston: Little, Brown and Company, 1969.

Brewer, E. "Some Intimation and Some Induction." *Character Potential*, 1974, 6(4):200-206.

_____. "The Religioning Process in Future Form of Ministers in the Military." *Military Chaplain Review*, 1978 (Winter):59-74.

Cavan, R. S., E. W. Burgess, R. J. Havighurst, and H. Goldhammer. *Personal Adjustment in Old Age*. Chicago: Science Research Associates, 1949.

Cook, J. "An Application of the Disengagement Theory of Aging to Older Persons in the Church." Ph.D. dissertation, University of Michigan, 1971.

Cumming, E., and W. E. Henry. *Growing Old*. New York: Basic Books, 1961.

Dumazedier, J. *Sociology of Leisure*. New York: Elsevier, 1974.

Feifel, H. "Religious Conviction and Fear of Death among the Healthy and the Terminally Ill." *Journal for the Scientific Study of Religion*, 1974, 13:353-60.

Fichter, J. H. "Profiles of Catholic Religious Life." *American Journal of Sociology*, 1952, 58:14549.

_____. *Social Relations in the Urban Parish*. Chicago: University of Chicago Press, 1954.

Fukuyama, Y. "The Major Dimensions of Church Membership." *Review of Religious Research*, 1961, 2:154-61.

Glock, C. Y. "The Role of Deprivation in the Origin and Evolution of Religious Groups." In *Religion and Social Conflict*, R. Lee and M. E. Marty (eds.), pp. 24-36. New York: Oxford University Press, 1964.

Glock, C. Y., and R. N. Bellah. *The New Religious Consciousness*. Los Angeles: University of California Press, 1976.

Glock, C. Y., and R. Stark. *Christian Beliefs and Anti-Semitism*. New York: Harper and Row, 1966.

Goody, J. "Aging in Non-Industrial Societies." In *Handbook of Aging and the Social Sciences*, R. H. Binstock and E. Shanas (eds.), pp. 117-29. New York: Van Nostrand Reinhold, 1976.

Gray, M., and D. O. Moberg. *The Church and the Older Person*. Grand Rapids, Mich.: William B. Eerdmans, 1962.

Hall, G. S. *Senescence, the Second Half of Life*. New York: Appleton and Company, 1922.

Havighurst, R. J., and R. Albrecht. *Older People*. New York: Longmans, Green and Company, 1953.

Heenan, E. R. "Aging in Religious Life." *Review for Religious Research*, 1968, 27:1120-27.

Hendricks, J., and C. D. Hendricks. *Aging in Mass Society: Myths and Realities*. Cambridge, Mass.: Winthrop Press, 1977.

Heyman, D. K. and D. Giantuco. "Long Term Adaptation by the Elderly to Bereavement." *Journal of Gerontology*, 1973, 28:359-62.

Himmelfarb, H. S. "Measuring Religious Involvement." *Social Forces*, 1975, 53:607-18.

Hoge, D. R. "A Validated Intrinsic Religious Motivation Scale." *Journal for the Scientific Study of Religion*, 1972, 11:369-76.

Hunter, W. W., and H. Maurice. *Older People Tell Their Story*. Ann Arbor, Mich.: University of Michigan, Division of Gerontology, 1953.

Jeffers, F. C., and A. Verwoerdt. "How the Old Face Death." In *Behavior and Adaption in Late Life*, E. W. Busse and E. Pfeiffer (eds.), pp. 163-81. Boston: Little, Brown and Company, 1969.

Johnson, B. "On Church and Sect." *American Sociological Review*, 1963, 28:539-49.

Kimmel, D. *Adulthood and Aging*. New York: John Wiley and Sons, 1974.

King, M. B. "Measuring the Religious Variable: Nine Proposed Dimensions." *Journal for the Scientific Study of Religion*, 1967, 6:173-90.

King, M. B., and R. A. Hunt. *Measuring Religious Dimensions*. Dallas: Southern Methodist University, Studies in Social Science, publication number 1, 1972.

Kivett, V. R., J. A., Watson, and J. C. Bush. "The Relative Importance of Physical, Psychological, and Social Variables to Locus of Control Orientation in Middle Age." *Journal of Gerontology*, 1977, 32:203-10.

Lazerwitz, B. "Some Factors Associated with Variation in Church Attendance." *Social Forces*, 1961, 39:301-9.

Longino, C. F., and G. C. Kitson. "Parish Clergy and the Aged: Examining Stereotypes." *Journal of Gerontology*, 1976, 31:340-45.

Lowenthal, M., and B. Robinson. "Social Networks and Isolation." In *Handbook of Aging and the Social Sciences*, R. H. Binstock and E. Shanas (eds.), pp. 432-56. New York: Van Nostrand Reinhold, 1976.

Maves, P. B. "Aging, Religion and the Church." In *Handbook of Social Gerontology*, C. E. Tibbitts (ed.), pp. 698-749. Chicago: University of Chicago Press, 1960.

Moberg, D. O. "Religion and Personal Adjustment in Old Age: A Study of Some Aspects of the Christian Relation to Personal Adjustment of the Aged in Institutions." Ph.D. dissertation, University of Minnesota, 1951.

_____. "The Integration of Older Members in the Church Congregation." In *Older People and Their Social World*, A. M. Rose and W. A. Peterson (eds.), pp. 125-40. Philadelphia: F. A. Davis, 1965.

_____. "Religiosity in Old Age." In *Middle Age and Aging*, B. L. Neugarten (ed.), pp. 497-508. Chicago: University of Chicago Press, 1968.

_____. "Religion in the Later Years." In *The Daily Needs and Interests of Older People*, A. M. Hoffman (ed.), pp. 175-91. Springfield, Ill.: Charles C. Thomas, 1970.

Moberg, R. "The Attitudes of Ministers toward Older People." Ph.D. dissertation, Boston University, 1969.

Moody, R. *Life after Life*. Covington, Ga.: Mocking Bird Press, 1975.

National Council on the Aging. *The Myth and Reality of Aging in America*. Washington, D.C.: National Council on the Aging, 1975.

Neugarten, B. L. *Middle Age and Aging*. Chicago: University of Chicago Press, 1968.

Orbach, H. L. "Aging and Religion." *Geriatrics*, 1961, 16:534-40.

O'Reilly, C. T. "Religious Practice and Personal Adjustment of Older People." *Sociology and Social Research*, 1957, 43:119-21.

Palmore, E. "Sociological Aspects of Aging." In *Behavior and Adaptation in Late Life*, E. W. Busse and E. Pfeiffer (eds.), pp. 207-50. Boston: Little, Brown and Company, 1969.

_____. *Normal Aging*. Durham, N.C.: Duke University Press, 1970.

_____. *Normal Aging II*. Durham, N.C.: Duke University Press, 1974.

Payne, B. P. *The Meaning and Measurement of Commitment to the Church*. Atlanta: Georgia State University, special publication number 13, 1966.

_____. "Age Differences in the Meaning of Leisure Activities." Paper presented to the 26th Annual Meeting of the Gerontological Society, Miami Beach, November 7, 1973(a).

_____. "Voluntary Associations of the Elderly." Paper presented to the Society on the Study of Social Problems, New York, August 27, 1973(b).

_____. "Religious Life Review." Field notes, 1977.

_____. "Religious Life of the Elderly: Myth or Reality." In *Spiritual Well-being of the Elderly*, J. A. Thorson and T. C. Cook (eds.), pp. 218-29. Springfield, Ill.: Charles C. Thomas, 1980.

Payne, B. P., and F. Whittington. "Older Women: An Examination of Popular Stereotypes and Research Evidence." *Social Problems*, 1974, 23:488-504.

Payne, R., B. P. Payne, and R. D. Reddy. "Social Background and Role Determinants of Individual Participation in Organized Voluntary Action." In *Voluntary Action Research: 1972*, D. M. Smith, R. D. Reddy, and B. R. Baldwin (eds.), pp. 207-500. Lexington, Mass.: D. C. Heath and Company, 1972.

Payne-Pittard, B. "Nonassociational Religious Participation." In *Participation in Social and Political Activities*, D. H. Smith, S. Macaulay, and associates (eds.), pp. 214-43. San Francisco: Jossey-Bass, 1980.

Pfeiffer, E., and G. C. Davis. "The Use of Leisure Time in Middle Life." *The Gerontologist*, 1971, 11 (3):187-95.

Pittard, B. (Payne). "The Meaning and Measurement of Commitment to the Church." Ph.D. dissertation, Emory University, 1963.

Riley, M. W., and A. Foner. *Aging and Society* (vol. 1). New York: Russell Sage Foundation, 1968.

Robinson, J. P., and P. Shaver. *Measures of Social Psychological Attitudes*. Ann Arbor, Mich.: Institute for Social Research, University of Michigan, 1973.

Schuyler, J. "Religious Observance Differentials by Age and Sex in a Northern Parish." *American Catholic Sociological Review*, 1959, 20 (2):124-31.

Starbuck, E. D. *The Psychology of Religion: An Empirical Study of the Growth of Religious Consciousness*. New York: Walter Scott, 1911.

Stark, R. "Age and Faith: A Changing Outlook as an Old Process." *Sociological Analysis*, 1968, 29:1-10.

Taietz, P., and O. F. Larson. "Social Participation and Old Age." *Rural Sociology*, 1956, 21: 229-38.

Tibbitts, C. E. (ed.). *Handbook of Social Gerontology*. Chicago: University of Chicago Press, 1960.

Waterman, L. "Religion and Religious Observance in Old Age." In *Living Through the Older Years*, C. E. Tibbitts (ed.), pp. 99-112. Ann Arbor, Mich.: University of Michigan Press, 1949.

Wingrove, C. R., and J. P. Alston. "Age, Aging, and Church Attendance." *The Gerontologist*, 1971, 11(4):345-58.

————. "Cohort Analysis of Church Attendance 1939-69." *Social Forces*, 1974, 53(2): 324-31.

Woodruff, D. S., and J. Birren. *Aging: Scientific Perspectives and Social Issues*. New York: Van Nostrand Reinhold, 1975.

Abstracts

RELIGIOSITY

H. L. Orbach, 1961

Definition of Concept or Variable

Participation in religious bodies through attendance and involvement in ceremonial worship is the most crucial and sensitive indicator of overt religiosity.

Description of Instrument

This single-item indicator measures the extent of church attendance on a five-point scale ranging from once a week to never.

Method of Administration

No special skills are needed to administer this item in interview or questionnaire form.

Context of Development

The item was included as part of the Detroit Area Study, 1952-1957.

Sample

The item was used on a pooled sample (N = 6,911) of the University of Michigan's Detroit Area Study for the years 1952-1957. Each of the yearly surveys was a three-stage area probability sample designed to accurately indicate the character of the sample universe. The pooled sample included 855 respondents age 60 to 74 and 132 respondents age 75 and older.

Usability on Older Populations

No problems were reported with respondents age 60 and older.

Sensitivity to Age Differences

Respondents aged 75 and older reported less frequent attendance than those of other ages, although a plurality of those 75 and older reported weekly attendance (Orbach, 1961).

General Comments and Recommendations

The religious attendance index is the most frequently used item in measuring age and religiosity, either as a separate item or in summary scales. There are wide variations in the categories of responses and in the weighting of the categories.

Reference

Orbach, H. L. "Aging and Religion." *Geriatrics*, 1961, 16:534-40.

Instrument

See Instrument V2.8.I.a.

INTRINSIC RELIGIOUS MOTIVATION SCALE

D. R. Hoge, 1972

Definition of Cencept or Variable

Instrinsically motivated individuals are those who find that their primary motive is religion and that all other needs are regarded as being of less ultimate significance. Those who embrace their creed lightly or selectively shape it in order to meet their primary needs are instrumentally motivated (Hoge, 1972; Kivett, Watson, and Bush, 1977). Hoge explained the variable as one of motivation and not behavior, cognitive style, or perception, i.e., as not inferred from theological position or external behavior (Hoge, 1972).

Description of Instrument

This scale of 10 items in Likert form, with four responses from strongly agree to strongly disagree, measures the dimension of ultimate (intrinsic) versus instrumental religious motivation. The scale was developed from 30 items, including 8 with highest item-to-scale correlations in the Allport and Ross (1967) study, and 22 new items pretested on 51 subjects who fit the intrinsic-extrinsic extremes of the continuum. This was repeated with 42 additional subjects using the same selection procedure. From the items in the final validation study that had highest item-to-item and item-to-scale correlation, a 10-item scale was identified.

Method of Administration

The scale is self-administered within a larger questionnaire. No specific time requirements are given in the instructions.

Context of Development and Subsequent Use

Hoge developed the scale as a project carried out in a seminar at Princeton Theological Seminary. It was a part of a larger study of religion and prejudice conducted by Hoge and Carroll (no date), Kivett, Watson, and Bush (1977) used the scale in research on the physical, psychological, and social predictors of locus of control among middle-aged adults.

Sample(s):

Hoge (1972) developed the instrument on two purposive samples of 51 and 42 adults.

Kivett, Watson, and Bush (1977) reported using this measure on a sample of 337 adults aged 45 to 65.

Scoring, Scales Norms, and Distribution

Item responses are scored as follows: (1) strongly agree, (2) agree (4) disagree, (5) strongly disagree. Items 8, 9, 10 are reversed prior to summation.

Items means range from 1.71 to 2.40 for items 1 to 7 and 3.88 to 4.33 for items 8 to 10 (before reversal). There is a strong tendency to report an intrinsic orientation to religion (Hoge, 1972).

Formal Tests of Reliability/Homogeneity

Kuder-Richardson formula 20 reliability is .901. Item-to-item correlations range from .132 (items 5 by 9) to .716 (items 2 by 7); of the 45 item-to-item correlations, 22 are stronger than .5 (Hoge, 1972).

Formal Tests of Validity

Item-total correlations, after the specific item was deleted from the scale, range from .48 to .80, with an average correlation of .65 (Hoge, 1972).

Correlations of the Intrinsic Religious Motivation Scale with other measures of religiosity range from .388 to .874 (Hoge, 1972).

Usability on Older Populations

Kivett, Watson, and Bush (1977) used the scale with a sample of persons 45 to 65 years of age and found that religious motivation was an important predictor of perceived locus of control, regardless of the relative influence of other variables.

General Comments and Recommendations

The Intrinsic Religious Motivation Scale is unique in that it is not based on church attendance, theological stance, or other organizational activities. Therefore, it has more universality than other measures and examines religion as a source or a prime mover, rather than as a set of specific acts or perceptions. The scale's uniqueness, coupled with its high reliability and validity, makes it a valuable tool for researchers who want to study the role of religion for older persons.

References

Allport, G., and J. M. Ross. "Personal Religious Orientation and Prejudice." *Journal of Personality and Social Psychology*, 1967, 5:432-43.

Hoge, D. R. "A Validated Intrinsic Religious Motivation Scale." *Journal for the Scientific Study of Religion*, 1972, 11:369-76.

Hoge, D. R., and J. W. Carroll. "Religiosity and Prejudice in Northern and Southern Churches." Unpublished paper, Princeton Theological Seminary, no date.

Kivett, V. R., J. A. Watson, and J. C. Bush. "The Relative Importance of Physical, Psychological, and Social Variables to Locus of Control Orientation in Middle Age." *Journal of Gerontology*, 1977, 32:203-10.

Instrument

See Instrument V2.8.I.b.

RELIGIOUS DISAFFILIATION

H. M. Bahr and T. Caplow, 1973

Definition of Concept or Variable

Religious Disaffiliation measures variation in church affiliation, religiosity, and participation throughout life. Disaffiliation is a type of retreatism characterized by retirement or withdrawal from what is difficult, dangerous, or disagreeable; it can also denote a place of seclusion, privacy, safety, or refuge. Furthermore, it is characterized by a coming out of circulation, a step from activity into inactivity or from active to passive service. Religious disaffiliation is the cessation of ties or marginal membership in a church without joining and/or participating in another religious group, and a devaluation of religious principles as life-guiding principles (Bahr and Caplow, 1973).

Description of Instrument

A sequence of 18 questions designed to yield retrospective data on affiliation and participation, together with 2 questions from Angell's (1962) study of moral norms, were used as a measure of religiosity by Bahr and Caplow (1973). The first affiliation question ascertains whether the respondent ever attended religious services, with other questions devoted to religious preference, participation in rituals, respondent's age, and length of attendance.

The questioning continued until the respondent reported all episodes of regular attendance and specified their duration. The disaffiliation instrument appears in Appendix II of *Old Men Drunk and Sober* (Bahr and Caplow, 1973).

Method of Administration

Interviews were administered originally in residences, cubicles in institutions, and neighborhood public rooms. The retrospective nature of the questions relies on probing questions and requires experienced interviewers trained in interviewing older, poor, and slightly disoriented adults.

Context of Development

The index was developed as a part of the Columbia Bowery Project, a study of homelessness and disaffiliation conducted by the Bureau of Applied Research at Columbia University. The project was expanded in 1976 to include disaffiliated women, elderly people in nursing homes, and other groups indirectly related to the original target population.

Samples

Four random samples were drawn from men residing in New York City, which resulted in a total of 621 interviews. Two samples were of the homeless men residing in the Bowery (N = 203) and Camp LaGuardia (N = 199), an institution for homeless men 60 miles from Manhattan. Two samples were of settled men in the Park Avenue area (N = 104) and in Park Slope (N = 125), a low-income area. The major characteristics of three of the samples are reported in Bahr and Caplow (1973, pp. 41-42).

Scoring, Scale Norms, and Distribution

Disaffiliation was determined by church attendance: (1) sporadic or not-at-all attenders (disaffiliates) and (2) regular or often attenders (affiliates). Age and disaffiliation were determined by dividing lifetime profiles into 10-year intervals from 15 to 65 years of age. These period variations determined congruence with the following models (Bahr and Caplow, 1973): (1) traditional—sharp decline in religious activity between the ages of 18 and 30, the lowest level is reached between ages 30 and 35, and there is a steady increase in religious activity beyond age 35 until old-age; (2) lifetime stability—no difference in participation throughout the life cycle; (3) family cycle—participation increases after marriage and peaks (with Protestants) at the time children are 5 years old or older and decreases when children are no longer in the home; and (4) progressive disengagement—attendance and participation decrease after middle-age.

Regular-church-attendance profiles varied from 35% to 50% at age 20 to between 20% and 40% at age 65. The highest rates of participation were from the low-income (Park Slope) settled sample, and the lowest rates were from the upper-income (Park Avenue), settled sample. There was no evidence in any of the noninstitutionalized samples that church attendance increases with age. A slight increase is noted for the institutionalized sample of persons between ages 50 and 65. The hypothesized traditional and family-cycle patterns of lifelong affiliation received no support in these data, but the stability hypothesis was supported from the skid-row sample and the disengagement hypothesis was supported in the noninstitutionalized sample.

Formal Tests of Reliability and Homogeniety

No specific information is available on the measure's reliability. However, other items on the schedule were checked against official records for discrepancies. Discrepancy rates were highest (almost 70%) for questions requiring a specific date and lowest for lifetime-identity items such as religious preference (6% to 12%) or ever-married status (7% to 8%).

Formal Tests of Validity

None of the available information about the measure is directly applicable to its validity. However, analysis of the discrepancies of other questions with organizational records suggests that item complexity is the major source of discrepancy.

Usability on Older Populations

The instrument was developed specifically for use with men of all ages, including homeless old men. It was used in a later study of single women of all ages (Bahr and Garrett, 1976). The recall of the older men was not significantly different from that of the younger men.

Sensitivity to Age Differences

The samples of noninstitutionalized men were subjected to gross, dichotomous age control (men under 50 and men over 50). Substantial differences in participation were found between younger and older men during the 25-year period between the ages of 20 and 45 years.

General Comments and Recommendations

The disaffiliation index allows less expensive and shorter-time-frame research than longitudinal studies. In studies of religion and aging, additional items need to be developed to measure religiosity and differences in the function of religion throughout the life cycle.

References

Angell, R. C. "Preferences for Moral Norms in Three Problem Areas." *American Journal of Sociology*, 1962, 67:650-60.

Bahr, H. M. "Aging and Religious Disaffiliation." *Social Forces*, 1970, 49:59-71.

Bahr, H. M., and T. Caplow. *Old Men Drunk and Sober*. New York: New York University Press, 1973.

Bahr, H. M., and G. R. Garrett. *Women Alone*. Lexington, Mass.: D. C. Heath and Company, 1976.

Bahr, H. M., and K. C. Houts. "Can You Trust a Homeless Man? A Comparison of Official Records and Interview Responses by Bowery Men." *Public Opinion Quarterly*, 1971, 35: 374-82.

Instrument

See Instrument V2.8.I.c.

SOCIAL INTEGRATION OF THE AGED IN CHURCHES

D. O. Moberg, 1965

Definition of Concept or Variable:

An age-integrated church is one in which older people are expected to be integral parts of a church that provides no speical age-segregated programs for the elderly.

Description of Instrument

In this longer personal interview, 31 questions with nested items are concerned with religion. These questions address these areas: (1) church friendship network, (2) devotional activities, (3) church membership and participation, (4) leadership roles, (5) church-group memberships and participation, (6) evaluation of church activities, (7) age composition of church groups, (8) feelings of involvement in the church, (9) attitudes toward religion, and (0) reactions to various aspects of the church program. A modified Burgess-Cavan-Havighurst Attitude Inventory (1948), including the religion subscale, was also included. (See the abstract for the Attitude Inventory in Chapter 5 of Volume 1.)

Method of Administration

No time estimate is given for this personal interview.

Context of Development

The instrument was developed to study the social policy statement and recommendation of the 1961 White House Conference on Aging that "every effort shall be made to see that these (special services, educational materials, and programs for the aged) do not involve an unnecessary separation from the mainstream of familial or congregational life." Support was provided by a research grant from the Hill Family Foundation and the Kansas City Association of Trusts and Foundations through the Midwest Council for Social Research on Aging. The study questions the philosophy of social integration in congregations.

Sample

Four churches from one Protestant denomination in the Minneapolis-St. Paul area were identified as having the most complete patterns of involvement of members past the age of 65. Two of these were chosen for the study. The chief criteria in the selection were basic similarities in history, size, location, denominational cooperation, and theological perspectives and a difference in their orientation toward senior citizens. A purposive sample of 55 older adults in the Senior Club Church and 76 older adults in a conventional church were interviewed. The respondents' ages ranged from 65 to over 90.

Usability on Older Populations

The use of the measure is restricted to use with adults aged 65 and older. No problems have been reported.

General Comments and Recommendations

Moberg (1965) reported that inconsistencies in response noted by interviewers, together with the small, selective nature of the sample, suggest that further reliability and validity testing of this exploratory instrument should be conducted before it is used widely.

References

Burgess, E. W., R. S. Cavan, and R. J. Havighurst. *Your Activities and Attitudes*. Chicago: Science Research Associates, 1948.

Moberg, D. O. "The Integration of Older Members in the Church Congregation." In *Older People and Their Social World*, M. Rose and W. A. Peterson (eds.), pp. 125-40. Philadelphia: F. A. Davis, 1965.

Instrument

See Instrument V2.8.I.d.

RELIGIOUS COMMITMENT

C. Y. Glock and R. Stark, 1966; R. Stark, 1968

Definition of Concept or Variable

Glock and Stark (1966) originally defined religious commitment as a complex phenomenon with five dimensions of religiosity: belief, ritual, experience, knowledge, and consequence. Stark (1968) studied three of the dimensions—belief, ritual, and experience—in his work on age and faith.

Description of Instrument

The items that measure the dimension are a part of a larger questionnaire containing over 500 items. For measures of age and faith, Glock and Stark selected the following subscales: (1) orthodoxy index: a measure of belief that consists of four weighted multiple-choice items; (2) ritual involvement and devotionalism: a measure consisting of four involvement items with frequency or intensity of feeling as the response; (3) experience: three items identifying subjective experiences constitute a religious experience index.

Method of Administration

The measure is self-administered through a mailed survey. The time of administration should be 10 minutes or less.

Context of Development

The indexes of religiosity were constructed as a part of the Christian beliefs study conducted in 1965 at the University of California, Berkeley.

Sample(s)

The random sample was of the church-member population of four counties in the San Francisco area. All the Protestant and Catholic congregations in the area were included in the sampling frame. Mailed questionnaires were sent to 3,000 persons selected from 97 Protestant congregations and 21 Catholic parishes; 2,326 Protestants and 545 Roman Catholics returned the questionnaires (Glock and Stark, 1966).

Telephone interviews were conducted with random samples of Protestant and Catholic nonrespondents to assess the return-rate bias.

Scoring, Scale Norms, and Distribution

The instrument is scored by simple addition. On the orthodoxy index, 1 point is scored for certainty of Christian position (responses 1a, 2a, 3d, and 4a); other responses are scored 0. Scores range from 0 to 4. Persons who fail to answer any of the four questions are not scored. On the ritual involvement index, persons who attend church every (or nearly every) week (a, b) and who say grace at least once a week (a, b) are classified as involved. On the devotionalism index, persons who feel that prayer is extremely important (2a) and pray privately at least once a week (13 f, g) are scored high; medium when they are devotional in either item; and low when they are not devotional on both items. On the experience index, Persons who think they have experienced all three states are scored high; medium when they claim to have had one or two of the three experiences; and low when they have had none of these experiences.

Usability on Older Populations

The sample included adults 18 to over 70 years of age. No difficulty was reported with using the measure on the older respondents, but it is restricted to use with Christian (church) samples.

Sensitivity to Age Differences

Stark (1968) reported that: (1) a meaningful shift in orthodoxy with age occurs between the ages of 40 and 50 years in the conservative and moderate Protestant groups; (2) the relationship between age and ritual participation is slight; (3) private devotionalism increases with age; and (4) the tendency to have religious experiences does not increase with age.

General Comments and Recommendations

The Glock and Stark (1966) indexes were designed to measure commitment to the Christian faith and the organized Christian churches. The one significant age effect Stark identified is on the devotional index, which includes only two items related to one devotional activity —private prayer. Generalizations about increasing piety with age or the function of religion for older persons based on this limited and narrow index must be tentative. Researchers are encouraged to use (within the cited limitations) the selected items from Glock and Stark's Dimensions of Religious Commitment in the study of age and religiosity.

References

Glock, C. Y., and R. Stark. *Christian Beliefs and Anti-Semitism*. New York: Harper and Row, 1966.

Stark, R. "Age and Faith: A Changing Outlook as an Old Process." *Sociological Analysis*, 1968, 29:1-10.

Instrument

See Instrument V2.8.I.e.

RELIGIOUS COMMITMENT

B. Pittard, 1963

Definition of Variable or Concept

The concept of commitment is defined by a cluster of categories that form three levels of commitment: (1) the individual, which represents the internalized aspects of commitment, e.g., beliefs in, feelings for, and impulse toward God, Christ, and church; choices of personal moral code, and a sense of personal responsibility for the achievement of the goals of the religious organization; (2) the collective, which represents the communal and relational aspects, e.g., feelings of closeness to sources of power and relevance for performance of social roles outside the church; and (3) the actional, which represents involvement in the ritual and activities of the organization (Payne, 1966).

Description of Instrument

This Likert-type scale of 24 items was designed to measure three conceptual dimensions of commitment. Respondents indicate their opinion on a five-point scale from strongly agree to strongly disagree.

Method of Administration

The instrument can be self-administered or included in an interview. Approximately 20 to 30 minutes are required for completing the items.

Context of Development and Subsequent Use

The scale was developed for the Protestant Parish Study supported by the National Division of the Board of Missions of the United Methodist Church. The original scale of 40 items was administered to a test sample and then revised to 24 items; the revision was administered to a national sample of Methodists in 1967. The original 40-item scale was included in King and Hunt's (1969) development of the dimensions of commitment. The revised scale was included in the misdemeanant study of the Georgia Committee of the National Council on Crime and Delinquency (Pittard, 1969) and in the Georgia State Longitudinal Study of the Older Volunteer (1974-1978) conducted by Payne and Bull (Payne and Mobley, 1977).

Sample(s)

The 1962 sample included rural Methodist church members in Georgia (N = 123) and urban Methodist church members in downtown Atlanta (N = 281). The ages of the respondents ranged from 15 to 85 years.

The 1967 national sample (Pittard, 1969; Payne and Mobley, 1977) consisted of 1,118 Methodist church members stratified by geographical region and size of church. Respondents ranged from 15 to 75 years of age and over, with 10% over 65 years of age.

The longitudinal sample included a volunteer panel from senior centers in Atlanta (N = 125) and Kansas City (N = 68) and the Andrus Gerontology Center volunteers (N = 38).

Between 1974 and 1978, a random sample of Retired Senior Volunteer Program (RSVP) volunteers was studied in Atlanta (N = 100) and Kansas City (N = 100). Ages ranged from 50 to 92 years.

Scoring, Scale Norms, and Distribution

Items 1, 5, 10, 14, 17, 18, 19, 23, 24 are reversed in scoring so that a response of strongly agree receives 5 points. The following scores are possible: (1) a total commitment score that is derived from the simple summation of the 24 items (range of 24 to 120) and (2) three subscales that range from 8 to 40. Items 1 through 8 are summed for the individual dimension, items 9 through 16 are summed for the communal dimension, and items 17 through 24 are summed for the actional dimension.

The total scale and three subscale scores are converted to a 5-point scale by dividing the scores by the number of applicable items. In the 1962 sample, 27.7% of the respondents reported low (1.0 through 3.34), 44.6% reported medium (3.35 through 3.76), and 27.7% reported high (3.77 through 5.0) commitment scores.

Formal Tests of Reliability

Intra- and interdimension correlations were analyzed in revising the scale and subscales from 40 to 24 items. Each item in the 24-item scale is significantly related to items in the same subscale.

Formal Tests of Validity

Ten judges evaluated an initial item pool of 100 for content and ranked each item on a five-point scale of low to high commitment (Payne, 1966). These 100 items were pretested with a sample of 50 respondents aged 15 to 50, and 40 items were chosen as the most discriminating.

Usability on Older Populations

The scale is usable for functionally capable older populations. Forced choice responses may result in some subject ambivalence.

Sensitivity to Age Differences

Studies report a significant relationship between age and commitment (Payne, 1966; Payne and Mobley, 1977). The relationship is not linear. Commitment declines for the young adult (20 to 24 years of age), increases until mid-life, and then begins to decline.

General Comments and Recommendations

Payne and Mobley (1977) recommended that reducing the forced choices from 50 to 4 ([1] strongly agree, [2] somewhat agree, [3] somewhat disagree, [4] strongly disagree]) would increase the measure's usability with all age-groups and the elderly in particular. They reported that items 6, 9, and 15 show a period effect, and they recommended that these items be dropped and new items developed. For use with elderly subjects, and for more sensitivity to age differences, the new items should identify informal religious participation activities and reflect the religious experiences, beliefs, and activities and the use of religion in coping unique to older persons. The length and wording of the items make this test appropriate for use with a variety of older populations.

References

King, M. B., and R. A. Hunt. "Measuring the Religious Variable: Amended Findings." *Journal for the Scientific Study of Religion*, 1969, 8:321-23.

Payne, B. P. *The Meaning and Measurement of Commitment to the Church*. Atlanta: Georgia State University, special publication number 13, 1966.

Payne, B. P., E. D. C. Brewer, T. Runyon, and H. McSwain. *The Protestant Parish*. Atlanta: Communicative Arts Press, 1969.

Payne, B. P., and M. Mobley. "Age and Period Effects in Religious Commitment Scales." Paper presented to the Annual Meeting of the Society for the Scientific Study of Religion, Chicago, October 27-30, 1977.

Pittard, B. B. (Payne). "The Meaning and Measurement of Commitment to the Church." Ph.D. dissertation, Emory University, 1963.

_____. "Commitment to Religion and the Church: A Study Using a National Sample." Paper presented to the annual meeting of the Society for the Scientific Study of Religion, Boston, October 1969.

_____. "Profile of the Convicted Misdemeanant, Atlanta Metropolitan Area, 1965-1967." Paper presented to the Fourteenth Annual Conference on Corrections, Tallahassee, Fla., February 11, 1969.

Instrument

See Instrument V2.8.I.f.

DIMENSIONS OF RELIGION

M. B. King, 1967; M. B. King and R. A. Hunt, 1969; 1972; 1975

Definition of Concept or Variable

Religion has a number of dimensions. King (1967) proposed 9 dimensions of religion; King and Hunt (1969) revised this number to 11 and then 10 (King and Hunt, 1972; 1975) constructs to measure the source and consequences of individual differences in religious behavior.

Description of Instrument

Factor analysis was applied to 121 items, some collected from other religiosity studies and some developed for this study (King, 1967); and 9 constructs that were relatively consistent across 3 analyses emerged. King and Hunt (1969) used an item scale analysis on these same data to propose 11 deminsions measured by 61 alternative response items. King and Hunt (1975) proposed the 10 dimensions that will be reviewed in this abstract: (1) creedal assent, (2) devotionalism, (3) church attendance, (4) organizational activity, (5) financial support, (6) orientation to religion: growth and striving, (7) orientation to religion: religious despair, (8) salience: behavior, (9) salience: cognition, and (10) active regulars.

The last three dimensions (8, 9, and 10) are composite scales that include items from the prior dimensions. King and Hunt (1975) also reported on three cognitive-style scales that are not reviewed here; however, their earlier work (1972) examined several additional dimensions not included in the 1975 national replication. Two are measures of congregational involvement and are largely composed of items from the 10 scales. They are: (1) the index of general activity, and (2) the index of belief and commitment. Other dimensions included in the 1972 report included: (1) religious knowledge, (2) extrinsic orientation to religion (Allport items), and (3) extrinsic orientation to religion (original items). Thus, a total of 15 dimensions of religion are included in this instrument.

Method of Administration

The instrument is self-administered and requires 20 to 25 minutes to complete.

Context of Development and Subsequent Use

A pilot study conducted in 1965 (King, 1967; King and Hunt, 1969) and a larger study in 1968 (King and Hunt, 1972) of religiosity were partially supported by the Graduate Council of the Humanities at Southern Methodist University and agencies of several Protestant denominations. The 1965 questionnaire used 121 items from the research literature on religiosity, including Fukuyama (1961), Glock (1954), Lenski (1961) Demerath (1965), Allport (1960), Brown (1964), Feagin (1964), Fichter (1953; 1954), Maranell (no date), Pittard (1963), and Whitman (1957; 1962). The 1968 questionnaire is a revision based on factor analysis and item analysis and some rewording of the items.

The national replication study (King and Hunt, 1975) included 98 items, of which 61 items represented 8 basic religious scales and 3 cognitive-style scales. An additional 37 items were developed by Hoge that measured priorities for an individual's congregation and several independent variables (King and Hunt, 1975, p. 14).

Sample(s)

The 1965 and 1968 samples were homogeneous and locally representative of each denomination. The purpose of the studies was to identify dimensions and develop scales. The 1965 sample examined six methodist congregations; the 1968 sample included six Disciples congregations, four Lutheran-Missouri Synods, five Presbyterian congregations, and six United Methodist congregations. The size of the congregation determined the proportion of members selected. Names were selected randomly from an alphabetical roster, with 1,356 cases selected by this method.

The national replication sample was a Presbyterian panel selected by stratified random procedures. Questionnaires were mailed to a representative 1,990 lay persons; only 872 provided usable responses. Nonrespondents were overrepresented among infrequent church attenders, males, and less-educated persons (King and Hunt, 1975, p. 15).

Scoring, Scale Norms, and Distribution

A scoring key is incorporated into the items listed in the instrument. A raw score is the sum of the item responses for each dimension. Standard scores with a mean of 50.0 and a standard deviation of 10 are also computed within each dimension. Table 8-2 lists the standardized means by age and the overall (raw) means and standard deviations (King and Hunt, 1972).

Formal Tests of Reliability

For the 1965 data (King and Hunt, 1969), Cronbach's alpha ranged from .681 to .906, with an average of .791. In the 1968 data (King and Hunt, 1972), alpha ranged from .715 to .872; some specific estimates for each scale for the 1968 and 1973 data accompany the instrument.

Formal Tests of Validity

King (1967) suggested 11 dimensions based on a literature review, and many of these dimensions have emerged empirically in factor analyses of the data. Cross-loading of the items suggests some confounding of the measures, however.

TABLE 8-2
Means, Standard Deviations, and Standardized
Mean Scale Scores by Age, 1968 Sample

The Scales N =	Under 21 145	21-34 369	35-54 547	55 and Over 289[a]	Raw Mean	Standard Deviation
I. Creedal Assent	45.2[b]	48.8	50.3	53.4	25.2	3.76
II. Devotionalism	47.3	47.0	50.1	54.9	15.8	3.77
IIIA. Church Attendance	49.3	48.9	50.1	51.3	9.1	2.70
IIIB. Organizational Activity	49.2	49.4	49.9	51.4	13.7	4.81
IIIC. Financial Support	46.0	46.1	51.1	54.7	13.1	3.79
IV. Religious Knowledge	46.9	50.2	50.8	49.9	20.6	13.20
VA. Growth and Striving	45.0	46.8	50.4	55.8	17.2	3.87
VB. Extrinsic Orientation	48.6	47.1	48.7	56.5	17.1	4.68
VIA. Salience: Behavior	47.7	47.8	49.5	54.7	13.4	4.37
VIB. Salience: Cognition	45.6	47.7	50.5	54.1	16.4	3.26
VII. Proreligious Response Set	46.0	47.4	49.6	55.9	20.2	4.66

a. Six respondents omitted the item.
b. The means of transformed scores: where for 1,356 cases mean = 50.0 and standard deviation = 10.0. Differences between means of about 5.0 and greater are probably statistically significant at the .05 level.

SOURCE: M. B. King and R. A. Hunt. *Measuring Religious Dimensions: Studies of Congregational Involvement*. Studies in Social Science, number 1. Dallas: Southern Methodist University, 1972. This table was constructed from Table IV-13 (p. 123) and Table V-10 (p. 136). Reprinted by permission of authors.

Usability on Older Populations

Persons aged 65 and older were included in the sample, and no problems were reported. The length of the instrument and the forced choice reponses limit its usefulness with some older people. The item content restricts the use of this instrument to Protestant populations.

Sensitivity to Age Differences

In general, older persons score higher on these measures of religiosity. (See Table 8-2.) However, it remains to be determined whether this is an age, period, or cohort effect.

General Comments and Recommendations

This scale includes the most discriminating items from the major studies of religiosity and have been submitted to rigorous factor analysis. Although the scale is biased toward church-related religiosity, it provides a more extensive measure of informal and privatized (Glock's devotional) religiosity.

References

Allport, G. "Religion and Prejudice". In *Personality and Social Encounter*, G. Allport (ed.), pp. 257-67. Boston: Beacon Press, 1960.

Brown, L. B. "Classification of Religious Orientation." *Journal for the Scientific Study of Religion*, 1964, 4:91-99.

Demerath, N. J. *Social Class in American Protestantism*. Skokie, Ill.: Rand McNally, 1965.

Feagin, J. R. "Prejudice and Religious Types." *Journal for the Scientific Study of Religion*, 1964, 4:3-13.

Fichter, J. H. "The Marginal Catholic: An Institutional Approach." *Social Forces*, 1953, 32: 167-73.

───────. *Social Relations in the Urban Parish*. Chicago: University of Chicago Press, 1954.

Fukuyama, Y. "The Major Dimensions of Church Membership." *Review of Religious Research*, 1961, 2:154-61.

Glock, C. Y. *Toward a Typology of Religious Orientation*. New York: Bureau of Applied Social Research, Columbia University, 1954.

King, M. B. "Measuring the Religious Variable: Nine Proposed Dimensions." *Journal for the Scientific Study of Religion*, 1967, 6:173-90.

King, M. B., and R. A. Hunt. "Measuring the Religious Variable: Amended Findings." *Journal for the Scientific Study of Religion*, 1969, 8:321-23.

───────. *Measuring Religious Dimensions: Studies of Congregational Involvement*. Studies in Social Science, number 1. Dallas: Southern Methodist University, 1972.

───────. "Measuring the Religious Variable: National Replication." *Journal for the Scientific Study of Relition*, 1975, 14:13-22.

Lenski, G. *The Religious Factor*. Garden City, N.Y.: Doubleday, 1961.

Maranell, G. M. "An Instrument for the Measurement of Some Dimensions of Religiosity or Religious Attitudes." Fayetteville, Ark.: University of Arkansas, no date.

Pittard, B. B. (Payne). "The Meaning and Measurement of Commitment to the Church." Ph.D. dissertation, Emory University, 1963.

Whitman, F. L. "Subdimensions of Religiosity as Related to Race Prejudice." M.A. thesis, Indiana University, 1957.

───────. "Subdimensions of Religiosity and Race Prejudice." *Review of Religios Research*, 1962, 3:166-74.

Instrument

See Instrument V2.8.I.g.

MEASURES OF RELIGIOUS INVOLVEMENT

H. S. Himmelfarb, 1975

Definition of Concept or Variable

Religious involvement is defined conceptually by a typology of religious involvement that includes four general orientations to religiosity: (1) supernatural, (2) communal, (3) cultural, and (4) interpersonal. The religious involvement scale is designed to measure the type, frequency, and intensity of religious involvement in nine dimensions and three subdimensions identified by the typology.

Description of Instrument

The scale consists of 54 Likert and 7 Guttman items designed to measure the dimensions of religious involvement.

Method of Administration

The scale is administered as a mailed questionnaire.

Context of Development and Subsequent Use

Developed as a part of a larger study of American religious life at the University of Chicago, the scale emphasized the development of a typology as a means of defining and classifying dimensions of religious involvement and the synthesis of previous work in a fairly comprehensive manner.

Sample

Persons having distinctively Jewish names in the Chicago Jewish schools (to assure a substantial number of cases with some secondary and higher Jewish education) were sampled. A 30% response rate yielded a total sample of 1,278, of which 234 (approximately 18%) were from the school alumni sample. Himmelfarb (1975) reported that the sample tended to be more middle-aged (25 to 55 years old), educated, professional, wealthy, and religiously committed than a more representative sample of Chicago Jews.

Scoring, Scale Norms, and Distribution

Respondents were asked to strongly agree, agree, disagree, or strongly disagree with statements in the following areas: (1) doctrinal-experiential, (2) associational, (3) fraternal, (4) parental, (5) ideological, (6) intellectual-esthetic, and (7) ethical-moral. Summary measures for each of these dimensions are obtained by standardizing each item and weighting each variable by its factor score coefficient and summing across these products for each factor. The items and their corresponding weights accompany the instrument.

The devotional-ritual observance items were scored as a Guttman scale, with 1 point allocated for practicing each ritual. The items and the rankings of items' difficulty accompany the instrument.

Formal Tests of Reliability/Homogeneity

A nine-factor solution emerged from a factor analysis of the data. Two of the factors (factors II and V) form a Guttman scale. The Guttman devotional-ritual scale yielded a .91 coefficient of reproducibility and a .72 coefficient of scaleability (Himmelfarb, 1975).

Formal Tests of Validity

The eight dimensions exhibited intercorrelations in the range of .25 to .66. A second-order factor analysis of these eight dimensions resulted in a single-factor solution, with all eight scales loading on that factor by at least .48. Communalities ranged from .23 to .70 in this analysis, and a total of 48.5% of the variance was explained (Himmelfarb, 1975).

The eight scales were correlated with an ordinal measure of denominational identification (i.e., nondenominational, reform, reconstructionist, conservative, traditional, and orthodox). Spearman rank-order correlations ranged from .31 to .72.

For construct validity, denominational identification among American Jews formed a simple ordinal scale of religious involvement. Each of the scales is correlated with denominational self-identification.

Usability on Older Populations

The usefulness of the scale is limited to a Jewish sample.

General Comments and Recommendations

One major criticism of most religiosity scales and commitment tests (Fukuyama, 1961; Glock and Stark, 1966; King and Hunt, 1969; Pittard, 1963) is their bias toward a Christian population. This Jewish religiosity scale provides an appropriate measure for a neglected segment of the older population. The typology and dimensions provide a synthesis and a scheme for a universal interpretation of religiosity. In future research on religiosity and the elderly that includes an interfaith sample, Christian and Jewish scales measuring the same dimension should be included (e.g., Glock and Stark's communal dimension and Himmelfarb's communal dimensions). Utilizing these in the same instrument makes it possible to employ specific measures of religiosity appropriate for different faith groups. Thus, the possibility of error in labeling items "not applicable" or the confusion resulting from items irrelevant to specific faiths is eliminated.

References

Fukuyama, Y. "The Major Dimensions of Church Membership." *Review of Religious Research*, 1961, 2:154-61.

Glock, C. Y., and R. Stark. *Christian Beliefs and Anti-Semitism.* New York: Harper and Row, 1966.

Himmelfarb, H. S. "Measuring Religious Involvement." *Social Forces*, 1975, 53:607-18.

King, M. B., and R. A. Hunt. "Measuring the Religious Variable: Amended Findings." *Journal for the Scientific Study of Religion*, 1969, 8:321-23.

Pittard, B. (Payne). "The Meaning and Measurement of Commitment to the Church." Ph.D. dissertation, Emory University, 1963.

Instrument

See Instrument V2.8.I.h.

ATTITUDES TOWARD THE CHURCH AND RELIGION

B. D. Bell, 1971

Definition of Concept or Variable

Religiosity is the degree of religious interest or belief manifested by a church member; it is defined by scores on two subscales: (1) attitudes toward the church and (2) attitudes toward religion. Church participation is defined as attendance at worship services.

Description of Instrument

The two Likert-type subscales were a part of a social participation interview. The 12 items on Attitudes toward the Church measure membership behavioral expectations; the two items on Attitudes toward Religion measure doctrinal orthodoxy.

Method of Administration

Although they were originally part of a personal interview, the attitude tests were self-administered.

Context of Development and Subsequent Use

Developed as a part of the larger research project for a master's thesis at Kansas State University, the items were based on the positions of the United Methodist Church.

Sample

A purposive sample of 60 male members of a United Methodist church in Manhattan, Kans., was drawn. Typical respondents were white-collar workers married and living with their spouses and in relatively good health.

Sensitivity to Age Differences

The measures of religiosity and church participation correlated with age, but not with family life stage.

Summary Assessment of Reliability and Validity

Its limited sample and denominational biases limit the usefulness of the instrument. The family-life-cycle explanation of church participation seems limited, and this study is too restricted to determine the value of the life-cycle measure. Albrecht (1959) did find that life-cycle stage related to religiosity. More research, both cross-sectional and longitudinal, is needed to test the reliability and validity of the life-cycle stage's influence on religious participation.

References

Albrecht, R. "The Meaning of Religion to Older People — The Social Aspect." In *Organized Religion and the Older Person*, D. L. Scudder (ed.), pp. 53-70. Gainesville, Fla.: University of Florida Press, 1958.

_____. *A Profile of East Alabama Families.* Alabama Agricultural Experiment Station, 1959.

Bell, B. D. "Church Participation and the Family Life Cycle." *Review of Religious Research*, 1971, 13 (1):57-64.

Instrument

See Instrument V2.8.I.i.

Instruments

V2.8.I.a

RELIGIOSITY

H. L. Orbach, 1961

About how often, if ever, have you attended religious services in the past year? (1) once a week or more, (2) two or three times a month, (3) once a month, (4) a few times a year or less (5) never.

SOURCE: H. L. Orbach. "Aging and Religion." *Geriatrics*, 1961, 16:534. Reprinted from *Geriatrics* © 1961, by Harcourt Brace Jovanovich, Inc.

V2.8.I.b

INTRINSIC RELIGIOUS MOTIVATION SCALE

D. R. Hoge, 1972

Instrument: (Stimulus direction noted in parthentheses)

1. My faith involves all of my life. (I)
2. One should seek God's guidance when making every important decision. (I)
3. In my life I experience the presence of the Divine. (I)
4. My faith sometimes restricts my actions. (I)
5. Nothing is as important to me as serving God as best I know how. (I)
6. I try hard to carry my religion over into all of my other dealings in life. (I)
7. My religious beliefs are what really lie behind my whole approach to life. (I)
8. It doesn't matter so much what I believe as long as I lead a moral life. (E)
9. Although I am a religious person, I refuse to let religious considerations influence my everyday affairs. (E)
10. Although I believe in my religion, I feel there are many more important things in life. (E)

SOURCE: D. R. Hoge. "A Validated Intrinsic Religious Motivation Scale." *Journal for the Scientific Study of Religion*, 1972, 11:371. Reprinted by permission of the author and publisher.

V2.8.I.c

RELIGIOUS DISAFFILIATION

H. M. Bahr and T. Caplow, 1973

DISAFFILIATION INDEX

Item 1

Have you ever attended church or synagogue services, either as a child or as an adult? (Do not include attendance at mission services.)

a. No (end interview)

b. Yes

Item 2

What is your religious preference?

a. Protestant: What denomination?

b. Catholic

c. Greek or Russian Orthodox

d. Jewish

e. Other (specify) (skip to question 5)

f. No preference (skip to question 5)

Item 3

(If Catholic or Greek or Russian Orthodox) Did you take first communion?

(If Protestant) Were you ever confirmed, or baptized at any time besides at birth?

(If Jewish) Were you every Bar Mitzvahed? (skip to question 5)

a. No (skip to question 5)

b. Yes

Item 4

At what age?

Item 5

Do you recall how old you were the first time you went?

Item 6

When was the last time you went? (date or age)

Item 7

Has there ever been a time, from your childhood until now, when you went to church regularly —say, almost every week?

a. No (ask question 8, then skip to question 13)

b. Yes (skip to question 9)

Item 8

Could you give me a general idea about how much you have attended church throughout your life? (probe for changes)

Item 9

How old were you when you first began to go that often?

Item 10

How long did that last?

Item 11

Was there another time after that when you went almost every week?

a. No

b. Yes (ask "when?" and "how long did that last?" for each period)

Item 12

Since then, how often have you gone? (probe for changes)

Item 13

Did you ever have any special duties or position in the church (such as committee member, elder, choir boy, or altar boy)?

a. No (skip to question 16)

b. Yes

Item 14

What did you do?

Item 15

When was that?

Item 16

As an adult, has your name ever acutally been on the membership rolls of any particular church?

a. No (end interview)

b. Yes.

Item 17

When did you join? (date or age)

Item 18

How long were you a member (Probe: any other churches?)
(ask questions 17 and 18 for each)

Item 19

What do you feel are the most important things in life?

Item 20

Do you have any guiding principle (or principles) in life? What is it?

SOURCE: H. M. Bahr and T. Caplow. *Old Men Drunk and Sober*, pp. 366-68. New York: New York University Press, 1973. © by New York University, used by permission of the authors and New York University Press.

V2.8.I.d

SOCIAL INTEGRATION OF THE AGED IN CHURCHES

D. O. Moberg, 1965

1. Would you say that you have ____close friends? (Insert the total number of close friends.)
2. How many of these persons attend the same church as you do? ____
3. We know that people differ a great deal in their devotional activities. I would like to ask you a few questions about how often you engage in certain activities. (This applies to religious activies which occur outside the church.)

	At least twice each day	At least once each day	At least twice each week	At least once each week	Less than once each week	Never
a. How often do you *listen to religious programs* on radio or television?						
b. How often do you *read the Bible*?						
c. How often do you *read other religious materials* like magazines, papers, or books?						
d. How often do you *say grace* or have prayer before meals, either aloud or silently?						
e. How often do you *pray*, other than grace at meals?						

4. Are you a church member now?
   _____yes
   _____no (skip to question 25)

5. Of what church are you a member?_____

6. When did you join this church?_____ (skip to question 26)

7. Have you ever been a church member?
   _____yes
   _____ no (skip to question 30) (If no) Why?_____

8. Of what churches were you *formerly* a member?_____

9. How long were you a member of these churches?_____ (List total years for all former churches together.)

10. When did you stop belonging to the last church? _____

11. *Why* did you drop or change your membership?_____

12. In an average month, how many times do you attend:
    (a). Sunday morning worship service?_____(times per month)
    (b). Sunday School?_____(times per month)
    (c). Sunday evening service?_____(times per month)
    (d). Midweek service?_____(times per month)

13. What offices or other positions do you now hold in the church? List each. (Include: usher, Sunday school teacher, etc., as well as offices held, but do *not* incude organization offices, e.g., president of the women's society.)

14. What organizations in the church do you attend? (Ask the following questions for each organization they attend.)

(1) Name of organization or activity	(2) How many times per month do you attend	(3) What offices do you now hold in this organization	(4) How many committees are you on in this organization?	(5) Are you now about as active, more active, or less active in this organization than in your 50's?			(6) Are most of the people who attend this organization			
				More now	Less now	Same now	Young	Middle aged	Older adult	Elderly
WOMAN's SOCIETY										
MEN'S BROTHER-HOOD										
SENIOR CITIZEN'S GROUP										
OTHER (list)										

15. Do you engage in any other church related activities? (Church visitation, service projects, denominational projects, etc.) (List each.)

16. Do you usually attend church business meetings?
    _____yes, always
    _____no, never
    _____sometimes

17. Which church activities do you enjoy the most? (This may include services; meetings of organizations; service projects; or any other church-related activities.)

18. Do you prefer to have separate activities in church for people your age or do you prefer activities in which all ages participate?
    _____prefer separate activities
    _____prefer integrated activities
    _____prefer some of each
    _____makes no difference

19. Do you think that there ought to be more organizations and activities in your church for people of your age group?
    _____yes Comments:
    _____no
    _____don't know or uncertain

20. How often do you feel that you are left out of things at church?
    _____often
    _____sometimes
    _____never

21. Would you like to take a more active part in church?
    _____ yes
    _____ no

22. Why don't you (want to) take a more active part? Because:
    _____ younger members won't let you
    _____ other people are more competent
    _____ of failing health
    _____ there are no activities for people your age
    _____ people don't want you
    _____ you don't have enough time
    _____ other (list)

23. Were you more active or less active in *church activities* in your early fifties than you are now?
    _____ more active then   Why?
    _____ less active then
    _____ same

24. Please name the church activities in which you were active during your early fifties but in which you no longer take part.

25. Which of these reasons describe why you quit holding such positions?
    _____ I was nominated but not elected
    _____ I was not wanted when I got old
    _____ I thought someone else should take their turn
    _____ I thought someone else could do the work better
    _____ I wanted a rest from church work
    _____ I was not able to do the work because of illness or disability
    _____ I had too many family responsibilities
    _____ I had too many other community and club activities
    _____ No one is allowed to serve consecutive terms
    _____ I changed to a different church
    _____ My elected term expired
    _____ Other reasons (list)

26. Do you listen to religious programs on radio or television more or less now than you did in your early fifties?
    _____ more now
    _____ less now
    _____ same

27. Do you read the Bible more now or less now than you did in your early fifties?
    _____ more now
    _____ less now
    _____ about the same

28. Do you read other religious materials more or less now than you did in your early fifties?
    _____ more now
    _____ less now
    _____ about the same

29. Do you say grace or have prayer before meals more often or less often now than in your early fifties?
    _____ more now

_____ less now

_____ about the same

30. Do you pray more or less now than you did in your early fifties?

_____ more now

_____ less now

_____ about the same

31. If you had a chance to live your life over again, would you be

_____ more religous?

_____ less religious?

_____ or just as religious as you were?

SOURCE: D. O. Moberg. "The Integration of Older Members in the Church Congregation." In _Older People and Their Social World_, A. M. Rose and W. A. Peterson (eds.), p. 127. Philadelphia: F. A. Davis, 1965.

V2.8.I.e

RELIGOUS COMMITMENT

C. Y. Glock and R. Stark, 1966; Stark, 1968

I. Belief Dimension

A. Orthodoxy Index

1. Which of the following statements comes closest to expressing what you believe about God? (Please check only one answer.)

   a) I know God really exists and I have no doubts about it.

   b) While I have doubts, I feel that I do believe in God.

   c) I find myself believing in God some of the time, but not at other times.

   d) I don't believe in a personal God, but I do believe in a higher power of some kind.

   e) I don't know whether there is a God and I don't believe there is any way to find out.

   f) I don't believe in God.

   g) None of the above represents what I believe. What I believe about God is

   _____

   (please specify)

2. Which of the following statements comes closest to expressing what you believe about Jesus? (Check only one answer.)

   a) Jesus is the Divine Son of God and I have no doubts about it.

   b) While I have some doubts, I feel basically that Jesus is Divine.

   c) I feel that Jesus was a great man and very holy, but I don't feel Him to be the Son of God any more than all of us are children of God.

   d) I think that Jesus was only a man although an extraordinary one.

   e) Frankly, I'm not entirely sure there was such a person as Jesus.

   f) None of the above represents what I believe. What I believe about Jesus is

   _____

   (please specify)

3. The Bible tells of many miracles, some credited to Christ and some to other proph-

ets and apostles. Generally speaking, which of the following statements comes closest to what you believe about Biblical miracles? (Check only one answer.)

a) I'm not sure whether these miracles really happened or not.
b) I believe miracles are stories and never really happened.
c) I believe the miracles happened, but can be explained by natural causes.
d) I believe the miracles actually happened just as the Bible says they did.

4. The Devil actually exists. (Check how certain you are this is true.)

a) Completely true
b) Probably true
c) Probably not true
d) Definitely not true

II. Ritual Dimension

A. Ritual Participation Index

1. How often do you attend Sunday worship services? (Check the answer which comes closest to describing what you do.)

a) Every week
b) Nearly every week
c) About three times a month
d) About twice a month
e) About once a month
f) About every six weeks
g) About every three months
h) About once or twice a year
i) Less than once a year
j) Never

2. How often, if at all, are table prayers or grace said before or after meals in your home?

a) We say grace at all meals.
b) We say grace at least once a day.
c) We say grace at least once a week.
d) We say grace, but only on special occasions.
e) We never, or hardly ever, say grace.

B. Devotionalism Index

1. How often do you pray privately? (Check the answer which comes closest to what you do.)

a) I never pray, or only do so at church services.
b) I pray only on very special occasions.
c) I pray once in a while, but not at regular intervals.
d) I pray quite often, but not at regular times.
e) I pray regularly once a day or more.
f) I pray regularly several times a week.
g) I pray regularly once a week.

2. How important is prayer in your life?

a) Extremely important
b) Fairly important

      c) Not too important

      d) Not important

III. Experiential Dimension

    A. Religious Experience Index

        Listed below are a number of experiences of a religious nature which people have reported having. Since you have been an adult have you ever had any of these experiences, and how sure are you that you had it?

	Yes, I'm sure I have	Yes, I think I have	No
*A feeling that you were somehow in the presence of God . . .	_____	_____	____
*A sense of being saved in Christ . . .	_____	_____	____
*A feeling of being punished by God for something you had done . . .	_____	_____	____

SOURCE: C. Y. Glock and R. Stark. *Christian Beliefs and Anti-Semitism*. New York, Harper and Row, 1966, p. 215.

V2.8.I.f

RELIGIOUS COMMITMENT

B. Pittard, 1963

Below are some statements about religion with which some people agree and others disagree. Give us your opinion about these statements, that is, whether you agree or disagree with them as they are stated. Your replies will be treated confidentially and you need not sign your name. Please read each statement and circle the appropriate number to represent your opinion, as follows:

           Circle 1 for Strongly Agree
           Circle 2 for Agree
           Circle 3 for Uncertain
           Circle 4 for Disagree
           Circle 5 for Strongly Disagree
           (Circle *one* number for each statement)

(1) 1 2 3 4 5 There is no meaning in life apart from a relationship to God in Christ.

(2) 1 2 3 4 5 It doesn't matter where you go to church; the important thing is to believe.

(3) 1 2 3 4 5 Keeping the "golden rule" is all that is necessary to live the Christian life.

(4) 1 2 3 4 5 The principles I have come to believe in are quite different from those held by most church members.

(5) 1 2 3 4 5 I feel closest to God in a worship service.

(6) 1 2 3 4 5 A Buddhist can live just as good a life as a Christian and his religion helps him as much as any other religion.

(7) 1 2 3 4 5 Being good is not related to what one believes.

(8) 1 2 3 4 5 The idea of a personal God is an outworn concept.

(9) 1 2 3 4 5 There is nothing wrong with social drinking.

(10) 1 2 3 4 5 The future of the church looks very bright.

(11) 1 2 3 4 5 We spend too much time in the church talking about money.

(12) 1 2 3 4 5 All I know about the church is what I read in the bulletin.

(13) 1 2 3 4 5 I often feel like an outsider in my church.

(14) 1 2 3 4 5 Today there are as many dependable ties between members of the church as ever.

(15) 1 2 3 4 5 "Blue laws" closing some businesses and recreational facilities on Sunday are out of date.

(16) 1 2 3 4 5 There is little chance of becoming a member of the official board or governing body of the church for most members.

(17) 1 2 3 4 5 Baptism is essential to membership in the church.

(18) 1 2 3 4 5 In case of conflict between a church meeting and a social engagement, I would generally go to the church meeting.

(19) 1 2 3 4 5 Every person planning marriage should have counseling by the minister.

(20) 1 2 3 4 5 Participation in a Bible study and prayer group helps me feel closer to God.

(21) 1 2 3 4 5 I find my personal needs met in groups outside the church.

(22) 1 2 3 4 5 I don't think classes in the church school are important or necessary for adults.

(23) 1 2 3 4 5 The major source of satisfaction in my life comes from my church activities.

(24) 1 2 3 4 5 Out daily work is service to God.

SOURCE: B. B. (Payne) Pittard. "The Meaning and Measurement of Commitment to the Church." Ph.D. dissertation, Emory University, 1963.

V2.8.I.g

DIMENSIONS OF RELIGION

M. B. King, 1967; M. B. King and R. A. Hunt, 1969; 1972; 1975

Item-Scale[1]
Correlations
1973 1968

		I. Creedal Assent (.84; .83)[2]
.68	.65	I believe in God as a Heavenly Father who watches over me and to whom I am accountable.[3,10]
.66	.70	I believe that the Word of God is revealed in the Scriptures.[10]
.65	.58	I believe that Christ is a living reality.[10]
.63	.58	I believe that God revealed Himself to man in Jesus Christ.[10]
.58	.54	I believe in salvation as release from sin and freedom for new life with God.
.55	.58	I believe in eternal life.[10]
(.42)[4]	.53	I believe honestly and wholeheartedly in the doctrines and teachings of the Church.
		II. Devotionalism (.84; .85)
.79	.74	How often do you pray privately in places other than at church?[5]
.70	.73	How often do you ask God to forgive your sin?

Item-Scale[1] Correlations		
1973	1968	
.63	.63	When you have decisions to make in your everyday life, how often do you try to find out what God wants you to do?
.59	.65	Private prayer is one of the most important and satisfying aspects of my religious experience.[10]
.53	.59	I frequently feel very close to God in prayer, during public worship, or at important moments in my daily life.

III. Church Attendance (.82; .82)

.71	.64	If not prevented by unavoidable circumstances, I attend church: (More than once a week-Twice a year or less)[11]
.67	.69	During the last year, how many Sundays per month on the average have you gone to a worship service? (None-Three or more)[11]
.65	.71	How often have you taken Holy Communion (The Lord's Supper, The Eucharist) during the past year?[11]

IV. Organizational Activity (.81; .83)

.71	.69	How would you rate your activity in your congregation? (Very active-Inactive)[11]
.64	.63	How often do you spend evenings at church meetings or in church work?[11]
.60	.59	Church activities (meetings, committee work, etc.) are a major source of satisfaction in my life.
.56	.55	List the church offices, committees, or jobs of any kind in which you served during the past twelve months (Coded: None-Four or more)[11]
.50	.57	I keep pretty well informed about my congregation and have some influence on its decisions.
.49	.59	I enjoy working in the activities of the Church.

V. Financial Support (.73; .73)

.61	.56	Last year, approximately what percent of your income was contributed to the Church? (1% or less-10% or more)
.49	.40	During the last year, how often have you made contributions to the Church IN ADDITION TO the general budget and Sunday School? (Regularly-Never)
.47	.51	During the last year, what was the average MONTHLY contribution of your family to your local congregation? (Under $5-$50 or more)
.46	.48	In proportion to your income, do you consider that your contributions to the Church are: (Generous-Small)
.45	.53	I make financial contributions to the Church: (In regular, planned amounts-Seldom or never)

VI. Religious Despair (.79; .77)[6]

.62	.56	My personal existence often seems meaningless and without purpose.
.62	.56	My life is often empty, filled with despair.
.55	.55	I have about given up trying to understand "worship" or get much out of it.
.50	.49	I often wish I had never been born.
.47	.47	I find myself believing in God some of the time, but not at other times.
.47	.38	Most of the time my life seems to be out of my control.
.42	.45	The Communion Service (Lord's Supper, Eucharist) often has little meaning to me.

VII. Orientation to Growth and Striving (.79; .81)

.61	.60	How often do you read the Bible?
.60	.61	How often do you read literature about your faith (or church)? (Frequently - Never) [A-F] [7]
.60	.54	The amount ot time I spend trying to grow in understanding of my faith is: (Very much - Little or none)
.57	.57	When you have decisions to make in your everyday life, how often do you try to find out what God wants you to do? (II) [8]
.53	.59	I try hard to grow in understanding of what it means to live as a child of God.
.44	.52	I try hard to carry my religion over into all my other dealings in life. [A-F]

COMPOSITE RELIGIOUS SCALES

A. Salience: Behavior (.80; .83)

.67	.68	How often in the past year have you shared with another church member the problems and joys of trying to live a life of faith in God?
.58	.59	How often do you talk about religion with your friends, neighbors, or fellow workers?
.57	.60	How often have you personally tried to convert someone to faith in God?
.54	.54	How often do you read the Bible? (VII)
.49	.57	When faced with decisions regarding social problems how often do you seek guidance from statements and publications provided by the Church?
.49	.53	How often do you talk with the pastor (or other official) about some part of the worship service: for example, the sermon, scripture, choice of hymns, etc.
.43	.49	During the last year, how often have you visited someone in need, besides your own relatives?

B. Salience: Cognition (.84; .81)

.66	.59	Religion is especially important to me because it answers many questions about the meaning of life. [A-F] [10]
.63	.64	I try hard to grow in understanding of what it means to live as a child of God. (VII)
.59	.64	My religious beliefs are what really lie behind my whole approach to life. [A-F]
.59	.54	I frequently feel very close to God in prayer, during public worship, or at important moments in my daily life. (II)
.56	(*)[9]	I often experience the joy and peace which come from knowing I am a for-given sinner.
.55	(*)	When you have decisions to make in your everyday life, how often do you try to find out what God wants you to do? (II, VII)
.53	(*)	I believe in God as a Heavenly Father who watches over me and to whom I am accountable. (I)
.52	.56	I try hard to carry my religion over into all my other dealings in life. [A-F] (VII)

C. The Active Regulars (.86; .84)

(In 1968, called Index of Attendance and Giving)

.77	.60	If not prevented by unavoidable circumstances, I attend church: (More than once a week - Twice a year or less). (III)

Item-Scale[1] Correlations		
1973	1968	
.68	.57	How would you rate your activity in your congregation? (Very active-Inactive) (IV)
.67	.66	How often have you taken Holy Communion (The Lord's Supper, The Eucharist) during the past year? (III)
.60	.69	During the last year, how many Sundays per month on the average have you gone to worship service? (None-Three or more) (III)
.55	(*)	How often do you spend evenings at church meetings or in church work? (IV)
.55	(*)	Church activities (meetings, committee work, etc.) are a major source of satisfaction in my life. (IV)
.54	(*)	During the last year, how often have you made contributions to the Church IN ADDITION TO the general budget and Sunday School? (Regularly-Never) (V)
.47	.54	I make financial contributions to the Church: (In regular, planned amounts-Seldom or never) (V)
.46	.54	Last year, approximately what percent of your income was contributed to the Church? (1% or less-10% or more) (V)
(.42)	.52	During the last year, what was the average MONTHLY contribution of your family to your local congregation (Under $5-$50 or more) (V)

1. The correlation coefficient of each item with the scale, the item itself having been dropped from the scale for that computation.
2. The coefficients of homogeneity (Cronbach's alpha) obtained for the scale in 1973 and 1968, respectively.
3. Unless otherwise indicated, the items were statements to which one responded with one of four degrees of assent: "Strongly agree", "Agree", "Disagree", "Strongly disagree".
4. Values in parentheses indicate items in the matrix but below the cut-off point for that year. The correlation is given so that the reader may evaluate the decision not to include that item.
5. A number of "how often" questions had as alternatives "Regularly", "Fairly frequently", "Occasionally", and "Seldom or never".
6. The 1968 scale was developed only for Presbyterian-U.S. members. However, similar scales are based on members of all four denominations.
7. Items indicated by [A-F] appear in Feagin's (1964) scale of Gordon Allport's Intrinsic Religion.
8. Items which have appeared on a preceding scale are indicated by the number of that scale.
9. An asterisk (*) indicated an item in the 1968 matrix, but not included in the maximally homogeneous scale for that year.

SOURCE: M. B. King and R. A. Hunt. "Measuring the Religious Variable: National Replication." *Journal for the Scientific Study of Religion*, 1975, 14:19-21.

VIII. Religious Knowledge [(.769) Response options in parentheses]

1. Which of the following were Old Testament Prophets?
   (Deuteronomy; Ecclesiastes; Elijah; Isaiah; Jeremiah; Leviticus)
2. Which of the following books are included in the Four Gospels?
   (James; John; Mark; Matthew; Peter; Thomas)
3. Which of the following were among the Twelve Disciples of Christ?
   (Daniel; John; Judas; Paul; Peter; Samuel)

4. Which of the following acts were performed by Jesus Christ during His earthly ministry?
   (Resisting the temptations of Satan; Healing ten lepers; Leading His people against the priests of Baal; Parting the waters to cross the Red Sea; Overcoming Goliath; Turning water into wine)
5. Which of the following men were leaders of the Protestant Reformation:
   (Aquinas; Augustine; Calvin; Cranmer; Hegel; Luther)
6. Which of the following principles are supported by most Protestant denominations?
   (Bible as the Word of God; Separation of Church and State; Power of clergy to forgive sins; Final authority of the Church; Justification by faith; Justification by good works)
7. Which of the following books are in the Old Testament?
   (Acts; Amos; Galatians; Hebrews; Hosea; Psalms)
8. Which of the following denominations in the United States have bishops?
   (Disciples; Episcopal; Lutheran; Methodist; Presbyterian; Roman Catholic)

IX. Orientation to Religion: Extrinsic (Allport) (.734)

1. It is part of one's patriotic duty to worship in the church of his choice.[12]
2. The Church is most important as a place to formulate good social relationships.
3. The purpose of prayer is to secure a happy and peaceful life.
4. Church membership has helped me to meet the right kind of people.[12]
5. What religion offers me most is comfort when sorrows and misfortunes strike.
6. One reason for my being a church member is that such membership helps to establish a person in the community.
7. Religion helps to keep my life balanced and steady in exactly the same way as my citizenship, friendships and other memberships do.

X. Extrinsic: Original (.715)

1. The Church is important to me as a place where I get strength and courage for dealing with the trials and problems of life.
2. The more I support the Church financially, the closer I feel to it and to God.
3. Church is important as a place to go for comfort and refuge from the trials and problems of life.

INDEXES OF CONGREGATIONAL INVOLVEMENT: 1968

XI. Index of General Activity [(.856) See also footnote 11]

1. During the last year, how many times per month on the average did you attend Sunday School or some equivalent educational activity?

XII. Index of Belief and Commitment [(.872) See also footnote 10]

1. I know that I need God's continual love and care.
2. I know that God answers my prayers.
3. Property (house, automobile, money, investments, etc.) belongs to God; we only hold it in trust for Him.

SOURCE: M. B. King and R. A. Hunt. *Measuring Religious Dimensions: Studies of Congregational Involvement.* Studies in Social Science, number 1. Dallas: Southern Methodist University, 1972. Reprinted by permission.

EDITOR'S NOTE: This instrument was compiled from information contained in both sources.

Editor's Notes:

10. Item also loads on the *Index of Belief and Commitment* but is not listed with that scale.
11. Item also loads on the *Index of General Activity* but is not listed with that scale (see below).
12. Item also loads on the *Extrinsic: Original* scale but is not included with the items listed on that scale.

V2.8.I.h

MEASURES OF RELIGIOUS INVOLVEMENT

H. S. Himmelfarb, 1975

DOCTRINAL-EXPERIENTIAL

*50. All religions have within them elements of faith which are accepted in varying degrees by its members. We would like to know what you believe. Please indicate your agreement or disagreement with the statements listed below by using the following number guide:

    1-Strongly disagree
    2-Moderately disagree
    3-Moderately agree
    4-Strongly agree

		.Factor Score Coefficient
I believe in a God who created the Universe	1 2 3 4	.162
I believe in a God who is continually guiding the universe	1 2 3 4	.169
I believe that the Torah was given by God	1 2 3 4	.170
I believe that God gave us a method for interpreting the Torah which is reflected in Rabbinic Law (Talmud)	1 2 3 4	.168
I believe that the Jews are a chosen people	1 2 3 4	.142

3a. Please circle the number which best describes the extent of your agreement or disagreement with the following statements:

    1-Strongly disagree
    2-Mostly disagree
    3-Mostly agree
    4-Strongly agree

During my life I have seen God perform miracles	1 2 3 4	.124

64g. Please indicate whether you agree or disagree with the following statements:

I trust God to guard and protect me from harm.   .150

    1-Strongly disagree
    2-Mostly disagree
    3-Mostly agree
    4-Strongly agree

At times, I have had a sense that God was near	1 2 3 4	.142

IDEOLOGICAL

49. Below is a list of types of aid that American Jews give to Israel. Using the following guide, please indicate whether or not you feel a personal obligation to help Israel in this manner.

    1-Strong obligation *not* to aid in this way
    2-Moderate obligation *not* to aid in this way
    3-Indifferent about this type of aid
    4-Moderate obligation to aid in this way
    5-Strong obligation to aid in this way

a. Give money for Israel	1 2 3 4	.274

*Item number of Study of American Life Questionnaire.

.Factor
Score
Coefficient

    b. Raise money for Israel . . . . 1 2 3 4   .287

    c. Seek to influence U.S. foreign policy in favor of Israel . . . . . 1 2 3 4   .270

    d. Belong to Zionist organization . . . . 1 2 3 4   .236

    e. Give Israeli financial needs priority over local
        Jewish causes . . . . 1 2 3 4   .221

ASSOCIATIONAL

39. What proportion of last year's meetings did you attend in
the one Jewish organization in which you were most active?   .515
None of the meetings. 1
Some of the meetings. 2
Most of the meetings 3
All of the meetings 4

40. Were you an officer in any Jewish organizations last year?
No 1   Yes 2

INTELLECTUAL-ESTHETIC

44c. For the next several questions, please use the following key:
        0-Can't speak this language
        1-Never, or almost never
        2-A few times a year
        3-Once or twice a month
        4-Several times a month
        5-Once or twice a week
        6-Daily, or nearly every day

    How often do you *read* a novel or short story on a Jewish topic
    or read a biography of a Jew. . . . . 0 1 2 3 4 5 6   .288

47. What proportion of the following items in your home are Jewish in character?
        1-Do not have any of these items
        2-None, or almost none, of them
        3-Some of them
        4-Most of them
        5-All, or almost all, of them

    Paintings, wall decorations, and other art objects . . . . 1 2 3 4 5   .326
    Books . . . . 1 2 3 4 5   .337
    Records . . . . 1 2 3 4 5   .326

FRATERNAL

32. What proportion of the following is (or was) Jewish?
        1-Does not apply to me
        2-None, or almost none
        3-Some
        4-About half
        5-Most
        6-All, or almost all

    a. Neighborhood in which you presently live. . . . . 1 2 3 4 5 6   .573
    b. Neighbors who visit you at home . . . . 1 2 3 4 5 6   .573

PARENTAL

63. Please indicate the extent to which you (would) encourage or discourage your children to do any of the following:

    1-Strongly discourage
    2-Moderately discourage
    3-Moderately encourage
    4-Strongly encourage

		.Factor Score Coefficient
a.	Learn about Judaism 1 2 3 4	.152
b.	Attend synagogue 1 2 3 4	.201
c.	Participate in Jewish organizations 1 2 3 4	.204
d.	Associate primarily with Jewish friends 1 2 3 4	.185
e.	Date Jews only 1 2 3 4	.208
f.	Marry within the faith 1 2 3 4	.200
g.	Attend a Jewish school for at least eight years 1 2 3 4	.186

ETHICAL-MORAL

3g. Please circle the number which best describes the extent of your agreement or disagreement with the following statements:

    1-Strongly disagree
    2-Mostly disagree
    3-Mostly agree
    4-Strongly agree

Even though a person has a hard time making ends meet, he should still try to give some of his money to help the poor . . . . 1 2 3 4   .394

75. Last year, into which group shown did your contributions to charity fall?

Under $10 01	$300-$499 06
$10-$49 02	$500-$999 07
$50-$99 03	$1,000-$1,999 08
$100-$199. 04	$2,000-$4,999 09
$200-$299. 05	$5,000-$9,999 10

76. What percentage of the charity that you donated last year was given to Jewish causes? . . . . _____%   .486

DEVOTIONAL

21. Listed below are a few ritual observances which are primarily observed in the home. By using the following number code, please tell us whether these observances were usually practiced in your parents' home while you were growing up, and whether they are practices in your home at the present time.

    1-Usually not practiced
    2-Usually practiced

	Your Home	Guttman Rank: least difficult item
c. Use of two sets of dishes for milk and meat products . . .	1 2	5

		Your Home	Guttman Rank: least difficult item
e. No bread eaten in home on Passover		1 2	3
f. Lighting of Hanukkah candles.		1 2	1

25. We would like to know when and how religious observance changes for most people. Therefore, we have selected some other ritual observances which are less related to the home and more individual in character. By using the number key to question 21, we would appreciate you telling us whether or not the observances listed below . . . [are] you practice now.

	Your Home	item
a. Fast on Yom Kippur	1 2	4
d. No movies or other recreational activities attended on the Sabbath	1 2	6
e. Attend synagogue services on High Holidays	1 2	2

SOURCE: H. S. Himmelfarb. "Measuring Religious Involvement." *Social Forces*, 1975, 53: 607-18.

V2.8.I.i

ATTITUDES TOWARD THE CHURCH AND RELIGION

B. D. Bell, 1971

Attitudes toward the Church

Of the following statements please check in the "Agree" column those which accurately express YOUR VIEWPOINT OF THE CHURCH. Check in the "Agree in Part" column for all statements with which you are in substantial agreement, *but* about which you have some doubt. Use the "Do Not Agree" column for all statements which, from your point of view, *do not* suit the church. There are *no correct replies* to these statements. I am interested only in your true feelings with respect to the statements presented. You are requested to refrain from consulting other persons while filling out this list. In answering these questions or responding to these statements, I *do not* want you to put down what you think you *should* believe or what you feel most people believe, but simply *what you actually believe* about each statement.

	Agree	Agree in Part	Do Not Agree
1. I take part in the church's activities just for the sake of participating. I really enjoy doing things with the people in my church.	a ( )	b ( )	c ( )
2. The church's activities may or may not be enjoyable in and of themselves, but I get a great deal of satisfaction from knowing that, in the long run, worthwhile and desirable results are accomplished.	a ( )	b ( )	c ( )
3. At least some of the important activities of the church are concerned with members of the congregation pretty exclusively.	a ( )	b ( )	c ( )
4. I receive as much or more pleasure from the attainment of the goals established by the church			

	Agree	Agree in Part	Do Not Agree
as from participation in the church's various activities.	a ( )	b ( )	c ( )
5. The activities of the church in which I take part are valuable in and for themselves regardless of any other purpose they may accomplish.	a ( )	b ( )	c ( )
6. I participate in the church because it attempts to accomplish purposes for which I stand.	a ( )	b ( )	c ( )
7. Some of the activities of my church allow me to be myself and have a really enjoyable time.	a ( )	b ( )	c ( )
8. Some of our activities represent an attempt to influence in one way or another the actions of persons in our congregation.	a ( )	b ( )	c ( )
9. One of the purposes of the church is to promote activities for members and others interested in these activities.	a ( )	b ( )	c ( )
10. A major reason why I participate in the activities of the church is because the church seeks to bring about goals which I consider desirable.	a ( )	b ( )	c ( )
11. Taking part in the activities of the church is enjoyable in itself. I get a great deal of enjoyment out of doing these things.	a ( )	b ( )	c ( )
12. One of the purposes of the church is to change or to affect in some way the behavior of persons outside the congregation.	a ( )	b ( )	c ( )

Attitudes toward Religion

Below is a list of statements concerning religion. Please read all statements very *carefully* and respond to ALL of them on the basis of YOUR OWN TRUE beliefs, *without* consulting any other persons. Your name will not appear anywhere on this questionnaire and therefore you are assured complete anonymity with respect to your answers. You are encouraged to be perfectly frank and honest in your replies. The interviewer is not interested in obtaining any particular responses, but rather in *your true feelings* with respect to the statements presented. There are *no correct answers* as such to any of these statements. Again, you are asked to respond to these statements in terms of what *you* actually believe about each statement.

	Definitely Agree	Agree Somewhat	Undecided	Disagree Somewhat	Definitely Disagree
1. The practice of infant baptisim should be retained in the church.	a ( )	b ( )	c ( )	d ( )	e ( )
2. Church members should read the Scriptures regularly.	a ( )	b ( )	c ( )	d ( )	e ( )
3. Church members should abstain from *all* forms of gambling.	a ( )	b ( )	c ( )	d ( )	e ( )
4. Jesus Christ rose from the dead, took again His body, and ascended into Heaven.	a ( )	b ( )	c ( )	d ( )	e ( )

	Definitely Agree	Agree Somewhat	Undecided	Disagree Somewhat	Definitely Disagree
5. I believe in the Second coming of Christ and His ultimate judgment of all men.	a ( )	b ( )	c ( )	d ( )	e ( )
6. There is a life after death.	a ( )	b ( )	c ( )	d ( )	e ( )
7. When a person is planning to be married he should consult his pastor.	a ( )	b ( )	c ( )	d ( )	e ( )
8. The Holy Scriptures contain all things necessary to salvation.	a ( )	b ( )	c ( )	d ( )	e ( )
9. There is one true God who reveals himself as the Trinity: Father, Son, and Holy Spirit.	a ( )	b ( )	c ( )	d ( )	e ( )
10. Religious people should try to spread the teachings of the Scriptures.	a ( )	b ( )	c ( )	d ( )	e ( )
11. We have no power to do good works, pleasant and acceptable to God, without the grace of God by Christ.	a ( )	b ( )	c ( )	d ( )	e ( )
12. Church members should attend church once a week if possible.	a ( )	b ( )	c ( )	d ( )	e ( )
13. Every person should participate in at least one church activity.	a ( )	b ( )	c ( )	d ( )	e ( )
14. Church members should totally abstain from the use of alcoholic beverages.	a ( )	b ( )	c ( )	d ( )	e ( )
15. The offering of Christ is that perfect redemption, propitiation, and satisfaction for all the sins of the whole world.	a ( )	b ( )	c ( )	d ( )	e ( )
16. It is possible in this life for all men to obtain a state of perfect love, righteousness, and true holiness.	a ( )	b ( )	c ( )	d ( )	e ( )
17. Church members should support the church with their prayers.	a ( )	b ( )	c ( )	d ( )	e ( )

	Definitely Agree	Agree Somewhat	Undecided	Disagree Somewhat	Definitely Disagree
18. Church members should establish a regular prayer and devotional life.	a ( )	b ( )	c ( )	d ( )	e ( )
19. We are accounted righteous before God only for the merit of our Lord and Savior Jesus Christ.	a ( )	b ( )	c ( )	d ( )	e ( )
20. Church members should establish a regular prayer and devotional life.	a ( )	b ( )	c ( )	d ( )	e ( )
21. Jesus Christ was the son of God.	a ( )	b ( )	c ( )	d ( )	e ( )
22. Children should be brought up in the church.	a ( )	b ( )	c ( )	d ( )	e ( )
23. Jesus was born of a virgin.	a ( )	b ( )	c ( )	d ( )	e ( )
24. I believe in Original Sin which is the corruption of the nature of every man, whereby man is of his own nature inclined to evil.	a ( )	b ( )	c ( )	d ( )	e ( )
25. The Old Testament is not contrary to the New; for both in the Old and New Testaments everlasting life is offered to mankind by Christ.	a ( )	b ( )	c ( )	d ( )	e ( )

SOURCE: B. D. Bell. "Church Participation and the Family Life Cycle." *Review of Religious Research*, 1971, 13 (1):58.

Chapter 9

Friends, Neighbors, and Confidants

George R. Peters

Despite the recognition of the important part friends, neighbors, and confidants play in the lives of many older people (Lowenthal, 1968), comparatively few studies on these important relationships exist. As a consequence, findings on the friendships of older people are scattered, frequently lack rigorously developed conceptual frameworks, and are often only adjunctive considerations to the interests of the researchers. Riley (1968) reinforced this conclusion when she noted that suggestive insights are afforded by data of national scope and by analyses of selected samples but that beyond several identified tendencies our knowledge of friendship and neighboring in old-age is meager.

There are significant exceptions to the conclusion just noted. The work of Babchuk and Bates (1963) and their students on the primary friendships of married couples, the work of Lopata (1973) on the social roles of friends and neighbors as sources of support in widowhood, the work of Rosow (1967) on friendship and neighboring in age-segregated residences, and the work of Rosenberg (1970) on working-class friendships provide detailed information focusing specifically on friendship and neighboring relations. Although it does not examine friendship and neighboring among older people, the work of Laumann (1973) also provides a seminal analysis of such relationships. There is good reason to believe that the conceptual framework and analysis design employed by Laumann should be applicable to older populations. Nonetheless, as Lowenthal and Robinson (1976) noted, most studies of friendship among older persons focus on the scope of networks and the frequency of interaction rather than on the quality of dyadic friendships. They expressed concern over how little attention has been paid to individual preferences for, and participation in, dyadic friendships as compared with group friendships across the adult life cycle, and to the sex differences therein. To these sentiments must be added other concerns. Much of the extant work treats friendship and neighboring in global terms, assuming that the concepts have a common meaning for all concerned, including the respondent. Largely ignored is the great need to engage in conceptual clarification, which would carefully delineate the dimensions of friend, neighbor, and confidant relationships worthy of study, differentiate them from one another and other types of relationships, and thereby suggest areas for systematic measurement development. Unfortunately, one is often left with the impression that "a friend is a friend" who is sometimes a neighbor, sometimes a relative who is also a friend, sometimes a fellow worker, sometimes an acquaintance, and sometimes a person with whom one has a highly intimate relationship. Occasionally, such diverse relationships are treated as equivalent. More frequently, the connotative differences among them are recognized by researchers, but rigorous denotative distinctions are lacking. Thus, much of the research that focuses on friendship and neighboring functions with a crude definition of the relationships and, in the main, seeks to establish the correlates (including age) of the relationships. Research that either implicitly or explicitly treats friendship and neighboring as independent variables too typically employs only a crude definition of the concepts and usually operationalizes a highly limited number of dimensions of the relationships (e.g., number of friends, frequency of contact).

The foregoing comments have relevance for the state of instrument development in the area. In general, the level, rigor, and sophistication of measurement devices are relatively low. Scales are almost nonexistent. Index development, to the extent that it occurs, typically combines scores from a limited number of dimensions across several types of interpersonal relationships, rather than focusing on friendship, neighboring, or confidant relations exclusively. Most frequently employed are batteries of items viewed by the researchers as conceptually related to one another and to the research problem being investigated. As it has already been noted, depending on the interest of the researcher, only a limited number of dimensions of the relationships are tapped by the items. Researchers also employ single-item indicators that tap one aspect of the relationships examined and treat these as more complete measures of the relationships than their limited focus merits.

Unfortunately, little careful and rigorous attention has been given to replication in studies of friendship, neighboring, and confidant relations. Thus, on some dimensions (e.g., frequency of contact) researchers frequently drop or reword items. On the other dimensions (e.g., confiding) different versions of a single-item indicator may be used. Where attempts are made to examine specific areas of shared confidences, one finds different aspects of the confidant dimension being tapped, which probably reflect more the personal preferences or interests of the researchers than a systematic attempt to fully delineate the confidant relationship.

Few researchers have described in detail the instrument-development procedures that result in the measurement devices they employ. This fact, and the fact that no national norms on the various dimensions of friendship, neighboring, and confidant relationships currently exist, make difficult any assessment of the state of knowledge on friendship, neighboring, and confidant relations beyond the confines of the specific and limited samples studied by researchers.

Measurement of Dimensions

Despite the problems of measurement and the questionable comparability of research in the area, a number of dimensions of friend, neighbor, and confidant relations have been identified. These are listed next and will be observed in the measures that are reviewed later.

Frequency of Interaction and Shared Activities

Frequency of interaction and shared activities is the most frequently measured dimension. Typically, respondents are asked to indicate how frequently they see their friends and neighbors. Researchers sometimes distinguish between mode of contact (e.g., face-to-face, telephone, letters) and context of contact (e.g., respondent's or friend's home, work place, in an organizational context). Often, respondents are asked to compare present frequency of interaction with frequency at an earlier time or age. Less frequently, respondents are asked to identify specific activities in which they engage with friends or neighbors.

Number of Friends/Neighbors

A measure of the number of friends/neighbors is obtained nearly as often as frequency of contact with friends and neighbors. Typically, respondents are simply asked to indicate the number of friends or neighbors they have, although different researchers assign different labels to the terms *friend* and *neighbor*. Thus, the question may be stated in terms of friends, good friends, close friends, very closest friends, etc., but usually without providing the respondent with a definition of what is meant by any of the terms. Depending on the researcher's preference, a respondent may be asked to respond in general terms about his or her friends in general, in detail about a selected number of friends named (e.g., three closest friends), or in detail about all friends named.

Intimacy or Affect

The dimension of intimacy or affect is recognized as both a highly important component of the friend and neighbor relationships and the most underdeveloped area of measurement. This dimension is of crucial significance because it provides a potential basis for distinguishing highly intimate and presumably important relations from more casual associations. This dimension is recognized by researchers when they ask respondents to identify their "very closest" friends and then focus most of the questions on such relationships. Intimacy is a multidimensional construct. Typical attempts at identifying dimensions of intimacy include assessing a respondent's ability to identify specifically X number of very close friends and his or her willingness to share confidences (usually stated in a global single question and occasionally in terms of a series of areas in which confiding may occur); researchers also sometimes present respondents with a hypothetical scale of closeness and ask them to place their friends along that scale or request that respondents select from their "close friends" those they consider to be their "very closest friends."

Attraction

Assessments of attraction seek to identify the processes of friendship formation, structural constraints on friendship and neighboring relations, the effect of certain losses (e.g., death of spouse or friend, retirement) in the lives of older people on friendship and neighboring relations, and the mechanisms of involvement in close relationships (e.g., reciprocity and commitment). Respondents are asked how the relationship was formed, who initiated it, and where and when the friend was met. Often, information on demographic or social status is requested in regard to the friend or neighbor, allowing the researcher to designate the extent to which friendships are homogeneous. As a rule, the information sought is not sufficient to describe friendship formation in other than global terms. Exceptions are Lopata's (1973) study of widows and Laumann's (1973) Detroit Area Study of men aged 21 to 64, in which the formation and maintenance of friendships among particular categories of persons are described in detail.

Spontaneity

Spontaneity is a dimension infrequently tapped but long recognized as a characteristic of more intimate ties. Explicit attention is given to this dimension by Babchuk and Bates (1963).

Assistance/Support

In the dimension of assistance/support the strong propensity for exchange between friends and neighbors is recognized and attempts are made to delineate areas in which exchanges occur. Usually, friends and neighbors are considered to be among the potential providers of support and assistance, together with other sources such as spouses and children. Given the comparative framework used in studies of this dimension, it is often difficult to determine to what extent friends and neighbors would be or are used as sources of support.

Attitudes toward Friendship and Neighboring

Attitudes toward friendship and neighboring are most frequently tapped by questions concerning a felt desire for more friends; the satisfaction with the current number of, and relations with, friends; the importance and functions of friends; and retrospective comparisons of present with past friends and neighbors.

Instruments Reviewed

I do not divide the instruments in this chapter into measures of friendship, neighboring, and confidant relationships, or along the lines of the dimensions just described. (See Table 9-1.) Because the instruments reported, for the most part, represent batteries of items that touch upon each of the relationships and dimensions in varying degrees and are considered as conceptually related components, any attempt to demarcate conceptual boundaries would be artificial at best. Therefore, it is necessary to depart from a format more appropriate to a presentation of separate scales and indexes.

Cavan, Burgess, Havighurst, and Goldhammer's (1949) Battery of Adult Activities with Friends and Index of Attitudes toward Friends is a multidimensional instrument designed to measure personal adjustment in old age. Quite aside from their relevance to the construct of personal adjustment, the items tap a number of important dimensions of friendship. These include measures of number of friends, confiding in friends, frequency of contact with friends, and reasons for not seeing friends. Attitudinal items tap feelings about present number of

TABLE 9-1
Measures Reviewed in Chapter 9

Instrument	Author(s)	Code Number
a. Friends, Neighbors, and Neighbor/Friends	Rosow (1967)	V2.9.I.a
b. Primary Friendship	Babchuk and Bates (1963)	V2.9.I.b
c. Urban Social Networks	Laumann (1973)	V2.9.I.c
d. Neighborhood Integration Measures	Fellin and Litwak (1963)	V2.9.I.d
e. Interaction and Homophily in Frienship	Rosenberg (1970)	V2.9.I.e
f. Interpersonal Contacts	Reiss (1959)	V2.9.I.f
g. Weiss's Intimacy Ranking Scale	Weiss (1977)	V2.9.I.g
h. Neighborhood Social Intimacy Scale	Smith, Form, and Stone (1954)	V2.9.I.h
i. Confidants, Neighbors, and Friends	Bultena et al. (1971)	V2.9.I.i
j. Friends and Neighbors	Peterson, Hadwin, and Larson (1968)	V2.9.I.j
k. Informal Social Relations	Bell and Boat (1957)	V2.9.I.k
l. Interaction with Friends	Kutner et al. (1956)	V2.9.I.l

friends, desire for more contact with friends, loneliness, and the contribution of friendship to a sense of happiness. The items were subjected to a rigorous and systematic scale-development procedure, in both their selection and later use. (The full Activity Inventory is reviewed in Chapter 2 of this volume; the Attitude Inventory, in Chapter 5 of Volume 1.)

Rosow's (1967) Friends, Neighbors, and Neighbor/Friends instrument constituted the basis for his book, *Social Integration of the Aged*. The 19 items measure several aspects of friendship and neighboring, globally conceived. These include number of friends, number of local friends, number of newly formed friendships, attraction to neighbor/friends, frequency of contact with neighbor/friends, desire for new friends, helping patterns, and the salience of friends. Rosow's work has proved to be seminal, at least in the context of the effects of age concentration or density on friendship formation.

The work of Babchuk and Bates (1963) and their students on primary friendships represents one of the few attempts to focus in detail solely on friendship relations. The items examine a number of dimensions of close friendships, including number of friends, attraction, intimacy (affect), frequency of contact, shared activities, and spontaneity in friendship relations. Although originally it was conceived as a means of studying the friendships of married couples, the approach has been adapted to single persons as well (Peters, 1968). The items have been used with a number of samples. The items were derived from a critical theoretical treatment of Cooley's conceptualization of the primary-group concept (Bates and Babchuk, 1961).

The 35 items developed by Laumann (1973) were employed in his study of urban social networks. The items tap many of the dimensions of friendship relationships. These include number of close friendships, frequency of contact with close friends, measures of the closeness (intimacy) of friendships, relationships of close friends to respondent, length of time the friends have been known, residence of friends, extent to which close friends of a respondent are close friends of one another, frequency with which close friends see one another at the same time, organizational context for meeting close friends, and the role played by homogeneity in attraction between friends. Laumann's work represents an important contribution to understanding the structure of social relations in urban areas. Of special significance is his sophisticated analysis framework and design that examine the multidimensionality of social networks through the techniques of smallest space analyses. The items included in this chapter do not exhaust the theoretically grounded questions about social networks raised by Laumann and expressed in additional items in his full schedule. The reader is encouraged to examine Laumann's work for a fuller understanding of his conceptual and methodological framework.

The Neighborhood Integration battery developed by Fellin and Litwak (1963) includes measures relevant to five dimensions of neighborhood integration. These include the dimensions of neighborhood cohesion; present, past, and future orientations to the neighborhood; husbands' orientation to interpersonal relations on the job; attitudes toward discussion of personal problems with neighbors; and attitudes toward strangers in the neighborhood. This work bears on the relationship between neighborhood and mobility and is concerned with identifying mechanisms that speed the socialization of newcomers and thereby maintain cohesion under conditions of turnover in membership.

The measures of Interaction and Homophily in Friendship (Rosenberg, 1970) were developed in the context of a larger study on the influence of the density of age and social class peers, socioeconomic status, and neighborhood social structure on neighborhood interaction with friends. The 15 items contained in the instrument measure a quantitative aspect of friendship relations and the presence of homophilous or heterophilous friendship ties. The study's particular concern with the working class in a large city raises questions about the applicability of its results to other settings, and yet the items and the approach used by Rosenberg could be fairly easily used with other study populations.

Reiss's (1959) Interpersonal Contacts index employs a time-budget approach that ascertains the allocation of time (in minutes) to different types of personal contacts. The measure distinguishes among contacts with intimate kin, close intimate friends, close associates, good friends, casual acquaintances, cordial recognitions, and pure clients. The measure does not tap the qualitative aspects of the various relationships, but it does appear to provide a fairly accurate means of recording actual contacts.

Weiss's Intimacy Ranking Scale (WIR) (Weiss, 1977) is a recently developed scale that attempts to measure the level of interpersonal intimacy perceived within opposite-sex and same-sex relationships. It employs a multidimensional approach that identifies the 16 independent intimacy statements that make up the scale. It was developed in an explicit attempt to extend the work of Lowenthal (1968) on the importance of intimacy as a buffer in adaption to stress in old age. The scale was rigorously developed, and early results suggest that it taps important aspects of intimate relations.

The four-item, Guttman-type Neighborhood Social Intimacy Scale developed by Smith, Form, and Stone (1954) measures knowledge of friends in the neighborhood, extent of contact with neighborhood friends, and sense of attachment to the neighborhood. The scale is easy to administer. To my knowledge, the scale has not been widely used, but it does tap limited but important aspects of neighboring relations.

In their study of life after 70 in Iowa, Bultena and associates (1971) developed a battery of items measuring aspects of the relationships of confidants, neighbors, and friends. The dimensions tapped in the battery include specification of the presence of absence of a confidant, relationship of confidant to respondent, events leading to the development (or loss) of a confidant relationship, and frequency of contact with confidants. In addition, 16 items relating to friendship and neighboring relations are included.

The Peterson, Hadwin, and Larson (1968) battery of items on Friends and Neighbors is taken from a larger study of retirement community in-movers. The battery measures several aspects of friendship and neighboring relationships, with an emphasis on the differential life satisfaction of a group of persons before and after moving into an age-segregated community. The items measure a number of dimensions of friendship relations, including number of close friends, number of close friends similar in age to respondent, attraction to friends, frequency of contact with close friends, activities shared with friends, present friendship relations compared to those at an earlier age, and orientation toward forming friendships. The neighboring items include measures of number of neighbors known well, exchange patterns, and desire for more contact with neighbors.

The battery developed by Bell and Boat (1957) measures participation in four types of informal social relations. Bell and Boat were interested in relations among neighbors, friends, co-workers, and relatives as they are influenced by family and economic status in urban areas. Their approach seems to be usable on other populations and settings. The items measure both quantitative and, to a limited degree, qualitative aspects of the target relationships.

Kutner and associates (1956) focused on interaction with friends in a 13-item battery measuring presence of local and nonlocal friends, frequency of contact with friends, selected characteristics of friends, how friends were met, and desire for new friends. An isolation index can be constructed from the items dealing with interaction with relatives and friends. The battery is limited in scope but has been shown to be usable with older populations.

Recommendations

Suggestions for the development of measures of friendship, neighboring, and confidant relationships follow from the comments introducing this section. Some initial steps that researchers should take in the future are these. First, adequate measurement ultimately reflects careful and systematic beginnings from theoretically and logically sound conceptual frameworks. Conceptual work is greatly needed in this area before significant advances in instrument development can be made. Conceptualization is not totally lacking (e.g., Bates and Babchuck [1961] and colleagues on primary friendships, Lopata [1973] on social roles of friend and neighbor, McCall and associates [1970] on friendship and other intimate social relationships within a symbolic interactionist framework). Researchers should examine more systematically and critically the potential inputs of balance models (Newcomb, 1956; 1961) or exchange models (Thibaut and Kelley, 1959; Homans, 1961) to measuring and conceptualizing the relations considered here. Such work should reduce the uncritical and global usage of the terms *friend*, *neighbor*, and *confidant* that characterize much of the literature. It would delineate the dimensions of the relationships in analytical terms amenable to measurement and avoid the largely descriptive approach now taken. It would allow for differentiations among the relationships, thereby reducing the perhaps unfortunate tendency to treat them as essentially equivalent in form and function. Much needed is work that focuses explicitly on the relationships instead of treating them as adjuncts to more central research interests.

Second, it would be very useful if researchers provided explicit descriptions of the procedures they employed to develop and test their measures. There is a great need to give more attention to the issues of reliability and validity. This is true whether the measure takes the form of a scale, an index, or a single-item indicator. Progress could be realized if measures proven effective were standardized by different researchers. The need for replication is obvious in the literature. Further, there is a need for the development of norms regarding the relationships, preferably national in scope, but at least sufficiently precise and standardized in form so that comparisons between samples could be made. Finally, it is my opinion that some of the measures currently existing could, with work, be developed to higher and more powerful levels of measurement. Although few scales of friendship, neighboring, and confidant relationships now exist, there is no good reason to believe that such measures could not be developed.

REFERENCES

Babchuk, N. "Primary Friends and Kin: A Study of the Associations of Middle Class Couples." *Social Forces*, 1965, 43:483-93.

Babchuk, N., and J. A. Ballweg. "Black Family Structure and Primary Relations." *Phylon*, 1972, 33:334-47.

Babchuk, N., and A. P. Bates. "Primary Relations of Middle Class Couples: A Study in Male Dominance." *American Sociological Review*, 1963, 28:377-84.

Bates, A. P., and N. Babchuk. "The Primary Group: A Reappraisal." *Sociological Quarterly*, 1961, 2:181-91.

Bell, W. "The Utility of the Shevky Typology for the Design of Urban Subarea Field Studies." *Journal of Social Psychology*, 1958, 47:71-83.

Bell, W., and M. D. Boat. "Urban Neighborhoods and Informal Social Relations." *American Journal of Sociology*, 1957, 62:391-98.

Booth, A. "Sex and Social Participation." *American Sociological Review*, 1972, 37:183-92.

Booth, A., and N. Babchuk. "Seeking Health Care from New Resources." *Journal of Health and Social Behavior*, 1972, 13:90-99.

Bultena, G. L., E. A. Powers, P. Falkman, and D. Frederick. *Life after 70 in Iowa*. Sociology Report number 95, Ames, Iowa: Iowa State University, 1971.

Cavan, R. S., E. W. Burgess, R. J. Havighurst, and H. Goldhammer. *Personal Adjustment in Old Age*. Chicago: Science Research Associates, 1949.

Fellin, P. A. "A Study of the Effects of Reference Group Orientations and Bureaucratic Careers on Neighborhood Cohesion." Ph.D. dissertation, University of Michigan, 1961.

Fellin, P. A., and E. Litwak. "Neighborhood Cohesion under Conditions of Mobility." *American Sociological Review*, 1963, 28:364-76.

Force, M. T., and W. Bell. "Social Structure and Participation in Different Types of Formal Associations." *Social Forces* 1956, 34:345-50.

Homans, G. F. *Social Behavior: Its Elementary Forms.* New York: Harcourt, Brace and World, 1961.

Kutner, B., D. Fanshel, A. M. Togo, and T. S. Langner. *Five Hundred Over Sixty: A Community Survey on Aging.* New York: Russell Sage Foundation, 1956.

Laumann, E. O. *Bonds of Pluralism: The Form and Substance of Urban Social Networks.* New York: John Wiley and Sons, 1973.

Lemon, B. W., V. L. Bengtson, and J. A. Peterson. "An Exploration of the Activity Theory of Aging: Activity Types and Life Satisfaction among In-Movers to a Retirement Community." *Journal of Gerontology*, 1974, 27:511-23.

Litwak, E. "Primary Group Instruments of Social Control." Ph.D. dissertation, Columbia University, 1958.

Litwak, E., and I. Szeleni. "Primary Group Structures and Their Functions: Kin, Neighbors, and Friends." *American Sociological Review*, 1969, 34:465-81.

Lopata, H. Z. *Widowhood in an American City.* Cambridge, Mass.: Schenkman, 1973.

Lowenthal, M. F. "Interaction and Adaption: Intimacy as a Critical Variable." *American Sociological Review*, 1968, 33:20-30.

Lowenthal, M. F., and B. Robinson. "Social Networks and Isolation." In *Handbook of Aging and the Social Sciences*, R. H. Binstock and E. Shanas (eds.), pp. 432-56. New York: Van Nostrand Reinhold, 1976.

McCall, G. J., M. M. McCall, N. K. Denzin, G. D. Suttles, and S. B. Kurth. *Social Relationships.* Chicago: Aldine, 1970.

Newcomb, T. "The Prediction of Interpersonal Attraction." *American Psychologist*, 1956, 11:575-86.

_____. *The Acquaintance Process.* New York: Holt, Rinehart and Winston, 1961.

Peters, G. R. "Primary Friendship in the College Community: A Study of the Associations of Male Students." Ph.D. dissertation, University of Nebraska, 1968.

Peters, G. R., and M. Kaiser. *Growing Older in Manhattan: Aging in a Small Urban Community.* Manhattan, Kans.: Kansas State University, Department of Sociology and Anthropology, 1972.

Peterson, J. A., T. Hadwin, and A. Larson. *A Time for Work, a Time for Leisure: A Study of Retirement Community In-Movers.* Los Angeles: Andrus Gerontology Center, University of Southern California, 1968.

Reiss, A. J., Jr. "Rural-Urban and Status Differences in Interpersonal Contacts." *American Journal of Sociology*, 1959, 65:182-95.

Riley, M. W., and A. Foner. *Aging and Society* (vol. 1). New York: Russell Sage Foundation, 1968.

Rosenberg, G. S. *The Worker Grows Old.* San Francisco: Jossey-Bass, 1970.

Rosow, I. *Social Integration of the Aged.* New York: Free Press, 1967.

Smith, J., W. H. Form, and G. P. Stone. "Local Intimacy in a Middle-Sized City." *American Journal of Sociology*, 1954, 60:276-84.

Thibaut, J. W., and H. H. Kelley. *The Social Psychology of Groups* (1st ed.). New York: John Wiley and Sons, 1959.

Weiss, L. J. "Interpersonal Intimacy: An Intervening Factor in Adaptation to Stress." Paper presented to the 30th Annual Meeting of the Gerontological Society, San Francisco, November 18-22, 1977.

Abstracts

FRIENDS, NEIGHBORS, AND NEIGHBOR/FRIENDS

I. Rosow, 1967

Definition of Variable or Concept

This battery of items measures several aspects of friendship and neighboring, as they are globally conceived. However, Rosow (1967) offers no formal conceptual definition of *friend* or *neighbor*. He was concerned about patterns of active friendship with neighbors; thus, his concept was of *neighbor/friend*. This term refers to "local" persons who are neighbors by virtue of residing in the same dwelling unit as a respondent, persons with whom the respondent has contact, and persons identified by the respondent as the "neighbors he/she is friendliest with."

Description of Instrument

The battery consists of items designed to measure a number of dimensions of local friendship relationships. These include number of friends, number of friends living in the neighborhood, number of new friendships formed during the past year, detailed information on neighbor/friends, desire for new friends, role models, and helping patterns. Additionally, there are three projective stories designed to measure "competitive loyalties" to family, friends, and neighbors. The three projective stories present separate problematic situations. The stories pair three groups—family, friend, and neighbor—and force the respondent to choose one of each pair. By using this procedure, Rosow (1967) attempted to develop a picture of the relative salience of family, friends, and neighbors as reference groups to the respondent. An index was developed showing for each reference group the proportion of choices given that group in the responses made to the projective stories. The resultant index is called the salience index.

Method of Administration

The items are administered as part of a longer interview.

Context of Development

The items (with others) were developed to test the effects of age concentration on local friendships. Rosow (1967) wanted to observe the effect that different concentrations of aged residents in apartments has on old people's local friendship activity and embeddedness in local friendship groups. Numerous structural, demographic, interpersonal, and personal correlates of the local friendship relation were examined.

Sample

A purposive sample of 1,200 middle- and working-class elderly people whose age qualified them for social security was studied, with 90% of the sample 65 years or older. The sampling units were apartment buildings. Respondents were drawn from several hundred buildings in the Cleveland metropolitan area. An additional 63 residents from four retirement hotels were interviewed. Additional details on sampling can be found in Rosow (1967). With respect to concentration of aged residents, three subsamples—normal (1-15% of households had an aged member), concentrated (33-49%) of households had an aged member), and dense (over 50% of households had an aged member)—were examined.

Norms and Scoring

Responses to the items measuring the frequency of contact with neighbor/friends and the desire for new friends are used to classify respondents into five types. First, contact with neighbors (CN) is trichotomized in low (0-1 contacts; $N = 650$), medium (2-3 contacts; $N = 146$), and high (4 or more contacts; $N = 404$). Desire for new friends (NF) is a simple yes-no variable. The five types are: (1) cosmopolitan, *low* on CN and *no* on NF ($N = 361$); (2) phlegmatic, *low* on CN and *no* on NF *and* with no good friends at all ($N = 41$); (3) isolated, *low* on CN and *yes* on NF ($N = 224$); (4) sociable, *high* on CN and *no* on NF ($N = 274$); and (5) insatiable, *high* on CN and *yes* on NF ($N = 120$). The medium category on CN was excluded from the typology and subsequent analyses (Rosow, 1967, p. 108). Average "saliences," developed from responses to the projective stories are: (1) family ($\overline{X} = .72$), (2) neighbors ($\overline{X} = .46$), and (3) friends $\overline{X} = .30$) (Rosow, 1967).

The remainder of the items are used, in the general sense, as a battery; descriptive statistics were provided by Rosow (1967).

Usability on Older Populations

The instrument is usable on older populations.

Sensitivity to Age Differences

Rosow (1967) reported that greater age strongly sensitizes members of both social classes to increased age density, markedly so in the working class. As density increases, active neighboring increases significantly more for those persons who are 75 years old or older compared to those who are less than 75 years old.

General Comments and Recommendations

Rosow's instrument is a useful set of items when it is employed within conceptual frameworks similar to the original study's. Little information has been provided on the qualitative aspects of friendship and neighboring.

Reference

Rosow, I. *Social Integration of the Aged.* New York: Free Press, 1967.

Instrument

See Instrument V2.9.I.a.

PRIMARY FRIENDSHIP

N. Babchuk and A. P. Bates, 1963

Definition of Concept or Variable

These measures of primary friendship are derived from a theoretical assessment made by Bates and Babchuk (1961) of Cooley's primary-group construct. Babchuk and Bates (1963, p. 377) defined primary friendships as those "in which members are predisposed to enter into a wide range of activities (within limits imposed by such factors as member interests, sex, age, financial resources, etc.), and their predisposition to do so is associated with a predominance of positive affect."

Description of Instrument

The instrument contains 11 items asked about local friends and 13 items asked about nonlocal friends. Four items measure either closeness of any given friendship or reported changes in friendship patterns. The items are asked in regard to all friends identified by respondents. Subsets of items focus on dimensions of the friendship relation and can be analyzed separately or combined into overall friendship scores. However, the researchers have not yet developed summary indexes.

The instrument measures a number of theoretically relevant dimensions: (1) number of close friends, (2) residence of friend, (3) length of time known, (4) where friend was met, (5) affect (intimacy), (6) shared activities, (7) frequency of contact, and (8) spontaneity in the relationship. Item-response categories vary according to the question.

Method of Administration

The instrument is administered by interview. If the instrument is to be employed with married couples, as originally conceived, the interviewer should be aware that: (1) husbands and wives can be interviewed separately or simultaneously, but they should be interviewed independently by two interviewers; (2) the questions in the battery are asked in regard to all friendship units cited by respondents; and (3) a prior determination should be made by the interviewer(s) about whether the friendship ties of the couple units will be discussed with the couple after separate or simultaneous interviews. (See Babchuk and Bates [1963] and Babchuk [1965].) Experience has shown that, though the items themselves are not threatening, the issues raised by them may relate to sensitive areas. The researcher should be aware of this and be prepared to deal with it. The interviews take about two and a half hours when the procedures just discussed are followed.

Context of Development

The battery was developed in an attempt to measure the dimensions of the close friendship relations of married couples.

Samples

Table 9-2 summarizes the characteristics of the samples on which the instrument has been used.

TABLE 9-2
Primary Friendship Samples

Researcher(s)	Sample Size	Age Range	Race
Babchuk and Bates (1963)[a]	39	20-40	White
Babchuk (1965)[b]	39	19-58	White
	39	22-55	White
Babchuk and Ballweg (1972)[c]	74	Not reported	Black
Booth and Babchuk (1972)[d]	800	45+	White
Peters and Kaiser, (1972)[e]	124	65-93	White (98%) and non-white (2%)

a. Married couples constituted the sample unit. Thus, the number of 39 refers to the number of couples. Both husband and wife were interviewed. Respondents were purposively drawn from two midwestern communities.
b. Two samples of married couples were drawn. One sample was purposive, and the second was randomly selected from a middle-class, homogeneous census tract in a midwestern city.
c. Married couples constituted the sample unit. Both husband and wife were interviewed. Respondents resided in 13 census tracts containing 97% of the black population (1960 census) in a midwestern city (population approximately 350,000). Two blocks were randomly selected from each of the 13 tracts, and persons in each of the dwelling units were contacted according to a cluster sampling procedure.

d. Noninstitutionalized adults residing in two midwestern communities were sampled. The sample was drawn by sampling from a list (city directory) and sampling areas.

e. Respondents were randomly drawn from a county assessor's records and a city directory.

NORMS

The normative data presented in Tables 9-3 and 9-4 are selective rather than exhaustive. The data in Tables 9-3 and 9-4 summarize friendship as it is measured by the battery.

TABLE 9-3
Summary of Friendship Choices Reported by Three Samples

Sample/Choice	Units on which Couples Agree			Units Listed by Husband but not Wife			Units Listed by Wife but not Husband		
	Couples	Single	Total	Couples	Single	Total	Couples	Single	Total
Babchuk and Bates (1963, p. 379):									
Local friends	49	37	86	28	25	53	22	18	40
Nonlocal friends	17	15	32	15	19	34	18	14	32
Babchuk (1965, p. 486):									
Local friends	55	15	70	24	16	40	25	9	34
Nonlocal friends	49	14	63	17	9	26	24	10	34
Local friends	66	3	69	53	8	61	43	9	52
Nonlocal friends	43	4	47	24	8	32	49	13	62
Babchuk and Ballweg (1972, p. 340):									
Lower-class local friends	27	10	37	41	37	78	37	37	74
Lower-class nonlocal friends	3	3	6	9	6	15	19	4	23
Working-class local friends	26	6	32	28	8	36	26	18	44
Working-class nonlocal friends	2	0	2	6	4	10	1	1	2
Middle-class local friends	16	0	16	12	8	20	10	4	14
Middle-class nonlocal friends	2	0	2	2	0	2	3	1	4

NOTE: All data are in frequencies and refer to friendship units cited. A unit may be a couple or a single person. Thus, a married couple named as a friendship equals one friendship unit. The total is the sum of units cited.

TABLE 9-4

Characteristics of Friendship Relations Reported by Men and Women,
Means and Standard Deviations

Friends	Males	Females	p^*
Opposite sex	14.8 (275)	9.4 (525)	.01
	23.1	19.2	
Same age	54.2 (275)	60.9 (525)	.05
	38.5	39.3	
Having weekly contact	13.4 (275)	28.2 (525)	.01
	26.9	34.7	
Spontaneous activities	46.3 (275)	59.9 (525)	.01
	42.0	41.2	
Confiding in each other	37.7 (275)	52.8 (525)	.01
	42.7	43.1	

NOTE: The percentage of respondent's friends in each of the categories indicated was computed. The means of these values comprise the first entries in the table. Standard deviations are listed below the means. The number upon which the mean is based appears in parentheses. *One-way analyses of variances were computed to obtain the probability of the observed differences.

SOURCE: A. Booth. "Sex and Social Participation." *American Sociological Review*, 1972, 37:186. Used by permission of author and publisher. For nonprofit use only.

Other data on distributions of friendship relations can be obtained from the sources cited in the references.

General Comments and Recommendations

Although the instrument has not been subjected to rigorous scaling procedures, it does appear to tap relevant dimensions of the friendship relation. Work by Peters (1968) on a youthful population has indicated that some dimensions (confiding and shared activities) of the battery are amenable to scale development.

References

Babchuk, N. "Primary Friends and Kin: A Study of the Associations of Middle Class Couples." *Social Forces*, 1965, 43:483-93.

Babchuk, N., and J. A. Ballweg. "Black Family Structure and Primary Relations." *Phylon*, 1972, 33:334-47.

Babchuk, N., and A. P. Bates. "Primary Relations of Middle Class Couples." *American Sociological Review*, 1963, 28:377-84.

Bates, A. P., and N. Babchuk. "The Primary Group: A Reappraisal." *Sociology Quarterly*, 1961, 2:181-91.

Booth, A. "Sex and Social Participation." *American Sociological Review*, 1972, 37:183-92.

Booth, A., and N. Babchuk. "Seeking Health Care from New Resources." *Journal of Health and Social Behavior*, 1972, 13:90-99.

Peters, G. "Primary Friendship in the College Community: A Study of the Association of Male Students." Ph.D. dissertation, University of Nebraska, 1968.

Peters, G., and M. Kaiser. *Growing Older in Manhattan: Aging in a Small Urban Community*. Manhattan, Kans.: Kansas State University, Department of Sociology and Anthropology, 1972.

Instrument

See Instrument V2.9.I.b.

URBAN SOCIAL NETWORKS
E. O. Laumann, 1973

Definition of Concept or Variable

The measures presented here allow for a multivariate, multidimensional approach to the study of social networks. Laumann (1973) was concerned with the analysis of friendship networks in macrostructural and microstructural terms. Microstructure refers to the pattern or structure of relations among individual actors. The aggregation into categories of individual actors who share similar social positions allows the description of the characteristic pattern of relationships among these categories and thereby describes the macrostructure of a community or society. Macrostructure can be described as the differential likelihood of specific relationships (in this case friendships) being formed among social positions. Social network refers to a specific set of linkages among a defined set of persons, with the additional property that the characteristics of these linkages as a whole can be used to interpret the social behavior of the persons involved. Within this framework, friendship denotes a voluntarily formed and maintained relationship between two persons who, more or less, regard themselves as having a special, affectively toned relationship of mutual trust and esteem.

Description of Instrument

A number of dimensions of friendship networks and relations are measured by Laumann's (1973) 35 items: (1) number of close friendships, (2) frequency of contact with close friends, (3) measures of closeness (intimacy) of friendships, (4) relationships of close friends to respondents, (5) length of time friends have been known, (6) residence of friends, (7) extent to which close friends of respondents are close friends of one another, (8) frequency with which friends see one another at the same time, (9) organizational contexts for meeting close friends, and (10) respondents' perception of friends' status on selected ascribed attributes (e.g., age, religious preference, nationality) and achieved criteria (e.g., occupation, education). A procedure for identifying friends to be interviewed is also included, as are 2 items concerning relations with neighbors.

The 35 items are abstracted from a longer interview schedule. However, the theoretical and analytic model employed by Laumann requires that the full schedule be used if the issues raised in his study are to be addressed. For example, if the underlying dimensionality of the ethnoreligious and occupational macrostructures (as they relate to friendship choices) are to be examined and interpreted, data on the relevant demographic and social characteristics of *both* respondent and friend (minimally as perceived by respondent) must be gathered. Laumann's theoretic and empirical concern with the concept of distance and its measurement —both as an appropriate analogy to physical distance (social quantities bearing a resemblance to physical distance) and in the development of a metric that satisfy the properties of a metric space—required the types of information contained in his full schedule (Laumann, 1973, Appendix C).

Method of Administration

The items are administered by interview. The entire schedule (which includes the 35 friendship items) requires approximately 85 minutes to administer.

Context of Development

The items were developed out of concern with the form and substance of urban social structures through mutual positive orientations and attractions, namely, friendship relations.

However, the procedures he proposed to describe structure do not require that the structures be of this type, nor should they be applicable *only* to urban social structures. The framework synthesizes the perspectives of three disparate and rather independently developed theoretical and research traditions. These were described and discussed as the "stratification tradition," the "sociometric tradition," and the (social) "network approach." Of concern to Laumann was the identification of the consequences of certain "formal" properties of social structures, such as their homogeneity of composition, density of interaction, and interconnectedness of "net" for the functioning of the system.

Sample

A multistage probability sample was drawn from that part of the Detroit SMSA that was tracted in 1950, plus some additions that took into account more recent suburban population growth. Within each dwelling unit having one or more eligible respondents, one person was selected at random for interview. Interviews with 985 white men aged 21 to 64 were obtained, of which 28 were double weighted, yielding a final set of 1,013 cases for use in analysis. Further details on sampling design are found in Laumann (1973, Appendix B).

Norms and Scoring

Laumann's concern with the structure of urban social networks and the concept of distance between various social (i.e., ethnic, religious, and occupational) groups led him to apply smallest space analyses to matrices composed of indexes of dissimilarity. The smallest space solution then locates the social groups in a multidimensional (Euclidean) space in which the Euclidean distance *between* groups represents a conception of social distance analogous to physical distance.

In order to assess the distance between social groups, Laumann first computed indexes of dissimilarity based on the contrast of the conditional probabilities of a given groups's friends with the probability distribution of all friends reported in the sample. The index of dissimilarity is computed as:

$$\text{ID} = \tfrac{1}{2} \left[\sum_{i=1}^{i} | (x_{ai} - x_{bi}) | \right]$$

where i indicates the number of groups (i.e., 22 ethnic groups [p. 48]; either 15 [p. 56] or 27 [pp. 62-63] ethnoreligious groups, and 16 occupational groups), x_{ai} indicates the probability distribution of *one group 's* friends, and x_{bi} indicates the probability distribution of *all* friends in the sample. In short, the index of dissimilarity is the sum across groups of the absolute values of differences in the distribution of friends and serves as a measure of proximity between pairs of groups.

The smallest space solutions applied to the dissimilarity matrices fits an m-dimensional space and determines the goodness of fit between the dissimilarity data and the hypothesized m-dimensional structure. Assuming a good fit (as expressed by the coefficient of alienation), distance *between* groups is computed as the Euclidean distance:

$$d_{AB} = \sqrt{\sum_{i=1}^{n} (X_{Ai} - X_{Bi})^2}$$

where d_{AB} indicates the Euclidean distance, i indicates the number of dimensions in the smallest space solution, X_{Ai} is the ith coordinate for group A, and X_{Bi} is the ith coordinate in smallest space for group B. These distances can be correlated with social status, size of group, or self-selection ratios.

The homogeneity of a respondent's friendship group is measured by summing the Euclidean distances between groups derived from the smallest space solutions. A person who has three friends who are drawn exclusively from his or her own group will have maximum homogeneity — a sum of 0 — while the larger the sum, the more heterogeneous the friendship networks. Measures of ethnoreligious and occupational homogeneity are developed.

Laumann differentiated between "completely interlocking," "partially interlocking," and "radial" friendship networks through the question that determined which of the respondent's three closest friends were good friends of one another. A radial network is one in which ego engages in three discrete dyadic relations with his or her friends; a partially interlocking network is one in which at least two of the friends are good friends of one another and have common interaction with ego; a completely interlocking network is one in which all three of the friends are good friends of one another and have common interaction with ego.

Laumann presented numerous tables relating homogeneity and type of friendship networks to demographic characteristics of associational networks, attitudes, etc. The interested reader is referred to his presentation of these data (Laumann, 1973).

Formal Tests of Reliability/Homogeneity

The goodness of fit of a given smallest space solution is expressed as a coefficient of alienation ranging from 0.00 to 1.00. The coefficients of alienation for one-, two-, and three-dimension solutions, respectively, by social group are: (1) 22 ethnic groups (.322, .187, .128), (2) 15 religious groups (.283, .180, .077), (3) 27 ethnoreligious groups (.377, .202, .132), and (4) 16 occupational groups (.270, .122, .077). A coefficient of alienation of .15 or less indicates an acceptable (rule-of-thumb) fit (Laumann, 1973).

Formal Tests of Validity

Lauman (1973) examined the accuracy with which respondents reported the social attributes (age, occupation, education, political party preference, religious preference, ethnic origin) of their friends. To do this a randomly drawn subsample of the friends ($N = 118$) was interviewed by telephone. Though variations in accuracy on some variables occurred, statistically significant mean differences were not obtained on the six social attributes.

Usability on Older Populations

Although Laumann did not study an older population, there is no good reason to believe that his approach would be unusable for older populations.

Sensitivity to Age Differences

Laumann (1973) reported that the older the respondent, the less likely the reciprocation of friendship choices. Respondents are unlikely to distort reports of friends' ages. Age is unrelated to the two measures of homogeneity for the total sample. However, occupational heterogeneity is associated with older age among those having some high school education or less. Among high school graduates, older men are associated with greater homogeneity of friendship networks. Only among Protestants is older age associated with occupational heterogeneity. Finally, younger respondents tend to have closer ties with friends than older respondents.

General Comments and Recommendations

Although the items and measures described in this section have not been applied to older populations, the level of rigor and sophistication of Laumann's approach demanded that they be included in this chapter. It would be useful to apply the procedures used by Laumann to an older population. The reader is reminded that only those items specifically relating to friends are included in the instrument. A replication of Laumann's approach would require the use of his entire schedule.

References

Laumann, E. O. "Friends of Urban Man: An Assessment of Accuracy in Reporting Their Socioeconomic Attributes, Mutual Choice, and Attitude Agreement." *Sociometry*, 1969, 32:54-69.

_____. *Bonds of Pluralism: The Form and Substance of Urban Social Networks*. New York: John Wiley and Sons, 1973.

Instrument

See Instrument V2.9.I.c.

NEIGHBORHOOD INTEGRATION MEASURES

P. A. Fellin and E. Litwak, 1963

Definition of Concept or Variable

This battery contains a number of measures of neighborhood integration. Neighborhood integration is defined in terms of the extensiveness of group contacts within the membership group. Fellin and Litwak were interested in the frequency of contact with neighbors and the development of affective relations. A basic assumption of the study was that the more people meet with neighbors on a voluntary basis, the more likely they are to engage in diffuse and affective relations.

Description of Instrument

Five dimensions of neighborhood integration are measured: neighborhood cohesion (10 items); present, past, and future orientation to neighborhood (12 items); husband's orientation to interpersonal relations on the job (3 items); attitudes toward discussion of personal problems (1 item); and attitudes toward strangers (5 items). The attitudes toward strangers items can also be treated as a measure of attitudes toward neighboring.

Method of Administration

The items are part of a larger interview schedule.

Context of Development

The battery was developed in the context of a study of the relationship between neighborhood cohesion and mobility. Fellin and Litwak were concerned with the mechanisms that speed the socialization of newcomers and thereby maintain cohesion under conditions of membership turnover. These mechanisms are examined from two perspectives: (1) those where the focus is on the attributes of the mobile person and (2) those where the focus is on the structure of the host group. Of particular interest is the relationship between neighborhood cohesion and mobility among respondents differentially classified as bureaucrats, entrepreneurs, and white-collar or manual workers.

Sample

The respondents in the original sample were 275 white women from the suburban Detroit area. The sample was purposive, selected for replication of Litwak's (1960) study in Buffalo, N.Y. Respondents ranged in age from less than 29 to 45 years old and older. Occupational categories (measured by husbands' occupation) included: (1) bureaucratic ($N = 91$), (2) business-professional ($N = 76$), (3) white-collar ($N = 42$), and (4) manual ($N = 66$). Further details on sampling procedure are reported in Fellin (1961, pp. 112-29).

Norms

Fellin and Litwak (1963) presented a number of cross-tabulations of relevance to the items contained in the battery. Average number of neighbors known for each occupational group are as follows: bureaucratic, $\bar{X} = 12.5$; business-professional, $\bar{X} = 9.8$; white-collar, $\bar{X} = 7.3$; and manual, $\bar{X} = 8.8$.

Formal Tests of Validity

For the three items measuring neighborhood orientation, three additional items were developed for past, present, and future neighborhood reference orientation as a validity check on the original items. Litwak (1960) stated that all but one yielded the same results as the original items, indicating that the original findings and the replication were not just a consequence of question wording. However, statistical results on validity tests have not been provided. Neither has it been made apparent which item failed to produce results similar to the original items.

Usability on Older Populations

The instrument appears to be highly usable.

Sensitivity to Age Differences

For the bureaucratic and combined white-collar/manual groups, the number of friends increases slightly, to age 40, and then it tapers off. Until they reach their 30s, entrepreneurs report more friends; this trend is followed by a decline to age 40, and there is a slight increase thereafter (Fellin and Litwak, 1963, p. 367).

General Comments and Recommendations

The battery of items taps important dimensions of the neighboring relationship and appears to be adaptable to older populations.

References

Fellin, P. A. "A Study of the Effects of Reference Group Orientations and Bureaucratic Careers on Neighborhood Cohesion." Ph.D. dissertation, University of Michigan, 1961.

Fellin, P. A., and E. Litwak. "Neighborhood Cohesion under Conditions of Mobility." *American Sociological Review*, 1963, 28:364-76.

Litwak, E. "Primary Group Instruments of Social Control." Ph.D. dissertation, Columbia University, 1958.

————. "Reference Group Theory, Bureacratic Career, and Neighborhood Primary Group Cohesion." *Sociometry*, 1960, 23:72-84.

Instrument

See Instrument V2.9.I.d.

INTERACTION AND HOMOPHILY IN FRIENDSHIP

G. S. Rosenberg, 1970

Definition of Concept or Variable

The instrument measures aspects of social interaction with friends among older people. Rosenberg (1970) was interested in examining the influence of density of age and social class peers in the respondents' neighborhoods on neighborhood social interaction with friends. Friendship was not conceptually defined by Rosenberg, and qualitative aspects of friendship were not tapped.

Description of Instrument

The instrument consists of 15 items that measure number of friends, frequency of interaction with friends, place of residence of friend, length of time the friend has been known, whether the friends are presently living, and number of new friends made. Status homophily/heterophily was measured by asking the respondent to indicate for each friend: age, occupation, work status, and marital status.

Method of Administration

The items are part of a larger interview schedule.

Context of Development

The instrument was developed in the context of a larger study of the relationships between poverty and old age and between poverty and social isolation from friends and kin among white, working-class respondents living in a large city in the United States.

Sample

The sample consisted of 1,596 noninstitutionalized working-class persons residing in Philadelphia. The respondents ranged in age from 45 to 79 years, with 42% aged 65 and over. About 35% of the sample reported poverty incomes, and 57% were females. The sample was disproportionately of immigrant and foreign stock (29% were born outside the United States).

Norms and Scoring

Rosenberg's (1970) scoring conventions followed his theoretical interest in examining the influence of network homogeneity and the social composition of neighborhoods on neighborhood social interaction with friends. Much of his analysis concerned three patterns of interaction: isolation, having friends beyond the neighborhood, and having friends within the neighborhood. An isolate was a person who had not visited or spoken to a friend or neighbor during the week preceding the interview. About 33% ($N = 533$) of the respondents were identified as isolates. Approximately 44% ($N = 702$) of the sample had conversed with only one or two friends during that period, and about 12% ($N = 192$) had contact with three or more friends. Of those who had contact, 27% ($N = 141$) had all their friends living outside the immediate neighborhood.

Usability on Older Populations

The instrument is usable on older populations.

Sensitivity to Age Differences

Several of Rosenberg's (1970) findings are relevant to age differences. First, the older the neighborhood, the more likely working-class people of any age are to have age peers as friends; but those most likely to have age-homophilous relations under the most favorable local conditions are people who are themselves old, i.e., over 65. Second, friendship pairs often span the conventional dividing line between middle and old age, thus indicating lack of homogeneity. The aged as a group in the working class cannot be considered a separate enclave of the society. Finally, age-homogeneous, informal participation seems to be related to socioeconomic rank rather than age. Role sets of the poor are somewhat more homophilous than those of the solvent, and the poor are more likely to make friends with people older than themselves.

General Comments and Recommendations

The results from Rosenberg's use of the measures are applicable to one social class group in large urban settings. Their applicability, within the conceptual framework employed by Rosenberg, needs to be examined for other settings. Measures of the qualitative aspects of friendship relations could be usefully added.

Reference

Rosenberg, G. S. *The Worker Grows Old*. San Francisco: Jossey-Bass, 1970.

Instrument

See Instrument V2.9.I.e.

INTERPERSONAL CONTACTS

A. J. Reiss, 1959

Definition of Concept or Variable

Reiss (1959) contrasted personal contacts that are anonymous, segmental, and impersonal in nature with those that are intimate and personal. He used the terms *interpersonal* and *personal* interchangeably, although by his approach it is evident that he preferred the latter concept. The focus is on face-to-face contact.

Description of Instrument

A time-budget, or time-diary, approach is used in Reiss's instrument. The time budget is recorded in minutes for the workday. The allocation of an individual's time during a single day is taken as a measure of the amount and kind of personal contact. Reiss (1959) obtained a budget of time for the nearest previous workday and the last full day off.

The time budget opens with the statement: "Now, we would like to know how you spent your time yesterday. We want to know just how much time you spent doing different things during the day and whom you spent it with. Suppose we begin with the time you got up yesterday:

1. What time did you get up? _____
2. What did you do when you first got up? _____
3. Did you spend the time with anyone, or were you more or less alone? _____
4. Whom were you with? _____
5. How close are they to you? _____

SOURCE: A. J. Reiss, Jr. "Rural-Urban and Status Differences in Interpersonal Contacts." *American Journal of Sociology*, 1959, 65:182-95. Reprinted by permission of publisher, The University of Chicago Press.

Each new activity or block of time is similarly explored until the respondent says he or she went to bed. Locus of the activity or the block of time during which it occurred is also noted.

Interviewers are specifically instructed to get information that is coded into one of the following mutually exclusive categories.

1. Intimate kinships, such as nuclear family members and extended kin members.
2. Close intimate friends, friends defined as "very close," "my best friend," etc.
3. Close associate or client, a close friend deriving from a work context, whether or not that person is actually seen at work.
4. Good friend, a friend defined as "close," "just a good friend," etc.
5. Distant associate or casual acquaintance, either a fellow worker who is not defined as a friend or a person with whom respondent has a "speaking acquaintance."
6. Cordial recognition, defined as a person whom respondent recognizes in address, or "just someone to whom I say 'hello.' "
7. Pure client, defined as a person whom respondent does not know personally, but a person with whom contact is made or with whom interaction takes place in a client relationship.

For analytical purposes, time spent in categories 1 through 4 can be summed and defined as "primary contacts"; categories 5 through 7, as "secondary contacts"; and categories 6 and 7, as "impersonal contacts."

Since the respondent is asked about his or her total time awake, an additional category of "no personal contact" is provided. An additional coding convention concerns time allocation to one of three contexts: (1) time spent at work on the job, (2) time spent in exposure to mass media, and (3) time spent in places where secondary contacts are probable. Secondary contacts are defined as relatively anonymous, segmental, and impersonal interpersonal relations. Operationally, secondary contexts are those in which contacts with persons falling into categories 5 through 7 are likely to occur. Reiss (1959) argued that persons need not have experienced any personal contact to be active in a situation. For example, a person can spend time in the intimate setting of the home without contacting family or friends or in the supermarket without speaking to others. Consequently, classification into situations is independent of the classification for interpersonal contacts. Accordingly, the same period of time can be coded for both the contact class and the situation class.

Method of Administration

The time budget is administered by interivew. Conceivably, respondents could be trained to keep the time budget themselves over a period of time, thereby reducing the need to depend on recall.

Context of Development

The procedure was developed as a means of testing hypotheses about differences in types of interpersonal contacts among urban, rural-nonfarm, and rural farm residents.

Sample

Residents of high and low socioeconomic status classified as rural farm (RF), rural non-farm (RNF), and urban residential made up the six populations sampled. The urban population of the Nashville, Tenn., SMSA was classified into white-collar and manual-worker census tracts and four white-collar and three manual-worker tracts were randomly selected. A 25% random sample of dwelling units yielded 176 high-status and 75 low-status respondents. The rural nonfarm and rural farm respondents were selected from a county south of the Nashville SMSA. Within the county, two village communities located at a maximum distance from the Nashville city center were selected, together with the rural area within a 4-mile radius of the communities. The area around the major traffic artery from the central city of these areas was also included in the area sampled. A regularly employed person aged 20 to 65 from every fourth dwelling unit with a male head was interviewed. This yielded an RNF sample with 27 high-status and 24 low-status respondents, and the RF sample included 28 high-status and 21 low-status respondents.

Norms

Reiss (1959, p. 188) reported means and standard deviations for each of the six samples for the seven contact areas, as well as the summary primary contact, secondary contact, and impersonal contact dimensions. In brief, the measure showed that respondents spent the most time in work-related situations, followed by the amount of time in contact with intimate kin. Geographic and status differences are presented.

Usability on Older Populations

The instrument can be used on older populations.

General Comments and Recommendations

This measure allocates daily contact time to persons with whom the respondent has a particular qualitative relationship and to types of social situations. Neither the quality and contact of the interaction nor the broad range of structural characteristics that affect the social allocation of time are examined. The procedure seems sound and should be developed with these additional considerations.

Reference

Reiss, A. J., Jr. "Rural-Urban and Status Differences in Interpersonal Contacts." *American Journal of Sociology*, 1959, 65:182-95.

Instrument

See the description of the instrument given above.

WEISS'S INTIMACY RANKING SCALE (WIR)

L. J. Weiss, 1977

Definition of Concept or Variable

This scale measures the level of interpersonal intimacy perceived within opposite-sex and same-sex relationships and focuses on spouses and friends.

Description of Instrument

A multidimensional approach was used to establish the 16 independent intimacy statements that comprise the scale. The ranking scale measures intimacy for four criterion groups: male friendship, male spouse, female friendship, and female spouse.

Method of Administration

The WIR is administered for each of the four criteria group relationships. It has been included as a part of a larger interview schedule.

Context of Development

The scale was developed by Weiss (1977) in the context of a larger longitudinal study of transitions at the University of California at San Francisco. The scale was employed as a partial test of the hypothesis that intimacy acts as a buffer in an individual's adaption to stress for the older subsamples studied.

Sample

The sample consisted of 171 men and women drawn from the University of California at San Francisco's Human Development Research Program. The respondents were mainly white, middle- and lower-middle-class people living in San Francisco.

Norms and Scoring

Intimacy-level scores are based on rankings of the 16 statements contained in the scale. Respondents are asked to rank the 16 items by importance for their closest friend (or spouse). A 1 equals the most important and a 16 the least important rank. Table 9-5 shows the areas that are most important for each criterion group. Scores are derived in terms of the ranking of these dimensions.

TABLE 9-5
Definition of Criterion Groups for the WIR

Male Friendship Intimacy	Male Spouse Intimacy	Female Friendship Intimacy	Female Spouse Intimacy
Confides in	Emotional attraction	Supportive	Emotional attraction
Comfortable	Confides in	Dependable	Likes me
Dependable	Comfortable	Likes me	Confides in
Respect	Sexual satisfaction	Confides in	Supportive
Supportive	Likes me		Respect
Knows me	Supportive		
Likes me			

SOURCE: L. J. Weiss, Jr. "Interpersonal Intimacy: An Intervening Factor in Adaptation to Stress." Paper presented to the 30th Annual Meeting of the Gerontological Society, San Francisco, November 18-22, 1977. Reprinted by permission of author.

A level of intimacy score is determined from the 16 dimensions contained within WIR by the summation of inverted ranks of only the appropriate dimensions for the four criteria groups and is standardized according to a mean of 50 and a standard deviation of 10. A higher score indicates greater intimacy. Scores ranged from 22 to 77 for the sample described.

Formal Tests of Reliability/Homogeneity

Test-retest reliability on a sample of 45 respondents over a 30-day interval was examined. The level of intimacy with a close friend ($r = .77; r = .67$) or a spouse ($r = .72; r = .71$) was relatively stable for males and females, respectively (Weiss, 1977).

Formal Tests of Validity

The 16 items of the WIR were selected from a pool of 26 items suggested in the literature. A pretest with colleagues of the investigator suggested this reduction. These 16 were then reviewed by a panel of 35 social scientists who ranked each item in order of importance for an *ideal* opposite-sex and an *ideal* same-sex intimate relationship. This panel determined the four conceptual clusters of male/female friendship intimacy and male/female spousal intimacy already noted.

Convergent validity was examined by correlating a single-item indicator of intimacy with WIR scores. Pearson correlations ranged from .64 to .74 in a sample of 44 men and women (Weiss, 1977).

Usability on Older Populations

The instrument can be used on older populations.

Sensitivity to Age Differences

Results indicate both age and sex differences throughout the adult life cycle.

General Comments and Recommendations

The scale is relatively new and has not yet been submitted to extensive testing on a range of populations. However, its rigorous development and promising early results suggest that it taps certain important aspects of intimate relations.

Reference

Weiss, L. J., Jr. "Interpersonal Intimacy: An Intervening Factor in Adaptation to Stress." Paper presented to the 30th Annual Meeting of the Gerontological Society, San Francisco, November 18-22, 1977.

Instrument

See Instrument V2.9.I.g.

NEIGHBORHOOD SOCIAL INTIMACY SCALE
J. Smith, W. H. Form, and G. P. Stone, 1954

Definition of Concept or Variable

Although they did not explicitly define intimacy, Smith, Form, and Stone equated intimacy with friendship and more specifically with the ability to identify "best" friends.

Description of Instrument

This four-item Guttman-type scale measures knowledge of people (friends) in the neighborhood, extent of contact with neighborhood friends, and sense of attachment to neighborhood. Originally, the scale contained six items, two of which were dropped as a result of the scalogram analysis. The responses to the six items were trichotomized and subjected to a Guttman-scale analysis. Ultimately, four items (one trichotomous and three dichotomous) were found to scale (Smith, Form, and Stone, 1954).

Method of Administration

The scale can be administered in either a questionnaire or an interview format.

Context of Development

The scale was developed in the context of a long-term research project on various aspects of urban life. One broad question raised in the research concerns the issue of urban integration. Specifically, the investigators asked how metropolitan residents form informal, intimate, and diffuse social relationships that are crucial for a sense of identification, involvement, and integration when the social structure depends on a functional specialization for its persistence (Smith, Form, and Stone, 1954, p. 276).

Sample

Area probability procedures were used to draw two samples of 573 and 125 residents of a midwestern metropolitan area with a total population of around 140,000 and a central city of about 100,000. The scale was developed on the basis of a randomly selected sample of the interviews (N = 116).

Norms and Scoring

The four items are scored as a Guttman scale with the cutoff points and observed distribution shown in Table 9-6.

TABLE 9-6
Neighborhood Social Intimacy Scale

Question	Intimate (+)	Intermediate (0)	Nonintimate (−)
Know each other	Quite well, very well	Fairly well	Not at all, not so well
Know name	One or more		None
Visit	About half or more		None, a few
Stay here	Yes		No, don't know

Ideal Scale Types	Patterns of Responses 1 2 3 4	Number of Cases
I	+ + + +	34
II	0 + + +	19
III	0 − + +	12
IV	0 − − +	16
V	− − − +	14
VI	− − − −	21

SOURCE: J. Smith, W. H. Form, and G. P Stone. "Local Intimacy in a Middle-Sized City." *American Journal of Sociology*, 1954, 60:278. Reprinted by permission of author and publisher. For nonprofit use only.

Formal Tests of Reliability/Homogenity

The coefficient of reproducibility was .894.

Usability on Older Populations

The instrument is usable for older populations.

General Comments and Recommendations

This short and infrequently used scale measures limited aspects of local ties with friends.

Reference

Smith, J., W. H. Form, and G. P. Stone. "Local Intimacy in a Middle-Sized City." *American Journal of Sociology*, 1954, 60:276-84.

Instrument

See Instrument V2.9.I.h.

CONFIDANTS, NEIGHBORS, AND FRIENDS

G. L. Bultena, E. A. Powers, P. Falkman, and D. Frederick, 1971

Definition of Concept or Variable

This battery measures aspects of an individual's relationships with confidants, neighbors, and friends. A confidant is defined as "a person with whom one can enjoy an intimate relationship and in whom he can confide about personal problems" (Bultena et al., 1971, p. 35).

Description of Instrument

The battery contains six items pertaining to the respondent's present confidants and five items pertaining to his or her past confidants. Respondents are asked to indicate the presence or absence of a confidant and, if a present or past confidant is identified, to specify the confidant's relationship to the respondent; the confidant's gender and age; frequency of contact, and events leading to the development (or loss) of the confidant relationship. An additional 16 items relating to neighboring and friendship relationships are included. These items on neighbors and friends seek the same types of information as are sought on confidants.

Method of Administration

The battery is administered by interview. The items were originally part of a larger interview schedule, and the total interview time averaged about 2 hours.

Context of Development

The battery was employed in a restudy of a sample of older people in Iowa. The original study was completed in 1960. The restudy occurred in 1970.

Sample

Respondents in 1970 were 611 older Iowans who had participated in the 1960 study. The 1960 study included 1,359 randomly selected noninstitutionalized persons aged 60 and over in representative Iowa counties. The 1970 restudy focused on 5 of the original 13 counties. Approximately 44% of the 1960 respondents were available for restudy.

Norms

Bultena and associates (1971) reported that 54% of the respondents identified a confidant and 14% named two such persons. Of the confidants identified, 64% were friends or neighbors and 36% were siblings or other relatives of the respondents. The majority of the confidants (84%) were of the same sex as the respondents, about 50% were within 10 years of the respondents' age, and 64% were within 15 years of the age of the respondents. Twenty-eight percent of the confidants were seen daily and 70%, at least weekly. Only 10 confidants were seen less than once a month. One-third (36%) of the respondents indicated that they had lost a confidant and 16% reported losing two such persons. Death accounted for 67% of the losses, and the residential mobility of confidants accounted for an additional 22%.

General Comments and Recommendations

The items tap only limited aspects of the confidant relationship. Though the items permit confidants to be identified, specify certain characteristics of confidants, and provide a measure of frequency of contact with confidants, the qualitative aspects of the confidant relation are not examined. Similar comments apply to the neighbor and friend items.

Reference

Bultena, G. L., E. A. Powers, P. Falkman, and D. Frederick. *Life after 70 in Iowa*. Sociology Report Number 95. Ames, Iowa: Iowa State University, 1971.

Instrument

See Instrument V2.9.I.i.

FRIENDS AND NEIGHBORS

J. A. Peterson, T. Hadwin, and A. Larson, 1968

Definition of Concept or Variable

This battery of items measures several aspects of friendship and neighboring relation-ships. Though no conceptual definition of friendship or neighboring is presented, item con-tent indicates that the investigators were interested in the losses of friends and neighbors as they related to increasing age and residential mobility.

Description of Instrument

The battery consists of 14 items pertaining to friendship, 8 items pertaining to neigh-bors, and 11 items pertaining to the influence of friends and neighbors on the respondent's decision to move into the retirement community studied. The friendship items measure number, frequency of contact, activities, geographic location, and age homogeneity of cur-rent friends. Present friendship relations are also contrasted with past relations, and the respondent's orientation toward friendship formation is also assessed.

The neighboring items measure number of neighbors, patterns of exchange, and desire for more contact with neighbors.

Method of Administration

The items are administered as part of a larger interview schedule.

Context of Development

The battery is part of a larger study of life satisfaction of older persons before and after moving into an age-segregated community.

Sample

The sample consisted of 182 males and 229 females systematically selected from a larger population of persons who were potential in-movers to Laguna Hills Leisure World, a retirement community located in southern California. Respondents ranged in age from 52 years to 75 years and older, and all were Caucasian (Peterson, Hadwin, and Larson, 1968).

Norms and Distribution

Numerous distributions are found in Peterson, Hadwin, and Larson (1968). In brief, 40.5% report fewer friends than at age 45, about 50% see their friends as much as they would like, and 41.9% feel that their capacity to make friends is about the same as it was at age 45.

Usability on Older Populations

The measure can be used on older populations.

General Comments and Recommendations

This instrument measures only a limited number of dimensions of the friendship and neighbor relationship, and many of the items are retrospective. The items concerning in-fluence of friends and neighbors on the decision to move deserve further testing and stan-dardization.

References

Lemon, B. W., V. L. Bengtson, and J. A. Peterson. "An Exploration of the Activity Theory of Aging: Activity Types and Life Satisfaction among In-Movers to a Retirement Com-munity." *Journal of Gerontology*, 1974, 27:511-23.

Peterson, J. A., T. Hadwin, and A. Larson. *A Time for Work, a Time for Leisure: A Study of Retirement Community In-Movers.* Los Angeles: Andrus Gerontology Center, University of Southern California, 1968.

Instrument

See Instrument V2.9.I.j.

INFORMAL SOCIAL RELATIONS

W. Bell and M. D. Boat, 1957

Definition of Concept or Variable

This battery of items measures informal social participation with neighbors, friends, co-workers, and relatives. Bell and Boat (1957) viewed these as primary social contacts, and they were concerned with the incidence of such relations in urban areas as a function of the social type of a neighborhood.

Description of Instrument

The battery consists of 22 items measuring both the quantitative and qualitative dimension of informal social relations. For each of the four types of informal groups, measures of frequency of contact are obtained. Measures of intimacy included number of close personal friends in each group, extent to which persons depend on group members for support in times of illness, and whether association with group members occurs in respondents' homes. Respondents were also asked where they met their friends and the extent to which association with group members yielded material benefits.

Method of Administration

The items are administered as part of a larger interview schedule.

Context of Development

The instrument was developed as a part of a study of social participation in urban settings (Bell and Boat, 1957). The investigators compared male residents of four different types of neighborhoods with respect to the amount of socializing they did, the nature of their informal contacts, the source of their friendships, and their personal relations in formal associations. The four neighborhoods varied by family status and economic status.

Sample

A probability sample (N = 701) of males over the age of 21 was drawn from four systematically selected census tracts in San Francisco. Each tract represented a different family-economic-status-type neighborhood (Shevky and Bell, 1955): (1) Mission, a low-rent, rooming-house neighborhood (N = 172; low family-low economic status); (2) Outer Mission, a neighborhood of low-rent, detached houses (N = 170; high family-low economic status); (3) Pacific Heights, a high-rent, apartment-house neighborhood (N = 191; low family-high economic status); and (4) St. Francis Wood, a neighborhood of high-rent, detached houses (N = 168; high family-high economic status) (Bell and Boat, 1957).

Norms and Scoring

The response categories for the frequency-of-contact items permit the construction of an index of informal social participation by simply summing frequency of participation in the four informal groups—neighbors, co-workers (outside of work), relatives (other than those living with the respondent), and friends (other than those who are neighbors, co-workers, and relatives).

Table 9-7 shows the percentage distribution of adult males by frequency of participation in all informal groups.

TABLE 9-7
Frequency of Participation in All Informal Groups
(in percentages)

Frequency of Informal Group Participation	Low Family-Low Economic Status (Mission)	Low Family-High Economic Status (Pacific Heights)	High Family-Low Economic Status (Outer Mission)	High Family-High Economic Status (St. Francis Wood)
More than once a week	44.2	50.3	55.3	45.8
About once a week	18.0	13.1	16.5	28.0
A few times a month	18.6	22.5	17.0	17.2
About once a month	8.1	3.1	3.5	2.4
A few times a year	6.4	6.3	6.5	4.8
About once a year	1.8	4.2	0.6	1.2
Never	2.9	0.5	0.6	0.6
Total	100.0	100.0	100.0	100.0
(N)	(172)	(191)	(170)	(168)

SOURCE: W. Bell and M. D. Boat. "Urban Neighborhoods and Informal Social Relations." *American Journal of Sociology*, 1957, 62:392. Reprinted by permission of authors and publisher, the University of Chicago Press.

Usability on Older Populations

The scale is usable for older populations, although items on co-workers may have to be used retrospectively with retired older persons.

General Comments and Recommendations

Although the battery was developed to test particular conceptual issues related to urban life, there is no reason to believe they would not be usable with other populations. Only a limited number of the more qualitative dimensions of informal ties are tapped by the items.

References

Bell, W. "The Utility of the Shevky Typology for the Design of Urban Subarea Field Studies." *Journal of Social Psychology*, 1958, 47:71-83.

Bell, W. and M. D. Boat. "Urban Neighborhoods and Informal Social Relations." *American Journal of Sociology*, 1957, 62:391-98.

Force, M. T., and W. Bell. "Social Structure and Participation in Different Types of Formal Associations." *Social Forces*, 1956, 34:345-50.

Shevky, E., and W. Bell. *Social Area Analysis*. Palo Alto, Calif.: Stanford University Press, 1955.

Instrument

See Instrument V2.9.I.k.

INTERACTION WITH FRIENDS

B. Kutner, D. Fanshel, A. M. Togo, and T. S. Langner, 1956

Definition of Concept or Variable

This battery of items measures aspects of contact with friends. The investigators (Kutner et al., 1956) apparently were interested in "close" friendships, frequency of contact with friends, and the formation of new friendships.

Description of Instrument

The battery contains 10 items measuring presence of local and nonlocal friendships, frequency of contact with friends or relatives, characteristics of friends, how friends were met, and desire for new friends. An isolation index is constructed from the items dealing with interaction with relatives and friends. Friends and neighbors are also two possible alternatives included in a larger list of sources of support (not included here). (See Kutner et al., 1956.)

Method of Administration

The items are administered as part of a larger interview schedule.

Context of Development

The items were developed in a comprehensive survey of the needs of older people in the Kips Bay-Yorkville Health District of New York City.

Sample

A stratified sample of 500 respondents aged 60 years or older was studied. The sample was stratified by socioeconomic status: low status (N = 297), middle status (N = 148), and high status (N = 55). Respondents ranged in age from 60 to 90, with the average age slightly under 70 years.

Norms and Scoring

An index of social isolation is based on items dealing with the degree of contact with friends or relatives. A score of 1 point each was given for: (1) seeing children at least once a month, (2) seeing other relatives at least once a month, (3) having very close friends who are still living, (4) having personal friends, and (5) having made new friends. For purposes of analysis, scores less than 2 were combined into a "limited" interpersonal relations group and those with scores of 3 to 5 into a "broad" interpersonal relations group.

Persons who live alone, are older, and are of low socioeconomic status are more likely to have limited or isolated interpersonal relations (Kutner et al., 1956, p. 110).

Usability on Older Populations

The battery can be used with older populations.

General Comments and Recommendations

The battery is limited in scope, but it has proved to be usable with older populations.

Reference

Kutner, B., D. Fanshel, A. M. Togo, and T. S. Langner. *Five Hundred Over Sixty: A Community Survey on Aging*. New York: Russell Sage Foundation, 1956.

Instrument

See Instrument V2.9.I.l.

Instruments

V2.9.I.a

FRIENDS, NEIGHBORS, AND NEIGHBOR/FRIENDS

I. Rosow, 1967

1. About how many good friends would you say that you have now?_____

2. How many of your good friends live in this neighborhood or section of town?_____

3. How many new friendships have you made during the past year?_____

4. How many of your new friends live in this neighborhood?_____

5. Is the number of neighborhood friends that you have now more, about the same, or less than ten years ago?
   More
   Same
   Less
   Still none

6. Now, who are the neighbors you are friendliest with?
   (Obtain following information on first three—or fewer—persons mentioned.)
   6a. Name(s)
   6b. Sex
   6c. Age
   6d. Marital status
   6e. Where he/she resides
   6f. Occupation

7. How frequently do you visit with, do things with, or spend time with _____ ?
   Name

   (Ask only of persons identified in item 6) (Coded as follows by weekly contact)
   0-1
   2-3
   4+

8. Do you ever wish that you had more friends?
   Yes
   No

9. Is there any old person—any old person at all—that you admire a lot now? (Open-ended —coded as follows)
   Public figure/celebrity
   Other stranger
   Spouse, other household member
   Neighbor
   Relative, friend (not neighbor)
   Other acquaintance
   Nobody

10. If older people have problems, who do you think should help them out and see that they are taken care of? (Open-ended—coded as: self, family, friends, neighbors, formal organization, government, other)

11. Now, who do you think would tend you if you get sick and need care? (Open-ended— coded as: self, spouse, other household member, daughter, other relative, neighbor, other friend; apartment management, social service, other).

Projective Stories—Forced choice between paired groups associated with each story.

12. *The Anniversary (Family-Friend):* Mrs. Johnson was a widow living alone and she received two invitations for *the same day.* One was from her oldest daughter, who was making a big family reunion on her own twenty-fifth wedding anniversary. And Mrs. Johnson's children and relatives would all be there. But, on the same day, her closest friends were celebrating their fiftieth wedding anniversary and at their party she would be able to see all her friends who were still alive.

Her daughter lived too far away for Mrs. Johnson to go to both affairs, even though she wanted to. Both her family and her friends wanted her to come very badly and they would feel hurt and insulted if she did not. She did not want to hurt anybody's feelings, but Mrs. Johnson still had to decide which affair to go to.

Which one do you think she should choose—her *family* or her *friends*?

13. *The Grandson (Family-Neighbor):* Mr. Green's grandson, Bobby, was becoming a wild boy who was always getting into trouble. His last stunt got him arrested and the judge let him off with a warning because it was his first offense. The old man was worried that Bobby was headed for serious trouble if someone did not straighten him out. His neighbor agreed with him and urged Mr. Green to help the boy. But Mr. Green's son, Bobby's father, disagreed and was sure the boy would settle down if people left him alone without meddling.

Mr. Green did not know what to do. If his son was right and he tried to help, then it would be interfering. His son would get mad and maybe not have any more to do with Mr. Green. But if his neighbor was right and he did not help, then Bobby might get into worse trouble.

Whose judgment should Mr. Green take—his *son's* or his *neighbor's?*

14. *The Prize (Friend-Neighbor):* Mr. Samson was a widower who won first prize in a newspaper contest—a trip to California with all expenses paid for *two people*. He did not know whom to invite to go with him, but he finally narrowed it down to either his next door neighbor or another old friend in town. Both these men were retired widowers like himself and Mr. Samson knew that they would both like to go with him.

Mr. Samson and his old friend had been very close for years, but they did not see much of each other since his friend moved away. As for his neighbor, the two to them got along fine together and were a big help to each other as they grew older.

In this case, whom do you think Mr. Samson should invite—his old *friend* or his *neighbor?*

SOURCE: I. Rosow. *Social Integration of the Aged.* New York: Free Press, 1967; and personal communication, 1978.

V2.9.I.b

PRIMARY FRIENDSHIP

N. Babchuk and A. P. Bates, 1963

1. Will you list the initials of the persons *you and your wife* (husband) *both consider* to be very close friends. I don't want their names or who they are. If you and your wife (husband) include other *couples* among your very close friends, will you please consider them as a unit in making your list. The list should not include relatives.
   A. Identify whether friendship is local or non-local, friend's sex, and note if a single friend or a married couple (both of whom are listed) as in the following example:

Male	Female
XX	YX - local married couple
AA	- non-local, single
	DD - local, single
CB	BB - non-local, married couple

   B. Ask the following questions for each friend mentioned.

Local Friendships

1. When did you first become acquainted with ( )? (Note date for each person.)
2. How did you first become acquainted with ( )? (Probe for whether husband or wife initiated the friendship.)
3. About how often do you and your spouse see ( )? (Reference is to friendship unit, whether couple or single person.)

4. (Hand card to respondent.) From the following list, could you tell me the numbers of the kinds of things you do when you and your spouse get together with ( ).
   1. Play cards
   2. Play games (other than cards)
   3. Go out to a restaurant for dinner
   4. Dine at home
   5. Go to movies
   6. Go to concerts
   7. Picnic
   8. Go to sports events
   9. Belong to same organization
   10. Vacation with
   11. Watch TV
   12. Listen to music
5. Have you ever exchanged intimate confidences with ( )?
   ____Yes
   ____No
6. In an emergency situation would you feel free to borrow quite a large sum of money from ( )?
   ____Yes
   ____No
7. When you don't decide together as a couple, are you or your spouse more likely to suggest that you get together with ( )?
8. When you and your spouse are with ( ), who is most likely to suggest things to do?
9. Have you and your spouse ever done things with ( ) on the spur of the moment?
   ____Yes
   ____No
10. Whom would you and your spouse together consider to be your three closest friends? (Answers should list single individuals from those listed above.)

Non-local Friendships

1. When did you first become acquainted with ( )? (Note date for each person.)
2. How did you first become acquainted with ( )? (Probe for whether husband or wife initiated the friendship.)
3. Do you:
   a) Correspond with ( )?
   ____Yes
   ____No
   b) Occasionally visit with ( )?
   ____Yes
   ____No
4. About how often *did* you and your spouse used to see ( )?
5. (Hand card to respondent.) From the following list, could you tell me the numbers of the kinds of things you used to do when you and your spouse got together with ( ).
   1. Play cards
   2. Play games (other than cards)
   3. Go out to a restaurant for dinner
   4. Dine at home
   5. Go to movies
   6. Go to concerts
   7. Picnic

8. Go to sports events
9. Belong to same organization
10. Vacation with
11. Watch TV
12. Listen to music

6. Did you ever exchange intimate confidences with ( )?
___Yes
___ No

7. In an emergency situation would you have felt free to borrow quite a large sum of money from ( )?
___Yes
___ No

8. When you didn't decide together as a couple, were you or your spouse more likely to suggest that you get together with ( )?

9. When you and your spouse were with ( ) who was most likely to suggest things to do?

10. Did you and your spouse ever do things with ( ) on the spur of the moment?
___Yes
___ No

Ask of all respondents:

1. Some persons we know are close and personal while others are somewhat more distant and impersonal. Let us say the number "1" represents a person with whom you have a very close and personal relationship, while a number "5" is a person with whom you have a distant relationship. Where would you place _____ on such a scale?

2. Two years ago was the number of close friends you had the same, greater, or less than now?
___Same
___Greater
___Less

3. Five years ago was the number the same, greater, or less?
___Same
___Greater
___Less

4. How about the past ten years?
___Same
___Greater
___Less

SOURCE: N. Babchuk and A. P. Bates. "Primary Relations of Middle Class Couples." *American Sociological Review*, 1963, 28:377-84. Reprinted by permission of author and publisher. For nonprofit use only.

V2.9.I.c

URBAN SOCIAL NETWORKS

E. O. Laumann, 1973

1. Of the seven days in the week, generally speaking, on how many do you spend at least an hour or two with friends (not counting those persons who live right here with you)?
_____ days in a week.

2. Here are some questions on things that concern you directly—such as friends. Some people think of themselves as having a large number of people they are really close and friendly with. Which of these do you feel comes closer to yourself?

1. One or two.
2. Three or four.
3. Large number (go to 2a).
   2a. How many friends would you say you have of this sort_____No. of friends.
3. Now would you think of the three persons* who are your closest friends and whom you see most often. They can be relatives or non-relatives, as you wish. I'd like to ask several questions about each, such as how long you have known them, so for convenience could you give me just their first name?
   First_____
   Second_____
   Third_____
4. Are any of the persons named relatives of yours? (If yes, determine exact relationship and enter in 4a.)
   1. yes   2. no
   4a. Relationship to R.
   First_____ no_____yes_____relationship
   Second_____ no_____yes_____relationship
   Third_____ no_____yes_____relationship
5. For each of these three persons, would you say he/she is a very close personal friend, or a good friend, or more than an acquaintance? Take_____first.
   A. 1. Very close personal 2. Good friend 3. Acquaintance
   B. 1. Very close personal 2. Good friend 3. Acquaintance
   C. 1. Very close personal 2. Good friend 3. Acquaintance
6. About how long have you known _____? (Repeat for each person.)
   A._____years
   B._____years
   C._____years
7. Could you tell me how old_____is? (Repeat for each person—ask R to guess if exact age unknown.)
   A._____years

*Laumann refers only to "men" in this and following questions. I have substituted the term "person."

   B._____years
   C._____years
8. What is the main job of each person? Take _____first. (Repeat for each person. If retired, indicate and obtain last job. Probe for specific codable occupations, e.g., lathe operator, bank teller, and for self employment.)
                    self-employed
   A._____ 1. Yes 2. No
   B._____ 1. Yes 2. No
   C._____ 1. Yes 2. No
9. How many years of school did_____finish? (Repeat for each person.)

A. 0-8 grades	9-11 some high school	12 high school graduate high school diploma? yes no	vocational training high school diploma? yes no
13-15 some college	16 college graduate college degree yes no	17 or more graduate training	

B. Repeat above for B.

C. Repeat above for C.

10. Do you know what_____'s religious preference is? (Repeat for each person. Where "PROTESTANT," obtain Denomination. Encourage R to guess if necessary: "Well, what is your guess?")*

   A._____

   B._____

   C._____

11. Do you happen to know the original nationality of_____? (Repeat for each person. Encourage R to guess if necessary. If "American," probe for original nationality besides American.")*

   A._____

   B._____

   C._____

12. Is_____generally a Republican or generally a Democrat? (Repeat for each person. Encourage R to guess if necessary.)*

   A. 1. Republican 2. Democrat 3. Independent

   B. 1. Republican 2. Democrat 3. Independent

   C. 1. Republican 2. Democrat 3. Independent

*For Q's 10, 11, 12, if R resists at all, indicate reason for each question but persist.

*10._____
_____
_____

*11._____
_____
_____

*12._____
_____

13. Do any of the persons live in this neighborhood—say, within 10 minutes of here—or do they live somewhere else in the area, or outside of the area? (If asked to clarify "10 minutes," indicate that any means of transportation is acceptable. If asked "the area" interviewer should be prepared to define.)

14. Do you often get together with all three of your best friends at the same time?

   1. Yes

   2. No (if no go to 14a).

      14a. Do you often get together with two of them at the same time?

      1. Yes

      2. No

15. Of your three best friends, how many of them are good friends with one another?

   1. All three of them

   2. Two of them (go to 15a)

   3. None of them

   15a. Circle which two: A B C

16. Where do you most often meet with each of them? At one of your homes or somewhere else? Take_____ first.

   A. At homes (go to 16a)   somewhere else (go to 16b)

      16a. Is that mainly at   16b. Where most often

      1. R's home   is that?_____

      2. A's home   _____

      3. Both equally

   B. At homes (go to 16a')   somewhere else (go to 16b')

      16a'. Is that mainly at   16b'. Where most often

      1. R's home   is that?_____

2. B's home   _____

3. Both equally   _____

C. At homes (go to 16a″)   somewhere else (go to 16b″)

16a″. Is that mainly at   16b″. Where most often

1. R's home   is that?_____

2. C's home   _____

3. Both equally   _____

17. Do you see _____ regularly where you work—that is, at least once or twice a week?

A. 1. Yes 2. No

B. 1. Yes 2. No

C. 1. Yes 2. No

18. All in all, how often do you usually get together with _____ (ourside of work)? (Code for each person as follows)

1. More than once a week

2. Once a week

3. Two or three times a month

4. Once a month

5. Several times a year

6. Rarely

A. _____

B. _____

C. _____

19. (If R married) when you and one or more of your best friends get together, would you say that your spouses are usually along, sometimes along, or rarely along?

1. Usually

2. Sometimes

3. Rarely

4. Never

20. Now, I have two questions about neighbors. First of all, which of the following would best describe the relations you have with your several nearest neighbors? (Put list on card, hand to R and read alternatives.)

1. Often visit one another in each other's homes

2. Frequent casual chatting in the yard or if you happen to run into each other on the street.

3. Occasional casual chatting in the yard or if you happen to run into each other on the street.

4. Hardly know my neighbors.

21. Now let's consider a specific neighbor—the neighbor nearest to your house. (Interviewer: Help R determine neighbor in nearest dwelling unit with separate front entrance. If no choice on basis of distance can be made, pick neighbor living to *right* of R's house/apt. as you enter. If that choice is not appropriate, indicate situation and choose among equally close neighbors by chance method.) What is that neighbor's main job at the present time? (Be specific, e.g., used car salesman, high school teacher. Describe and check.)

1. Self-employed

2. Not self-employed

22. Now here is a list of clubs and organizations that many people belong to. Please look at this list (show card), and tell me which of these kinds of organizations you belong to, if any. Are there any you're in that are not on this list? (Check at left where appropriate,

then ask 23 and 24 for each organization R mentioned.)

23. Would you say that you are very involved or not very involved in _____ ?
(Check response in involvement column question 23.)

24. Do you usually meet any of the three friends you mentioned in meetings of _____ ?
(Check all responses in "friend memberships" column question 24.)

	Q23 Involvement	Q24 Friendship Membership
a. Church-connected Groups (but not the church itself)	1. Very 2. Not	A B C None
b. Labor Unions	1. Very 2. Not	A B C None
c. Veterans' Organizations	1. Very 2. Not	A B C None
d. Fraternal Organizations or Lodges	1. Very 2. Not	A B C None
e. Business or Civic Groups	1. Very 2. Not	A B C None
f. Parent-Teachers Association	1. Very 2. Not	A B C None
g. Community Centers	1. Very 2. Not	A B C None
h. Organizations of People of the Same Nationality	1. Very 2. Not	A B C None
i. Sports Teams	1. Very 2. Not	A B C None
j. Country Clubs	1. Very 2. Not	A B C None
k. Youth Groups (Scout Leaders, etc.)	1. Very 2. Not	A B C None
l. Professional Groups	1. Very 2. Not	A B C None
m. Political Clubs or Organizations	1. Very 2. Not	A B C None
n. Neighborhood Improvement Association	1. Very 2. Not	A B C None
o. Charity or Welfare Organizations	1. Very 2. Not	A B C None
p. Other (specify) _____	1. Very 2. Not	A B C None
q. Other (specify) _____	1. Very 2. Not	A B C None

(If none go to question 25.)

25. Now here's a list of several problems that might come up in a person's life. (Present card.) Some people would ordinarily want to discuss some of these with their friends; others would ordinarily prefer not to. In each, if this were a problem for you, would you ordinarily discuss it with your friends, or would you ordinarily rather not?
(Spouse is not counted as a friend—if spouse given, probe for friends.)

a. What kind of car to buy? 1. Discuss 2. Not discuss
b. Who to vote for for President 1. Discuss 2. Not discuss
c. Troubles between you and your spouse 1. Discuss 2. Not discuss
d. Difficulties at work with your boss 1. Discuss 2. Not discuss
e. A serious personal medical problem 1. Discuss 2. Not discuss

26. One of the things we're interested in is whether people tend to have friends that have the same interests and backgrounds as they do. With this in mind, we've asked you

some questions about your three closest friends. But to get a more accurate picture we'd also like to phone one of your friends and ask him a few questions too. We'd like to pick this friend by chance. Let's see, the first two friends you mentioned were:

A. (Heads)_____

B. (Tails) _____

We'll let A be heads and B be tails. Let's flip a coin to see which friend is the one which we'd like to get information about. Could you give me (selected friend's) last name and address? We won't mention your name, of course, and please don't tell that we'll be calling.

A or B_____
Name

_____
Address

_____   _____
Phone

SOURCE: E. O Laumann. *Bonds of Pluralism: The Form and Substance of Urban Social Networks.* New York: John Wiley and Sons, 1973, pp. 262-93. Reprinted by permission of author and publisher.

V2.9.I.d

NEIGHBORHOOD INTEGRATION MEASURES

P. A. Fellin and E. Litwak, 1963

Measures of Neighborhood Integration

1. How many neighbors do you know well enough to call on?_____
2. How many neighbors do you know well enough to spend an afternoon or evening with? _____
3. How many neighbors do you know well enough to call by their first names?_____
4. How often do you borrow things from one another such as books, dishes, etc.?_____
5. How often do you talk with neighbors about dressing for an important occasion?_____
6. How often do you talk with neighbors about entertaining friends?_____
7. How often do you talk with neighbors about the sex education of the children?_____
8. How often do you talk with neighbors about disagreements with in-laws?_____
9. How often do you talk with neighbors when you are worried or upset?_____
10. How often do you talk with neighbors about getting advice on getting a job? _____

The following response categories apply to questions 4-10:

Always
Sometimes
Seldom
Never
Don't know

Husband's Orientation to Interpersonal Relations on the Job

1. On your husband's present job, how often does he have to make new friends and leave old ones?
2. Does your husband have the kind of job where he is:
   a. working with someone else at every stage
   b. or is it the kind of job where he does the job more or less on his own and then someone else carries on?
3. Would you say your husband's job is the kind where a person has to talk things over on a friendly basis with his fellow workers if the work is to go ahead smoothly?

The following response categories apply to the items 1 and 3:

Always
Sometimes
Seldom
Never
Don't know

Neighborhood Reference Orientation

1. Past neighborhood orientation
    a. Were you near houses of good friends?
    b. At that time of your life, how close were your neighbors to what you think neighbors should be like?
    c. Was thinking about how your neighbors might handle problems like furnishing a house, controlling children, or dealing with in-laws:
    a. helpful to you
    b. harmful
    c. or wouldn't you think about it?
    d. Have you gotten any ideas from your neighbors about the following things: caring for children?

Response categories for items 1a and 1d are:
Always
Sometimes
Seldom
Never
Don't know

Response categories for item 1b were not available.

2. Present neighborhood orientation
    a. Are you near houses of good friends?
    b. At your present time of life, how close are your neighbors to what you think neighbors should be like?
    c. Would thinking about how your neighbors might handle problems like furnishing a house, controlling children, or dealing with in-laws be:
    a. helpful to you?
    b. harmful?
    c. or wouldn't you think about it?
    d. Have you gotten any ideas from your neighbors about the following things: caring for children?

Response categories for items 2a and 2d are:
Always
Sometimes
Seldom
Never
Don't know

Response categories for item 2b were not available.

3. Future neighborhood orientation
    a. Is there a good chance your husband will take a job out of town?
    b. How long do you expect to stay in this neighborhood?
    c. Do young couples just starting out have to expect to move around quite a bit or not before settling down?
    d. If people have to move around some before settling down, is it generally a good or bad idea to make friends in a temporary neighborhood?

Response categories for items 3a, 3c, and 3d are:

Always
Sometimes
Seldom
Never
Don't know

Response categories for item 3b were not available.

Attitude toward Discussion of Personal Problems

1. Do you think a person who has personality problems like being shy or losing his temper can or cannot talk about these problems with neighbors?

Always
Sometimes
Seldom
Never
Don't know

Attitudes toward Strangers (Neighboring)

"In general which, if any, of the following attitudes do you think a person should take toward new neighbors?"

1. Go over to their house after they move in and offer help.
2. Go over to their house and introduce yourself, but do not offer help unless they ask for it.
3. Don't go over unless invited, but be friendly.
4. Don't become too friendly until you have had some time to see what kind of people they are.
5. Stay away from all newcomers and keep to lifetime friends.

Finally, an item tapping the extent to which friends of the wife are shared by the husband.

1. Think of the friends you see most often. Are these the same friends your husband will see most often or not?

Always
Sometimes
Seldom
Never
Don't know

SOURCE: P. A. Fellin and E. Litwak. "Neighborhood Cohesion under Conditions of Mobility." *American Sociological Review*, 1963, 28:364-76. Reprinted by permission of authors and publisher. For nonprofit use only.

V2.9.I.e

INTERACTION AND HOMOPHILY IN FRIENDSHIP

G. S. Rosenberg, 1970

1. Thinking back over the past seven days, could you tell me which of your friends or neighbors you have visited with or talked to? (IF RESPONDENT WORKS, EXCLUDE VISITS DURING WORKING HOURS, BUT INCLUDE TELEPHONE CALLS—LIST NAMES IN LINE 1) (PROBE—Anyone else?) (COMPLETE THE LISTING OF FRIENDS AND THEN FOR EACH LISTING, ASK Q.'s 2-11)
2. About how old do you think_____is? (WRITE IN AGE IN LINE 2)
3. How far from you does_____live? (CIRCLE IN LINE 3)
4. How often do you get together with_____? (CIRCLE IN LINE 4)
5. What does_____do for a living . . . (his) (her) usual job? (GET SPECIFIC OCCUPATION, NAME OF COMPANY—WRITE IN LINE 5)

6. Does he/she usually have a job? (CIRCLE IN LINE 6)
7. Does his job mainly involve working with his hands? (CIRCLE IN LINE 7)
8. Is your (husband) (wife) usually present when you see _____ ? (CIRCLE IN LINE 8)
9. How many years have you known _____ ? (WRITE IN YEARS IN LINE 9)
10. Is _____ married, widowed, divorced, separated or never married? (CIRCLE IN LINE 10)
11. Is _____ working full time, part time, or not working? (CIRCLE IN LINE 11)

	(WRITE IN NAMES—ONE NAME PER COLUMN)								
Line 1 Q. 1	Name None								
Line 2 Q. 2	Age								
Line 3 Q. 3	Less than 1 block	1	1	1	1	1	1	1	1
	1-5 blocks	2	2	2	2	2	2	2	2
	Over 5 blocks	3	3	3	3	3	3	3	3
Line 4 Q. 4	Several times per yr.	1	1	1	1	1	1	1	1
	1-2 times per month	2	2	2	2	2	2	2	2
	1-2 times per week	3	3	3	3	3	3	3	3
	3 or more times per wk.	4	4	4	4	4	4	4	4
Line 5 Q. 5	Occupation (Duties & Company)								
Line 6 Q. 6	Yes	1	1	1	1	1	1	1	1
	No	2	2	2	2	2	2	2	2
Line 7 Q. 7	Yes	1	1	1	1	1	1	1	1
	No	2	2	2	2	2	2	2	2
Line 8 Q. 8	Spouse usually present	1	1	1	1	1	1	1	1
	Spouse not present	2	2	2	2	2	2	2	2
Line 9 Q. 9	Number of years known								
Line 10 Q. 10	Married	1	1	1	1	1	1	1	1
	Widowed	2	2	2	2	2	2	2	2
	Divorced	3	3	3	3	3	3	3	3
	Separated	4	4	4	4	4	4	4	4
	Never married	5	5	5	5	5	5	5	5
Line 11 Q. 11	Full time	1	1	1	1	1	1	1	1
	Part time	2	2	2	2	2	2	2	2
	Not working	3	3	3	3	3	3	3	3

12. Of those friends you used to see a lot, or phone or write to frequently in the past 5 years, have any passed away during these past 5 years

                                 Yes   1

(SKIP TO Q. 16) No   2

13. What were their names? Any other? (RECORD IN COLUMN 1 BELOW)
14. (FOR EACH LISTING) In what year did _____ pass away? (RECORD IN COLUMN 2 BELOW)
15. Have you found another friend to help make up that loss? (CIRCLE CODE IN COLUMN 3 BELOW)

Question 13	Q. 14	Question 15	
Column 1	Col. 2	Column 3	
First Name	Year	Found New Friend	Did Not
		1	2
		1	2
		1	2
		1	2
		1	2
		1	2
		1	2
		1	2
		1	2
		1	2

16. Of those friends you need to see a lot, or phone or write to frequently in the past 5 years, have you lost touch with any of them because you, he/she, moved away?

           Yes   1

(SKIP TO Q. 20) No   2

17. What were their names? (RECORD IN COLUMN 1 BELOW)
18. (FOR EACH LISTING) In what year did you or (he) (she) move away? (RECORD IN COLUMN 2 BELOW)
19. Did you find a new friend to replace _____ ? (CIRCLE CODE IN COLUMN 3 BELOW)

Question 17	Q. 18	Question 19	
Column 1	Col. 2	Column 3	
First Name	Year	Found New Friend	Did Not
		1	2
		1	2
		1	2
		1	2
		1	2
		1	2
		1	2
		1	2
		1	2
		1	2

SOURCE: G. S. Rosenberg, personal communications, 1978. Used with permission.

V2.9.I.f

INTERPERSONAL CONTACTS

A. J. Reiss, Jr., 1959

See the description of the instrument in the abstract.

V2.9.I.g

WEISS'S INTIMACY RANKING SCALE

L. J. Weiss, 1977

Respondents are asked to complete the following for both their closest friend and spouse — where both relationships are relevant.

Here are 16 statements which represent different attributes or qualities which some people consider important in interpersonal relationships.

Please number each statement in terms of *what you would consider the MOST IMPORTANT*. (Put a 1 next to the most important attribute, and so on through number 16 which would be the least important attribute.) Respondents are asked to rank in order the items in terms of specific intimate relations they have.

_____ I respect him or her
_____ Is dependable and trustworthy
_____ Is supportive and accepting
_____ Likes me
_____ Knows me well
_____ Provides sexual satisfaction
_____ Is comfortable and easy to be with
_____ Would help me out in a crisis
_____ Is someone I can confide in
_____ Shares activities with me
_____ Is physically attractive
_____ Is enjoyable, entertaining company
_____ Has similar attitudes (ideas, values, morals, ethics)
_____ We feel a strong emotional attraction for each other
_____ Has similar interests
_____ Has a similar or complementary personality

SOURCE; L. J. Weiss, Jr. "Interpersonal Intimacy: An Intervening Factor in Adaptation to Stress." Paper presented to the 30th Annual Meeting of the Gerontological Society, San Francisco, November 18-22, 1977. Reprinted by permission of author.

V2.9.I.h

NEIGHBORHOOD SOCIAL INTIMACY SCALE

J. Smith, W. H. Form, and G. P. Stone, 1954

1. How well do you think the people in this neighborhood know each other?
   ___+___ Very well
   ___+___ Quite well
   ___0___ Fairly well
   ___-___ Not so well
   ___-___ Not at all

2. About how many of them would you say you know by name?

    + = One or more

3. About how many do you spend a whole afternoon or evening with every now and then?

    + = About half or more

4. If you had your choice would you continue living in this neighborhood?

    _____+_ Yes

    _____-_ No

    _____-_ Don't know

[The authors employed two additional questions with the scale items which the reader might consider for use in conjunction with the scale. These items were not submitted to scalogram analysis. Respondents were asked to:]

1. Name your three best friends.

2. Provide the addresses of the three persons designated as best friends.

[Respondents were asked not to consider only local (within the neighborhood) relationships in designating best friends.]

SOURCE: J. Smith, W. Form, and G. P. Stone. "Local Intimacy in a Middle-Sized City." *American Journal of Sociology*, 1954, 60:278. Reprinted by permission of authors and publisher. For nonprofit use only.

V2.9.I.i

CONFIDANTS, NEIGHBORS, AND FRIENDS

G. L. Bultena, E. A. Powers, P. Falkman, and D. Frederick, 1971

Confidants

1. Is there any one person you feel particularly close to?

    We are thinking of someone other than your husband/wife or a child whom you share your innermost feelings with; someone you feel you can really depend on; in other words, someone who is closer to you than "just" a friend.

    _____ No   (go to 2)

    _____ Yes   List no more than 2 persons. If respondent lists more than 2, check here___
                    and ask: Is one or two of these persons particularly close to you?

           _____No (go to 2)

           _____Yes

    1A.   What is this person's relationship to you? (Record below)

    1B.   Determine sex of confidant(s).

    1C.   What is his/her approximate age?

    1D.   About how often do you *talk* to him/her?

    1E.   Was there anything in particular that happened in your life that led you to establish such a close relationship with this person, such as your moving to a new community; a decline in your health; the loss of a spouse; or something like that?

Present Confidants

A. Relationship	(1)	(2)
Brother/sister, other relative	___	___
Friend	___	___
Neighbor	___	___
Other (specify)	___	___

B. *Sex*
    Male   ———   ———
    Female   ———   ———
C. *Age*   ———   ———
D. *Frequency of Contact*
    Every day   ———   ———
    Every week   ———   ———
    Several times a month   ———   ———
    Monthly   ———   ———
    Less often   ———   ———
E. *Events Leading to the Establishment*
    of Confidant (Record all responses)
    Residential mobility   ———   ———
    Decline in health   ———   ———
    Loss of spouse   ———   ———
    Loss of children   ———   ———
    Loss of friends   ———   ———
    New acquaintances   ———   ———
    Other (specify)   ———   ———
    Other (specify)   ———   ———
    Don't know   ———   ———

2. *Has* there been any one person that you enjoyed a particularly close relationship to, but who is no longer close to you? This would be someone other than your husband/wife or a child with whom you shared your innermost feelings; someone you felt you could really depend on.

———No

———Yes   Record the following information on no more than 2 persons. If the person lists more than 2 persons check here——— and ask: Was one or two of these persons particularly close to you?

———No

———Yes

2A.   What *was* this person's relationship to you? (Record below)
2B.   Determine sex of confidants.
2C.   What *was* his/her age relative to your own? Would you say this person was: older, about your age, or much younger than yourself?
2D.   What led to your no longer having this person close to you?

Past Confidants

A. *Relationship*   (1)   (2)
    Brother/sister, other relative   ———   ———
    Friend   ———   ———
    Neighbor   ———   ———
    Other (specify)   ———   ———
B. *Sex*
    Male   ———   ———
    Female   ———   ———
C. *Age Relative to Respondent*
    Older   ———   ———
    About the same age   ———   ———
    Younger   ———   ———
D. *Loss of Confidant*

Residential mobility of confidant _____   _____
Residential mobility of respondent _____   _____
Death of confidant _____   _____
Other (specify) _____   _____

Neighbors and Friends

1. Would you say that you know most, some, only a few, or none of your neighbors by their first name?

_____ Most

_____ Some

_____ Few

_____ None

2. About how many of the people in this neighborhood are in your age group: Would you say that it is none, only a few, or most of them?

_____ None

_____ Few

_____ Some

_____ Most

_____ Don't know

3. Are there enough friendly neighbors around here?

_____ Yes

_____ No

_____ Other (specify)

4. Are there any relatives, close friends or neighbors that you spend some time visiting with every day or nearly every day? (Do not include children, siblings, or persons in household.)

_____ No (go to 5)

_____ Yes

4A. What are their first names? (List below: ask C-D for each)

4B. Ask sex if unclear from name.

4C. Is _____ a relative, close friend, or neighbor? (Code R-relative; N-neighbor; F-friend)
        Name

4D. What is _____ approximate age?
        Name

Daily Interaction

Name	Sex	Relationship R,F, N	Age
1.			
2.			
3.			
4.			

5. Are there any special friends, neighbors, or other relatives that you visit with regularly each week, but whom you are not likely to visit with every day?

_____ No (go to 6)

_____ Yes

5A. What are their first names? (List below: ask C-D for each)

5B. Ask sex if unclear from name.

5C. Is _____ a relative, close friend, or neighbor?
        Name
    (Code R-relative; N-neighbor; F-friend)

5D. What is _____ approximate age?
        Name

Weekly Interaction
Relationship

Name	Sex	R,F,N	Age

1.
2.
3.
4.
5.
6. Would you say that in the last few years the amount of contact you have with your friends, neighbors, and relatives has remained about the same, has been increasing, or has been declining?

_____ Increasing (ask 6A)

_____ About the same (go to 7)

_____ Declining (ask 6A)

6A.   What are the reasons for this increase/decrease in the amount of contact you have with your friends, neighbors, and relatives?_____

_____

7. Would you like to have more contact with your friends, neighbors, and relatives than you have now; do you feel that the amount of contact now is about right; or would you like to see your friends less often?

_____ Want more contact

_____ About right

_____ Less often

_____ Other (specify)

SOURCE: G. L. Bultena, E. A. Powers, P. Falkman, and D. Frederick. *Life after 70 in Iowa.* Sociology Report numer 95. Ames, Iowa: Iowa State University, 1971, pp. 114, 123-25, 142-43.

V2.9.I.j

FRIENDS AND NEIGHBORS

J. A. Peterson, T. Hadwin, and A. Larson, 1968

Friends

1. How many friends do you have that you would call really close friends, people you can confide in and talk over personal matters with? (Get a specific number if possible)_____
2. How many of these people are about your age? Would you say:

_____ 1. Most of them

_____ 2. Some of them

_____ 3. Very few of them

3. Do these people live in your immediate neighborhood, nearby in Los Angeles or Orange County, or in some other area?

_____ 1. Neighborhood

_____ 2. Los Angeles or Orange County

_____ 3. Other (specify) _____

4. About how often do you get together with your close friends? Would you say you see them almost every day, several times a week, several times each month, or once a month or less?

_____ 1. Almost every day

_____ 2. Once a week

_____ 3. Few times a month

_____ 4. Once a month or less

5. What kinds of things do you usually do with your friends? _____

6. Do you wish you could see more of your close friends than you do, or would you like more time to yourself?
   _____ 1. See more of close friends
   _____ 2. See them right amount
   _____ 3. Have more time to self

7. Do you now have more friends whom you see regularly as compared to when you were 45 years of age, or fewer now? (If less than 50, 10 years ago)
   _____ 1. More now
   _____ 2. About the same
   _____ 3. Fewer now

8. Would you say you are the kind of person who meets a lot of people?
   _____ 1. Yes (Go to Question 10)
   _____ 2. No (Go to Question 9)

9. Would you say you make friends of most of the people you do meet or just a few of them?
   _____ 3. Makes friends of most.
   _____ 4. Makes friends of just a few.
   [Skip to Q. 11]

10. Would you say you make friends of most of the people you meet or just a few of them?
    _____ 1. Makes a lot of friends
    _____ 2. Makes just a few friends

11. Would you say you make friends more easily or less easily compared to when you were 45? (If less than 50, 10 years ago)
    _____ 1. More easily now
    _____ 2. About the same
    _____ 3. Less easily now

12. Did you at any time before you were 45 years of age yourself have a close relationship with an older person that you thought led a useful and happy life? (Either friend or relative)
    _____ 1. Yes (Go to Question 13)
    _____ 2. No (Stop)

13. Who was that (relationship)? _____

14. Did this person actually live with you, or was it someone that you just saw fairly often?
    _____ 1. Lived with respondent
    _____ 2. Saw often only

Neighbors

1. Let's talk a little about your neighbors. Do you know any of your neighbors well enough to talk to them when you meet them on the street?
   _____ 1. Yes (Go to Question 2)
   _____ 2. No (Go to Question 4)

2. About how many do you know well? _____

3. How often do you and your neighbors: read list below. Probe for how often.

	Daily	Once or Twice a Week	Once or Twice a Month	Less than Once a Month	Never
3a. Loan each other					

		Daily	Once or Twice a Week	Once or Twice a Month	Less than Once a Month	Never
	things or do favors for each other	5	4	3	2	1
3b.	Visit with each other	5	4	3	2	1
3c.	Ask each other for advice on problems	5	4	3	2	1

4. Would you like to get together with neighbors more often than you do, or would you like more time to yourself?
   _____ 1. More often with neighbors
   _____ 2. See them right amount
   _____ 3. More time alone

5. Do you now get together with your neighbors more or less often than you did when you were 45?
   _____ 1. More now (Go to Question 6)
   _____ 2. Less now (Go to Question 6)
   _____ 3. No change (Stop)

6. Why is that? _____

Influences on decision to move

1. Did anyone who is not a relative, like one of your friends or neighbors, help you in your decision to move?
   _____ 1. Yes (Go to Question 2)
   _____ 2. No (Go to Question 4)

2. Who was that? Was that a friend, a neighbor, or someone else?
   _____ 1. Friend
   _____ 2. Neighbor
   _____ 3. Someone else (specify) _____

3. In what way did they help? _____
   _____ (Go to Question 7)

4. Have you ever discussed moving into this retirement community with any of your friends and neighbors?
   _____ 1. Yes (Go to Question 5)
   _____ 2. No (Go to Question 7)

5. Who was that? Was that a friend, a neighbor, or someone else?
   _____ 1. Friend
   _____ 2. Neighbor
   _____ 3. Someone else (specify) _____

6. How did they seem to feel about it? _____
   _____

7. Is there anyone you know who is planning to move into the same retirement community?
   _____ 1. Yes (Go to Question 8)
   _____ 2. No (Go to Question 9)

8. Who is that? Is it a friend, a relative, or someone else?
   _____ 1. Friend
   _____ 2. Relative (specify) _____
   _____ 3. Someone else (specify) _____
   _____ (Go to Question 10)

9. Would you feel happier about this move if someone you know were moving in too?
   _____ 1. Yes
   _____ 2. No
10. Does anyone that you already know *already* live in such a community?
    _____ 1. Yes (Go to Question 11)
    _____ 2. No (Stop)
11. Who is that? Is it a friend, relative, or someone else?
    _____ 1. Friend
    _____ 2. Relative (specify) _____
    _____ 3. Someone else (specify) _____

SOURCE: J. A. Peterson, T. Hadwin, and A. Larson. *A Time for Work, A Time for Leisure: A Study of Retirement Community In-Movers.* Los Angeles: Andrus Gerontology Center, University of Southern California, 1968. Reprinted from pp. 11, 12, 18, and 23 of the appendix by permission of the author and the Andrus Gerontology Center.

V2.9.I.k

INFORMAL SOCIAL RELATIONS

W. Bell and M. D. Boat, 1957

1. How frequently do you get together informally with neighbors?
   _____ More than once a week
   _____ About once a week
   _____ A few times a month
   _____ About once a month
   _____ A few times a year
   _____ About once a year
   _____ Never
   How frequently do you get together informally with co-workers?
   _____ More than once a week
   _____ About once a week
   _____ A few times a month
   _____ About once a month
   _____ A few times a year
   _____ About once a year
   _____ Never
   How frequently do you get together informally with friends?
   _____ More than once a week
   _____ About once a week
   _____ A few times a month
   _____ About once a month
   _____ A few times a year
   _____ About once a year
   _____ Never
   How frequently do you get together informally with relatives?
   _____ More than once a week
   _____ About once a week
   _____ A few times a month
   _____ About once a month
   _____ A few times a year
   _____ Never

2. How many close personal friends do you have among your *type of group*? (Neighbors, co-workers, friends, relatives) _____

3. How many persons among your *type of group* could you call on to take care of you if you were sick for even as long as a month? _____

4. Apart from the enjoyment you get out of it, does your participation with *type of group* yield material benefits? _____

5. How many of your "close personal friends" have you met:
   _____ In the neighborhood
   _____ At work

6. How many of your "close personal friends" belong to formal associations of which you are a member? _____

7. Do most of your associations with *type of group* occur at your home or elsewhere? ___
*Questions 2-4 and 7 are asked for each group.

SOURCE: W. Bell and M. D. Boat. "Urban Neighborhoods and Informal Social Relations." *American Journal of Sociology*, 1957, 62:391-98. Reprinted by permission of authors and publisher, the University of Chicago Press.

V2.9.I.1

INTERACTION WITH FRIENDS

B. Kutner, D. Fanshel, A. M. Togo, and T. S. Langner, 1956

1. Do you go around with a certain bunch of close friends who visit each other or do things together?
   _____ Yes
   _____ No

2. Would you say that most of your *close* friends are living, only some of them, or almost none?
   _____ Most
   _____ Some
   _____ None

3. Do you have any close friends here in the *community* whom you occasionally talk over personal matters with?
   _____ Yes: About how many _____
   _____ No: Do you have *any* friends here in the *community* you see from time to time in a friendly way?
       _____ No (go to 6)
       _____ Yes: About how many _____

4. Now, think of the friend that you know best here in the *community*. How often do you get to see that friend?
   _____ At least once a week
   _____ Every two or three weeks
   _____ About once a month
   _____ Less frequently

5. Have you made any new friends here in the *community* in recent years:
   _____ No (go to 6)
   _____ Yes B. Think of the closest new friend you have made in recent years. How long have you known this friend? _____
       C. Is this person a man or woman? _____
       D. Is he/she about your age, younger, or older than you? _____
       E. How did you happen to meet this friend?

_____Through work
_____Through a club
_____Through another friend
_____Through a relative
_____We were neighbors
_____Other (specify) _____

6. How often do you find yourself wishing you meet (more) new friends?
_____ Often
_____ Sometimes
_____ Hardly ever

Items on children and other relatives (used with above items in computing isolation index):

7. How many living children do you have? (omit if never married)
_____ None
_____ One
_____ Two
_____ Three
_____ Four or more

8. How often do you see them? (ask about one seen most frequently)
_____At least once a week
_____Every two or three weeks
_____About once a month
_____Less frequently

9. About how many close relatives do you have who live here?
_____None
_____One
_____Two
_____Three
_____Four or more

10. How often do you see them? (ask about one seen most frequently)
_____At least once a week
_____Every two or three weeks
_____About once a month
_____Less frequently

SOURCE: B. Kutner, D. Fanshel, A. M. Togo, and T. S. Langner. *Five Hundred Over Sixty*. New York: Russell Sage Foundation, 1956, pp. 286-88. Reprinted by permission of publisher.

Chapter 10

Voluntary Associations

C. Neil Bull

Participation in voluntary associations has been shown to play a major role in most societies. Such organizations have been shown to be important agents in supporting normative order (Babchuk and Edwards, 1965), integrating people into a community (Hausknecht, 1962), improving the quality of community services (Young and Larson, 1965), providing leisure-time activities (Godbey and Parker, 1976), providing for volunteer roles (Smith, 1973), and developing political resources (Cutler and Mimms, 1977). It is, therefore, important to know who participates in voluntary associations and why there is differential participation by certain segments of the population. Investigations of the rates of participation of the elderly, both as members and as volunteers, are seen as an area of growing importance. This chapter initially will look at instruments used to measure participation in voluntary organizations and then at instruments directed at the role of the volunteer.

Participation in Voluntary Associations

Formal voluntary organization, voluntary group, and *voluntary association* are terms used interchangeably in the literature. They refer to a group that is freely brought together for a specific purpose, has some sort of charter and rules, is generally long lasting, and is nonprofit in nature (for more detail see Scott, 1957). However, the lack of a standard definition of what constitutes a voluntary organization has had a marked effect on the research. The major difficulty revolves around the freedom of choice in joining or leaving an organization, and two main classes of organization are affected: those associated with work and those with religion. First, membership in a union or a professional association is often a prerequisite for employment, and continued membership is required while the job is held. As a result, there often is little freedom of choice as to membership in these organizations, given that a certain job is selected. Second, membership in a religious organization is usually chosen first for people by their parents, but the freedom to join or leave increases with age. These two difficulties raise the question of whether unions, professional associations, and religious organizations should be classified as voluntary organizations. Some studies include them and others do not; this makes comparisons in the number of memberships difficult.

Most studies try to tap the dimension of membership by using questions on affiliations. Again, however, measurement problems have plagued the field, producing very diverse estimates of the percentage of the general population having at least one membership.

Participation can be measured minimally by the number of organizations to which a person belongs. Most often, investigators use only one of two questions to obtain such information and, as noted, may include or exclude unions, professional associations, and participation in formal church ceremonies. This measure (number of affiliations) taps the lowest level of intensity of affiliation and perhaps produces overestimates of the number of memberships. As a result, nominal participation is not a useful index. Many studies have also included measures concerned with the frequency of attendance at meetings over a given time interval (e.g., the number of hours spent at meetings during the last month or the number of times meetings were attended during the last month) together with a measure dealing with the number of past or present offices or committee memberships held. Each of these measures can be used to form an ordinal measure of participation. Two important works formed the basis for necessary developments in the field: first, the Social Participation Scale developed by Chapin (1947) and reviewed in Chapter 2 of this volume and, second, the Institute for Social Research at the University of Michigan's work, *A Social Profile of Detroit: 1952*, a classification scheme that was to be used later in the "aided recall" technique.

It would appear cogent that in measuring memberships the following guidelines should be followed: (1) unions should be excluded; (2) among church-related groups, only those in which membership is not religiously compelled should be included (such as committees, auxiliaries, etc.); and (3) some measure of intensity of involvement must be included.

Probably the best method to be used is that of aided recall, in which a list of the various types of organizations is handed to the respondent and subsequent questions on each organization are used to elicit the respondent's degree of involvement and how he or she came to join the organizations. The best example of this approach is that provided by Babchuk and Booth (1969).

Almost all research on membership in voluntary associations uses questions that are readily applicable to all age-groups, with the exception of persons under the ages of eight or nine. Little seems to be required to adapt questions specifically to an aged population, with the possible exception of including an expanded section on past memberships when a history of voluntary participation is of interest. However, it should be noted that there is a growing number of age-specific organizations for the elderly (e.g., the Grey Panthers, the American Association of Retired Persons [AARP]) and specific questions may be needed to sharpen this area of research.

A different approach has been to classify voluntary organizations by their functions in society. Jacoby and Babchuk (1963) looked at the differences between instrumental and expressive organizations.

Volunteerism

A distinction must be made between a volunteer and a voluntary participant. A volunteer is a person who gives his or her time to help operate a voluntary organization or who works without pay in such health-related organizations as hospitals and nursing homes. The voluntary participant, however, is more likely to attend functions of voluntary organizations with no other intended commitment. Volunteerism among the elderly has gained popularity since the federal government has become increasingly involved in creating voluntary agencies and has recognized the significant contribution older volunteers can make as in extending social programs and services. Good examples are the Foster Grandparents Program, the Retired Senior Volunteer Program, the Senior Companion Program, and the Service Corps of Retired Executives.

As with the area of membership in voluntary associations, research on volunteerism has focused on the social correlates of volunteerism. The variables of age, sex, marital status, socioeconomic status, race, and health have been used to predict the degree of, and potential for, volunteering. As an independent variable, volunteerism has been examined as a correlate of the degree of life satisfaction, especially among the elderly.

A further refinement of the concept of volunteerism has been the attention to the degree of satisfaction with the volunteer role. Often, volunteer-satisfaction scales are used to consider the relationships among role continuity, social integration, the age homogeneity of people served, the types of community functions being served, and the volunteers' satisfaction with the role of volunteer. The importance of the increase in voluntary services of various types will probably attract higher rates of volunteering among the elderly, and the importance of adequately measuring volunteer satisfaction will become more important.

Conclusion

It should be noted that there are several publications that bear directly on both voluntary organizations and volunteerism. The Association of Voluntary Action Scholars publishes the *Journal of Voluntary Action Research* and a more practical journal entitled *Volunteer Administration*. The instruments reviewed in this chapter are listed in Table 10-1.

TABLE 10-1
Measures Reviewed in Chapter 10

Instrument	Author(s)	Code Number
I. History of Participation in Voluntary Associations		
a. Volunteer History	Payne and Bull (1974-1976)	V2.10.I.a
b. History of Voluntary Organization Participation	Peterson (1976)	V2.10.I.b
II. General Level of Participation in Voluntary Associations		
a. Activity and Organizational Inventory	Pihlblad (1976)	V2.10.II.a
III. Specific Indexes of Participation in Voluntary Associations		
a. Voluntary Association Participation	Booth and Babchuk (1972)	V2.10.III.a
b. Voluntary Association Participation	S. J. Cutler (1972)	V2.10.III.b
c. Voluntary Association Participation	Powers (1962-1974)	V2.10.III.c
d. Participation of Older Persons in Voluntary Associations	N. E. Cutler (1977)	V2.10.III.d
IV. Volunteer Satisfaction		
a. Volunteer Satisfaction Index	Payne and Bull (1974-1977)	V2.10.IV.a

TABLE 10-1 — *Continued*

Instrument	Author(s)	Code Number
b. Role Continuity and Satisfaction in the Volunteer Role	Kaplan (1976)	V2.10.IV.b
V. Volunteer Participation Rate		
a. Volunteer Participation	NCOA (1975)	V2.10.V.a

References

Babchuk, N., and A. Booth. "Voluntary Association Membership: A Longitudinal Analysis." *American Sociological Review*, 1969, 34:31-45.

Babchuk, N., and J. N. Edwards. "Voluntary Associations and the Integration Hypothesis." *Sociological Inquiry*, 1965, 35:149-62.

Chapin, F. S. *Experimental Designs in Social Research*, pp. 195-97. New York: Harper, 1947.

Cutler, N. E., and G. E. Mimms. "Political Resources for the Elderly: The Impact of Membership in Non-political Voluntary Associations upon Political Activity." Paper presented to the Annual Meeting of the American Political Science Association, Washington, D.C., September 1-5, 1977.

Godbey, G., and S. Parker. *Leisure Studies and Services: An Overview*. Philadelphia: W.B. Saunders, 1976.

Hausknecht, M. *The Joiner: A Sociological Description of Voluntary Association Memberships in the United States.* New York: Bedminister Press, 1962.

Institute for Social Research. *A Social Profile of Detroit: 1952.* Ann Arbor, Mich.: Institute for Social Research, University of Michigan, 1952.

Jacoby, A. P., and N. Babchuk. "Instrumental and Expressive Voluntary Associations." *Sociology and Social Research*, 1963, 47:461-71.

Scott, J. C., Jr. "Membership and Participation in Voluntary Associations." *American Sociological Review*, 1957, 22:315-26.

Smith, D. H. "The Impact of the Voluntary Sector on Society." In *Voluntary Action Research*, D. H. Smith (ed.), pp. 387-99. Lexington, Mass.: D. C. Heath, 1973.

Young, R. C., and O. F. Larson. "The Contribution of Voluntary Organizations to Community Structures." *American Journal of Sociology*, 1965, 71:178-86.

Abstracts

VOLUNTEER HISTORY

B. P. Payne and C. N. Bull, 1974-1976

Definition of Variable or Concept

A history of participation in the volunteer role since 1920 to the present covering type of organization, work done, and the age-group worked with in the organization is measured by this instrument.

Description of Instrument

This battery of questions examines participation in nine types of voluntary organizations over three historic periods: 1920-1940, 1940-1960, and 1960 to present.

Method of Administration

The battery is included as part of an interview.

Context of Development and Subsequent Use

The index of previous volunteer experience served as a predictor of present volunteer involvement and as a test of the continuity of the volunteer role.

Sample

This index was used on two samples. The first was a Kansas City sample (N = 58), which was upper-class and white and had an age range of 55 to 82. A similar sample from Atlanta (N = 51) was also drawn.

Scoring, Scale Norms, and Distribution

A five-point index, on which 1 is scored for low previous involvement and 5 for high previous involvement, is developed. Coding is done as follows: (1) 1961 to present only; (2) 1941 to 1960 only; (3) 1920 to 1940 only; (4) 1920 to 1969, or 1941 to present, or 1920 to 1940 and 1961 to present; and (5) 1920 to present.

Usability on Older Populations

No problems were encountered in these two samples.

General Comments and Recommendations

This is one of the few attempts to systematically evaluate a history of voluntary participation in an elderly population. More work is required to evaluate the type of volunteer work done.

References

Work is continuing on this project.

Instrument

See Instrument V2.10.I.a.

HISTORY OF VOLUNTARY ORGANIZATION PARTICIPATION

W. A. Peterson, 1976

Definition of Variable or Concept

The instrument assesses the number of organizations belonged to or dropped between the ages of 40 and 50 and organizations joined since age 50.

Description of Instrument

An open-ended question allows for the designation of six organizations joined between ages 40 and 50 and six after age 50, together with level of organizational activity defined as "very active," "active," or "member only."

Method of Administration

The measure is part of an interview.

Context of Development and Subsequent Use

The instrument was designed to assess changes in involvement patterns of older people, and it was first developed for the 1970 study of the Problems and Potentials of Older People. This instrument was used in an assessment of special programs in segregated retirement communities.

Sample

A 10% random sample of all residents in a retirement community was carried out in January and February of 1975. This procedure yielded a sample of 150 persons over age 60 (median age category of 75 to 79; males constituted 34% of the sample).

Distribution

Tables 10-2 and 10-3 show the distributions of organizational activities for persons aged 50 years.

TABLE 10-2
Type of Organizational Activities at Age 50

Organization	Total	First Mentioned	Second Mentioned	Third Mentioned
Professional	6.9	7.5	4.4	9.3
Church	21.3	31.8	15.4	5.5
Business	3.6	2.3	3.3	7.4
Social (cards/hobby/study)	20.2	14.4	25.3	25.9
Charity (civic/music/Red Cross)	11.2	6.8	13.2	18.5
Fraternal	28.8	31.1	30.7	20.4
Senior Citizen, AARP, etc.	.7	.8	—	1.9
Union	5.1	3.8	5.5	7.4
Political	2.2	1.5	2.2	3.7
Total (N)	277	132	91	54

TABLE 10-3
Change in Participation in Organizations Since 50

Change	Number	Percent
Increased activity	12	8.6
No change in activity	44	31.7
Less activity	83	59.7
Total respondents	139	100.0

SOURCE: Tables 10-2 and 10-3 are from W. A. Peterson, L. W. Phelps, and C. F. Longino, Jr. "John Knox Village Residents: Exploring The Tangibles and Intangibles of Retirement Living." Report for the Institute for Community Studies, Kansas City, Mo., 1976. Reprinted by permission of authors.

Usability on Older Populations

No problem has been encountered in using the the measure with an older population.

General Comments and Recommendations

This set of two questions allows an assessment of participation from middle age on, as well as an assessment of change in participation. The items have been used in more than one study and could be made (with the inclusion of a clearer assessment of involvement) into an index or a scale.

Reference

Peterson, W. A., L. W. Phelps, and C. F. Longino, Jr. "John Knox Village Residents: Exploring the Tangibles and Intangibles of Retirement Living." Report for the Institute for Community Studies, Kansas City, Mo., 1976.

Instrument

See Instrument V2.10.I.b.

ACTIVITY AND ORGANIZATIONAL INVENTORY

C. T. Pihlblad, 1976

Definition of Variable or Concept

Organizational involvement is a component of what persons do with their time.

Description of Instrument

In this battery, several indicators deal with membership in social, civic, and business organizations; involvement in church or religious organizations; and involvement with organizations for "people your age."

Method of Administration

The items are included as part of an interview.

Context of Development and Subsequent Use

The battery was developed as part of a longitudinal study to observe and describe changes over an 8-year period (1966-1974) in the lives of the elderly living in small towns.

Sample

From the 1966 sample of 1,700 persons aged 65 and older and residing in towns with populations from 250 to 5,000 in the state of Missouri, reinterviewing was carried out with 568 persons during the winter and spring of 1973 and 1974. The subsample was 69% of those surviving, and it had a median age of 79.

Scoring, Scale Norms, and Distribution

According to the data from the 1966 study, about 75% of both sexes said that they belonged to no social organizations, 90% belonged to no political or civic groups, but 5% had memberships in business or professional societies. In the 1973-1974 sample, one-third claimed membership in some social or civic group, although of these one-fourth said they never attended meetings. One-fifth claimed regular attendance, and one-half attended at least once a month. In both samples there was decreased participation with age.

Usability on Older Populations

No problems were encountered in using the instrument with an older population.

Sensitivity to Age (Including Social Age) Differences

The investigators indicated there was a sharp decrease in participation between T_1 and T_2 in social or civic groups. In 1974, 1 in 20 respondents belonged to American Association of Retired Persons or the National Retired Teachers' Association.

General Comments and Recommendations

These questions are not an adequate measure of associational participation.

Reference

Pihlblad, C. T., R. Hessler, and H. Freshley. "The Rural Elderly, 8 Years Later." Report, University of Missouri at Columbia, 1976.

Instrument

See Instrument V2.10.II.a.

VOLUNTARY ASSOCIATION PARTICIPATION

A. Booth and N. Babchuk, 1972

Definition of Variable or Concept

This instrument measures the number, type, frequency, change, and age homogeneity of participation in voluntary organizations. Also included are the dimensions of reason for joining or dropping organizations within the past 2 years and influence of media, friends, etc., on decision to join.

Description of Instrument

This battery includes aided recall questions on number of memberships, length of membership, degree of involvement in terms of hours spent being an officer, and whether the organization is for persons over 60 or retired. A second set of questions deals with mode of entering an organization and information on organizations a person might wish to join, with a single item identifying the most important association for the respondent.

Method of Administration

The battery is included as part of an interview.

Context of Development and Subsequent Use

The instrument was included as part of a larger study concerning the impact of aging on health-care decision making (Booth and Babchuk, 1972a; 1972b).

Sample

A random sample of noninstitutionalized adults 45 years old and older in Lincoln and Omaha, Neb., was drawn from the city directories and an area probability sample in each city. As a result, 300 respondents were selected from Lincoln; and 500, from Omaha. The number of respondents aged 64 and older was 272 for both samples combined.

Scoring, Scale Norms, and Distribution

The numbers of memberships are summed for each individual as are the numbers of hours spent per month on association activities. The data are reported as mean scores for subpopulations. Also, mean participation rates by type of organization are given, with emphasis on "Instrumental-Instrumental Expressive-Expressive" (Booth, 1972, p. 188).

Formal Tests of Validity

The instrument has predictive validity in that this measure has been used in several studies and has been shown to correlate with other variables, as the investigators hypothesized. For example, the data show that healthy, middle-aged, highly educated, native-born, white-collar, and upwardly mobile members of the labor force belong to more formal voluntary groups than persons in other categories.

Usability on Older Populations

No problem was reported with using the instrument on an older population.

General Comments and Recommendations

This collection of questions is probably the best one available in the field. However, little work has been done on indexing, scaling, or reliability.

References

Booth, A. "Sex and Social Participation." *American Sociological Review*, 1972, 37:183-92.
Booth, A., and N. Babchuk. "Informal Medical Opinion Leadership among Middle Aged and Elderly." *Public Opinion Quarterly*, 1972a, 36:87-96.

————. "Seeking Health Care from New Resources." *Journal of Health and Social Behavior*, 1972b, 13:90-99.

Instrument

See Instrument V2.10.III.a.

VOLUNTARY ASSOCIATION PARTICIPATION

S. J. Cutler, 1972

Definition of Variable or Concept

The number of memberships in voluntary association and the respondent's associated level of involvement are assessed.

Description of Instrument

This battery of questions asking whether respondents belong to each of 16 types of voluntary associations was based on the Michigan Survey Instrument. For each type, when membership was indicated, respondents were asked whether they were "very involved" or "not very involved." Also, when membership was indicated, a question was used to elicit the respondent's frequency of attendance.

Method of Administration

The battery is included as part of an interview.

Context of Development and Subsequent Use

The instrument was used in a study of the correlates of membership in voluntary associations, with the elderly as a specific subpopulation. The study was replicated in 1973 by Bull and Aucion (1975).

Sample

Cutler (1972) studied 170 older persons in Ohio with an average age of 74; Bull and Aucion's (1975) replication included 97 older persons in Kansas City.

Scoring, Scale Norms, and Distribution

A measure of number of different associations is computed through summation of the number of groups checked, yielding a measure theoretically ranging from 0 to 16. A measure of organizational involvement is obtained by summing the organizations with which the respondent was "very involved," yielding a measure ranging from 0 to 16. A single-item indicator of frequency of attendance at organization meetings is scored as follows: 0 for respondent does not belong to an organization; 1 for respondent never attends meetings, and 2 for respondent attends a few times a year or less, 3 for once a month, 4 for two or three times a month, 5 for once a week, and 6 for more than once a week.

The three components are then summed to form one measure of participation, which theoretically ranges from 0 to 38. Cutler and Bull trichotomozed this measure in low (0-3), medium (4-8), and high categories, with Cutler (1973) reporting 32.7%, 35.2%, and 32.1% of the sample in each group, respectively. Bull and Aucion (1975) reported 30.9%, 36.1%, and 33.0% of his sample in each of the respective categories.

Formal Tests of Validity

Replication by Bull and Aucion (1975) showed the index to produce results very similar to Cutler's.

Usability on Older Populations

No problems have been encountered in using the instrument with older populations.

General Comments and Recommendations

This useful index has been shown to be replicable. It could be improved by adding an attendance component for each membership in place of the component of overall attendance.

References

Bull, C., and J. B. Aucion. "Voluntary Association Participation and Life Satisfaction: A Replication Note." *Journal of Gerentology*, 1975, 30:73-76.

Cutler, S. J. "The Availability of Personal Transportation, Residential Location, and Voluntary Association Participation among the Aged." Paper presented to the 25th Annual Meeting of the Gerontological Society, San Juan, Puerto Rico, December 17-21, 1972.

_____. "Voluntary Association Participation and Life Satisfaction: A Cautionary Research Note." *Journal of Gerontology*, 1973, 28:96-100.

Instrument

See Instrument V2.10.III.b.

VOLUNTARY ASSOCIATION PARTICIPATION

E. A. Powers, 1964-1974

Definition of Variable or Concept

Continuity between voluntary-association participation rates in 1964 and in 1974, including level of participation, is measured by this instrument.

Description of Instrument

A battery of questions asks those who belonged to voluntary associations in 1964 what their level of participation was in 1974. The level of participation runs from membership to holding office or committee membership. Also included is a battery of questions dealing with organizations belonged to at present but not earlier. As many or as few organizations as are appropriate may be examined.

Method of Administration

The instrument was originally part of an interview, for which information from the 1964 interview membership had been recorded on the 1974 schedule before the interview.

Sample

The data were collected in nonmetropolitan areas in the state of Iowa. The sample consisted of males employed in one of five occupational groups (farmers, small businessmen, factory workers, self-employed workers, and salaried professionals). The sample size was 1,333 in 1974, with all respondents over age 60 at that time.

Usability on Older Populations

No problems were encountered in this study.

General Comments and Recommendations

This technique is useful for a panel design. The items tap the number and intensity of organizational participation as well as the organizations added or dropped.

References

None at this time.

Instrument

See Instrument V2.10.III.c.

PARTICIPATION OF OLDER PERSONS IN VOLUNTARY ASSOCIATIONS

N. E. Cutler, 1977a; 1977b

Definition of Variable or Concept

Membership and activity level in voluntary associations are measured by this instrument.

Description of Instrument

The respondent is handed a card on which there is a list of 17 types of voluntary associations. After saying he or she belongs to a given type, the respondent is asked about his or her level of activity: "not very active," "fairly active," or "very active."

Method of Administration

The data are collected by a personal interview; no time requirements are specified.

Context of Development and Subsequent Use

The instrument was part of a national survey of the adult electorate collected in 1972 by the Center for Political Studies, Institute for Social Research, University of Michigan.

Sample

The instrument was used with a national sample of 2,705 respondents, with 349 respondents aged 60 to 69 and 279 respondents aged 70 and older.

Scoring, Scale Norms, and Distribution

The number of memberships is summed to provide an individual score. No distributions of number of memberships or level of participation are given (Cutler, 1977a; 1977b).

However, 50.8% of the sample belonged to religious groups, and 74.9% belonged to at least one organization.

Usability on Older Populations

No problems were mentioned in the study.

General Comments and Recommendations

The checklist strategy is one of the standard ways to measure participation in voluntary associations, with the checklist approach being better then simple open-ended questions. The measure of degree of participation is poor, since the categories of participation are very subjective.

References

Cutler, N. E. "Patterns of Membership in Voluntary Associations among Older Persons in the Central States." Report number 1 by the Andrus Gerontology Center, University of Southern California, Los Angeles, January 1977(a).

————. "Toward an Age-Appropriate Typology for the Study of the Participation of Older Persons in Voluntary Associations." Report by the Andrus Gerontology Center, University of Southern California, Los Angeles, June 1977(b).

Instrument

See Instrument V2.10.III.d.

VOLUNTEER SATISFACTION INDEX

B. P. Payne and C. N. Bull, 1974-1977

Definition of Variable or Concept

Based on several dimensions of work satisfaction, the index taps areas dealing with training, remuneration, responsibility, contact with people, and recognition in the volunteer role.

Description of Instrument

The Likert scale of 25 items uses a five-point response pattern of "very satisfied" to "very dissatisfied."

Method of Administration

The items are included as part of an interview.

Context of Development and Subsequent Use

The measure was used in a longitudinal study of volunteers to investigate the correlates of volunteer satisfaction.

Sample

The instrument has been used in Kansas City and Atlanta on panels of volunteers and on groups of RSVP (Retired Senior Volunteer Program) volunteers. The age range was 55 to 82, with predominately upper-middle-class whites included in the sample (see Table 10-4).

TABLE 10-4
Sample Sizes for Panel Studies

	1974	1975	1976	1977
Kansas City (panel)	68	58	54	55
Kansas City (RSVP)	—	—	—	90
Atlanta (panel)	—	—	70	58
Atlanta (RSVP)	—	—	100	76

Scoring and Distribution

Mean scores for 22 of the 25 items are listed in Table 10-5.

TABLE 10-5
Scores of Volunteer Satisfaction for Volunteers in Shepherd's Centers
and the Retired Senior Volunteer Program (RSVP)

Volunteer-Satisfaction Items	RSVP Atlanta ($N = 100$)	RSVP Kansas City ($N = 90$)	Life Enrichment (Oak Grove), Atlanta ($N = 21$)	Northside Shepherd's Center (Home Park), Atlanta ($N = 49$)	Shepherd's Center, Kansas City ($N = 68$)
1. Contact with program recipients	1.64	1.55	1.43	1.74	1.50
2. Reporting hours	3.17	1.75	2.19	3.60	2.07
3. Training you received	1.99	1.78	1.71	1.74	1.62
4. Money you received for expenses	2.16	1.59	2.14	2.35	2.13
5. Contract with program staff	1.70	1.64	1.62	1.96	1.55

TABLE 10-5—*Continued*

Volunteer-Satisfaction Items	RSVP Atlanta ($N = 100$)	RSVP Kansas City ($N = 90$)	Life Enrichment (Oak Grove), Atlanta ($N = 21$)	Northside Shepherd's Center (Home Park), Atlanta ($N = 49$)	Shepherd's Center, Kansas City ($N = 68$)
6. Recognition for being a volunteer from the community, neighbors, or state	2.33	1.75	2.87	2.35	1.66
7. Contact with other volunteers	1.81	1.54	1.48	1.96	1.54
8. Ways the volunteer program made use of your skills and talents	1.89	1.76	1.86	1.89	1.72
9. Supervision or direction you recieved	2.03	1.72	2.24	1.94	1.87
10. The particular kind of work you did as a volunteer	2.09	1.63	2.48	1.92	1.58
11. Progress made by recipients you helped	2.03	1.96	2.38	1.88	1.76
12. Thanks from the recipients personally	2.03	1.73	2.14	1.90	1.32
13. Chances you have had to help make policy decisions	2.29	1.79	1.81	2.50	2.00
14. Demand made upon your time by recipients	2.07	1.75	2.19	2.02	1.97
15. Physical work involved	2.03	1.88	2.14	1.98	1.81
16. Chance to be your own boss	2.07	1.75	2.29	1.98	1.60

TABLE 10-5—*Continued*

Volunteer-Satisfaction Items	RSVP Atlanta (N = 100)	RSVP Kansas City (N = 90)	Life Enrichment (Oak Grove), Atlanta (N = 21)	Northside Shepherd's Center (Home Park), Atlanta (N = 49)	Shepherd's Center, Kansas City (N = 68)
17. Personal satisfaction of helping others	1.77	1.41	1.81	1.76	1.19
18. Chance to be promoted from the volunteer organization	2.13	1.72	2.05	2.16	1.75
19. Chance for recognition from the volunteer organization	2.03	1.72	2.01	2.00	1.83
20. Chance to participate in planning	2.16	1.90	2.00	2.22	1.84
21. Reporting to fellow volunteers	2.21	1.87	2.20	2.22	1.71
22. Opportunity to do something about the problems of the elderly	1.80	1.95	1.95	1.74	1.85

SOURCE: Payne and Bull, 1977.

NOTE: Score is the mean: lowest volunteer satisfaction is scored 5; highest volunteer satisfaction is scored 1. All scores are for time 1 interviews. Time 1 for the Shepherd's Center, Kansas City, was 1974; for RSVP, 1976; and for Northside and Life Enrichment, 1977.

Usability on Older Populations

No problems were encountered in using the instrument with older populations.

General Comments and Recommendations

Payne and Bull's work represents a first attempt to tap some of the dimensions surrounding the role of volunteer and the satisfaction derived from the role. The instrument is still in the construction stage. Several methodological problems yet to be overcome involve the halo effect and the nonapplicability of some of the items in certain volunteer settings.

Reference

Payne, B., and C. N. Bull. "Critical Issues in Volunteer Satisfaction." Paper presented to the Thirtieth Annual Meeting of the Gerontological Society, San Francisco, November 18-22, 1977.

Instrument

See Instrument V2.10.IV.a.

ROLE CONTINUITY AND SATISFACTION IN THE VOLUNTEER ROLE

B. I. Kaplan, 1976

Definition of Variable or Concept

The components of the volunteer role and the degree of volunteer satisfaction are assessed.

Description of Instrument

This interview instrument deals with the following aspects of the volunteer role: time spent, choice of work versus volunteer role, volunteer's perception of prestige related to agency structure, working conditions, volunteer's relations with others, agency management, supervision, training, recognition of contribution, and volunteer/staff relations. The instrument includes an index of volunteer satisfaction with 20 Likert-type questions. Only a synopsis of this extensive instrument can be reproduced here.

Method of Administration

An entire interview schedule is composed of these items.

Context of Development and Subsequent Use

The instrument was designed at the University of Southern California School of Social Work and the Andrus Gerontology Center to test older volunteer's perception of role continuity and agency structure as they relate to satisfaction in the volunteer role.

Sample

The study was carried out in Los Angeles, where 100 volunteers from 18 inner-city agencies were interviewed. The volunteers were all aged 55 and older.

Scoring, Scale Norms, and Distribution

There is no information on scoring and distribution available at this time, but an index of satisfaction that uses Likert scale is probably employed.

General Comments and Recommendations

The instrument includes a series of good questions tapping important areas of the volunteer role. Replication of the satisfaction measure is needed to make sure that the scale discriminates. In addition, assessment of the psychometric properties of the other dimensions (e.g., time, working conditions) would be very useful.

Reference

Kaplan, B. I. "Role Continuity and Satisfaction in the Volunteer Role." Paper presented to the 29th Annual Meeting of the Gerontological Society, New York, October 13-17, 1976.

Instrument

See Instrument V2.10.IV.b.

VOLUNTEER PARTICIPATION

National Council on the Aging, 1975

Definition of Variable or Concept

The instrument assesses the number of persons doing volunteer work, the type of volunteer work being done, and attitudes toward older people's volunteering, plus types of volunteer work persons might like to do.

Description of Instrument

The battery of questions distinguishes those who volunteer and those who would like to volunteer; it includes a classification of 18 types of volunteer work and a battery of eight questions with a five-point scale ("agree strongly" to "disagree strongly") on attitudes toward volunteer work by persons 65 years old and older.

Method of Administration

The personal interviews conducted by Louis Harris and Associates required an unknown amount of time to complete.

Context of Development and Subsequent Use

The interviews were part of the larger study called "The Myth and Reality of Aging in America." A participation section was used to estimate the amount of volunteering and the potential for volunteering in the elderly population.

Sample

A national sample completed in May through July of 1974 resulted in a sample of 2,797 for the elderly population (NCOA, 1975). Special sample characteristics were an oversample of 2,400 persons 65 and over and an oversample of 200 blacks 65 and over. The sampling used a multistage, random cluster sample of households stratified by geographic region and size of place (city, suburb, town, rural area). The sample was 59% female and 90% white.

Scoring, Scale Norms, and Distribution

Frequencies of response types were used as descriptive statistics showing the number of persons participating, the type of work done, the potential for a volunteer force, the reasons for not volunteering, and attitudes toward people over 65 as volunteers.

Usability on Older Populations

Since the overall refusal rate was only 2%, difficulties in use with older populations are unlikely.

General Comments and Recommendations

This battery of items has potential for generating descriptive statistics on the number of volunteers and the potential volunteers among the aged. Unfortunately, it does not assess the level of involvement.

Reference

National Council on the Aging. *The Myth and Reality of Aging in America.* Washington, D. C.: National Council on the Aging, 1975.

Instrument

See Instrument V2.10.V.a.

Instruments

V2.10.I.a

VOLUNTEER HISTORY

B. P. Payne and C. N. Bull, 1974-1976

1. What other volunteer work have you done throughout your life? We are interested in *all* the volunteer work that you did for *three months or more*.
   (FOR EACH AREA MENTIONED, ASK A-C)
   A. What type of organization did you work for?
   B. What kind of work did you do?
   C. What age group did you work with?

EDITOR'S NOTE: Questions are asked for each of three periods of time, (1) 1920-1940, (2) 1941-1960, (3) 1961-present.

Types of Volunteer Organizations
   A. Health (hospitals, mental health clinics, March of Dimes, other health drives)
   B. Education (teacher's aid, tutor, etc.)
   C. Justice (court volunteer, legal aide)
   D. Citizenship (scout leader, VFW officer)
   E. Recreation (activity leader, Little League coach)
   F. Social and Welfare (home for the aged)
   G. Civic and Community Action (consumer group, environmental protection)
   H. Religious (usher, choir, Sunday school teacher)
   I. Political (fund raiser, pollwatcher, campaign worker, etc.)

SOURCE: B. P. Payne and C. N. Bull, personal communications about work in progress, 1976.

V2.10.I.b

HISTORY OF VOLUNTARY ORGANIZATION PARTICIPATION

W. A. Peterson, 1976

A-11. Thinking back to when you were younger, 40-50 years of age, what church groups, lodges, clubs, unions, other organizations did you belong to then?
   (FOR EACH MEMBERSHIP MENTIONED, ASK *A* AND *B*.)
   A. How active were you then? Were you very active, active, or just a member?
       (1) Very Active   (2) Active   (3) Member Only
   B. Are you *now* very active, active, or just a member?
       (1) Very Active   (2) Active   (3) Member Only   (4) Inactive/Drop
A-12. Are there church groups, lodges, clubs, senior citizens' groups, organizations, to which you now belong which you did not belong to at age 50?
   (FOR EACH MEMBERSHIP MENTIONED, ASK *A* AND *B*.)
   A. Are you very active, active, or just a member?
       (1) Very Active   (2) Active   (3) Member Only
   B. At what age did you start?   (ACTUAL YEARS)

SOURCE: W. A. Peterson, L. W. Phelps, and C. F. Longino, Jr. "John Knox Village Residents: Exploring the Tangibles and Intangibles of Retirement Living." Report for the Institute for Community Studies, Kansas City, Mo., 1976. Reprinted by permission.

V2.10.II.a

ACTIVITY AND ORGANIZATIONAL INVENTORY

C. T. Pihlblad, 1976

1. What kinds of activities do you generally do in order to keep yourself busy or to entertain yourself? (INTERVIEWER: PROBE FOR HANDWORK, YARD, GARDENING,

GAMES, WALKS, RELIGIOUS SERVICES, TELEVISION, READING, OTHER THINGS?
ALSO RECORD SOLITARY ACTIVITIES VS. ACTIVITIES WITH OTHERS, WHICH AC-
TIVITIES ARE MOST ENJOYED.)

2. Do you belong to any church or religious organization?
    ___Yes   ___No (SKIP TO 3)
    a. What denomination to you belong to? _____
    b. How often did you attend during the past year?
          ___ More than once weekly   ___Weekly   ___About once a month
          ___Few times a year   ___Never
    c. Are you now more or less active in church than you were seven years ago?
          ___More   ___Less   ___ About the same
    d. What social activities connected with the church do you attend?
          ___None   ___(Specify)_____
    e. How do you get to church?   (Specify conveyance or walking) _____
          (If car, who drives?) _____
    f. How often does the (minister/priest) or visitation committee visit you?
          ___ Weekly   ___ Monthly   ___ Yearly   ___ Never
3. Is your religion important to you now?
    ___Yes (CONTINUE)   ___No (SKIP TO 4)
    a. Is it more or less important to you now than it was seven years ago?
4. Do you belong to any other social, civic, or business organizations?
    ___Yes (CONTINUE)   ___No (SKIP TO 5)
    a. How many meetings did you attend altogether during the past year?_____
    b. Approximately what percent of your close friends are members of this (these) organi-
        zation(s)?_____%
    c. Are you either more or less active in these groups than you were seven years ago?
          ___ More active   ___ Less active   ___ About the same
    d. How do you get to the meetings?   (Specify conveyance or walk)_____
          (If car, who drives?)_____
5. Do you belong to:
    a. The American Association of Retired Persons?   ___Yes ___No
    b. The National Retired Teachers Association?   ___Yes ___No
    c. A Senior Citizens' Group or Club?   ___Yes ___No
    d. Or any other organization for people your age? (Specify) _____

SOURCE: C. T. Pihlblad, R. Hessler, and H. Freshley. "The Rural Elderly, 8 Years Later."
Report, University of Missouri at Columbia, 1975.

V2.10.III.a

VOLUNTARY ASSOCIATION PARTICIPATION

A. Booth and N. Babchuk, 1972

VOLUNTARY ASSOCIATION AFFILIATION

1. Do you belong to any organizations similar to the ones on this list? HAND R SHEET A.
    Yes . . . . . . .1 ( )   No . . . . . . 2 ( ) SKIP TO 4
                    SHEET A

    CHURCH related group, such as: Board or standing committee
                                       Men's or women's group
                                       Voluntary service (choir, usher)

JOB related association, such as:	Farmers' organization
	Business or professional organization
	Labor union
RECREATIONAL group, such as:	Bowling league
	Woman's club
	Card club
	Golf club
FRATERNAL-SERVICE organization:	Masons or Eastern Star
	Service club (such as Lions or Rotary)
	Hospital auxiliary
CIVIC-POLITICAL group, such as:	Parent Teachers Association (PTA)
	Political party club
	Chamber of Commerce
OTHER organizations	Adult leader of a youth program (Boy Scouts, Campfire Girls)
	Veterans' organizations (Legion, V.F.W.)
	Board member of a community agency

2. IF YES: What are the names of these organizations? LIST EACH NAME IN SPACE PROVIDED BELOW (NO ABBREVIATIONS). ENTER TOTAL NUMBER. FOR EACH ORGANIZATION LISTED:

A. How long have you been a member of this organization? ENTER TWO-D NUMBER OF YEARS.

B. Do you now hold or have you ever held an office or served as a committee chairman in this organization? CODE 1-YES; 2-NO.

C. How many hours a month (including meetings) do you spend on activities related to this organization? ENTER TWO-D NUMBER OF HOURS.

   ASK ONLY FOR APPROPRIATE NUMBER OF YEARS:

   C.1 Two years ago was the number of hours the same, greater, or less? CODE 1-SAME; 2-GREATER; 3-LESS.

   C.2 Five years ago were the hours the same, greater or less? CODE AS ABOVE.

   C.3 What about 10 years ago? CODE AS ABOVE.

D. IF R 60 OR OVER ASK: Is this organization especially for persons who are 60 or retired? CODE 1-YES; 2-NO.

E. How many times a year does this group meet? ENTER TWO-D NUMBER.

F. CODE ACCORDING TO TYPE

   1. CHURCH
   2. JOB
   3. RECREATIONAL
   4. FRATERNAL-SERVICE
   5. CIVIC-POLITICAL GROUP
   6. ADULT LEADER OF YOUTH PROGRAM
   7. OTHER

G. IF MORE THAN ORGANIZATION: If you had to drop all of these groups but one, which one would you continue to belong to?

3. Do any of the organizations to which you belong sometimes take a stand on housing, better government, school problems, or other public issues?

   Yes. . . . . .1 ( )   No . . . . .2 ( )

   3.1 IF YES: Which one(s)? RECORD NAMES.

4. During the past two years, did you think seriously about joining an organization and then decide *not* to?

        Yes . . . . 1 ( )   No . . . . . . 2 ( ) SKIP TO 5

    4.1 IF YES: What was the name of the organization? RECORD NAME, TYPE OR PURPOSE AND INDICATE IF FOR AGED.

    4.2 IF YES: What events or considerations led you to decide against joining the organization? (PROBE FOR DETAIL.)

5. Are there any organizations you would like to join?

        Yes . . . . 1 ( )   No . . . . . . 2 ( ) SKIP TO 6

    5.1 IF YES: What are the names of these groups? RECORD NAME, TYPE OR PURPOSE, AND INDICATE IF FOR AGED.

    5.2 IF MORE THAN ONE: Which group are you most interested in joining? CHECK GROUP ABOVE.

    5.3 IF YES: What has prevented you from joining this organization so far?

6. In the past two years have you dropped your membership in any organization?

        Yes . . . . .1 ( )   No . . . . .2 ( )

    6.1 IF YES: Which one(s)? RECORD NAME, TYPE OR PURPOSE, AND INDICATE IF FOR AGED.

    6.2 SELECTING ORGANIZATION DROPPED MOST RECENTLY OR ONLY ONE DROPPED, ASK: What factors led to your decision to drop your membership in (ORGANIZATION)?

        PROBE FOR SPECIFIC EVENTS, CONDITIONS, OR CIRCUMSTANCES. RECORD NAME OF ORGANIZATION ALONG WITH R'S RESPONSE.

7. IF R HAS REPORTED AN ORGANIZATION THAT HE JOINED IN THE PAST TWO YEARS, ASK QUESTIONS 7.1-20. (SEE ITEM 2A.) ASK ABOUT MOST RECENT *AGED* ORGANIZATION OR IF NONE, ASK ABOUT MOST RECENT ORGANIZATION JOINED. CHECK CATEGORY R FALLS INTO.

    R Did not join group in past two years SKIP TO 21 . . . . 1 ( )

    Recently joined group for aged . . . . 2 ( )

    Recently joined non-aged group. . . . . 3 ( )

    7.1 IF MORE THAN ONE ASK: Which organization (for older persons IF R REPORTED ASSOCIATION FOR AGED) did you join most recently? OTHERWISE CONFIRM ORGANIZATION R JOINED DURING PAST TWO YEARS AND RECORD NAME.

8. Now I would like to discuss (ONLY/OR MOST RECENTLY JOINED AGED OR OTHER GROUP).

How many months ago did you decide to join this group? ENTER TWO-D NUMBER.

9. I'd like you to think back to the time before you made a firm decision to join the organization. How long before you decided to join did you first know about the organization? ENTER NUMBER OF DAYS, MONTHS, OR YEARS—WHICHEVER IS APPROPRIATE—AND CHECK TIME CATEGORY.

    Days . . .1 ( )   Months . . 2 ( )   Years. . . 3 ( )   No time elapsed. . . 4 ( )

    9.1 Where did you get this information?

10. How long before you decided to join did you actually begin to think about and make plans to join? ENTER NUMBER OF DAYS, MONTHS, OR YEARS—WHICHEVER IS APPROPRIATE—AND CHECK TIME CATEGORY.

    Days . . .1 ( )   Months . . 2 ( )   Years. . . 3 ( )   No time elapsed. . . 4 ( )

11. I would like to ask you about this period—that is, from the time you first began thinking about joining to the time when you decided to join. Could you tell me some of the reasons why you felt it would be worthwhile to join the group that you thought about

during that period? PROBE: What features of the organization attracted you?

11.1 Which one of the above factors weighed most heavily in your decision to join?

12. Describe any disadvantages you thought about before reaching a decision to join. IF NONE, RECORD NONE.

13. During this period did you happen to see anything in a newspaper, magazine, or on TV, or did you hear anything on the radio about the organization? IF YES: How many times did that happen altogether? ENTER TWO-D NUMBER.

14. During this period did you happen to see any brochures, announcements, or application forms for the organization before deciding to join? IF YES: About how many would that be? ENTER TWO-D NUMBER.

15. Do you recall any formal announcements made by someone in a meeting of some kind? IF YES: On about how many different occasions did that happen? ENTER TWO-D NUMBER.

16. During this period did you talk with anyone at all or did anyone speak with you about the organization before you decided to join? This includes phone calls, personal corresdence, conversation in small groups, and so on. If YES: How many people did you talk with altogether? ENTER TWO-D NUMBER.

17. IF MORE THAN ONE OF ITEMS 13-16 WERE ANSWERED AFFIRMATIVELY: During this period what was your first source of information about the organization:

Media . . . . . 1 ( )
Brochure . . . . . 2 ( )
Announcement during formal meeting . . . . . 3 ( )
Personal contact . . . . . 4 ( )
Don't recall . . . . . 5 ( )

18. IF R DID NOT REPORT TALKING WITH ANYONE IN QUESTION 16 GO ON TO ITEM 21. OTHERWISE SAY: On this sheet of paper would you list the initials of all the people that you talked with about the organization before you actually decided to join. I don't need to know their names or who they are. You may keep the sheet when we are through. HAND R SHEET B AND WAIT FOR R TO MAKE LIST.

18.1 Now, then, number the names. WAIT FOR R TO NUMBER.

18.2 How many people have you listed? ENTER TWO-D NUMBER. IF NUMBER IS LESS THAN OR EXCEEDS THE NUMBER REPORTED IN ANSWER TO QUESTION 16 SAY: I think I must have recorded the wrong number of persons earlier. PROCEED TO CLARIFY AND OBTAIN ADDITIONAL INFORMATION FOR QUESTION 16.

19. Were you a member of a group the individual was considering at that time?

Yes. . . . . . . .1 ( )   No . . . . . . .2 ( ) FINISH

20. How many hours per month, including meetings, did you spend on the organization? ENTER TWO-D NUMBER.

21. Were you or had you ever been an officer, committee chairman or committee member of_____(ASSOCIATION)? ENTER THE NUMBER OF OFFICES OF EACH TYPE R HAS HELD IN THE BRACKET NEXT TO THE OFFICE.

Officer ( )   Committee chairman ( )   Committee member ( )   Other (specify) ( )

22. In your judgement, which of the following qualities was it important for members to have? Tell me whether you think each quality was very important, somewhat important, or of little importance.

22.1 The individual should be able to get along extremely well with other members.

Very important 1 ( ) Somewhat important 2 ( ) Of little or no importance 3 ( )

22.2 The member should have personal contacts that would help the organization accomplish its goals

Very important 1 ( ) Somewhat important 2 ( ) Of little or no importance 3 ( )

22.3 The new member should have some ability or skill that would have the effect of advancing the objectives of the association

Very important 1 ( ) Somewhat important 2 ( ) Of little or no importance 3 ( )

22.4 Are there any other important qualifications a new member should have?

Yes . . . . . . 1 ( )　　　　　　No . . . . . . 2 ( )

22.4A IF YES: What are they?

23. Which of these qualities did the person with whom you spoke have? ENTER A NUMBER *ONE* IN THE APPROPRIATE BRACKETS.

Compatible. . . .( )　　　Contacts . . .( )　　　Skill . . .( )　　　Other . . . ( )

SOURCE: A. Booth and N. Babchuck. "Informal Medical Opinion Leadership among Middle Aged and Elderly." *Public Opinion Quarterly*, 1972, 36:87-96. Reprinted by permission.

V2.10.III.b

VOLUNTARY ASSOCIATION PARTICIPATION

S. J. Cutler, 1972

1. I have here a list of clubs and organizations that many people belong to. As I read down the list, whould you please tell which of these kinds of organizations you belong to, if any.

CHECK AT *LEFT* WHERE APPROPRIATE, THEN ASK 1a. FOR *EACH* ORGANIZATION R MENTIONS.

1a. Would you say you are very involved in or not very involved in _____?

(CHECK RESPONSE IN "INVOLVEMENT" COLUMN BELOW)

		Involvement	
_____	1. Church-Connected Groups (but not the church itself)	1. Very	0. Not
_____	2. Labor Unions	1. Very	0. Not
_____	3. Veterans' Organizations	1. Very	0. Not
_____	4. Fraternal Organizations or Lodges	1. Very	0. Not
_____	5. Business or Civic Groups (not professional associations)	1. Very	0. Not
_____	6. Community Centers	1. Very	0. Not
_____	7. Organizations of People of the Same Nationality	1. Very	0. Not
_____	8. Recreation Clubs	1. Very	0. Not
_____	9. Country Clubs	1. Very	0. Not
_____	10. Youth Groups (Scout Leaders, etc.)	1. Very	0. Not
_____	11. Professional Associations	1. Very	0. Not
_____	12. Political Clubs or Organizations	1. Very	0. Not
_____	13. Neighborhood Improvement Associations	1. Very	0. Not
_____	14. Charity or Welfare Organizations	1. Very	0. Not
_____	15. Retirement or Golden Age Clubs and Associations	1. Very	0. Not

Are there any others you belong to that are not on the list?

_____ 16. Other (specify) _____　　1. Very　　0. Not

_ _ _ None (F NONE, TERMINATE)

2. All in all, how often do you attend meetings of (this/these) organizations? More than once a week, once a week, two or three times a month, about once a month, a few times a year or less, or never? (REPEAT IF NECESSARY)

1. More than once a week　　2. Once a week　　3. Two or three times a month　　4. Once a month　　5. A few times a year or less　　6. Never

SOURCE: S. J. Cutler. "Voluntary Association Participation and Life Satisfaction: A Cautionary Research Note." *Journal of Gerontology*, 1973, 28:96-100. Reprinted by permission of author and publisher.

V2.10.III.c

VOLUNTARY ASSOCIATION PARTICIPATION

E. A. Powers, 1964-1974

1. In 1964 you indicated you belonged to (GIVE NAME OF EACH LISTED AND FOR EACH ONE ASK APPROPRIATE QUESTION; SKIP TO Q3 IF NO 1964 ORGANIZATIONS).
   a. Are you a member now?   (1) No   (2) Yes ASK b AND c
   b. Do you hold an office or committee membership?   (1) No   (2) Yes
   c. Do you attend any meetings?   (1) No   (2) Yes ASK d
   d. Do you attend less than half the meetings or half or more?
                   (1) Less than half   (2) Half or more

2. Do you presently belong to any other organizations?
                   (1) No FINISH   (2) Yes ASK a,b,c
   a. What is the name of the organization(s) you now belong to that you didn't in 1964? (ENTER EXACT NAME)
   b. Do you hold an office or committee membership?   (1) No   (2) Yes
   c. Do you attend any meetings   (1) No   (2) Yes ASK d
   d. Do you attend less than half the meetings or half or more?
                   (1) Less than half   (2) Half or more

3. In 1964 you indicated you did not belong to any organizations. Do you belong to any now?
                   (1) No FINISH   (2) Yes ASK a,b,c
   a. What is the name of the organization(s) you now belong to (ENTER EXACT NAME)
   b. Do you hold an office or committee membership?   (1) No   (2) Yes
   c. Do you attend any meetings?   (1) No   (2) Yes ASK d
   d. Do you attend less than half the meetings or half or more?
                   (1) Less than half   (2) Half or more

SOURCE: E. A. Powers, personal communication, 1976.

EDITOR'S NOTE: These questions were asked for as many organizations as were applicable to the respondent.

V2.10.III.d

PARTICIPATION OF OLDER PERSONS IN VOLUNTARY ASSOCIATIONS

N. E. Cutler, 1977

1. Here is a list of some kinds of organizations to which people may belong. Just tell me the letter on the card of any type of organization that you belong to. If you belong to any that are not on this list, tell me about those too.

                (INTERVIEWER HANDS SHOW CARD TO RESPONDENT)

2. Also, select the statement at the bottom of the card that best tells how active you are in each of the organizations you belong to.

	Not Very Active	*Fairly Active*	*Very Active*
A) Fraternal lodges			
B) Business groups			

	Not Very Active	Fairly Active	Very Active

C) Professional groups

D) Farm organizations

E) Church or religious groups

F) Neighborhood associations (including scout troops)

G) Social or cardplaying groups (including hobbies, college alumni)

H) Athletic clubs or teams

I) Cooperatives

J) Political clubs or organizations

K) Charity or social welfare organizations

L) Veterans' organizations

M) Civic groups

N) Special interest groups or lobbies

O) Ethnic, racial or nationality associations

P) Labor unions

Q) Other (organizations)

SOURCE: N. E. Cutler. "Patterns of Membership in Voluntary Association among Older Persons in the Central States." Report number 1 by the Andrus Gerontology Center, University of Southern California, Los Angeles, January 1977. Reprinted by permission of author.

V2.10.IV.a

VOLUNTEER SATISFACTION INDEX

B. P. Payne and C. N. Bull, 1974-1977

Now, please think back over your experience (work) as a volunteer during the past year. Using the responses on this card, please tell me how satisfied you are with each of these aspects.

1. Contact with program recipients.
2. Reporting of hours
3. Training you received
4. Money you received for expenses
5. Contact with program staff
6. Recognition for being a volunteer from the community, neighbors or state
7. Contact with other volunteers
8. Ways the volunteer program made use of your skills and talents
9. Supervision or direction you received
10. The particular kind of work you do as a volunteer
11. Progress made by recipients you helped
12. Thanks for the helping of recipients from them personally
13. Chances you have had to help make policy decisions
14. Demands made upon your time by recipients
15. Physical work involved.
16. Chance to be your own boss
17. Personal satisfaction of helping others
18. Chance to be promoted from within the organization
19. Chance for recognition from the volunteer organization
20. Opportunity for getting your ideas into organization decisions
21. Chance to be involved in the planning of programs
22. Reporting to fellow volunteers
23. Executing your own ideas
24. Opportunity to discuss problems of the elderly
25. Opportunity to do something about the problems of the elderly

All questions are answered with these response options: (1) very satisfied, (2) satisfied, (3) uncertain, (4) dissatisfied, (5) very dissatisified, (6) no response.

SOURCE: B. Payne and C. N. Bull. "Critical Issues in Volunteer Satisfaction." Paper presented to the 30th Annual Meeting of the Gerontological Society, San Francisco, November 18-22, 1977.

V2.10.IV.b

ROLE CONTINUITY AND SATISFACTION IN THE VOLUNTEER ROLE

B. I. Kaplan, 1976

SYNOPSIS OF INSTRUMENT

I. Volunteer role information
    A. Duration of service
    B. How was agency chosen

II. Relation of role in this agency to other volunteer roles
    A. Whether volunteer work was done before this job
    B. Continuity of aspects of service from other volunteer work to this job
        1. Concrete services
        2. Community services
        3. Counseling
        4. Administrative services
        5. Clerical/maintenance services

III. Relative importance of this job (single Likert item)

IV. Family status information
    A. Current employment
    B. Lifetime employment
    C. Work preferred but not pursued
    D. Extent to which present volunteer role fulfills aspirations in (IV-C).
    E. Respondent's educational level
    F. Marital status
    G. (2 questions) Children
    H. Spouse's current employment
    I. Spouse's lifetime employment
    J. Spouse's educational level

V. Family roles information: continuity of roles from family life to volunteer work
    A. Planning of educational, recreational, cultural activities
    B. Money and household management
    C. Maintenance of kinship relations
    D. Organization of social functions
    E. Emotional support
    F. Counseling

VI. Continuity of work roles from paid employment to volunteer work
    A. Hours/days of employment
    B. Specific assigned task involvement
    C. Group work
    D. Leadership functions
    E. Skill acquisition
    F. Increasing responsibility
    G. Feelings of accomplishment

H. Requirements of dress and grooming

I. Friendship opportunities

J. (Open-ended question) Other aspects of continuity

VII. Comparison of paid and volunteer work

A. Preference ordering of means of recognition in paid work

B. Preference ordering of means of recognition in volunteer work

C. Rating of how most people compare paid to volunteer work as to importance

VIII. Volunteer's estimate of his and others' perceptions of the agency's prestige/importance

A. His own perception

B. Community members'

C. Agency executives'

D. Staff members'

E. Other volunteers'

F. His perception of the importance of his own contribution

IX. Adequacy of working conditions

A. Work space

B. Location

C. Esthetics of workspace

D. Availability of equipment

E. Socializing opportunities

F. (Distinct item) Selection of space, location, or esthetics as feature most usefully changed in present agency

X. Volunteer relationships

A. Frequency of working with same group

B. How many volunteers known by name

C. How well volunteers get along

D. Out-of-agency social contact with volunteers

E. Importance of opportunities to socialize among volunteers

XI. Agency management: respondent's estimate of the importance, desirable frequency, and best purpose

A. Meetings of volunteers

B. Supervision

C. Education and training

D. Intraorganizational upward movement of volunteers

Along with two questions on each of the above, regarding

(1) How the agency manifests these features and

(2) the respondent's personal experience of them

XII. Means of recognizing volunteers' contributions

A. Importance of a system of recognition

B. Categories of workers subject to such a system

C. Frequency or regularity of recognition

D. Respondent's own experience with recognition of his contributions

E. Selection of a single most important means of recognition

XIII. Volunteer-staff relationships: frequency, regularity, or perceived importance

A. Volunteer's consultation with staff

B. Teamwork with professional staff member

C. Attendance at staff meetings

D. Knowing names of staff members

    E. Personal contact with staff member outside of agency

    F. Opportunities for volunteers and staff to work together

XIV. Index of satisfaction: 20 Likert-format items
    1 referring to objective conditions of work
    5 referring to boredom or interest
    10 referring to pleasure or enjoyment
    2 referring to satisfaction
    2 referring (perhaps ambiguously) to motivational levels

 XV. A single item asking respondent to estimate the priority of his volunteer job among all his other activities

XVI. Questions on demographic and socioeconomic attributes of respondent

SOURCE: Abstracted from B. I. Kaplan. "Role Continuity and Satisfaction in the Volunteer Role." Paper presented to the 29th Annual Meeting of the Gerontological Society, New York, October 13-17, 1976.

V2.10.V.a

VOLUNTEER PARTICIPATION

National Council on the Aging, 1975

24b. Apart from any work you're paid for, do you do any volunteer work, or not?

                      Do volunteer work . .   (SKIP TO 24f)
                      Don't do volunteer work. .   (ASK 24c)

24c. (IF "DON'T DO VOLUNTEER WORK" IN 24b—OTHER SKIP TO 24f) Would you like to do some volunteer work, or not?

                      Would like to . . . . . _____ (ASK 24d)
                      Would not like to . . . _____ } (SKIP TO
                      Not sure . . . .   _____ {   (25)

24d. (IF "WOULD LIKE TO" IN 24c) What's keeping you from doing volunteer work? Anything else?

24e. What kind of volunteer work would you like to do? Anything else? (MULTIPLE RECORD IF NECESSARY. PROBE FULLY, FINDING OUT THE NATURE OF THE WORK AND THE KIND OF ORGANIZATION WOULD LIKE TO WORK FOR, IN ORDER TO CATEGORIZE CORRECTLY BELOW)

24f. (ASK IF "DO VOLUNTEER WORK" IN 24b—OTHERS SKIP TO 25) What kind of volunteer work do you do? Anything else? (MULTIPLE RECORD IF NECESSARY. PROBE FULLY, FINDING OUT THE NATURE OF THE WORK AND THE KIND OF ORGANIZATION WORK FOR, IN ORDER TO CATEGORIZE CORRECTLY BELOW)

	24e. Volunteer Work Would Like to Do	24f. Volunteer Work Do
Administration and organization in volunteerism (e.g., information and referral services, released time volunteer assignments, summer volunteer opportunities, directories of community volunteer opportunities	_____	_____

	24e. Volunteer Work Would Like to Do	24f. Volunteer Work Do
Civic affairs (e.g., voter registration, lobbying and advocacy activities).	_____	_____
Consumer services (e.g., financial and budget counseling, consumer complaints, consumer education)	_____	_____
Cultural activities (e.g., teaching art, theatre for young people, general enrichment opportunities, museum tours, sponsoring art centers)	_____	_____
Education (e.g., teacher aides, tutoring—kindergarten through high school, adult literacy, programs for dropouts, English as a second language, library services, story hours, raising scholarship money for needy students, setting up preschools)	_____	_____
Employment and jobs (e.g., career counseling, placement services, upgrading skills).	_____	_____
Entrepreneurship (e.g., technical and/or financial advice to struggling businesses, management training, assisting minority businessmen).	_____	_____
Family, youth and children-oriented services (e.g., programs for foster children, teaching home management skills, working in residential facilities for dependent children, multi-faceted youth service programs, day care services, involving parents in their children's development)	_____	_____
Give-away programs (e.g., providing emergency food/clothes/household equipment, holiday gift bureaus, thrift shops).	_____	_____
Health and mental health (e.g., working in hospitals and clinics, programs for the emotionally ill, disease prevention, alcoholism, drug abuse prevention, family planning, suicide prevention)	_____	_____
Housing (e.g., improving existing structures in rundown areas, non-profit programs to build new houses, home maintenance assistance)	_____	_____
Interracial/interethnic/intergroup relations (e.g., formation of coalitions among religious denominations to tackle common problems, preparation of literary material to improve minority images)	_____	_____
Legal rights, law enforcement and crime prevention (e.g., working with juveniles to prevent delinquency, probation/parole programs, legal services, programs in juvenile institutions and prisons, helping former prisoners return to the community, police-community relations).	_____	_____

	24e. Volunteer Work Would Like to Do	24f. Volunteer Work Do
Nutrition (e.g., teaching food selection and preparation, school lunch programs, meals-on-wheels, food distribution programs).	_____	_____
Physical environment (e.g., anti-pollution efforts through research/data gathering/code enforcement, conservation education and practices, developing playgrounds and parks, cleanup campaigns, recycling centers)	_____	_____
Psychological/social support services (e.g., big brother or big sister programs, friendly visiting to the home-bound, programs in nursing homes, aiding unwed mothers, hot-line counseling, telephone reassurance for shut-ins, outreach programs to find people in need)	_____	_____
Recreation (e.g., coaching in sports, teaching arts and crafts, developing club facilities)	_____	_____
Transportation (e.g., driving the aged/ill/handicapped or others in need)	_____	_____

25. (ASK EVERYONE) I'd like to read you some things people have said about volunteer work. For each, please tell me if you tend to agree strongly, agree somewhat, disagree somewhat or disagree strongly? (READ STATEMENTS AND RECORD BELOW FOR EACH ONE)

	Agree Strongly	Agree Somewhat	Disagree Somewhat	Disagree Strongly	Not Sure
1. People with unused skills and talents should make use of them by doing volunteer work	____	____	____	____	__
2. If someone's work is valuable, he should be paid for it	____	____	____	____	__
3. Doing volunteer work is a good way for people to keep themselves busy and active	____	____	____	____	__
4. People over 65 usually make good volunteer workers.	____	____	____	____	__
5. Volunteer work is essential to meet the community's needs and everyone should do his share.	____	____	____	____	__
6. Most jobs saved for volunteer workers are routine and boring, and not very rewarding.	____	____	____	____	__
7. People doing volunteer work often get in the way and slow things down more than they help out	____	____	____	____	__

	Agree Strongly	Agree Somewhat	Disagree Somewhat	Disagree Strongly	Not Sure
8. People over 65 usually have some skills and talents that they could make good use of by doing volunteer work	_____	_____	_____	_____	___

SOURCE: Reproduced with permission from the *Codebook for "The Myth and Reality of Aging,"* a survey conducted by Louis Harris and Associates for the National Council on the Aging; prepared by the Duke University Center for the Study of Aging and Human Development under a grant from the Edna M. Clark Foundation, 1976.

Chapter 11

Leisure Activities

C. Neil Bull

Engaging in leisure implies performing an activity for its own sake, i.e., performing it because of its intrinsic value for the individual. The concept of leisure encompasses a multitude of possible activities, since what is rewarding to one person may be viewed by another with apathy or aversion. Thus, the question of leisure inherently involves a consideration of individual differences in the preferred modes of behavior.

Given the vast array of possible leisure activities, it is not surprising that leisure is often vaguely defined. Typically, leisure is studied as a residual phenomenon, i.e., time that is "free" from work and other obligatory activities such as sleeping, eating, and the like (Kleemeier, 1961). Since work is a major factor in conceptions of leisure in this sense, those persons who are older and who have retired necessarily have large amounts of leisure time, because only the obligatory activities of daily living remain. Hence, gerontological researchers have been quite concerned about the allocation of leisure time by older persons and the impact that leisure has on their lives.

Treating leisure as a residual phenomenon leaves much to be desired, for this implicitly assumes that people are alienated from their work. Though this concern may be less problematic in researching the leisure patterns of older, retired adults, other difficulties remain. The vast array of possible leisure (i.e., self-rewarding) activities could certainly include virtually any facet of social participation and social integration, as well as recreative activities and hobbies. Consequently, it is important to note that many other areas of social role participation reviewed in this volume of *Research Instruments in Social Ger-*

ontology are conceptually relevant to the study of leisure, including religious participation (Chapter 8 in this volume), friendship and neighborhood networks (Chapter 9), and memberships in voluntary associations (Chapter 10), as well as interaction with the family (Chapters 3, 4, and 5). Indeed, one of the earliest studies of the leisure patterns of older adults was the Cavan, Burgess, Havighurst, and Goldhammer (1949) study of personal adjustment, which included a series of questions on leisure as part of the Activity Inventory. (See Chapter 2 in this volume.) The interested reader would certainly benefit from examining these conceptually related chapters, since I have tried to limit this chapter to the general issues of recreation, use of the media, hobbies, vacations, and similar aspects of leisure.

Measurement of Leisure in Gerontological Research

Measures of leisure behavior have most commonly been used to test propositions concerning disengagement, activity-continuity, and activity-substitution theories. Furthermore, they have been used to test for crises in the life cycle, especially at the time of retirement. As such, leisure behavior has been utilized as both an independent variable—predictive of morale, life satisfaction, adjustment, or outlook on life (Cavan et al., 1949; Peterson, Phelps, and Longino, 1976; Sherman, 1974)—and a dependent variable to be explained (Gordon, Gaitz, and Scott, 1976; Sherman, 1974) within these theoretical contexts. Leisure behavior is often used descriptively to answer practical questions concerning housing and other program developments (Lawton, 1978). Differential participation by age, often with a special emphasis on specific subareas of leisure participation and/or frequency (e.g., watching television, reading newspapers, engaging in or viewing sports activities), has been examined (Payne, 1973a; 1973b).

From a measurement perspective, however, several critical questions pertinent to theory emerge. First, *what* should be measured? Is the simple *occurrence* of a behavior sufficient, or are measures of the *frequency* of participation needed to adequately test theoretical concerns? Measures of frequency are usually constructed along one of two forms: frequency of participation within a given time period (e.g., times per month) or time spent in a given behavior within a specified time frame (e.g., minutes per day). The latter approach partially approximates time-budget methodologies, differing most notably in that time-budget methods chart all activities for a given day and the more limited leisure measures focus only on the time devoted to specific recreative activities. Cowgill and Baulch (1962) used a variant of this approach, but they also included measures of membership in voluntary associations and the like. Nevertheless, measures of frequency and duration enable the researcher to tap quantitative variation in the degree of activeness, and they also allow the development of summary scales.

Two other factors often considered in deciding what to measure are the locus of a leisure activity and its social context. Does the activity take place within the home or outside of the home? Are activities social forms of leisure, or does one engage in solitary activities? Once again, the use of these additional questions can further refine the conceptualization of leisure activities and thus facilitate scale development.

Some research has implicitly or explicitly assessed the value of a given leisure behavior. A researcher explicitly determines value by asking about the importance of a behavior or by asking persons to rank their favorite (say, the top five) leisure activities. Implicitly, value is used to limit the number of different leisure behaviors research can pursue by asking respondents to think only of their favorite leisure activities. In a related vein, measures of attitudes toward leisure or satisfaction derived from leisure tap another cognitive component of the general leisure domain. These tend to focus on self-defined leisure and do not necessarily stress specific behaviors; rather, they address the entire set of behaviors.

The last facet of the "what to measure" issue concerns the time element so important to gerontological research. Since age-related research often must focus on questions of change over time and since longitudinal research is complex, with its payoffs distant, investigators often are compelled to use retrospective questions about past levels of participation to assess the critical issue of change. The use of retrospective techniques is problematic; certainly, further studies of the reliability and validity of these procedures are needed.

The second critical question to emerge regarding the measurement of leisure assumes that behavioral data are the primary focus. Since such a diverse range of behaviors are included in the general leisure domain, researchers often code these discrete activities into a more limited set of categories. Thus, the rules for categorization become important, since this procedure aims to capture the meaningful differences in the content of leisure. For example, the discrete activities of gardening and stamp collecting may be combined into a category called hobbies. Other researcher-defined categorization schemes include the differentiation of active and passive forms of leisure, the consideration of the locus of leisure activities (e.g., activities within the dwelling unit versus those engaged in out of doors), and the social context in which activities occur, as in the differentiation of solitary from social forms of leisure (see the earlier discussion of what to measure).

On a more abstract level, Gordon, Gaitz, and Scott (1976, pp. 314-15) proposed a continuum of intensity of expressive involvement. Beginning with the action theory perspective of Parsons (1951a; 1951b; 1959), Gordon, Gaitz, and Scott defined leisure as "discretionary personal activity in which *expressive* meanings have primacy over *instrumental* themes" (italics added). By focusing on one of the Parsonian pattern variables and integrating this with Gross's (1961) and Dumazedier's (1967) conceptualizations of the functions of leisure, Gordon, Gaitz, and Scott proposed a five-step ordering of the objectives of leisure. These five steps vary according to the intensity of expressive involvement, and they include (from very low to very high involvement): (1) relaxation, (2) diversion, (3) development, (4) creativity, and (5) sensual transcendence. These five steps *do not* represent an ordering of values, but rather they focus on the intensity of expressive involvement in discretionary personal activity. Indeed, more intense activities could well be negatively valued insofar as high cost, severe guilt, and physical injury may result from them (Gordon, Gaitz, and Scott, 1976, p. 316).

It is not the theme of this section to advocate one technique for categorization of leisure activities over another; such choices are inherently the province of theoretically guided researchers. Rather, my goal here is to illustrate the range of categorization schemes available for grouping discrete leisure behaviors into sets amenable to statistical analyses.

The final critical theme to emerge from this review of gerontological measures of leisure revolves around the broad question of how to measure leisure. In its simplest (and least effective) form, leisure activity has been assessed, for example, by the single question "What kinds of activities do you generally do in order to keep yourself busy?" The question may be completely open ended, or a list of possible leisure behaviors may be included. The inclusion of an activity list decreases potential problems with recall, but such lists are never complete or representative of the total pool of possible leisure activities, and thus responses may be biased. In order to minimize this bias, open-ended lists may be used that allow the respondent to add activities not on the main list of behaviors. However, any movement toward open-ended procedures is likely to result in increased coding costs.

Generally, the research strategy used in obtaining greater specificity regarding leisure behaviors is adding questions that focus on the frequency, locus, social context, and value of these behaviors. The questions used apply readily to almost all age-groups, including the elderly, and age-related trends do emerge. (See Riley and Foner, 1968, pp. 511-35, for an excellent review.) The issue here involves not the *dimensions* of leisure, but the use of survey-based questions to assess types and degrees of leisure participation.

Since leisure is such a diffuse concept involving many possible behaviors, the use of one-shot survey questions to be completed in the homes of respondents *during* the interview requires some element of shared meaning as to what leisure is. The use of lists of possible behaviors increases the degree to which interviewer and interviewee are talking about the same behaviors, but it ignores some aspects of the meaning of leisure. Furthermore, measures of frequency are likely to be subject to memory and desirability bias.

As an alternative to the use of questions about leisure, it is possible to use time-budget methodologies to chart the typical or randomly selected weekday or weekend as to the types of behavior engaged in and the relative amount of time devoted to each behavior. Although such studies are not restricted to the measurement of leisure behaviors, they certainly address some critical facets of the conceptual domain.

Apparently, extensive time-budget studies of the elderly have not been conducted. The Multinational Comparative Time-Budget Study (Szalai, 1972) specifically omitted households in which all members were retired. Similarly, other valuable studies in this area (e.g., Lundberg, Komarowski, and McInerny, 1934; Sorokin and Berger, 1939; Converse and Robinson, 1966) focused on populations other than the aged.

Though studies using time budgets produce results rich in detail, time-budget methodology is not a panacea for the problem of measuring leisure. A high degree of cooperation from respondents is needed, accurate description of a complex activity in only a few words is required, and memory is still a factor. Indeed, Robinson and Converse (1972, p. 21) noted that the majority of time-budget studies "seem haphazardly executed and/or confined to relatively narrow classes of activities." These problems limit the usefulness of the procedure.

Review of Instruments

Table 11-1 lists the instruments reviewed in this chapter. The instruments have been grouped into four broad domains, although I hasten to point out that there are no clear-cut divisions between these areas. The primary thrust of gerontological research has been on leisure behaviors—an individual's present activities and past history of activities. Media use, though representing a behavioral component, is represented as a special subclass in order to highlight the distinctiveness of this activity group from the other domains. The cognitive component of leisure, (i.e., attitudes and satisfactions) is comparatively less researched, with relatively few research instruments in existence. All of the measures use survey research procedures, including the interviewer-rating scales of Havighurst (1957a; 1957b).

In reviewing these instruments, it has become clear that there is a

TABLE 11-1
Measures Reviewed in Chapter 11

Instrument	Author(s)	Code Number
I. Multidimensional Measures of Leisure		
a. Leisure Activities	Havighurst (1957)	V2.11.I.a
b. Leisure Time	Gordon, Gaitz, and Scott (1976)	V2.11.I.b
II. General Leisure Inventories		
a. Leisure Participation	NCOA (1975)	V2.11.II.a
b. Leisure Time Behavior	Payne (1973)	V2.11.II.b
c. Leisure Activity Score	Sherman (1973)	V2.11.II.c
d. Leisure Participation	Havens and Thompson (1973-1977)	V2.11.II.d
e. Use of Leisure Time	Duke Longitudinal Study of Adaptation (1968)	V2.11.II.e
III. History of Leisure		
a. Leisure Activities	Committee on Research and Development Goals in Social Gerontology (1971)	V2.11.III.a
b. Free Time Activities	Peterson, Phelps, and Longino, (1976)	V2.11.III.b
c. Past Leisure Participation	Payne and Bull (1976)	V2.11.III.c.
IV. Media Use		
a. Communications Activity	Graney and Graney (1974)	V2.11.IV.a
b. Media Habits	Canadian Radio-Television Commission (1974)	Not reproduced
V. Leisure Attitudes and Satisfaction		
a. Elderly Leisure Attitude Scale	Teaff, Ernst, and Ernst (1975)	V2.11.V.a
b. Leisure Activities and Satisfaction	Powers (1964-1974)	V2.11.V.b

lack of solid theoretical work that has been translated into reliable and valid empirical measures. To the extent that theory about the leisure behavior of older adults has been developed, it has stressed the relationships *between* constructs (e.g., activity and morale) and ignored the relationships between the empirical indicators and the theoretical constructs of leisure. The dimensions of leisure participation (i.e., incidence, frequency, social context, locus, and value) are usually treated as distinct constructs, and yet theoretical work *could* produce the rules of correspondence that would link these dimensions into a sophisticated summary index. Though these rules of correspondence would necessarily be complex, one relatively succinct recommendation can be made. At the very least, adequate measurement would require the incorporation of measures of frequency or duration of leisure behavior as well as simple incidence measures. This would enable researchers to determine the degree of participation or relative commitment to one activity vis-à-vis another. Moreover, the rules of correspondence between theory and data are apt to be simple additive functions in linking the incidence and frequency dimensions, while complex nonadditive or differentially weighted functions are likely to be required in combining the social context, locus, and value dimensions. In short, linking incidence and frequency represents a reasonable first step in producing theoretically based summary measures.

Assessment of the measurement properties of these instruments has also been lacking. Instrument reliability and validity studies are vitally needed. Test-retest reliabilities are especially pertinent for behavioral data, as are studies of the accuracy of retrospective-question techniques. Though the time interval for test-retest studies should be quite short (e.g., two weeks) in order to minimize true age-related change (see Wheaton et al., 1977, for a general discussion of reliability and stability in panel research), the elapsed time interval for an analysis of the accuracy of retrospective questions must be considerably longer. To assess the accuracy of retrospective questions requires the use of a time 1 measure of present activity level and a time 2 measure of past history of participation, with a lag effect in the history measure equal to the interval between time 1 and time 2. Making studies that assess the degree of convergence between methods (e.g., open ended, aided recall, time budget, etc.) would be an excellent first step in determining validity. More important to the question of validity, however, is the assessment of the isomorphism between theoretical concepts and empirical indicators.

Summary

Considerable descriptive data are available about the leisure activities of older persons. Refinements are needed, however, in both the conceptual explication of the leisure variable—especially in differentiating leisure from other facets of social participation—as well as the specific techniques of measurement. Clearly, a greater connection between conceptualization and theory, on the one hand, and conceptualization and measurement techniques, on the other, is indicated. I hope that this review of research procedures facilitates the development of this connection by providing baseline data for researchers to use in constructing new instruments.

References

Cavan, R. S., E. W. Burgess, R. J. Havighurst, and H. Goldhammer. Personal Adjustment in Old Age. Chicago: Science Research Associates, 1949.

Converse, P. E., and J. P. Robinson. "1965/66 Survey Research Center Study." Ann Arbor, Mich.: Institute for Survey Research, University of Michigan, 1966.

Cowgill, D. O., and N. Baulch. "The Use of Leisure Time by Older People." The Gerontologist, 1962, 2(1):47-50.

Dumazedier, J. Toward a Society of Leisure. (S. E. McClure, trans.) New York: Free Press, 1967.

Gaitz, C. M., and C. Gordon. "Leisure and Mental Health Late in the Life Cycle." Psychiatric Annals, 1972, 2:38ff.

Gordon, C., C. M. Gaitz, and J. Scott. "Leisure and Lives: Personal Expressivity across the Life Span." In Handbook of Aging and the Social Sciences, R. H. Binstock and E. Shanas (eds.), pp. 310-37. New York: Van Nostrand Reinhold, 1976.

Graney, M. J. "Communication Uses and the Social Activity Constant." Communication Research, 1975, 2:347-66.

Graney, M. J., and E. E. Graney. "Communications Activity Substitutions in Aging." Journal of Communication, 1974, 24(4):88-96.

Gross, E. "A Functional Approach to Leisure Analysis." Social Problems, 1961, 9:2-8.

Havighurst, R. J. "The Leisure Activities of the Middle-aged." American Journal of Sociology, 1957a, 63:152-62.

————. "The Social Competence of Middle-aged People." Genetic Psychology Monographs, 1957b, 56:297-375.

Hearn, H. L. "Career and Leisure Patterns of Middle-aged Urban Blacks." The Gerontologist, 1971, 2(4, part 2):21-26.

Kleemeier, R. W. "Time, Activity, and Leisure." In Aging and Leisure, R. W. Kleemeier (ed.), pp. 243-72. New York: Oxford University Press, 1961.

Lawton, M. P. "Leisure Activities for the Aged." The Annals of the American Academy of Political and Social Science, 1978, 438:71-80.

Lopata, H. Z., and F. Steinhart. "Work Histories of American Urban Women." The Gerontologist, 1971, 2(4 part 2):27-36.

Lundberg, G., M. Komarowski, and M. McInerny. Leisure: A Suburban Study. New York: Columbia University Press, 1934.

Murray, J. R., E. A. Powers, and R. J. Havighurst. "Personal and Situational Factors Producing Flexible Careers." The Gerontologist, 1971, 2(4, part 2):4-12.

Neulinger, J. *The Psychology of Leisure.* Springfield, Ill.: Charles C. Thomas, 1974.

Oliver, D. B. "Career and Leisure Patterns of Middle-aged Metropolitan Out-Migrants." *The Gerontologist,* 1971, 2(4 part 2):13-20.

Parsons, T. A. *The Social System.* New York: Free Press, 1951a.

————. *Toward a General Theory of Action.* Cambridge, Mass.: Harvard University Press, 1951b.

————. "An Approach to Psychological Theory in Terms of the Theory of Action." In *Psychology: The Study of a Science* (vol. 3), S. Koch (ed.), pp. 612-711. New York: McGraw-Hill, 1959.

Payne, B. P. "Adult Patterns of Leisure in the Piedmont Region." Report under contract with the National Park Service No. S-O-S 201-S-O-5-500. Atlanta: Sociology Department, Georgia State University, 1973a.

————. "Age Differences in the Meaning of Leisure Activities." Paper presented to the 26th Annual Meeting of the Gerontological Society, Miami Beach, November 14, 1973(b).

Peterson, W. A., L. W. Phelps, and C. F. Longino, Jr. "John Knox Village Residents: Exploring the Tangibles and Intangibles of Retirement Living." Report for the Institute for Community Studies, Kansas City, Mo., 1976.

Pfeiffer, E., and G. C. Davis. "The Use of Leisure Time in Middle Life." In *Normal Aging II,* E. Palmore (ed.), pp. 232-43. Durham, N.C.: Duke University Press, 1974.

Pihlblad, C. T., R. Hessler, and H. Freshley. "The Rural Elderly, 8 Years Later." Report, University of Missouri at Columbia, 1975.

Pollack, O. *Social Adjustment in Old Age, a Research Planning Report.* New York: Social Science Research Council, 1948.

Riley, M. W., and A. Foner. *Aging and Society.* (vol. 1). New York: Russell Sage Foundation, 1968.

Robinson, J. P., and P. E. Converse. "Social Change Reflected in the Use of Time." In *The Human Meaning of Social Change,* A. Campbell and P. E. Converse (eds.), pp. 17-86. New York: Russell Sage Foundation, 1972.

Sherman, S. R. "Methodology in a Study of Residents of Retirement Housing." *Journal of Gerontology,* 1973, 28:351-58.

————. "Leisure Activities in Retirement Housing." *Journal of Gerontology,* 1974, 29: 325-35.

Sorokin, P., and C. Berger. *Time Budgets of Human Behavior.* Cambridge, Mass.: Harvard University Press, 1939.

Szalai, A. *The Use of Time.* The Hague: Mouton, 1972.

Wheaton, B., B. Muthén, D. F. Alwin, and G. F. Summers. "Assessing Reliability and Stability in Panel Models." In *Sociological Methodology 1977,* D. R. Heise (ed.), pp. 84-136. San Francisco: Jossey-Bass, 1977.

Abstracts

LEISURE ACTIVITIES

R. J. Havighurst, 1957

Definition of Variable or Concept

Leisure is seen as having several dimensions. Significance refers to the value or importance attached to leisure in the person's life; content refers to the nature or type of leisure activity engaged in; and the meaning of leisure refers to the motives or reasons for engaging in leisure. Leisure role performance refers to competence in filling the leisure role.

Description of Instrument

The significance dimension is composed of 19 variables which were rated by disinterested people who read the entire interview schedule; 13 of these variables were applied to the two favorite leisure activities of the respondent, while the six remaining were applied to the entire leisure life of the respondent. Content of leisure refers to the two preferred leisure activities which were placed in eleven categories (e.g., travel, watching sports). The meaning of leisure measure consists of 12 statements from which the respondent selects the three which are most applicable to each of his/her two favorite leisure activities (i.e., a total of six statements). The measure of leisure role performance is a rating scale ranging from 0 (apathetic, bored) to 9 (is well known among associates for the competence in a particular leisure activity).

Method of Administration

The significance and role-performance variables are rated by persons familiar with the entire interview schedule. The content and meaning dimensions are directly included as part of a longer (2-hour) interview schedule.

Context of Development and Subsequent Use

The significance variables were developed from the discursive writings of sociologists interested in leisure (e.g., Clarke, 1956) and from selected interviews (Havighurst, 1957a, p. 153). The meaning dimension was initially examined during research in New Zealand, where pilot interviews and a literature review led to the development of 16 meanings statements (Donald and Havighurst, 1959, p. 355). The content categories simply were convenient descriptive categories for frequently mentioned activities (Havighurst, 1961, p. 315). The leisure-role-performance measure drew upon the writings of social philosophers and ethical leaders, as well as social scientists who wrote about the social definitions of excellent, average and poor role performance.

It should be noted that a number of other social roles are rated; these are very similar to Havighurst and Albrecht's (1953) measure. (See Chapter 2 in this volume or Havighurst, 1957b, pp. 349-60.) Similarly, other questions concerned with leisure (e.g., television watched, books read) were included in the study and used in making the ratings. They are not included with the instrument since they appeared to be only tangentially relevant to the major dimensions of leisure. The interested reader is referred to Havighurst (1957b, pp. 362-63).

Sample

The social role interview was administered to a stratified random sample of 124 women and 110 men aged 40 to 70 (Havighurst, 1957a).

Scoring, Scale Norms, and Distribution

The significance variables are rated on five-point scales, and the content and meaning dimensions are analyzed as percentage distributions. Apparently, summary measures can be developed from the significance variables (probably with simple additive techniques), although the exact details are not available. (See Havighurst, 1961, pp. 327-30.) Donald and Havighurst (1959, p. 357) presented percentage distributions for the meaning distributions for the meaning dimension, and Havighurst (1957b, p. 316) reported an average score of 5.02 for men and 4.73 for women on the role-performance measure.

Formal Tests of Reliability/Homogeneity

Havighurst (1957a, p. 156) reported that complete agreement between two raters ranged from 28% to 93%, with an average of 56%, for the significance variables. The average agreement within 1 point was 89% (range of 70% to 100%).

Homogeneity is examined as part of a principal components analysis of 24 variables, including 14 of the significance variables. Five components that account for 71% of the total variance emerge. Factor loadings for the significance variables range from –.70 to .42 (Havighurst, 1961, p. 327).

Havighurst (1957b, p. 309) reported that Spearman-Brown reliabilities between raters for the social-role measures range from .86 to .95, but an exact coefficient for the leisure role is not given.

Usability on Older Populations

The items appear to be applicable across all age-groups, including the elderly.

Sensitivity to Age Differences

Age correlates with only one of the significance variables (i.e., expansion versus constriction of interests [Havighurst, 1961, p. 325]), although a somewhat stronger relationship emerges between age and content (Havighurst, 1957a, p. 157), and no relationship is noted between age and meaning (Donald and Havighurst, 1959, p. 357; Havighurst and Feigenbaum, 1959, p. 396).

General Comments and Recommendations

Havighurst's work represents one of the few attempts to examine several different facets of the leisure domain. Though these instruments require further examination for their reliability and validity, they do present an interesting alternative to the standard incidence and frequency measures. It should be noted, however, that these measures may be biased by middle-class definitions. This is especially true of the role-performance measure.

References

Clarke, A. C. "Leisure and Levels of Occupational Presitge." *American Sociological Review*, 1956, 21:301-7.

Donald, M. N., and R. J. Havighurst. "The Meanings of Leisure." *Social Forces*, 1959, 37: 355-60.

Havighurst, R. J. "The Leisure Activities of the Middle-aged." *American Journal of Sociology*, 1957a, 63:152-62.

————. "The Social Competence of Middle-aged People." *Genetic Psychology Monographs*, 1957b, 56:297-375.

————. "The Nature and Values of Meaningful Free-Time Activity." In *Aging and Leisure*, R. W. Kleemeier (ed.), pp. 309-44. New York: Oxford University Press, 1961.

Havighurst, R. J., and R. Albrecht. *Older People*. New York: Longmans, Green and Company, 1953.

Havighurst, R. J., and K. Feigenbaum. "Leisure and Life-style." *American Journal of Sociology*, 1959, 64:396-404.

Instrument

See Instrument V2.11.I.a.

LEISURE TIME

C. Gordon, C. M. Gaitz, and J. Scott, 1976

Definition of Variable or Concept

This instrument measures patterns of participation in 17 categories of leisure activities and differentiates between active versus passive leisure, homebound versus external behavior, and social versus individual patterns. The concept of expressivity and the amount of pleasure received from leisure participation is also relevant to this instrument.

Description of Instrument

A battery of questions covers 17 categories of leisure activity, asking about rate of participation, enjoyment from activity, and perceived level of competency. A separate battery of 21 questions on participation in activities specific to the Houston area, a battery of 18 activities scored according to importance to respondent, and an open-ended question on the need for training in leisure skills are also included.

Method of Administration

Structured interviews are used to gather these data.

Context of Development and Subsequent Use

The principal focus of this study was the relationship of leisure and mental health. Age and life stage were seen as key independent variables that shape individuals' leisure choices and satisfactions (Gordon, Gaitz, and Scott, 1976).

Sample

A probability sample stratified by race, gender, occupation and age of adults in Houston, Tex. (N = 1,375), was interviewed between November 1969 and February 1970. The sample size within each stratum was determined by quotas. Respondents aged 65 to 74 numbered 242; those over 75 numbered 218 (Gordon, Gaitz, and Scott, 1976).

Scoring, Scale Norms, and Distribution

Participation in the 17 categories of leisure is scored as percentage participating at each stage of the life cycle. Activities are assigned to five levels of increasing intensity of expressive involvement and then related to percentage participation of life-cycle stage. The leisure-pleasure score, which includes the self-rated importance, enjoyment, and the frequency of participation in activities, is presented by Gordon, Gaitz, and Scott (1976). No scoring technique is given, although their data indicate that index scores could run from 40 to 204.

Usability on Older Populations

No problems were noted with the study's older population.

Sensitivity to Age (Including Social Age) Differences

Gordon, Gaitz, and Scott (1976, pp. 326-28) reported that participation declines with age in 8 of the 17 areas (e.g., dancing, drinking, traveling, reading); that it is fairly stable in 7 areas (e.g., television viewing, entertaining); and that it increases for solitary activities and, for males, cooking.

General Comments and Recommendations

The several batteries of questions used in the study cover a good range and depth of leisure behaviors. The inclusion of perceived level of competence adds strength to the participation rates. The index of pleasure is important and needs further replication.

References

Gaitz, M., and C. Gordon. "Leisure and Mental Health Late in the Life-Cycle." *Psychiatric Annals*, 1972, 2:38ff.

Gordon, C., C. M. Gaitz, and J. Scott. "Leisure and Lives: Personal Expressivity across the Life Span." In *Handbook of Aging and the Social Sciences*, R. H. Binstock and E. Shanas (eds.), pp. 310-37. New York: Van Nostrand Reinhold, 1976.

Instrument

See Instrument V2.11.I.b.

LEISURE PARTICIPATION

National Council on the Aging, 1975

Definition of Variable or Concept

The involvement of older people in active, constructive activities or passive, sendentary activities and the beliefs of others as to whether the elderly participate in active or passive leisure are tapped by this measure.

Description of Instrument

This battery of questions includes nested subquestions concerning a number of leisure activities, including sports, gardening, voluntary organizations, media use, and religious participation in various leisure activities as well as his or her attendance. Finally, 10 items are concerned with the portrayal of older persons on television.

Method of Administration

Personal interviews were conducted by the Harris organization.

Context of Development and Subsequent Use

The questions were used in the larger study on "The Myth and Reality of Aging in America" (NCOA, 1975), with the leisure-participation section used to look at the assumptions people hold about older people. The responses are compared with the actual participation rates of an elderly population.

Sample

The national sample of 4,254 persons was conducted in 1974. It included oversamples of the noninstitutionalized population aged 65 and older, persons aged 55 to 64, and blacks. The sample included 2,797 persons aged 65 and older. (For further details, see NCOA, 1975, pp. v-vii and Appendexes I-III.)

Scoring, Scale Norms, and Distribution

This instrument is not scored as a battery. Rather, the percentage responses to items are used as descriptive of leisure participation. The NCOA report (1975) presented numerous cross-tabulations comparing older persons' activities with the opinions the public aged 18 to 64 has of older persons' activity levels (1975, pp. 57, 59-60, 109, 175-79, 183-85, 187-88, 191, 193-94, 197-202, 206-9).

Usability on Older Populations

A refusal rate of 2% was noted for this survey. Response rates for individual items vary considerably.

Sensitivity to Age Differences

The percentage responses to individual items are related to age throughout the report. The nature of that relationship is highly dependent on the type of leisure activity being assessed.

General Comments and Recommendations

This extensive battery of items constitutes a partial inventory of leisure behaviors. Some of the items are redundant.

References

National Council on the Aging. *The Myth and Reality of Aging in America.* Washington, D.C.: National Council on the Aging, 1975.

_____.*Codebook for "The Myth and Reality of Aging,"* a survey conducted by Louis Harris and associates for the National Council on the Aging; prepared by the Duke University Center for the Study of Aging and Human Development, 1976.

Instrument

See Instrument V2.11.II.a.

LEISURE TIME BEHAVIOR

B. P. Payne, 1973a; 1973b

Definition of Variable or Concept

Patterns of adult leisure, rank order of leisure behavior by level of enjoyment, place where favorite activity occurs, with whom such activity takes place, and the meaning of the activity are measured by this instrument.

Description of Instrument

This battery of questions codes the respondent's favorite leisure activity into 1 of 72 categories (with room for "other" responses). Data regarding the location of the activity, reasons for participation, and the social context of leisure are also gathered.

Method of Administration

Data are gathered as part of a telephone interview, with the section on leisure behavior taking about 5 minutes to administer.

Context of Development and Subsequent Use

Payne's study was a systematic replication of the North Pacific Border Study (Field, 1971). Payne (1973a) looked at the effects of age differences in the meaning of leisure activities as part of a study of adult patterns of leisure in the Piedmont region; the study was requisitioned by the National Park Service.

Sample

The study was carried out in the Piedmont area of Virginia and North Carolina. A multistage probability sample using 150 sampling points resulted in a sample of 1,500 households, with respondents aged from 17 to 85. Of the respondents 118 were 65 years old or older.

Scoring, Scale Norms, and Distribution

This instrument is not scored as a battery. Percentages of respondents mentioning each activity as the most enjoyable are presented (Payne, 1973b, pp. 16-17).

Usability on Older Populations

No problems were encountered with the older respondents in this study.

Sensitivity to Age Differences

Preferences for the more active participant sports and outdoor activities declined with age in this cross-sectional study (Payne, 1973b, p. 19).

General Comments and Recommendations

This instrument uses the standard technique employed to inventory leisure behavior. There are few if any scales made from this information. The range of possible activities included in this study is extensive; however, it is not exhaustive.

References

Field, D. R. "Interchangeability of Parks with Other Leisure Settings." Paper presented to the AAAS Symposium, Philadelphia, December, 1971.

Payne, B. P. "Adult Patterns of Leisure in the Piedmont Region." Report under contract with the National Park Service No. S-O-S 201-S-O-5-500. Atlanta: Sociology Department, Georgia State University, 1973a.

_____. "Age Differences in the Meaning of Leisure Activities." Paper presented to the 26th Annual Meeting of the Gerontological Society, Miami Beach, November 14, 1973(b).

Instrument

See Instrument V2.11.II.b.

LEISURE ACTIVITY SCORE

S. R. Sherman, 1973

Definition of Variable or Concept

Frequency of involvement in leisure activities is used as a measure of activity level.

Description of Instrument

This index of participation in 12 leisure activities includes a probe for 4 more activities; responses are used to form an index of participation. A battery of questions concerning the number of club memberships, frequency of participation, and location of club ("on site" or not) is also included in this interview schedule.

Method of Administration

The leisure items should take about 5 minutes to administer by interview.

Context of Development

The measure was developed as part of the California study of housing environments for the elderly in good health (Sherman, 1974). Leisure participation was included to determine whether leisure patterns in retirement-housing environments differ from those in dispersed housing.

Sample

From lists of six retirement-housing sites 10 residents were selected by choosing every Nth individual (N = total/100 following a random start), which resulted in a total of 600 respondents. A control sample of 600 respondents matched on sex, working status, marital status, age, income, occupation, housing (rental versus ownership), household composition, and number of children was used. The matches were selected from a large pool of respondents used by a local newspaper for market-survey analysis and supplemented by a sample from specific census tracts. Interviews were carried out in November 1965 to January 1966 and again 2 years later ($N = 1,200$ at T_1 and $N = 952$ at T_2). The age range of respondents from the retirement was 45 to over 91, with a mean of 73.06 years; the range for the matching sample was 45 to over 95, with a mean of 72.7 years (Sherman, 1973, pp. 353-57).

Scoring, Scale Norms, and Distribution

The items on the activity index are dichotomized, with "often" and "sometimes" scored 1 and "never" scored 0. Items are then summed, yielding an index with a range from 0 to 16. The scores on the battery for club memberships are treated as percentage frequencies. Item responses for both times 1 and 2 are presented by Sherman (1974, pp. 328-29).

Usability on Older Populations

The instrument was well recieved, with low refusal rates.

General Comments and Recommendations

This is one of the few indexes used to date with time-1 and time-2 data and measures of stability or changeover. The 2-year period could be examined to begin to assess the reliability of the index.

References

Sherman, S. R. "Methodology in a Study of Residents of Retirement Housing." *Journal of Gerontology*, 1973, 28:351-58.
————. "Leisure Activities in Retirement Housing." *Journal of Gerontology*, 1974, 29: 325-35.
Walkley, R. P., W. P. Mangum, Jr., S. R. Sherman, S. Dodds, and D. M. Wilner. *Retirement Housing in California*. Berkeley, Calif.: Diable Press, 1966.

Instrument

See Instrument V2.11.II.c.

LEISURE PARTICIPATION

B. Havens and M. Thompson, 1973-1977

Definition of Variable or Concept

Participation rates and satisfaction with a select group of leisure activities are measured by this instrument.

Description of Instrument

This battery of items covers 21 activity areas (e.g., music, art, and theater). The respondent is asked in general, "What are the most important things that you do?" and then "What additional things which you are not now doing would you like to do?" For each response the respondent is asked supplemental questions (1) on participation during last week, (2) on level of satisfaction, and (3) whether lack of participation is a problem. A separate series of questions deals with the role of residence councils in some leisure activities.

Method of Administration

These items are included as part of an interview schedule.

Context of Development and Subsequent Use

A large study conducted for the Province of Manitoba on the needs and priorities of the elderly included these items. The primary thrust of the full study was policy related.

Sample

A provincewide area probability sample of persons over 65 ($N = 3,558$) was combined with a random sample of persons living in facilities for the elderly ($N = 1,249$).

Scoring, Scale Norms, and Distribution

This instrument is not scored as a battery. Havens and Thompson reported percentages of the level of participation and the degree of the problem with nonparticipation.

Usability on Older Populations

No problems were mentioned in this large sample study.

General Comments and Recommendations

This battery taps general leisure participation as well as work and housework. The response categories used are arbitrary.

Reference

"Aging in Manitoba. Volumes I-IX." Winnipeg: Manitoba Department of Health and Social Development, 1973-1977.

Instrument

See Instrument V2.11.II.d.

USE OF LEISURE TIME

Duke Longitudinal Study of Adaptation, 1968

Definition of Variable or Concept.

Allocation of time and the use of free time by the middle-aged are examined within the changing sociohistorical context of increasing amounts of time not devoted to work.

Description of Instrument

The battery of questions asks about the number of hours per day spent on 14 activities ranging from eating to yard care, with the inclusion of an open-ended question on "other leisure" activities. Four questions assess vacation behavior, and six questions assess attitudes toward, and satisfactions derived from, leisure activities.

Method of Administration

Data are collected by personal interview.

Context of Development and Subsequent Use

The leisure questions were part of a longitudinal study focusing on adaptation during middle age and the preretirement years. The study's emphasis was on adaptation to potentially stressful events (e.g., death of spouse, illness, retirement).

Sample

A random sample stratified by age and gender was taken of members of a health insurance association in Durham, N.C. This procedure generated a pool of 2,000 persons, about half of whom refused to participate; illiterate, black, and institutionalized or homebound persons were excluded. Quotas were established for each of 10 age-gender cohorts, so that approximately 40 persons in each cohort could be retested after 5 years. Persons were contacted and scheduled in a random order until the quotas were filled. This resulted in a sample of 502 men and women aged 45 to 69, who were tested from August 1968 to April 1970; and 443 survivors had been retested by March 1972. Further information on the sample is presented by Palmore (1974, pp. 203-96).

Scoring, Scale Norms, and Distribution

The battery on activities is scored as the actual number of hours per day or week an individual spent in an activity; Pfeiffer and Davis (1974, p. 236) analyzed these data in terms of the average number of hours per week for each sex. The vacation and satisfaction questions are presented as percentage distributions broken down by age and gender (Pfeiffer and Davis, 1974, pp. 238-40).

Usability on Older Populations

No problems were mentioned by any of the investigators.

Sensitivity to Age Differences

Men 66 to 71 years old were more likely than other males to report that they had too much free time, that work was more satisfying than leisure, and that they wanted to continue work in the absence of financial need. Women aged 46 to 55 were more likely than other females to report having too little free time.

General Comments and Recommendations

This battery of questions covers only a sample of possible leisure behaviors; this may preclude scale formation. The questions on vacations and satisfaction with leisure are very general and probably could not be scaled.

References

Palmore, E. "Design of the Adaptation Study." In *Normal Aging II*, E. Palmore (ed.), pp. 291-96. Durham, N.C.: Duke University Press, 1974

Pfeiffer, E., and G. C. Davis. "The Use of Leisure Time in Middle Life." In *Normal Aging II*, E. Palmore (ed.), pp. 232-43. Durham, N.C.: Duke University Press, 1974.

Instrument

See Instrument V2.11.II.e.

LEISURE ACTIVITIES

Committee on Research and Development Goals in Social Gerontology, 1971

Definition of Variable or Concept

Leisure is defined as taking part in noneconomic endeavors (i.e., as a residual phenomenon).

Description of Instrument

A battery of 4 questions with 10 nested subquestions asks the respondent and his or her spouse to rank their favorite leisure activities, the age at which they were most active, and the reasons for changes in activity levels.

Method of Administration

It requires about 5 minutes to administer the leisure items during a personal interview.

Context of Development and Subsequent Use

Developed by a team of social scientists interested in flexible careers and life-styles, this instrument was used to test developmental conceptions of work and leisure during the adult portion of the life cycle.

Scoring, Scale Norms, and Distribution

Descriptive data on the favorite leisure activities of respondents are presented.

Sample

Oliver (1971) studied 30 Caucasians aged 44 to 66 who were in-migrants to the Ozarks region of Missouri. Hearn (1971) studied 22 blacks aged 50 to 70 in Kansas City, Mo. Lopata (1971) studied 20 Chicago women (predominantly widows) aged 62 to 87. All samples were purposive.

Usability on Older Populations

No problems were encountered in the studies using the instrument.

General Comments and Recommendations

This instrument sees a useful method of eliciting rankings of favorite leisure behaviors. Such information is rarely used as an index or scale.

References

Hearn, H. L. "Career and Leisure Patterns of Middle-aged Urban Blacks." *The Gerontologist*, 1971, 11 (4, part 2):21-26.

Lopata, H. Z., and F. Steinhart. "Work Histories of American Urban Women." *The Gerontologist*, 1971, 11 (4, part 2):27-36.

Murray, J. R., E. A. Powers, and R. J. Havighurst. "Personal and Situational Factors Producing Flexible Careers." *The Gerontologist*, 1971, 11 (4, part 2):4-12.

Oliver. D. B. "Career and Leisure Patterns of Middle-aged Metropolitan Out-Migrants." *The Gerontologist*, 1971, 11 (4, part 2):13-20.

Instrument

See Instrument V2.11.III.a.

FREE TIME ACTIVITIES

W. A. Peterson, L. W. Phelps, and C. F. Longino, Jr., 1976

Definition of Variable or Concept

This instrument is an inventory of free-time activities and involvement with the media. Present participation rates are compared with those at age 50 years (as measured by recall methods).

Description of Instrument

The battery of 24 questions assesses the degree of involvement in leisure at age 50 and at present, with probes designed to further probe for reasons why change may have occurred, and the respondent's age during that change.

Method of Administration

Personal interviews 60 minutes long were used to gather all the data in this study. No estimate of the time requirements for the leisure items is availabe.

Context of Development and Subsequent Use

Designed to assess changes in leisure behavior, the instrument is currently being used in a larger study of special programs developed in age-segregated retirement communities.

Sample

The sample was a 10% sample of all the residents of a retirement community. The 150 interviews were carried out in 1975. The respondents ranged in age from 60 to over 90, with 60% of the respondents female.

Scoring, Scale Norms, and Distribution

Descriptive statistics of the percentage of persons participating in leisure activities are given. A cumulative index to designate low, medium, and high activity levels is also developed, but exact scoring procedures are not available.

Usability on Older Populations

No problems were encountered with the older population in the study.

General Comments and Recommendations

This instrument is a battery of questions covering the major areas of leisure participation.

The battery has been used as an index, and it has the potential of being made into a scale.

Reference

Peterson, W. A., L. W. Phelps, and C. F. Longino, Jr. "John Knox Village Residents: Exploring the Tangibles and Intangibles of Retirement Living." Report for the Institute for Community Studies, Kansas City, Mo., 1976.

Instrument

See Instrument V2.11.III.b.

PAST LEISURE PARTICIPATION

B. P. Payne and C. N. Bull, 1976

Definition of Variable or Concept

The respondent's history of participation and cessation of leisure activities during school or college, after school or college, and at present is measured by this instrument.

Description of Instrument

A battery of four items allows for the listing of four hobbies or leisure activities during each of three stages of life.

Method of Administration

These questions take 5 minutes to administer as part of an interview.

Context of Development and Subsequent Use

The instrument was used to examine the relative effect of learning new leisure activities (i.e., socialization) as contrasted to the carryover of preretirement activities for adults who have retired.

Sample

The instrument was used during the second year of a longitudinal study of older volunteers ($N = 58$) in 1975 in Kansas City, Mo. The respondents had an age range of 55 to 82, and they were white, upper-middle-class, and in excellent health.

Scoring

The data are coded into 88 separate activities.

Usability on Older Populations

No problems were encountered with the study's older population.

General Comments and Recommendations

This series of open-ended questions only begins to tap a life history of leisure activities. Much more work on large populations will be required to standardize this measure.

Reference

None is available at this time.

Instrument

See Instrument V2.11.III.c.

COMMUNICATIONS ACTIVITY

M. J. Graney and E. E. Graney, 1974

Definition of Variable or Concept

Media use as a subarea of leisure participation is measured by this instrument.

Description of Instrument

This battery of preestablished categories concerns the frequency of participation per day, week, and month in watching television, listening to radio, and reading books, magazines, and newspapers; it is included with questions on visiting patterns, religious participation, and membership in voluntary associations.

Method of Administration

Data are gathered as part of an interview.

Context of Development and Subsequent Use

The battery was used in a panel study undertaken to learn more about the characteristics of elderly persons residing in public housing (Graney and Graney, 1974).

Sample

The all-female panel was interviewed in 1968 ($N = 60$) and again in 1972 ($N = 46$) in Minneapolis. The panel was composed of elderly women selected by the Metropolitan Housing and Redevelopment Authority. The ages of the women ranged from 62 to 89 in 1968.

Scoring, Scale Norms, and Distribution

Participation is scored as high, medium, or low for each activity. Cutoff points are listed with the instrument.

Formal Tests of Reliability/Homogeneity

The average correlation among the media-use variables (i.e., television, radio, reading) in 1968 was .47 (Graney, 1975, p. 354).

Usability on Older Populations

No problems were encountered in this study.

Sensitivity to Age Differences

Analysis of these longitudinal data indicates that change in radio listening is inversely related to change in religious attendance and friend visiting and that change in visiting is inversely related to telephone use, thus providing evidence of activity substitution (Graney and Graney, 1974, pp. 93-94).

Direct relationships among measures of change are noted for the following pairs: (1) visiting neighbors-organization memberships, (2) television viewing-telephone use, (3) television viewing-organization participation, (4) radio listening-organization membership and participation, and (5) organization membership-organization participation (Graney and Graney, 1974, pp. 93-94).

General Comments and Recommendations

The battery only looks at frequency of participation in broad categories of media use. It omits information on types of program watched, time at which participation occurred, and person with whom participation occurred.

References

Graney, M. J. "Communication Uses and the Social Activity Constant." *Communication Research*, 1975, 2:347-66.
Graney, M. J., and E. E. Graney. "Communications Activity Substitutions in Aging." *Journal of Communication*, 1974, 24(4):88-96.

Instrument

See Instrument V2.11.IV.a.

MEDIA HABITS

Canadian Radio-Television Commission, 1974

Definition of Variable or Concept

The use of media (both amount and type) with *media* defined as television, radio, newspapers, and magazines, is measured by this instrument as major components of leisure time.

Description of Instrument

The entire interview (except the questions on demographics) is concerned with the media. Each media type is covered in turn, with questions dealing with ownership, access, type of program, degree of use, time of day used, and enjoyment from programs or reading materials.

Method of Administration

Personal interviews are used to collect the data.

Context of Development and Subsequent Use

The survey was carried out for the Communications Committee of the Toronto Area Presbytery of the United Church of Canada, with the assistance of the Canadian Radio-Television Commission, the Ontario Ministry of Community and Social Services, and the Department of National Health and Welfare. The focus of the study was on assessing the use of the media by an elderly population.

Sample

The data were collected in Toronto, Canada, in 1973. The sample was based on a list of persons 65 and older who subscribed to the Ontario Hospital Insurance Plan (an almost universal list). A probability sample of 1,554 was drawn, with a final sample of 522 being interviewed. The age ranges of the respondents were 65 to 69 (39%), 70 to 74 (27%), 75 to 79 (15%), and over 80 (17%). The sample was 45% male.

Scoring and Distribution

Percentages of response types are presented as descriptive participation rates and participation preferences.

Usability on Older Populations

No problems were stated; however, a refusal rate of 29% was noted.

General Comments and Recommendations

This instrument is a straightforward descriptive measure of media participation. The length of the instrument may preclude its use in studies in which media use is an ancillary focus.

Reference

Canadian Radio-Television Commission. "Reaching the Retired: A Survey of the Media Habits, Preferences, and Needs of Senior Citizens in Metro Toronto." Canadian Radio-Television Commission, Information Canada. Document Number BC 92-9/1974.

Instrument

This instrument is too long to be reproduced here.

ELDERLY LEISURE ATTITUDE SCALE

J. D. Teaff, N. W. Ernst, and M. Ernst, 1975

Definition of Variable or Concept

Attitudes toward leisure are measured by five dimensions: (1) desired leisure, (2) perceived leisure, (3) self-definition through leisure or work, (4) affinity for leisure, and (5) society's role in leisure planning.

Description of Instrument

The scale is a modified 26-item version of the original Neulinger and Breit (1971) leisure attitude scale. The items were modified for length, clarity of directions, and complexity to facilitate their use with older respondents.

Method of Administration

Teaff, Ernst, and Ernst (1975) used a questionnaire format in their study; the instrument could easily be used with personal interviews.

Context of Development and Subsequent Use

This modified measure was developed in a methodological study determining items suitable for an elderly leisure attitude scale.

Sample

The modified scale was used with a nonrandom sample of participants in the Foster Grandparents Program (N = 93) and the AARP chapter (N = 36) in Dallas, Tex.

Scoring, Scale Norms, and Distribution

Factor scores are constructed by standardizing each item to a Z score, multiplying the score by its factor loading, and summing across items in the factor (Neulinger, 1974, p. 183). Factor loading for the Teaff, Ernst, and Ernst (1975) analysis are included with the instrument. Items are scored for each factor when the loading exceeds .40 (Neulinger, 1974, p. 181) or .30 (Teaff, Ernst, and Ernst, 1975, p. 2) *and* when the difference between factor loading exceeds .10.

Formal Tests of Validity

The modified instrument yielded factors very similar to Neulinger's analysis; none of the factors had to be renamed.

Usability on Older Populations

The modified scale, tailored to an elderly population, seems very good. However, it is recommended that the scale be used only on better-educated older subjects because of its complex item working.

General Comments and Recommendations

The modified scale is a very important measure of leisure attitudes, which has been used with, and adapted for, an elderly population.

References

Neulinger, J. *The Psychology of Leisure*. Sprinfield, Ill.: Charles C. Thomas, 1974.

Neulinger, J., and M. Breit. "Attitude Dimensions of Leisure: A Replication Study." *Journal of Leisure Research*, 1971, (3): 108-15.

Teaff, J. D., N. W. Ernst, and M. Ernst. "An Elderly Leisure Attitude Schedule." Paper presented to the 28th Annual Meeting of the Gerontological Society, Louisville, October 26-30, 1975.

Instrument

See Instrument V2.11.V.a.

LEISURE ACTIVITIES AND SATISFACTION

E. A. Powers, 1964-1974

Definition of Variable or Concept

Attitudes toward leisure activities and the role of leisure in the life of the older person are measured by this instrument.

Description of Instrument

This battery includes eight questions about the respondent's favorite leisure activity, leisure satisfaction, amount of time spent on leisure, and respondent's leisure activity compared to his or her activities with family, work, and community.

Method of Administration

The battery is administered as part of a longer interview.

Context of Development and Subsequent Use

The measure was used as part of a longitudinal study of men who were employed in 1964 and 60 years or older in 1974.

Sample

The sample included 1,332 nonmetropolitan Iowa males employed in one of five occupational groups (farmers, small businessmen, factory workers, self-employed workers, and salaried professionals) in 1964; all were over age 60 during the second interview in 1974.

Usability on Older Populations

No problems were encountered in the longitudinal study of middle-aged and aging males.

General Comments and Recommendations

This battery starts to look at different facets of leisure. Measuring the degree of involvement in leisure (i.e., either time spent or financial resources committed) would go a long way toward improving this measure.

Reference

None is available at this time.

Instrument

See Instrument V2.11.V.b.

Instruments

V2.11.I.a

LEISURE ACTIVITIES

R. J. Havighurst, 1957

I. Rating Scales for Significance Variables
   Applicable to specific activities. These are five-point scales, with definitions of each point on the scale.

   A. Autonomy versus other-directed
      (1) Chooses activity with purpose and regard for its function in one's personal life;
      (2) acts on own initiative, without much reflection on the function of the activity;

    (3)   activity represents a weak but visible choice;

    (4)   chooses activity but is pushed toward it by circumstances of his position; activity related to work;

    (5)   activity determined by others or by propinquity.

B. Creativity (new solution, novel behavior)

    (1)   Produces new and interesting results (material, non-material, makes things, arranges things, does things with and through people);

    (2)   there is an element of novelty, though not to a high degree; alters approach to activity occasionally;

    (3)   some evidence of variety through choice; behavior not completely stereotyped;

    (4)   relies on habit, with occasional innovations;

    (5)   rote activity (TV several hours a day, routine newspaper reading).

C. Enjoyment versus time-killer

    (1)   Gets strong pleasure out of activity;

    (2)   gets mild pleasure out of activity;

    (3)   enjoys it slightly but sees it mainly as a time-filler;

    (4)   enjoyable partly because it allows escape from unpleasantness;

    (5)   time-killer, no enjoyment.

D. Development of talent

    (1)   Activity develops or maintains outstanding talent;

    (2)   activity develops or maintains positive and fairly complex ability;

    (3)   activity develops or maintains a fairly complex ability at a mediocre level;

    (4)   activity requires a perceptible amount of complex ability;

    (5)   activity requires no complex ability.

E. Possibility for future versus limited to present

    (1)   Activity promises to be more rewarding in the future;

    (2)   activity will grow slightly in reward value;

    (3)   activity will continue to be rewarding;

    (4)   activity will continue but will lose reward value;

    (5)   activity must soon be abandoned and will have no valuable effect in the future.

F. Instrumental versus expressive

Instrumental: Manipulation of the object world to meet human needs.

Expressive: Expressing emotion as an end in itself. Showing affection, appreciation, enjoyment. Supportive, acceptive behavior.

    (1)   Makes or produces something for a useful purpose or for pleasure of others; production is essential in process; may or may not be pleasurable;

    (2)   plays a game or participates in an activity for some goal beyond the game or activity (church committee, philanthropic board);

    (3)   does something for a goal beyond the activity but gets a great deal of pleasure out of it also; balance between product and process;

    (4)   does something for pleasure of self, with an element of pleasure for others or of use for others;

    (5)   does something for the sheer pleasure of it or associates with others in a pleasure-seeking activity; focus is on pleasure for self.

G. Physical energy input

    (1)   Maximum physical activity; physical activity is of the essence;

    (2)   physical activity is considerable;

    (3)   active but limited;

    (4)   physically passive but requires effort to participate (e.g., going to baseball game);

    (5)   physically passive, purely spectator, at home.

H. Relation of leisure to work: complementary-competitive

    (1)   Recreation grows out of work and makes work more successful, e.g., reading for a scholar;

    (2)   recreation helps in career but also enjoyable in itself, e.g., play golf or cards for the sake of "contacts";

    (3)   fits in with expectation of general occupational status—appropriate for a person with this kind of job;

    (4)   no relation between recreation and work; non-congruent and has no function by being non-congruent;

    (5)   recreation offsets work—a real relief and contrast; requires a shift of roles from the work-roles, e.g., going fishing to be alone.

J. Gregarious versus solitary

    (1)   Essentially gregarious;

    (2)   mainly gregarious but occasionally alone;

    (3)   balanced, e.g., swimming, movies;

    (4)   mainly solitary, occasionally involves social interaction;

    (5)   essentially solitary.

K. Service versus pleasure

    (1)   Primarily to serve others;

    (2)   service to others with an element of self-development or pleasure;

    (3)   primarily to develop one's self or do something useful for one's self;

    (4)   pleasure, with an element of self-development;

    (5)   primarily for personal pleasure.

L. Status, prestige

    (1)   Builds up general social prestige;

    (2)   brings prestige in present, immediate status group;

    (3)   has mild prestige value;

    (4)   has no prestige value;

    (5)   reduces general prestige.

M. Relaxation from anxiety-arousing tensions

    (1)   Provides no relaxation;

    (2)   provides a trace of relaxation;

    (3)   partial escape from tension of life but not a complete letdown;

    (4)   somewhat relaxing; minimal tension;

    (5)   gives complete relaxation from tension, e.g., minister who goes fishing.

N. Ego-integration versus role diffusion

    (1)   Activity develops the individual as an integrated person;

    (2)   helps one to maintain one's level of integration or life-style;

    (3)   fits neatly into established life-style; congruent with life-style;

    (4)   represents a mild discontinuity in life-style;

    (5)   definitely disintegrative; does not fit the person's life-style.

General rating scales for nature and use of leisure

  I. Financial cost

    (1)   A great deal, e.g., golf at a private country club, $500+;

    (2) costs something but not much, $100-$500, e.g., golf at a municipal course, television;

    (3) costs little or nothing, less than $100, e.g., playing cards without gambling, fishing (locally).

II. Feeling of much versus little leisure
    (1) A lot of leisure, almost too much;
    (2) plenty of spare time—a feeling of relaxation—can play whenever I like;
    (3) some leisure—taken as a matter of course, would prefer more;
    (4) "I have to fight for leisure time"; very little spare time;
    (5) no spare time at all.

III. New experience versus repetition
    (1) Always looking for new experience in leisure; tends to drop an activity after a while because it loses its novelty;
    (2) has done at least one new thing in leisure time recently;
    (3) feels no need for novelty but can accept it; has at least one habitual activity;
    (4) slightly resistive to novelty;
    (5) likes to do things over and over; has a routine for leisure, and enjoys it, e.g., long-time gardener or card player.

IV. Vitality versus apathy
    (1) Vigorous, active, pleasure-seeking in use of leisure;
    (2) different from 1 in having lesser degree of vigor (or related to fewer activities);
    (3) finds leisure agreeable but not exciting;
    (4) feels that leisure is uninteresting;
    (5) apathetic—expects and gets nothing from leisure.

V. Expansion versus constriction of interests and activities
    (1) Leisure pattern shows expansion of interests and activities, high level;
    (2) shows active interest or vigor in things he does, but no expansiveness;
    (3) leisure pattern shows plateau of interests and activities;
    (4) imminent decrease but still seems on plateau;
    (5) decreasing range of interests in leisure.

VI. Things versus other values
    (1) Predominant interest in things versus social relations or other non-material values; is definitely interested in handling or working with objects;
    (2) more interest in things than non-material values, may have perfunctory interest in television, watching sports, or playing games, along with an active interest in working with things;
    (3) balance of interests between things and non-material values; has at least one strong interest in making, collecting, or cultivating material objects;
    (4) more interest in non-material than in material things, that is, more interest in social relations, music, reading, than in working with things;
    (5) no interest in material objects or in working with materials.

SOURCE: R. J. Havighurst. "The Leisure Activities of the Middle-aged." *American Journal of Sociology*, 1957, 63:154-56. Reprinted by permission of author and publisher, the University of Chicago Press.

II. Leisure Role Interview Schedule.

43. In this interview we want especially to know about your spare time activities—the kinds of things you do when you aren't working. What kinds of things do you do in your spare

time?

ACTIVITY (DESCRIPTION)_____

Why liked?_____

With whom?_____

How much time?_____

(LATER) Meanings Code   (1)_____ (2)_____ (3)_____

(REPEAT ACTIVITY DESCRIPTION FOUR TIMES)

44. Of the things we have talked about which is most important?_____
    Which is second most important?_____

45. (INTERVIEWER: CHOOSE TWO IF POSSIBLE OF THESE ACTIVITIES LISTED
    ABOVE. SHOW THE RESPONDENT THE ATTACHED CHECK LIST AND ASK RE-
    SPONDENT TO CHECK THE ONES WHICH MOST NEARLY EXPRESS HIS REASONS
    FOR LIKING THIS ACTIVITY. RECORD THE LETTERS IN THE LAST SPACE UN-
    DER ACTIVITY.)

    To the Respondent: I have here a list of reasons people give for doing various things in
    their spare time. These are reasons given by people in Chicago, in New Zealand, and
    other places. Will you look at this list and tell me the reasons you would pick for _____
    _____(NAME OF ACTIVITY)_____

    Which of these reasons is most important? Second most important? Third most impor-
    tant?

MEANINGS OF LEISURE ACTIVITIES

Instructions: Place a (1) in front of the statement which best describes your reason for liking
this activity. Place a (2) in front of the statement which applies second. Place a (3) in front
of the statement which applies third.

_____ Z. I feel that I am being creative.

_____ Y. It gives me a chance to achieve something.

_____ X. It gives me more standing with other people.

_____ W. It makes the time pass.

_____ V. It gives me new experience; I feel I learn something from it.

_____ U. It makes me popular among other people.

_____ T. It helps me financially.

_____ S. I feel I can respect myself for doing these things.

_____ R. I like it because I like to do things that will be of benefit to society.

_____ Q. It is a welcome change from my work.

_____ P. I like it because it brings me into contact with friends.

_____ O. I like it just for the pleasure of doing it, that's all.

46. How have you changed in the way you spend your spare time in the last ten years?
    Are there things which you enjoy doing now that you didn't used to enjoy? What are
    they?_____
    Are there things which you used to enjoy doing that you don't enjoy now? What are
    they?_____

47. (IF NOT VISIBLE) Do you have television?
    What television shows do you watch?_____

48. How much time do you spend listening to the radio?_____
    What programs?_____

49. Are you interested in sports?_____
    What kind of sports?_____
    Do you ever play yourself?_____

50. Are ther (other kinds of) outdoor activities that you like? (Fishing, camping, hunting, etc.)_____
    About how much are you able to?_____

51. How often do you go to the movies?_____
    What kind of movies do you like?_____

52. What do you read in the newspaper? (What parts of the newspaper are you most interested in?)_____

53. What magazines do you read regularly?_____

54. Do you ever read books?_____
    What books have you read recently?_____

55. Do you like music?_____What kind of music do you like?_____

56. What do you do when you are on vacation?_____
    This year?_____ Last year?_____

57. What do you do around the house?_____
    How much responsibility do you have for keeping house?_____
    Do you do much fixing and decorating around the house?_____

58. How old are you now?_____

59. How is your health?_____

60. Since you have been grown up, what have been the important changes in your health (illnesses, operations)?_____

61. Are you more or less satisfied with your health than you were ten years ago?_____

SOURCE: R. J. Havighurst. "The social Competence of Middle-aged People." *Genetic Psychology Monograph*, 1957, 56:362-63. Reprinted by permission of author and publisher, the Journal Press.

III. Content of Leisure Categories

1. Participation in formal groups—social clubs, fraternal organizations, church groups, discussion groups, or adult education classes
2. Participation in informal groups—sociability stressed, and no rules or organization, no fixed meeting times, etc.—such groups are card-playing cliques, neighborhood groups, tavern groups
3. Travel for the sake of enjoying travel
4. Participation in sports
5. Watching sports (not on TV)
6. Television and radio
7. Fishing and hunting (mainly fishing)
8. Gardening—flowers or vegetables or landscaping
9. Manual-manipulative activities—sewing and handwork for women, do-it-yourself carpentry and home repairs, woodworking, etc., for men
10. Imaginative—almost entirely reading but might include music and art-apprecciation activity
11. Visiting relatives and friends—travel may be involved, but the main object is visiting

SOURCE: R. J. Havighurst, "The Leisure Activities of the Middle-aged." *American Journal of Sociology*, 1957, 63:156-57. Reprinted by permission of author and publisher, the University of Chicago Press.

IV. Leisure Role Performance Rating Scale

a. High 8-9. Spends enough time at some leisure activity to be rather well known among his associates in this respect. But it is not so much the amount of leisure activity as the quality of this activity which gives him a high rating. He has one or more leisure activities for which he gets public recognition and appreciation, and which gives him a real sense of accomplishment.

Chooses his leisure activities autonomously, not merely to be in style. Gets several of the following types of satisfaction from leisure: feeling of being creative, novel and interesting experience, sheer pleasure, prestige, friendship, sense of being of service.

b. Above Average 6-7. Has 4-5 leisure activities. Leisure time is somewhat patterned indicating that he has planned his life to provide for the satisfaction of the needs met through these activities.

Leisure interests show some variety. Displays real enthusiasm for one or two of these—talks about them in such a way as to indicate that he has put considerable energy into acquiring proficiency or the requisite understanding and skills involved in this activity. Prides himself in this activity.

c. Medium 4-5. Has two or three leisure activities which he does habitually and enjoys mildly—reading, TV, radio, watching sports, handwork, etc. May do one of these things well or quite enthusiastically, but not more than one. Gets definite sense of well-being from leisure activities, and is seldom bored with leisure.

Leisure activities are somewhat stereotyped—do not have a great deal of variety.

d. Below Average 2-3.

(1) Tends to take the line of least resistance in leisure time. Needs to be stimulated. Looks for time-fillers.

(2) May have very little spare time. What he has is taken up with activities related to his job or profession or with work around the house which is viewed as obligatory and not a positive leisure-time pursuit.

e. Low 0-1.

(1) Apathetic in leisure. Does nothing and makes no attempt to find outside interests.

(2) Tries anxiously to find interesting things to do and fails to find them. Is bored by leisure and hurries back to work. Dislikes vacations, and cannot relax.

SOURCE: R. J. Havighurst. "The Social Competence of Middle-aged People." *Genetic Psychology Monographs*, 1957, 56:356-57. Reprinted by permission of author and publisher, the Journal Press.

V2.11.I.b

LEISURE TIME

C. Gordon, C. M. Gaitz, and J. Scott, 1976

29. A. We are particularly interested in what people do for leisure—that is, what they do in their non-working time.

For example, how much do you enjoy getting out into the country or to the beach —camping, fishing, walking in the woods, etc.? Would you say that you enjoy this type of activity very much, pretty much, not very much, or not much at all?

Very much. 1
Pretty much 2

Not very much 3
Not much at all 4
Don't know 5

B. In the last 2 or 3 years, about how many times have you gone on an outing like this?

More than 10 times 6
5-9 times 7
1-4 times 8
Never 9

C. How good do you think you (are/would be) at this type of activity — very good, pretty good, not very good, or not at all good?

Very good 1
Pretty good 2
Not very good 3
Not much at all 4
Don't know 5

---

30. A. How much do you enjoy things like sewing, mending, decorating, fixing, building, or working in the yard? Do you enjoy these kinds of things very much, pretty much, or not much at all?

Very much 1
Pretty much 2
Not very much 3
Not at all 4
Don't know 5

B. In the last year or so, how often have you done things like this — every day, few times a week, every week, few times a month, every month, or less often than that?

Every day 1
Few times a week 2
Every week 3
Few times a month 4
Every month 5
Less often than that 6

C. How good do you think you (are/would be) at any of these kinds of activities? Would you say very good, pretty good, not very good, or not good at all?

Very good 1
Pretty good 2
Not very good 3
Not good at all 4
Don't know 5

---

31. A. Do you enjoy looking at paintings or listening to music very much, pretty much, not very much, or not much at all?

Very much 1
Pretty much 2
Not very much 3
Not much at all 4
Don't know 5

B. How often in the last year have you engaged in this type of activity—would it be every day, a few times a week, every week, a few times a month, or less often than that?

Every day 1
A few times a week 2
Every week 3
A few times a month 4
Less often than that 5

C. How much do you know about art or music—a great deal, a moderate amount, or very little?

A great deal 6
A moderate amount 7
Very little 8
Don't know 9

32. A. How much do you enjoy doing things like singing, drawing or painting, or playing a musical instrument? Would you say very much, pretty much, not very much, or not much at all?

Very much 1
Pretty much 2
Not very much 3
Not much at all 4
Don't know 5

B. How often in the last year have you participated in any of these kinds of activities— every day, a few times a week, every week, a few times a month, every month, less often than that, or never?

Every day 1
A few times a week 2
Every week 3
A few times a month 4
Every month 5
Less often than that 6
Never .7

C. How good do you think you (are/would be) at any of these things, like drawing, singing, or playing an instrument? Would you say very good, pretty good, not very good, or not good at all?

Very good 1
Pretty good 2
Not very good 3
Not good at all 4
Don't know 5

D. Which one of the kinds of music listed on this card is closest to being your favorite? (CIRCLE ONE.)

Country and western 01
Religious 02
Semi-classical 03
Popular or musical comedy 04
Folk or rock 05

Rhythm and blues 06
Mexican 07
Dixieland or jazz 08
Classical 09
Don't know 10

33. A. And how much do you enjoy traveling to other cities (aside from your job)? Would
     you say you enjoy traveling very much, pretty much, not very much, or not at all?

     Very much. 1
     Pretty much 2
     Not very much 3
     Not at all. 4
     Don't know 5

     B. (Aside from your job) in the last three years how many times have you traveled to
     other cities?

     7 or more 1
     4-6. 2
     2-3 trips 3
     1 trip 4
     None 5

     C. How good do you think you (are/would be) at planning a trip—that is, like making
     reservations, buying tickets, or figuring out which way to go? Would you say very
     good, pretty good, not so good, or not good at all?

     Very good 1
     Pretty good 2
     Not so good 3
     Not good at all 4
     Don't know 5

     D. Do you (have/think you would have) a lot of trouble, some trouble or no trouble at
     all in finding your way around a strange town or area?

     A lot 6
     Some 7
     None at all. 8
     Don't know 9

34. A. How much do you enjoy going out for an evening to a place where you can dance
     or drink? Would you say very much, pretty much, not very much, or not at all?

     Very much. 1
     Pretty much 2
     Not very much 3
     Not at all. 4
     Don't know 5

     B. In the last year, about how often have you gone out for this type of evening—2-3
     times a week or more, once a week, few times a month, or once a month or less?

     2-3 times a week or more 1
     Once a week. 2
     Few times a month 3

Once a month or less 4

Never .5

C. For the most part, is going out like this very dangerous, somewhat dangerous, only slightly dangerous, or not dangerous at all?

Very dangerous 1

Somewhat dangerous 2

Only slightly dangerous 3

Not dangerous at all 4

Don't know 5

D. Would you say you are a very good drinking companion, about average as a drinking companion, or not very good at this sort of thing?

Very good drinking companion 6

About average as a drinking companion . .7

Not very good at this sort of thing 8

Don't know 9

E. How well do you know how to dance? Do you dance very well, pretty well, about average, not so well, or not at all?

Very well. 1

Pretty well. 2

About average 3

Not so well. 4

Not at all. 5

35. A. How about movies? Do you enjoy going to the movies very much, pretty much, not very much, or not at all?

Very much. 1

Pretty much 2

Not very much 3

Not at all. 4

Don't know 5

B. In an average six-month period, how many times do you go to the movies?

More than 12 times. 1

6-12 times. 2

2-5 times. 3

Once 4

Never .5

36. A. Now how much do you enjoy either having people at your house for an evening or going to someone else's house—very much, pretty much, not very much, or not at all?

Very much. 1

Pretty much 2

Not very much 3

Not at all. 4

Don't know 5

B. On the average, how often do you get together like this? Is this more than once a week, once a week, few times a month, or once a month or less?

More than once a week. 1
Once a week. 2
Few times a month 3
Once a month or less 4
Never. 5

C. How good are you at talking with people — that is, just being sociable? Would you say you are very good, pretty good, about average, or below average at this?

Very good 1
Pretty good 2
About average. 3
Below average 4
Don't know 5

37. A. In general, how much do you enjoy reading — very much, pretty much, not very much, or not at all?

Very much. 1
Pretty much 2
Not very much 3
Not at all. 4
Don't know 5

B. Have you read and finished any book within the last year?

Yes 8
No 9

C. How many books do you have in the house?

None 1
1-5 2
6-20 3
21-50. 4
51-100. 5
101-250 6
Over 250. 7

D. Which one of the newspaper sections listed on this card is your favorite? (CIRCLE ONE.)

Front page. 01
Editorial page 02
Comics. 03
Horoscope 04
Features such as Dear Abby 05
Women's section (food, fashion) 06
Sports section 07
Business section. 08
Neighborhood news. 09
Other (SPECIFY). 10
Don't know 11

E. 1. Now, aside from the newspaper, which one of these items comes closest to being your favorite reading matieral? First, read through this entire list. (HAND RESPONDENT CARD F, AND GIVE HIM TIME TO READ ALL THE ITEMS CAREFULLY.)

2. Now, which one would you say is your favorite?

Papers or magazines of your
national or ethnic group 01
Magazines like Life and Look 02
Reader's Digest 03
Magazines like Harper's, New
Yorker 04
Magazines like Women's Day, Ladies
Home Journal 05
Magazines like True, Popular Mechanics,
Sports Illustrated 06
Magazines like Time and Newsweek . . . 08
Detective or mystery novels 08
Magazines like True Romance 09
Professional literature related to
your work 10
Science fiction. 11
The Bible or other religious material . . . 12
Serious fiction books. 13
Serious non-fiction books 14
Don't know 15

F. In general, how would you rate your intellectual ability—that is, how smart you are. Would you rate yourself very high, pretty high, about average, or not very high at all?

Very high 1
Pretty high. 2
About average 3
Not very high at all 4
Don't know 5

---

38. A. How much do you enjoy talking about local or national problems and issues? Would you say you enjoy it very much, pretty much, not very much, or not at all?

Very much. 1
Pretty much 2
Not very much 3
Not at all. 4
Don't know 5

B. As you recall, during the last year, how often would you say that you've talked about these things? Would you say more than once a week, once a week, a few times a month, or less than once a month?

More than once a week. 1
Once a week 2
Few times a month 3
Once a month 4
Less than once a month 5
Never. 6

C. How good are you at understanding or discussing these kinds of issues and problems? Would you say you are very good, pretty good, about average, or not too good?

Very good 1
Pretty good 2
About average 3
Not too good 4
Don't know 5

---

39. A. How do you feel about sports or exercise? Do you enjoy taking part in this type of thing very much, pretty much, not very much, or not at all?

Very much. 1
Pretty much 2
Not very much 3
Not at all. 4
Don't know 5

B. In the last six months, how often would you say you've taken part in something like this? Would you say every day, a few times a week, every week, a few times a month, once a month, or less often than that?

Every day 1
A few times a week. 2
Every week 3
A few times a month 4
Once a month 5
Less often than that 6
Never. 7

C. Overall, how good are you at sports for someone your age — very good, pretty good, not very good, or not good at all?

Very good 1
Pretty good 2
Not very good 3
Not good at all 4
Don't know 5

---

40. A. And how about watching sporting events, either live or on TV — how much do you enjoy doing that — very much, pretty much, not very much, or not at all?

Very much. 1
Pretty much 2
Not very much 3
Not at all. 4
Don't know 5

B. How often in the last six months have you either gone to a game or watched one on TV — every day, a few times a week, every week, a few times a month, once a month, or less often than that?

Every day 1
A few times a week. 2
Every week 3
A few times a month 4
Once a month 5
Less often than that 6
Never. 7

C. Do you know a lot, a little, or hardly anything about the players, performers or teams in the world of sports?

A lot 1
A little 2
Hardly anything. 3
Don't know 4

41. A. Over the last year or so, how many times have you engaged in the use of firearms in sports like hunting, or target practice?

3 or more times 6
1-2 times. 7
Never .8

B. How much (do you/do you think you would) enjoy the use of firearms?

Very much. 1
Pretty much 2
Not very much 3
Not at all 4
Don't know 5

42. A. How much do you enjoy cooking, baking, barbecuing—fixing food for yourself, your family, or friends? Would you say you enjoy it very much, pretty much, not very much, or not at all?

Very much. 1
Pretty much 2
Not very much 3
Not at all 4
Don't know 5

B. How often do you actually fix food for yourself, family, or friends?

Every meal. 1
Once a day. 2
Once a week or so. 3
Once a month or so. 4
Once a year or so 5
Never .6

C. How good (are you/do you think you would be) at this sort of thing, very good, fairly good, about average, not very good?

Very good 1
Fairly good 2
About average 3
Not very good. 4
Don't know 5

43. A. On the whole, how much do you enjoy having time to be alone to think, daydream, plan or just do nothing—very much, pretty much, not very much, or not at all?

Very much. . . . . .(ASK B-D). 1
Pretty much . . . . .(ASK B-D). 2
Not very much . . .(GO TO C). 3

Not at all . . . .(GO TO C). 4
Don't know . . . . .(GO TO C). 5

IF ENJOY AT ALL:

B. Does anyone else mind that you enjoy being alone?

Yes 6
No 7
Don't know 8

C. How often during the past year or so have you had a chance to be alone — very often, fairly often, not very often, or not at all?

Very often 1
Fairly often 2
Not very often 3
Not at all 4

D. How often do you have trouble finding satisfying things to do when you are alone — often, sometimes, seldom, or never?

Often 5
Sometimes 6
Seldom 7
Never 8

44. A. Do you have a television set?

Yes 1
No 2

B. (Even though you don't have one) About how many hours would you say you watch TV on an average day?

Never watch . . . . .(GO TO Q.45). 4
Less than 1 hour 5
1 hour-less than 2 hours 6
2 hours-less than 4 hours 7
4 or 5 hours 8
More than 5 9

IF WATCH AT ALL, ASK C-G:

C. Do you usually watch alone or with someone else?

Alone 1
Someone else 2
Don't know 3

D. Which one of these would you say is your favorite kind of program, the kind you try not to miss. (CIRCLE ONE.)

Detective or adventure 01
Daytime stories 02
News, documentaries, or discussions . . . 03
Variety shows with a lot of guests 04
Movies 05
Comedies 06
Westerns 07
Sports 08

Plays or other cultural events 09
Other (SPECIFY). 10
Don't know 11

E. When you're not at home, how often do you talk with others about what you've seen on TV, often, occasionally, seldom or never?

Often. 1
Occasionally 2
Seldom .3
Never 4

F. In general, do you think the kinds of programs on TV should be decided by the TV networks or by the people who watch TV?

Networks. 5
Watchers 6
Don't know 7

G. When you watch TV, do you ever feel you ought to be doing something else, but can't tear yourself away?

Yes (ASK H). 1
NO (GO TO Q. 45) 2

H. *IF YES TO G:* Would you say you feel that way often, occasionally, or only now and then?

Often. 6
Occasionally 7
Only now and then 8

---

45. A. We're interested in the clubs and organizations that people belong to and how they feel about them.

Altogether, how many clubs or organizations are you a member of?

0 . . . .(ASK C-D) 1
1 . . . .(ASK B-D) 2
2 or 3 . . . .(ASK B-D) 3
4 or 5 . . . .(ASK B-D) 4
6 or more . . . . .(ASK B-D) 5

B. Are these (is this) social clubs for enjoyment, organizations for some civic or other purpose, or some of each?

Social. 6
Civic or other purpose 7
Some of each 8

C. (Whether or not you belong at present) how much do you enjoy getting together with other people in clubs and organizations—very much, pretty much, not very much or not at all?

Very much. 1
Pretty much 2
Not very much 3
Not at all. 4
Don't know 5

D. When in comes to leading or speaking out in clubs or organizations, do you think you have a lot of ability, a moderate amount, or not so much?

A lot 6
A moderate amount 7
Not so much. 8
Don't know 9

E. How about just getting the work done in a club or organization—that is, being a good follower or helping to encourage others? How much ability do you have (think you have) . . . would you say a lot, a moderate amount, or not so much?

A lot 1
A moderate amount 2
Not so much. 3
Don't know 4

46. A. I'm going to read to you a list of places which people in Houston sometimes visit. As I read them please tell me which ones you have ever been to.

READ FIRST ITEM AND CIRCLE ONE CODE UNDER A. IF "BEEN TO" ASK B BEFORE READING NEXT ITEM. IF "NEVER BEEN TO" READ NEXT ITEM.

B. FOR EACH ITEM CODED "BEEN TO" ASK: How long ago were you last there?

Have you every been to:	A.		B.			
	BEEN TO (ASK B)	NEVER BEEN TO (NEXT ITEM)	Less than a week ago	Less than a month ago (more than a week)	Several months ago	Over a year ago
Sea Arama	(1)	2	3	4	5	6
The Gulf (Galveston or other beaches)	(1)	2	3	4	5	6
The New Alley Theatre (plays)	(1)	2	3	4	5	6
Jones Hall (symphony and ballet)	(1)	2	3	4	5	6
A swimming pool	(1)	2	3	4	5	6
The music theater in Sharpstown (musicals)	(1)	2	3	4	5	6
A downtown movie	(1)	2	3	4	5	6
A neighborhood movie or drive-in	(1)	2	3	4	5	6
A lake or river	(1)	2	3	4	5	6
The Astrodome	(1)	2	3	4	5	6
Astroworld	(1)	2	3	4	5	6
An air-conditioned shopping mall (center)	(1)	2	3	4	5	6
The Fine Arts Museum, or the Contemporary Arts Museum	(1)	2	3	4	5	6
Miller Theater in Hermann Park (free concerts, meetings, plays)	(1)	2	3	4	5	6
The mountains	(1)	2	3	4	5	6

	A.		B.			
	BEEN TO (ASK B)	NEVER BEEN TO (NEXT ITEM)	Less than a week ago	Less than a month ago (more than a week)	Several months ago	Over a year ago
NASA	(1)	2	3	4	5	6
Planetarium or Museum of Natural Sciences	(1)	2	3	4	5	6
Golf courses	(1)	2	3	4	5	6
San Jacinto	(1)	2	3	4	5	6
The zoo	(1)	2	3	4	5	6
Any city park	(1)	2	3	4	5	6

47. We have talked about a lot of things people like to do. Now, aside from enjoyment, I'd like to find out how important each of these activities is to you.

First, getting away from the city, out into the country or the woods. Would you say this is very important, somewhat important, not too important, or not important at all, as far as you're concerned? (READ EACH ITEM AND CIRCLE APPROPRIATE CODE.)

	Very important	Somewhat important	Not too important	Not important at all
Getting away from the city, etc.	1	2	3	4
Things liek sewing, fixing, building	5	6	7	8
Looking at art or listening to music	1	2	3	4
Traveling	5	6	7	8
Going out dancing or drinking	1	2	3	4
Visiting with relatives, friends, or neighbors, in your home or theirs	5	6	7	8
Reading	1	2	3	4
Discussing important issues	5	6	7	8
Watching sports	1	2	3	4
Taking part in sports or exercise	5	6	7	8
Cooking, preparing food	1	2	3	4
Having time to be alone	5	6	7	8
Watching TV	1	2	3	4
Singing, drawing, playing a musical instrument, etc.	5	6	7	8
Use of firearms in target practice or hunting	1	2	3	4
Going to movies	5	6	7	8
Being a member of a club or organization	1	2	3	4
Church or religious activities	5	6	7	8

SOURCE: C. Gordon, personal communications, 1977.

V2.11.II.a

LEISURE PARTICIPATION

National Council on the Aging, 1975

5a. Now I'm going to read you some things that other people have said they do with their time. For each, would you tell me whether you personally spend a lot of time, some but not a lot, or hardly any time at all doing that? (READ LIST AND RECORD BELOW FOR EACH ITEM)

5b. And how much time do you think most people over 65 spend (READ LIST)—a lot of time, some but not a lot, or hardly any time at all? (RECORD BELOW FOR EACH ITEM ON LIST)

	5a. You Personally			
	5b. Most people Over 65			
	A Lot	Some but Not a Lot	Hardly Any at All	Not Sure
ITEM LIST FOR 5a, b.				
1. Participating in recreational activities and hobbies				
2. Participating in fraternal or community organizations or clubs				
3. Socializing with friends.				
4. Sitting and thinking.				
5. Caring for younger or older members of the family.				
6. Participating in political activities. . . .				
7. Sleeping				
8. Watching television				
9. Working part-time or full-time.				
10. Doing volunteer work				
11. Participating in sports, like golf, tennis or swimming.				
12. Just doing nothing				
13. Reading				
14. Going for walks				
15. Gardening or raising plants.				

27a. (ASK EVERYONE) I'm going to read you a list of places people sometimes go. For each please tell me whether it is convenient for you to go there, or not. (READ LIST AND RECORD BELOW FOR EACH ITEM)
(1) Convenient   (2) Not Convenient   (3) Not Sure

27b. In the last year or so, have you been to (READ LIST), or not? (RECORD BELOW FOR EACH ITEM ON LIST)
(1) Have Been To   (2) Have Not Been To   (3) Not Sure

27c. (ASK FOR EACH "HAVE BEEN TO" IN 27b) When did you last attend (*ITEM*)—(1)

Within Last Day or Two, (2) Within Last Week or Two, (3) A Month Ago, (4) 2-3 Months Ago, (5) Longer Ago Than That, (6) Not Sure. (READ LIST AND RECORD FOR EACH ITEM)

ITEM LIST FOR 27a,b, c.

1. A movie
2. A museum
3. A live theatre, dance or musical concert performance
4. Places to shop
5. (ASK IF 55 TO 64 YEARS OLD) A senior citizens center or Golden Age Club
6. A sports event
7. A restaurant
8. A community or neighborhood center or recreation center
9. A church or synagogue
10. A library
11. A doctor or clinic
12. A public park
13. The home of a neighbor
14. The home of a relative

27d. (ASK IF "55 to 64" *AND* "HAVE NOT BEEN TO SENIOR CITIZENS' CENTER OR GOLDEN AGE CLUB" IN 27b, ITEM #5 — OTHERS SKIP TO 28a) Would you like to attend a snior citizens' center or Golden Age Club, or not?

Would like to attend. . . . . _____ (ASK 27e)

Would not like to attend . . . . _____ (ASK 27f)

Not sure. . . . . _____ (SKIP TO 28a)

27e. (IF "WOULD LIKE TO ATTEND" IN 27d) What's keeping you from attending a senior citizens' center or Golden Age Club? Anything else?

27f. (IF "WOULD NOT LIKE TO ATTEND" IN 27d — OTHERS SKIP TO 28a) Why aren't you interested in attending a senior citizens' center or Golden Age Club? Any other reason?

28a. (ASK EVERYONE) Do you ever spend any time (READ LIST), or not? (RECORD BELOW FOR EACH ITEM ON LIST) (1) Do, (2) Don't, (3) Not sure.

28b. (FOR EACH ACTIVITY "DO" IN 28a) About how much time did you spend yesterday (*activity*)? (RECORD BELOW FOR EACH APPLICABLE ITEM) (1) None, (2) 1 hour, (3) 2 hours, (4) 3 hours, (5) 4 hours, (6) 5 hours, (7) More than 5 hours, (8) Not sure.

ITEM LIST FOR 28a,b.

1. Listening to radio
2. Watching television
3. Reading newspapers
4. Reading magazines
5. Reading books

28c. (ASK EVERYONE) The media sometimes show older people. On the whole, when they show older people, would you say (READ LIST) usually give a fair picture of what older people are like, do they make older people look better than they really are, or worse than they really are? (RECORD BELOW FOR EACH ITEM ON LIST)

	Fair Picture	Better than Really Are	Worse than Really Are	Not Sure
1. Radio programs	_____	_____	_____	_____

	Fair Picture	Better than Really Are	Worse than Really Are	Not Sure
2. Television progams	_____	_____	_____	_____
3. Television commercials.	_____	_____	_____	_____
4. Newspapers	_____	_____	_____	_____
5. Magazines	_____	_____	_____	_____
6. Books.	_____	_____	_____	_____

28d. (ASK IF "DO WATCH TELEVISION" IN 28a, #2—OTHERS SKIP TO 29a) Now I'd like to read you some statements people have made about the way people over 65 are shown in television programs and commercials. For each, would you tell me whether you tend to agree strongly, agree womewhat, disagree womewhat, or disagree strongly? (READ STATEMENTS AND RECORD BELOW FOR EACH)

	Agree Strongly	Agree Somewhat	Disagree Somewhat	Disagree Strongly	Not Sure
1. Television usually makes older people look old-fashioned and narrow-minded	_____	_____	_____	_____	_____
2. Television usually makes older people look sick and helpless.	_____	_____	_____	_____	_____
3. Television usually makes older people look wise and full of good advice . .	_____	_____	_____	_____	_____
4. Television usually makes older people look success-full at what they do. . . .	_____	_____	_____	_____	_____
5. On the whole, television treats older people with respect	_____	_____	_____	_____	_____
6. Television usually makes older people look pushy and meddling into their family's business	_____	_____	_____	_____	_____
7. Television usually makes older people look untidy and not very pleasant to look at	_____	_____	_____	_____	_____
8. Television usually makes older people look like they are an important part of the family.	_____	_____	_____	_____	_____
9. Television usually makes older people look useless and in everyone's way . .	_____	_____	_____	_____	_____

	Agree Strongly	Agree Somewhat	Disagree Somewhat	Disagree Strongly	Not Sure
10. On the whole, television programs show young people, not older people	_____	_____	_____	_____	____

28e. Do you ever see any older people in television programs or commercials that you particularly look up to or admire, or not?

See . . . . ._____ (ASK 28f)

Don't see. . . . ._____

Not sure . . . . ._____ (SKIP TO 29a)

28f. (IF "SEE OLDER PEOPLE" IN 28e) Who is that person? Anyone else?

SOURCE: Reproduced with permission from *Codebook for "The Myth and Reality of Aging,"* a survey conducted by Louis Harris and Associates for the National Council on the Aging; prepared by the Duke University Center for the Study of Aging and Human Development under a grant from the Edna M. Clark Foundation, 1976.

V2.11.II.b

LEISURE TIME BEHAVIOR

B. P. Payne, 1973

1. To start off, thinking about the activities you do for enjoyment when not on a regular job, what one activity do you consider most enjoyable? (CIRCLE ONLY ONE. IF RESPONDENT MENTIONS ACTIVITY NOT NAMED IN ANY OF THE THREE LISTS BELOW, WRITE IN UNDER "OTHER.")

ACTIVITIES (NON-SPORTS)

01 DID ART/CRAFT WORK
02 ATTENDED CLUB/MEETING
03 COOKED
04 ATTENDED CONCERTS, PLAYS, LECTURES
05 ENTERTAINED GUESTS
06 DID GARDENING
07 WENT OUT (e.g., FOR DINNER, DANCING, ETC.)
08 DID MECHANICAL WORK OR REPAIR
09 ATTENDED MOVIE, DRIVE-IN MOVIE
10 PLAYED MUSICAL INSTRUMENT, LISTENED TO MUSIC
11 PLAYED CARDS OR GAMES
12 LISTENED TO RADIO
13 READ
14 DID SEWING
15 DID SHOPWORK
16 SHOPPED
17 WATCHED T.V.
18 VISITED FRIENDS, WENT TO PARTIES

19 DID VOLUNTEER SERVICE WORK
20 WORKED AROUND THE HOUSE
ATTENDED SPORTS EVENTS
30 ATTENDED BASEBALL GAME
31 ATTENDED BASKETBALL GAME
32 ATTENDED FOOTBALL GAME
33 ATTENDED GOLF MATCH
34 ATTENDED HOCKEY MATCH
35 ATTENDED HORSE RACE
36 ATTENDED STOCK CAR RACE
PARTICIPATED IN SPORTS/OUTDOOR ACTIVITIES
50 PLAYED BASEBALL/SOFTBALL
51 PLAYED BASKETBALL
52 WENT TO THE BEACH
53 WENT BIKE RIDING
54 WENT BOATING (MOTOR)
55 WENT BOATING (SAIL)
56 WENT BOWLING
57 WENT CAMPING
58 WENT FISHING

59 PLAYED GOLF	66 PLAYED TOUCH FOOTBALL
60 HIKED	67 WENT SNOW SKIING
61 PLAYED HOCKEY	68 WENT SWIMMING
62 WENT HORSEBACK RIDING AND	69 WENT WATER SKIING
PARTICIPATED IN HORSE-	70 WALKED, JOGGED
RELATED ACTIVITIES	71 VISITED A ZOO
63 WENT HUNTING	72 VISITED A MUSEUM
64 VISITED PARKS	*OTHER (SPECIFY)*
65 PLAYED TENNIS	

2. The most recent time you _____ , where did it take place?
   (FILL IN FROM QUESTION 1)

   1. RESPONDENT'S HOME OR CLOSE BY IN NEIGHBORHOOD.
   2. FRIEND'S/RELATIVE'S HOME.
   3. AT A PARK.
   4. BEACH, RIVER, LAKE, ETC.
   5. STADIUM, TRACK, FIELD FOR ATHLETICS, ETC.
   6. SCHOOL, COLLEGE, UNIVERSITY, ETC.
   7. OTHER (SPECIFY) _____ .
   0. DON'T KNOW.

(IF "BEACH, RIVER, LAKE, ETC." ON QUESTION 2, ASK):

3. Was this _____ located in a park, or not?
   (FILL IN FROM QUESTION 2)

   1. YES, IN PARK
   2. NO, NOT IN PARK
   3. OTHER (SPECIFY) _____
   0. DON'T KNOW

4. On this last occasion, did you (go) (do it) alone, or with one or more people?
   1. ALONE (SKIP TO Q.9)
   2. WITH OTHER PERSON(S)

(IF "WITH OTHER PERSON(S)" ON Q. 4, ASK):

5. With whom did you (go) (do it)?
   1. SPOUSE
   2. CHILD(REN)
   3. BROTHER(S), SISTER(S)
   4. PARENT(S)
   5. OTHER FAMILY
   6. FRIEND(S)
   7. NEIGHBOR(S)
   8. OTHER (SPECIFY) _____

6. Counting yourself, how many were in you group in total? (IF RESPONDENT CAN'T
   RECALL, ASK: Would you tell me just approximately how many?)

   _____ FILL IN NUMBER
   1. CIRCLE IF APPROXIMATE
   2. DON'T KNOW

7. Have you done this other times with the same group or was this the first time?
   1. FIRST TIME
   2. OTHER TIMES ALSO

3. OTHER TIME(S) WITH SOME OF THE SAME GROUP
4. OTHER (SPECIFY)_____

8. While you were involved in this activity, did other people join you and become part of your group?

   1. YES
   2. NO
   3. DON'T KNOW

9. People participate in activities for a variety of reasons. In order to learn the reason why you_____ on the most recent occasion, I am going to read
   (FILL IN FROM QUESTION 1)
   you a list of statements. We realize that not all of these may apply, but would you please tell me which *one* best describes the reason why you did it?

(INTERVIEWER: READ STATEMENTS 1-5 FIRST, THEN RECORD RESPONDENT'S ANSWER.)

   1. I enjoy being with the people I was with.
   2. It is important to be seen doing the right things.
   3. I like the feeling I get out of the activity.
   4. I believe you ought to have a leisure time activity.
   5. It is important to be seen with the right people.

(INTERVIEWER: DO NOT READ STATEMENTS 6, 7 AND 0.)

   6. IT IS JUST SOMETHING TO DO.
   7. NONE OF THE ABOVE.
   0. DON'T KNOW

10. Now think back to about five years ago. If I had asked you then what activity you considered most enjoyable, do you think your answer would have been the same as now, or different?

    1. SAME
    2. DIFFERENT
    3. DON'T KNOW

11. Now, try to imagine five years ahead. If, about five years from now, I were to ask you what activity you considered most enjoyable, do you think your answer would be the same as now, or different?

    1. SAME
    2. DIFFERENT
    3. DON'T KNOW

Now, for our last few questions, let's talk about parks.

12. When was the last time you went to a park, any park?

    1. LESS THAN A WEEK AGO.
    2. ONE WEEK TO LESS THAN ONE MONTH AGO.
    3. ONE MONTH TO LESS THAN THREE MONTHS AGO.
    4. THREE MONTHS TO LESS THAN SIX MONTHS AGO.
    5. SIX MONTHS TO ONE YEAR AGO.
    6. MORE THAN ONE YEAR AGO.
    7. NEVER.
    0. DON'T REMEMBER.
    (INTERVIEWER: CIRCLE NUMBER OF STATE IN WHICH THIS INTERVIEW IS

BEING CONDUCTED:)

13. I'm going to read you the name of some places that are in (NAME OF STATE). As I
read each name, please tell me whether you *have* or have *not* been in that place *within
the past twelve months.* (READ EACH PLACE ON EXHIBIT A, NATIONAL PARKS,
AND CIRCLE BELOW IN TURN THE ANSWER FOR EACH.)

PARK NUMBER   *1 2 3 4 5 6 7 8 9 10 11 12 13 14 15 16 17 18 19*

Have you been in
that place 1 1 1 1 1 1 1 1 1 1 1 1 1 1 1 1 1 1 1

Have not been in
that place 2 2 2 2 2 2 2 2 2 2 2 2 2 2 2 2 2 2 2

Don't know 0 0 0 0 0 0 0 0 0 0 0 0 0 0 0 0 0 0 0

(INTERVIEWER: ASK IF MORE THAN ONE NATIONAL PARK NAMED IN QUES-
TION 13:)

14. You mentioned that you've been to (READ ALL NATIONAL PARKS NAMED). Which
one of these parks have you visited most recently? (RECORD PARK NUMBER AND
NAME.)

NUMBER_____ NAME _____

15. The last time you were in (NAME OF ONLY MOST RECENT PARK), did you take
part in any of the following activities? As I read each activity, please tell me whether
or not you took part in that activity.

1. Stopping at the visitors' center.
2. Talking with a ranger.
3. Taking self-guided walks or drives over nature or historical trails.
4. Purchasing food at a food service facility, for example, restaurant, snack.
5. Reading roadside exhibits.
6. Reading park brochures or maps.
7. Viewing slides or movie show about park.
8. Viewing exhibits.
9. Asking for information.
0. Taking guided tours.
X. Purchasing gifts or souvenirs.
V. OTHER ANSWER (SPECIFY) _____

SOURCE: B. P. Payne. "Adult Patterns of Leisure in the Piedmont Region." Report under
contract with the National Park Service No. S-O-S 201-S-O-5-500. Atlanta: Sociology Department, Georgia State University, 1973, Appendix IV. Reprinted by permission of author.

V2.11.II.c

LEISURE ACTIVITY SCORE

S. R. Sherman, 1973

24. A. Now I would like to ask you about some of your present activities. Do you often,
sometimes, or never:

	(OFTEN)	(SOMETIMES)	(NEVER)
a. watch TV or listen to the radio?	3	2	1
b. play cards?	3	2	1

	(OFTEN)	(SOMETIMES)	(NEVER)
c. read books, magazines, or newspapers?	3	2	1
d. go to lectures or concerts?	3	2	1
e. go to the theatre or movies?	3	2	1
f. travel or go on tours?	3	2	1
g. go for rides or walks?	3	2	1
h. do arts and crafts or fix things?	3	2	1
i. participate in church activities?	3	2	1
j. do volunteer work?	3	2	1
k. garden?	3	2	1
l. sing or play a musical instrument?	3	2	1

B. Are there any activities or pastimes in which you participate that I have left out?

    1. no (SKIP TO Q. 25.)

    2. yes (GO TO Q. 24.c)

C. What are they?   D. Do you do this?

	(OFTEN)	(SOMETIMES)	(NEVER)
_____	3	2	1
_____	3	2	1
_____	3	2	1
_____	3	2	1

SOURCE: S. R. Sherman, personal communication, 1977.

V2.11.II.d

LEISURE PARTICIPATION

B. Havens and M. Thompson, 1973-1977

1. In order to serve the desires of people, we need to know what you are doing and what you would like to do:

    a) p What are the most important things that you do? (CODE THE FIRST THREE MENTIONED WITH 1's IN COLUMN (a), THE 4th-6th AS 2's AND THE 7th-9th AS 3's.) What additional things which you are not now doing, would you like to do? (CODE ALL MENTIONED HERE AS 5's IN COLUMN (a); ALL OTHERS NOT ALREADY CODED MUST HAVE 0's IN COLUMN (a).)

        FOR EACH OF THOSE ACTIVITIES CODED 1 IN COLUMN (a)—ASK QUESTIONS b) & c) (CODE AS INDICATED IN COLUMNS (b) & (c).) FOR THOSE ACTIVITIES CODED 5 IN COLUMN (a)—ASK QUESTION d) ONLY. (CODE AS INDICATED IN COLUMN (d).)

    b) p Have you participated in this activity within the past week? '

            1. Yes   5. No   3. Don't know

    c) How satisfied are you with your participation in this activity?

            1. Extremely satisfied

            2. Somewhat satisfied

            3. Neutral

            4. Somewhat unsatisfied

            5. Extremely unsatisfied

    3) Do you consider this lack of participation a problem?

1. No problem
2. Slight problem
3. Neutral
4. Somewhat of a problem
5. Extreme problem

	P (a) CODE 1,2 3,5 OR 0	P (b) PARTICIPATION IN PAST WEEK	(c) LEVEL OF SATISFACTION	(d) VIEWED AS A PROBLEM
ACTIVITIES				
Visit family or relatives				
Visit friends or neighbors				
Telephone conversation with friends/relatives				
Radio or T.V.				
Walk, shop or drive				
Light housework or gardening				
Heavy housework or yardwork				
Collecting hobbies (INCLUDING PET CARE AND OUTDOOR ACTIVITIES)				
Handwork hobbies (INCLUDING CARVING AND SEWING)				
Sports or games (INCLUDING BOWLING, SHUFFLEBOARD, FOOTBALL, HOCKY)				
Church related activities				
Music, art, theatre				
Reading or writing				
Organized or informal multi-age social recreation groups (INCLUDING EDUCATIONAL ACTIVITIES)				
Formal or informal social groups for aged				
Service, fraternal or legion organizations				
Formal or informal community volunteer work				
Politically related activities				
Mass activities (BINGO, COMMUNITY CLUB)				
Travel (TRIPS, SEASONAL CAMPING)				
Work (INCLUDING OCCASIONAL SEASONAL, PART-TIME, OR FULL-TIME)				

2.____ If you had a choice of participating in activities you enjoy, would you prefer to do them with people mostly younger than you, or with people mostly around your age?

        3. With younger people mainly
        1. With people of all ages
        3. With people your own age
        5. Cannot participate in activities
           (FOR WHATEVER REASON)
        4. By self, without other people

IF IN A FACILITY OTHER THAN GENERAL HOSPITAL ASK:

3.____ Does this facility have a residents' council or a committee of residents?

Ps   1. Yes
              5. No

IF YES (1) ASK (a) & (b)
IF NO (5) ASK:

_____ Would you and other residents be interested in having a council or committee?

        1. Yes
        2. No

_____ Ps (a) Does the council have any funds available to it?

        1. Yes
        2. No

IF (1) YES ASK:

_____ What is the major source of these funds?

Ps   3. Provided by facility
            2. From sale of residents' products
            3. From residents' social functions.
            1. From sales in facility shops

    (b) In which of the following areas is the council involved?

    (IN HOUSING UNITS WHERE ALL RESIDENTS HAVE INDEPENDENT MEALS, SCORE YES (1) FOR LETTERS d. & e.)

			YES	NO
_____ Ps	a.	Movies, games, parties, special day celebrations and other entertainment for residents in facilities	1	5
_____ Ps	b.	Attending outside theatre, sporting events, concerts and other community events	1	5
_____ Ps	c.	Tourist trips or tours	1	5
_____ Ps	d.	Assisting with menu planning	1	5
_____ Ps	e.	Meal hours	1	5
_____ Ps	f.	Activity schedules	1	5
_____ Ps	g.	Operating shops	1	5
_____ Ps	h.	Gardening	1	5

    (CODE IN 8-70 MORE THAN 4 1's = 1
                    4 1's = 2
            2 OR 3 1's = 3
               1 1 = 4
               0 1's = 5)

4. _____ Is there an adequate garden or park area easily accessible to you from this facility?

Ps
1. Yes-adequate
2. Yes-inadequate
4. No-desired
4. No-undesired

5. _____ Is there an adequate porch or all-weather walk area easily accessible to you from this facility?

Ps
1. Yes-adequate
2. Yes-inadequate
3. No-desired
4. No-undesired

6. _____ Do you and/or any other residents attend day centres, clubs or societies outside the facility? (CONSIDER AS AN OUTSIDE DAY CENTRE, A CENTRE WITHIN THE FACILITY WHICH HAS ONE THIRD OR MORE OF ITS MEMBERSHIP FROM OUTSIDE THE FACILITY)

Ps
1. Yes, most of the residents
2. Yes, many residents
3. Yes, some residents
4. Yes, but few residents
5. None

If 1-3 ASK (a):

_____ (a) How did you and/or any other residents happen to start attending such centres or clubs?

Ps
1. Some of us started on our own due to interest
2. The staff and the facility got some of us interested and helped me get started (MADE ARRANGEMENTS)
3. The centres or clubs got some of us interested and helped me get started (MADE ARRANGEMENTS)

SOURCE: B. Havens, personal communications, 1976.

V2.11.II.e

USE OF LEISURE TIME

Duke Longitudinal Study of Adaptation, 1968

1. How many hours a day do you usually spend:
   a. Eating
   b. Dressing, bathing, and personal care
   c. Working (or housework) including travel to work
   d. (If working) How many days per week?

   During the last typical week, how many hours did you spend:
   e. Watching TV or listening to radio
   f. Reading newspapers, magazines, or books
   g. Playing a sport or working on a hobby
   h. Watching a sports even such as a baseball or football game (not on TV)
   i. Attending church or other meetings
   j. Doing volunteer work for church, other organizations, or relatives
   k. Visiting, telephoning, or writing friends or relatives, parties, eating out, or entertaining

l. Yard care, gardening, repairing, building, mending, sewing, and other such activities

m. Other leisure activities. Specify:

n. Just sitting around doing nothing, taking it easy

2. With whom do you spend most of your free time?
   (1) By myself
   (2) With my wife (husband)
   (3) With my children
   (4) With my wife (husband) and children
   (5) With friends or relatives of my own sex
   (6) With friends or relatives of the opposite sex
   (7) With friends or relatives of mixed sex
   (8) Don't know

3. How much vacation time did you take during the twelve months just passed?
   (0) No vacation—Skip to 11
   (1) Less than a week
   (2) About one week
   (3) About two weeks
   (4) About three weeks
   (5) About four weeks
   (6) More than a month
   (7) Don't know

4. What did you do on your vacation? (If you did more than one thing, what did you do for the biggest part of it?)
   (1) I travelled for pleasure (includes visiting friends and relatives)
   (2) I travelled on business
   (3) I just took it easy around the house
   (4) I tried to catch up on my usual work
   (5) I worked around the house, or yard, building, repairing, fixing up
   (6) I spent it on self improvement (took lessons, courses)
   (7) I did volunteer work
   (8) Other. Specify:
   (9) Don't know

5. How much money did you spend on vacations during the last year including costs of vacation equipment, travel, lodging, and meals?
   (1) $ 0-50
   (2) $ 50-100
   (3) $100-200
   (4) $200-500
   (5) $500-2,000
   (6) More than $2,000
   (7) Don't know

6. Looking back on it, was it money well spent, or do you think you should have spent it on something more useful?
   (1) It was money well spent
   (2) I should have spent it on something more useful
   (3) Don't know

7. When was the last time you really had fun?
   - (1) Within the last day
   - (2) Within the last week
   - (3) Within the last month
   - (4) Within the last 6 months
   - (5) Within the the last year
   - (6) More than a year ago
   - (7) Don't know

8. Are you satisfied with the amount of free time you have now, or do you feel you have too much free time or too little free time?
   - (1) I am satisfied with the amount of free time I now have
   - (2) I have too much free time
   - (3) I have too little free time
   - (4) Don't know

9. If your job would permit you an additional day off each week, how would you spend most of that time?
   - (0) Watching TV or listening to radio
   - (1) Reading newspapers, magazines, or books
   - (2) Playing a sport or working on a hobby
   - (3) Attending sports events or meetings
   - (4) Doing volunteer work for church, other organization
   - (5) Visiting, telephoning, or writing friends or relatives, parties, eating out, or entertaining
   - (6) Yard care, gardening, repairing, building, mending, sewing, and other such activities
   - (7) Self improvement (taking courses, lessons)
   - (8) Catching up on my work
   - (9) Other. Specify:

10. If you did not actually have to work for a living, would you still work?
    - (1) Yes
    - (2) No
    - (3) Don't know

11. What is more satisfying to you, your work or your leisure activities?
    - (1) Both are equally satisfying
    - (2) My work is more satisfying to me
    - (3) My leisure activities are more satisfying to me
    - (4) Don't know

12. What is your definition of leisure activity? Choose one:
    - (1) Anything that is not work
    - (2) Anything you don't have to do
    - (3) Anything that is fun to do ›
    - (4) Anything that is relaxing
    - (5) Free time
    - (6) Other. Specify:
    - (7) Don't know

SOURCE: L. George, personal communications, 1976.

V2.11.III.a

LEISURE ACTIVITIES

Committee on Research and Development Goals in Social Gerontology, 1971

5. Favorite Personal Leisure Activities of Respondent: Please list your most favorite free time activities, over your life, in the following table. Note the ages at which you were most actively involved in each activity, also if you have changed your participation in each activity, also if you have changed your participation in each and if yes, why.

Respondent Leisure Activity	Age Most Active	Change	Reasons for Change
1.		Yes/No	
2.		Yes/No	
3.		Yes/No	
4.		Yes/No	
5.		Yes/No	

6. Spouse's Favorite Leisure Activities: List the most favorite free time activities of your spouse over the years. Do this in terms of your impressions. Note the ages of most active participation, changes, if any, and reasons for the change.

Spouse Leisure Activity	Age Most Active	Change	Reasons for Change
1.		Yes/No	
2.		Yes/No	
3.		Yes/No	
4.		Yes/No	
5.		Yes/No	

7. What have been the major leisure activities in which your family has engaged, for example, on vacations? Have there been changes in these activities? Yes/No. If yes, why?

8. For your current job (or last job if retired), how many weeks of vacation do you get each year? What are your current major vacation activities? Have there been any changes in your vacation activities over the years? Why?

SOURCE: J. R. Murray, E. A. Powers, and R. J. Havighurst. "Personal and Situational Factors Producing Flexible Careers." *The Gerontologist*, 1971, 11 (4, part 2):11-12.

V2.11.III.b

FREE TIME ACTIVITIES

W. A. Peterson, L. W. Phelps, and C. F. Longino, Jr., 1976

E-28. Now, I'd like to mention a few things people spend time with, and ask you whether you have these things and how much you use them?

Do you have (take) a_____ ? (SEE LIST; IF YES ASK a, b, and c.)

    (1) Yes   (2) No

  a. On an average day, about how many hours per day do you use (LIST)?

        _____ (CODE ACTUAL HOURS)

  b. Is this more or less than you did at age 50?

    (1) More   (2) Less

c. What are your major *current* (interests, topics, persons) on _____ (LIST)? _____

ITEM LIST FOR E-28:

    1. TELEVISION;   2. RADIO;   3. TELEPHONE;   4. NEWSPAPER
    5. MAGAZINES OR BOOKS.

E-29. (IF R DOES NOT HAVE OR TAKE *ANY* OF THE ABOVE) Would you like to have: television, radio, telephone, newspapers, magazines, books? Why don't you have (or take) them? (ALSO PROBE ACCESS OF SOMEONE ELSE'S TELEPHONE OR NEWSPAPER, AND PROBE PAST INTEREST AND USE.)

F-3. There are a number of other things that you might do in your free time. For instance, when you were 50 years of age, did you go to (LIST)?

        (1) Yes   (2) No

a. Were you then: (1) Very active; (2) Active; (3) Occasionally Active; (5) Not at All Active?

b. How about now. Are you: (1) Very Active; (2) Active; (3) Occasionally Active; (5) Not at All Active?

IF CHANGE BETWEEN AGE 50 AND PRESENT, ASK c AND d.

c. At what age did you change your activity level?_____(CODE AGE)

d. Why did you change?

ITEM LIST FOR F-3:

  1. Sports events: football, basketball, baseball, bowling games, stock care races, etc.;
  2. Movies, plays, musical events;
  3. Political meetings and rallies;
  4. American Royal, state fair, carnivals, rodeos, holiday parades;
  5. Special church events, revivals, etc.;
  6. Just go out of doors to watch people go by, children playing, cars, etc.;
  7. Hunting, fishing, camping, pool, etc.;
  8. Bowling, golfing, billiards, pool, etc.;
  9. Family picnics, group picnics;
10. Church, club or lodge, veterans, social, suppers, dances, etc.;
11. Dancing, night clubs, taverns, etc.;
12. Informal neighborhood visiting and gossiping;
13. Gardening, yardwork, houseplants;
14. Walking or jogging in the neighborhood;
15. Hobbies—making and fixing;
16. Hobbies—collecting;
17. Vacation trips, Sundays, holidays, etc.;

(ITEMS 18-23, OUT OF TOWN TRIPS:)

18. Visiting friends, relatives;
19. Business
20. Shopping
21. Conventions, special meetings;
22. Entertainment—social;
23. Other (SPECIFY);
24. Pets.

SOURCE: W. A. Peterson, L. W. Phelps, and C. F. Longino, Jr. "John Knox Village Residents: Exploring the Tangibles and Intangibles of Retirement Living." Report for the Institute for Community Studies, Kansas City, Mo., 1976, appendix.

V2.11.III.c

PAST LEISURE PARTICIPATION

B. P. Payne and C. N. Bull, 1976

We would also like to ask you some questions about your past leisure activities.

1. During the time you were in school or college were there any sports, hobbies, or other leisure activities in which you participated? (RECORD A MAXIMUM OF FOUR AC—TIVITIES.)
2. a) Which of the activities listed above did you participate in after school?_____

   _____

   b) Which ones have you dropped?_____

3. After school, what leisure activities, sports, or hobbies did you pick up? (RECORD A MAXIMUM OF FOUR ACTIVITIES.)
4. a) Of the activities listed above, in which ones are you still participating?_____

   _____

   b) Which ones have you dropped?_____

SOURCE: B. P Payne and C. N. Bull, 1977, work in progress.

V2.11.IV.a

COMMUNICATIONS ACTIVITY

M. J. Graney and E. E. Graney, 1974

1. About how many hours would you say you watch TV on a day like yesterday?
   ( ) hours
2. About how many hours would you say you listened to the radio yesterday?
   ( ) hours
3. About how many hours would you say you read yesterday?
   ( ) hours
4. Do you visit with your neighbors in the building often?
   more than once a day ( ), daily ( ), less than daily ( ), never ( )
5. All in all, how often do you see any of your friends and relatives in the Twin Cities—I mean people you know pretty well?
   several times a week ( ), about once a week ( ), several times a month ( ),
   never ( )
6. Do you recall about how many phone calls you made and received yesterday?
   ( ) calls in and out
7. Do you go to church (or temple)? If yes, about how often?
   more often than weekly ( ), weekly ( ), monthly ( ), less often than month-ly ( ), never ( )
8. Do you attend meetings of any clubs, civic groups, or other organizations? If yes, which ones? If yes, do you attend these kinds of meetings often?
   weekly ( ), monthly ( ), less often than monthly ( )

SOURCE: M. J. Graney and E. E. Graney. "Communications Activity Substitutions in Aging." *Journal of Communication*, 1974, 24 (4): 91-92.

V2.11.IV.b

MEDIA HABITS

Canadian Radio-Television Commission, 1974

This instrument is too long to reproduce here.

V2.11.V.a

ELDERLY LEISURE ATTITUDE SCALE

J. D. Teaff, N. W. Ernst, and M. Ernst, 1975

Below are listed a number of free time activities. Using the scale values given, indicate what in your opinion society's position regarding these activities should be:

This activity should be:	SCALE VALUES
very strongly encouraged	7
strongly encouraged	6
encouraged	5
neither encouraged nor discouraged	4
discouraged	3
strongly discouraged	2
very strongly discouraged	1

FREE TIME ACTIVITIES: YOUR POSITION

1. activities emphasizing mental endeavors such as studying, taking adult education courses, etc. . .   _____

2. activities involving active participation in social affairs, such as volunteer work, club activities, etc. . .   _____

3. activities that consist basically of doing nothing, such as writing, painting, or playing an instrument . . .   _____

4. activities involving productive efforts, such as certain hobbies like woodworking, leather tooling, sewing, etc. . .   _____

5. activities involving physical exercise, such as sports and calisthenics, hunting and fishing, or just walking . . .   _____

Given the most ideal conditions of any society you can think of, how many weeks of vacation should a person get who has been employed by a company for 10 years?
Number of Weeks_____

How many weeks of vacation per year would you like to have?
Number of Weeks_____

How many days per week would you want to spend working for a living?
Number of Days _____

Given the present state of our society, what should be the *workweek*, that is, how many days per week should be spent working for a living?
Number of Days

Below are listed a number of statements. Indicate your own position on each of these by using the number of the label which comes closest to your opinion.

LABELS

7 . . . . . I agree very strongly
6 . . . . . I agree strongly
5 . . . . . I agree moderately
4 . . . . . I am undecided, uncertain or don't know
3 . . . . . I disagree moderately
2 . . . . . I disagree strongly
1 . . . . . I disagree very strongly

Assign numbers
here

1. My personal ambitions can be more fully realized on the job than in my free time . . .   _____

2. Very little of my free time is actually leisure . . . _____

3. I would prefer to be famous for something I had done on my job (like an invention) rather than for something I had done in my free time (like crossing the ocean in a rowboat) . . . _____

4. I always seem to have more things to do than I have time for . . . _____

5. It is more important for me to be good at my free time activities than at my work activities . . . _____

6. I have enough leisure . . . _____

7. My leisure activities are more satisfying to me than my work . . . _____

8. I would like to have more free time than I have now . . . _____

9. My leisure activities express my talents and capabilities better than does my job . . . _____

In our society nearly everybody works. Now, assume that you were given the chance to live a life of complete leisure, never again having to work for a living. Indicate on the scales below how you think you might feel about certain aspects of such a life.

1. How much would you like to lead such a "life of leisure"?
   _____ not at all _____ probably dislike it _____ uncertain _____ would like
   _____ like it very much _____ extremely so _____ would be the fulfillment of my greatest dreams

2. How long could you "stand" such a life?
   _____ for a month or less _____ half a year _____ one year
   _____ two years _____ five years _____ ten years _____ forever

3. Would you feel "guilty" about living such a life of leisure?
   _____ not at all _____ probably not _____ uncertain _____ somewhat
   _____ quite a bit _____ very much _____ extremely so

4. If you had (or have) children, would you like them to live such a life of leisure?
   _____ certainly not _____ probably not _____ uncertain _____ somewhat
   _____ quite a bit _____ very much _____ extremely so

5. How much of your free time activities could be called "killing time"? (PERCENT)
   _____ None _____ 10 _____ 20 _____ 30 _____ 40 _____ 50
   _____ 60 _____ 70 _____ 80 _____ 90 _____ All

If you were to divide your time into two parts: one work time and the other free time—how much time would you want for each?

Let the bar below represent your time. Draw a line dividing the bar according to the way you would divide your time between work time and free time. Label the work part "W" and the free time part "F."

Check the statement below which best describes you:
_____ My leisure time is always filled with thousands of things I want to do
_____ I usually have no trouble finding things to do during my leisure time
_____ I sometimes do not know what to do in my leisure time
_____ I usually do not know what to do in my leisure time
_____ I sometimes feel quite bored during my leisure time
_____ I usually feel quite bored during my leisure time
_____ I always feel quite bored during my leisure time

If you were to describe yourself to someone in terms of what is most important to you about yourself, how much would you talk about your work and how much would you talk about your free-time activities? Indicate your position by checking below:

_____ talk only about work _____ talk mostly about work _____ talk a little more about work than free time
_____ talk equally about work and free time _____ talk a little more about free time than work
_____ talk mostly about free time _____ talk only about free time

FACTOR ANALYSIS OF LEISURE ATTITUDES

FACTOR 1 — Amount of Work or Vacation Desired

Variable	Loading	Mean	S.D.
9 Given the present state what should be the work week.	.95	4.90	5.83
8 How many days per week would you want to work . .	.93	4.83	5.46
6 Given the most ideal conditions, how many weeks of vacation should a person have	.91	3.42	3.20
7 How many weeks of vacation would you like to have .	.78	3.78	6.68

FACTOR 2 — Amount of Perceived Leisure

Variable	Loading	Mean	S.D.
13 I always have more things to do than I have time for .	.63	5.68	1.95
24 Free time vs. work time allotment (graph)	.63	36.45	18.25
11 Little of my free time is actually leisure	.59	5.08	2.01
12 Prefer fame for job activity rather than something done in leisure	.49	5.12	2.13
10 Ambitions more realized on job than in free time . . .	.48	5.40	1.95
25 Self-description through free-time activities	.46	5.16	2.31
23 How much free time is "killing time"	.46	2.16	3.92

FACTOR 3 — Self-Definition through Leisure or Work

Variable	Loading	Mean	S.D.
18 Leisure activities express talents better than job	.79	3.17	2.04
16 Leisure activities more satisfying than work	.79	3.08	2.10
26 Describing self, how much talk about work, how much talk about free-time activities	.58	3.28	1.42
17 I would like to have more free time than I have	.38	3.28	2.25
14 More important to be good in free time than work activities	.33	3.27	2.12

FACTOR 4 — Affinity for Leisure

Variable	Loading	Mean	S.D.
22 Would you like children to live life of leisure	.80	1.34	1.17
19 How much would you like to lead a "life of leisure" .	.79	1.69	1.43
20 How long could you "stand" such a life	.78	1.84	1.81
21 Would you feel "guilty" about living such a life	.36	4.08	2.46

FACTOR 5 — Society's Role in Leisure Planning

Variable	Loading	Mean	S.D.
2 Participation in social affairs	.74	5.63	1.50
5 Physical exercise	.70	5.59	1.78
1 Mental endeavors	.70	5.95	1.41
4 Productive efforts	.59	5.68	1.39

SOURCE: J. D. Teaff, N. W. Ernst, and M. Ernst. "An Elderly Leisure Attitude Schedule." Paper presented to the 28th Annual Meeting of the Gerontological Society, Louisville, October 26-30, 1975, appendix.

V2.11.V.b

LEISURE ACTIVITIES AND SATISFACTION

E. A. Powers, 1964-1974

Now let's talk about some of your leisure activities.

201. Do you feel you have:
   1 _____ too much leisure time,
   2 _____ too little leisure time, or
   3 _____ are you satisfied with the amount of leisure time you have now?

202. What is your favorite leisure activity? _____
   IF R WORKING FULL-TIME, CONTINUE WITH Q.203.
   IF R NOT WORKING FULL-TIME, GO TO NEXT PAGE, Q. 206.
   IF YOU DO NOT REMEMBER IF R IS WORKING, GO TO PAGE 2, Q.1.

203. Would you say your favorite leisure activity:
   1 _____ provides satisfaction you don't get from your work, or
   2 _____ provides satisfaction similar to what you get from your work, or
   3 _____ provides satisfaction similar to what you get from your work, but which work
           never provides enough of?

204. Would you say your favorite leisure activity:
   1 _____ is similar to your work activities, or
   2 _____ is different from your work activities?

205. How often do you use this favorite leisure activity to "let off steam" which is created
   at work? Would you say:
   1 _____ all of the time,
   2 _____ some of the time, or
   3 _____ none of the time?

206. How satisfied are you with the amount of time you spend on your favorite leisure
   activity?
   1 _____ very satisfied,
   2 _____ satisfied,
   3 _____ dissatisfied, or
   4 _____ very dissatisfied?

207. Would you like to spend more, the same or less time on your favorite leisure activity?
   1 _____ more time in the activity
   2 _____ same amount of time in the activity
   3 _____ less time in the activity

208. We have talked about four areas, among others: family, work, leisure and community.
   a. Which one of these activities do you enjoy *most*? Would you say:
   1 _____ family,
   2 _____ work,
   3 _____ leisure, or
   4 _____ community?
   b. Which one of these activities would you *most* like to devote more time to?
   1 _____ family
   2 _____ work
   3 _____ leisure
   4 _____ community
   c. Which one of these activities provides you the *greatest* sense of accomplishment?
   1 _____ family
   2 _____ work
   3 _____ leisure
   4 _____ community

SOURCE: E. A. Powers, personal communication, 1977.

Indexes

Index of Subjects

Index of Names

David J. Mangen is assistant professor of gerontology and sociology at the Leonard Davis School of Gerontology, University of Southern California. He is associate editor of *Research on Aging: A Quarterly of Social Gerontology*.

Warren A. Peterson is director of the Centers on Aging Studies, University of Missouri-Kansas City and University of Missouri-Columbia, and professor of sociology at University of Missouri-Kansas City.